Human Development and Interaction in the Age of Ubiquitous Technology

Hakikur Rahman
BRAC University, Bangladesh

A volume in the Advances in Human and Social
Aspects of Technology (AHSAT) Book Series

Information Science
REFERENCE
An Imprint of IGI Global

Published in the United States of America by
  Information Science Reference (an imprint of IGI Global)
  701 E. Chocolate Avenue
  Hershey PA, USA 17033
  Tel: 717-533-8845
  Fax: 717-533-8661
  E-mail: cust@igi-global.com
  Web site: http://www.igi-global.com

Library of Congress Cataloging-in-Publication Data

Names: Rahman, Hakikur, 1957- editor.
Title: Human development and interaction in the age of ubiquitous technology
  / Hakikur Rahman, editor.
Description: Hershey, PA : Information Science Reference, [2016] | Includes
  bibliographical references and index.
Identifiers: LCCN 2016010960| ISBN 9781522505563 (hardcover) | ISBN
  9781522505570 (ebook)
Subjects: LCSH: Information technology--Economic aspects. | Information
  technology--Social aspects. | Human-computer interaction.
Classification: LCC HC79.I55 H864 2016 | DDC 303.48/34--dc23 LC record available at https://lccn.loc.gov/2016010960

This book is published in the IGI Global book series Advances in Human and Social Aspects of Technology (AHSAT) (ISSN: 2328-1316; eISSN: 2328-1324)

British Cataloguing in Publication Data
A Cataloguing in Publication record for this book is available from the British Library.

All work contributed to this book is new, previously-unpublished material. The views expressed in this book are those of the authors, but not necessarily of the publisher.

For electronic access to this publication, please contact: eresources@igi-global.com.

Advances in Human and Social Aspects of Technology (AHSAT) Book Series

Ashish Dwivedi
The University of Hull, UK

ISSN: 2328-1316
EISSN: 2328-1324

MISSION

In recent years, the societal impact of technology has been noted as we become increasingly more connected and are presented with more digital tools and devices. With the popularity of digital devices such as cell phones and tablets, it is crucial to consider the implications of our digital dependence and the presence of technology in our everyday lives.

The **Advances in Human and Social Aspects of Technology (AHSAT) Book Series** seeks to explore the ways in which society and human beings have been affected by technology and how the technological revolution has changed the way we conduct our lives as well as our behavior. The AHSAT book series aims to publish the most cutting-edge research on human behavior and interaction with technology and the ways in which the digital age is changing society.

COVERAGE

- Human Rights and Digitization
- Technoself
- Gender and Technology
- End-User Computing
- Technology Dependence
- Cyber Behavior
- Computer-Mediated Communication
- ICTs and social change
- Activism and ICTs
- Philosophy of technology

IGI Global is currently accepting manuscripts for publication within this series. To submit a proposal for a volume in this series, please contact our Acquisition Editors at Acquisitions@igi-global.com or visit: http://www.igi-global.com/publish/.

Titles in this Series

For a list of additional titles in this series, please visit: www.igi-global.com

Defining Identity and the Changing Scope of Culture in the Digital Age
Alison Novak (Rowan University, USA) and Imaani Jamillah El-Burki (Lehigh University, USA)
Information Science Reference • copyright 2016 • 316pp • H/C (ISBN: 9781522502128) • US $185.00 (our price)

Gender Considerations in Online Consumption Behavior and Internet Use
Rebecca English (Queensland University of Technology, Australia) and Raechel Johns (University of Canberra, Australia)
Information Science Reference • copyright 2016 • 297pp • H/C (ISBN: 9781522500100) • US $165.00 (our price)

Analyzing Digital Discourse and Human Behavior in Modern Virtual Environments
Bobbe Gaines Baggio (American University, USA)
Information Science Reference • copyright 2016 • 320pp • H/C (ISBN: 9781466698994) • US $175.00 (our price)

Overcoming Gender Inequalities through Technology Integration
Joseph Wilson (University of Maiduguri, Nigeria) and Nuhu Diraso Gapsiso (University of Maiduguri, Nigeria)
Information Science Reference • copyright 2016 • 324pp • H/C (ISBN: 9781466697737) • US $185.00 (our price)

Cultural, Behavioral, and Social Considerations in Electronic Collaboration
Ayse Kok (Bogazici University, Turkey) and Hyunkyung Lee (Yonsei University, South Korea)
Business Science Reference • copyright 2016 • 374pp • H/C (ISBN: 9781466695566) • US $205.00 (our price)

Handbook of Research on Cultural and Economic Impacts of the Information Society
P.E. Thomas (Bharathiar University, India) M. Srihari (Bharathiar University, India) and Sandeep Kaur (Bharathiar University, India)
Information Science Reference • copyright 2015 • 618pp • H/C (ISBN: 9781466685987) • US $325.00 (our price)

Human Behavior, Psychology, and Social Interaction in the Digital Era
Anabela Mesquita (CICE – ISCAP/Polytechnic of Porto, Portugal & Algoritmi Centre, Minho University, Portugal) and Chia-Wen Tsai (Ming Chuan University, Taiwan)
Information Science Reference • copyright 2015 • 372pp • H/C (ISBN: 9781466684508) • US $200.00 (our price)

Rethinking Machine Ethics in the Age of Ubiquitous Technology
Jeffrey White (Korean Advanced Institute of Science and Technology, KAIST, South Korea) and Rick Searle (IEET, USA)
Information Science Reference • copyright 2015 • 331pp • H/C (ISBN: 9781466685925) • US $205.00 (our price)

www.igi-global.com

701 E. Chocolate Ave., Hershey, PA 17033
Order online at www.igi-global.com or call 717-533-8845 x100
To place a standing order for titles released in this series, contact: cust@igi-global.com
Mon-Fri 8:00 am - 5:00 pm (est) or fax 24 hours a day 717-533-8661

Table of Contents

Detailed Table of Contents

Chapter 1

Sylvain K. Cibangu, Loughborough University, UK

Since evolving into an established science in the 1990s, the field of information and communication technologies for development (ICT4D) has seen unprecedented and fast-growing rates of publication, curriculum venues, and development projects around the globe. To this effect, ICT4D literature is informed by a variety of theories (e.g., capability approach, livelihoods, participatory development, etc.). In the process of asserting its body of knowledge, however, ICT4D has tended to dismiss the theory of modernization. For example, under labels such as technology fix, technology transplant, a computer per child, etc., the theory of modernization has been equated with the failures of and threats against development. Consequently, the theory of modernization has lost its value among development practitioners and theorists. This chapter assesses the theory of modernization. There is no such thing as a developed nation without modernization. The chapter derives some points of departure for ICT4D research.

Chapter 2

Madhuri V. Tikam, H. R. College of Commerce & Economics, India

Information and Communication Technologies (ICT) are extremely influencing every discipline under the sun including Education. It is affecting every aspect of education from teaching-learning to assessment and evaluation. It improves the effectiveness of education. It aids literacy movements. It enhances scope of education by facilitating mobile learning and inclusive education. It facilitates research and scholarly communication. Impact of ICT and its potential for the education field is manifold. It positively affects all the stakeholders of the education field. The current chapter discusses the same along with the various challenges posed by ICT. The challenges include economical issues, educational and technical factors. Appropriate content, Design and workability of ICT also play a crucial role in adoption of ICT in the education field. The chapter delineates in brief the challenges and probable solutions.

Chapter 3

Lester Leavitt, Florida Atlantic University, USA

This chapter explains the theory behind an information communication technology (ICT) being developed to provide marginalised populations with a tool for uniting the voices of progressive-minded activists. The theory suggests that with this technology, seemingly incompatible progressive groups might enlarge their campaigns for social equity, creating a global, heterogeneous network. The ICT allows for the capture of crowd-sourced artistic creativity, and through algorithms that have been shaped by academics in public administration, makes content retrievable as pluralistic, policy-supporting narrative threads. The new narratives should also work to alter the discourse within communities by diminishing the worldview threats associated with zero-sum ideology. This ICT is seen as vital because of how powerful lobbyists (funded by global elites) have consistently been successful in skewing the outcomes of policymaking decisions and elections. The system is firmly rooted in the small-group, consensus-building organisational theories of respected authors dating back to the 1970s.

Chapter 4

Geeta Nair, H R College of Commerce & Economics, India
Robert Hindle, University of Manchester, UK

The present research paper discusses the pivotal role of Information and Communication Technology (ICT) in education which is gaining currency in the new era of globalism as the telecom revolution has hastened the pace of globalization and vice-versa; along with the catalyst role ICT-enabled education plays in promoting inclusive growth and human development for all. These smart tools of the emerging smart economy would help to promote mass literacy and also narrow inter, as well as intra-generational gaps. Most importantly, it will provide 'second opportunities' to the generation that missed them in the first place, thus helping adult learners, particularly the employed and women; thus attempting to reduce gender inequities; particularly in South Asia and the Indian sub-continent. The case study of the famous open University, namely Indira Gandhi National Open University (IGNOU) in India is being studies as a case of sustainable development and inclusive growth as it 'reaches the unreached' and untouched and marginalized segments of society.

Chapter 5

Sarika Sawant, SHPT School of Library Science, SNDT Women's University, India

Collaborative learning experiences not only promotes critical thinking and reflection in students but also encourages them to develop a sense of community, thus enabling the creation of an environment in which further collaborative work can take place. While technologies to facilitate collaborative learning include a range of features and functionalities, this paper focuses on ten types of tools that deal with idea generation and brainstorming, mapping, design, online group work and document collaboration, and online communication. The present paper explains the online collaboration with its features, preparation required by institution and role of teacher presence in online learning. It highlights on ten different tools based on its function with suitable examples. It also explores paradigm shift from academic librarian to blended librarian, it's possible hurdles and benefits. The blended librarian is versed in both print and online tools and can help faculty meet course goals, regardless of the medium or technology. The paper concludes with how idea of online collaborative learning methodology is likely to evolve and make significant benefits to education, and probably to post educational business collaboration as well.

Chapter 6

Jorge Bernardino, Polytechnic of Coimbra - ISEC, Portugal
Pedro Caldeira Neves, Polytechnic of Coimbra - ISEC, Portugal

The importance of supporting decision making for improving business performance is a crucial, yet challenging task in enterprise management. The amount of data in our world has been exploding and Big Data represents a fundamental shift in business decision-making. Analyzing such so-called Big Data is becoming a keystone of competition and the success of organizations depends on fast and well-founded decisions taken by relevant people in their specific area of responsibility. Business Intelligence (BI) is a collection of decision support technologies for enterprises aimed at enabling knowledge workers such as executives, managers, and analysts to make better and faster decisions. We review the concept of BI as an open innovation strategy and address the importance of BI in revolutionizing knowledge towards economics and business sustainability. Using Big Data with Open Source Business Intelligence Systems will generate the biggest opportunities to increase competitiveness and differentiation in organizations. In this chapter, we describe and analyze four popular open source BI systems – Jaspersoft, Jedox, Pentaho and Actuate/BIRT.

Chapter 7

Sarika Sawant, SHPT School of Library Science, SNDT Women's University, India

E-learning includes several types of media that deliver text, audio, images, animation, and streaming video, and includes technology applications and processes such as audio or video tape, satellite TV, CD-ROM, and computer-based learning, as well as local intranet/extranet and web-based learning. E learning is a learner-friendly mode of learning, offering alternative, self-paced and personalised ways of studying. The present chapter explains the synchronous and asynchronous mode of e learning with its features. It also defines and summarises the impact of open source software on teaching and learning process. The numerous open source e learning tools are discussed with examples such as Open source LMS, Open source authoring tools, Open source audio editing software, Open source social bookmarking tools, Open source CMS etc. It also throws light on free e learning tools useful in e learning such as Slideshare, Youtube, Wikis, RSS, Wordpress etc. The search engines especially for academic purpose and for Open CourseWear are also discussed in the chapter. It identifies open courseware around the world spanning various subjects. The chapter concludes with e learning initiatives in India.

Chapter 8

Brian Semujju, Uganda Christian University, Uganda & University of Kwazulu-Natal, South Africa

This chapter discusses two issues prevalent in community media: Information communication technology (ICT) and Community participation. While several studies have explored community media and ICT in Uganda, the view that ICT has changed the way media operate to an extent of reversing the agenda-setting role to the listeners needed investigation. Using Kagadi-Kibale Community radio (KKCR), the chapter shows how ICT is spreading in one Ugandan region and the relationship that technology has with participation in community media activities. Findings show that there is need to redefine the relationship between ICT and geographically defined community media as usage of ICT is dependent on forces that still require decades to harmonize. The chapter therefore suggests that an alternative to community media, herein called Basic Media, is best suited to match the communication patterns of a developing world.

Chapter 9

Innovation is treated as a recognized driver of economic prosperity of a country through the sustained growth of its entrepreneurships. Moreover, recently coined term open innovation is increasingly taking the lead in enterprise management in terms of value addition. Foci of academics, researchers and practitioners nowadays are revolving around various innovation models, comprising innovation methods, processes and strategies. This chapter seeks to find out open innovation researches and practices that are being carried out circumscribing development of entrepreneurships, particularly the sector belonging to the small and medium enterprises (SMEs) through a longitudinal study. Along this context the chapter put forwards part of a continuous study investigating into researches in the area of open innovation for entrepreneurship development that are being carried out by leading researchers and research houses across the globe, and at the same time it also investigating open innovation practices that are being carried out for the development of entrepreneurships, emphasizing SMEs. Before conclusion the chapter has tried to develop a framework to instigate future research.

Chapter 10

A large number of ICT for development (ICT4D) projects experience a variety of challenges, especially when conducting field research with disadvantaged communities in developing nations. Using cluster analysis, this chapter identifies the six most common factors associated with a majority of ICT4D project challenges, and depicts the inter-relationship between these factors and over 100 distinct challenges reported by existing literature. In addition, based on the secondary analysis of 380 research artifacts in the ICT4D literature, this chapter proposes ways to manage the scope, time, costs, quality, human resources, communication, and risks for addressing ICT4D project challenges. Findings inform researchers of best practices for conducting ICT4D research with disadvantaged communities in developing nations.

Chapter 11

In spite of the increased acceptance by most of the corporate business houses around the world, the adaptation of strategies and concepts belonging to the newly evolved dimension of entrepreneurships, the opcn innovation (OI), countries in the East, West or South are yet to adapt appropriate strategies in their business practices, especially in order to reach out to the grass roots communities, or to the masses. So far, firms belonging to the small and medium sized enterprises (SMEs) sector, irrespective of their numbers and contributions towards their national economies are lagging behind far in accepting open innovation strategies for their business advancements. While talking about this newly emerged business dimension, it comprises of complex and dynamically developed concepts like, management of various aspects of intellectual property, administration of patents, copyright and trademark issues or supervision of market trend for minute details related to knowledge acquisition. All these issues are largely responsible to add value to the business plan in terms of economy or knowledge gain, and organizations acting in this aspect deserve comprehensive researches and investigations. As most of the developed countries are already in their advanced stage in adopting open innovation strategies, finding this as a weak link in terms of entrepreneurships in less developed countries, this chapter intends to seek answers related to the mentioned issues focusing adaption of open innovation strategies in developing and transitional economies. It is a study on business houses or national efforts from countries belonging to these categories, deducting from a longitudinal literature review. The chapter goes on looking into other aspects of business development incorporating various OI concepts, synthesizes to build a reasonable framework to be applicable in the target economies, points out to some future research aspects and concludes the finding of this research. This study expects to enhance knowledge of entrepreneurs, academics and researchers by gaining specific knowledge on trend of open innovation strategies in developing and transitional countries.

Chapter 12

While talking about successful entrepreneurship and value addition within an enterprise through innovation, one could realize that the innovation paradigm has been shifted from simple introduction of new ideas and products to accumulation of diversified actions, actors and agents along the process. Furthermore, when the innovation process is not being restricted within the closed nature of it, the process takes many forms during its evolution. Innovations have been seen as closed innovation or open innovation, depending on its nature of action, but contemporary world may have seen many forms of innovation, such as technological innovation, products/service innovation, process/production innovation, operational/ management/organizational innovation, business model innovation or disruptive innovation, though often they are strongly interrelated. Definition of innovation has also adopted many transformations along the path, incorporating innovations within the products, process or service of an enterprise to organizational, marketing, or external entities and relations. Nature and scope of agents and actors even varies widely within the innovation dynamics, when the open innovation techniques are being applied to enterprises, designated as the small and medium enterprises (SMEs). This study will conduct extensive literature review on various patterns of open innovation (crowdsourcing or collaborative), investigate case studies to learn about intricate issues surrounding their operational strategies (conducted by European Commission, OECD and similar institutions) and conduct surveys among selected SMEs (email, web based, egroups) in several phases. Research design includes formulation of strategies to resolve acquired research questions; collection and recording of the evidences obtained from the literature review or case studies or surveys; processing and analyzing gathered data and their appropriate interpretations; and publication of results. Analysis will include both qualitative (descriptive and exploratory) and quantitative (inferential statistics) methods.

Chapter 13

Christopher Chepken, University of Nairobi, Kenya

This chapter covers design experiences gained by working with two Non-Governmental organizations and one day-labour organization for the informal job seekers and employers—day-labour market (DLM). The three design architectures implemented for the DLM organizations are presented. On critically discussing the designs, it is found that even when users are portrayed as similar in the way they work and the things they do, their Information Management Systems (IMS) functional software requirements remain contextual up to the details. The synthesis of the designs shows that there is need to focus on the different functional information needs, including the ones that may seem insignificant even where non-functional requirements may be the same for seemingly similar users. From this argument, it is important that information systems designers, especially for Day labour market organizations, should go deeper into their users and beyond the "about us" information to understand the unique features and requirements of each user group. In conclusion, designers should not assume that seemingly similar organizations/users can be approached from the "one size fits all" IMS perspective.

Foreword

With the advancement of information and communication technology (ICT) the daily life pattern of human beings has improved dramatically. At the same time with the use of mobile technologies and social networks, communications have widened to a many-to-many format, connecting people beyond place and time. Technologies have become ubiquitous, supporting almost each and every aspect of human life; utilizing these technologies human development has advanced manifolds and evolving patterns.

Modern ICTs are being used in the classroom for versatile learning and out of the classroom for lifelong learning. Similarly, ICTs are being used in the field of scientific research, engineering science, medical science and health related issues, business entrepreneurship development, community development, socio-economic development and other fields. ICTs have improved peoples' way of life far more than ever before.

In these aspects, a book on human development and interaction, utilizing ubiquitous technologies, deserves the deepest attention from the perspectives of both research and practice. It is a pleasure to learn that IGI has taken the initiative to publish an edited book on this subject. I wholeheartedly wish this book great success and expect that it will serve as a valuable resource in current research on the topic.

Syed Saad Andaleeb
BRAC University, Bangladesh & Pennsylvania State University, USA

Syed Saad Andaleeb, *Ph.D. is Vice Chancellor at the BRAC University, Bangladesh, Distinguished Professor Emeritus at the Pennsylvania State University, and Editor of the Journal of Bangladesh Studies.*

Preface

PREAMBLE

UNDP has been defining human development as "the process of enlarging people's choices," said choices being allowing them to "lead a long and healthy life, to be educated, to enjoy a decent standard of living", as well as "political freedom, other guaranteed human rights and various ingredients of self-respect" (UNDP, 1997, p. 15). Human development is a well-being concept within a field of international development. It involves studies of the human condition with its core being the capability approach (Google/Wikipedia definition).

The word "ubiquitous" can be defined as "existing or being everywhere at the same time", "constantly encountered", and "widespread". When applying this concept to technology, the term ubiquitous implies that technology which is everywhere and we use it all the time (RECT, 2016). Ubiquitous technology is often wireless, mobile and networked, making its users more connected to the world around them and the people in it.

Along this discourse, human computer interaction (HCI) came into being with the mission of understanding the relationship between humans and computers. However, the relationship has altered radically with the changes in socio-technical arena that many researchers and practitioners are questioning about its domain and reach in upcoming years. Computer systems have entered into our lives in such a way that it appears that they are monitoring as well as guiding us, including the provision of providing all-out support in versatile forms (Sellen, Rogers, Harper & Rodden, 2009, Echeverria, Nussbaum, Calderon, Bravo, Infante & Vasquez, 2011, Jacko, 2012).

The contemporary world is changed by technologies which have profoundly transformed our living. Computers are increasingly becoming part of our daily environments, in public places like airports and shopping malls, or in private places such as our home and office. This transformation has extended our minds to become open to the world. With versatile usage of computers, it has become part and parcel of our livelihood and living (Rogers, 2009).

Simultaneously, with affordable computing devices, like mobile phones, accessibility has increased across the globe. More and more people are using computing devices to reach each other in various forms and natures. In the age of this technology era, through the utilization of social networks, the reach of usability has become ubiquitous in nature. A village farmer in the Amazon, a schoolchild in Nigeria, or an elderly person from Australia is communicating with each other uninterruptedly across the globe at any time, at any place.

Upholding these concepts and contexts, the book, has tried to include research topics and agendas on ubiquitous usage of technologies for human development. The book has incorporated topics from e-learning and e-business to topics on open innovation with emphasis on ICT4D.

ORGANIZATION OF BOOK CHAPTERS

Chapter one discusses about a specific trend in the aspect of information and communication technologies for development (ICT4D) that is modernization. Since evolving into an established science in the 1990s, the field of ICT4D has seen unprecedented and fast-growing rates of publication, curriculum venues, and development projects around the globe. To this context, ICT4D literature is informed by a variety of theories, such as capability approach, livelihoods, participatory development and others. In the process of asserting its body of knowledge, however, ICT4D has tended to overlook the theory of modernization. For example, under labels such as technology fix, technology transplant, a computer per child, etc., the theory of modernization has been equated with the failures of and threats against development. At the same time, the theory of modernization has lost its value among development practitioners and theorists. This chapter assesses the theory of modernization. The author argues that there is no such thing as a developed nation without modernization. The chapter derives some points of departure for contemporary ICT4D research.

Information and Communication Technologies (ICT) are tremendously influencing every discipline under the sun including Education. It is affecting every aspect of education from teaching-learning to assessment and evaluation. It improves the effectiveness of education. It aids literacy movements. It enhances scope of education by facilitating mobile learning and inclusive education. It facilitates research and scholarly communication. Impact of ICT and its potential for the education field is manifold. It positively affects all the stakeholders of the education field. Chapter two discusses the various aspects of ICT in education along with the various challenges posed by ICT. Author argues that the challenges include economical issues, educational and technical factors. Author further argues that appropriate content, design and workability of ICT also play a crucial role in adoption of ICT in the education field. The chapter delineates in brief the challenges and probable solutions.

Chapter three explains the theory behind an information communication technology (ICT) being developed to provide marginalized populations with a tool for uniting the voices of progressive-minded activists. The theory suggests that with this technology, seemingly incompatible progressive groups might enlarge their campaigns for social equity, creating a global, heterogeneous network. The author emphasizes that the ICT allows for the capture of crowd-sourced artistic creativity, and through algorithms that have been shaped by academics in public administration, makes content retrievable as pluralistic, policy-supporting narrative threads. In this aspect, the new narratives should also work to alter the discourse within communities by diminishing the worldview threats associated with zero-sum ideology. This ICT is seen as vital because of how powerful lobbyists have consistently been successful in skewing the outcomes of policymaking decisions and elections. The author also emphasizes that the system is firmly rooted in the small-group, consensus-building organizational theories of respected authors dating back to the 1970s.

The use of Information and Communication Technology (ICT) in education, which is gaining momentum in the new era of globalism as the telecom revolution has hastened the pace of globalization and vice-versa; along with the catalyst role ICT-enabled education plays in promoting inclusive growth and human development for all. Chapter four discusses the use of ICT in the Indian classroom. Author argues that ICT in education is becoming universally popular and widespread as people across the length and breadth of the globe are looking at ways and means to improve educational access through modern technology and techniques. Along this context, author further argues that emerging economy like India embarked on their 'New Economic Policy' in 1991 with the help of accelerating economic growth facilitated by modern technology and communication systems in almost all areas ranging from banking to trade to education.

Collaborative learning experiences not only promotes critical thinking and reflection in students but also encourages them to develop a sense of community, thus enabling the creation of an environment in which further collaborative work can happen. While technologies to facilitate collaborative learning include a range of features and functionalities, chapter five focuses on ten types of tools that deals with idea generation and brainstorming, mapping, design, online group work and document collaboration, and online communication. This chapter explains the online collaboration with its features, preparation required by institution and role of teacher presence in online learning. It highlights various tools based on its function with suitable examples. It also explores paradigm shift from academic librarian to blended librarian, possible hurdles and benefits. The blended librarian is versed in both print and online tools and can help faculty meet course goals, regardless of the medium or technology. The chapter concludes with how the idea of an online collaborative learning methodology is likely to evolve and make significant benefits to education, and probably to post-educational business collaboration as well.

New advances of Information and Communication Technologies (ICT) continue to rapidly transform how business is performed and change the role of information systems in business and our daily life. In this context, the importance of supporting decision making for improving business performance is becoming crucial and at the same time, a challenging task in enterprise management. The amount of data in our world has been exploding and Big Data represents a fundamental shift in business decision-making. Analyzing such so-called Big Data is becoming a keystone of competition and the success of organizations which depend on fast and well-founded decisions taken by relevant people in their specific area of responsibility. Business Intelligence (BI) is a collection of decision support technologies for enterprises aimed at enabling knowledge workers such as executives, managers, and analysts to make better and faster decisions. Chapter six reviews the concept of BI as an open innovation strategy and address the importance of BI in revolutionizing knowledge towards economics and business sustainability. Authors emphasize that using Big Data with Open Source Business Intelligence Systems will generate the biggest opportunities to increase competitiveness and differentiation in organizations. In this chapter, authors describe and analyze four popular open source BI systems - Jaspersoft, Jedox, Pentaho and Actuate/BIRT.

E-learning includes several types of media which delivers text, audio, images, animation, and streaming video, and includes technology applications and processes, such as audio or video tape, satellite TV, CD-ROM, and computer-based learning, as well as local intranet/extranet and web-based learning. E learning is a learner-friendly mode of learning, offering alternative, self-paced and personalized ways of studying. Chapter seven explains the synchrosdnous and asynchronous mode of e learning with its available features. It also defines and summarizes the impact of open source software on teaching and learning process. The numerous open source e learning tools are being discussed with examples, such as Open source LMS, Open source authoring tools, Open source audio editing software, Open source social bookmarking tools, Open source CMS and others. It also throws light on free e learning tools useful in e learning such as Slideshare, Youtube, Wikis, RSS, Wordpress etc. The search engines especially for academic purposes and for Open CourseWear are also discussed in the chapter. Furthermore, it identifies open courseware around the world spanning various subjects. The chapter concludes with various e learning initiatives in India.

Chapter eight discusses about two issues that are prevalent in community media, such as Information communication technology (ICT) and Community participation. While several studies have explored community media and ICT in Uganda, the view that ICT has changed the way media operate to an extent of reversing the agenda-setting role to the listeners needed further investigation. Using Kagadi-Kibale Community radio (KKCR), the chapter shows how ICT is spreading in one Ugandan region and the relationship that technology has with participation in community media activities. Findings of this research show that there is need to redefine the relationship between ICT and geographically defined community media as usage of ICT is dependent on forces that still require decades to harmonize. The chapter, therefore, suggests that an alternative to community media, herein called Basic Media, is best suited to match the communication patterns of a developing world.

Along the context of ICT4D, innovation is treated as a recognized driver of economic prosperity of a country through the sustained growth of its entrepreneurships. Moreover, recently coined term open innovation is increasingly taking the lead in enterprise management in terms of value addition. Foci of academics, researchers and practitioners nowadays are revolving around various innovation models, comprising innovation methods, processes and strategies. Chapter nine seeks to find out various open innovation researches and practices that are being carried out circumscribing development of entrepreneurships, particularly the sector belonging to the small and medium enterprises (SMEs) through a longitudinal study. Along this context, the chapter put forwards part of a continuous study investigating into researches in the area of open innovation for entrepreneurship development that are being carried out by leading researchers and research houses across the globe, and at the same time it is also investigating open innovation practices that are being carried out for the development of entrepreneurships, emphasizing on SMEs. Before conclusion the chapter has tried to develop a framework to instigate future research.

It is well known that a large number of ICT for development (ICT4D) projects experience a variety of challenges, especially when conducting field research with disadvantaged communities in developing nations. Using cluster analysis, chapter ten identifies the six most common factors associated with a majority of ICT4D project challenges, and depicts the inter-relationship between these factors and over 100 distinct challenges reported by existing literature. In addition, based on the secondary analysis of 380 research artifacts in the ICT4D literature, this chapter proposes ways to manage the scope, time, costs, quality, human resources, communication, and risks for addressing ICT4D project challenges. Findings of the research inform researchers about the best practices for conducting ICT4D research with disadvantaged communities in developing nations.

In spite of the increased acceptance by most of the corporate business houses around the world, the adaptation of strategies and concepts belonging to the newly evolved dimension of entrepreneurships, the open innovation (OI), countries in the East, West or South are yet to adapt appropriate strategies in their business practices, especially in order to reach out to the grass roots communities, or to the masses. So far, firms belonging to the small- and medium-sized enterprises (SMEs) sector, irrespective of their numbers and contributions towards their national economies are lagging behind far in accepting open innovation strategies for their business advancements. While talking about this newly emerged business dimension, it is comprised of complex and dynamically developed concepts like, management of various aspects of intellectual property, administration of patents, copyright and trademark issues or supervision of market trend for minute details related to knowledge acquisition. All these issues are largely responsible to add value to the business plan in terms of economic or knowledge gain, and organizations acting in this aspect deserve comprehensive research and investigation. As most of the developed countries are already in the advanced stage in adopting open innovation strategies, finding this as a weak link in terms of entrepreneurships in less developed countries, chapter eleven intends to seek answers related to the mentioned issues focusing adaption of open innovation strategies in developing and transitional economies. It is a study on business houses or national efforts from countries belonging to these categories, deducting from a longitudinal literature review. The chapter goes on looking into other aspects of business development incorporating various OI concepts, synthesizes to build a reasonable framework to be applicable in the target economies, points out to some future research aspects and concludes the finding of this research. This study expects to enhance knowledge of entrepreneurs, academics and researchers by gaining specific knowledge on trends of open innovation strategies in developing and transitional countries.

While talking about successful entrepreneurship and value addition within an enterprise through innovation, one could realize that the innovation paradigm has been shifted from simple introduction of new ideas and products to accumulation of diversified actions, actors and agents along the process. Furthermore, when the innovation process is not being restricted within the closed nature of it, the process takes many forms during its evolution. Innovation has been seen as closed innovation or open innovation, depending on its nature of action, but the contemporary world may have seen many forms of innovation, such as technological innovation, products/services innovation, process/production innovation, operational/management/organizational innovation, business model innovation or disruptive innovation, though often they are strongly interrelated. Definition of innovation has also adopted many transformations along the path, incorporating innovations within the products, process or service of an enterprise to organizational, marketing, or external entities and relations. Nature and scope of agents and actors even vary widely within the innovation dynamics, when the open innovation techniques are being applied to enterprises, designated as small and medium enterprises (SMEs).

Researching in this paradigm, one has to look for some underlying issues that should be attended through responding to research questions as the research continues. Among many of the fundamental questions on innovation advancement for SMEs development there are a few, how to acquire precise information on the flow-chart of their business operations, gain knowledge on specific parameters of their business processes, utilizing existing potential capacities to extend their knowledge towards successful innovation acquisition and dissemination, and to extend their knowledge platform through various capacity development initiatives. They aggregate further, when issues of opportunities and challenges are being researched along the path of SME development through open innovation. Along these aspects, chapter twelve ascertains diverse aspects of opportunities and challenges surrounding the open innovation processes, and designs action plans to empower SMEs in reaching out to the grass roots communities utilizing open innovation strategies. Primary focus of this research is to enable SMEs in finding out their innovation potentiality and empower them through various capacity development initiatives. However, the specific focus will adhere to adaptable technology transfer through open innovation. Along the route to justify the research potential and validate the research hypotheses (whether this research will add any economic value or knowledge gain), this study will conduct an extensive literature review on the various patterns of open innovation (crowdsourcing or collaborative), investigate case studies to learn about intricate issues surrounding their operational strategies (conducted by European Commission, OECD and similar institutions) and conduct surveys among selected SMEs (email, web based, egroups) in several phases. Research design includes the formulation of strategies to resolve acquired research questions; collection and recording of the evidences obtained from the literature review or case studies or surveys; processing and analyzing gathered data and their appropriate interpretations; and publication of results. Analysis included both qualitative (descriptive and exploratory) and quantitative (inferential statistics) methods.

Chapter thirteen covers design experiences gained by working with two non-governmental organizations and one day-labor organization for the informal job seekers and employers—day-labor market

(DLM). The three design architectures implemented for the DLM organizations are presented. On critically discussing the designs, it is found that even when users are portrayed as similar in the way they work and the things they do, their Information Management Systems (IMS) functional software requirements remain contextual up to the details. The synthesis of the designs shows that there is a need to focus on the different functional information needs, including the ones that may seem insignificant even where non-functional requirements may be the same for seemingly similar users. From this argument, it is important to note that information systems designers, especially for Day labor market organizations, should go deeper into their users and beyond the "about us" information to understand the unique features and requirements of each user group. The chapter concludes that designers should not assume that seemingly similar organizations/ users can be approached from the "one size fits all" IMS perspective.

CONCLUSION

Including research and case studies ranging from e-learning to open innovation, this book has created a separate sphere of study in the aspect of ICT4D. The book will find importance not only in the research arena to researchers, but also in the practical world to practitioners. The book stands on its own with the inclusive research potential and innovative study.

Hakikur Rahman
BRAC University, Bangladesh
February 2016

REFERENCES

Echeverria, A., Nussbaum, M., Calderón, J. F., Bravo, C., Infante, C., & Vásquez, A. (2011). Face-to-face collaborative learning supported by mobile phones. *Interactive Learning Environments*, *19*(4), 351–363. doi:10.1080/10494820903232943

Jacko, J. A. (Ed.). (2012). *Human Computer Interaction Handbook: Fundamentals, Evolving Technologies and Emerging Applications*. CRC Press. doi:10.1201/b11963

RECT. (2016). What. Retrieved from http://www.rcet.org/ubicomp/what.htm

Rogers, Y. (2009). *The changing face of human-computer interaction in the age of ubiquitous computing*. Berlin, Heidelberg: Springer. doi:10.1007/978-3-642-10308-7_1

Sellen, A., Rogers, Y., Harper, R., & Rodden, T. (2009). Reflecting human values in the digital age. *Communications of the ACM*, *52*(3), 58–66. doi:10.1145/1467247.1467265

UNDP. (1997). Human Development Report 1997.

Acknowledgment

Editor gladly acknowledges the relentless support and generous assistance from all authors that are involved in the accumulation of manuscripts, revision and finalization of various studies and research outcomes, without which the project could not have been satisfactorily accomplished.

Special thanks go to the enthusiastic and brilliant publishing team at the IGI Global. Particularly to Eleana Wehr for her suggestions, supports, feedbacks and co-operations for keeping the project on schedule, and to Mehdi Khosrow-Pour, Jan Travers and Caitlyn Martin for their continuous professional guidance. Finally, sincere thanks go to my family, friends and colleagues for their love and support.

Hakikur Rahman
BRAC University, Bangladesh
February 2016

Chapter 1
The Contribution(s) of Modernization Theory to ICT4D Research

Sylvain K. Cibangu
Loughborough University, UK

ABSTRACT

Since evolving into an established science in the 1990s, the field of information and communication technologies for development (ICT4D) has seen unprecedented and fast-growing rates of publication, curriculum venues, and development projects around the globe. To this effect, ICT4D literature is informed by a variety of theories (e.g., capability approach, livelihoods, participatory development, etc.). In the process of asserting its body of knowledge, however, ICT4D has tended to dismiss the theory of modernization. For example, under labels such as technology fix, technology transplant, a computer per child, etc., the theory of modernization has been equated with the failures of and threats against development. Consequently, the theory of modernization has lost its value among development practitioners and theorists. This chapter assesses the theory of modernization. There is no such thing as a developed nation without modernization. The chapter derives some points of departure for ICT4D research.

INTRODUCTION[1]

Technology has been the product and conduit of human wellbeing throughout recorded history. In recent decades, ICT4D has seen its body of literature grow at an indescribable speed.[2] From a vast array of disciplines, various theories have been imported and implemented in an attempt to best accommodate the goals, scopes, and benefits of development in our poverty-plagued world. Chief among imported theories are the capability approach, livelihoods, participatory development, and modernization theory (Clark, 2006, 2007; Fuchs, 2013; Heeks, 2006, 2007; 2010a, 2010b, 2014c, 2014d; Heeks and Molla, 2009; Harriss, 2014; Jacobsen, 2015; Kleine, 2009, 2013; Mosse, 2013; Potter, Binns, Smith, & Elliott, 2008; Potter, Conway, Evans, & Lloyd-Evans, 2012; Sandum, 2010; Unwin, 2009a, 2009b, 2009c, 2009d; Williams, 2014). In the meantime, modernization theory has come to represent the failures of and threats against

DOI: 10.4018/978-1-5225-0556-3.ch001

development practice (He, 2012a, 2012b; Marsh, 2014; Peet & Hartwirck, 2015). In the same vein, it is not uncommon that development is viewed as philanthropic and/or rural work comprised of small-scale endeavors, with concepts such as micro-finance, small-scale enterprise, micro-credit, micro-loan, etc. For better or worse, the dominance of statistical (sweeping) generalization has left a significant impact on much of the research into ICT4D and its corollary ICT [Information and Communication Technology] (see May, Dutton, & Munyakazi, 2014, p. 50). This chapter is not claiming to dismiss micro-level data, especially with regard to micro-analysis, rather it is calling into question the ways in which modernization theory has been shunned altogether. For example, there is no such thing as a developed society or nation without modernization. The chapter seeks to map the history of development to best capture the moves or patterns in which modernization theory is seen to be rooted.

Background

Development is a concept hailed from a variety of fronts. A glaring example is with Village Phone, a development project founded by Nobel Prize Muhammad Yunus in Bangladesh in 1981 to provide rural women with micro-credits (Aminuzzaman, 2002; Aminuzzaman, Baldersheim, & Jamil, 2003; *Bank for the Poor*, 2014; Singhal, Svenkerud, Malaviya, Rogers, & Krishna, 2005; Yunus, 2007). The Bangladesh project has been copied and pasted in developing countries around the world. Despite the buzz about rural micro-credits, Bangladesh remains one of the poorest nations in the world, and its human conditions continue to deteriorate (Legge, 2014). Although not the topic of this chapter, micro-credit has been misrepresented and misdiagnosed as the prescription of development required of all societies. More pertinently, Abraham (2011) warned,

If I were to make the argument that the use of credit cards [micro-credit] led to ... the removal of poverty in the US, that will be a fairly laughable proposition... People overpromised in terms of what micro-finance could do... Often in time, people misdiagnosed survival [in rural areas] as entrepreneurship.

No country has become developed by the mere distribution of micro-credits. In other words, just like any micro-project, micro-credit cannot replace development nor eradicate poverty. As has been remarked about entrepreneurship, micro-credit is only a fraction of, if not a diversion from, what development entails for modern day societies.

To add to the challenge, no sustainable development has ever occurred without broad-based undertakings to improve people's living conditions. This does not mean that small-scale enterprises cannot make a difference, but that due to its complex nature, development requires authors to think big. With simplistic and charity-limited views of development, ICT4D authors cannot think big. The main reason might be the deification of information access and usage. Looking at the status of ICT4D projects sponsored by the Canadian IDRC [International Development Research Centre] around the world, Diga (2013a) reminded us,

However, the key assumption underlying this work [ICT4D] – that the poor could be moved out of poverty simply by providing them with ICT and information access and usage – was a limited one. Just comparing the haves and have-nots was not enough to understand the broader development issues of poverty. As work in this field moved forward, the effects of ICTs on the lives of the poor were identified as key issues that were missing and that required the attention of researchers in this area. (p. 127)

Although needed in rural areas, access to and usage of information technologies do not converge to replace the work of modernization hitherto neglected. The mere implementation of information technologies is not the solution either (Diga, 2013b, p. 156). A broader and multi-faceted view of modernization has the potential to substantially change the lives of the poor.

For ease of discussion, two concepts central to this chapter need to be clarified, namely: modernization and development. Modernization has preoccupied humans under different circumstances, at different times, and in different spaces. In more ways than one, the concept development has been envisaged as the endeavor to modernize people's lives. As Currie-Alder, Kanbur, Malone, and Medhora (2014) wrote, "concern over development has been with us as long as people have existed, for it is fundamentally about *the improvement of the human condition* [emphasis added]" (p. 3). The need to improve human conditions has always preoccupied humans.

Besides the literary meaning reserved for the historical period of Modern Times, *The Oxford American dictionary* (1999) defines the verb modernize as the endeavor to adapt to modern needs and habits, and the adjective modern as that which is of the present and recent times. To modernize simply means to improve and/or adapt the conditions of societies. The word modernization comes from the Latin adjective *modus*, meaning: of the present, of just now, etc. or *modernus*, meaning: things or institutions of the present. Several Latin words derive from this adjective, such as the noun *moderamen*, meaning: management, direction, control, etc., the verb *modero,* and its participle *moderatus*, meaning to manage, moderate, keep within due bounds, etc. The underlying meaning (Lewis & Short, 1879) is that of management, order, bounds, extent, etc. Interestingly, the Greek word μέδομαι [medomai] from which the Latin words cited above derived has stronger connotations. Medomai (Liddell & Scott, 1843/1996) means to provide for, be mindful of, to plan, contrive, devise, etc. With these etymologies one can get an idea of what modernize tends to imply. Modernization is the extent to which one manages, provides for, and plans welfare in response to people's needs and habits. At varying degrees, the connotations drawn from the etymology and semantics of the word modernization resonate in the discussions that have characterized the efforts of development over time.

The second and last theme to define is development. Different understandings of development have been adopted by researchers, based on selected research questions and proposed theories. Thus, a clarification of the term development is needed for our discussion. A thorough analysis of social science literatures reveals five key conceptions of development: (a) psychological, (b) infrastructural, (c) philanthropic, (d) economic, and (e) journalistic. First, the psychological conception defines development as the unfolding and the optimal manifestation of human personality (Greve, 2001; Kalsched, 2013; Lerner, 2001; Harris & Butterworth, 2002; Thornton, 2008). Second, the infrastructural conception describes development as the product of urbanization and/or infrastructure and facility construction (Perry, 2001). The infrastructural conception has led to the English word developer, which means constructor. Third, the philanthropic conception, most common in development studies, takes development to mean humanitarian and/or rural work undertaken with new digital technologies for the welfare of people in developing countries (Clark, 2006, 2007; Elliott, 2008; Heeks, 2007, 2010a, 2010b, 2014a, 2014b, 2014c, 2014d; Heeks & Jagun, 2007; Heeks and Molla, 2009; Jagun, 2007; Kleine, 2009, 2013; Duncombe, 2012a, 2012b; Heeks, Subramanian, & Jones, 2013; Mohan, 2008; Potter, Binns, Smith, & Elliott, 2008; Potter, Conway, Evans, & Lloyd-Evans, 2012; Thirlwall, 2008; Smith, 2013; Unwin, 2009a). Fourth, the economic conception of development involves specific metrics, such as GDP, GNP, medical care, currency, salary, etc. (Ashraf, Weil, & Wilde, 2013; Henderson, Storeygard, & Weil, 2012; Kanbur, 2002; Sandum, 2010; Weil, 2012). Fifth and last, the journalistic conception of development concerns the unfolding of events, achievements, and phenomena (Sheller, 2015; Xiong *et al.*, 2014). Inexplicably, attempts to conceptualize development come to us in silos. In other words, all too often, the conceptions of development outlined above remain buried in separate bodies of work, which do not cite nor learn from each other.

In addition, much of recent literature takes development to be a holistic process (Acemoglu & Robinson, 2013; Buenstorf, 2012; Currie-Alder, Kanbur, Malone, & Medhora, 2014; Harriss, 2014; Giugale, 2014; Lockner, 2013; Mosse, 2013; Liddy, 2013; Peet & Hartwick, 2015; Potter, Conway, Evans, & Lloyd-Evans, 2012; Smith, 2012; Williams, 2014; Yamarik & Ghosh, 2015). This book chapter presents development as an integrated phenomenon needed to achieve the wellbeing of individuals and their societies. For example, in a state-of-art description of development, Kleine (2013) argued, "Sen's understanding focuses on freedom of choice in the personal, economic, and political spheres, making it a remarkably *holistic approach to human development* [emphasis added]" (p. 4). In slightly different terms, Giugale (2014) reiterated Kleine's remark, saying, "at its most basic level, economic development is the process through which a community creates material wealth and uses it to improve the well-being of its members. This calls for many interrelated ingredients" (p. 1). Perhaps the major reason is that the limitations of economic development have caused authors to engage with broader perspectives of development. The measurements of poverty are one of the areas in which traditional economic development has proven to be unproductive (Alkire *et al.*, 2015; Alkire, Roche, & Sumner, 2013; Chambers & Von Medeazza, 2013; Dulani, Mattes, & Logan, 2013; Hofmeyr, 2013; Mattes, 2008; Mattes & Bratton, 2009).

Subsequently, the holistic approach calls authors to undertake synergic work. As Currie-Alder, Kanbur, Malone, and Medhora (2014) reminded us, "thinking on development is pulling together, breaking out of disciplinary silos and drawing on ideas, concepts, and theories across the natural and social sciences" (p. 2, also see Giugale, 2014, p. 1). Not surprisingly, ICT4D has been criticized for its parochial or bubble-centered research. Heeks (2014d) noted,

Alongside these specific topics, the paper diagnoses a set of cross-cutting issues. It recognises the need for practice to break out of the "ICT4D bubble" and engage more with the development mainstream through a reorientation of ICT4D's scope, language and worldview. (p. 1)

As shown below, the realm of development and of its corollary modernization proves to be multi-faceted and cross-disciplinary. Development is taken in this chapter in a broad sense to mean people's holistic and integrated welfare. Put differently, it can be said that development

simply suggests improvement in the conditions and quality of life of the population. Greater levels of wealth, technological advancement, and public policies permit people to live better, to consume more, to feed themselves better, and to get sick less frequently. (Filguiera, 2001, pp. 3583-3584)

These definitions recollect specific reactions and positions that have emerged in the history of the concept development. After the introduction, the present chapter is divided into three phases: (a) history of development, (b) modernization theory, and (c) practical consequences.

HISTORY OF DEVELOPMENT

Although the term development has been a subject of debate in the last few decades, it traces back to Antiquity, with the idea that humans have the tendency to progress and/or deteriorate. Despite its roots in Antiquity, our concept of development continues to be reminiscent of and synonymous with the notion of the West. Yet, ancient cultures around the globe have presented humans as en route to a better state of living, both on earth and after death. For instance, Buddhism teaches that *Nirvana* is the ultimate stage of wellbeing (Amstrong, 2001). Civilization was another term used by authors to indicate wellbeing. Thorough review of historical materials reveals that different peoples developed and exemplified the idea of civilization, such as the Ethiopians, Egyptians, Arabs, Babylonians, Indians, and Greeks.

The earliest record of development is that of the civic work undertaken in ancient Egypt by the official Nefer-seshem-re (2,345 BC). Apparently living in an affluent and more advanced city, and conscious of undignified poverty, Nefer-seshem-re pointed to development that includes both the spiritual and material dimensions of human dignity. As he related his experience,

I have left my city, I have come down from my province, having done what is right (maat)... I spoke maat and did maat. I spoke well and I reported well... I rescued the weak from the hand of one stronger than he when I was able. I gave bread to the hungry, clothing (to the naked), a landing for the boatless. I buried him who had no son, I made a boat for him who had no boat. (Lichtheim, 1973, p. 17)

The official's concern for the relief of his constituents from deprivation and destitution is clear in the above statement. The official did not delight in the mere provision of bread to the poor, but he lived and strove for justice first, protected the vulnerable from mistreatment, did the burial for the poor who was unable to do so, provided the transportation means to the person who had none, etc. Therefore, development was thought to involve material, ethical, emotional, and spiritual obligations.

In the 5th century BC, appalled at widespread misery, suffering, and absurd deaths, Buddha (Amstrong, 2001) suggested radical management and progressive monitoring of greed as the best way of ensuring wellbeing. In his *Laws*, Plato (5-4th c. BC, 1967) made extensive use of the concept development and/or non-development, so to speak, with words such as modern, progress, movement, etc. Plato wrote, "that from which one should always observe the progress of States as they move towards either goodness or badness" (III, 676a). Nations were seen to have progressed as developed and non-developed. The idea of a nation's choice to opt or not opt for development is clear here. Plato considered his contemporaries as modern or more advanced. "For none of them [individuals of past societies] had the shrewdness of the modern man to suspect a falsehood; but they accepted as true the statements made about gods and men, and ordered their lives by them" (III, 679c). History was seen as a passage from a low to a high status. Perhaps the most influential author of development/progress was the 5th-century Greek thinker Heraclitus with his famous idea "that all things move and nothing remains still... you cannot step twice into the same stream" (Plato, 5-4th c. BC, 1921, 402a). The word development is not literally used, but the point made here implies a process with which (social) reality changes for better or worse. Movement is presented to be universal in nature (e.g., individuals, societies, facts, ideas, etc.).

As in Antiquity, the Middle Ages saw the expansion of technology and human values and ideals (Burke, 1999; Copenhaver & Schmitt, 2002). In the Middle Ages, for example, the press and public buildings (e.g., museums, cathedrals, universities, etc.) witnessed tremendous modernization across Europe. Up to this point in history, modernization displays a distinct flavor of universal human values and works. Only in the 1700s and onward, with the Modern Times, more specifically, with the Industrial Revolution, did the concept development start to crystallize around Western societies and ideologies.

Historically, modernization is the process of change towards those types of social, economic, and political systems that have developed in Western Europe and North America from the seventeenth century to the nineteenth and have then spread to other European countries and in the nineteenth and twentieth centuries to the South American, Asian, and African continents. (Eisenstadt, 1966, p. 1)

From the 18th century on, the imitation of Western societies has gained prestige among development authors. Modernization or a nation's progress was thought to be exemplified by the industrial achievements implemented in England (Kumar, 2005; Wagner, 2001). This was a major turning point for the interpretation of the term development. It was exactly in this context that the British economist Adam Smith (1723-1790) wrote his seminal book, *Wealth of Nations* (Smith, 1776/1961), to inquire about the ways in which nations could manage the trade of goods to increase their wealth. Smith's book (book 1), for example, posits that civilization started around the Mediterranean Sea (i.e., Western Europe). Smith's work is considered to be the masterpiece of international development. It is important to clarify that the concept international development, very commonly used in lieu of development studies, came into play to emphasize the welfare of and trade between nations, not societies and/or individuals. It is also important to keep in mind that development has to engage individuals' daily lives.

For better or worse, the most decisive factor in the westernization of development lies in the idea of the stage-like evolution of societies that dominated the 19th century. The book published by the American anthropologist and legal expert Lewis H. Morgan (1818-1881) argued that societies follow three stages: savagery, barbarism, and civilization (Morgan, 1877/1985). Civilization was presented by Morgan to be the ultimate stage characterized by Western writing and technology. This book left an immense impact on social theorists, with the belief that Western societies were the accomplished beacon of societal evolution. To a great extent, development theories will not escape this influence. The Western stage-compounded scheme of development received a greater focus from the Morganian presentation of societies. However, it should be noted, although it is not always acknowledged, that not all authors cherished and centered the idea of stages exclusively on Western societies. The French sociologist Emile D. Durkheim (1858-1917), with his work on the division of labor (Durkheim, 1893/2007), presented societies as organisms involved in a process of evolution from a primitive to a modern state. Durkheim understood the evolution of societies as that of biological organisms which interact with their environment. Such evolution had nothing to do with being Western or non-Western. The German philosopher Karl H. Marx (1818-1883) explained modernization to the extent that the modes of technology production are owned and managed by the proletariat. Marx thought that modern progress would be an empowerment of the proletariat. Though he mainly analyzed firms in Western societies, Marx (1847/1955, 1867/1977) saw the end of oppression and exploitation through the proletariat's ownership and leadership as the makers of development, irrespective of whether it was a Western or non-Western society. Marx devoted extensive attention to poverty in Europe and around the world. As one can see, while the idea of stages for societies' evolution received greater attention in the 19th century, it was not, and should not, be equated with the West. It is inexplicable that this non-Westernized and universal dimension of development, apparent since Antiquity (as discussed above), escapes development authors when it comes to modernization theory.

The Westernized view of development has dominated the social sciences for a long time. Consequently, development carries the meaning of Westernization. A plain proof of Westernization is seen when Nisbet

(1969) postulated, "developmentalism is one of the oldest and most powerful of all Western ideas; very little in the Western study of social change, from the early Greeks down to our own day, falls outside the perspective of developmentalism" (p. vii). This includes progress, process, evolution, continuity, system, and the like. Beyond a shadow of doubt, Nisbet (1986) persisted, "development, as I have suggested, is not only an old idea of Western thought, it is one of the master ideas of the West, to be found in virtually every major system since the time of the Eleatic [pre-Socratic of Elea, a city in ancient Greece] philosophers" (p. 42). Note how the Egyptian, Platonian, and Buddhist portions were left out, let alone the West-crystallized idea of development is not confirmed by a thorough analysis of ancient writings. For instance, Aristotle and other ancient Greek philosophers expressed a great admiration for the Egyptian civilization. A number of Greek philosophers enjoyed travelling to Egypt (Bernal, 2000; Meltzer, 2000; Vrettos, 2001). Moreover, civilizations such as the Babylonians, Maya (Peru), Monomotapa (Africa), and others reflected significant aspects of development (Diehl, 2004; Haughton, 2007; Shank, 2000; Wilmot, 1896; Wright & Zegarra, 2000). It follows that development/modernization is not and should not be a Western idiosyncrasy. One of the consequences of development's westernization was that literature has equated development with a stage-structured phenomenon or with the idea of evolution centered on Western Europe. North America can be considered as the product of Western Europe.

The question as to why modernization continued to be centered on Western Europe finds part of its answer in the aftermath of World War II. After World War II, the successful reconstruction of war-devastated countries in Europe reinforced the Industrial Revolution-inherited perception of development. Todaro (1997) replicated this perception, saying,

When interest in the poor nations of the world began to materialize following the Second World War, economists in the industrialized nations were caught off guard. They had no readily available conceptual apparatus with which to analyze the process of economic growth in largely peasant, agrarian societies characterized by the virtual absence of modern economic structures. But they did have the recent experience of the Marshall Plan, under which massive amounts of U.S. financial and technical assistance enabled the war-torn countries of Europe to rebuild and modernize their economies in a matter of a few years... was it not true that all modern industrial nations were once underdeveloped agrarian societies?... The utility of massive injection of capital and the historical pattern of the now developed countries – was too irresistible to be refuted by scholars, politicians, and administrators in rich countries [emphasis added]. (p. 71)

In this sense, development consists of a uniform and linear formula that all nations, at the example of successfully rebuilt European countries, had to follow in order to access modernity. For this very reason, "development then became a mechanism for the extension to the Third World of the dominant economic rationality of the West" (Escobar, 2005, p. 141). Development was an economic recipe to be transplanted to developing countries.

Nevertheless, at the turn of the second half of the 20th century, postmodernism (Rosenau, 1995; Ward, 2003) put Western-propelled ideas (e.g., development) under attack. In essence, postmodernists rejected the idea of centralized authority and truth, and defended individuality and locality as the referent of truth and progress. The rise of postmodernism constitutes another decisive factor in the de-westernization of development. As apparent below, development detractors have foregrounded locally managed organizational leadership in rejection of a European-imported and top-down imposed authority through which development was undertaken or proposed. A decentralization of authority therefore has been seen as one of the key paths toward the welfare of those concerned.

The history of development has provided us with a broader background of modernization theory. As is now clear, our notion of development has shifted over time, often returning to the language and culture of the West. In sum, development discussions have engaged a wide range of concerns and themes from Antiquity to the present era, all of which provide materials for modernization. The Industrial Revolution, the idea of stage-driven evolution of societies, and the rebuilding of World War II-destroyed nations in Europe have played a major role in the germination and interpretation of modernization theory.

MODERNIZATION THEORY

As an articulated social doctrine, modernization theory took shape after World War II. Modernization theory has unfolded along the lines of four major strides. Although instigated by the same goal, namely development, the four strides of modernization theory had developed under different circumstances, for different purposes, and with different proponents. First, one of the most well-known examples of modernization theory is the Green Revolution. Despite criticism, the Green Revolution's development impact has gained fame across the globe (Perkins, 1997). Thanks to technological advances, the Green Revolution helped make high yielding grains available around the world. The project arguably started in Mexico in the first half of the 1940s, with technology as a central focus at each stage toward development. In the 1940s, Borlaug (2000a, 2000b) propounded modernization theory on the basis of technology-propelled high yielding grains. This model focused more on technology and science than on Western societies, and the exemplary experiment was that of Mexico and China. Under the banner of Green Revolution, the goal of the project was to allow greater agricultural productivity around the world. In his late writing, Borlaug (2000b) vigorously defended the importance of technology-improved agricultural yields. Borlaug wrote,

The breakthrough in wheat and rice production in Asia in the mid-1960s, which came to be known as the Green Revolution, symbolized the process of using agricultural science to develop modern techniques [emphasis added] for the Third World. It began in Mexico with the "quiet" wheat revolution in the late 1950s. During the 1960s and 1970s in India, Pakistan, and the Philippines received world attention for their agricultural progress (Table 1). Since 1980, China has been the greatest success story. Home to one-fifth of the world's people, China today is the world's biggest food producer. With each successive year, its cereal crop yields approach that of the United States. (p. 4)

While the statement relates to food production, it involves modern techniques as the key element of development. When implemented, these techniques precipitate core aspects of development. Borlaug (2000b) elaborated,

China has been more successful in achieving broad-based economic growth and poverty reduction than India. Nobel Economics Laureate, Professor Amartya Sen, attributes this to the greater priority the Chinese government has given to investments in rural education and health care services. Nearly 80 percent of the Chinese population is literate while only 50 percent of the Indian population can read and write. (p. 6)

Modernization theory is clearly presented to be a successful tool with which to develop human societies. The second stride of modernization theory took place in the 1950s and 1960s. The 1950s and 1960s saw a greater emphasis placed on modernization as a stage-driven and Western Europe-modeled enterprise. Noted authors of this Western-revived trail of modernization theory were P. Berger, B. Berger, and Kellner (1973), Huntington (1968), Organski (1965), and Rostow (1960). This school of thought led critics in the late 1960s and the 1970s to simply equate development with Western domination and interests (Escobar, 1995). With varied hardships such as lack of infrastructure, health services, security, and sanitation system, people's lives in rural areas displayed distinct determinants whose forces needed a salvation plan. According to its Western-focused logic, modernization theory implies that the greater is the technology, the greater is the development. Conceived of as a step-by-step process, modernization theory served to lay out the plans as to how non-Western or developing nations would copy and paste Western societies. As Kiely (2006) summarized,

Modernization theory was the dominant sociological theory of development for much of the 1950s and 1960s. Its principal claim was that development was a process in which 'societies' – defined as nations states – pass through similar stages of development on the road to an end state... The claims of modernization theory can be traced back to the nineteenth and eighteenth centuries... Modernization theorists argued that development represented a transition from tradition to modernity. This was achieved through copying at least some of the (perceived) characteristics of Western societies, such as the development of entrepreneurship and the borrowing of advanced technology. Enhanced contact with the West was considered desirable as it hastened the transition to modernity. (p. 395)

As seen above, the Westernization of development, inherited primarily from the 19th century, was presented as integral to modernization, although development is not a phenomenon limited to Europe and North America. It is important to bear in mind that this is how a great many development critics have viewed, and still view, development processes (detail below).

Two important consequences can be derived from the Westernization of development. First, although they are not always clearly outlined, the consequences that exclusively culminate in the emulation of the West- proposed stages, also called carriers or packages of modernization (P. Berger, B. Berger, & Kellner, 1973), become the major conditions of development success. The success is determined in the way in which the stages are either conceptualized or implemented. On this note, there are no preset preferences, depending on what Western sector and/or society one is interested in (e.g., city planning, transportation, education, hospital, bank, etc.). Usually, stages are conceived in advance and imposed on or applied to societies afterward, irrespective of local conditions and circumstances. The second consequence involves the leadership and organization. Modernization theorists of the second stride tend to impose what is commonly known as the top-down hierarchy. The reason being, the proposed stages and the leadership are coming from above and outside. The immediate result is that local realities are largely ignored or at least minimized.

One can easily anticipate the reaction of critics. As Mohan (2008) argued, "'normal' development is characterized by biases – Eurocentricism, positivism and top-downism – which are disempowering... The tendency is to equate development with the modernity achieved by 'Western' societies and to copy them through planning by experts" (p. 46). Modernization has been equated with imposed leadership and predetermined packages of development. Packages were described as technology fix, technology implant, or technology answer (Verzola, 2006). Inspired by postmodernism (see above), critics have propounded locality and bottom-up authority and organization as the best way of ensuring development.

Critics have propagated non-Western principles in rebuttal against development since development epitomizes a Western agenda, ideology, and/or interests.

[Critics] argue that the development project is inherently Western and based on the exercise of power over subject peoples in the South... [Critics] suggest that an alternative is support for social movements that are said to reject the inherent Westernization of the development project, and which support a variety of alternatives to the homogenising discourse of development. (Kiely, 2006, p. 398)

According to this approach, the freer developing nations are from the oppression of the West, the more opportunity they gain for development. Freedom from Western exploitation is thought to provide more opportunities of self-ruled development. Not only technology, but Western values and ideas were applied to non-Western societies. Williams (2001) denounced "a wholesale attempt at transplanting Western values to Third World countries in terms of models of economic and political development. Non-Western nations," Williams clarified, "[are] to glide smoothly towards democracy under the same preconditions experienced in the West" (p. 312). To date, such anti-Western development criticism continues to gain currency in a shaky world economy by calling into question the interests of the West. As Harrison and Huntington (2000) noted, 'the liberal and democratic capitalist model of the West...offers the best way of organizing a society that humankind has been able to devise" (p. 167). In this context, critics have found development to be a conduit of Western domination insofar as economic models of the West are read as a panacea for improving the conditions of non-developed societies.

In the field of ICT4D, where many development projects have been met with failure, the rejection of the development concept has received rapid acceptance. Poignantly, Escobar (1995) criticized Western imperialism for its *developmentalist* guise. He observed,

The discourse and strategy of development produced its opposite: massive underdevelopment and impoverishment, untold exploitation and oppression, the debt crisis, the Sahelian famine, increasing poverty, malnutrition, and violence are the only most pathetic signs of the failure of forty years of development. (p. 4)

From a different angle, Esteva (1987) argued, you "must be either very dumb or very rich if you fail to notice that development stinks" (p. 135). It is critical "to resist," Esteva went on, "the destruction of their [the poor or minorities'] local spaces by modernizers and developers (sustainable or other, including the proponents of green or eco-development)" (Esteva & Prakash, 1998a, p.10). The criticism radically rejected all development-related terms such as sustainable, green, ecosystem, developed countries, Third World, globalization, etc.

Not surprisingly, in the late 1990s, interest in development has significantly diminished. Escobar (1992) claimed, "the dream of development is over" (p. 419). One further discredit on the word development is its association and equation with colonization. Development should aim for the liberation of the poor from colonization (the West) in order to produce the best results. Consequently, development was separated from the concept modernization. As Kiely (2006) stated, "a commitment to development needs to be separated from a commitment to modernization theories, and the debate continues to take place *within* [italics in original] rather than outside the discourse of development" (p. 399). Development has been reassessed at the exclusion of modernization. The dissociation of development with modernization/colonization implied a prior rapport with and/or equation made between modernization and Western domination (as shown earlier). Meanwhile, in the process of revised development, criticism of Western domination can obscure uncritical populism and local dynamics of oppression and repression. Recall that, as also argued earlier, according to Marx, for example, the elimination of oppression and repression (not only that of the West) constituted the goals of modernization in the 19th century.

The third stride of modernization theory, yet often forgotten, is that of contemporary non-Western societies, the most illustrious of which is Japan. Japan has used motored-vehicle technology to significantly improve the wellbeing of its population. Eisenstadt noted,

In the first decades of the twentieth century it [Japan] could compare very well with any Western country on indices of "modernization," urbanization, levels of education, communication, and the like... From the 1950s on, Japan constituted a major focus in the burgeoning studies of modernization. (1996, pp. 2-3)

The exact details as to how a technology-driven development can be applied to all societies remain an interesting question for modernization researchers. Japan embodies a potent illustration of non-Westernized modernization of our times. Indeed, "relatively quickly, however, it was noted not only that Japan," as Eisenstadt (1996) emphasized, "became the sole non-Western country to become fully and relatively successfully industrialized and modernized" (p. 3). But Eisenstadt (1996) went on to say "that it [Japan] appeared to organize its life in *ways radically different from the West* [emphasis added]" (p. 3). For concision reasons, this book chapter has not included several cases of emerging non-Western developed societies such as South Korea, Hong Kong, Thailand, and Malaysia. Nor has this book chapter considered instances of modernization in Antiquity such as Egypt, Maya, Monomotapa, China, etc. (Diehl, 2004; Haughton, 2007; Rojas, 2010; Shank, 2000; Vrettos, 2001; Waldron, 1983, 1990; Wilmot, 1896; Wright & Zegarra, 2000). It bears noting that ancient Egypt, a case of its kind in recorded history, with its gigantic pyramids, was a superpower for two millennia, not to mention the Great Wall of China whose work (of more than 6,250.00 km [3,883.57 mi] masonry) involved unparalleled large-scale modernization, engineering planning, and technology supply.

The fourth and last stride of modernization is that of multiple paths of modernization, also called multiple modernities (Escobar, 2010; Martinelli, 2015; Trakulhun & Weber, 2015). The goal is to propose a broader realm of modernization paths, of which Western societies represent only a fraction. It is inexplicable that this strand of multiple modernities has remained unknown in ICT4D literature. It follows that ICT4D research continues to relay simplistic and skewed views of modernization theory. Meanwhile, one of the most vocal figures of the multipath scheme of modernization, is Escobar (2010), who was not long ago the staunchest opponent of modernization theory. In his reassessment of modernization theory, all too forgotten, Escobar reinstated the concept development. Escobar (2010) wrote,

It has been said of the notion of post-development (Escobar 1995) that it pointed at a pristine future where development would no longer exist. Nothing of the sort was intended with the notion, which intuited the possibility of visualizing an era where development ceased to be the central organizing principle of social life [emphasis in original] and which, even more, visualized such a displacement as already happening in the present. (2010, p. 11)

Development remains a central theme with which to organize and improve social reality. The goal is to allow development endeavors that embrace alternative and plural modernizations in contrast to Euro-centric modernization. To explain, the modernization line of thought "could be moving at the very least beyond the idea of a single, universal modernity and towards a more plural set of modernities" (Escobar, 2010, p. 3). While modernization has been understood as Western development, it has become a development program of multiple modernities. Present at all times and under different circumstances, and vivid at the core of human actions struggling between the old and the new, modernity presents a spectrum too complex to be limited to a single facet of human existence, be it the North America or Western Europe. The point being, "Western modernity is simply one modernity among others" (Mouzelis, 1999, p. 143). Modernization is thus the idea that sets of broad social transformations or industrializations, namely: education, health, housing, water supply, transportation, electricity, food supply, clothing, etc. have integrated or linked local particular entities with the state entity. An important dimension of this broad-based integration was that local and private individuals are given sovereignty over the political order – through critical and rational discussion over matters of general interest. These all-encompassing social transformations "although fully institutionalized in the West, have a more universal character" (Mouzelis, 1999, p. 142). It is also worth noting that "no society can advance or even survive in the present world without acquiring the broad economic, political, cultural, and social modern features" (Mouzelis, 1999, p. 151). One major advantage of this stride of modernization is its insistence on the universal character of modernization. This allows authors to criticize any violation of basic human rights, monopoly of the political order by the state, fraudulent elections, repressive use of military force, and undemocratic access and exercise of power seen in a number of non-Western societies or modernities.

As a line of thought, multiple modernities are not recent; they go as far back as Antiquity with the notion of progress and movement being universal in all things and people. In 1993, for example, as modernization theory was gaining in prominence, Habermas cautioned against exaggeration, saying,

I think that instead of giving up modernity and its project as a lost cause [of development], we should learn from the mistakes of those extravagant programs which have tried to negate modernity... The project of modernity has not yet been fulfilled... The project aims at a differentiated relinking of modern culture with an everyday praxis...under the condition that societal modernization will also be steered in a different direction.... out of ... an almost autonomous economic system and its administrative complements. (pp. 106-107)

As clear from the cited statement, modernization is essential to people's development and is intended to take different directions and praxes. Authors should not deprive the world's poorest from modernity. Note that there is alarming and increasing evidence of poverty within rich and poor nations alike (see Jarrett, 2013, p. 3). Therefore, development means multiple, multidirectional, communicative, and interactive modernization, based on people's needs, situations, cultures, etc. Sustained inquiry into the development of Japan and other newly industrialized nations of South East Asia, not to mention cases of Antiquity (discussed above), can supply ICT4D with constructs and variables different from those of the West.

Curiously enough, plural modernities are best translated by new ICTs (i.e., social media, mobile technologies, virtual communities, etc.) in the sense that ICTs resist the full-fledged Euro-modernization plan of development. In effect, the information age represents a trail of modernity couched in the Enlightenment dream that knowledge/information is a power with which to dominate natural forces and improve individuals' lives and their societies. As Escobar (2009) elaborated,

[ICTs and] cyberspace can be seen as a de-centralised archipelago of relatively autonomous zones in which communities create their own media and process their own information... ICTs and cyberspace tend to promote the creation of networked cultures without the homogenised identities assumed by the mass media, they foster routes for the circulation of ideas that are not so subject to centralised controls and the irruption of subcultures that are aware of the need to re-invent social and political orders [modernities]. (p. 394)

ICTs provide a plural platform of modernization wherein development can be experienced differently by different people. Modernity no longer translates domination and colonization, but rather it consists of collegially created and shared life-worlds. Already propelled by Habermas (1981, 1993), the idea of multiple modernities has been explored by Arnason (2002) in relation to the Japanese experience. Euro-modernity represents all but one way of being modern. As Martinelli (2015) put it, "modernity has gone global and at the same time takes different forms" (p. 5). One key idea behind this argument is that, "global modernity unifies and divides the globe in new ways" (Dirlik, 2003, p. 277). More interestingly, even in Europe, a monolithic euro-modernity is being shown counterproductive to a prosperous European Union (Sen, 2011). To be productive, discussions of modernity require more informed and informative research about the literature surrounding it.

PRACTICAL CONSEQUENCES

Several practical consequences can be derived to advance ICT-related research. It should now become clear that the four strides of modernization theory speak to a vast array of modernization paths and theorists who readily escape hasty accounts of development. Inexplicably, the most common interpretation of modernization has been that of Western-stages model, which leaves aside invaluable development literatures. Much of this interpretation came, to use Fuchs' (2013) characterization, "as the ICT4D 'storm' was building" (p. 5). It is important to take a fuller picture of modernization theory in order to provide firmer and fairer arguments of development. For the sake of this discussion, I have selected the three most important arguments of modernization theory. First, modernization is integral to social reality and its management as seen in the history of development from Antiquity to date. To modernize is simply to provide for and manage our wellbeing in its varied facets. To this end, technology can and should be the answer. Examples where technology is the answer include: housing, cooking, transportation, health, bridge, dam, etc.

The second argument concerns organizational leadership. Met with great fanfare, bottom-up leadership has been hailed as the most empowering organizational style among development practitioners and theorists (Prahalad, 2005). However, this is a simplistic view of human societies. Indeed, as Palmer, Dunford, Rura-Polley, and Baker (2001) insisted,

Centralized procedures are still necessary parts of an organization's operations... [The reason being] innovations [e.g., modernization] are systemic and in need of strategic coordination to enable them to be achieved successfully, something which is more difficult in a decentralized, virtual organizational setting. (p. 192)

There is no such thing as a developed society without strong and centralized authority and leadership. It is erroneous to argue that development is incompatible with centralized (top-down) authority. Van den Ham (2004) and Castells (2010), for example, showed successful instances of top-down-driven development. Centralized authority does not mean, although it can, authoritarianism. Democratic and alternating mandates ensure that those in power are accountable and removable, and their good actions can be evaluated and affirmed for the greater good of the community. While acknowledging the utility of centralized organizational style, Castells (2010) posited, "their main distinctive trend [of South Korean enterprises] is that all firms in the network are controlled by a *central* holding company... The central holding company," Castells specified, "is backed by government banks and by government-controlled trading companies... Most of the firms... are relatively sizeable, and they work under the coordinated *initiative of the top, centralized management* [emphasis added]" (pp. 191-192). This is not to say that decentralized organization cannot foster wellbeing, but that development very well engages centralized leadership. Accountable and term-restricted leaders implement and pursue coordinated and consulted initiatives of development.

The third and last argument relates to infrastructures. It is problematic that development authors have made micro-projects and –finances the center stage of development studies, leaving infrastructures (macro-projects) to the discretion of politicians and affluent donors. No one can manage and develop a society without infrastructures, however expensive and demanding they can be. So long as they are not researched from various fronts and disciplines (besides engineering), infrastructures will remain prohibitively expensive. It is also problematic that macro-projects of development have been scarce around the world and in ICT4D literature. This is largely due to the silos of conceptions from which ICT authors have been assessing and repudiating the concepts development and modernization. No developed societies have developed with mere humanitarian and philanthropic projects. This is not to disregard, for example, the wonderful work of humanitarian helpers in times of disaster. Rather, modernization needs broader and stronger insights, commitments, and analyses of our societies. To give another example, it should make sense that, in conformity with environmental requirements/challenges, NGOs put their energy and time together to build dams and highways across developing countries.

CONCLUSION

It is completely unfair to continue to see modernization theory as the villain of development. From its etymology and semantics to Antiquity and present times, modernization theory graces us with invaluable meanings, which make it a robust tool of development research and practice. In lieu of hasty, fragmentary, and condemnatory accounts, modernization theory lays claim to ICT4D sustained inquiry and in-depth discussions. Development is not quintessentially synonymous with the West, nor is locality exempt from the structures of oppression and repression. This is not to say that colonialism and/or imperialism do not exist, but that the modernization of our world cannot fare well with simplistic views of development. Modernization is a multi-paths forum in which researchers are called to manage the wellbeing of societies by responding and catering to people's needs and habits. With modernization, researchers are encouraged to keep societies and their activities within due bounds. Not one author or practitioner can develop the world without modernization theory, or help the world's poorest with mere philanthropic gestures and wishes. Just like any scientific theory, modernization theory calls for more informative, broader, and firmer inquiries into people's wellbeing within both rich and poor nations. To this end, silo-lodged, charity-dependent, and modernization-demonizing conceptions of development are neither helpful for ICT4D and ICT uses nor conducive to the improvement of people's lives. Micro-projects should be paired with and integrated into comprehensive macro-development projects.

REFERENCES

Abraham, R. (2011). The poor are no different from us. *The Economist*. Retrieved from http://www.economist.com/blogs/banyan/2011/10/reuben-abraham-market-solutions

Acemoglu, D., & Robinson, A. J. (2013). *Why nations fail: The origins of power, prosperity and poverty*. London: Profile Books.

Alkire, S. et al.. (2015). *Multidimensional poverty index: Measurement and analysis*. New York, NY: Oxford University Press. doi:10.1093/acprof:oso/9780199689491.001.0001

Alkire, S., Roche, M. J., & Sumner, A. (2013). Where do the world's multidimensionally poor people live? *Oxford University Department of International Development OPHDI Working Papers No 61*. Retrieved from http://www.ophi.org.uk/resources/ophi-working-papers/

Aminuzzaman, M. S. (2002). Cellular phones in rural Bangladesh: A study of the Village Pay Phone of Grameen Bank. In A. Goldstein & D. O'Connor (Eds.), *Electronic commerce for development* (pp. 161–178). Paris: OECD.

Aminuzzaman, S., Baldersheim, H., & Jamil, I. (2003). Talking back! Empowerment and mobile phones in rural Bangladesh: A study of the village phone scheme of Grameen Bank. *Contemporary South Asia*, *12*(3), 327–348. doi:10.1080/0958493032000175879

Armstrong, K. (2001). *Buddha*. New York, NY: Penguin.

Arnason, P. J. (2002). Multiple modernities and civilizational contexts: Reflections on the Japanese experience. In J. P. Arnason (Ed.), *The peripheral centre. Essays on Japanese history and civilization* (pp. 132–157). Melbourne, Australia: Trans Pacific Press.

Ashraf, Q. H., Weil, D. N., & Wilde, J. (2013). The effect of fertility reduction on economic growth. *Population and Development Review*, *39*(1), 97–130. doi:10.1111/j.1728-4457.2013.00575.x PMID:25525283

Bank for the poor. (2014). *Grameen Bank*. Retrieved from http://www.grameen.com/

Berger, L. P., Berger, B., & Kellner, H. (1973). *The homeless mind: Modernization and consciousness*. Oxford, UK: Penguin.

Bernal, M. (2000). Animadversions in the origins of Western science. In M. H. Shank (Ed.), *The scientific enterprise in Antiquity and the Middle Ages* (pp. 72–83). Chicago: Chicago University Press.

Borlaug, E. N. (2000a). Ending world hunger: The promise of biotechnology and the threat of antiscience zealotry. *Plant Physiology*, *124*(2), 487–490. doi:10.1104/pp.124.2.487 PMID:11027697

Borlaug, E. N. (2000b). *The Green Revolution revisited and the road ahead*. Retrieved from http://nobelprize.org/nobel_prizes/peace/laureates/1970/borlaug-lecture.pdf

Buenstorf, G. (Ed.). (2012). *Evolution, organization, and economic behavior*. Northampton, MA: Edward Elgar. doi:10.4337/9780857930897

Burke, P. (1999). *The European Renaissance: Centres and peripheries*. New York, NY: Blackwell.

Castells, M. (Ed.), (2010). The information age: Economy, society and culture (Vol 1, 2nd ed., with a new preface). Malden, MA: Blackwell.

Chambers, R., & Von Medeazza, G. (2013). Sanitation and stunting in India: Undernutrition's blind spot. *Economic and Political Weekly*, *48*(25), 15–18.

Cibangu, K. S. (2013). A reconsideration of modernization theory: Contribution to ICT4D's research. *International Journal of Information Communication Technologies and Human Development*, *5*(2), 86–101. doi:10.4018/jicthd.2013040106

Clark, A. D. (Ed.), (2006). *The Elgar companion to development studies*. Northampton, MA: Edward Elgar. doi:10.4337/9781847202864

Clark, A. D. (2007). Adaptation, poverty and well-being: Some issues and observations with special reference to the capability approach and development studies. *Work Paper Series 081 Global Poverty Research Group University of Manchester*. Retrieved from http://www.gprg.org/pubs/workingpapers/pdfs/gprg-wps-081.pdf

Copenhaver, P. B., & Schmitt, B. C. (2002). *Renaissance philosophy (Foreword by P.O. Kristeller)*. New York, NY: Oxford University Press.

Currie-Alder, B., Kanbur, R., Malone, M. D., & Medhora, R. (2014). The state of development thought. In B. Currie-Alder, R. Kanbur, D. M. Malone, & R. Medhora (Eds.), *International development: Ideas, experience, and prospects* (pp. 1–16). New York, NY: Oxford University Press. doi:10.1093/acprof:oso/9780199671656.003.0001

Diehl, A. R. (2004). *The Olmecs: America's first civilization*. London: Thames and Hudson.

Diga, K. (2013a). Access and usage of ICTs by the poor (Part I). In L. Elder, H. Emdon, R. Fuchs, & B. Petrazzini (Eds.), *Connecting ICTs to development: The IDRC experience* (pp. 117–135). New York, NY: Anthem Press.

Diga, K. (2013b). Local and economic opportunities and ICTs: How ICTs affect livelihoods (Part II). In L. Elder, H. Emdon, R. Fuchs, & B. Petrazzini (Eds.), *Connecting ICTs to development: The IDRC experience* (pp. 137–160). New York, NY: Anthem Press.

Dirlik, A. (2003). Global modernity? Modernity in an age of global capitalism. *European Journal of Social Theory*, *6*(3), 275–292. doi:10.1177/13684310030063001

Dulani, B., Mattes, R., & Logan, C. (2013). After a decade growth in Africa, little change in poverty at the grassroots. *Afrobarometer Policy Paper No 1*. Retrieved from http://www.afrobarometer.org/files/documents/policy_brief/ab_r5_policybriefno1.pdf

Duncombe, R. (2012a). Understanding mobile phone impact on livelihoods in developing countries: A new research framework. *IDPM Development Informatics Working Paper no.48*. Retrieved from http://www.sed.manchester.ac.uk/idpm/research/publications/wp/di/index.htm

Duncombe, R. (2012b). Mobile phones for agricultural and rural development: A literature review and future research directions. *IDPM Development Informatics Working Paper no.50*. Retrieved from http://www.sed.manchester.ac.uk/idpm/research/publications/wp/di/index.htm

Durkheim, E. (2007). *De la division du travail social*. Paris: PUF. (Original work published 1893)

Eisenstadt, S. N. (1966). *Modernization: Protest and change*. Englewood Cliffs, N.J: Prentice-Hall.

Eisenstadt, S. N. (1996). *Japanese civilization: A comparative view*. Chicago: University of Chicago Press.

Elliott, A. J. (2008). Development and social welfare/human rights. In V. Desai & R. B. Potter (Eds.), *The companion to development studies* (2nd ed., pp. 40–45). London: Hodder Education.

Escobar, A. (1992). Reflections on "development,": Grassroots approaches and alternatives politics in the Third World. *Futures, 24*(5), 411–436. doi:10.1016/0016-3287(92)90014-7

Escobar, A. (1995). *Encountering development: The making and unmaking of the Third World*. Princeton, NJ: Princeton University Press.

Escobar, A. (2005). Economics and the space of modernity: Tales of markets, production and labour. *Cultural Studies, 19*(2), 139–175. doi:10.1080/09502380500077714

Escobar, A. (2009). Other worlds are (already) possible: Self-organization, complexity, and post-capitalist cultures. In J. Sen & P. Waterman (Eds.). *World social forum: Challenging empires* (pp. 393-404). New York, NY: Black Rose.

Escobar, A. (2010). Latin America at crossroads: Alternative modernizations, post-liberalism, or post-development? *Cultural Studies, 24*(1), 1–65. doi:10.1080/09502380903424208

Esteva, G. (1987). Regenerating people's space. *Alternatives, 10*(3), 125–152. doi:10.1177/030437548701200106

Esteva, G., & Prakash, S. M. (1998). *Grassroots post-modernism: Remaking the soil of cultures*. London: Zed.

Filgueira, H. C. (2001). Social development. In N. J. Smelser & P. B. Baltes (Eds.), *International encyclopedia of the social and behavioral sciences* (Vol. 6, pp. 3583–3587). New York, NY: Elsevier. doi:10.1016/B0-08-043076-7/03343-X

Fuchs, R. (2013). From heresy to orthodoxy: ICT4D at IDRC. In L. Elder, H. Emdon, R. Fuchs, & B. Petrazzini (Eds.), *Connecting ICTs to development: The IDRC experience* (pp. 1–17). New York, NY: Anthem Press.

Giugale, M. M. (2014). *Economic development: What everyone needs to know*. New York, NY: Oxford University Press.

Greve, W. (2001). Successful human development: Psychological conceptions. In N. J. Smelser & P. B. Baltes (Eds.), *International encyclopedia of the social and behavioral sciences* (Vol. 10, pp. 6970–6974). New York, NY: Elsevier. doi:10.1016/B0-08-043076-7/01693-4

Habermas, J. (1993). Modernity an incomplete project. In T. Docherty (Ed.), *Postmodernism: A reader* (pp. 98–109). New York, NY: Harvester Wheatsheaf.

Habermas, J., & Ben-Habib, S. (1981). Modernity versus postmodernity. *New German Critique, NGC, 22*(22), 3–15. doi:10.2307/487859

Harris, M., & Butterworth, G. (2002). *Developmental psychology: A student's handbook*. New York, NY: Psychology Press.

Harrison, L., & Huntington, P. S. (2000). *Culture matters*. New York, NY: Basic Books.

Harriss, J. (2014). Development theories. In B. Currie-Alder, R. Kanbur, D. M. Malone, & R. Medhora (Eds.), *International development: Ideas, experience, and prospects* (pp. 35–49). New York, NY: Oxford University Press. doi:10.1093/acprof:oso/9780199671656.003.0003

Haughton, B. (2007). *Hidden history: Lost civilizations, secret knowledge, and ancient mysteries (foreword by F. Joseph)*. Franklin Lakes, NJ: The Career Press.

He, C. (2012a). Introduction. In C. He (Ed.), *Modernization science: The principles and methods of national advancement* (pp. 1–65). New York, NY: Springer. doi:10.1007/978-3-642-25459-8_1

He, C. (2012b). History of Modernization. In C. He (Ed.), *Modernization science: The principles and methods of national advancement* (pp. 153–180). New York, NY: Springer. doi:10.1007/978-3-642-25459-8_3

Heeks, R. (2006). Analysing the software sector in developing countries using competitive advantage theory. *IDPM Development Informatics Working Paper no.25*. Retrieved from http://www.sed.manchester.ac.uk/idpm/research/publications/wp/di/index.htm

Heeks, R. (2007). Theorizing ICT4D research. *Information Technologies and International Development, 3*(3), 1–4. doi:10.1162/itid.2007.3.3.1

Heeks, R. (2010a). Do information and communication technologies (ICTs) contribute to development? *Journal of International Development, 22*(5), 625–640. doi:10.1002/jid.1716

Heeks, R. (2010b). Development 2.0: The IT-enabled transformation of international development. *Communications of the ACM, 53*(4), 22–24. doi:10.1145/1721654.1721665

Heeks, R. (2014a). From the MDGs to the post-2015 agenda: Analysing changing development priorities. *IDPM Development Informatics Working Paper no.56*. Retrieved from http://www.sed.manchester.ac.uk/idpm/research/publications/wp/di/index.htm

Heeks, R. (2014b). Future priorities for development informatics research from the post-2015 development agenda. *IDPM Development Informatics Working Paper no.57*. Retrieved from http://www.sed.manchester.ac.uk/idpm/research/publications/wp/di/index.htm

Heeks, R. (2014c). ICTs and poverty eradication: Comparing economic, livelihoods and capabilities models. *IDPM Development Informatics Working Paper no.58*. Retrieved from http://www.sed.manchester.ac.uk/idpm/research/publications/wp/di/index.htm

Heeks, R. (2014d). ICT4D 2016: New priorities for ICT4D policy, practice and WSIS in a post-2015 world. *IDPM Development Informatics Working Paper no.59*. Retrieved from http://www.sed.manchester.ac.uk/idpm/research/publications/wp/di/index.htm

Heeks, R., & Jagun, A. (2007). Mobile phones and development: The future in new hands? *Id21 Insights, 69*, p. 1. Retrieved from http://www.id21.org/insights/insights69/insights69.pdf

Heeks, R., & Molla, A. (2009). Impact assessment of ICT-for-development projects: A compendium of approaches. *IDPM Development Informatics Working Paper no.36*. Retrieved from http://www.sed.manchester.ac.uk/idpm/research/publications/wp/di/index.htm

Heeks, R., Subramanian, L., & Jones, C. (2013). Understanding e-waste management in developing countries: Building sustainability in the Indian ICT sector. *IDPM Development Informatics Working Paper no.52*. Retrieved from http://www.sed.manchester.ac.uk/idpm/research/publications/wp/di/index.htm

Henderson, V. J., Storeygard, A., & Weil, N. D. (2012). Measuring economic growth from outer space. *The American Economic Review, 102*(2), 994–1028. doi:10.1257/aer.102.2.994 PMID:25067841

Hofmeyr, J. (2013). *Africa rising? Popular dissatisfaction with economic management despite the decade of growth. Afro Barometer Policy Paper No2*. Retrieved from http://www.afrobarometer.org/files/documents/policy_brief/ab_r5_policybriefno2.pdf

Huntington, P. S. (1968). *Political order in changing societies*. New Haven, CT: Yale University Press.

Jacobsen, J. (2015). Revisiting the modernization hypothesis: Longevity and democracy. *World Development, 67*, 174–185. doi:10.1016/j.worlddev.2014.10.003

Jagun, A. (2007). Micro-enterprise and the "mobile divide": New benefits and old inequalities in Nigeria's informal sector. *Id21 Insights, 69*, p. 2. Retrieved from http://www.id21.org/insights/insights69/insights69.pdf

Jarrett, S. (2013). From poverty traps to indigenous philanthropy: Complexity in a rapidly changing world. *University of Sussex IDS [Institute of Development Studies] Working Paper No 425*. Retrieved from http://www.ids.ac.uk/files/dmfile/Wp425.pdf

Kalsched, D. (2013). *Trauma and the soul: A psycho-spiritual approach to human development and its interruption*. New York, NY: Routledge.

Kanbur, R. (2002). Economics, social science and development. *World Development, 30*(3), 477–486. doi:10.1016/S0305-750X(01)00117-6

Kiely, R. (2006). Modernization theory. In D. A. Clark (Ed.), *The Elgar companion to development studies* (pp. 395–399). Northampton, MA: Edward Elgar.

Kleine, D. (2009). ICT4What? Using the choice framework to operationalise the capability approach to developemnt. *Proceedings of the Doha Conference.* Retrieved from http://www.cs.washington.edu/education/courses/cse590f/09sp/ictd09/Kleine.pdf

Kleine, D. (2013). *Technologies of choice: ICTs, development, and the capabilities approach.* Cambridge, MA: MIT.

Kumar, K. (2005). *From post-industrial to post-modern society: New theories of the contemporary world* (2nd ed.). Malden, MA: Blackwell.

Legge, J. (2014). La frontière la plus meurtrière au monde. *La Libre Belgique.* Retrieved from http://www.lalibre.be/actu/international/la-frontiere-la-plus-meurtriere-au-monde-52975d703570386f7f3695ab

Lerner, M. R. (2001). History of developmental sciences. In N. J. Smelser & P. B. Baltes (Eds.), *International encyclopedia of the social and behavioral sciences* (Vol. 11, pp. 3615–3620). New York, NY: Elsevier. doi:10.1016/B0-08-043076-7/00057-7

Lewis, T. C., & Short, C. (1879). *A Latin dictionary: Founded on Andrews' edition of Freund's Latin dictionary: Revised, enlarged, and in great part rewritten.* Oxford, UK: Clarendon Press.

Lichtheim, M. (1973). Ancient Egyptian literature.: Vol. 1. *The Old and Middle Kingdoms.* Berkeley, CA: University of California Press.

Liddell, G. H., & Scott, R. (1996). *A Greek-English lexicon* (9th ed.). New York, NY: Oxford University Press. (Original work published 1843)

Liddy, M. (2013). Education about, for, as development. *Policy and Practice: A Development. Educational Review, 17,* 27–45.

Lockner, O. A. (Ed.). (2013). Steps to local government reform: A guide to tailoring local government reforms to fit regional governance communities in democracies. Bloomington, IN: iUniverse.

Marsh, M. R. (2014). Modernization theory, then and now. *Comparative Sociology, 13*(3), 261–283. doi:10.1163/15691330-12341311

Martinelli, A. (2015). Global modernization and multiple modernities. In A. Martinelli & C. He (Eds.), *Global modernization review: New discoveries and theories revisited* (pp. 5–24). Hackensack, NJ: World Scientific.

Marx, K. (1955). *The poverty of philosophy.* Moscow: Progress Publishers. (Original work published 1847)

Marx, K. (1977). *Capital: A critique of political economy* (B. Fowkes, Trans.). New York, NY: Vintage. (Original work published 1867)

Mattes, R. (2008). The material and political bases of lived poverty in Africa: Insights from the Afrobarometer. *Afrobarometer Working Paper No. 98.* Retrieved from http://www.afrobarometer.org/files/documents/working_papers/AfropaperNo98.pdf

Mattes, R., & Bratton, M. (2009). Poverty reduction, economic growth and democratization in Sub-Saharan Africa. *Afrobarometer Briefing Paper No.68.* Retrieved from http://www.afrobarometer.org/files/documents/briefing_papers/AfrobriefNo68.pdf

May, J., Dutton, V., & Munyakazi, L. (2014). Information and communication technologies as a pathway from poverty: Evidence from East Africa. In E. O. Adera, T. M. Waema, J. May, O. Mascarenhas, & K. Diga (Eds.), *ICT pathways to poverty reduction: Empirical evidence from East and Southern Africa* (pp. 33–52). Ottawa, Canada: IDRC. doi:10.3362/9781780448152.002

Meltzer, S. E. (2001). Egyptology. In D. B. Redford (Ed.), *The Oxford encyclopedia of ancient Egypt* (Vol. 1, pp. 448–458). New York, NY: Oxford University Press.

Mohan, G. (2008). Participatory development. In V. Desai & R. B. Potter (Eds.), *The companion to development studies* (2nd ed., pp. 45–50). London: Hodder Education.

Morgan, H. L. (1985). *Ancient society.* Tucson, AZ: University of Arizona Press. (Original work published 1877)

Mosse, D. (2013). The anthropology of international development. *Annual Review of Anthropology, 42*(1), 227–246. doi:10.1146/annurev-anthro-092412-155553

Mouzelis, N. (1999). Modernity: A non-European conceptualization. *The British Journal of Sociology, 50*(1), 141–159. doi:10.1080/000713199358851 PMID:15266678

Nisbet, A. R. (1969). *Social change and history: Aspects of the Western theory of development.* New York, NY: Oxford University Press.

Nisbet, A. R. (1986). *The making of modern society.* New York, NY: Wheatsheaf.

Organski, F. K. A. (1965). *The stages of political development.* New York, NY: Alfred A. Knopf.

Palmer, I., Dunford, R., Rura-Polley, T., & Baker, E. (2001). Changing forms of organizing: Dualities in using remote collaboration technologies in film production. *Journal of Organizational Change Management, 14*(2), 190–212. doi:10.1108/09534810110388081

Peet, R., & Hartwick, E. (2015). *Theories of development: Contentions, arguments, alternatives* (3rd ed.). New York, NY: The Guilford Press.

Perkins, H. J. (1997). *Geopolitics and the Green Revolution: Wheat, genes, and the Cold War.* New York, NY: Oxford University Press.

Perry, C. D. (2001). Infrastructure investment. In N. J. Smelser & P. B. Baltes (Eds.), *International encyclopedia of the social and behavioral sciences* (Vol. 11, pp. 7486–7489). New York, NY: Elsevier. doi:10.1016/B0-08-043076-7/04411-9

Plato. (5-4th c. BC, 1921). Cratylus (Vol. 12, H.N. Fowler, Trans.). Cambridge, MA: Harvard University Press.

Plato. (5-4th c. BC, 1967). Laws (Vols. 10 & 11, R.G. Bury, Trans.). Cambridge, MA: Harvard University Press.

Potter, B. R., Binns, T., Smith, W. D., & Elliott, A. J. (2008). *Geographies of development: An introduction to development studies* (3rd ed.). London: Pearson.

Potter, R., Conway, D., Evans, R., & Lloyd-Evans, S. (2012). *Key concepts in development geography.* Thousand Oaks, CA: Sage. doi:10.4135/9781473914834

Prahalad, K. C. (2005). *The fortune at the bottom of the pyramid: Eradicating poverty through profits.* Upper Saddle River, NJ: Pearson.

Rojas, C. (2010). *The Great Wall: A cultural history.* Cambridge, MA: Harvard University Press.

Rostow, W. W. (1960). *The stages of economic growth: A non-communist manifesto.* New York, NY: Cambridge University Press.

Sandum, A. (2010). *Economics evolving: A history of economic thought.* Princeton, NJ: Princeton University Press.

Sen, K. A. (2011). L'euro fait tomber l'Europe. *Le monde.* Retrieved from http://www.lemonde.fr/imprimer/article/2011/07/02/1543995.html

Shank, H. M. (2000). Introduction. In M. H. Shank (Ed.), *The scientific enterprise in Antiquity and the Middle Ages* (pp. 1–19). Chicago: Chicago University Press. Random House.

Sheller, M. (2015). News now. *Journalism Studies, 16*(1), 12–26. doi:10.1080/1461670X.2014.890324

Singhal, A., Svenkerud, J. P., Malaviya, P., Rogers, M. E., & Krishna, V. (2005). Bridging digital divides: Lessons learned from the IT initiatives of the Grameen Bank in Bangladesh. In O. Hemer & T. Tufte (Eds.), *Media and glocal change: Rethinking communication for development* (pp. 427–433). Göteborg, Sweden: NORDICOM.

Smith, A. (1961). *An inquiry into the nature and causes of the wealth of nations.* London: Penguin. (Original work published 1776)

Smith, B. M. (2012). Reimagining development education for a changing geopolitical landscape. *Policy and Practice: A Development. Educational Review, 15,* 1–7.

Smith, C. L. (2013). The great Indian calorie debate: Explaining rising undernourishment during India's rapid economic growth. *University of Sussex Institute of Development Studies [IDS] Working Papers No 430.* Retrieved from http://opendocs.ids.ac.uk/opendocs/bitstream/handle/123456789/2877/Wp430.pdf?sequence=1

The Oxford American dictionary and language guide. (1999). New York, NY: Oxford University Press.

Thirlwall, P. A. (2008). Development and economic growth. In V. Desai & R. B. Potter (Eds.), *The companion to development studies* (2nd ed., pp. 37–40). London: Hodder Education.

Thornton, S. (2008). *Understanding human development: Biological, social and psychological processes from conception to adult life.* New York, NY: Palgrave Macmillan.

Todaro, P. M. (1997). *Economic development* (6th ed.). New York, NY: Addison Wesley.

Trakulhun, S., & Weber, R. (2015). Modernities: Editors' introduction. In S. Trakulhun & R. Weber (Eds.), Delimiting modernities: Conceptual challenges and regional responses (pp. ix-xxiv). Lanham, MD: Lexington Books.

Unwin, T. (2009a). Development agendas and the place of ICTs. In T. Unwin (Ed.), *ICT4D: Information and communication technology for development* (pp. 7–38). New York, NY: Cambridge University Press.

Unwin, T. (2009b). ICT4D implementation: Policies and partnerships. In T. Unwin (Ed.), *ICT4D: Information and communication technology for development* (pp. 125–175). New York, NY: Cambridge University Press.

Unwin, T. (2009c). Conclusions. In T. Unwin (Ed.), *ICT4D: Information and communication technology for development* (pp. 360–375). New York, NY: Cambridge University Press.

Unwin, T. (2009d). Information and communication in development practices. In T. Unwin (Ed.), *ICT4D: Information and communication technology for development* (pp. 39–75). New York, NY: Cambridge University Press.

Van den Ham, A. (2004). Local area development planning and management in the province of West Java and the province of the special territory of Aceh, Indonesia. In A. Van den Ham & J. Veenstra (Eds.), *Shifting logic in area development practices* (pp. 255–340). Burlington, VT: Ashgate.

Verzola, R. (2006). Technology issues and the new ICTs. *Leonardo, 39*(4), 311–313. doi:10.1162/leon.2006.39.4.311

Vrettos, T. (2001). *Alexandria*. New York, NY: The Free Press.

Wagner, P. (2001). Modernity: One or many? In J. R. Blau (Ed.), *The Blackwell companion to sociology* (pp. 30–42). Malden, MA: Blackwell.

Waldron, N. A. (1983). The problem of the Great Wall of China. *Harvard Journal of Asiatic Studies, 43*(2), 643–663. doi:10.2307/2719110

Waldron, N. A. (1990). *The Great Wall of China: From history to myth*. Cambridge, MA: Harvard University Press.

Weil, N. D. (2012). *Economic growth* (3rd ed.). New York, NY: Pearson.

Williams, D. (2014). The study of development. In B. Currie-Alder, R. Kanbur, D. M. Malone, & R. Medhora (Eds.), *International development: Ideas, experience, and prospects* (pp. 21–34). New York, NY: Oxford University Press. doi:10.1093/acprof:oso/9780199671656.003.0002

Williams, H. (2001). Hindsight after the Cold War: Samuel Huntington, the social sciences and development paradigms. *Dialectical Anthropology, 26*(3/4), 311–324. doi:10.1023/A:1021224219580

Wilmot, A. (1896). *Monomotapa (Rhodesia): Its monuments, and its history from the most ancient times to the present century (with preface by H.R. Haggard)*. London: Fisher Unwin.

Wright, R. K., & Zegarra, V. A. (2000). *Machu Picchu: A civil engineering marvel*. Reston, VA: ASCE. doi:10.1061/9780784404447

Xiong, B., Ren, K., Shu, Y., Chen, Y., Shen, B., & Wu, H. (2014). Recent developments in microfluidics for cell studies. *Advanced Materials, 26*(31), 5525–5532. doi:10.1002/adma.201305348 PMID:24536032

Yamarik, S., & Ghosh, S. (2015). Broad versus regional integration: What matters more for economic development? *The Journal of International Trade & Economic Development: An International and Comparative Review*, 24(1), 43–75. doi:10.1080/09638199.2013.868024

Yunus, M. (2007). *Creating a world without poverty: Social business and the future of capitalism*. New York, NY: Public Affairs.

KEY TERMS AND DEFINITIONS

Development: Integrated or holistic phenomenon needed to achieve the wellbeing of individuals and their societies.

Green Revolution: Production of high-yielding grains that are part of the modernization program that started in Mexico in the late 1950s and was pursued in Pakistan and India in the 1960s and 1970s in China in the 1980s.

Modernity: Broad-based set of social transformations that were institutionalized in Western Europe and constitute the core areas of industrialization for Western as well as non-Western societies, etc.

Modernization: Endeavor to manage, provide for, and plan welfare in response to people's needs and habits.

Modernize: Improve and/or adapt the living conditions of societies. From the Latin verb, *modero*: manage, moderate, keep within due bounds, etc.

Postmodernism: Current that rejects central authority and truth, and defended individuality and locality as the referent of truth and progress.

ENDNOTES

[1]   This is an updated version of my article (Cibangu, 2013) published in the *International Journal of Information Communication Technologies and Human Development*. Newer arguments and sources have been added to strengthen the earlier work.

[2]   Fuchs (2013) provided an informative background as to how ICT4D took shape

Chapter 2
ICT Integration in Education
Potential and Challenges

Madhuri V. Tikam
H. R. College of Commerce & Economics, India

ABSTRACT

Information and Communication Technologies (ICT) are extremely influencing every discipline under the sun including Education. It is affecting every aspect of education from teaching-learning to assessment and evaluation. It improves the effectiveness of education. It aids literacy movements. It enhances scope of education by facilitating mobile learning and inclusive education. It facilitates research and scholarly communication. Impact of ICT and its potential for the education field is manifold. It positively affects all the stakeholders of the education field. The current chapter discusses the same along with the various challenges posed by ICT. The challenges include economical issues, educational and technical factors. Appropriate content, Design and workability of ICT also play a crucial role in adoption of ICT in the education field. The chapter delineates in brief the challenges and probable solutions.

INTRODUCTION

"Education for All" is a global movement led by UNESCO (United Nation educational, Scientific and Cultural Organization), aiming to meet the learning needs of all children, youth and adults by 2015.It faces three major challenges:

1. Providing access to all
2. Improving learning environment
3. Measuring learning outcomes.

To succeed in "Education for All" movement, access to education should be provided to all irrespective of gender, physical, geographical, language, economical, social or any other barrier. The poorest people, residents of remote areas, and the most disadvantaged populations - for example, girls and members of ethnic and religious minorities, physically challenged people are the main category of people to whom

DOI: 10.4018/978-1-5225-0556-3.ch002

education should reach. To deal with varied needs of learners from different stratum is a complex issue to handle in a traditional mode of teaching learning. It demands for an open and flexible approach of education and distance or virtual modes of learning. These advanced demands of education delivery cannot be met in the developed and developing world without the help of Information and Communication Technologies (ICT) (UNESCO, 2009). The impact of ICT on trainers, learners, researchers and the entire learned society is tremendous. It is changing the contours of the education delivery system in the world by enhancing access to information for all. It also ensures effective and inclusive education. ICT supports the concept of open learning where the thrust is upon enhanced student access and the development of student autonomy.

ROLES OF ICT IN EDUCATION

ICT can play varied roles in developing an effective learning environment. It helps in offering access as well as enhances the learning environment. It acts as a teacher and explains core content concepts and addresses misconceptions. It acts as a stimulant and fosters analytical thinking and interdisciplinary studies. It networks a learner with the peers and experts and develops collaborative atmosphere. It plays the role of a guide and mentor by providing tailor made instructions to meet individual needs. Online learning facilitates learning through digital mode. With the help of multimedia, it enhances effectiveness of teaching-learning and hence proves crucial for early learners, slow learners and differently abled learners. Studies of the effect of technology-enhanced instruction on achievement and studies of student attitudes regarding learning with technology have been reported (Salaberry, 2001). These include increased motivation, improvement in self-concept and mastery of basic skills, more student-centered learning and engagement in the learning process, and more active processing, resulting in higher-order thinking skills and better recall (Brownlee-Conyers, 1996; Chenoweth, Ushida & Murday, 2006; Dwyer, 1996; McGrath, 1998; Stepp- Greany, 2002, Weiss, 1994). Additionally, there seems to be a beneficial multimedia effect, especially for low achieving students, when it is used to illustrate concepts and organize factual information (Nowaczyk, 1998).

Modern ICT tools not only deliver the content but also replicate formal learning experience via virtual learning. The intention of virtual classrooms is to extend the structure and services that accompany formal education programs from the campus to learners. The benefits of integration of ICT in education are depicted in Figure 1.

ICT also addresses the need of mobile learning. It offers independent space and flexibility that comes from working away from the learning institute or tutor. It makes education accessible to all, irrespective of geographical barriers or resource constraints. Learners from remote areas, working people who want to learn further and update their knowledge and differently-abled students who find travelling an issue of concern - benefit from the mobile learning mode. As per Scott Motlik's technical evaluation report on "Mobile Learning in Developing Nations"; by comparison, mobile phone technology is widespread, easy to use, and familiar to learners and instructors (Motlik, 2008). An exploratory study of unsupervised mobile learning in rural India conducted by Anuj Kumar and his colleagues showed a reasonable level of academic learning and motivation among rural children who were voluntarily engaged in mobile learning. (Kumar, 2010). Similarly a study by Douglas Mcconatha, Matt Praul, and Michael J. Lynch, revealed that the use of mobile learning can make a positive and significant difference in the outcome performance than traditional methods of class lectures, notes and reviews (Mcconatha, 2008). Dr. Fahad N. Al-Fahad's

Figure 1. Benefits of ICT

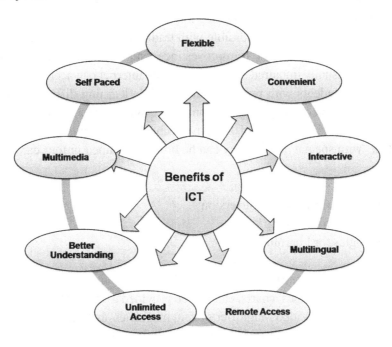

study about students' attitudes and perceptions towards the effectiveness of mobile learning in King Saud University, Saudi Arabia, also supported that m learning makes the learners truly engaged learners who are behaviorally, intellectually and emotionally involved in their learning task. (Al-Fahad, 2009).

A lot of educational resources are available in m-learning formats. Google books have worked with major publishers to bring pages, chapters and books in mobile readable format. It also offer mobile version of book search since February 2009. Other publishers like Amazon, EBL, BBC, etc. also provide mobile collection of e-books and/or audio books to their users. Databases like JSTOR, LexisNexis, EBSCO, etc. are available on mobile devices. Many libraries all over the world like California State University, Fullerton Pollak Library, National University of Singapore Libraries; Public Library Münster, Germany; University of Virginia Library; Washington State University Libraries; London School of Economics, United Kingdom; etc. offer mobile based library services. Many mobile service provider companies are providing educational programs via mobiles. E.g. Tata Docoma launched mobile sex education program – Sparsh, they also offers programs like English Seekho, Storytelling via mobile. Universities like S.N.D.T. Women's University, Indira Gandhi Open University, etc. are developing tie ups with mobile service provider companies to offer distance education programs with the help of mobile phones. Publishers like Tata McGraw Hill also initiated mobile based courses like TOPCAT. Thus, ICT offers possibilities of transforming the learning paradigm and bringing knowledge to those who have not earlier been able to participate in education.

ICT and Inclusive Education

Inclusion helps to involve the identification and minimizing of barriers to learning. It encourages participation and maximizing of resources to support learning. This participation is irrespective of the gender, age, ability, ethnicity or impairment of learners. ICT proves a boon in such circumstances. It unlocks the hidden potential of those who have communication difficulties. It enables students to demonstrate achievement in ways which might not be possible with traditional methods by developing tailor-made tasks to suit individual skills and abilities. It improves independent access to students to educate themselves at their own pace. Visually impaired students using the internet can access information alongside their sighted peers while students with profound and multiple learning difficulties can communicate more easily besides gaining interest in education, confidence and social credibility at school and in their communities (UNESCO, 2006). An array of Assistive technology is available for supporting inclusive education for students with special needs. They can be broadly grouped in four categories:

1. Assistive technologies for Magnification
2. Assistive technologies for Format Conversion
3. Assistive technologies for Reading
4. Assistive technologies for Learning

Assistive technologies for Magnification include computers having larger screen so that magnified images of text as well as photographs, charts, etc. can be provided to the partially sighted. Software like Optelec's ClearView+ Desktop Video Magnifier system magnifies anything under the viewfinder from 2 to 50 times its original size. It has a specially designed monitor and lighting design for optimum visual enhancement and the entire unit can be controlled with a single button, and can be customized to meet the exact needs. The advanced versions like Optelec Compact + Portable Magnifier, Bonita (Portable mouse Magnifier), etc. are more powerful, smaller, portable and user friendly devices which can be used anywhere and anytime. It has six viewing modes (full color, high contrast black/white, white/black, yellow/black, yellow/blue and full color without light - ideal for magnifying displays such as the screen of your mobile phone). An integrated writing function enables a person to write while viewing what is being written. It is best suited for persons with low vision for attending to their daily reading-writing tasks.

Assistive technologies for Format Conversion used to digitize the notes, question papers, etc. Software like EasyConverter, Zoom Ex instant reader, etc. can convert any printed text into multiple accessible formats such as speech, large print, sound, text files and Braille versions within seconds. The speech mode offers a choice of accents; one can even select Indian Accent for better understanding which meet the needs of dyslexic, visually impaired and learning disabled students.

Software like JAWS (Jobs Access with Speech), KURZWEIL, SARA (Scanning and Reading Appliance), Dolphin Easy Reader, etc. convert the computer into a talking machine by providing the user with access to the information displayed on the screen via text to speech mode. They provides users with document creation, editing as well as study skills capabilities for preparing notes, summarizing and outlining the text. This software are multilingual and interactive. They allow the users to make their talking book directly from plain text.

Assistive technologies for Learning include hardware and software which assists the users with special needs to create their own information resource and learn by their own. Software like Talking Typing Teacher, Touch Typing Tutor reads out the text as it is typed on the keyboard. Recorders like Angel player, Victor Stream Reader and Digital Voice recorder can be used to record information which can be played back according to the need of the individual. Specially designed keyboards like Easy Link 12, allows the Braille user to effortlessly control PDA, PC and smartphone. It can be connected to a smartphone to send / receive SMS. Software like Spell well software used to learn spellings and pronunciation of different words. With the advancement of ICT, mainstream education became available, accessible, affordable and appropriate for students with disabilities. ICT removes the hindrance in accessing higher education and motivates the disabled students to pursue higher education by making them self-reliant (Tikam, M. & Lobo, A. (2012).

ICT and Evaluation

Education and Evaluation goes hand in hand. ICT aids and speeds the process while maintaining transparency and accuracy. ICT offers a chance to treat every student as an individual and offer a tailor made solution for each. E.g. Reading Assessment software like AceReader takes into account the existing skills of a student as an individual and develops advanced assessments based on previous results. As a result, the coursework per student differs and caters their personalized needs. The ICT based evaluation proves exceedingly useful for distance education students where lack of feedback may de-motivate the students. The use of software like 'MarkIt' - used widely in Australia, provides students information about their various performances consistently. It also offers details about performance of their peers, plus the capacity for markers to enter detailed and consistent feedback at all stages of the marking process (Don, 2000). Such software enhances the inclusiveness and give rise to healthy competitions.

Computer based concept mapping with automated scoring helps summative assessment of critical and creative thinking about complex relationships. A large number of students can be analyzed for different sets of skills simultaneously with the help of ICT. ICT based evaluation avoids time-consuming manual data transcription and recoding before statistical analysis. Built-in error control in ICT based evaluation methods reduces administrative errors. As a result, assessment becomes speedy and transparent. Data analysis programs facilitate the tutor and learner to monitor their progress and understand the different facets of performance. Visual representations and study of different relations of evaluations are made easy by ICT. It facilitates teachers in understanding the difficulties faced by students in a particular area and helps in developing suitable measures. Overall, ICT offers greater flexibility, improved reliability and enhanced effectiveness to the assessment process.

ICT and Research

ICT offers a range of products to aid research work at every stage. It has tools for searching and keeping updated. It has tools for collaboration and communication. The introduction of the Open Access Resource initiative by ICT makes the sharing of scholarly ideas at a global level easy. Budapest Open Access Initiative of Open Society Institute (OSI) activated this initiative in December 2001. It makes peer-reviewed journal articles and un-reviewed preprints that [scholars] might wish to put online for comment or to alert colleagues to important research findings freely available on the public internet, permitting any user to read, download, copy, distribute, print, search, or link to the full texts of these articles, crawl them for indexing, pass them as data to software, or use them for any other lawful purpose, without financial, legal, or technical barriers other than those inseparable from gaining access to the internet itself. The only constraint on reproduction and distribution, and the only role for copyright in this domain, should be to give authors control over the integrity of their work and the right to be properly acknowledged and cited (BOAI, 2011). It impacts the education field a lot as more and more researchers have started publishing and the latest updates in a subject field become available to all across the globe in real time. Initiatives like DOAJ, Google Books reveals a large database of scholarly communication to the researchers irrespective of subject, language and geographical barrier. Search engines like Google, Yahoo aids to search the required information in fraction of seconds. Tools like RSS, wikis, bookmarks helps to remain updated in one's field. Programs like Freesummarizer or Greatsummary helps to Summarize any text online in just a few seconds. Mind mapping tools like Freemind, Mindmeister helps to manage the knowledge base as well as the project progress.

For developing and conducting survey, survey tools like Survey Monkey (www.surveymonkey.com), Zoomerang (www.zoomerang.com), Survey Gizmo (www.surveygizmo.com), PollDaddy(www.polldaddy.com) helps a lot. They offer extensive reporting, with a flexible cross-tabulation report and advanced logic features like question and answer piping, randomization, text analysis for open responses, and integration with statistical software like IBM's SPSS. To conduct complex data mining and analysis, statistical software like Analytica, Matlab +Statistics toolbox, SPSS, etc. are very useful. One can use social media tools like Linkendin, skype, slideshare, etc. to share and disseminate the ideas and views. There are a few all in one solution like Zotero [zoh-TAIR-oh] are available for researchers which free, help to collect, organize, cite, and share research sources. Once the final research paper is ready, one can use bibliographic tools like Easybib (www.easybib.com), noodletools (www.noodletools.com/), Bibme (www.bibme.org), Google Docs Bibliographic Template, etc. to build their bibliography in APA, MLA, AMA, and Chicago Style. ICT became an integral part of the research and scholarly communication. It contributes positively to the all stages of research and impacts the scholarly world remarkably.

CHALLENGES OF E-LEARNING

The benefits of ICT in education are manifold. It improves efficiency and accessibility both in learning and teaching by deepening understanding and providing new ways of interacting. ICT makes education convenient, consistent and flexible. It provides a single experience that accommodates the three distinct learning styles of auditory learners, visual learners and kinesthetic learners. It increases motivation and social skills. It aids in collaborative learning and self-evaluation. However, it also poses a range of challenges in terms of i) Economical Issues ii) Education iii) Technical Factors iv) Content v) Workability and vi) Design (see: Figure 2).

1. Economical Issues

Telecommunications infrastructure is limited in most developing countries and costs are exceedingly high and are only affordable to a few. Bandwidth costs as well as transmission costs incurred by Internet Service Providers (ISP) are high and passed on to users which make the cost of online access prohibitively expensive for most. As per International Telecommunication Union's (ITU) latest figures, mobile broadband is still much more expensive in developing countries (see Figure 3).

Fixed-broadband prices drop by 82% between 2008 and 2012 which results into rise in fixed broadband penetration. However, it is too low in developing countries with compared to developed countries (see: Figure 4).

Further, telephone lines are generally undependable, while electricity supply can be erratic. In rural areas, infrastructure is almost non-existing and services are generally too expensive for poor populations. The cost of internet access at all levels makes it inaccessible for a majority of the population. Computers and modems are imported from industrialised countries with accompanying increases in transportation

Figure 2. Challenges of E-Learning

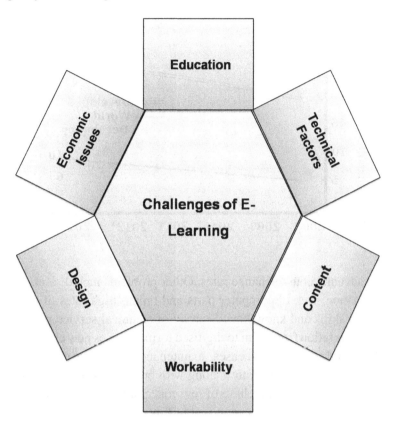

Figure 3. Price of mobile-broadband services, early 2013
Source: ITU World Telecommunication /ICT Indicators database, 2014

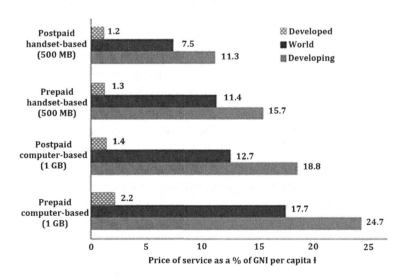

Figure 4. Fixed broadband penetration
Source: *ITU World Telecommunication /ICT Indicators database, 2014*

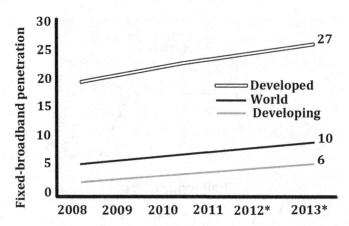

and duty as well as disadvantageous exchange rates. Other problems include lack of access to training, lack of technical information, lack of computer parts and repair, high rates of technological obsolescence and lack of human skills and know-how. Scarcity of technical service providers allows them to charge higher rates. The migration from print to digitised formats raises new challenges of copyright and ownership. Costs of copyright, software licenses, maintenance, leasing equipment, staff development and training should be taken into consideration along with other costs. Policies for pricing, copyright, export procedures, assistance with the purchase of low cost computers and communications subsidies, free training programmes and scholarships are possible ways to deal with this barrier. Lower-cost and lower-maintenance networking technologies should be examined.

2. Education

ICT requires that users have some skills and no one should assume that by providing the facilities, everyone in the community will immediately embrace the technology. Without a formal user education program some users are at risk of relying solely on 'trial and error' familiarisation with the ICT, or not at all. Research study confirms that a degree of search modification is available for those users who can interpret the various data elements available. ICT can be made easier to use through improved training and documentation that is based on information seeking behavior, with the caveat that good training is not a substitute for good system design. A linear approach should be followed to determine what should be covered in a user education program by turning to studies of how users fail to use ICT. Some basic technical expertise to take care of maintenance of ICT is a must along with the capability of effective use of ICT. Lack of skills, interest, time and support of the tutor kills all motivation of users. In addition, ICT is ever-changing. Yesterday's latest knowledge becomes obsolete today. It demands a continuous learning scenario and a lot of resources.

3. Technical Factors

The findings showed that users value the ability to communicate and economy of time over expense and the complexity of ICT. In the University of the South Pacific survey almost 90% of users preferred to usc ncw tcchnologies, particularly computers and multimedia for their studies and work instead of using traditional methods. Keeping aside the cost and user willingness factors in effective use of ICT technical factors like content - its quality, level, authenticity, currency and purpose, the metadata, data mining and other management tools for content analysis, design and workability affect the utilization of ICT. The unavailability of appropriate technology, access facilities, handling, maintenance, storage, problems from actual usage and lack of relevant software/courseware make ICT daunting. (Mahajan, 2002).

4. Content

The quality of information content is the most important evaluation criterion for any information resource. For effective use of information content in local languages, level of information, its currency, objective and the cognitive approach of the users become essential. Scanning millions of documents -- even if those documents are the fundamental documents of a nation -- is a useless enterprise unless one also figures out how to create interpretive structures that a researcher can navigate unassisted (Day, 1998). The Content of E learning will be meaningful only if it is authentic, accurate, in local language and in proper context. It should be supported with appropriate metadata, data mining, management tools, etc.

5. Design

The designing of ICT - quality and quantity of graphic and multimedia content, inclusion of links, inter-activity and complexity become very important issues while using any type of ICT. Numerous studies have shown that users prefer ICT with a high percentage of graphic and multimedia content to those that are overwhelmingly composed of written text but demand that they should have a relatively low percent-age of advertising content. To appeal to users to use ICT more prominently proper attention should be paid to clear and easily understandable graphics and high quality audio and video components. Various aspects of general design, such as the physical placement of items on the screen page, the use of appeal-ing colors, and the use of easily readable type fonts are of considerable importance in the use of ICT. Pleasing, appealing, attention-grabbing, but not distracting design is essential. Easy to read (based on font appearance, size, and color) and un-lengthy text (to avoid excessive scrolling) is necessary. Proper navigational help and Graphical User Interfaces make the use of ICT user friendly and help users a lot. Weakness at this stage forms a major barrier in extensive and effective use of ICT. The quality, quantity and context of links to additional resources play a very crucial role in the use of ICT. The numbers of links, the topicality of links and discrediting resources with unrelated links are important considerations.

One advantage of electronic resources over paper-based materials is the opportunity for increased interactivity. The users prefer highly interactive sites to non-interactive sites and favors a method for contacting the authoring/sponsoring body for questions and comments. If an information resource is too complex, most juvenile users will abandon it in favor of a more simply organized tool. Inclusion of more sophisticated software for automatic correction of search term spellings and format errors and automatic search aids will improve the efficiency of ICT and will generate more relevant results. It should be able to provide user assistance so that fewer headings get lost due to typos, dead forms, etc. It should have the potential to correct user input, better browsing displays and more cross-references. It should attempt to make searching easier and more effective for untrained users by automating some of the "intelligent" judgments and activities of experienced search intermediaries. This includes relevant feedback, stemming or truncation, finding synonyms, applying Boolean operators, and ranking some index terms as more important than others. Easy navigation, clear designing, proper links, automatic and intelligent search functions make ICT an enjoyment to use (Hidreth, 2001).

6. Workability

The overall workability of ICT is affected to a greater extent on the basis of loading speed, workability of links, media, formats and security issues. A common complaint with juvenile ICT users is lengthy loading time. Single pages with numerous large graphics, especially animated pictures, often load excessively slowly. Downloading large audio and video files can also be annoyingly slow. Slow loading is a source of considerable frustration for users. Downloading one week's tutorial material usually takes more than two weeks due to some links being timed out, slow connection time, etc. In addition dead links, links incompatible with most personal computer systems annoy the users a lot. Numerous inoperative links indicate that a resource is poorly maintained, casting doubt on the quality of its information (Kole, 2001).

Different aspects of media used in ICT like fragility, lifetime, and unavailability of required form of media, related technology and other resources affect the successful long term use of ICT. Even worse than media problems are the problems of formats on the media, because there are a great many more formats than there are media. There is no Universal Preservation Format (UPF). Converting between these formats may face problems of unexact representation of the original data and scarcity of general conversion package. (Lesk, 1995) Requirement of proprietary software and helper applications or plug-ins prevent the exhaustive use of ICT. The fear about data security and lack of user skills adds to the problem. Rising destructive devices like e-bomb, flash bombs, war scripts, denial of service tools and viruses, identity revealing sites like WHOIS, inability of system designers to incorporate security features cause crisis (Anonymous, 1998). Unclear copyright rules and product liability can lead organisations to a fear of punishment for providing access to erroneous, libelous, or pornographic information and will cause hindrance about use of ICT. (Trilokekar, 2000)

ICT should be compatible with most personal computer systems, demand no special proprietary software, browsers, helper applications or plug-ins. To be successful, users must have or need to be trained in a basic system expertise, minimum skills or naive information seeking strategies, some cognitive approach, fundamental subject access and domain knowledge. Keeping oneself abreast of information about technology, security measures, legal issues will be beneficial.

GUIDELINES FOR DEVELOPING A DIGITAL CONTENT POLICY

To avail the benefits of ICT integration in the education, one needs a strong Digital Content Policy which defines guidelines to select / deselect digital content. A written Digital Content Policy is a valuable tool for better management of digital content. The digital content policy should guide about how to negotiate for what the organisation and its users want. It should take care about various aspects of collection development in detail. A list of important issues is given below:

1. **Selection Related:**
   ◦ The digital collection and services should aim to support the vision and mission of the parent organization.

○ It should keep pace with changes in research, teaching, information technology and scholarly communication. Necessary changes should be adopted accordingly.

○ Care should be taken to verify that the subscribed information is not available via free access.

○ While offering links to free E-content it should be made sure that they are complete and legible.

○ Efforts should be made to join appropriate consortia to acquire required information at the best deal and bargain for requisite number of licenses.

○ In the beginning of any new digitization project, one should verify that they are not duplicating the process. One should check the copy created by various partnerships, including the Google and OCA mass digitization projects. Once satisfied that it's a firsthand effort then an expert committee should be appointed to handle the project. Clear documentation about required output format, time schedule, etc. should be made.

2. **Budget Related:**

○ While defining the budget for digital content alongwith the cost of digital content, make provision for the required hardware and software cost, storage and maintenance cost, preservation cost, etc. Also keep in mind the lawyer's fees required for the better license negotiations.

○ Decide your preference for payment schemes i.e. whether it will be flat rate, pay-per-use, subscription basis, etc.

3. **Vendor Related:**

○ The vendor of the electronic resource should be established and reliable.

○ The vendor should offer product demonstrations, training, required documentations, accurate professional customer and technical support.

○ The vendor should be ready for customization and should offer modes for usage assessment.

○ Clarify in advance that how the vendor will address downtime when access to the content will not be possible? Or if some of the content is removed from the database?

○ Know the details about updates - how often will updates to the electronic material will be provided and how will these updates be delivered.

4 **Use Related:**

○ Licenses should define "Authorized Users", "Authorized Sites" and "Fair Use" concepts as broadly as possible.

○ While defining the authorized users keep in mind all types of users like students, staff, alumni, visiting faculty, public, Inter organisation loan partners, etc.

○ Also define Authorized sites - their geographical territory i.e. will access from same building, campus, area, city, state or will access the data from anywhere in the world.

○ Describe the prospective usage of the digital content - whether the content will be printed, downloaded, stored electronically, e-mailed to others, etc.

○ Specify with the vendor whether the content will be used internally, externally, via website, intranet, blog, etc.

○ Identify whether the content will be accessed from a single machine, from the LAN, etc. and number of Concurrent users i.e. how many people will access the content simultaneously.

○ Be clear about the ability to make a copy for inter organisation loan? By e-mail or by print?

5. **License Related:**

○ Decide the suitable duration of the license;

     ○   Ask for different terms and conditions for renewal procedures (like partial, consequent, automatic, etc.)

     ○   Define the circumstances under which the license would be terminated.

     ○   Decide which state/province and country's law would govern the license.

     ○   Try to specify the special circumstances which should be addressed by the license to avoid future chances of breaking the license agreement.

     ○   Define in advance the required archival rights after the termination of the license.

6. **Organisation Related:**

     ○   Decide who will negotiate and sign the license, who will monitor that the terms and conditions in the license agreement are met during the duration of the license and if not who will take the required action.

     ○   Know in detail whether the authentication of authorized users is necessary, what are the required steps and resources to do so and whether the vendor will set this up.

     ○   Recognize the mechanism to ensure user confidentiality and the fair use of the digital content as per the defined terms and conditions of the license.

7. **Maintenance and Preservation Related:**

     ○   When acquiring licensed e-content it should meet the current standards, however these may change from time to time.

     ○   The digital material should be compatible across different platforms (PC, Mac, etc.)

     ○   Digital material should receive the same priority for acquisition, cataloging, and processing as other print materials.

     ○   Every organisation is committed to branding and promoting of digital assets effectively to its user community.

     ○   Organisation should offer not only the required hardware and software but it should also give appropriate metadata and user training.

     ○   Educating users about fair use of E content is necessary.

     ○   Regular assessment of usage is a must. Updating the links and contents with timely needs is necessary.

     ○   Effort should be made to identify and acknowledge the owner/creator of the Internet resource of provided links.

8. **De-Selection Related**

     ○   Similar to print collection, e content should be assessed on a regular basis.

     ○   The materials which are not compatible with existing hardware and software, materials available in obsolete formats and platforms, and/or not supported by the vendors should be withdrawn.

     ○   Outdated or inaccurate materials, materials damaged beyond repair and if duplicate content is available in preferred formats, then such e contents should be removed.

     ○   The links provided to the resources which are no longer available or maintained or which are no longer current, reliable or relevant should be deleted from time to time.

     ○   Licenses should be modified with the help of usage statistics.

     ○   Whenever necessary the format migration should be done.

GUIDELINES FOR ADOPTING ICT BASED TRAINING

For effective adoption of ICT based training a few essential factors must be considered so that maximum benefits can be derived. Kailash Srivastava (2004) enumerates some of the important aspects to be considered while adopting ICT based technology:

1. **Learning Objectives:** Training programmes are designed to meet the organizational goals. While developing or selecting an appropriate digital content or course, one has to keep in mind the mission and goals of the organization and whether the learning objectives are in line with current, specific goals of the organisation.
2. **Instructional Design:** Instructional design must match with learning objectives. It should match with the requirements of both the users and the organisation. As per the need, a self directed, task specific, learn-by-doing method should be adopted.
3. **Appropriate Media:** Introducing ICT in Education does not mean converting print resource into a digital one. To enhance the value of digital content, one must use appropriate media along with text. It makes the training program more interesting and effective.
4. **Engaging and Interactive Methodologies:** The ICT based training sessions should use variety of interactive media such as video, audio, animation, etc. The interaction engages the participants in realistic situations and facilitates learning by doing.
5. **Realistic Examples and Solutions:** Use the realistic examples and solutions which match the users' needs, situations and culture. A special attention to be provided to this issue while delivering the ICT based education as its access does not have any geographical boundaries. However, one should keep in mind that the users relates to the program only when there is a link between what they lean and real life.
6. **User-friendly Navigation:** Effective technology based learning is highly intuitive, enabling the learner to navigate through the program quickly and easily. E.g. Users should be able to quit the program at any time and then return later to the exact point in the program.
7. **Skilled Application Assessment:** A good ICT based training program should be bundled with an adept assessment or evaluation module.
8. **Tracking Capabilities:** An efficient ICT based training program should be able to compile critical information and facilitate analysis. Effective technology based training can track results individually, departmentally and organizationally.
9. **Multiple Deployment Options:** Most organisations have a wide variety of technological platforms. To make the ICT based training program accessible to maximum number of users in the organization it should have multiple deployment options such as CD-ROM based, Internet based, Intranet based, etc. It facilitates the users to adopt the required mode as per their requirement and vailable resources.

CONCLUSION

The impact of ICT on the education sector is tremendous. It improves the effectiveness and inclusiveness of education. It saves resources and enhances access. However, it poses many challenges. While for many ICT offers a promise of greater inclusion of previously marginalized groups (whether marginalized by gender, disability, distance, language, culture, race, age or economic status), their use also brings with it very real dangers of increasing the marginalization of such groups inside the education system. Required policies and infrastructure in place can act as a catalyst for ICT penetration. Cognitive knowledge of both, the content designers and learners enhances the ICT applications and usability. It is essential to focus on ICT workability in terms of economical, technical, legal and ethical aspects to boost its applications in various fields including Education. An in depth research about various aspects of ICT and its impact on education is a must.

REFERENCES

Al-Fahad, F. (2009). Students' attitudes and perceptions towards the effectiveness of mobile learning in king Saud University, Saudi Arabia. *The Turkish Online Journal of Educational Technology, 8*(2). Retrieved November 18, 2012, from http://www.tojet.net/articles/8210.pdf

Berthon, H., & Webb, C. (2000). The Moving Frontier: Archiving, Preservation and Tomorrow's Digital Heritage. Paper presented at VALA 2000 - 10th VALA Biennial Conference and Exhibition, Melbourne, Victoria, 16 - 18 February, 2000. Retrieved from http://www.nla.gov.au/nla/staffpapers/hberthon2.html

Björk, B.-C., Welling, P., Laakso, M., Majlender, P., Hedlund, T., ... (2010). Open Access to the Scientific Journal Literature. *PLoS ONE, 5*(6). Retrieved from www.plosone.org/article/info:doi/10.1371/journal.pone.0011273

BOAI: Budapest Open Access Initiative. (Last revised December 16, 2011). Frequently Asked Questions. Retrieved from http://www.earlham.edu/~peters/fos/boaifaq.htm

Brownlee-Conyers, J. (1996). Voices from networked classrooms. *Educational Leadership, 54*(3), 34–37.

Chenoweth, N. A., Ushida, E., & Murday, K. (2006). Students learning in hybrid French and Spanish courses: An overview of language online. *CALICO Journal, 24*(1), 115–145.

Crawford, W. (2011). *Open access: what you need to know now.* USA: ALA Publishing.

Day M. (1998). Electronic Access: Archives in the New Millennium. Reports on a conference held at the Public Record Office, Kew on 3-4 June 1998 *Ariadane (16).*

Diwan, P., Suri, R. K., & Kaushik, S. (2000). *IT Encyclopaedia.com* (Vol. 1-10). New Delhi: Pentagon Press.

Don Dingsdag, D., Armstrong B. & Neil, D. (2000). *Electronic Assessment Software for Distance Education Students.*

Douglas, M., Praul, M., & Lynch, M. (2008). Mobile learning in higher education: an empirical assessment of a new educational tool. *The Turkish Online Journal of Educational Technology, 7*(3). Retrieved from http://www.tojet.net/articles/732.pdf\

Dwyer, D. (1996). A response to Douglas Noble: We're in this together. *Educational Leadership, 54*(3), 24–27.

Freedman, A. (1996). *The computer desktop encyclopedia.* New York: AMACOM.

Hidreth, C. (2001). Accounting for user's inflated assessment of online catalogue search performance and usefulness an experimental study. *Information Research, 6* (2). Retrieved from http://www.informationR.net/ir/6-2/paper101.html

International Telecommunication Union (ITU). (2013). *The world in 2013: ICT facts and figures.* Retrieved from https://www.itu.int/en/ITU-D/Statistics/.../facts/ ICTFactsFigures2014-e.pdf

Johnson, L., Smith, R., Willis, H., Levine, A., & Haywood, K. (2011). *The 2011 Horizon Report.* Austin, Texas: The New Media Consortium.

Kanugo, S. (1999). *Making IT work.* New Delhi: Sage Publications.

Khona, Z. (2000, September18). Copyright: A safeguard against piracy. *Express Computer, 11*(28), 15.

Kole, E. S. (2001). Internet Information for African Women's Empowerment. Paper presented at the seminar 'Women, Internet and the South', organized by the Vereniging Informatie en International Ontwikkeling (Society for Information and International Development, VIIO), 18 January 2001, Amsterdam. Retrieved from http://www.xs4all.nl/~ekole/public/endrapafrinh.html

Kumar, A. (1999). *Mass Media.* New Delhi: Anmol.

Kumar, A., ... (2010). An exploratory study of unsupervised mobile learning in rural India. Retrieved from http://www.cs.cmu.edu/~anujk1/ CHI2010.pdf

Lesk, M. (1995). *Keynote a*ddress: preserving digital objects: recurrent needs and challenges. Papers from the National Preservation Office Annual Conference - 1995 Multimedia Preservation: Capturing The Rainbow. Retrieved from http://community.bellcore.com/lesk/auspres/aus.html)

Mahajan, S. L. (2002). Information Communication Technology in distance education in India: A challenge. *University News, 40*(19), 1–9.

Maximum security: a hacker's guide to protecting your internet site and network. (1998). New Delhi: Techmedia.

Mcconatha, D., Praul, M., & Lynch, M. (2008). Mobile learning in higher education: An empirical assessment of a new educational tool. *The Turkish Online Journal of Educational Technology* – TOJET, 7 (3). Retrieved from http://davidwees.com/etec522/sites/default/files/mobile%20learning%20in%20 higher%20education.pdf

McGrath, B. (1998). Partners in learning: Twelve ways technology changes the teacher-student relationship. Technological Horizon. *Education, 25*(9), 58–62.

Motlik, S. (2008). Mobile Learning in Developing Nations. *International Review of Research in Open and Distance Learning, 9*(2).

Nowaczyk, R. (1998). Student perception of multimedia in the undergraduate classroom. *International Journal of Instructional Media, 25,* 367–368.

Salaberry, M. (2001). The use of technology for second language learning and teaching: A retrospective. *Modern Language Journal, 85*(1), 41–56. doi:10.1111/0026-7902.00096

Srivastava, K. (2004). Technology based training: Issues and concerns. In E learning and technology: New opportunities in training and development by Reddy, S. (ed.): Hyderabad: ICFAI Books, p. 3 – 18.

Stepp- Greany, J. (2002). Student Perceptions on Language Learning in a Technological Environment: Implications for the New Millennium. *Language Learning & Technology, 6*(1), 165–180.

Strigel, C. (2011). *ICT and the Early Grade Reading Assessment: From Testing to Teaching.* Retrieved from https://edutechdebate.org/reading-skills-in-primary-schools/ict-and-the-early-grade-reading-assessment-from-testing-to-teaching/

Tikam, M., & Lobo, A. (2012). Special Information Center for Visually Impaired Persons – A Case Study. *International Journal of Information Research, 1*(3), 42–49.

Traxler, J. (2007). Defining, discussing and evaluating mobile learning: The moving finger writes and having writ . . .. *International Review of Research in Open and Distance Learning, 8*(2). Retrieved from http://www.irrodl.org/index.php/irrodl/ article/ view/346/875

Trilokekar, N. P. (2000). *A practical guide to information technology act, 2000: Indian cyber law.* Mumbai: Snow White Publications.

UNESCO. (2006). *ICTs in education for people with special needs united nations educational, scientific and cultural organizationunesco institute for information technologies in education specialized training course.* Moscow: UNESCO. Retrieved from http://iite.unesco.org/pics/publications/en/files/3214644.pdf

UNESCO. (2009). *Guide to measuring Information and Communication Technologies (ICT) in education.* Canada: UNESCO Institute for Statistics.

Valk, J., Rashid, A., & Elder, L. (2010). Using Mobile Phones to Improve Educational Outcomes: An Analysis of Evidence from Asia. *The International Review of Research in Open and Distance Learning, 11*(1). Retrieved from http://www.irrodl.org/index.php/ irrodl/article/view/794/1487

Weiss, J. (1994). Keeping up with the research. *Technology and Learning, 14*(5), 30–34.

World Bank. (2002). *Information and Communication Technologies: a World Bank group strategy.* Washington: World Bank.

Yadava, J. S., & Mathur, P. (1998). Mass communication: the basic concepts: Vol. 1 & 2. New Delhi: Kanishka.

ADDITIONAL READING

Ahmed, S. & Singh, M. (2010). Multimedia in Teacher Education Empowering Accessible, Flexible and innovative learning, *Shikshak - Shikha Shodh Patrika, 4*(1), 32-33.

Alexander, S, (2001). E-learning developments and experiences, *Education + Training, 43*, (4-5), 240-248.

Arora, J., Trivedi, K. J. & Kembhavi, A., 2013. Impact of access to e-resources through the UGC-INFONET Digital Library Consortium on research output of member universities. Current Science, February, 104(3).

Baral, A K. (2008, March 10). E-learning and its prospects. *Employment News, 1.*

Barth, M. & et al. (2000). Developing Key Competencies for Sustainable Development in Higher Education, *International Journal of Sustainability in Higher Education,* Retrieved November 18, 2012, from emaraldinsight.com.

Dhar, B. B. (2002). *The importance of ICT in teaching: is it growing?* Delhi: Association of Indian Universities.

Holmes. (2000). *Comparative International Research on Best Practice and Innovation in Learning Consultative Workshop for Developing Performance Indicators for ICT in Education,* UNESCO-Bangkok.

Ignacimuthu, S., Devi, T., & Sarukesi, K. (2002). *Practical Steps for Aligning Technology with Higher Education.* Delhi: Association of Indian Universities.

Kaur, N. (2007, February). E-resources and collection development: emerging issues for the academic libraries. Paper published in 5th International CALIBER -2007, Panjab University, Chandigarh, 08-10 February, 2007. Retrieved from http://iam.inflibnet.ac.in:8080/dxml/bitstream/handle/1944/1435/599-607.pdf? sequence=1

Kozma, R. B. (2005). National Policies that connect ICT-based Education Reform to Economic and Social Development. *An Interdisciplinary Journal on Humans in ICT Environments, 1*(2), 117–156. doi:10.17011/ht/urn.2005355

Kumar, H., et. al. (2006). Using Blogs for Extending Library Services. *University News, 48*(12), 16.

Mislevy, R., Steinberg, L., Almond, R., Haertel, G., & Penuel, W. (2003). Improving educational assessment. In G. Haertel & B. Means (Eds.), *Evaluating Educational Technology: Effective Research Designs for Improving Learning* (pp. 149–180). New York: Teachers College Press.

Mui, Y. H., Kan, E., & Chun, T. Y. (2004). National policies and practices on ICT in education: Singapore. In T. Plomp, R. Anderson, N. Law, & A. Quale (Eds.), *Cross-national information and communication technology policies and practices in education* (pp. 495–508). Greenwich, Connecticut.

Publications, C. (2001). *The copyright act 1957: with short notes.* Mumbai: Current Publications.

UNESCO. (2003). *Developing and Using Indicators of ICT Use in Education.* Paris: UNESCO.

Venna S. K. (2010). Teacher Education some qualitative consideration, *Shikshak - Shikha Shodh Patrika, 4*(1), 10.

Wagner, D., Day, B., James, T., Kozma, R., Miller, J., & Unwin, T. (2005). Monitoring and Evaluation of ICT in Education Projects: A Handbook for Developing Countries. Washington, DC: infoDev /World Bank. Retrieved from http://www.infodev.org/en/Publication.9.html

Waight, C. et al.. (2004). Recurrent themes in e-learning: A narrative analysis of major e-learning report. *The Quarterly Review of Distance Education, 5*(3), 195–203.

Williams, E. B. (2001) "Crossing Borders: Women and Information and Communications Technologies in Open and Distance Learning in the South Pacific" Paper presented at a symposium "Identifying Barriers Encountered by Women in the use of Information and Communications Technologies (ICTs) for Open and Distance Learning in the South Pacific" Organised by: The Commonwealth of Learning: The Open Polytechnic of New Zealand, New Zealand. May 7-11, 2001 Retrieved from http://www.colorg/wdd/ BarriersICT_Africa_report.pdf

Zha, X., Li, J., & Yan, Y. (2012). Understanding Usage Transfer from Print Resources to Electronic Resources: A Survey of Users of Chinese University Libraries. *Serials Review*, *38*(2), 93–98. doi:10.1080/00987913.2012.10765435

KEY TERMS AND DEFINITIONS

Digital Content: Digital Content includes products available in digital form. It typically refers to music, information and images that are available for download or distribution on electronic media.

E- Learning: "E - Learning can be defined as 'learning facilitated and supported through the use of information and communications technology'. It can cover a spectrum of activities from the use of technology to support learning as part of a 'blended' approach (a combination of traditional and e-learning approaches), to learning that is delivered entirely online. Whatever the technology, however, learning is the vital element."

Inclusive Education: Inclusive education defined as including traditionally excluded or marginalized groups or making the invisible visible. The most marginalized groups are often invisible in society: disabled children, girls, children in remote villages, and the very poor. These invisible groups are excluded from governmental policy and access to education. Inclusive education seeks to address the learning needs of all children, youth and adults with a specific focus on those who are vulnerable to marginalisation and exclusion.

Information and Communications Technology (ICT): Refers to all the technology used to handle telecommunications, broadcast media, intelligent building management systems, audiovisual processing and transmission systems, and network-based control and monitoring functions. Although ICT is often considered an extended synonym for information technology (IT), its scope is broader.

M Learning: Mobile learning is broadly defined as the delivery of learning content to learners utilizing mobile computing devices.

Metadata: Metadata is data about data. It includes navigational aids, discovery aids, access counts, guest lists, data bases, combing screens, e-mails, chat group references, how to recover the data stored on the medium and to enable the construction of reading devices etc.

APPENDIX

Table 1. 21 ICT Tools for Education

Sr. No	Tool	Description
1.	Classtools.net	Create free educational games, activities and diagrams
2.	Delicious	Save all your favourite web sites to del.icio.us so you can access them from any computer any time.
3.	Dropbox	Store your files online and access from anywhere
4.	Facebook	A social utility that connects people with friends and others who work, study and live around them.
5.	Gnowledge	A free-to-use education platform where everyone can create, publish, share and take tests, exercises and assignments.
6.	Google Earth	Maps and information from around the world
7.	GoogleDocs	Create and share your work online and access your documents from anywhere.
8.	ISSUU	A digital publishing platform that makes it simple to publish magazines, catalogs, newspapers, books, and more online.
9.	Moodle	Create on-line course content for your students.
10.	Picasa	Organise, Edit, Create & Share your photos
11.	PlanBoard	It's an online lesson planner made for teachers. Create, share, and manage lesson plans with simple and easy to use lesson plan templates.
12.	Prezi	Make zooming presentations. Use text, pictures and insert videos and PDF's
13.	Primarywall	Web-based sticky note tool designed for schools that allows pupils and teachers to work together in real-time
14.	Slideshare	For creating and sharing presentations.
15.	Storybird	Make stories in minutes.
16.	Voice Thread	Participate in discussions about images, documents or videos
17.	Voki	Create a speaking avatar
18.	Wikis	an application, typically a web application, which allows collaborative modification, extension, or deletion of its content and structure
19.	Wordpress	Start blogging
20.	Youtube	Hosts user-generated videos. Includes network and professional content.
21.	Zamzar	web application to convert files

Table 2. 21 ICT Tools for Inclusive Education

S. No.	Tool	Description
		For Magnification
1	Computers having larger screen	Magnifies images of text as well as photographs, charts etc can be provided to the partially sighted.
2	Optelec's ClearView+ Desktop Video Magnifier	Magnifies anything under the viewfinder from 2 to 50 times its original size. It has a specially designed monitor and lighting design for optimum visual enhancement and the entire unit can be controlled with a single button, and can be customized to meet the exact needs.
3	Optelec Compact + Portable Magnifier	The smallest and most user-friendly devise that can be used anywhere and anytime. It has six viewing modes (full color, high contrast black/white, white/black, yellow/black, yellow/blue and full color without light - ideal for magnifying displays such as the screen of your mobile phone). An integrated writing function enables a person to write while viewing what is being written. It is best suited for persons with low vision for attending to their daily reading-writing tasks.
4	Bonita (Portable mouse Magnifier)	Designed for people with low vision. It is a powerful, portable, hand-held electronic reading aid which when moved over a page can capture its image as well as magnify it.
		For Format Conversion
5	Simple Scanners	Used to digitize the notes, question papers, etc
6	Braille embosser	A printer that can be used to print the Braille documents which can be converted from .xls or .doc files into the Braille format with the help of WinBraille 5.1 software. This embosser is capable of printing a single sheet of paper on both the sides.
7	EasyConverter	Creates Large Print, MP3, DAISY and Braille versions of learning materials that can either be scanned from paper, or input from Word, PDF, html or text files and can meet the needs of dyslexic, visually impaired and learning disabled students.
8	Duxbury Braille Translator for windows (DBT 10.7 SR1)	Provides translation and formatting facilities to automate the process of conversion from regular print to Braille (and vice versa), and also provides word-processing facilities for working directly in the Braille as well as the print. **'Fonts'** are used for displaying the Braille. This software is designed so that it can be effectively used by both people knowing Braille as well as those who do not know Braille.
9	Zoom Ex instant reader	A portable device having a highly sensitive camera that can scan images, It can convert any printed text into multiple accessible formats such as speech, large print, sound or text files within seconds. The speech mode offers a choice of accents, one can even select Indian Accent for better understanding.
		For Reading
10	JAWS (Available in Ver13.0, Ver 10.0 and Ver 8.0)	A screen reading software, it converts the computer into a talking machine by providing the user with access to the information displayed on the screen via text to speech made. It also allows comprehensive keyboard interaction with computer.
11	KURZWEIL software	Used for scanning and reading the text. This software reads aloud text in a variety of accents so that the sound can be modified to suit individual preferences.
12	SARA (Scanning and Reading Appliance)	Used for scanning text and then to read it aloud. SARA stores the contents of hundreds scanned pages and can be used to read selected pages.
13	Dolphin easy readers	A software digital talking book player, it allows the user to read and listen to content through a combination of text, audio and images. One of the main advantages of using EasyReader is that the content becomes easy to navigate through, where a reader can skip through sections of their content and place bookmarks to highlight areas of interest.
14	Optelec ClearReader+	A high tech reader with which a visually impaired person can read any kind of printed material. It has a high quality multi-lingual speech output and includes fast text recognition.
15	Open book software	Used to scan, read and change the size & colours of the font according to the student's vision capacity.
16	Dolphin Cicero	Allows scanning and listening to printed documents. It also allows converting the message into speech, large print, or Braille.

continued on following page

Table 2. Continued

S. No.	Tool	Description
17	SightSavers Dolphin Pen	A lightweight pen drive with a screen magnifier and screen reader software, with Braille support.
18	Angel player	Used as a recorder to record and playback the recorded notes. It has different features such as Daisy reader, Ebook, Recording, Radio and Music Player (mp3 files support).
19	Talking Typing Teacher	It reads out the text as it is typed on the keyboard. It is complete interactive software which has both sound and full color animations. This helps students having low vision as well as the visually challenged students to learn typing on the computer and develop speed in a systematic matter.
20	Touch Typing Tutor	A software that activates the screen of a normal computer so that it works like a touch pad by touching the virtual keyboard on the screen one can type out required materials without using keyboard. This software is useful for improving the speech and accuracy of the individual.
21	Spell well software	Used to learn spellings and pronunciation of different words

Table 3. 21 ICT Tools for Evaluation

S. No	Tool	Description
1	Classdojo	ClassDojo helps teachers improve behavior in their classrooms quickly and easily. It also captures and generates data on behavior that teachers can share with parents and administrators. Teachers can use this app to give students real-time feedback while in class - it will sync with the main ClassDojo website. Better learning behaviors, smoother lessons, and hassle free data and it's free for teachers!
2	College Biology Self-Efficacy Instrument	The instrument may lead to further understanding of student behavior, which in turn can facilitate the development of strategies that may increase students' desire to understand and study biology. More specifically, by using the self-efficacy tool as a pre- and posttest indicator, instructors can gain insight into whether students' confidence levels increase as they engage in more complex tasks during the course, and, in addition, what type of teaching strategies are most effective in building confidence among students to achieve biological literacy.
3	Critical Thinking in Everyday Life	This tool is part of a larger evaluation system used to measure the life skills of decision making, critical thinking, problem solving, goal setting, communication, and leadership. The life skills (i.e., decision making, critical thinking, communication, problem solving, and goal setting) selected for this overall measure were thought to be the most commonly identified life skills emphasized in 4-H youth development curricula and program activities.
4	Edmodo	Edmodo is a fantastic tool for collecting student work and assigning quizzes. Students can quiz from Socrative's free iPad app or website, making this tool PC and Mac friendly. All of the data collected can be exported into spreadsheets, making it easy to access and analyze results.
5	Education Galaxy	Education Galaxy also offers diagnostic testing. There is a free version for teachers that doesn't include all of the bells and whistles as the paid version, but still provides diagnostics by standard and skill and prescribes a learning path for instruction based on test results.
6	ForAllRubrics	This software is free for all teachers and allows you to import, create and score rubrics on your iPad, tablet or smartphone. You can collect data offline with no internet access, compute scores automatically and print or save the rubrics as a PDF or spreadsheet.
7	Googleforms	A Google Drive app that allows you to create documents that students can collaborate on in real time using smartphones, tablets and laptops.
8	I>Clicker	A device that helps facilitate all student response to polls, questions and other teacher-led discussions.
9	iClicker	This audience response system is engaging and helps teachers gain real-time feedback on the status of their students' learning. Classes can use their own devices with iClick GO, or they can use specialized remotes if personal or one to one devices aren't allowed in class.

continued on following page

Table 3. Continued

S. No	Tool	Description
10	InfuseLearning	A platform by which teachers can engage all students on any device, getting valuable formative feedback along the way.
11	iReady	This program provides adaptive diagnostic testing and will report on student mastery down to the sub-skill level. The program is adapted by state and district standards, as well as by which Common Core test your state has adopted (if it *has* adopted one). One of the more reasonably priced products out there, the cost is $6 per student, and there are tests for both math and reading diagnostics. For an additional fee ($30 per student for the school year), schools can pay for prescribed personalized lessons based on the student's diagnostic results.
12	Padlet	This app works as a virtual wall or bulletin board where students can collaborate and add ideas in the form of text and multimedia. Padlet can be used as a formative assessment by asking students to answer questions about a topic or to create graphic organizers about what they're learning.
13	Quizlet:	Build flashcards, quizzes, games, and tests in the app. It's free and simple to get started and you have access to the sets created by other users. For $25 per year you can add data tracking, like class progress on the study sets you've created or assigned. You can also add images and voice recording. But even without the bells and whistles, the Quizlet experience makes testing more enjoyable.
14	Reading Horizons	The online software is a yearly subscription that gives a child (ages 4-9) an online, self-directed solution to receiving the fundamental skills of reading (teaches the entire Discovery program through self-directed software).
15	Socrative	Socrative lets teachers engage and assess their students with educational activities on tablets, laptops and smartphones. Through the use of real time questioning, instant result aggregation and visualization, teachers can gauge the whole class' current level of understanding.
16	STAR Early Literacy	STAR Early Literacy assess students' early literacy skills in preparation for reading. SEL identifies student reading levels (e.g. Emergent Reader) and provides student performance results for pre-K through third grade students.
17	STAR Math	The purpose of STAR Math assists to assess student mathematics skills. An approximate students can complete the assessment in less than 12 minutes measure of each students' math level.
18	STAR Reading	STAR Reading helps to assess student reading skills. The assessment provides an approximate measure of each students' reading level.
19	testdyslexia. com	This free and confidential screening assessment will give a profile of learning strengths and weaknesses, including a measure of severity of symptoms.
20	TodaysMeet	This online collaboration tool allows educators to create a "room" in which students can share ideas, answers and thoughts to lectures and lessons. Educators can view student responses in real time for evidence of learning.
21	tv	Bubblr allows users to create trivia quizzes based on YouTube videos. You can play challenges created by other users, or create your own trivia challenges for students. This site helps students get used to being tested on multi-media stimuli, something that is popular in the Common Core tests.

Table 4. 21 ICT Tools for Research

Sr. No.	Tool	Description
For Search/ Organisation		
1	DeweyDigger	Explore knowledge via the Dewey Decimal Classification
2	Findhow	Find how to do things. This site gives you access to trusted, reliable How-To content on the Interne
3	infoplease	General searches plus almanacs, biographies, dictionaries, encyclo pedia, spelling.
4	Livebinders	Collect resources, organize them and add the livebinder button your browser toolbar
5	Nibipedia	Video search.
6	PDFCatch	Ebook, PDF search engine.
For Survey/ Statistics / Display		
7	DataPlot	"a free, public-domain, multi-platform (Unix, VMS, Linux, Windows 95/98/ME/XP/NT/2000, etc.) software system for scientific visualization, statistical analysis, and non-linear modeling. The target Dataplot user is the researcher and analyst engaged in the characterization, modeling, visualization, analysis, monitoring, and optimization of scientific and engineering processes." (Free, multi-platform)
8	Diagrammr	Create visual diagrams, flow charts, brainstorms from text.
9	Poll Daddy	Create your surveys and polls using our custom templates or create your own. Use reporting engine to aggregate, print and export your results.
10	Statistical Lab:	"an explorative and interactive tool designed both to support education in statistics and provide a tool for the simulation and solution of statistical problems."
11	SurvyeMonkey	Design survey, collect responses, analyse results.
For Quoting and Referencing		
12	APA website citation	Create your APA website citation
13	Citation Maker	Create records for books, web sites, interviews, images, music and sound effects, videos and animation, and more. Records can be formatted in either APA or MLA format.
14	Citation Wizard	Automatically generates citations according to MLA style speficiations. In addition to instant citation generation, it allows you to create an entire bibliography document from scratch! You will be able to begin a document, add entries to it, and save the document to your computer.
15	Easybib	Free automatic bibliography and citation maker. Search for your source, build your bibliography, print or export it.
16	Zotero	Free, easy-to-use Firefox extension to help you collect, manage and cite your research sources.
For Anti-plagiarism Check		
17	Anti-Plagiarism	A versatile tool to deal with World Wide Web copy-pasting information from the assignment of authorship.
18	DupliChecker	A 100% free, easy to operate and fast tool.
19	Paper Rater	It offers three tools: Grammar Checking, Plagiarism Detection and Writing Suggestions.
20	PlagiarismChecker	PlagiarismChecker.com makes it simple for educators to check whether a student's paper has been copied from the Internet. Users can also use the "Author" option to check if others have plagiarized their work online.
21	Viper	It is a fast plagiarism detection tools with the ability to scan your document through more than 10 billion resources, such as academic essays and other online sources, offering side-by-side comparisons for plagiarism.

Chapter 3

Information Communication Technology and the Street-Level Bureaucrat:
Tools for Social Equity and Progressive Activism

Lester Leavitt
Florida Atlantic University, USA

ABSTRACT

This chapter explains the theory behind an information communication technology (ICT) being developed to provide marginalised populations with a tool for uniting the voices of progressive-minded activists. The theory suggests that with this technology, seemingly incompatible progressive groups might enlarge their campaigns for social equity, creating a global, heterogeneous network. The ICT allows for the capture of crowd-sourced artistic creativity, and through algorithms that have been shaped by academics in public administration, makes content retrievable as pluralistic, policy-supporting narrative threads. The new narratives should also work to alter the discourse within communities by diminishing the worldview threats associated with zero-sum ideology. This ICT is seen as vital because of how powerful lobbyists (funded by global elites) have consistently been successful in skewing the outcomes of policymaking decisions and elections. The system is firmly rooted in the small-group, consensus-building organisational theories of respected authors dating back to the 1970s.

INTRODUCTION

If nothing else, what engaged citizens should have learned from the global protests in 2011 is that young people are frustrated at their prospects for the future. Estimates are that on the weekend of November 12 - 13 that year, "Occupy" actions (organized by groups that trace their origins to the "Occupy Wall Street" movement, the European austerity protests, and the Arab Revolutions) took place in 951 cities and 82 countries (Rogers, 2011). Nevertheless, very little *structural* change has taken place in the years

DOI: 10.4018/978-1-5225-0556-3.ch003

since the 2011 protests. This chapter proposes that the failure of these and other contemporary efforts to change the governing paradigm has actually been a failure to identify hierarchical authority as the problem, in spite of numerous theorists who have pointed to this over the decades. The theory suggests that unsuccessful efforts to alter the structural dynamics of governing also can be traced to an inability to *extract the institutional memory* (specifically, the media material that is used to impact policymaking) *and its custodians* from the grasp of the hierarchy.

What will be shown is that current cloud technology not only makes change like this possible, but once the theory expands upon what the available options are the possibility emerges whereby the algorithms that give the policymaking institutional memory its utility could also be engineered to provide a functional *direct democracy system* (Leavitt, 2013, p. 458). This chapter will demonstrate this by first explaining how the ICT works within the most basic organisational unit of community governance, at which point it becomes apparent that through the algorithms of the institutional memory database, a global network could emerge organically. In support of taking this global view of a local problem, organisational theory expert Morgan wrote, "...we may be able to remove key problems [within our institutions] by changing the 'rules of the game' that produce them" (2006, pp. 332-333). Morgan, like Thayer 33 years before him, was referring to a complete restructuring of the hierarchical organisation, and by extension, the bureaucracy that controls which policy proposals are introduced, and which ones succeed (Thayer, 1973).

This chapter will first describe a new kind of organisational model that circumvents hierarchy (and the lobbyists that leverage it to their advantage). The chapter will then describe the stakeholders for this new global (virtual) institution and explore their relationships with each other as populations that have traditionally been kept hopelessly fragmented. With this foundation, the chapter will conclude by describing how a reengineered institutional memory for the agenda setting process could be blended with information communication technology to unify all of these global populations and provide them with the tools for not only improving policymaking outcomes, but also a tool for self-governance.

BACKGROUND

It was the famed sociologist Robert Michels who wrote in 1911 about the iron law of oligarchy. In that piece "... he developed the view that modern organizations typically end up under the control of narrow groups, even when this runs against the desires of the leaders as well as the led. ... Despite the best intentions, these organizations seemed to develop tendencies that gave their leaders a near monopoly of power (Morgan, 2006, p. 296)." In similar ways, modern theories about these organisational elites continue to underscore why the problems with government and public administration are what they are today (Farazmand, 1999, p. 325; Chen, 2009, p. 451; Thayer, 2002, pp. 107-115). This introduces the much larger debate about the stratospheric increase in the wealth of the global elite, all in a time when middle-class wealth is stagnating, which was the topic of Piketty's bestseller, *Capital in the Twenty-first Century* (2014, p. 24).

Balancing social equity in the face of poorly-regulated capitalism will be a growing problem unless something is done to devolve the power downward once again; into the hands of the electorate where it was designed to be by the eighteenth-century engineers of democracy. Public administration, as an academic field, has tried to facilitate this process over the years, and in the 1960s (notably with the Minnowbrook

I Conference in 1968) leaders became very vocal in proposing that the field assume an *advocacy* role in the defence of social equity for vulnerable and marginalised populations (Gooden & Portillo, 2011, pp. 1-14). This, however, never happened, and in light of the severity of the current crisis of social inequity, academics are asking why. The failure, in the view of many, is blamed on a kind of wandering in the wilderness where everyone was scrambling to offer a more palatable free-market alternative form of government. Farazmand wrote of this period by stating how "organizational eclecticism" has prevailed for four decades now. The title of Farazmand's article sums up his thoughts well as he asks, "Can we go home now?" (Farazmand, 2013, p. 219).

Statement of Purpose

This chapter argues that in order to facilitate this return to our "home" (i.e. the ideals of the 1960s), public administration needs to become far more multidisciplinary, enlarging our scope to include inquiry into social psychology, media and communication, and as advocated by this chapter, information systems that can be employed at the grassroots level. With improved tools, street-level bureaucrats, community organizers, social entrepreneurs, and any other progressive political activist will be far better equipped to fix the problems where they are first experienced. What arguably will emerge from the information communication technology being proposed here is a mechanism for creating an efficient heterogeneous network (Leavitt, 2013, p. 460; Sandström & Carlsson, 2008, p. 507) that is simultaneously *local* at the most basic of levels, yet *global* in its scope and reach; a process now referred to as "*glocalization*" (Hong & Song, 2010).

Before this glocalization can emerge it will be vital that the citizens of less-powerful nations become as informed as possible in what their role is as a member of "the polis," with *polis* being defined in the context that Deborah Stone used it in *Policy Paradox*; as "an entity small enough to have very simple forms of organization yet large enough to embody the elements of politics" (2002, p. 17). Having said that, however, the theories that trace the extent of control held by the global elite continue to show that there is a lack of a clear, practical method whereby oppressed populations can effectively participate. Such a mechanism has to exist before equal and fair access to the democratic process can be restored for marginalised populations (El-Mahdi, 2009, p. 1011). Because it hopes to do this, the ICT introduced within this chapter could be summarized as an effort to engineer a new paradigm for accessible democracy. For the sake of simplicity, the author has adopted the name *MOCSIE Systems* for this ICT.

MOCSIE is an acronym for Media Omniverse Collective for Social Initiative and Enterprise. It is an information system that has been six years in development, first as a media technology project as the capstone project of the author's bachelor's degree in multimedia journalism, and more recently as an integration of several technologies into a comprehensive ICT platform.

Changing the Rules of the Game

Morgan and Thayer are not the only ones who have tried to bring in a new paradigm for how our public institutions are constituted. In the preface to his current edition of Public Organization, Denhardt writes, "As a theory of organization, [the history of past efforts of the field has] limited itself to instrumental concerns expressed through hierarchical structures, failing to acknowledge or to promote the search for alternative organizational designs." His tone is almost as serious as Thayer's as he underscores how scrious hc is by adding, "If democracy is to survive in our society, it must not be overridden by the false promises of hierarchy and authoritarian rule. Democratic outcomes require democratic processes" (Denhardt, 2011, pp. x-xi; emphasis in original).

While Morgan and Denhardt are current in the field, Thayer's views are almost 40 years old, but nevertheless, they have shaped the engineering of this proposed information system because he was one of the earliest, and arguably the most strident, in strongly advocating for a new paradigm that abandoned hierarchy. Thayer's suggestion was that society and its institutions be guided by an "almost infinite number of small groups" instead of a hierarchy (1973, p. 171). Being a visionary, Thayer did not concern himself with how these groups would be connected to each other because, like many of his era, he anticipated that the computer would soon make the impossible, possible, so he simply set out ideas for what "should be," not what was practical at the time. As a starting point he set out to identify the ideal group size for consensus-building. As he traced the history of human civilization he found that most tasks seemed naturally suited for a small group process, and that the natural affinity was to gravitate into these small groups when work becomes especially challenging and the risk of an incorrect decision increases (1973, p. 8). He concludes on this topic by affirming that, "While common sense would seem to dictate that there can be no 'magic' number, five appears so often in so many environmental situations to carry persuasion with it" (Thayer, 1973, p. 8). In the references at the back of his book he cites over a dozen studies that support this number (p. 199).

Figure 1 shows what might best be described as a community oversight organisation that brings together 18 individuals and gives them a mandate to unify all of the policymaking needs of any number of local nonprofits and government agencies. These people can be thought of as the street-level bureaucrats of today. These people also happen to be the bureaucrats that are furthest removed from the policymaking decisions that, nevertheless, impact their daily work the most. Experience has shown that even when those street-level bureaucrats furthest from the centre attempt to effect policy change, their ideas carry little weight as they advocate for change to their superiors; a process that Hal Rainey calls "…information leakage as lower-level officials communicate up the hierarchy" (Rainey, 2009). Figure 1 is a bit misleading though because it makes no attempt to distinguish which level of government these 18 individuals report to.

Figure 1. Traditional hierarchy at the street-level-bureaucrat level

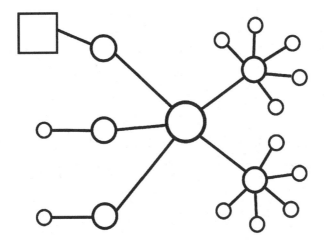

In practice, in most Western democracies they will likely be divided into one of six divisions of government that are represented by Figure 2. Street-level bureaucrats in traditional departments will find themselves reporting up a hierarchy to superiors who are in federal, state (or province), county (or equivalent), city, or school district administrative roles. At the street-level it is even more complicated because of the involvement of the nonprofit sector, which is represented by the sixth column in Figure 2. As noted in the right-hand sidebar of Figure 2, authority flows downward in these silos, but the decision-makers are furthest from the point of delivery for public goods and services, which is a violation of Mary Parker Follet's *Law of the Situation*, in which she stated, "My solution is to depersonalize the giving of orders, to unite all concerned in a study of the situation, to discover the *law of the situation*, and obey that." (1926; emphasis added).

What is outlined in this chapter is a new authority structure as represented by Figure 3, which shows how individuals who choose to collaborate or otherwise work together can bridge the dividing lines between the levels of government at the point of contact with the citizens, creating an *informal institution*. In today's climate, where governments are deeply divided ideologically, they will only be able to do this if they have a new kind of information communication technology that will create a completely new institutional memory. This is what will allow for the uniting of the *citizens* with the *street-level*

Figure 2. The six silos of governance and their reliance upon hierarchical power

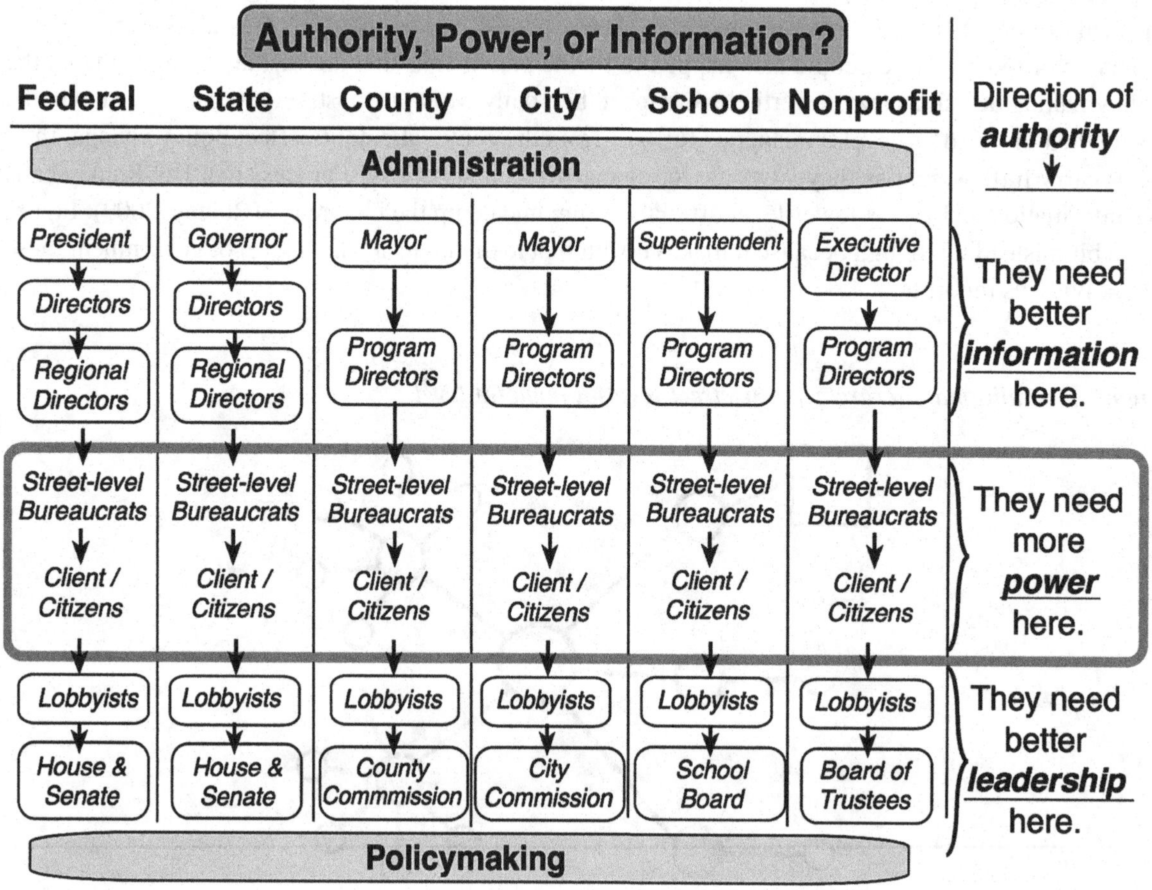

bureaucrats, *community organizers*, and the *nonprofit sector*. Note how the reconfigured organisational model that has been superimposed on the left side of Figure 3 represents the same 18 individuals that were illustrated with a hierarchical model in Figure 1. What should be immediately evident with this inset is that, even though every position is in an identical position to Figure 1 (remove all of the connecting lines), the superimposed model in Figure 3 operates with four linked groups, and is therefore free of a hierarchical structure. The "juggler" role (the individual in the middle) will be explained further along in the chapter when the first hypothesis is introduced, but suffice it to say at this point that this is the individual who brings the other 17 together without pursuing any kind of leadership authority.

ENVISIONING "GLOCALIZATION"

The goal of this redesign for governance was to propose new relationships between existing people at the community level so that they would merge Thayer's small-group, consensus-building ideals (1973, p. 171) with Follet's *Law of the Situation*. The inset in Figure 3 outlines four such groups that are captured in more detail in Figure 4, but this chapter is about much more than reconfiguring community organisations. It is about creating a completely re-imagined institution that comes together organically *without creating a hierarchy*, which is what the stacking mechanism represented by Figure 4 is meant to illustrate. This, of course, is where the new paradigm can be imagined best if viewed through the lens of a virtual (cloud-based) institution. As a model for scalability, it is important to note that so long as the "institutional memory" is digital, and resident in the cloud, that same ICT that would serve a single organisation with 18 individuals in it (the inset of Figure 3) could be launched from enterprise-level platforms to serve thousands of city-based units simultaneously.

Figure 3. Allowing for the formation of an informal institution over the provision of public goods and services

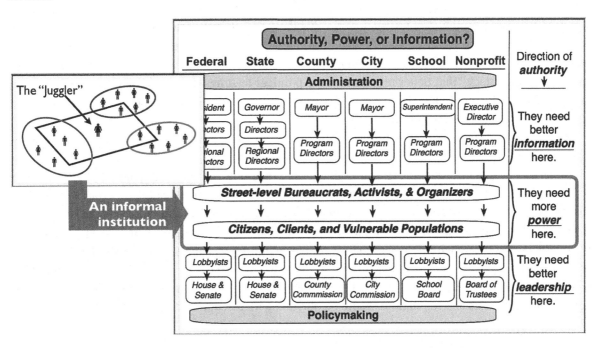

Figure 4. The stacking mechanism of the MOCSIE Systems that precludes the formation of hierarchies

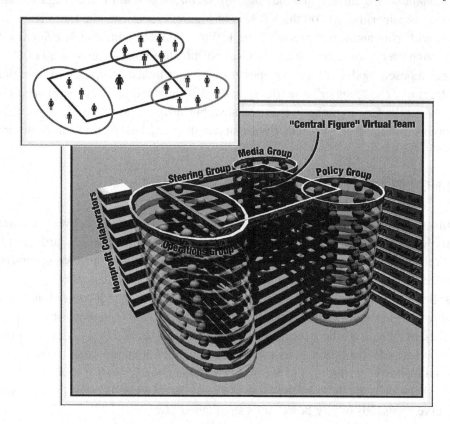

Figure 4 simply illustrates a stack of ten such "community-based" layers, but in truth there would be no defined limitation. The existence of the relationships between individuals in the vertical columns of Figure 4would not be impeded by political or geographical boundaries, and it could not be easily co-opted by any institutional elites because, in this day and age, the component parts of the informal institution could be easily tweaked and re-launched under a different name, and from another server. In other words, a group that is displeased with its current associations would simply "vote with their feet" and find a new "stack" that better represents their political leanings. It is important to note, however, that the new stack would likely still be tapping into the same institutional memory. The *data does not change*, just the associations within the stack.

Before leaving Figure 4, note that each of the four groups represent a different role within the new organisational structure. A policy group (right circle), with its six members, would oversee six all-encompassing social justice campaigns, a media group (top circle), with its six members, would oversee six all-encompassing genres of artistic creativity, an operations group (the oval in the front) would make sure that each unit runs smoothly, and a steering group of six that links the outer three groups (the square) would "govern" the community. The single, over-arching goal of the four groups at the community level is to *unify the discourse* within the community that each unit represents. According to Thayer's theory, when functioning without a hierarchy, "unity" would come by striving for *consensus*. In governing this way, no "authority" would swoop in to enforce or impose new governing regulations of policy. Instead, agreement on policies and regulations would be pursued with discourse. It is important to note that this theory is not proposing to redefine all public institutions. Policing, for example, requires unquestioned authority in exchange for respect for the citizens' right to due process. This theory, at this early stage, is only about *determining policies* that defend and advance social equity.

An important point that this chapter hopes to make later on through a sampling of literature on the global elite is that it is important to underscore how the MOCSIE Systems are not another social media site. As will be explained later, the fact that the media will be proactively and selectively solicited by politically motivated (*progressive*) social entrepreneurs and community activists elevates this information communication technology from being a simple crowd-sourcing social site to the point that it can be seen as a tool of democracy, free speech, and representative governance. It is not a passive system; it is an activist-driven, grassroots system for making the governing process truly, in every way, a consensus-building direct-democracy system.

The Twin Hypotheses

We live in a political climate where it is dangerous for a population to expose where they are most vulnerable because those in positions of power routinely exploit vulnerabilities, and the phenomenon is not limited to tyrannical regimes. In many cases, the policies of Western democracies have been incredibly oppressive and damaging to minority populations, and even women, who make up half the population! In reviewing the book, Globalization from Below, Peter Evans wrote, "Preoccupation with movement democracy is complemented by a profound distrust of established governance organizations" (2007, p. 62). It is noteworthy that he wrote that more than a year before the global financial crisis, and the book certainly foreshadowed the protests of 2011.

This chapter recognises that within this emerging information communication technology, at the nexus of organisational behaviour and policymaking, resides a paradox of vulnerability and trust. The importance of building in a mechanism to compensate for this was seen as critically important because the trust of the common person has routinely been violated; the most glaring example being the events of more than three decades that led up to the 2008 financial crisis, followed-up by a failure to prosecute a single elite individual for any kind of failing in what will likely go into the record books as the largest upward transfer of wealth in the history of humankind (Kolnick, 2012). Even beyond that, it has not seemed to matter whether a person lived in a democratic nation or one ruled by a dictator, because, in both cases, vulnerable people routinely have their trust in leadership violated. Mohamed Bouazizi, the individual credited with lighting the spark that fuelled all of the 2011 protests by setting himself on fire in a remote Tunisian town, should have been able to trust the police in his town to enforce the law equally. He was vulnerable to a corrupt system that was untrustworthy.

It is believed that the MOCSIE Systems can (and will) achieve wide-spread use, and the measures of this success will revolve around twin hypotheses, each in turn intended to mitigate the problems of vulnerability and trust. The central-figure hypothesis is proposed to test whether or not people can be motivated to contribute to the institutional memory, as well as to glean narrative content from it in supporting effective policy proposals in the agenda setting process. This behaviour will, of course, radiate out from those 18 individuals represented in Figures 3 and 4. There will, of course, be no organisation if nobody steps up to organize them, and this is where the central figure comes in, or, as pointed out in the inset of Figure 3, the "juggler." There will need to be a person – a social entrepreneur – who is so driven by a passion for social justice that she or he will be willing to persist with dogged determination in the daunting task of bringing together a team of 17 existing (preferably recognized and respected) community leaders for a unified purpose of improving policymaking decisions on behalf of a population.

This person will have to be a driven individual because, within marginalised populations, most people are reluctant to listen to the initial sales pitch for "yet another nonprofit advocacy group." History has told most marginalised people to mistrust newcomers and individuals with grandiose ideas. At the root of the problem is hegemony, a topic that will be covered in detail further along in this chapter, but for now, suffice it to say it is because of hegemony that there is so much distrust of upstart leaders who come into a community with big promises. Hegemony essentially is what convinces people to just accept things the way they are because, even if things are bad, they might get worse if you "jerk on the chain" of the powerful and wake the sleeping tiger. The *central figure* will not only need to overcome this age-old tactic of fragmentation, but they will also have to be the kind of person that Al Sharpton is, who captured the spirit of this chapter well by simply stating, "A lot of things were acceptable – until we *stopped* accepting it" (Sharpton, 2011).

While on the topic of hegemony, it needs to be pointed out that, for centuries now, philosophers and theorists have advocated that hegemonic narratives be deconstructed. While that might be one tactic of the proposed MOCSIE Systems, it will not be the main tactic. Hugh Miller suggests an approach that differs from most others in that he advocates for the displacement of harmful narratives like those advanced under the umbrella of hegemony. This displacement is accomplished by putting forth a new narrative that tells a more compelling story of how things should be different than they are (Miller, 2012, p. 108). The proposed tactics through which this will be done will be explained later in this chapter.

The second hypothesis, referred to as the collective-thought hypothesis, supports two ideas. First, as noted above, most marginalised populations know that they are vulnerable when the dominant group concentrates its power in a hierarchy, so in constructing a new paradigm an easily demonstrated alternative to hierarchy must first be put into place before existing opinion leaders will recommend to the community that they put their trust in the charismatic central figure who will necessarily emerge as their spokesperson. Undeniably, charisma makes a person a natural at leading and organising, but that charisma can be frightening to a population that has previously been sucked in by charisma and suffered as a result. To make matters worse for this central figure, the "capture" of a charismatic leader is a common practice of organisational elites who swoop in and make promises of greatness to those who rise to the top and, with the promise of money and/or power, turn them against the people that gave them their trust (Farazmand, 1999; Thayer, 2002). The *collective-thought hypothesis* supports making this central figure just another voice in one of the four consensus-building groups of the MOCSIE Systems organisational model (Figures 3 and 4). The very design of the model is engineered to circumvent this.

Second, in addition to placing the central figure into the steering group (the linking square of Figures 3 and 4), rather than giving her or him a position in a hierarchy, the collective-thought hypothesis also relates to how the community-based governing unit is structured so as to germinate a consensus-building process for framing and contextualizing the growing repository of records in the institutional memory, enabling users from within the community to effectively *displace* those harmful, socially constructed narratives that are rooted in, and defended by, hegemony. Again, it is important to note that *displace* was used in that sentence, not *deconstruct*.

Space does not permit more detailed coverage of what leadership qualities the central figure (the *juggler*) will need to possess in order to accomplish the daunting task before them, but Figure 5 represents six very specific, multidisciplinary talents that the *MOCSIE Systems* proposes to teach in what is

Figure 5. The complex, multidisciplinary leadership role of the central figure or "juggler"

Item #3: The Disconnect   Item #4: The Campaigns

Item #2: Empathy

Item #5: The Missing Activists

Item #1: The Echo Chamber

Item #6: Marketable Multimedia

Imagine a Person Capable of Juggling Diverse Responsibilities

intended to be a certificate program for individuals seeking leadership skills in social equity activism. They include skills in media, communication, sociology, political science, social psychology, information systems, artistic creativity, and of course, public administration.

Preparing a regimen for training this new breed of political activist is an integral part of the *MOCSIE Systems*. Again, citing Peter Evans from 2007, he predicted that the globalisation movement that was started by capitalists would eventually divide the elite class and open a window of opportunity for global solidarity (2007, p. 64). Seven years later, political scientist Randall Schweller dedicated an entire book to expanding this idea, referring to the phenomenon of destabilising the hegemonic forces as "global entropy." In his book he documents just how ripe the world is for chaos if a new global power structure is not put into place quickly (2014). It is the opinion of this author that both of these men are correct. The window of opportunity is wide open at the moment, but the counter-hegemonic voices have yet to coalesce. The *juggler* role was engineered into this socio-technical system as the catalyst for the unification of progressive voices precisely because it was seen as the only kind of a leader capable of not only surviving, but also *thriving*, in the face of this entropy that Schweller describes so succinctly.

Nowhere was the *absence* of this leadership talent more evident than in the wake of the protest movements of 2011 when we, as researchers, found ourselves combing through hundreds of web pages simply to excavate any semblance of a narrative thread that would support the kind of policy change capable of satisfying the protestors' demands. The material was there because the protestors had been very faithful in holding their daily "circle time" (an Occupy Wall Street term) and drafting manifestos, so they had enormous amounts of "information." What they lacked was the "system" to make it usable.

Overcoming the Instability of Funding

In the non-profit sector, grant making is just another institution of hierarchy. Even if this were not a problem unto itself, grant funding is notorious for its instability because, by its very nature, it lacks a guarantee that it will be there from one year to the next. In light of this, grant funding is currently only being pursued to fund the development of the *MOCSIE Systems* software and a start-up year of operations. Beyond that, the MOCSIE Systems have been structured in such a way that they should be self-funded by traffic to the global domain. Even at that, a monetized web domain will be just one of four revenue streams designed into the model. Items that are expected to be for sale through an online store are things like limited edition art prints, books, CD's, DVD's, postcards, bumper stickers, mugs, t-shirts, other apparel, bookmarks, and other related items. Additionally, revenue streams will also be realized from symposia, exhibitions, tours, and public speaking engagements by members of the collective. Finally, tuition fees from a future online university will round out the income streams.

Although the ultimate self-funding model is still being engineered, it is the intent of the model that any profits be shared in similar ways to how the farmer's cooperatives structured their marketplace more than a century ago; specifically, that members of the collective who have converted their talent into revenue streams should be compensated relative to their contribution. The difference, of course, is that in this collective no capital will have to be tied up in real estate. With its own revenue streams, it is hoped that the global institution will enjoy complete autonomy.

THE STAKEHOLDERS

When it is proposed that this new model for governance be self-funding, most listeners interpret that to mean that it will look and "feel" like a business, and a business necessarily has stakeholders. From that perspective, then, the stakeholders of the MOCSIE Systems will be any marginalised or oppressed population, no matter where they might be located. If they are capable of generating a message in support of a desired policy change (i.e. media, in any of six genres), and they can somehow get that media into the institutional memory of the MOCSIE Systems, then they are, by definition, one of its stakeholders.

Further to that, if you are a member of an oppressed or marginalised population, then you are also a survivor of abuse. Continuing on in this vein, survivors of abuse will always benefit by belonging to a therapy group. In this regard, the MOCSIE Systems will be seen by its stakeholders as a kind of mental health organisation, and that is a wonderful thing. For this reason, the ICT database, by itself, will be engineered so that it can be accessed by the most vulnerable and marginalised people who stand the most to gain by affiliating themselves with it.

As it relates to how crowd-sourcing of media might be considered an exercise of mental health therapy, research supports the fact that by simply having a validating outlet through which one can recount one's abuse (i.e. their marginalization), a person begins the healing process and ends the cycle of submitting to further abuse. Studies show that survivors of abuse who do not talk about it impair their recovery (Lepore, Ragan, & Jones, 2000; Hemenover, 2003; Ruggiero et al., 2004). One psychologist writes, "Those who have survived [traumatic events] learn that their sense of self, of worth, of humanity, depends upon a feeling of connection to others. The solidarity of a group provides the strongest protection against [...] despair" (Herman, 1997). Countless web pages have already become invaluable as virtual support groups to meet the demand, but, similar to the narratives of the 2011 protest movements, as a system it is hopelessly fragmented. That kind of data is invaluable in the policymaking process, but again, the data, as currently constituted, does not lend itself for use within an ICT. It is part of the web, but it is not useable in the ways outlined for the institutional memory that this chapter advocates.

Cast in this light, the amazing thing is that by its mere existence, the MOCSIE Systems could arguably qualify as a resounding success even if no data is ever *retrieved* from its database. Therefore, even though the topic of societal abuse (and its victims) will not come up again in this chapter, it needs to be understood that from a mental health standpoint, anything that alters the discourse inside a person's own head will be therapeutic, and the natural outcome of that is that those loved ones and acquaintances of that individual will begin to hear a new discourse as well.

Also, by extension, when a victim of societal abuse is introduced to a fellow survivor with a similar story, they *also* start a conversation (in those vertical stacks shown in Figure 4). When provided with a safe, nurturing, and supportive environment, these conversations will build momentum. As *new narratives for living* emerge, a change within the community begins to evolve, even if the change is not immediately visible to outside observers. For the remainder of this chapter, even though it will primarily discuss the institutionalized, proactive role that the MOCSIE Systems will assume in resisting some of the most powerful forces on the planet, the change that occurs in the hearts and minds of its individual participants should never be overlooked or underestimated for the degree of its impact.

Collective Will and an End to Hierarchy

It should now be apparent that every element of the MOCSIE Systems is connected in some way to its institutional memory through its information communication technology. That is because, as shown by Figure 4, with its ten layers and 18 individuals in each layer, the institution per se *could not exist* outside of the ICT. It is, in the purest sense, a virtual institution that is cloud-resident. While the 18 individuals at the community level might see each other face-to-face on a daily basis, it is possible that most of the "work" that needs to be done is work that will require these individuals to be engaged with individuals in the vertical stack (the virtual realm) who are similarly situated in distance neighbourhoods. In other words, "going to work" will likely not require interaction on the horizontal layer (the real world) as much as it will require going online to interact with your colleagues in the vertical columns of the stacked organisations. Regardless, in this model, *a person's entire work environment is contained by the technology*, and therefore, so is the decision-making process that guides how its crowd-sourced content will be utilized; both as media, and as a policy-making tool.

Just to review then, when imagined as a matrix of 180 individuals, the Figure 4 representation of the MOCSIE Systems socio-technical model cannot be construed in any way to show a hierarchy. This should serve to reinforce how every decision is derived as a product of a *collective* effort. Similarly, the natural outcome of the work of the 180 individuals represented in Figure 4 will be that the supporting information that is guiding the policymaking process in ten cities (and by extension at the state or provincial level, and possibly at the federal level) will now be remarkably similar in each of the respective communities, regardless of where that community might be on the planet. For the sake of clarity, the model in Figure 4 was limited to ten horizontal (stacked) units, but in practice the composition of these stacks will be very organic, where affiliates can come and go based upon where they find their best allies. The stack will, of course, become unwieldy if it grows too "tall," and it is therefore anticipated that most groups will affiliate themselves formally with about a dozen companion organisations where the "fit" is well-matched to neighbourhood circumstances. The benefit, of course, comes from the feature that every group will have access to the same narrative threads emerging from the institutional memory and ICT, regardless of who generates them. Therefore, a national policy that is being worked on by hundreds of inner-city groups simultaneously could, in truth, be considered the outgrowth of several smaller "stacked" groups with 10 to 12 layers in each.

AN ALGORITHM FOR SOCIAL CONSTRUCTIONISM

From a postmodern perspective it needs to be understood that what we think of as "truth" is a social construct. In keeping with this logic, the political "left" and the political "right" are also social constructs. We only know how to define "conservative" and "progressive," or "liberal" and "libertarian," because of narratives that have been handed down to us from our parents, grandparents, schoolteachers, and the media, to name just a few sources. In church, as illustrated so well by the character Tevye in Fiddler on the Roof, we are taught that the only "tradition" worth preserving is the one that relates to our own culture (Stein, 1964). Edgar Schein wrote an entire book on "organizational culture" to put this into an institutional perspective (2010).

Based on these narratives, the deliberate progressive framing of this chapter advocates change from the traditional, which sets the stage for a confrontation with the conservative-minded. For a majority of conservatives, the leaders within their cultural institutions have typically framed change as a *worldview threat*. After all, from a governing perspective, nothing seems to propel a governing narrative within conservative crowds better than the fear that cherished traditions are being put at risk. This describes the ubiquity of the "Take our Country Back" narrative used by conservatives to motivate their electoral base in the United States.

Given this understanding as a starting point, we can better understand governing narratives as they are now constituted in many parts of the world. What we have in many countries is a dialectical discourse; dialectical inasmuch as there are frequently two completely opposite dominant narratives. For this chapter, the dialectical nature of them can be thought of in terms of the viewpoints being 180° opposed to each other. In zero-sum terms, if one is correct, the other has to be wrong by default, which is why it is so easy to motivate conservatives with a worldview threat.

What is not implied with a vision of dialectical narratives is that there should be 178° of possible compromise between the two polar opposites; possibilities that will only be considered in a spirit of compromise, and which, in postmodernist terms, can only be realized by swaying public opinion in such a way that diversity or pluralism are also not framed as a worldview threat to conservatives. As shown in Figure 6, this principle might be more easily understood if the reader imagines a protractor overlaid onto a dialectical line between the political foes of the left and right.

At this point the nature of writing in policymaking terms becomes very reductionist, grossly oversimplifying the algorithms that will go into engineering the information communication technology, but it was felt that a simple discussion that conveys the idea of how narrative threads are germinated within the database was warranted.

Regardless of how similar or dissimilar other countries are to the United States, the *MOCSIE Systems* information communication technology could possibly provide the best way forward in countries where compromise has become impossible between ideological extremists who are now painting politics as a zero-sum game that should be approached with the same zeal as religious fundamentalism. With alarming regularity across the globe, when it comes to policymaking and the agenda setting process it is becoming increasingly clear that we, as citizens of these countries, will have to define the new governing narratives on behalf of, and for the benefit of, our legislative bodies. This discussion therefore now turns toward a discussion of how computer algorithms might be able to suggest viable and nonviable narratives as policy proposals by generating narrative threads that approximate what was illustrated by Figure 6. Again, as a reminder, this chapter takes a simplistic approach to what will inevitably be a multi-year process of refining incredibly complex software.

Figure 6. Measuring the viability of ideographs for their potential to support policy proposals

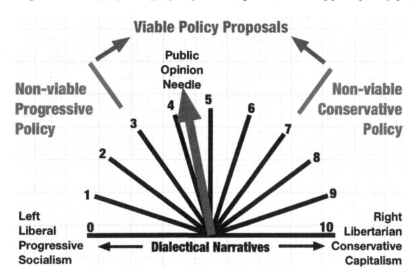

A "Consultable Record"

In the same year that Thayer published his book, back in a period when computer memory was still being loaded with punch cards, Clifford Geertz, one of the most influential cultural anthropologists of the 20th century (Shweder and Good, 2005), wrote about the importance of having a "consultable record of what man has said" (Geertz, 1973, p. 30). In 2000, Dvora Yanow elevated this thinking when she suggested that by, "Observing what people do and how they do it, listening to how they talk about the issue, reading what they read, and talking with them about their lives…", a person becomes more in tune with what the policymaking needs of a population are because they come to understand the true issues of concern. She continues by stating that, "Out of this growing familiarity, the researcher-analyst will be able to identify the overlappings and commonalities…" (Yanow, 2000, p. 37). Both of these academics were talking about the value of having access to *qualitative* information as "institutional memory" (Thayer, 1973, p. 171).

There is one important point that needs to be made here for the readers that do not understand the nature of policymaking. Governing policies are *not* fact-based. Good research does *not* determine the direction of policymaking in the same way that a compelling argument does, and this is why we have social *inequity* in every part of the world. This ICT promises to back good research up with the compelling arguments that it needs in order to get better policies through the agenda setting process. It is anticipated that this institutional memory will be full of compelling stories that not only outline the seriousness of societal problems, but also, it is felt that by linking similar stories into narrative threads, and subsequently linking them to a viable policy proposal that will fix that problem, a new kind of governing narrative will emerge.

The Ideographic Records

As described earlier, the records within the MOCSIE Systems are called ideographs, and in their raw form they will exist in isolation from each other, like the bricks in a brick wall that arrived neatly stacked on pallets. Without the proper fields within these records, there could be no algorithm with which the necessary narrative threads could be invoked through the query mechanism, therefore the goals of the emerging virtual governing institution could not be accomplished. The system will also somehow need to support those small-group decision-makers represented in Figures 3 and 4. As noted, one group (the policy group) is charged with putting forward policy proposals, and another (the media group) is charged with framing the media so that it provides compelling narratives to propel each policy proposal through the agenda setting process. Beyond that, the entire team of 18 individuals is charged with altering the discourse *within their own communities* so that marginalised populations begin to see themselves through a different lens as well. To do this manually would be an enormous task, but with a crowd-sourced institutional memory with properly engineered search algorithms that generate narrative threads, it is expected that this process will be no more complicated than searching for something inside Wikipedia.

Figure 7 provides a graphic illustration of the institutional memory that captures the top four drill-down tiers of the media campaigns (top left exploded box) as well as a similar drill-down mechanism into the policy campaigns (bottom left exploded box). Each starts in the first tier with these twelve all-inclusive groupings (recall Figure 4, with its six media leaders and six policy leaders) before being broken out in the second tier into *media genres* (on the top media campaigns half) and *sustaining institutions* (on the bottom policy campaigns half). Beyond that the units are referred to as "communities," which is a reflection of the research that supports the idea that "narrative communities" are, for many in the field of organisation theory, viable *institutions* unto themselves (Baker, 2006, p. 463; Schein, 2010, p. 70). This is why the individual elements of the second tier on the bottom half (i.e. one tier removed from the six policy campaigns) are referred to as *sustaining institutions* for the meta-narrative and micro-narrative communities (Leavitt, 2013, pp. 459-464).

Figure 7. Diagrammatic model of the institutional memory with associated heterogeneous policy networks

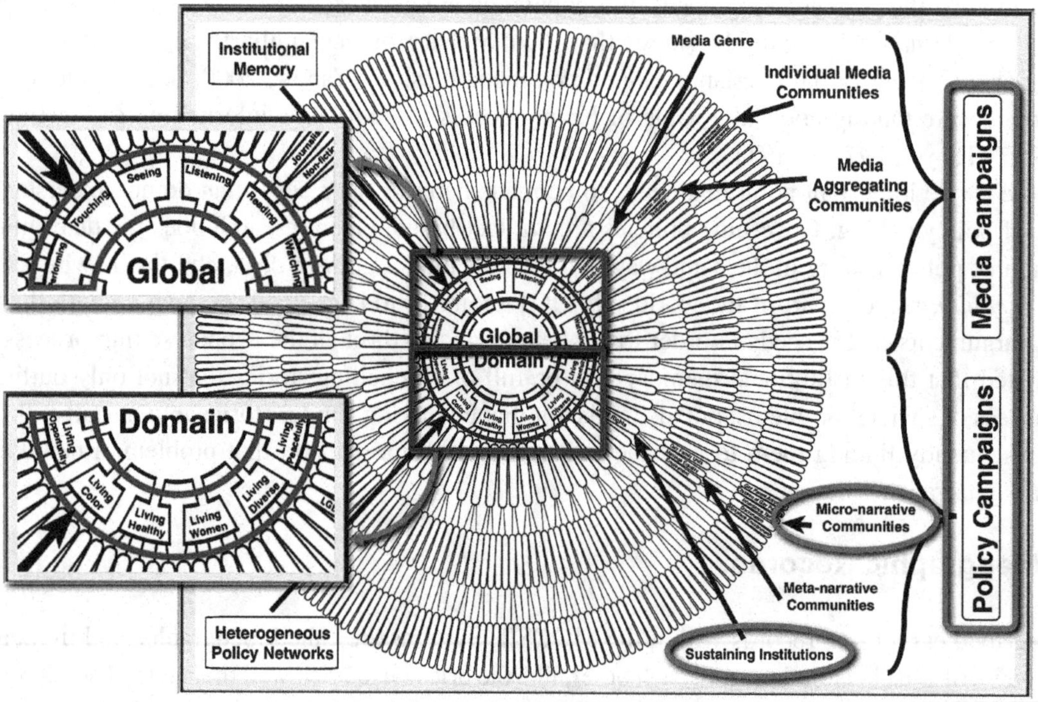

It is also important to note that the model is diagrammatic only insofar as it represents how people will intuitively think of the information communication technology. Technically though, only the top half refers to ideographs in the database, and is therefore referenced in the top left corner as the "institutional memory." What is represented in the bottom half of the diagram is *not* a separate database of ideographs, but rather it is merely an illustration of how heterogeneous the policy network is, which is why the bottom half is labelled in the bottom left corner as "heterogeneous policy networks."

Creating Emergent Narrative Communities

One thing that becomes critically important for this information system is that it will have a mechanism to inspire a spirit of compromise during the actual media linking or uploading (crowd-sourcing) process. The single best opportunity to change minds and have people look at the situation from "outside the box," so to speak, is to allow them to experience the elements of the algorithms while they are online contributing their media. For this reason each contributor will have to give their own ideograph a rating when they initially post it. Miller expressed the benefit of creating this kind of a "deciding moment" when he wrote that the goal is to get a person to think in their mind, "Most likely, I will do what I have done before, though maybe not this time" (Miller, 2012, p. 15; emphasis added). This is that instant in time when an emergent narrative community (Leavitt, 2013, pp. 461-462) can be germinated within the thoughts of an individual by the ICT algorithms.

Figure 8 illustrates how the mechanism works by comparing dialectic narrative communities that have differing opinions about homosexuality. Technically speaking, the narrative community on the right that suggests that people are "born gay" is not dialectical to the one on the left because it embraces pluralism and diversity. Nevertheless, the sustaining institution that maintains discipline in the monistic worldview narrative community on the left will interpret *any* narratives from the sustaining institutions on the right as a serious worldview threat. This is why, "Being gay is a lifestyle choice," is referenced as an *interpretive monopoly*. After all, the consequences to the sustaining institution would be enormous if sexual orientation is no longer seen as binary. Because of this, the harder the sustaining institutions on the right push *their* narrative, the more *threatened* the sustaining institutions on the left feel. This is where Miller's suggestion comes from where he advises against deconstructing these centuries-old narratives, referring to them as "ostensive." What he means by that is that the narratives are seen by conservative sustaining institutions as fixtures that cannot be challenged because they have *always been that way* (Miller, 2012, pp. 86-88).

The only way out of this stalemate then is to create a *new narrative* that is not a direct threat or challenge to the interpretive monopoly. This is what is illustrated at the bottom of Figure 8, referring to it as an "engineered shared premise." If done properly, with a new sustaining institution to nurture it, a new *emergent narrative community* will be germinated.

Programming Platform and Language

Work to-date on the prototype of the *MOCSIE Web* platform has been done in C# on a SQLServer platform. A pre-alpha version of the database storage and retrieval mechanism for the ideographs has been operational since mid-2012, and it also is providing an internal web page for selecting and viewing these ideographs. The official launch of a rudimentary beta release will not take place until mid-2015 and an enterprise level platform for the fully functional beta release is expected to take place in late-2015. This

Figure 8. Engineering a shared premise in an attempt to create an emergent narrative community

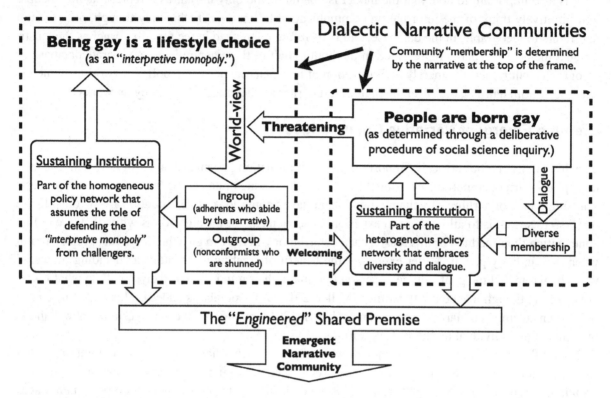

date could be advanced dramatically if approval is obtained to use overlays, allowing popular existing web content to be rated using the MOCSIE Systems algorithms without actually having to manually embed hyperlinks into the *MOCSIE Systems* records. Plans call for the MOCSIE Systems to be launched in conjunction with a language system that could make the ICT available in more than 11 languages on its launch date.

FUTURE RESEARCH DIRECTIONS

When Time magazine honoured "The Protestor" as The Person of the Year for 2011 (Andersen, 2011), the article mentioned the global scope of the phenomenon. As noted earlier, some estimated that the protests took place in 951 cities in 82 countries (Rogers, 2011). With this in mind, take another look at the 10 layers of city-based units that are represented in Figure 4. Now imagine 951 layers represented in Figure 4 instead of just ten. It is useful to also imagine how each of the 180 individuals represented in Figure 4 will not only be a crowd-source contributor to the proposed ICT database, but each of them will also be a conduit and custodian for the content, naturally helping to frame and contextualize the consensus-building (discourse-altering) nature of the content that is brought into the database from the grassroots of an entire neighborhood. This kind of networking would organically provide for an almost infinite sprawl of crowd-sourced material as digital content begins to aggregate from activists and community workers around the world.

With that in mind we can take this example even further. As illustrated in Figure 7, the *MOCSIE Systems* are intended to embrace media of all kinds, and would provide for visual art, photojournalism, blogs, novels, non-fiction books, podcasts, YouTube videos, and any number of hyperlinks to other content already on the web. It could also be something as simple as a cell phone image that was uploaded with a text message caption added at a later point. It is important to note that this kind of content is being generated already, and whether or not this database exists will neither accelerate nor diminish the rate at which this data is posted to the Internet. The only thing that this database will do is allow for it to be accessed through the query language of an information system, thus weaving it together into compelling narratives. As noted above, it will also allow the media to be evaluated by fellow contributors and the general public.

Discourse Structuration and Hegemony

With the above detailed description of both the institutional memory and the ideographs that are archived there, we can now move on to how ideographs and narratives will be utilized as media tools. To do this, this chapter will now delve deeper into the process of discourse structuration. The term was used by Hajer in 1993 in Discourse Theory in European Politics: Identity, Policy and Governance. Miller, in 2012, quotes Hajer as well, writing, "discourse-coalition is not so much connected to a particular person, but is related to practices in the context in which actors employ story lines and (re)produce and transform a particular discourse" (Miller, 2012, p. 33). Discourse structuration has never been a problem for the global elite, and it was Antonio Gramsci, the Italian political activist, who first described how power is retained by the ruling class by the way they structure the governing narratives to marginalise others, and therefore benefit them[selves] (Bates, 1975, p. 351; emphasis added).

Returning to the idea above about the "othering" tactic of hegemony, it needs to be underscored that those carefully structured narratives not only tell a population who they should hate (a process called framing), but also, embedded in that narrative, is a cleverly engineered narrative that instructs the oppressed to consent to their own marginalization; a process called quiescence (Gaventa, 1980, pp. v-xi; Scott, 1990, p. 71). That insidious narrative typically outlines the conditions under which certain benefits will inure to the submissive population so long as they cooperate with the elite (structuration; in this case by the oppressors). In many cases the only "benefit" promised is that, as bad as things might be, they at least will not get *worse*. What the MOCSIE Systems recognize is that, while the elite are already very good at doing this, there is nothing that stops the oppressed from *doing the same thing* to change the discourse so that a new narrative emerges that favours *them* instead of the elite.

Unfortunately, this will only happen if the fractured progressive activists can reach consensus on the topics that they want to be advanced. This is why the institutional memory and ICT cannot be under custodianship of a hierarchy, and it is also why these decisions are all placed into the hands of small groups instead of larger committees. The way the process is designed to work is that, once consensus on the best narratives for the new solidarity movement is reached, those communities that are represented by each city-based group, will, themselves, elevate this narrative to the forefront through a framing and contextualizing process of their own.

If it would help to provide an example of when the global population consented to their own oppression, a good case study would be the case of "trickle-down economics." With some powerful academics taking the helm, the idea of supply-side economics was pushed throughout Western democracies with religious-like zeal. As an ideology, or new paradigm if you will, it was pitched in the 1980s and 1990s by the likes of Ronald Reagan, Margaret Thatcher, Brian Mulroney, and the leaders of almost every other Western superpower. What this discourse told citizens is that if they would allow the super-rich to become obscenely-rich, then everybody would be better off. After all, these are the "job creators." Looking at the 2012 reincarnation of this trickle-down narrative it once again illustrates how marginalised populations are not monolithic (Wilkes, 2006, p. 510), and how the forces of hegemony can still advance their "divide and rule" tactic (Riggs, 1997, p. 354). This is why the ability to generate viable governing narratives is critically important at this juncture in history. The proverbial "99 percent" of the *Occupy* narrative had both framed and contextualized alternative (better) taxation narratives that provided compelling reasons for a more equitable tax structure, (and in the case of Europe, for softer austerity measures), but before the *Occupy* policy proposals would have a chance at becoming actual governing narratives they needed some kind of a vehicle to propel those narratives into mainstream thinking. A "governing narrative," in the context of this chapter is determined by whether or not the new policy-proposals of the counter-elite become viable (majority-supported) alternatives to the ideas being pushed by the global elite and their powerful lobbyists. In this regard, the 2011 protestors failed. The theory presented by this chapter suggests a reason as to why that happened.

CONCLUSION

As difficult as it was to keep the disparate parts of this chapter aligned, the one thing that should have been clear throughout is that the media that the counter-hegemonic forces need in order to support all of their policymaking endeavours is already out there, on the web, but it is simply too difficult to navigate to it. In this environment every person who seeks to create a narrative thread for a progressive policy endeavour is forced to start from scratch, which is really discouraging because the established governing narratives from the conservative side have decades, if not centuries, of history that have cemented policies into place. To make it worse, the conservatives' networks are incredibly homogeneous, making it easy for them to plug their "structural holes" and bring people into line with the hierarchy, while the progressive networks are heterogeneous, making them far less efficient (Sandström & Carlsson, 2008, p. 510).

In this climate, not only is it incredibly time consuming for a progressive to advance a policy proposal, but it is discouraging when the odds of succeeding are so low, and people disengage when they feel that their effort is not contributing to any kind of change. To make matters worse, in many instances, after a person puts in the effort to generate the kind of research needed to support a progressive policy argument, they find that there is no media channel through which one's finished product can be effectively disseminated in a way that it will have any impact on the agenda setting process of a government, whether local, provincial, or federal. Global endeavors in this current climate all require the resources of a benefactor like the Bill & Melinda Gates Foundation before a "good idea" will have any impact.

The claim made by this chapter is that until there is a single institutional memory that will serve to enlarge the problems faced by progressive-minded individuals, there will be no unifying force for global solidarity. However, the theory presented in this chapter suggests that once every social justice community begins drinking from the same well we will all have occasion to meet and collaborate in our work, and pluralism will no longer be seen as something to fear. Only then will there be spokespeople (the central figures) who are speaking with a clear, cohesive voice that the counter-hegemonic forces will rally behind.

A suitable metaphor for the current climate might be to liken the activity in the nonprofit sector to a bumper car arena in which every car has its steering wheel disconnected from the front wheel, but the gas pedal is held all the way to the floor. It is for this reason that the issue of *trust* comes into play. New nonprofits, with almost identical mission statements to an existing nonprofit, are incorporated every day, simply because the founders did not have the confidence that *somebody else* could do the job as effectively as they themselves could do it. In other instances it comes down to trust because much of the competition in the "third sector" is over who gets to stand at the microphone; an inherent flaw that is rooted in the hierarchical design of both large and small nonprofits.

Instead of allowing the above scenario to play out time and time again, imagine instead the collective thought of a community as it comes together in small, consensus-building groups. All it would take is to find that central figure; that one community leader with the skills of a juggler who is able to bridge the gap between vulnerability and trust so that the paradox can be reconciled. This will be the voice that actually "speaks," but the words invoked by that voice would be the words of the collective. The *narrative* will be one that was gleaned from the real-life experiences of a population that took the time to deposit their singular "voices" into an ICT database over which they held a measure of control.

Looking back in history, the consensus seems to be that it was the printing press that ushered in the Age of Enlightenment and broke the stranglehold that the absolute monarchs held over the merchant and peasant classes. Who's to say that the Internet and ubiquitous technology today do not offer us a similar opportunity for a *Second Age of Enlightenment*? As Argyriades wrote, in speaking of this comparison,

Debureaucratization, the Reformation movement of our times, confronts us with this challenge: it could compound the symptoms of disorganization, indeed ungovernability, passivity, exclusion, marginaliza- tion, alienation, and anomie, which can be found all around us—or it could pave the way for a more democratic, more open, self-directed, and self-governed human society. (Argyriades, 2010, p. 293)

To achieve this "self-directed, and self-governed human society" would be an ideal outcome for the MOCSIE Systems, and if one takes the time to read Frederick Thayer's book (1973), they might cap- ture this vision and see how the technology of today makes *possible* what was then *impossible*. In this twenty-first century revolution of intellectual development, what should be hoped for is the ability to *delegitimize* old paradigms that facilitate oppression and *displace* them with new ones that flatten the hierarchies of power. The challenge will be to not repeat the mistakes of the peasant revolutions of the 18th century. In the long history of humanity it has never been enough to simply topple a government, because a new oppressor always seems to be at the ready to jump into the vacuum of the old hierarchy and simply fill each void with a different face, but one equally willing to oppress and marginalise a new class of "othered" people. In those instances, for those who seek power, the old axiom of hierarchy still applies: "When you are in a race to climb a ladder, every kick is a step up."

If the marginalised and oppressed are to undertake a new kind of revolution, the new weapon that will allow the "peasants," to pull off a definitive and permanent victory will be a tool that alters narra- tives, because only narrative, as a weapon, will deploy new governing methodologies as an organic part of any protest movement. And yet, there will be no *uniform* governing narrative until there is solidarity among the progressive voices. And so, under a new paradigm, when a protest movement next emerges and begins to find traction, it must *first* make peace with the other progressive allies that it will need at the end of the day when the task of governing has been *earned*. In the history of humanity, that seems to be the one ingredient that is always missing, and so history continues to repeat itself. When the counter-hegemonic forces find a way to do this, then history might one day refer to *that* moment as the dawn of the Second Age of Enlightenment.

REFERENCES

Andersen, K. (2011, December 14). The protestor. *Time*.

Argyriades, D. (2010). From bureaucracy to debureaucratization? *Public Organization Review*, *10*(3), 275–297. doi:10.1007/s11115-010-0136-1

Baker, M. (2006). Translation and activism: Emerging patterns of narrative community. *The Massachusetts Review*, *47*(3), 462–484.

Bates, T. R. (1975). Gramsci and the theory of hegemony. *Journal of the History of Ideas*, *36*(2), 351–366. doi:10.2307/2708933

Chen, X. (2009). The power of "troublemaking". *Comparative Politics*, *41*(4), 451–471. doi:10.5129/0 01041509X12911362972557

Denhardt, R. B. (2011). *Theories of Public Organization* (6th ed.). Boston: Wadsworth.

El-Mahdi, R. (2009). Enough! Egypt's quest for democracy. *Comparative Political Studies*, *42*(8), 1011–1039. doi:10.1177/0010414009331719

Evans, P. (2007). The "movement of movements" for global justice. *American Sociological Association*, *62*(6), 62–64.

Farazmand, A. (1999). The elite question: Toward a normative elite theory of organization. *Administration & Society*, *31*(3), 321–352. doi:10.1177/00953999922019166

Farazmand, A. (2012a). Institutionalized chaos and transformation of governance and public administration: Explaining the global crisis of capitalism. *Public Organization Review*, *12*(4).

Farazmand, A. (2012b). Predatory globalization, global crisis of capitalism, and the deepening crisis of the state: Why has public administration failed to grasp its own identity? *Public Organization Review*, *12*(4).

Farazmand, A. (2013). Conclusion: Can we go home now? Roads taken, targets met, and lessons learned on governance and organizational eclecticism in the public arena. *Public Organization Review*, *13*(2), 219–228. doi:10.1007/s11115-013-0236-9

Follet, M.P. (1926). The giving of orders. *Scientific foundations of business administration*. 29-37.

Garrison, V. (2012, July 16). How I lost my fear of universal health care. RH Reality Check: Reproductive & Sexual Health and Justice News, Analysis & Commentary. Retrieved from http://www.rhrealitycheck. org/article/2012/07/12/how-i-lost-my-fear-universal-health-care

Gaventa, J. (1980). *Power and Powerlessness: Quiescence and Rebellion in an Appalachian Valley*. Chicago: University of Illinois Press.

Geertz, C. (1973/2000). *The interpretation of cultures: Selected essays by Clifford Geertz*. New York: Basic Books.

Gooden, S., & Portillo, S. (2011). Advancing social equity in the Minnowbrook tradition. *Journal of Public Administration: Research and Theory*, *21*(1), 1–14.

Hajer, M. A. (1993). Coalitions, practices and meaning in environmental politics: from acid rain to BSE. In D. Howarth & J. Torfing (Eds.), Discourse Theory in European Politics: Identity, Policy and Governance (Ch. 12, pp. 297-315). Hampshire, UK: Palgrave MacMillan.

Hemenover, S. H. (2003). The good, the bad, and the healthy: Impacts of emotional disclosure of trauma on resilient self-concept and psychological distress. *Personality and Social Psychology Bulletin*, *29*(10), 1236–1244. doi:10.1177/0146167203255228 PMID:15189585

Herman, J. (1997). *Trauma and recovery: The aftermath of violence – from domestic abuse to political terror*. New York: BasicBooks.

Hong, P. Y. P., & Song, I. H.In Han Song. (2010). Glocalization of social work practice: Global and local responses to globalization. *International Social Work*, *53*(5), 656–670. doi:10.1177/0020872810371206

Kolnick, J. (2012, September 26). Redistribution of wealth has gone upward, not down, since early '80s. *MinnPost*. Retrieved from http://www.minnpost.com/community-voices/2012/09/redistribution-wealth-has-gone-upward-not-down-early-80s

Leavitt, L. (2013). A purple primaries protocol for progressive policy victories in "deep-red" American states. *Administrative Theory & Praxis*, *35*(3), 457–465. doi:10.2753/ATP1084-1806350306

Lepore, S. J., Ragan, J. D., & Jones, S. (2000). Talking facilitates cognitive-emotional processes of adaptation to an acute stressor. *Journal of Personality and Social Psychology*, *78*(3), 499–508. doi:10.1037/0022-3514.78.3.499 PMID:10743876

Miller, H. T. (2004). The ideographic individual. *Administrative Theory & Praxis*, *26*(4), 469–488.

Miller, H. T. (2012). *Governing narratives: Symbolic politics and policy change*. Tuscaloosa: University of Alabama Press.

Morgan, G. (2006). *Images of organization, updated*. Thousand Oaks, CA: Sage.

Piketty, T. (2014). *Capital in the Twenty-First Century*. Cambridge, Mass: Belknap Press. doi:10.4159/9780674369542

Rainey, H. (2009). *Understanding and managing public organizations* (4th ed.). San Francisco, CA: John Wiley & Sons.

Riggs, F. W. (1997). Modernity and bureaucracy. *Public Administration Review*, *4*(57), 347–353. doi:10.2307/977318

Rogers, S. (2011, November 14). Occupy protests around the world: full list visualised. *The Guardian*. Retrieved from http://www.guardian.co.uk/news/datablog/2011/oct/17/occupy-protests-world-list-map#

Ruggiero, K. J., Smith, D. W., Hanson, R. F., Resnick, H. S., Saunders, B. E., Kilpatrick, D. G., & Best, C. L. (2004). Is disclosure of childhood rape associated with mental health outcome? Results from the national women's study. Child Maltreatment. *Journal of the American Professional Society on the Abuse of Children, 9*(1), 62–77.

Saez, E. (2012). *Striking it richer: the evolution of top incomes in the United States (updated with 2009 and 2010 estimates). Pathways Magazine.* Berkeley, CA: University of California – Berkley.

Sandström, A., & Carlsson, L. (2008). The performance of policy networks: The relation between network structure and network performance. *Policy Studies Journal: the Journal of the Policy Studies Organization, 36*(4), 497–524. doi:10.1111/j.1541-0072.2008.00281.x

Schein, E. H. (2010). *Organizational Culture and Leadership* (4th ed.). San Francisco, CA: Jossey-Bass.

Schweller, R. L. (2014). *Maxwell's Demon and the Golden Apple: Global Discord in the New Millennium.* Baltimore, MD: Johns Hopkins University Press.

Shafritz, J. M., & Russell, E. W. (2002). *Introducing Public Administration* (3rd ed.). New York: Longman.

Sharpton, A. (Performer) (2011). Acceptable [YouTube Video]. Retrieved from http://www.youtube.com/watch?v=3Hdr-ToihZc

Shweder, R. A., & Good, G. (2005). *Clifford Geertz by his Colleagues.* Chicago.

Stein, J. (1964). *The fiddler on the roof.* New York: Crown Publishers.

Stille, A. (2011, October 22). The paradox of the new elite. *New York Times.*

Stone, D. (2002). *Policy Paradox: The Art of Political Decision Making* (Revised ed.). New York: W.W. Norton.

Thayer, F. C. (1973). *An end to hierarchy! an end to competition!* New York: New Viewpoints.

Thayer, F. C. (2002). Elite theory of organization: Building a normative foundation. In A. Farazmand (Ed.), *Modern Organizations: Theory and Practice* (2nd ed., pp. 97–132). Westport, CT: Praeger.

Walsh, J. (2012). *What's the matter with white people: Why we long for a golden age that never was.* Hoboken, NJ: John Wiley & Sons.

Wilkes, R. (2006). The protest actions of indigenous peoples: A Canadian-U.S. comparison of social movement emergence. *The American Behavioral Scientist, 50*(4), 510–525. doi:10.1177/0002764206294059

Yanow, D. (2000). *Conducting interpretive policy analysis.* Thousand Oaks, CA: Sage. doi:10.4135/9781412983747

ADDITIONAL READING

Allport, G. (1954). *The Nature of Prejudice.* Reading, MA: Addison-Wesley Publishing.

Gaddis, J. L. (2002). *The Landscape of History.* New York: Oxford University Press.

Greene, J. (2013). *Moral Tribes: Emotion, Reason, and the Gap between Us and Them*. New York: The Penguin Press.

Hall, S. (1973). *Encoding and Decoding in the Media Discourse*.

Morçöl, G. (2012). *A Complexity Theory for Public Policy*. New York: Routledge.

Schneider, A., & Ingram, H. (1993). Social Construction of Target Populations: Implications for Politics and Policy. *The American Political Science Review*, *87*(2), 334–347. doi:10.2307/2939044

KEY TERMS AND DEFINITIONS

Central-Figure Hypothesis: Proposed by this theory to test whether or not people can be motivated to contribute to the institutional memory, as well as to glean narrative content from it, in supporting a more effective discourse aimed at improving the viability of policy proposals in the agenda setting process.

Collective-Thought Hypothesis: Supports two ideas. First, that most marginalised populations know that they are vulnerable when the dominant group concentrates its power in a hierarchy. This would suggest that, as part of constructing a new paradigm, an easily demonstrated alternative to hierarchy must first be put into place before existing opinion leaders will recommend to the community that they put their trust in the charismatic central figure who will necessarily emerge as their spokesperson. The collective-thought hypothesis supports making this central figure just another voice in one of the four consensus-building groups of the MOCSIE Systems organisational model. Second, in addition to placing the central figure into the steering group, rather than giving her or him a position in a hierarchy, the collective-thought hypothesis also relates to how the community-based governing unit is structured so as to germinate a consensus-building process for framing and contextualizing the growing repository of records in the institutional memory, enabling users from within the community to effectively *displace* those harmful, socially constructed narratives that are rooted in, and defended by, hegemony. Again, it is important to note that *displace* was used in that sentence, not *deconstruct*.

Emergent Narrative Community: A critically important concept for the information system described in this chapter. This "sense of community" (whether online or face-to-face) creates a "deciding moment" when an individual thinks in their mind, "Most likely, I will do what I have done before, though *maybe not this time*" (Miller, 2012, p. 15; emphasis added). This is that instant in time when an emergent narrative community (Leavitt, 2013, pp. 461-462) can be germinated within the thoughts of an individual by the ICT algorithms.

Glocalization: What arguably will emerge from the information communication technology being proposed here is a mechanism for creating an efficient heterogeneous network (Leavitt, 2013, p. 460; Sandström & Carlsson, 2008, p. 507) that is simultaneously *local* at the most basic of levels, yet *global* in its scope and reach; a process now referred to as "*glocalization*" (Hong & Song, 2010).

Institutional Memory: The theory presented in this chapter suggests that unsuccessful efforts to alter the structural dynamics of governing also can be traced to an inability to extract the institutional memory (specifically, the media material that is used to impact policymaking) and the custodians of that institutional memory from the grasp of the hierarchy.

Interpretive Monopoly: The concept that members of a group or class are bound by a single worldview that cannot be challenged without significant consequences. Narrative communities can be either monistic or pluralistic. Sustaining institutions for monistic narrative communities have a vested interest in claiming an interpretive monopoly that will protect their worldview. This is why, "Being gay is a lifestyle choice," is a classic interpretive monopoly for many religious narrative communities. After all, the consequences to some religions would be enormous if sexual orientation is no longer seen as binary. This is where Miller's suggestion comes from where he advises against *deconstructing* these centuries-old interpretive monopoly narratives, referring to them instead as "ostensive." What he means by that is that the narratives are seen by conservative sustaining institutions as fixtures that cannot be challenged because they have *always been that way* (Miller, 2012, pp. 86-88).

Narrative Community: A unit of society where people tend to share beliefs and a common worldview. Here they are referred to as "communities" because it is a reflection of the research that supports the idea that "narrative communities" are, for many in the field of organisation theory, viable *institutions* unto themselves (Baker, 2006, p. 463; Schein, 2010, p. 70). Recall as well that these narrative communities are germinated, nurtured, and protected by *sustaining institutions*. The research breaks these down as either meta-narrative or micro-narrative communities (Leavitt, 2013, pp. 459-464).

Social Entrepreneur: The theory developed in this chapter requires that there be a central figure who comes in to organize a new kind of sustaining institution capable of germinating pluralistic narrative communities (see *emergent narrative communities* above). This "juggler," or central figure, will have to be a very special kind of social entrepreneur who is so driven by a passion for social justice that she or he will be willing to persist with dogged determination in the daunting task of bringing together a team of 17 existing (preferably recognized and respected) community leaders for a unified purpose of improving policymaking decisions on behalf of a population. This person will have to be a driven individual because, within marginalised populations, most people are reluctant to listen to the initial sales pitch for "yet another nonprofit advocacy group." History has told most marginalised people to mistrust newcomers and individuals with grandiose ideas.

Sustaining Institution: Narrative communities cannot survive without sustaining institutions. As described above, these sustaining institutions can germinate, nurture, and protect either monistic narrative communities or pluralistic (*emergent*) narrative communities, which is why a complete understanding of what the motives are for each sustaining institution is essential in the research. One cannot fully understand the sustaining institution without first understanding who it is that benefits from the narratives that are germinated, nurtured, and protected. Hierarchical institutions almost always have sustaining institutions that support narratives that define why the power rightfully belongs with a privileged few in the top levels of the hierarchy.

Chapter 4
ICT in the Indian Classroom

Geeta Nair
H R College of Commerce & Economics, India

Robert Hindle
University of Manchester, UK

ABSTRACT

The present research paper discusses the pivotal role of Information and Communication Technology (ICT) in education which is gaining currency in the new era of globalism as the telecom revolution has hastened the pace of globalization and vice-versa; along with the catalyst role ICT-enabled education plays in promoting inclusive growth and human development for all. These smart tools of the emerging smart economy would help to promote mass literacy and also narrow inter, as well as intra-generational gaps. Most importantly, it will provide 'second opportunities' to the generation that missed them in the first place, thus helping adult learners, particularly the employed and women; thus attempting to reduce gender inequities; particularly in South Asia and the Indian sub-continent. The case study of the famous open University, namely Indira Gandhi National Open University (IGNOU) in India is being studies as a case of sustainable development and inclusive growth as it 'reaches the unreached' and untouched and marginalized segments of society.

INTRODUCTION

The present research paper discusses the use of Information and Communication Technology (ICT) in education which is gaining currency in the new era of globalism as the telecom revolution has hastened the pace of globalization and vice-versa; along with the catalyst role ICT-enabled education plays in promoting inclusive growth and human development for all. These smart tools of the emerging smart economy would help to promote mass literacy and also narrow inter, as well as intra-generational gaps. Most importantly, it will provide 'second opportunities' to the generation that missed them in the first place, thus helping adult learners, particularly the employed and women; thus attempting to reduce gender inequities.

DOI: 10.4018/978-1-5225-0556-3.ch004

ICT in education is defined in various ways and can be broadly categorized in the following manner as:

- ICT as a subject (i.e., computer studies)
- ICT as a tool to support traditional subjects (i.e., computer-based learning, presentation, research)
- ICT as an administrative tool (i.e., education management information systems/EMIS)
- ICT as a medium of knowledge exchange

Ms. Irina Bokova, Director-General of UNESCO, quoted the great Thai poet and teacher Sunthorn Phu who said that "With knowledge, you can stand on your own two feet" (Asia-Pacific Ministerial Forum on ICT in Education 2012 in Bangkok, Thailand). This is the heart of all education - to build confidence in young women and men and allow them to stand on their own two feet. Information and communication technologies can and must serve this essential goal. She further stated that, "We must ensure that information and communication technologies are accessible, that they bridge divides and favour inclusive education, that they draw on appropriate content, and that they support quality teaching. This requires effective capacity development and policy dialogue – this is why this annual forum is so important."

Technology plays an important role in all walks of human lives in modern times and the gap between the West and the East was largely explained by the digital divide. According to Vrasidas and McIssac (2001), international trends in the applications of ICTs in schools bear a direct relation with the teaching-learning environments and the development of schools. This is supported by documented evidence that rich nations provide adequate technology in schools as average public schools in the USA had 189 instructional computers with 98% of these having internet access & the number of students per computer with internet access was 3 in 2008 (Institute of Educational Sciences Report, 2010). Emerging trends show that students are more sophisticated in technology usage than their teachers in OECD nations, thereby widening the gap in knowledge, information, and its dissemination.

The learning of use of technology takes places in the following 6 stages:

- Awareness
- Learning
- Understanding and Application of the Process
- Familiarity and Confidence
- Adaptation to Other Contexts
- Creative Application to New Contexts (Russell, 1996)

Computer technology can be integrated into the curriculum of teachers through a 5 stage model constituting pre-integration, transition, development, expansion, and system wide integration (Toledo, 2005). To be successful, teachers also need to accept e-learning technology by updating knowledge and skills, creating right attitudes and values that blossom into a proactive personality, along with supportive institutional factors and infrastructure (Babiae, 2012).

UNESCO takes a holistic and comprehensive approach to promoting ICT in education as access; inclusion and quality are among the main challenges they can address and also contribute to universal access to education, equity in education, the delivery of quality learning and teaching, teachers' professional development and more efficient education management, governance and administration. UNESCO's global network of institutes and partners provide Member States with resources for elaborating ICT in education policies, strategies and activities. In particular, the UNESCO Institute for Information Technologies in Education (IITE), based in Moscow, specializes in information exchange, research and training on the integration of ICT in education while UNESCO's Open Educational Resources (OER) are teaching, learning or research materials that are in the public domain or that can be used under an intellectual property license that allows re-use or adaptation (e.g Creative Commons). The potential of opening up educational resources for use and adaptation by everyone, especially those in resource-poor environments, is a great opportunity to achieve quality education for all. Within a broad movement working to encourage creators of knowledge and information (including software), UNESCO has been active in promoting OER. The Communication and Information programme on OER allows learners, teachers, administrators and governments to freely access and create, as well as share open document-format educational resources. The UNESCO Education Sector focuses on promoting the introduction of OER in teacher education, HIV and AIDS and Literacy and education in post-conflict and post-disaster situations clearly bringing out far-ranging ramifications of this new mandate.

ICT IN EDUCATION

Information and Communication Technology has permeated in every walk of life affecting the technology fields such as launching satellites, managing businesses across the globe and also enabling social networking. There is a convergence of computer, communication, and content technologies known as ICT that have attracted attention of academia, business, government and communities to use it for innovative profitable propositions. 21st century is characterized with the emergence of knowledge based society wherein ICT plays a pivotal role. The National curriculum framework 2005 (NCF, 2005) has also highlighted the importance of ICT in school education. With this backdrop, major paradigm shift is imperative in education characterized by imparting instructions, collaborative learning, multi-disciplinary problem-solving and promoting critical thinking skills.

In order to be innovative and inclusive, learning and education strategies must recognize all places where learning takes place: at work, in the community, in the family, and in social and civic life. ICT has tremendously broadened the opportunities for people to acquire information, interact, network, address issues of common concern, generate income and participate in society. There is a risk that advanced technological requirements may lead to the exclusion of large numbers of people from sharing the advantages of the new global communication channels. It is UNESCO's concern to enable all people around the world to make use of the huge potential of ICT for learning and self-empowerment.

Open learning is a philosophy founded on the principle of flexibility concerning when, where and how the learner studies. This approach is especially relevant for learners who are physically and/or geographically challenged. Distance education is the use of specific instructional techniques, resources and media to facilitate learning and teaching between learners and teachers who are separated by time or place. Techniques, resources, and media are dependent on factors such as: subject matter; student needs and context; teacher skills and experience; instructional goals; available technologies; and institutional capacity. Despite the proliferation of technologies in education, distance education in developing economies is still heavily reliant on printed materials. In order to be innovative and inclusive, learning and education strategies must recognize all places where learning takes place: at work, in the community, in the family, and in social and civic life. ICT has tremendously broadened the opportunities for people to acquire information, interact, network, address issues of common concern, generate income and participate in society. However, there is a risk that advanced technological requirements may lead to the exclusion of large numbers of people from sharing the advantages of the new global communication channels. It is UNESCO's concern to enable all people around the world to make use of the huge potential of ICT for learning and self-empowerment.

The United Nations Global Alliance for ICT (Information & Communication Technology) and Development (UN GAID) hosted by the Government of Abu Dhabi discussed the role of ICT in achieving the development goals. Dignitaries including His Excellency Sheikh Nahyan Bin Mubarak Al Nahyan, the Minister of Higher Education and Scientific Research of the United Arab Emirates (UAE), UN representatives, and Jeffrey Sachs of Columbia University's Earth Institute (via video address) emphasized the importance of ICT in sustainable development.

How Does ICT Help Advance Sustainable Development?

As Jeffrey Sachs pointed out in his address, one main cause of poverty is isolation from the rest of the global community. Access to the internet and mobile networks can allow impoverished people around the world to access banking, medical services, and markets. Remote weather stations can be set up in new locations and connected via mobile networks to allow researchers to better study the local and global impacts of climate change.

The Importance of Access to the Internet

Providing laptops to students in the developing world like the program does, allows children in Uganda to communicate with children in the US and even to work on class projects together. The potential of such interaction is invaluable. Learning to use technology to expand the reach of a child in a small village in Africa expands the horizons of their possibilities infinitely. For the children in the developed world the lessons will also be of great value. Due to the importance of the transfer of knowledge, a dedicated news network, has been set up to help reach the Millennium Development Goals through the use of Information, Communication, and Technology (www.treehugger.com).

Access to Mobile Networks

In just the last two decades most of Africa has leapfrogged the communication infrastructure divide from having no telephones to having widespread cellular networks. This has allowed the rapid spread of mobile banking services, allowing people to make secure transactions and secure small business loans. Also being currently developed is a system that allows for minimally-trained local medical workers to easily diagnose malaria, obtain prescriptions, and register cases with mobile technology. Mobile networks can also help disseminate information by allowing farmers access to best practices for irrigation and fertilization. Unfortunately, cost is still a major barrier to the effective use of mobile technology. As Columbia University professor Graciela Chichilnisky suggested, African countries should monetize their extremely valuable mobile communication spectrum to invest in major infrastructure improvements.

Are There Downsides to Expanded Access to ICT?

Enabling access to ICT to over six billion people sounds like a nightmare in the making. There is certainly a need to have serious discussions about the environmental implications. Systems must be put in placc to allow for cffective recycling of laptops and mobile devices. There are also serious considerations around. Finally, in addition to connecting farmers and workers to markets, will access to ICT also move the rest of the world toward Western-style consumerism? Rather than fearing the consequences of others following in the West's destructive footsteps, it is our responsibility to lead by example and extend a hand to our global brothers and sisters to elevate their quality of life and alleviate extreme hardship. ICT, for the first time, makes this a possibility.

ICTs in Education for Sustainable Development

The increasing rate of information and communication technologies (ICTs) development and their widespread implementation across all sectors of the economic and social life brings about radical changes in the way we work, think, learn and communicate. There is not, however, a universally accepted definition of ICTs due to the fact that concepts, methods and applications related to ICT are constantly evolving and can be contextually interpreted and applied. A broad definition of ICT is concerned with the distinction between "old or traditional technologies" (radio, television, video, DVD, telephone, computers) and "new or modern technologies" (video conferencing, e-mail, cellular telephones, weblogs, Web 2.0, and other social networking software). An "old or traditional technology" might be a driving force for change in the right context in the same way as a "new or modern technology" could be a driving force in another context. No matter what technology development is, educational systems, worldwide, face the challenge of preparing citizens who need to be equipped with the necessary skills and competencies to transform current unsustainable practices. In this context, teachers are increasingly called upon to switch from roles of being knowledge transmitters towards taking more active roles as curriculum developers, knowledge constructors and transformative learning agents.

Three of the major forces shaping and driving the 21st century education are: 1) the development and diffusion of Information and Communication Technologies (ICTs); 2) the increasing demand for new educational approaches and pedagogies that foster transformative and lifelong learning and 3) the reorientation of educational curricula to address sustainable development (SD).

The link between ICT, transformative learning and sustainable development is being addressed by extensive debates and research which recognize the challenge new technologies bring to the reorientation of education towards learning to live sustainably. ICTs can thus be a context for ESD as well as ESD can be a context for ICT. More specifically:

- ESD themes integrated into the school curricula could provide a worthwhile context for ICTs in education. For example, social, economic and environmental issues can provide meaningful and challenging contexts for developing a wide range of ICT skills.
- ESD methods are conducive with constructivist and transformative learning theories, which can provide a context and rationale for using ICT-based learning tools such as concept mapping, modeling, and social networking.
- When considering areas such as cultural diversity and intercultural understanding, health, HIV/ AIDS, governance, natural resources, climate change, rural development, sustainable urbanization, poverty alleviation, corporate responsibility and accountability, there is potential to assess the impact of ICTs in these key sustainable development areas.

However, the so-called digital divide, especially for women and other disadvantaged groups, is still a problem that challenges educators and policy makers. Teachers have an opportunity to develop skills in problem definition and problem solving, to reflect on their students learning, knowledge and practices, and develop a deep understanding of the way students think and act on social and environmental issues. Some key questions that could be asked are:

- How can you use computerized graphic organizers to teach vocabulary relevant to environmental sustainability issues?
- Have you ever wanted to measure the effect you have on greenhouse gas emissions in your home and school?
- How can you use data handling tools (e.g. Excel) to construct knowledge and promote learning-based action on ESD local/global issues?
- How can you use computerized programs to assess your ecological footprint towards sustainable energy or water use, for example?

Let's take, for example, the last question set on the above list: "How can a teacher use ICTs to assess his/her students' ecological footprint towards sustainable water use?" The teacher can use various computerized programmes available for free in the Internet to calculate the person's impact on the environment. Using such tools together with social-dialogic teaching methods that could be also supported by new communication tools, such as chats and forums, the teacher activates students' prior knowledge and behaviours. This leads to reflect on perceptions and behaviours about water use and waste and make comparisons with other students, as well as going deeper in analyzing water uses/waste and the consequences on the environment. Questions such as: Why do people use water as though there is an unlimited resource? Are they aware of the water problems in the future, because of their current water consumption practices?

How personal water use and management of water can be addressed to avoid dramatic impacts on the environment, the economy and quality of life? In this way, technology helps not only to develop awareness about the environment, but also to create a learning environment that uses dialogue, negotiation and reflection, which could eventually lead to actions for building a more sustainable future (Makrakis, 2012).

ICT REVOLUTION IN ASIA

The ICT revolution catapulted the global South amongst the league of fast growing economies as a major force to reckon with. These game-changers and new rule-setters demonstrated their power as engines of global growth shifted from the North to the South. Gwang-Jo Kim, Director of UNESCO Asia and Pacific Regional Bureau for Education stated that, "Information and communication technologies (ICT), if used wisely, can contribute to universal access to quality education in formal, non-formal and informal education settings across sectors. However, ICT in education only works when it is closely aligned with a clear national vision, explicit implementation strategies, feasible action plans and solid monitoring and evaluation."

Each country is diverse and different; especially when it comes to the Asia-Pacific region. This scenario becomes more complex as they have varied educational contexts and unique challenges. In Asia and the Pacific, the status of integrating ICT in education varies widely – from least developed countries where electricity supply in schools is scarce, to middle income countries where there is high demand for assistance in developing effective ICT policies, to high income countries where concerns relate to the rapidly increasing harmful effects due to over-supply of, and easy access to ICT.

Lead nations like China have been promoting equity, aiming to narrow the digital divide among regions and schools, while Malaysia and Indonesia have set focus on improving quality of education through teacher development. Thailand is promoting "One Tablet Computer per Child" project, by supplying all Grade 1 primary students with a tablet computer in 2012, with an expansion of distribution channels to Grade 1 and secondary students next year. The onus is on providing free WIFI to be provided in future for every school and in many public areas to expand the coverage to 80 percent of population over the next three years, and to 95 percent of the population by the year 2020. Also, the Republic of Korea and Singapore have implemented comprehensive and evolving national technology strategies in education master plans.

Ms. Bokova strongly emphasized the role of teachers to maximize the use of technology for better learning stating that, "Technology can be a powerful education multiplier, but we must know how to use it. It is not enough to install technology into classrooms – it must be integrated into learning. Nothing can substitute for a good teacher. It is not technology itself that empowers people - empowerment comes from skills and knowledge," thereby reiterating that technology is just an enabler giving teachers the modern tools for smart teaching that could supplement or complement traditional 'chalk and talk' measures. UNESCO's activities in ICT in Education focus on supporting policy development for quality provision of ICT-enhanced higher education, open learning, distance education and dual/bimodal or mixed mode provisions (www.unesco.org).

India and the ICT Revolution

The Government of India has announced 2010-2020 as the decade of innovation. Reasoning and Critical thinking skills are necessary for innovation. Foundation of these skills is laid at school level. It is desirable that affordable ICT tools and techniques should be integrated into classroom instructions right form primary stage so as to enable students develop their requisite skills. Most of the tools, techniques and tutorials are available in Open domain and accessible on web. Further to circular number 7 dated 22 Feb 2010 wherein the NCERT had invited responses from teachers involved in the teaching and learning of Mathematics at the senior secondary stage to acquire the skills for using the World Wide Web, the CBSE would like to extend it to all subjects and all classes. At Primary and Upper Primary level, focus may be on simple access to information and trying to compile different views and analyze them to conclude in one's own way. At the Secondary level, gathering and structuring of data and computing to arrive at some reports may be taken up in any subject not necessarily Science and Mathematics. At the Senior Secondary level, when students are so exposed, they will get highly motivated to use ICT tools for taking up complex, multidisciplinary problems such as biochemistry, bioinformatics, environmental science, forensic science, nanotechnology, business intelligence etc. This may necessitate computing tools and techniques of generic nature as well as domain-specific. This is the time when the students and the teachers together will work in global competitive environment.

All assessments must inform teachers that using technology helps to create interest among learners as for example a quiz may be done online as part of formative assessment. Technology can greatly assist teachers in classrooms to teach difficult and abstract subject matter concepts effectively if the right digital instruction materials, supporting technology infrastructure and intensive training are provided to the teachers to support instruction through smart classrooms equipped with LCD projector.

The National Mission on Education through Information and Communication Technology (ICT) has been envisaged as a Centrally Sponsored Scheme to leverage the potential of ICT, in teaching and learning process for the benefit of all the learners in Higher Education Institutions in anytime anywhere mode. This is expected to be a major intervention in enhancing the Gross Enrolment Ratio (GER) in Higher Education by 5 percentage points during the XI Five Year Plan period (Ministry of HRD, Government of India, 2008).

The objectives of the National Mission on Education through ICT were stipulated to include the following:

- Building connectivity and knowledge network among and within institutions of higher learning in the country with a view of achieving critical mass of researchers in any given field;
- Spreading digital literacy for teacher empowerment;
- Development of knowledge modules having the right content to take care of the aspirations of academic community and to address to the personalized needs of the learners;
- Standardization and quality assurance of e-contents to make them world class;
- Research in the field of pedagogy for development of efficient learning modules for disparate groups of learners;
- Making available of e-knowledge contents, free of cost to Indians;
- Experimentation and field trial in the area of performance optimization of low cost access devices for use of ICT in education;
- Providing support for the creation of Virtual Technological University;
- Identification and nurturing of talent;
- Certification of competencies of the human resources acquired either through formal or non-formal means and the evolution of a legal framework for it; and
- Developing and maintaining the database with the profiles of our human resources.

The Mission has two major components:

- Providing connectivity, along with provision for access devices, to institutions and learners;
- Content generation.

It aims to extend computer infrastructure and connectivity to over 18000 colleges in the country including each of the departments of nearly 400 universities/deemed universities and institutions of national importance as a part of its motto to provide connectivity up to last mile. Therefore, the Mission, in addition to utilize the connectivity network of BSNL/MTNL and other providers, shall explore the possibility to provide connectivity utilizing Very Small Aperture Terminal (VSAT), Very Personal Network (VPN) and EduSat channels. It seeks to bridge the digital divide, i.e., the gap in the skills to use computing devices for the purpose of teaching and learning among urban and rural teachers/learners in Higher Education domain and empower those, who have hitherto remained untouched by the digital revolution and have not been able to join the mainstream of the knowledge economy so that they can make best use of ICT for teaching and learning. The Mission would create high quality e-content for the target groups. National Programme of Technology Enhanced Learning (NPTEL) Phase II and III will be part of the content generation activity. The peer group assisted content development would utilize the Wikipedia type of collaborative platform under the supervision of a content advisory committee responsible for vetting the content. Interactivity and problem solving approach would be addressed through "Talk to a Teacher" component, where the availability of teachers to take the questions of learners shall be ensured appropriately. The Mission also envisage, on line, for promoting research with the objective to develop new and innovative ICT tools for further facilitation of teaching and learning process. It plans to focus on appropriate pedagogy for e-learning, providing facility of performing experiments through virtual laboratories, on-line testing and certification, utilization of available Education Satellite (Edu-SAT) and Direct to Home (DTH) platforms, training and empowerment of teachers to effectively use the new method of teaching learning. Central Government would bear 75% of the connectivity charges for 5 years even for institutions not belonging to it. Renowned institutions would anchor various activities in their areas of excellence. The Mission would seek to enhance the standards of education, in Government as well as in private colleges. Enlistment of support and cooperation of States/Union Territories, Institutions and individual experts would be an integral part of the Mission.

Shri Arjun Singh, Minister for Human Resource Development, today launched the 'National Mission on Education through Information and Communication Technology at Sri Venkateswara University, Tirupati. Launching the Mission he said that the aim of this initiative is to address the goals of access, equity and quality in Higher Education and attempt to bridge the digital divide between urban and rural as well as between the rich and poor strata of society. 'National Mission on Education through Information and Communication Technology' is part of Ministry's such initiatives that will help the common man in his quest for education. A sum of Rs. 4,612 crore has been allocated for it in the 11th Plan. Chief Minister of Andhra Pradesh, Dr. Y.S. Rajasekhara Reddy and Smt. D. Purandeshwari, Minister of State of HRD, were also present on the occasion.

Emphasizing the importance of Information and Communication Technology (ICT) in the expansion of education in India, Shri Arjun Singh said that the Government is committed to make the best possible use of ICT not only for teaching and learning process but also to promote the research in all our institutions of higher learning, by providing access to research articles, journals and speedier interaction with their senior colleagues in various Universities and premier institutions. The continuous innovations are needed, to develop new ICT tools that may further facilitate the teaching, learning and research, reduce distance among researchers and faculty members with in the country and abroad, reduce the cost of education without compromising on the quality.

Shri Arjun Singh said that it is a momentous opportunity for all the teachers and experts in the country to pool their collective wisdom for the benefit of every Indian learner and, thereby, help in reducing the digital divide. The Mission proposes a collaborative approach for implementation of a programme involving both central and state governments, as well as aided and private institutions. Information and communication technologies (ICT) are increasingly being used to deliver on promises of universal education. Despite a growing number of ICT for education (ICT4E) initiatives in South Asia, there was no up-to-date and comprehensive information about the sector. To fill this gap, *info*Dev commissioned a survey of ICT4E in India and South Asia. The result includes country-level studies, sub-national reports for five Indian states, two detailed essays on distance education and teacher training in Pakistan, and five thematic essays on cross-cutting issues. Information and communication technologies (ICT) are important tools for delivering education around the world. However, despite the proliferation of initiatives that promote ICT4E, there was little guidance for policy-makers and donors on what is already being done and how well it works.

The lack of information affects planning, coordination and implementation. To address this problem, *info*Dev commissioned PricewaterhouseCoopers India to survey the experience of South Asia in ICT4E. The report is sub-divided as follows:

- An extended summary of the findings;
- Individual country-level reports for Afghanistan, Bangladesh, Bhutan, India, Maldives, Nepal, Pakistan, and Sri Lanka;
- Four state-level profiles from India - including Delhi, Karnataka, Rajasthan, and West Bengal;
- Two profiles of distance education and teacher training in Pakistan;
- Five thematic essays on gender equality, policy coherence, non-formal learning, capacity building, and primary and secondary schooling;
- A discussion of the methodology and database of consulted experts and documents.

In nearly all countries, *four main themes* emerge:

- The importance of ICTs for training teachers. Much of this takes the form of basic computer literacy instead of how to integrate computers into teaching methods, but the emphasis on building capacity is important.
- Secondly, providing and sustaining ICT infrastructure in schools, especially through public-private partnerships, is essential.
- Thirdly, while ICT is an important part of formal educational institutions, it can be just as powerful in non-formal education settings, creating the opportunity for life-long learning.
- Finally, several countries have very strong Open and Distance Learning initiatives that seek to provide mass education and overcome geographic or financial barriers.

Among the *key findings* is the importance of fostering an ICT 'ecosystem' with numerous constituent parts working in collaboration to provide opportunities for innovative educational approaches. ICTs can be seen as a platform to overcome the worst parts of education and learning while creating new opportunities and innovative ways to teach and learn. Meeting this demand can take many forms - from distance learning on a radio or TV, to newer devices like the widespread mobile phone. Through it all though, the importance of local context and systematic capacity building is key. Careful monitoring and evaluation, and coordination, are critical to success.

American higher education is undergoing substantial change in terms of the way colleges and universities are organized and function. This change is being driven by the combined forces of demographics, globalization, economic restructuring, and information technology – forces that will, over the coming decade, lead us to adopt new conceptions of educational markets, organizational structures, how we teach, and what we teach. This article describes these forces and speculates on their effects on higher education in the USA and other industrialized nations (Morrison, 2000). The focus of much e-learning activity is upon the development of courses and their resources. Successful e-learning takes place within a complex system involving the student experience of learning, teachers' strategies, teachers' planning and thinking, and the teaching/learning context. Staff development for e-learning focuses around the level of technological delivery strategies when other issues such as the teachers' conception of learning has a major influence on the planning of courses, development of teaching strategies and what students learn. This calls for a more comprehensive framework for the design, development and implementation of e-learning systems in higher education (Linn, 1998; Richardson, J. and Swan, K., 2003; Townsend, M. and Wheeler, S., 2004; Waight et al, 2004; Yancey, 2005).

Translating ICT-in-Education Policies into Action: Up to 2015 andBbeyond

United Nations Educational Scientific and Cultural Organization (UNESCO) and Intel; co-organized a two-day long South Asian Ministries of Education Forum (SAMF 2013) focused on 'Translating ICT-in-Education Policies into Action - up to 2015 and beyond' in New Delhi. SAMF2013 is a platform for officials from Afghanistan, Bangladesh, Bhutan, India, Maldives, Nepal, Pakistan and Sri Lanka to deliberate on ICT in Education Master Plans and share best practices. The delegates shared experiences and discussed strategies on the roles and uses of information and communication technologies in education.

The SAMF 2013 witnessed opening remarks by Mr. Shigeru Aoyagi, Director, UNESCO New Delhi and a Special Address by Debjani Ghosh, Managing Director, and Intel South Asia on Bilateral and Multilateral Regional Cooperation of the South Asian Ministries of Education on harnessing ICT use in and for Education. Dr. Shashi Tharoor, Hon'ble Minister of State for Human Resource Development, Government of India delivered the closing keynote address.

In the opening session of the two-day summit, Mr. Shigeru Aoyagi, Director, UNESCO New Delhi said "India along with the rest of South Asian countries has a rich history and expertise in education development, and governments as well as a number of premier educational institutions have been putting a strong focus on promoting Education for All. With rapid advancement of ICTs, the governments and institutes are currently working towards building an enabling ICT environment in education sector; but there are still many challenges yet to be addressed. Therefore, we aim to work together to achieve Education for All incorporating ICT in Education to ensure quality and inclusive education for every girl and boy and woman and man.

In his closing remarks, Dr. Shashi Tharoor, Hon'ble Minister of State for Human Resource Development, Government of India said "Effective, scalable and motivational education policies can result in the development of a nation by sowing seeds of learning and skills in the youth of any nation. Education transformation is a global priority and the use of ICT in and for education will be imperative for this transformation. I am delighted to be part of this conclave of the best minds from the South Asian region that have collectively discussed various actionable strategies on leveraging ICT for educational transformation." Closing his speech, he further added "I would like to commend UNESCO New Delhi and Intel India for coming forward to collaborate towards contributing to the growth of South Asia."

This South Asian Ministerial Forum focused on tracking progress on development of ICT use in Education in the South Asian countries and the latest National policies in this regard. It also outlined the need for strengthening the integration of ICT in Pedagogy and Teacher Professional Development as well as the development of a Master Plan for ICT in Education by establishing partnership within the country and collaborating at the sub-regional level. This forum helped delegates to familiarize themselves with the process of converting policies into action plans, identifying levers for change and finding ways of aligning ecosystems as well as designing strategies, schemes to accomplish their goals of providing quality education. UNESCO is tasked with coordinating progress to achieve by 2015 the six Education for All (EFA) goals agreed to by 164 countries at the World Education Forum in Dakar in 2000. The SAMF 2013 also discussed how to ensure that the issues around use of ICT in Education are effectively addressed and also have an appropriate place in the Post-2015 Development Agenda.

Ms. Debjani Ghosh, Managing Director, Intel South Asia said "Intel firmly believes in the transformative power of technology and that an effective education led transformation can help countries increase student competitiveness, build job skills and competencies, thus, support economic development and provide social cohesion. This can never be achieved in isolation and we all need to work together towards achieving sustainable social and economic growth and development through discourse over innovation, technology, and skills development. The need of the hour is policies and action plans aligned to education goals to ensure that all students obtain the skills necessary to succeed in a knowledge-based economy and society."

Given the rapid developments in ICT in recent years and the different forms of technologies that are available for use in education, policy makers are in need of a set of tools that can be used throughout the planning process to provide policy options regarding the effective use of ICT in education. The 'UNESCO ICT in Education Toolkit for Policy Makers, Planners and Practitioners' collaboratively developed by policy makers in the Asia Pacific region in response to the need for a systematic approach to integrating ICT into education at the national level. This South Asian Ministerial Forum had been initiated as a follow-up to the important discussions held at the Asia-Pacific Ministerial Forum on ICT in Education (AMFIE) in 2012, which was the third in the series of forums.

Integrated approach to use of technology in education has been used and researched for many years, but its adaptation in underprivileged settings in India has remained at the skill level or as a teaching tool. This approach may not be rare with international schools, but remains rare and novice in schools of poor students. Installing computers in schools of poor children has gained considerable momentum in India. Organisations with corporate partners have been loading government schools with computers and fancy software. Skill based focus is another big objective of the government and many corporate CSRs. Many believe that technology taught in schools where children from underprivileged backgrounds learn will assure skilled workforce in the future. However, there are numerous computer centres and institutes even in the most backward villages that can provide technological skills. It doesn't take a whole school life cycle to learn the computer basics and advanced functions. Such a skill based motive to connect schools with technology seems superficial and a weak technical rationality to bring in social change in education for the poor.

On the other hand, the National Policy on Information and Communication Technology (ICT) In School Education (2011-draft) is a comprehensive document that envisages such approaches discussed in this paper. But its implementation is more than challenging because of many factors. The most vigilant is access and digital divide. As per a NUEPA 2007 study report, 87 percent of the schools in India do not have a single computer. However, the model school concept announced by the Prime Minister promises an ICT infrastructure in schools. The most awaited Aakash will soon hit the schools. But at this juncture, it is more about access and the systemic approach for integration within the curriculum remains a consideration.

Although access to computers has been documented as influencing classroom use of computers, it is not a sufficient factor for use. The World Bank study (2011) suggested that merely putting computers in schools and training teachers to use them will not improve the learning levels in students. A two-year study conducted by the World Bank (2011) in Colombia where the computers were deputed in public schools from the year 2002 to 2008, showed no relationship between learning achievement and computers in the classroom. One of the obvious reasons or this as explained in the study was that the computers in the schools were used to learn computer systems and applications with no plan and efforts to integrate it with the teaching and learning in the classroom. Technology integration in education as explained above is a systemic process.

In the Indian context, the most prevailing factors besides access are:

- failure of understanding and implementing *constructivist pedagogy* in the education system,
- the overpowering attention on *economic value* of learning technology for these students,
- and most importantly, the lack of *capacity building* of teachers and school administrators in this area.

An exploratory study: A dip and analyse technique was used to explore computers in school projects initiated by three organisations. The designated Programme Officer explored three organizations in Western and Southern India that run computer assisted learning programmes in public or aided schools. These three organisations are very well known for technology in education projects in schools. Two of the three organisations have developed their own software to promote technology in schools.

A total of five government or government aided schools were visited. These schools had adopted computer aided activities implemented by the three organisations. The detailed observations at these three organisations are documented and available. In a nutshell, computers at these projects were used to inculcate either skills based intervention or in the form of CD based learning in government or aided schools. Two of the projects had computers in the computer labs managed by computer teacher. The activities were computer centred, where children were either playing educational games or learning software applications. In one of the projects, the teachers were using open share software to create teaching tools.

But even here, the students' use of computers to construct their own learning was not seen.

These observations indicated that they are merely witnessing a shift from teacher centred to computer centred learning. Integration of technology in both teaching and learning processes was not seen.

Even in the developed countries, integration of technology in the curriculum and school culture was not easy. It requires a systemic approach where all the stake holders in the education micro-systems are involved and engaged. In India, we are witnessing the issue at a very basic level. We have not yet reached the stage where we know what successful integration means and therefore, cannot answer if we have achieved it or not. The organizations and corporations have been stuffing their fancy software in computer labs, without making any impact in the teaching and learning processes in the classroom. As Zhao

(2003) claims that most software tools are rarely created as solutions to pedagogical problems. One of the reasons is their pre-occupation with learning outcomes than teaching and learning processes. The arguments raised here is not to attack educational software. It definitely has value in improving learning outcomes. The question here is why has the technology not been used as a tool to revitalise the teaching and learning pedagogy, student centred and constructive processes in classroom, and most importantly, why are computers an added layer and not integrated within the curriculum. This leads to understanding the concept of integrated approach to Technology in Education (ITE).

Use of Social Media in Education

This new trend is gaining currency among the youth worldwide and is indeed becoming an accepted way of expression, even in fields of education albeit opposition from the 'nay-sayers'. *Twitter* represents an excellent opportunity for classroom teachers. The sign up process is straightforward and allows the user to 'tweet' information of up to 60 characters- this is then read by anyone who signs up to 'follow' the user, viewed in a stream of information. A large number of news agencies, commentators, economists and bloggers tweet information daily. This can then be re-tweeted to other followers. Should I choose to follow Paul Krugman, for example, and feel one of his tweets could be of interest to my students, I can choose to re-tweet it to a 'list' of my students who have signed up to follow me on the site. On a daily basis, a teacher can tweet information to a class, say on homework deadlines, class activity or an item in the news.

Whether students choose to act on the information is, however, a matter for them, though a teacher could award prizes, or produce a weekly 'newsletter' of the best tweets from students via a file sharing website such as Storify (see below).

The hash tag (#) allows tweets to be sorted. I could for example search #Indian economy and find tweets posted on that topic. Tweets can also be sorted by 'favouring' them and returning to them later. Twitter helps support online tutoring and supports independent study though the tweeting of links to articles and video clips, as well as useful websites for exam skills or career options. There is also a group of teachers of economics and business who follow each other and share information and advice on teaching key topics. This is centred on Jim and Geoff Riley at www.tutor2u.net

Finally, twitter helps students keep up to date with the latest news via the smartphone App. Instant information is available from economic and financial institutions. These feeds can even be used by students in class. Students can reply to the economist or institution they follow- one of my students had a reply from David Smith (Times Economics correspondent) over a query about his book *Free Lunch*. The online polling website www.polleverywhere.com can also be used via students making their voting decisions via Twitter.

Storify allows its users to gather together information from other social media and to organise it with their own narrative. Writers can gather a set of tweets or a video embedded on Facebook. In this sense it is rather like an online student project on issues in the news. It could be used in economics for an online report say, on commentators' views of the budget and be open for view by other web users.

Pinterest allows the user to collect images and store them in sets of online notice boards. The principle is of the photo album- a set of images with some commentary from the collector. The user can upload photographs or web articles, providing they contain a useable image, with one photo chosen to identify the board. Users can put boards together individually or allow others to 'pin' on their boards. This is a great mechanism for teachers to collect resources and images from the web. An obvious use would be asking students to collect examples of demerit goods, a series of articles on quantitative easing or images associated with an economic boom or recession.

Blogging is a great mechanism for students to express their opinions and share these with others. Sites such as Word Press allow both teachers and students to writer newspaper 'leader' style columns that can be viewed and rated by others. These sites also allow additional contributions from other readers. They present a useful opportunity for teachers to develop the skills at the higher level of Bloom's taxonomy, such as evaluation and application.www.tutor2u.net now encourages economics students to submit articles for publication.

Some schools and Colleges now have their own *Facebook* page where students can share comments, video clips and 'likes' about topics or the institution in general. A caveat about social media is that staff and pupils must agree a code of conduct as to how the various sites are used. These might mean ensure all comments are purely education and topic related. Schools and Colleges can appoint an administrator to ensure this and set up appropriate firewalls to ensure access is limited to those desired. Social media are used by young people on a daily basis- indeed; many are more familiar with the application of these sites than the average teacher. However, they present a great opportunity for use to share information and opinions and activities such as 'pinning' and 'tweeting' can indicate students' understanding of a topic. They can also be used to stimulate student interest beyond the use of a core text or hand-out.

Social and digital media have shaped a transformational process in the way learning is developed by new teachers. An initial limited use of new media is followed by a period of expansion as more resources that are subject specific become available. Research (Hsu, 2011) has looked at the type of teachers who are likely to assign students ICT related activities and the nature of the tasks themselves. He found those teachers who infrequently use ICT in their own lives are less likely to use it with students. Hsu concludes that those staff who are competent in building websites are those most likely to assign ICT related tasks.

Wider Social Development

ICT can also have a significant role in poverty reduction (Tas, 2011). Students are able to work collaboratively across continents and within countries across mediums such as blogs, emails and Skype conversations. This supports the use of peer mentoring or the joint development of classroom and resources by teachers. Websites and social media channels offer a form of tutoring which allows students to access expertise beyond that provided from their original teacher.

In this context it is argued that ICT improves the monitoring ability of the Principal observing the agent. This could be teaching monitoring student attainment via their scores on a self-marked online test; a school observing the performance of teacher educators in a similar context; and/or a Local Authority comparing the performance of its schools and teachers over a period of time. Research (Dlodlo,2009) looked at the impact of ICT on female education in South Africa; others contrasted the use of ICT in education in urban and rural China, noting a widening gap in attainment and accessibility between such regions, noting the key variables in the acceptance and use of ICT as teaching practice, funding, equipment and the institutional educational framework. He proposes the development of ICT packages and approaches that are customised for use in rural areas, where teachers and students may have limited use and experience- he proposes that 'canned' products developed for wealthier schools must be adapted.

Changes in Relationships Among Teachers, Students, and Parents

In keeping with the new activities and roles for students, the teachers and students in the schools we visited reported that they were transforming how they interact. The changes in teaching practices in these schools are part of a broader change in relationships within the school and between the school and the community. The educators and students described changes in the ways they collaborate with each other that grew out of the new teaching practices (e.g., project based approaches, open-ended questions), integrating ICT into the schools (e.g., Internet research or presentations), or both. We noticed that teachers, students, and parents reported changes in three sets of relationships: (1) among the students; (2) between students and teachers; and (3) Between the school, the parents, and sometimes the community.

1. *Projects and ICT activities fostered collaborative relationships among students.* Many of the teachers and parents interviewed said that students were developing a range of social and interpersonal skills that they attributed to the projects and the new roles that students were taking on. As noted, students in every school were taking on new responsibilities as they worked on projects—leading teams, conducting research, writing reports, debating with peers, and making presentations to peers,

teachers, and parents. A Chilean fifth grade teacher explained how her students were developing the skills and maturity to work as a team, even across grade levels, because of the collaborative techniques she learned in the Essentials Course. Some of the parents also commented on their children's maturity and responsibility. A Turkish father noticed a change in his daughter's attitudes since doing the "Intel projects." He observed that before teachers participated in the Essentials Course, his daughter did not share her things with anyone. After her teachers participated in the Course, his daughter began to share more with friends and she enjoyed working in teams. The father also said that, as a result of her involvement in projects and team work, his daughter completed her school assignments independently at home and no longer asked him for help.

2. *New teaching strategies allowed teachers to develop more collaborative and inter-active relation-ships with their students.* The teachers reported that, as their teaching practices changed, their relationships with their students also became more open and supportive. Teachers began to allow more intellectual discussions between themselves and their students, and students were more will-ing to approach teachers and share concerns and opinions. The teachers and parents in Mumbai were, perhaps, the most eloquent. One group of teachers commented that, as children, they had been afraid of their teachers and they were happy that their students no longer "fear the teacher" but gladly ask questions and give opinions. The students we interviewed echoed these sentiments. A group of high school students from the school in Santiago, Chile explained that a good teacher is one who encourages students to disagree when they have a well-reasoned argument. A student from Mumbai shared a similar perspective: "I like that whenever I do a report I can include my own critical opinion—it is not just cut and paste. And I can learn many things outside of the textbook."

3. *Innovating with projects and ICT strengthened the relationships between the school, parents, and the community.* The parents we interviewed were excited by the introduction of community-focused projects and student research, and they expressed pride in what the schools were doing for their children with technology. A group of parents in India praised their school "because of the new technology, [the school] is innovative. They have very high performance, but it is not just academics-oriented." In the four public schools we visited, parents and the community had also initiated efforts to bring additional ICT resources to the schools by donating equipment or paying for improved Internet connections. However, the parents also remarked on the new teaching practices and what these changes mean for their children. All of the parents we interviewed commented on how the school was developing the whole child since the project work was supporting teamwork, independence, and self–confidence. Parents in India and Turkey highlighted their children's grow-ing confidence and independence to do research or make public presentations, and they also noted the caring relationships between students and teachers.

The author has also started using visuals and audios for her sessions which can be replicated on the College website via students and teachers email accounts. The dual advantage is that it provides revision sessions for those in class, as well as reference for those outside/absent from class. This creates 'win-win' situations for the learners and the teachers as new technologies that are cost and time effective get introduced. Figures 1 and 2 demonstrate sessions for our undergraduate students that were posted online for studying Producer's Equilibrium or Principle of Maximum Social Advantage (MSA).

This clearly demonstrates an effective application of technology to the traditional 'chalk and talk' technique that can modernize Indian class rooms.

Figure 1.

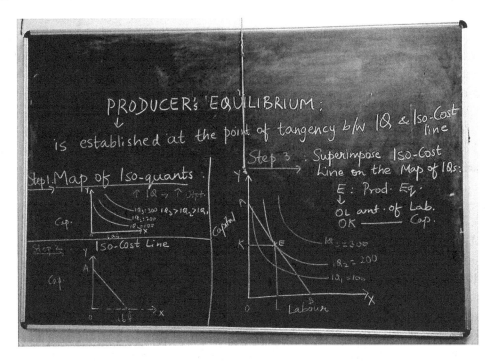

Figure 2.

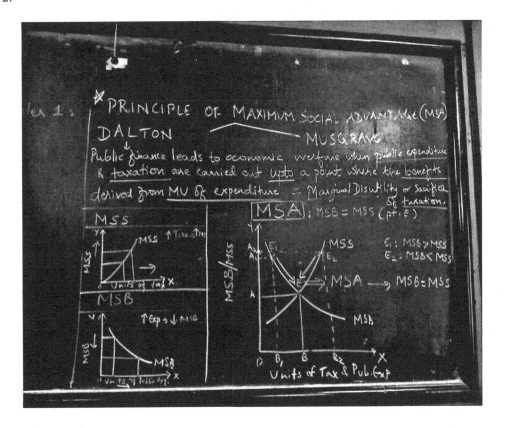

CONCLUSION

The above research paper showed the trajectory of ICT and its increased usage across the world in an era of globalism. Technology helps update, modernize, and revolutionalize knowledge, information teaching-learning processes et al that help to bridge the digital divide on multi levels-between the rich and poor nations, between the rich and poor classes within a nation, between the rural and urban areas, between the young and old population, between the first and second generation learners and teachers that have become the essence of the new knowledge economy comprising smart students, teachers, policy makers, and communities all woven together through the yarn of the world wide web (See Johnston, 2002; UNESCO, 2002, 2003; Becker, 2000; WestEd, 2002; Stats Canada, 2004; Barth, et al. 2000; Dawson et al, 2006; Aggarwal, A. and Regino Bento, 2002). Like any other innovation, this one too is a double-edged coin with its intrinsic advantages and disadvantages. It is for us to harness modern technologies and utilize the ICT revolution in education for modern global growth, interconnectedness, and inclusiveness that create 'win-win' situations for all stakeholders.

Quality in education through ICT and its awareness among stakeholders will have positive impact on the society. ICT can be helpful in quality and standards of education by implementing it in various phases of education. ICT can be employed in formal and Non-formal types of education and would eventually make the learners employable and socially useful part of the society. By employing ICT in teacher training can save a lot of money of the Government. Moreover, a lot of qualitative improvement can be seen as resource persons for the training can be best of the world. By employing ICT in administration can help in solving the problem of Absenteeism of students and teachers. Good quality content is one of the major issue and directly affects the standards of education and quality. By overcoming the certain challenges involved in the process of education can help a lot in this side. Conclusively a lot of quality improvement is possible after careful and planned implementation of ICT in education by various stakeholders.

Most of the operating Distance Education (DE) networks are facing a flak because education regulator University Grants Commission (UGC) in India does not recognize any course offered solely through the online mode.

Many universities are offering such degrees, even though "UGC has not yet recognized any University/Institution for offering distance education programmes solely through the online mode," writes SK Mishra, deputy director, UGC, in response to a question under the Right to Information Act.

U18 is an education technology and content services provider, working in collaboration with various University's (i.e. Universities recognized as per the University Grants Commission (UGC) Act of 1956), in the conduct of various distance education and professional continuing education programs that lead to the award of Diplomas and Degrees by the Universities directly, upon a successful completion by the enrolled candidate. U18 is by itself NOT a University, and is not to be interpreted as a University under the University Grants Commission Act, 1956 (www.U18edu.in).

The website of the Karnataka Stake Open University (KSOU), for instance, offers online, correspondence and regular face-to-face programmes in its distance learning package. "In online courses, you get an opportunity to view videos, take assignments, etc. anytime anywhere and from any device," is the message on the university's website. Students can take the course entirely online the website informs.

We are aware of the growing digital divide between the global North and the global South that needs to be addressed on an urgent basis; particularly in the area of ICT, distance and online learning in higher education. Expected conclusions clearly point to this gap due to an escalating mismatch between the rapidly growing demand for higher education on account of growing youth population and rising aspirations. This is largely unmet by the supply of higher education facilities in terms of quantity, quality, access, and relevance. In lieu of the above scenario, we recommend increasing use of modern technology that is cost-effective and reaches a larger audience thus, providing world-class education to our masses. This will make technology the great enabler of economic growth, knowledge creation and circulation; as well a tool of 'inclusive growth'. Data mining and studying of 'best practices' from the University of Mumbai, IGIDR, IGNOU, and YCMOU at the national level in India would enrich our research and provide plausible solutions for a modern and cost-effective interactive educational tool. This in turn can serve as a model that can be easily replicated by institutions of higher education. We can even suggest 'public-private partnerships' between technology-providing solutions/companies to work in synchronization with public/private educational institutions.

REFERENCES

Aggarwal, A., & Bento, R. (2002). Web-Based Education. Hershey, PA, USA: IGI Global.

Alexander, S. (2001). E-learning developments and experiences. *Education + Training, 43*(4-5), 240-248.

Barth, M. et al. (2000). Developing Key Competencies for Sustainable Development in Higher Education. *International Journal of Sustainability in Higher Education.*

Becker. (2000). *The Digital Disconnect: The Widening Gap Between Internet-Savvy Students and Their Schools.*

Dawson, S., Burnett, B., & O'Donohue, M. (2006). Learning Communities: An untapped sustainable comparative advantage for higher education. *International Journal of Educational Management, 20*(2), 127–139. doi:10.1108/09513540610646118

Dlodlo, N. (2009). Access to ICT education for girls and women in rural South Africa: A case study. *Technology in Society, 31*(2), 168–17. doi:10.1016/j.techsoc.2009.03.003

Erixon, P (2010). School subject paradigms and teaching practice in lower secondary Swedish schools influenced by ICT and media in *Computers & Education, 54*(4), 1212-1221.

Everywhere, P. live audience participation (2012). Retrieved from http://www.polleverywhere.com

Hsu, S. (2011). Who assigns the most ICT activities? Examining the relationship between teacher and student usage. *Computers & Education, 56*(3), 847–855. doi:10.1016/j.compedu.2010.10.026

Johnston. (2002). *Assessing the Impact of Technology in Teaching and Learning Changing the Conversation about Teaching, Learning and Technology: A Report on 10 Years of ACOT Research.*

Kumar, H., et al. (2006). Using Blogs for Extending Library Services. *University News, 48*(12), 16.

Light, D., Menon, R., & Shulman, S. (2009). *Training teachers across a diversity of contexts: An analysis of international evaluation data on the Intel Teach Essentials Course, 2006.* New York: EDC/Center for Children and Technology.

Linn, M. C. (1998). Instances of Distance Learning: Cognition and distance learning. *Journal of the American Society for Information Science*, *47*(11), 826–842. doi:10.1002/(SICI)1097-4571(199611)47:11<826::AID-ASI6>3.0.CO;2-4

Lv, J. (2011). ICT education in rual areas of southwest China: A case study of Zhongxian County, Chongqing. *Proceedings of the6th International Conference on Computer Science & Education* (pp. 681-685). IEEE doi:10.1109/ICCSE.2011.6028730

Makrakis. (2012). ICTs in Education for Sustainable Development. *UNESCO Ministry of HRD*.

Morrison, J. (Ed.), (2000) On the Horizon: US Higher Education in Transition. The Technology Source, 11(1), 6-10.

National Curriculum Framework. (2005). *Ministry of HRD*. Government of India.

Online degree courses from India. (2016). *U18edu.in*. Retrieved from www.U18edu.in

Richardson, J., & Swan, K. (2003). Examining social presence in online courses in relation to students' perceived learning and satisfaction. *Journal of Asynchronous Learning Networks*, *7*(1), 68–88.

Statistics Canada. (2004). *Literacy Scores, human capital and growth across 14 OECD countries*.

Tas, E. M. (2011). ICT Education for Development- a case study. *Procedia Computer Science*, *3*, 507–512. doi:10.1016/j.procs.2010.12.085

The exam performance specialists (2012). *Tutor2u.net*. Retrieved from http://www.tutor2u.net

Townsend, M., & Wheeler, S. (2004). Is there anybody out there? Teaching assistants' experiences of online learning. *The Quarterly Review of Distance Education*, *5*(2), 127–138.

Travis, J., & Price, K. (2005). Instructional culture and distance learning. *Journal of Faculty Development*, *20*(2), 99–103.

UNESCO. (2003). *Developing and Using Indicators of ICT Use in Education*. Paris.

UNESCO. (2015). Retrieved from http://unesco.org

Waight, C. et al.. (2004). Recurrent themes in e-learning: A narrative analysis of major e-learning report. *The Quarterly Review of Distance Education*, *5*(3), 195–203.

WestEd (2002), *The e Learning Return on our Educational Technology Investment—A Review of Findings from Research*

Yancey, K. (2005). The people's university. *Change*, (March-April), 13.

ADDITIONAL READING

These could be sourced from several UNESCO & OECD Reports on e-learning, social media, ICT, and the like, some of which are listed below:

E-learning Series on ICT in Education. (2009).

Fostering Digital Citizenship through Safe and Responsive Use of ICT: A Review of Current Status in Asia and the Pacific. (2014, December).

Quick Guide: ICT and Education at the OECD. (n. d.).

GuideQuickICT and Education at the UNESCO. (n. d.).

OECD. (2005, December). E-learning in Tertiary Education (Policy Brief).

Quality Assurance and Recognition. (n. d.). UNESCO.

KEY TERMS AND DEFINITIONS

ICT: Information and Communication Technology.

Iso-Quants (IQs): Are equal product curves used by producers while employing various factors of production like labour and capital used in different combinations to give the same amount of output.

Maximum Social Advantage (MSA): Concept of MSA was given by public economists Musgrave and Dalton indicating that the maximum social advantage from public expenditure will be maximized by taking the net of MSB over MSS as every public expenditure involves a benefit to society; while every tax levy has a sacrifice to be made by tax-payers. Thus, the ideal size of the Government's budget is determined by difference in both MSB and MSS.

MSB: Marginal Social Benefit.

MSS: Marginal Social Sacrifice.

OECD: Organization for Economic Cooperation and Development.

Open Educational Resources (OER): Are being used as a mass open learning platform accessible to all, thus becoming a good example of creative commons.

UNESCO: United Nation's Educational, Scientific and Cultural Organization.

Chapter 5
Collaborative Online Learning Tools and Types:
Few Perspectives of Its Use in Academic Library

Sarika Sawant

SHPT School of Library Science, SNDT Women's University, India

ABSTRACT

Collaborative learning experiences not only promotes critical thinking and reflection in students but also encourages them to develop a sense of community, thus enabling the creation of an environment in which further collaborative work can take place. While technologies to facilitate collaborative learning include a range of features and functionalities, this paper focuses on ten types of tools that deal with idea generation and brainstorming, mapping, design, online group work and document collaboration, and online communication. The present paper explains the online collaboration with its features, preparation required by institution and role of teacher presence in online learning. It highlights on ten different tools based on its function with suitable examples. It also explores paradigm shift from academic librarian to blended librarian, it's possible hurdles and benefits. The blended librarian is versed in both print and online tools and can help faculty meet course goals, regardless of the medium or technology. The paper concludes with how idea of online collaborative learning methodology is likely to evolve and make significant benefits to education, and probably to post educational business collaboration as well.

COLLABORATIVE LEARNING

Collaborative learning is a situation where students are able to socially interact with other students, as well as instructors. In essence, learners work together in order to expand their knowledge of a particular subject or skill.

Collaborative learning is based upon the principle that students can enrich their learning experiences by interacting with others and benefiting from one another's strengths. In collaborative learning situa-

DOI: 10.4018/978-1-5225-0556-3.ch005

tions, students are responsible for one another's actions and tasks which encourages teamwork as well (eLearning 101 – concepts, trends, applications, 2014).

Collaborative learning engages learners in knowledge sharing, inspiring each other, depending upon each other, and applying active social interaction in a small group. Therefore, collaborative learning depends upon the art of social interaction among learners rather than a mechanical process (Tu, 2004). The idea of group work in learning finds its root in work from the Russian psychologist Vygotsky (1978) who explored the causal relationships that exists between social interaction and individual learning providing a foundation of the social constructivist theory of learning (Muuro,Wagacha, Kihoro & Oboko, 2014).

Collaborative learning is based on the view that knowledge is a social construct. Collaborative activities are most often based on four principles:

- The learner or student is the primary focus of instruction.
- Interaction and "doing" are of primary importance
- Working in groups is an important mode of learning.
- Structured approaches to developing solutions to real-world problems should be incorporated into learning (Chandra, 2015).

A set of assumptions about the learning process according to Smith and MacGregor, (1992) underlies approaches to collaborative learning are as follows

- Learning is an active process whereby students understand the information and relate this new knowledge to the existing knowledge.
- Learning opens the door for the learner to actively engage his/her peers, and to process and produce information rather than simply remembering it.
- Learners benefit when exposed to people with diverse backgrounds & viewpoints.
- Learning flourishes in a social environment where conversation between learners takes place. During this process, the learner creates a framework and meaning to the discourse.
- In the collaborative learning environment, the learners are challenged both socially and emotionally as they listen to different perspectives, and are required to articulate and defend their ideas. In so doing, the learners begin to create their own unique conceptual frameworks and not rely solely on an expert's or a text's framework. Thus, in collaborative learning setting, learners have the opportunity to converse with peers, present and defend ideas, exchange diverse beliefs, question other conceptual frameworks, and be actively engaged.

Some activities or assignments well suited for collaborative learning include:

- Case studies
- Discussions
- Student-moderated discussions
- Debates
- Collaborative writing
- Collaborative presentation
- Games
- Demonstrations

Benefits of collaborative learning include:

- Development of higher-level thinking, oral communication, self-management, and leadership skills.
- Promotion of student-faculty interaction.
- Increase in student retention, self-esteem, and responsibility.
- Exposure to and an increase in understanding of diverse perspectives.
- Preparation for real life social and employment situations.

COLLABORATIVE ONLINE LEARNING

Collaborative learning can be conducted either offline or on the web, and can be done asynchronously or synchronously. It allows students to learn from the ideas, skill sets, and experience of others enrolled in the course. By engaging in a shared task (whether it be a project or lesson) students gain the opportunity to learn a variety of skills, such as group analysis and collaborative teamwork building skills.

In addition, even students who are unable to attend a live event online can participate in collaborative learning, using online forums, message boards, and other various posting sites that don't rely on real-time interaction (eLearning 101 – concepts, trends, applications, 2014).

Collaborative learning technologies range from communication tools that allow text, voice, or video chat to online spaces that facilitate brainstorming, document editing, and remote presentations of topics (Mallon & Bernsten, 2015)

Preparation Required by The Instructor/Trainer/Teacher to Implement Collaborative Online Learning

The right plans will help instructors to conceive and create interesting, informative learning coursework, activities and exercises that will fuel students' hunger for learning more. Also this will encourage them to open up towards their instructors and other students in their group who can ably support them by offering thoughtful advice and tips. So implementing right plans and using proper tools for implementing them, is a must for facilitating learning through online group collaboration.

- Course wise planning of the activities.
- Whenever teacher think about whether to introduce a new tool, activity or method into a course, it is important to consider its usefulness right form teaching style to its assessment method.
- Teacher need to invest as much time in advance as possible thinking through the new activity to balance interactivity and instructor workload.
- The more time teacher able to spend in advance, less time they will have to spend making important decisions about the course while it is in session. Online instruction can often mean more work for the instructor, but good course design and planning can help reduce the workload while the course is in session and can help make the quality of interaction between the instructor and the students more rewarding. Online discussions should not be viewed as an "add-on"; rather, they should replace something else.
- Plan to prepare the students for using the new tool or activity.

- Students cannot be expected to "know" how to discuss effectively either online or in person. Nor can one expect them to "know" how to work effectively in a group setting, particularly in a virtual group. The teacher need to prepare students for the work they will be doing. Also need to prepare them for working in groups by arranging workshop on group work to teach them how to work as a team in a face-to-face setting so groups can begin to understand the dynamics of their team and what their own role in the group will be (University of Waterloo, n.d.).
- Clear definition of expectations and purpose
- It needs to be clearly defined how a specific learning activity is relevant to the students and why being part of a group and working together will be beneficial for them. They need to be conveyed what is expected to be in the syllabus. It should very well define as what are the goals, learning objectives, & possible outcomes.
- Providing clear instructions to students in a group
- Smooth working in a group gets expected if students are clear about objectives of an activity. Teachers need to explain the purpose of an activity, provide specific due dates and necessary instructions. It is highly advised to set a due date around such time when course is nearing completion as this would enable students to get adjusted, be familiar with other students and cultivate rich relationships with them.
- Emphasis on keeping groups small
- To ensure active participation from students, it is better to make small sized groups which can be handled well. By larger groups, students tend to become unresponsive and do not actively contribute for any activity assigned.
- Close monitoring and support to be provided by teachers
- Timely help should be provided by the teaches to the students in case of any queries raised by the students. Especially weak students need support in a fast manner. Teachers can readily pass instructions to students in a group through synchronous video sessions.
- Defining etiquette guidelines for proper participation
- Guidelines need to be created for making students aware about how they can better participate in an online group. They need to be clear about how they should collaborate.
- Devising activities relevant to the topic
- Teachers should conceive such activities which are relevant and specific to the topic. These should be interesting not having general information so that students lose their interest. Activities that encourage exploration, improve engagement and relate with real life examples will invoke a much better response from the students. Keeping relevant links, images, quizzes, videos and other engaging, informative material will make a interesting learning process (Thomson, 2014).

Role of Teacher Presence in Facilitating an Effective Online Discussion

- Set-up expectations for the students engaged in the activity. Rules for posting in discussion such as grammatically correct language, informal expression and the use of slang and emoticons. Students may need a reminder of acceptable online behaviour; to be courteous and respectful in their communication style, content, and tone. Provide a rubric to help students understand how they are going to be assessed on in the discussion activity. Helping the students get started in their group activities online is an important first step in ensuring success. As they start to discuss online, drop into their discussions to provide focus to the discussion or to draw attention to particular concepts or information that is necessary to frame or pursue knowledge growth.

- Help students get started in their discussion. An online icebreaker activity can help students get to know each other online and reduce the awkwardness of discussing a topic with strangers. Alternatively arrange for your students to meet face-to-face as a group before they start their online discussion if that option is possible. Encourage students to draw on previous knowledge and experiences and respond to others' comments directly as they think critically about the discussion questions. E-mail people who are not participating to find out if they are experiencing technical difficulties with the online forum.

- Teacher's presence motivate and encourage students. Perhaps one of the most important aspects for the instructor who uses online discussions is teacher presence. This happens by posting the discussion questions, directing the groups in the discussions, and by providing feedback on how the discussion is going. Strategies include the following: ask questions (these are called "trigger questions"); give and ask for examples; identify students who are good at making connections between posts; create "weaving" posts to link other's good ideas together to advance the discussion, (example "V and X make a good point,... What do others think?"). When instructors explicitly recognize and reward this level of learning they can also encourage further knowledge growth.

- Provide direct instruction to the students. Direct instruction and feedback to the groups is sometimes necessary to keep them on track with the discussion. The instructor's comments and questions to the groups can be invaluable and can serve as a model for how the discussion should unfold.

- Provide access to resources. The instructor can provide access to a wealth of resources which students can be referred to for further individual or group study. Hyperlinks to online resources can be especially helpful, as they are easy for students who are already online to access.

- Provide technical assistance. The teachers may be asked to provide direct instruction about technical issues related to accessing the conferencing system, manipulation of the conferencing software, operation of other tools or resources and the technical aspects of dealing with any of the subject related tools and techniques. Have a plan in place to handle these requests.

- Practical considerations for facilitating online. It can become overwhelming to read through a busy discussion forum with lots of posts and replies. Teacher should ask students to create new threads if new topics evolve in the discussion. "Subscribing" to receive e-mail alerts of new postings can help participants keep up with a conversation without checking back into the discussion forum repeatedly (University of Waterloo, n.d.).

COLLABORATIVE ONLINE LEARNING TOOLS

Learning is no longer limited to classrooms now. The introduction of new technological tools has made it possible for far away located students to collaborate with their instructors and peers for learning new skills and acquiring enhanced knowledge, probably gain degree. Distance and time is no longer a barrier for imbibing knowledge. But for ensuring that students remain motivated and focused in their learning and gain the most from their interaction with their fellow students and instructors, proper strategies for learning activities need to be formulated and implemented. Otherwise, students will feel neglected and disengaged. For effective implementation of learning strategies, right aids need to be used. These online collaboration tools will enable students to communicate and collaborate quickly and easily. This will sustain their interest, improve focus and they would be able to contribute in best possible way and get quality results in turn.

Choosing precise tools is important for improved online collaboration for group learning. These online collaboration tools should have right functionality and should be easy to use. Only then students will feel confident and comfortable in carrying out their tasks and assignments (Thomson, 2014).

The enormous and distributed landscape of tools, makes it difficulty of finding one or a set of online learning tools to meet the requirements and it can be time intensive too.

While choosing for best online collaboration tool one can expect following features:

- Facilitate real-time and asynchronous text, voice, and video communication.
- Assist in basic project management activities.
- Support co-creation by enabling groups to modify output in real-time or asynchronously.
- Facilitate consensus building through group discussions and polling.
- Simplify and streamline resource management.
- Enable local and remote presentation archiving of completed projects (Carnegie Mellon University, 2009).

Online collaboration Tools can be divided into types according to its functions are as follows

- Collaboration Suites
- Course / Learning Management Systems
- Project Management Tools
- Wikis
- Real-Time Communications
- Collaborative Concept Mapping
- List/Task Management
- Presentation & Slide Sharing
- Collaborative Writing
- Creative/Design Collaboration

Collaboration Suites

An online collaboration suite provides an integrated set of web tools that span a range of collaboration needs. While not every collaboration suite includes the same capabilities, they often feature web tools for email, instant messaging, contact management, calendars, file sharing, document management, project management, portals, workspaces, web conferencing, and social media tools such as forums and wikis (McCabe, 2010).

Some examples are as follows.

Google http://www.google.com/intl/en/options/

It includes:

Google Apps offers web-based real-time collaboration: document, spreadsheet, presentation editing and more. It is free.

Google Drive is a file storage and synchronization service which enables user cloud storage, file sharing and collaborative editing. It is free.

Google Sites is a structured wiki- and web page-creation tool offered by Google as part of the Google Apps productivity suite.

Zimbra http://www.zimbra.com/

Zimbra is an open source unified collaboration platform for messaging, social and sharing. There is a free trial for Email and Collaborate option including an open source email and collaboration solution, Zimbra mobile and customer support and also a free edition of Build a Social Network which is a private social networking and online community solution, with full suite of social applications and built-in social analytics. Other options are paid.

Zoho http://www.zoho.com/

Zoho provides a wide, integrated portfolio of rich online applications for businesses. With more than 20 different applications spanning Collaboration, Business and Productivity applications, Zoho helps businesses and organizations get work done. Our applications are delivered over the internet, requiring nothing but a browser. This means you can focus on your business and rely on us to maintain the servers and keep your data safe.

Course / Learning Management Systems

An LMS is an integrated software environment supporting all these functionalities along with some mechanism for student enrolment into courses, general user management (including administrator, teacher, and student) and some important system functions like backup and restore. Some examples are as follows

Blackboard http://www.blackboard.com/

It is a virtual learning environment and course management system developed byBlackboard Inc. It is Web-based server software which features course management, customizable open architecture, and scalable design that allows integration with student information systems and authentication protocols. It may be installed on local servers or hosted by Blackboard ASP Solutions. Its main purposes are to add online elements to courses traditionally delivered face-to-face and to develop completely online courses with few or no face-to-face meetings.

Moodle https://moodle.org/

Moodle (Modular Object-Oriented Dynamic Learning Environment) Moodle is a Course Management System (CMS), also known as a Learning Management System (LMS) or a Virtual Learning Environment (VLE). It is an Open Source e-learning web application that educators can use to create effective online learning sites.

There are a range of potential applications of Moodle technology in education and training, delivery of learning materials and collaboration.

The basic features of Moodle include tools for creating resources and activities. These in turn provide the teacher managing the course various useful options. The Resources tab offers the teacher a choice of creating labels which are simply headings for each topic or week, creating text pages or web pages with a combination of text, images and links. Creating links to files or web sites/pages which can link to podcasts, videos and other files, creating directories which are folders one creates with a multitude of different files to be accessed by students or staff.

Another useful and collaborative section is the Activities tab which includes: assignments, chat, choice (one question with a choice of answers – answers are logged so statistics can be deducted), database which is a table created by the teacher and which is filled in by the students creating a database. Forum where everyone can post in response to discussion threads, glossary is a type of dictionary created by the teacher with terms used and their meanings.

Glossaries can also be an enjoyable, collaborative activity as well as a teaching tool. Lessons offer the flexibility of a web page, the interactivity of a quiz and branching capabilities. Quiz enables the creation of various types of quizzes, survey is a questionnaire which gathers feedback from students, wiki is a web page edited collaboratively.

Project Management Tools

Collaborative project management is based on the principle of actively involving all project members in the planning and control process and of networking them using information, communication, and collaboration modules. Management is not regarded as an activity reserved solely for managers but as an integral part of the project work of all team members.

ActiveCollab http://www.activecollab.com/

Active Collab offers features such as task management, collaboration, time tracking, and invoicing. It provides users with needed flexibility to manage virtual projects. Active Collab runs in the cloud like most browser apps today, but can also install it on server too.

Basecamp http://www.basecamphq.com/

Basecamp is an excellent online software package that makes project management and collaboration easy. Basecamp helps to manage multiple projects at a time with to-do lists, file sharing, chatting, messages, calendars and time tracking

Wikis

Wiki is a piece of server software that allows users to freely create and edit web page content using any web browser. Wiki supports hyperlinks and has a simple text syntax for creating new pages and crosslinks between internal pages on the fly.

Wiki is unusual among group communication mechanisms in that it allows the organization of contributions to be edited in addition to the content itself.

Like many simple concepts, "open editing" has some profound and subtle effects on Wiki usage. Allowing everyday users to create and edit any page in a Web site is exciting in that it encourages democratic use of the Web and promotes content composition by nontechnical users.

PBwiki http://pbwiki.com/

PBworks provides a broad set of collaboration products that help businesses work more efficiently and effectively. Products such as Agency Hub, Legal Hub, and Project Hub serve markets such as advertising and marketing agencies, law firms, and education, as well as the broader business market. Millions use PBworks each month for partner/client collaboration, new business development, project management, social intranets, and knowledge management.

PBworks allows multiple users to create and edit a website without any special software or web-design skills. The owner(s) of the wiki can track changes, moderate comments, and control who has access to the wiki. These features make PBworks a useful tool for collaborative writing projects. Also publish schedules, lectures, notes, and assignments. It enables collaborative group projects. Even it keeps parents involved and informed. Some more features include

- Create student accounts without requiring email addresses
- Automated notifications
- keep everyone up to date
- Edit and format wiki pages without learning how to code Grant access to people inside or outside your organization
- Store, discuss, search & share wiki pages, files, and documents
- Every wiki page or file, accessible by computer, smartphone, or tablet

Wikispaces http://www.wikispaces.com/

Wikispaces Classroom is a social writing platform for education. It is incredibly easy to create a classroom workspace where teacher and students can communicate and work on writing projects alone or in teams. Rich assessment tools gives the power to measure student contribution and engagement in real-time. Wikispaces Classroom works great on modern browsers, tablets, and phones. Some applications are as follows.

Some Social applications

- Create a safe, private network for your students
- Connect and communicate using a familiar newsfeed
- Monitor complete history of student discussions, writing, and file uploads

Writing

- Collaboratively edit pages using our visual editor
- Embed content from around the web, including videos, images, polls, documents, and more
- Comment on sections of text or the entire page

Projects

- Create individual or group assignments in seconds
- Choose to set assignment start and end dates, or create long-running projects
- At the end of the assignment, automatically publish projects to the entire class or students, parents, or others in your community

Real-Time Formative Assessment

- Watch student engagement in real time, literally as they type, without changing how you work
- Report on contributions to pages, discussions, and comments over time
- Focus on particular students, projects, or view reports across your entire class

Real-Time Communications

The real time communication is the communication in which sender and receiver exchange their information and data over a channel without any delay. Generally Real time communication (RTC) is called "live communication".

Characteristics of Real time communication:

- Timeliness
- Fast
- Low loss rate
- Low end to end delay
- Delivery of acknowledgement
- Peer to peer
- Cost effective

Some application of Real time communication (RTC)

- Instant messaging
- Internet telephony and voip
- Live video conferencing
- Teleconference
- Multimedia multicast
- Internet relay chat(IR)
- Amateur radio (Singh, & Passi, 2014)

Citrix GoToMeeting http://www.gotomeeting.com

Citrix GoToMeeting makes it simple and cost-effective to meet online with colleagues and customers. Best of all, meeting participants can share their webcams in high definition, so you can enjoy more personal interactions – without needing a complicated setup. You can meet from anywhere on any device – no training needed. Start a meeting and share your screen, video and audio with just a click. Show your screen, share your webcam and speak your mind.

GoToMeeting integrates everything – VoIP, telephone, HD video – for a clear and professional web conference. It's the next best thing to sitting at the same table.

It hosts over 30 million meetings a year. Each one is secured by end-to-end 128-bit AES encryption and backed by multiple datacenters around the globe

Skype http://www.skype.com/

Skype is an application that specializes in providing video chat and voice calls. Users can also exchange text and video messages, files and images, as well as create conference calls.

Skype is available on Microsoft Windows, Mac, or Linux, as well as Android, Blackberry, iOS and Windows smartphones and tablets. Skype is based on a freemium model. Much of the service is free, but users require Skype Credit or a subscription to call landline or mobile numbers.

Skype allows users to communicate by voice using a microphone, video by using a webcam, and instant messaging over the Internet. Skype-to-Skype calls to other users are free of charge, while calls to landline telephones and mobile phones (overtraditional telephone networks) are charged via a debit-based user account system called Skype Credit.

Skype boosts online group learning. Instructors can conduct video meetings with groups. They can also conveniently discuss progress or concerns with individual students through video meetings.

These online group collaboration tools have enabled smooth and fast communication, collaboration among distantly located students and their instructors. Thus students can gain more from the experience of their instructors. These tools along with instructional design and implementation strategies devised by instructors has led to enhancement of knowledge and sharpening of students' skills. This has allowed educational benefits to reach to more and more students globally beyond the confines of classrooms

BigMarker

This web conferencing service facilitates communication among learning group members through webinars. Webinars can be flexibly conducted from any location at present or in the future. Members can discuss over matters in real time. Members/contacts can be invited to participate in a webinar through automatic email invitations. Webinars can be tracked through calendar. Its live video chat feature enables synchronous communication among group members. Presentations, audio, chat and webcams can be effectively recorded for later viewing and sharing. So members missing the live events can view their recorded version and gain from them. Participation and attendance of group members in events can be effectively tracked through members page (Thomson, 2014).

Collaborative Concept Mapping

Concept mapping is a technique where users externalise their conceptual and propositional knowledge of a domain in a way that can be readily understood by others. It is widely used in education, so that a learner's understanding is made available to their peers and to teachers. There is considerable potential educational benefit in collaborative concept mapping (Martinez, Yacef & Kay, 2010)

Bubbl.us http://bubbl.us/

is a free online mind mapping tool that allows users to create colorful mind maps and even collaborate on a document. The interface is easy to use and includes several basic options. Maps can also be printed, emailed, downloaded as a graphic, or embedded into a website. This activity allows students to hone their skills for organizing and mapping ideas and collaborating with others.

Powered by Flash, Bubbl-us makes it easy for anyone to quickly start planning and sorting out their ideas through the use of linked text bubbles.

MindMeister https://www.mindmeister.com

MindMeister an online mind mapping and collaboration platform that runs in both web browser and mobile devices. It can be used for live or remote online collaboration. It's a great organizational tool for note taking, live collaborative story or concept mapping, and maps can easily be transformed into stand-alone or live presentations.

Slatebox https://www.slatebox.com

Slatebox is a slick tool for collaboratively creating mind maps and organizational charts. Slatebox offers a variety of good-looking templates and intuitive tools for designing and editing mind maps and charts. Creating a mind map is a simple matter of selecting a template and using the visual editor to place text and images in boxes. Those boxes can be resized and rearranged using the drag and drop editor. If you need more text boxes, simply add more.

List/Task Management

Task management is the process of managing a task through its life cycle. It involves planning, testing, tracking and reporting. Task management can help either individuals achieve goals, or groups of individuals collaborate and share knowledge for the accomplishment of collective goals

Remember the Milk https://www.rememberthemilk.com

Remember the Milk is available as a Web app, but not as a desktop app. You'll need an Internet connection to use it on the Web, i.e., there is no offline functionality. It formerly had offline features running through Google Gears, but with that program long gone and dead, offline functionality for Remember the Milk is, too.

On mobile devices, Remember the Milk is available on iOS, Android, and BlackBerry. It can also integrate with Gmail, Google Calendar, Outlook, Evernote, and Twitter.

In the app, you can create a task, assign a due date, attach notes (as typed text only, not uploaded files), and add tags. I like that you can also add a time estimate to any task, which isn't a feature I've seen in many task management apps for personal use, though it's more common among project management platforms.

Tasks can be grouped into Lists, sometimes called projects by other apps. For example, you might have a list for personal to-dos, family to-dos, and work tasks. Remember the Milk lets you share both individual tasks and lists with others. When you share a task or list, the collaborators have both read and write privileges. In the Web app, it's easy to spot a tab to the right of any task that's prominently labeled Share, though this feature is only in the Web app, not the mobile apps.

Thoughtboxes https://www.thoughtbox.es/

Thoughtboxes makes it easy to get organized, complete tasks, and collaborate.

- All your lists on one page
- Web-based, access anywhere
- Drag-and-drop controls
- Sharing & Collaboration

It breaks down bigger tasks into actionable steps, and so one see everything at a glance. It is available free of cost.

It manages a project, keep track of to-dos, or brainstorm a new idea. One can make lists public, or share them privately and collaborate with friends, family, or co-workers. Thoughtboxes is web-based, so there is nothing to download, and need to log on to access lists from anywhere.

Todoist: http://todoist.com/

Todoist is a cloud-based service, so all your tasks and notes from one app automatically sync to all the other places where you have Todoist installed.

To manage and conquer your to-dos, Todoist lets you create projects and add tasks to them. Projects can be color-coded to help you visually differentiate between them. Tasks can have subtasks, as well as due dates, reminders, flags noting the tasks' urgency, and more.

You can schedule a task to be recurring, and one neat feature is that Todoist lets you use natural language to set it up. For example, if you open the due date option on any task and type "every two weeks" or "every other Wednesday," Todoist will figure out what you want and schedule the task to recur accordingly. The natural-language input works on the Web, in the desktop apps, and in the mobile apps.

It has custom filter and good reminder options. Email notifications are included, as are a few notifications that are specific to mobile devices: push notifications, SMS notifications, and location-based reminders.

One can invite collaborators to access the tasks and projects, but need to sign up for a Todoist account

Presentation and Slide Sharing

Prezi https://prezi.com

It is a presentation tool that can be used as an alternative to traditional slide making programs such as PowerPoint It is a presentation resource, on a mission to reinvent how people share knowledge, tell stories, and inspire their audiences to act. The product employs a zooming user interface (ZUI), which allows users to zoom in and out of their presentation media, and allows users to display and navigate through information within a 2.5D or parallax 3D space on the Z-axis. Unlike slides, Prezi gives a limitless zoomable canvas and the ability to show relationships between the big picture and fine details. The added depth and context makes message more likely to resonate, motivate, and get remembered, whether it is bread-and-butter sales pitch, a classroom lecture, or a TED Talk to the world's foremost thinkers.

SlideShare http://www.slideshare.net/

SlideShare is a Web 2.0 based slide hosting service. Users can upload files privately or publicly in the following file formats: PowerPoint, PDF, Keynote or OpenDocument presentations. Slide decks can then be viewed on the site itself, on hand held devices or embedded on other sites. Although the website is primarily a slide hosting service, it also supports documents, PDFs, videos and webinars. SlideShare also provides users the ability to rate, comment on, and share the uploaded content.

The website gets an estimated 70 million unique visitors a month, and has about 38 million registered users. SlideShare was voted among the World's Top 10 tools for education & e-learning in 2010

SlideRocket www.sliderocket.com

Attractive and engaging presentations can be created with this web based presentation tool and can be accessed from anywhere. Members in a learning group can collaboratively work on one presentation document. Each document has got a specific URL which can be be submitted to an instructor for easy viewing. This application can be embedded within discussion forums of learning management system platforms or web pages. Themes, pictures, audio and others can be combined in a presentation. Presentations and slides can be shared and reused. Invites can be sent for sharing presentations. Data can be pulled in real time from Google Spreadsheets, Twitter live feeds and Yahoo. SlideRocket analytics helps to measure a presentation's effectiveness by giving information about who viewed it and what was their response (Thomson, 2014).

Collaborative Writing

Group writing assignments have traditionally been confined to a word processing program where one group member would attempt to record all of the group's ideas into one coherent product. However, having students write collaboratively online allows them to share ideas in real time, peer edit, contribute to the writing process from any computer with internet access and they can share their live edits with teachers/peers with a unique web address for their paper. Online, collaborative writing is an outstanding platform for a group writing assignment because it allows all group members to participate in the writing process. Whether students are working in a computer lab or from a computer in their home across globe, the writing process is extended beyond the classroom with online, collaborative writing. Along with group writing assignments, with online collaborative writing, students can share their work in real time and one can have the ability to read, critique, leave feedback and comments directly in their paper during the writing process.

Some of the key advantage of online, collaborative writing include:

- Live, real time feedback.
- Editable & accessible from any computer with an internet connection.
- Specific word processing programs are not necessary, allowing students without specific programs to access their work in multiple locations.
- Student work can be easily published and shared online.
- Revision history of writing and progress is easily accessible and viewable by both the student and teacher
- Accessibility: Online documents can be shared as viewable or editable (Collaborative Writing, n.d.)

Etherpad: http://etherpad.org/

Etherpad is an open-source writing platform, which has been forked for dozens of iterations, such as PiratePad. While not as robust as Google Docs, or as elegantly designed, the fact that Etherpad is open-source means that it can be customized to suit the needs of a specific organization or project.

Draft https://draftin.com/

A very simple tool for working with editors or getting feedback from peers on a piece of writing. Like Editorially, Draft has a clean interface that keeps the focus on the text itself. Includes robust version control, carefully tracking changes made to a document. Draft does not facilitate co-authoring, as much as it attempts to smooth out and enhance the relationship between writers and editors. And the best part: you can shut off your internal editor by using "Hemingway mode," which basically disables your "delete" button and allows only one way through to the completion of a piece of writing: forward.

Examples of Online Collaborative Writing in the Classroom

- The Great Immigration Debate is a Google Docs lesson designed to help students study a topic re-lated to patterns in immigration history, while gathering and analyzing data using primary source materials.
- Islamic Architecture is a Google Document resource created by students.(Collaborative Writing, n.d.)

Creative/Design Collaboration

Creative/Design Collaboration tools makes it easier and faster for designers to get feedback and approve artwork in a professional manner, and they come in all sort of forms, from free Android apps to Chrome extensions. These online tools allow designers to take part in collaborational work in real time. There are collaboration tools, from concept drafting and brainstorming to working on mock-ups and live project (He & Brandweiner, 2014)

ConceptShare http://www.conceptshare.com/

ConceptShare is a creative operations platform used by enterprises of all sizes to share, communicate and collaborate on creative work. ConceptShare helps eliminate the clutter, chaos and inefficiency of paper and email-based review and approval processes. Through the web-based system, users can initiate, track and report on reviews and approvals, and easily communicate clear and actionable feedback on project assets.

Red Pen: https://redpen.io/

Specifically created for designers, Red Pen lets you drag and drop your designs into a dashboard and invite specific colleagues (or even clients) to let you know their thoughts in real-time as you roll out your latest updates to a project. One of its best features is that it keeps track of the numerous versions made so you can always reclaim that earlier design if you changed you mind. Pricing starts at $20/month for 5 projects.

Stixy http://www.stixyexperience.com/work/stixy

Stixy helps users organize their world on flexible, shareable web-based bulletin boards called Stixyboards. Unlike most personal productivity or project management software, Stixy doesn't dictate how users should organize their information. Users can create tasks, appointments, files, photos, notes, and bookmarks on their Stixyboards, organized in whatever way makes sense to them. Then they can share Stixyboards with friends, family, and colleagues.

Some miscellaneous application that doesn't fit into above types useful in online collaborative learning are as follows

Twiddla http://www.twiddla.com/

Twiddla is a real-time web-based meeting tool that lets you "mark up websites, graphics, and photos, or start brainstorming on a blank canvas." This is a great alternative for those sometimes deadly boring online meetings in Adobe Connect and the like. No plug-ins. No sign-up. Just click, invite and go.

Synaptop https://www.synaptop.com

Synaptop lets students watch videos or lectures together, edit and annotate documents together, give presentations online, and store and share files. Plus, there are loads of apps, music, movies, games, and more.

Synaptop works similarly to Google Hangouts, but without the need for screensharing or downloads. Everything is done via the cloud. Classroom instructors and librarians can useSynaptop for Education for online presentations, webinars, or even online courses. And librarians can co-browse the web with students for remote reference help. This is a tool worth looking at. (Hovious, 2013).

Quick Screenshare screencast-o-matic.com

Screencast-o-matic is a screen capture software that can be used to create video from your screen (i.e. short lectures or course tours), and it doesn't require any downloading or installing

TogetherJS https://togetherjs.com/

TogetherJS is a service you add to an existing website to add real-time collaboration features. Using the tool two or more visitors on a website or web application can see each other's mouse/cursor position, clicks, track each other's browsing, edit forms together, watch videos together, and chat via audio and WebRTC

APPLICATIONS IN ACADEMIC LIBRARY: EVOLUTION OF ACADEMIC LIBRARIAN TO BLENDED LIBRARIAN

Academic librarians are equally important as teachers. The main aim of academic librarians is to help students and faculty to achieve academic success. But the situation has been changed where librarians can no longer in position themselves at service desks and wait for students and faculty to come to them but to proactively work to bring and provides best services to them. There is need to blend library and information services into the teaching and learning process by applying "design thinking," which involves, first and foremost, putting librarians in the place of the user in order to understand how the user can receive the "optimal learning experience." The blended librarian on today's campus seeks to meet the user on the user's terms.

The blended librarian is focused on course goals and learning objectives outside of the library and across the curriculum. Books, articles, and reserve readings (both electronic and print) may meet the needs of many faculty and students. But for instructors who seek to use new forms of multimedia—streaming video, podcasts, digitized images, 3-D animations, screencasts, etc.—to engage students and enhance the learning experience, the blended librarian is there to provide guidance and expertise, as well. Perhaps the learning objectives are more collaborative in nature and would benefit from social software in the form of wikis, blogs, video sharing, discussion forums, and other tools offered through a learning management system. The blended librarian is versed in both print and online tools and can help faculty meet course goals, regardless of the medium or technology.

Essentially, this is a new call to outreach. The blended librarian seeks to build new collaborations with students, faculty, staff, and other information and instructional technology professionals both in and outside of the classroom—in physical spaces and virtual environments—in order to match learners and teachers with the information tools they need (Sinclair, 2009).

There are a wide range of potential tools available, which has prompted some libraries to create guides to quality collaboration tools for their campus communities.

These guides, including the University of Queensland Library's Research Collaboration Tools and Harvard Law School Library's Collaboration Tools, suggest tools for a variety of applications.

Use of Collaborative Learning Tools in Providing Library Services

Library Instruction

In library instruction, online mind and concept mapping tools can be used to generate keywords for searches, to narrow down research topics, and for students in groups to give feedback on each other's topics. Fuchs (2014) describes a variety of possible uses of Padlet, including having students post terms they would use to search for their topic at the beginning of an instruction session. She points out that in addition to serving as a formative assessment, this activity engages students in peer learning and helps them to assess their own skills. The activity could be taken further by having students suggest additional terms for their peers and adding terms to the Padlet after the library instruction session.

Singapore Management University Library produces video tutorials and other online learning objects which promote self-paced learning in the use of library resources and aspects of the research process (Lee Yen, Yuyun, Sandra, Shameen, & Rajen, 2013)

Online Group Work and Collaboration

Document collaboration tools are widely used among librarians to work together on presentations and instructional materials, and they can be used in one-shot sessions as well. Bobish (2011) provides creative examples of how Web 2.0 tools can be used in library instruction. Many of his ideas, such as creating a research timeline or a collaborative bibliography or wiki, could easily be adapted for use with Google Docs or Padlet. Bilby (2014) reports on a collaborative student research project developed with the theology librarian at the University of San Diego that required students to create and share annotated bibliographies throughout the semester using Google Drive. Librarians can also use these tools to facilitate small group discussions about research strategies. For example, groups of students could be assigned websites to evaluate and could then post their evaluations, and review other group's evaluations.

Library Space, Facilities, and Services

In a flipped classroom and blended learning environment, students spend more time in collaborative learning spaces. The Singapore Management University Library provides such physical spaces especially for individual students and for collaborative study to the entire library community 24/7 open for them.

Bringing Real-Time Help to Patrons

Embedding live chat in specific web pages, to provide just-in-time services. The widget would also be mobile friendly and taps into the Singapore Management University library's extensive FAQ and Lib-Guides knowledge base, to provide a unified patron support service. Also uses a webinar platform to deliver research skills workshop (Lee Yen, Yuyun, Sandra, Shameen, & Rajen, 2013).

PROS AND CONS OF ONLINE COLLABORATIVE LEARNING

Technology comes with pros and cons so do online collaborative learning.

Pros are as follows:

- Many collaborations online tools are free to use & available 27/7 for everyone
- Students can actively exchange, debate and negotiate ideas within their groups increases students' interest in learning.
- Students may feel good to learn virtually in group instead of learning virtually alone which can be boring
- It can help to build a professional network
- Planning, working & submission of project can be done in time as everyone in group has to complete task in time
- Learning from other group members can be possible

Cons are as follows:

- Online collaborative tools are free tools but often disappear or become paid tools.
- Sometimes it is difficult to divide students into groups.
- Those tools offer anonymous participation, can lead to students starting conversations that are offensive or completely irrelevant to the topic
- Low or no participation of other group members
- Differences in skill/knowledge level of group members
- Delays in communication by some group members
- Some kind of hindrance due to not knowing group member personally

CONCLUSION

There is great potential for using online collaboration tools to engage students/researchers, provide an outlet for creative exploration of ideas. The variety of tools available means that there is a technology available for almost any classroom activity, right from idea generation and discussion at the beginning of a research project/assignment to its working, sharing to peer-review of research papers. For the effective collaborative learning, Muuro, Wagacha, Kihoro & Oboko (2014) has recommended that institutions should ensure their instructors do engage students in collaborative activities in their online courses and instructor's role is more emphasized during collaborative learning. Also find ways of motivating the students as well as teachers in order to increase their level of participation in collaborative learning. According to

Collaboration can be effectively used to improve the quality and quantity of education in online learning environments. There are numerous tools and methods that can be used to facilitate and stimulate collaboration in online education. The author has made an effort to list and define the most important of those tools and methods. These tools have evolved very recently and will continue to evolve as the time progresses. The online collaborative learning methodology is likely to evolve and make significant benefits to education, and probably to post educational business collaboration as well (Lark, n. d.)

REFERENCES

Advanced Online Collaboration. (n. d.). Where Creative Minds Meld. Retrieved from http://www.yorku.ca/dzwick/what_is_octopz.htm

Bell, S., & Shank, J. (2007). *Academic Librarianship by Design: A Blended Librarian's Guide to the Tools and Techniques*. Chicago: ALA.

Bilby, M. (2014, June 17-22). Collaborative Student Research with Google Drive: Advantages and Challenges. *Presentation at the annual conference of the American Theological Library Association*, New Orleans, LA. Retrieved from http://lanyrd.com/sctzbt

Bobish, G. (2011). Participation and Pedagogy: Connecting the Social Web to ACRL Learning Outcomes. *Journal of Academic Librarianship, 37*(1), 54–63. doi:10.1016/j.acalib.2010.10.007

Center for Teaching Excellence. Carnegie Mellon University. (2009). Collaboration tools. Teaching with Technology White Paper. Carnegie Mellon university. Retrieved from https://www.cmu.edu/teaching/technology/whitepapers/CollaborationTools_Jan09.pdf

Chandra, R. (2015). Collaborative Learning for Educational Achievement. *IOSR Journal of Research & Method in Education, 5*(3), 04-07. Retrieved from http://www.iosrjournals.org/iosr-jrme/papers/Vol-5%20Issue-3/Version 1/B05310407.pdf

Collaborative writing (n. d.). EdTechTeacher. Retrieved from http://tewt.org/collaborative-writing/

Cooper, B. B. (2015, November 18). The Science of Collaboration: How to Optimize Working Together. Retrieved from http://thenextweb.com/entrepreneur/2014/07/15/science-collaboration-optimize-working-together/

eLearning 101 – concepts, trends, applications. (2014). Epignosis. Retrieved from http://www.talentlms.com/elearning/

Fuchs, B. (2014). The Writing is on the Wall: Using Padlet for Whole-Class Engagement. LOEX Quarterly, 40(4), 7-9. Retrieved from http://uknowledge.uky.edu /libraries_facpub/240

He, J., & Brandweiner, N. (2014). The 20 best tools for online collaboration. *CreativeBloq.com*. Retrieved from http://www.creativebloq.com/design/online-collaboration-tools-912855

Hovious, A. (2013). 5 Free Real-Time Collaboration Tools. *Designer Librarian*. Retrieved from https://designerlibrarian.wordpress.com/2013/09/15/5-free-real-time-collaboration-tools/

Krongard, S., & McCormick, J. (2013). Real Time Visual Analytics to Evaluate Online Collaboration. *Presentation at the annual conference of NERCOMP*, Providence, RI. Retrieved from http://www.educause.edu/nercomp-conference/2013/2013/real-time-visual-analytics-evaluate-online-collaboration

Lark, J. (n. d.). Collaboration Tools in Online Learning Environments. *ALN Magazine*. Retrieved from www.nspnvt.org/jim/aln-colab.pdf

Mallon, M., & Bernsten, S. (2015). Collaborative Learning Technologies. Tips and Trends. ACRL Instruction Section, Instructional Technologies Committee, Winter. Retrieved from http://bit.ly/tipsandtrendswi15

Martinez, R., Yacef, K., & Kay, J. (2010). Collaborative concept mapping at the tabletop. Technical Report 657. University of Sydney. Retrieved from http://sydney.edu.au/engineering/it/research/tr/tr657.pdf

McCabe, L. (2010). What's a Collaboration Suite & Why Should You Care? *Small Business Computing*. Retrieved from http://www.smallbusinesscomputing.com/biztools/article.php/3890601/Whats-a-Collaboration-Suite--Why-Should-You-Care.htm

Murugan, S. (2013). User Education: Academic Libraries. *International Journal of Information Technology and Library Science Research*, 1(1), 1-6. Retrieved from http://acascipub.com/Journals.php

Muuro, M., Wagacha, W., Kihoro, R., & Oboko, J. (2014). Students' Perceived Challenges in an Online Collaborative Learning Environment: A Case of Higher Learning Institutions in Nairobi, Kenya. *The International Review of Research in Open and Distributed Learning*, 15(6). Retrieved from http://www.irrodl.org/index.php/irrodl/article/view/1768/3124

Nine Tools for Collaboratively Creating Mind Maps. (2010). Retrieved from http://www.freetech4teachers.com/2010/03/nine-tools-for-collaboratively-creating.html#.VubuNPl97IV

Sinclair, B. (2009). The blended librarian in the learning commons: New skills for the blended library. *College & Research Libraries News*, 70(9), 504–516. http://crln.acrl.org/content/70/9/504.full Retrieved October 27, 2015

Singh, S. P., & Passi, A. (2014). Real Time Communication. *International Journal of Recent Development in Engineering and Technology*, 2(3). Retrieved from http://www.ijrdet.com/files/Volume2Issue3/IJRDET_0314_23.pdf

Skype. (n. d.). *Wikipedia*. Retrieved from https://en.wikipedia.org/wiki/Skype

Slideshare. (n. d.). *Wikipedia*. Retrieved from https://en.wikipedia.org/wiki/SlideShare

Smith, B. L., & MacGregor, J. T. (1992). What is collaborative learning? In A. S. Goodsell, M. R. Maher, & V. Tinto (Eds.), *Collaborative Learning: A Sourcebook for Higher Education*. National Center on Postsecondary Teaching, Learning, & Assessment. Syracuse University.

Task management. (n. d.). Retrieved from Wikipedia: https://en.wikipedia.org/wiki/Task_management

Thomson, S. (2014). 6 Online Collaboration Tools and Strategies for Boosting Learning. Retrieved from http://elearningindustry.com/6-online-collaboration-tools-and-strategies-boosting-learning

Todoist. (2015). Retrieved from http://www.pcmag.com/article2/0,2817,2408574,00.asp

Tu, C.-H. (2004). *Online Collaborative Learning Communities: Twenty-One Designs to Building an Online Collaborative Learning Community* (p. 12). Libraries Unlimited Inc.

University of Waterloo. (n. d.). Collaborative online learning: fostering effective discussions. Retrieved from https://uwaterloo.ca/centre-for-teaching-excellence/teaching-resources/teaching-tips/alternatives-lecturing/discussions/collaborative-online-learning

Vygotsky, L. S. (1978). *Mind in society: The development of higher psychological processes*. Cambridge, UK: Harvard University Press.

Wiki. (n. d.). Retrieved from Wikipedia: http://wiki.org/wiki.cgi?WhatIsWiki

Yen, L. Yuyun, Sandra, Shameen, and Rajen. (2013). SMU Libraries' Role in Supporting SMU's Blended Learning Initiatives. Retrieved from http://library.smu.edu.sg/sites/default/files/library/pdf/Librarys_Role_in_Blended_Learning.pdf

ADDITIONAL READING

Academic Training Group, University of Kentucky. (2015). Adobe Connect Best Practices. Retrieved from http://www.uky.edu /acadtrain/connect/bestpractices

Amandolare, S. (2011). Using Collaborative Learning in Classrooms and Libraries. Retrieved from http://www.findingdulcinea.com/news/education/2010/march/Collaborative-Learning-Gaining-Traction-in-Classrooms-and-Libraries.html

An, H., Kim, S., & Kim, B. (2008). Teacher perspectives on online collaborative learning: Factors perceived as facilitating and impeding successful online group work. *Contemporary Issues in Technology & Teacher Education*, 8(1). Retrieved from http://www.citejournal.org/vol8/iss4/general/article1.cfm

Barkely, E. F., Cross, K. P., & Howell Major, C. (2005). *Collaborative learning techniques: A handbook for college faculty*. San Francisco: Jossey-Bass.

Black, A. (2005). The use of asynchronous discussion: Creating a text of talk. Contemporary *Issues in Technology and Teacher Education, 5*(1), 5-24. Retrieved from www.citejournal.org/articles/v5i1languagearts1.pdf

Brindley, J., Blaschke, L. M., & Walti, C. (2009). Creating effective collaborative learning groups in an online environment. *International Review of Research in Open and Distance Learning, 10*(3). Retrieved from http://www.irrodl.org/index.php/irrodl/article/view/675/1271

Bruffee, K. A. (1998). *Collaborative learning: Higher education, interdependence, and the authority of knowledge*. Baltimore: The Johns Hopkins University Press.

Byrne, R. (2014, November 19). Seven Free Online Whiteboard Tools for Teachers and Students. Free Technology for Teachers (Web log post), Retrieved from .[REMOVED HYPERLINK FIELD]http://www.freetech4teachers.com/2014/01/seven -free-online-whiteboard-tools-for.html

Capdeferro, N., & Romero, M. (2012). Are online learners frustrated with collaborative learning experiences? *International Review of Research in Open and Distance Learning, 13*(2), 26–44. Retrieved from http://www.irrodl.org/index.php/irrodl/article/view/1127

Cavalier, R. (2008). Campus conversations: Modeling a diverse democracy through deliberative polling. *Diversity and Democracy, 11*(1), 16–17.

Cavalier, R., & Bridges, M. (2007). Polling for an Educated Citizenry. *The Chronicle of Higher Education, 53*(20).

Center for Research on Learning and Teaching, University of Michigan. (2015). Teaching with Online Collaboration Tools: U-M Faculty Examples. Retrieved from [REMOVED HYPERLINK FIELD]http://www.crlt.umich.edu/oct

Chiong, R., & Jovanovic, J. (2012). Collaborative Learning in Online Study Groups: An Evolutionary Game Theory Perspective, Journal of Information Technology Education: Research, *11*, Retrieved from http://jite.informingscience.org/documents/Vol11/JITEv11p081-101Chiong1104.pdf

Curtis, D. D., & Lawson, M. J. (2001). Exploring collaborative online learning. *Journal of Asynchronous Learning Networks*, *5*(1), 21–34. Retrieved from http://wikieducator.org/images/6/60/ALN_Collaborative_Learning.pdf

Davis, B. G. (2009). *Tools for teaching* (2nd ed., pp. 190–221). San Francisco: Jossey-Bass.

Desanctis, G., & Gallupe, B. R. (1987). A foundation for the study of group decision support systems. *Management Science,* 33(5), 589-609. Retrieved from http://www.jstor.org/stable/2632288

Dooly, M. (Ed.), (2008). Telecollaborative Language Learning. A guidebook to moderating intercultural collaboration online. Bern: Peter Lang.

EDUCAUSE Learning Initiative. (2014). Cloud Storage and Collaboration. 7 Things You Should Know About…. EDUCAUSE. Retrieved from https://net.educause.edu/ir/library/pdf /ELI7108.pdf

Felder, R. M., Felder, G. N., & Dietz, E. J. (1998). A longitudinal study of engineering student performance and retention. V. Comparisons with traditionally-taught students. *The Journal of Engineering Education*, *87*(4), 469–480. doi:10.1002/j.2168-9830.1998.tb00381.x

Floyd, J. (2015, January 18). How to Use Google+ Hangouts in Higher Education: Distance Learning with Social Media. Retrieved from www.jeremyfloyd.com/2013/05 /how-to-use-google-hangouts-in-higher-education-distance-learning -with-social-media/

Forsyth, D. R. (2009). *Group dynamics*. Belmont, CA: Wadsworth Cengage Learning. doi:10.4135/9781412958479.n248

Harasim, L., Hiltz, S. R., Teles, L., & Turoff, M. (1998). *Learning networks: A field guide to teaching and learning online*. Cambridge: The MIT Press.

Hassanien, A. (2007). A qualitative student evaluation of group learning in higher education. *Higher Education in Europe,* *32*(2-3), 135-150. Retrieved from www.tandfonline.com/doi/pdf/10.1080/03797720701840633

Hershock, C., & LaVaque-Manty, M. (2012). Teaching in the Cloud: Leveraging Online Collaboration Tools to Enhance Student Engagement. CRLT Occasional Papers, No. 31. Ann Arbor, MI: Center for Research on Learning and Teaching, University of Michigan. Retrieved from http://www.crlt.umich.edu/sites /default/files/resource_files/CRLT_no31.pdf

Jahng, N., Chan, E. K. H., & Nielsen, W. S. (2010). Collaborative learning in an online course: A comparison of communication patterns in small and whole group activities. *Journal of Distance Education*, *24*(2), 39–58.

Jaques, D., & Salmon, G. (2007). Learning in groups: A handbook for facc-to-facc and online environments (4th ed.). UK, USA, and Canada: Routledge.

Kashorda, M., & Waema, T. (2014). E-readiness survey of Kenyan universities (2013) report. Kenya Education Network. Retrieved from ereadiness.kenet.or.ke:8080/ereadiness/2013/E-readiness%20 2013%20Survey%20of%20Kenyan%20Universities_FINAL.pdf

Kim, K. J., Liu, S., & Bonk, C. J. (2005). Online MBA students' perceptions of online learning: Benefits, challenges, and suggestions. *The Internet and Higher Education, 8*(4), 335–344. doi:10.1016/j. iheduc.2005.09.005

Klosowski, T. (2014, February 20). The Best Add-Ons for Google Drive. Lifehacker (Web blog post). Retrieved from http://lifehacker.com/the-best-add-ons-for -google-drive-1541643206.

Liu, S., Joy, M., & Griffiths, N. (2010, July 5-7). Students' perceptions of the factors leading to unsuccessful group collaboration. *Proceedings of the 2010 IEEE 10th International Conference on Advanced Learning Technologies (ICALT)*, Sousse, Tunisia (pp. 565-569).

Lomas, C., Burke, M., & Page, C. L. (2008). Collaboration Tools. ELI Paper 2. EDUCAUSE Learning Initiative. Retrieved from http://net.educause.edu/ir/library/pdf /eli3020.pdf

Mattar, J. A. (2010). Constructivism and connectivism in education technology: Active, situated, authentic, experiential, and anchored learning. *Technology (Elmsford, N.Y.), 2010*, 1–16.

Michaelsen, L. K., Knight, A. B., & Fink, L. D. (Eds.). (2004). *Team-based learning: A transformative use of small groups in college teaching*. Sterling, VA: Stylus.

Moller, L. (1998). Designing communities of learners for asynchronous distance education. *Educational Technology Research and Development, 46*(4), 115–122. doi:10.1007/BF02299678

North, A. C., Linley, P. A., & Hargreaves, D. J. (2000). Social loafing in a co-operative classroom task. *Educational Psychology, 20*(4), 389–392. Retrieved from http://www.pgce.soton.ac.uk/IT/Research/ Papers/Northetal2000SocialLoafing.pdf doi:10.1080/01443410020016635

Nyerere, J. A., Gravenir, F. Q., & Mse, G. S. (2012). Delivery of open, distance, and e-learning in Kenya. *International Review of Research in Open and Distance Learning, 13*(3), 185–205.

Palloff, R. M., & Pratt, K. (2005). *Collaborating online: Learning together in community. San Francisco.* CA: Jossey-Bass.

Palloff, R. M., & Pratt, K. (2007). *Building online learning communities: Effective strategies for the virtual classroom*. John Wiley & Sons.

Project-based learning. (2008, December 12). Wikipedia Retrieved from http://en.wikipedia.org/wiki/ Project-based_learning

Roberts, T. S., & McInnerney, J. M. (2007). Seven problems of online group learning (and their solutions). *Journal of Educational Technology & Society, 10*(4), 257–268.

Rossman, M.H. (1999, November). Successful Online Teaching Using An Asynchronous Learner Discussion Forum. *JALN, 3*(2).

Salmon, G. (2004). *E-moderating: the key to teaching and learning online* (2nd ed.). London: Routledge.

Siemens, G. (2005). Connectivism: A learning theory for the digital age. *International Journal of Instructional Technology and Distance Learning*, 2(1), 3–10.

Singh, H. K. (2005). Learner satisfaction in a collaborative online learning environment. Retrieved from http://asiapacific-odl.oum.edu.my/C33/F239.pdf

Song, L., Singleton, E. S., Hill, J. R., & Koh, M. H. (2004). Improving online learning: Student perceptions of useful and challenging characteristics. *The Internet and Higher Education*, 7(1), 59–70. doi:10.1016/j.iheduc.2003.11.003

Sours, T. J., Newbrough, J. R., Shuck, L., & Varma-Nelson, P. (2013). Supporting Student Collaboration in Cyberspace: A cPLTL Study of Web Conferencing Platforms. EDUCAUSE Review Online, Retrieved from http://www.educause.edu/ero/article/supporting-student-collaboration-cyberspace-cpltl-study-web-conferencing-platforms

Zorko, V. (2009). Factors affecting the way students collaborate in a wiki for English language learning. *Australasian Journal of Educational Technology*, 25(5), 645–665. doi:10.14742/ajet.1113

KEY TERMS AND DEFINITIONS

Academic Library: An academic library is a library which serves an institution of higher learning, such as a college or a university — libraries in secondary and primary schools are called school libraries. These libraries serve two complementary purposes: to support the school's curriculum, and to support the research of the university faculty and students.

Asynchronous Learning Model: In asynchronous mode of elearning generally teacher can post study material, an have announcements and calendar online, assignment posting, submission, and evaluation with feedback etc.

Blended Librarian: The Blended Librarian is the academic professional who offers the best combination of skills and services to help faculty apply technology for enhanced teaching and learning.

Collaborate: To collaborate is "to work jointly with others or together especially in an intellectual endeavor."

Collaboration Suites: An online collaboration suite provides an integrated set of web tools that span a range of collaboration needs.

Collaborative Project Management: Collaborative project management is based on the principle of actively involving all project members in the planning and control process and of networking them using information, communication, and collaboration modules.

Concept Mapping: It is a technique where users externalise their conceptual and propositional knowledge of a domain in a way that can be readily understood by others.

E-Learning: It is commonly referred to the intentional use of networked information and communications technology in teaching and learning.

Learning Management System: An LMS is an integrated software environment supporting all these functionalities along with some mechanism for student enrolment into courses, general user management (including administrator, teacher, and student) and some important system functions like backup and restore.

Online Learning/Virtual Learning/Distributed Learning/Web Based Learning: It refer to educational processes that utilize information and communications technology to mediate asynchronous as well as synchronous mode of learning and teaching activities.

Real-Time Communications: The real time communication is the communication in which sender and receiver exchange their information and data over a channel without any delay.

SlideShare: It is a Web 2.0 based slide hosting service.

Synchronous Learning Model: In the synchronous learning model (Online model), the students can attend 'live' lectures at the scheduled hour from wherever they are irrespective of their location forming a virtual classroom.

Task Management: Task management is the process of managing a task through its life cycle.

Wiki: Wiki is a piece of server software that allows users to freely create and edit web page content using any web browser.

Chapter 6
Decision–Making with Big Data Using Open Source Business Intelligence Systems

Jorge Bernardino
Polytechnic of Coimbra - ISEC, Portugal

Pedro Caldeira Neves
Polytechnic of Coimbra - ISEC, Portugal

ABSTRACT

The importance of supporting decision making for improving business performance is a crucial, yet challenging task in enterprise management. The amount of data in our world has been exploding and Big Data represents a fundamental shift in business decision-making. Analyzing such so-called Big Data is becoming a keystone of competition and the success of organizations depends on fast and well-founded decisions taken by relevant people in their specific area of responsibility. Business Intelligence (BI) is a collection of decision support technologies for enterprises aimed at enabling knowledge workers such as executives, managers, and analysts to make better and faster decisions. We review the concept of BI as an open innovation strategy and address the importance of BI in revolutionizing knowledge towards economics and business sustainability. Using Big Data with Open Source Business Intelligence Systems will generate the biggest opportunities to increase competitiveness and differentiation in organizations. In this chapter, we describe and analyze four popular open source BI systems - Jaspersoft, Jedox, Pentaho and Actuate/BIRT.

INTRODUCTION

New advances of Information and Communication Technologies (ICT) continue to rapidly transform how business is done and change the role of information systems in business and our daily life. The amount of data in our world has been exploding. Enterprises are flooded with ever-growing data of all types, easily amassing terabytes, even petabytes, of data. Analyzing such so-called Big Data is becoming a keystone of competition, new waves of productivity growth, and innovation. With the emergence

DOI: 10.4018/978-1-5225-0556-3.ch006

of new data collection technologies and analytical tools, Big Data offer an unprecedented opportunity to discover insights in new and emerging types of data, to make businesses more agile, and to answer questions that were previously considered beyond reach. Increasing competition, demand for profits, contracting economy, and savvy customers all require companies and organizations to make the best possible decisions. With the fast advancement of both business techniques and technologies in recent years, knowledge has become an important and strategic asset that determines the success or failure of an organization (Wit & Meyer, 2003). Studies show that a competitive advantage in the business environment depends on the accessibility to adequate and reliable information in shortest time possible and the high selectivity in the creation and use of information. An effective instrument to create, aggregate and share knowledge in an organization has therefore become a key target of management.

The need to implement decision support systems in organizations is an unavoidable reality (Arsham, 2015). Currently, the majority of organizations have Information Technology (IT) systems, designed to record and store massive amounts of data resulting from the operational activity (Kimberling, 2006). This data set has to be transformed in information and all that information will lead to knowledge useful for the organizations.

In addition, in a competitive environment, traditional decision-making approaches no longer meet the requirements of organizations for decision-making; organizations must make good use of electronic information system tools such as Business Intelligence (BI) systems to quickly acquire desirable information from huge volume of data to reduce the time and increase the efficiency of decision-making procedure. Different researchers have different definitions for business intelligence system, for example (Turban et al., 2008) defined the business intelligence system as "an umbrella term that encompasses tools, architectures, databases, data warehouses, performance management, methodologies, and so forth, all of which are integrated into a unified software suite".

Business Intelligence is one of the few forms of sustainable competitive advantage left (Burstein & Holsapple, 2008). For example, any two well-funded competitors in a market have near real access to capital, technology, market research, customer data, and distribution. People and the quality of the decisions that they make are the primary competitive differentiators in the Information Age (Lin et al., 2009). The implementation of BI components is the key to sustaining long-term competitive advantage.

Several studies have shown how IT investments impact enterprise performance (Popovič et al., 2010). In order to capture real benefits of BI investments, as an IT investment, these studies revealed that organizations have to make a great effort (Chamoni & Gluchowski, 2004). In the earlier steps of BI system implementation, the selection of the most convenient system is very important. Organizations implementing a BI solution need also to consider several factors such as: the scope of functionalities that each software provide; how each system fit within the organization's data model; and how expensive is the total cost of ownership (total cost of acquiring and implementing a BI solution).

In this work we describe the top key systems to implement open source BI in organizations: Jaspersoft, Jedox, Pentaho and Actuate/BIRT. In particular organizations which would like to enter into the new market and operate on a global scale. Thus, open source BI systems can trigger immense possibilities of accelerating knowledge acquisition, intensifying entrepreneurship development and improving business skills, therefore, leading to business sustainability. In this context open source BI can be seen as another form of open innovation, which can be used by business communities, especially among SMEs.

The rest of the chapter is organized as follows. First, we describe the problem of growing data volumes that organizations have to deal with. Second, we introduce the concept of BI and address the importance of BI in revolutionizing knowledge to enhance organization's response in making better and more efficient business decisions, also increasing innovation. Some BI resources are also introduced and we discuss the advantages of using the open source model. After, we present the top Business Intelligence software vendors to implement open BI in organizations. Some future research directions are also pointed out. Finally, the concluding remarks are presented in conclusions section.

SMARTER DECISIONS WITH BIG DATA

Business Intelligence (BI) provides a set of methodologies, processes, architectures, and technologies, which transform raw data into valuable information to enable more effective strategic, tactical, and operational insights and decision-making (Evelson & Norman, 2008). As we know, BI applications use data gathered from a data warehouse or a data mart. However, the situation begins to change when meeting the growing trend of Big Data. In recent years, with the widespread use of wiki and the popularity of micro blog and other Web 2.0 applications for business, there has been an explosive increase in the amount of data in different types of enterprises, which even exceeds the rate of Moore's Law. For example, Wal-Mart, one of the famous worldwide supermarkets, collects more than 2.5 petabytes (PB) of data every hour from its customer transactions, and it also has related 40 billion photos held by Facebook alone in order to facilitate the marketing. According to the International Data Corporation's (IDC) estimate, modern enterprises will need to manage, on average, 50 times more information by the year 2020 (Cisco, 2011), which is actually a great challenge for medium-sized and small enterprises. Thus, it can be seen that Big Data does move into enterprises.

A 2010 article suggests that data volume will continue to expand at a healthy rate, noting that "the size of the largest data warehouse triples approximately every two years" (Adrian, 2010). The data explosion is globally recognized as a key Information Technology (IT) concern. According to a Gartner study published in October of 2010, "47% of the respondents to a survey, ranked data growth in their top three challenges" (Mearian, 2010). As an example of rampant data growth, retailer Walmart executes more than 1 million customer transactions every hour, feeding databases estimated at more than 2.5 petabytes. Persistence is not a requirement either – a 2010 report suggests that by 2013, the amount of traffic flowing over the Internet annually will reach 667 exabytes (Cukier, 2010).

Structured information in databases is just the tip of the iceberg; some important milestones document the explosive growth of unstructured data as well: by the end of 2009, the amount of digital information was estimated to have grown to almost 800,000 petabytes (or 800,000,000,000 gigabytes), with an expectation that by the end of 2010 that amount would total approximately 1.2 million petabytes! At this rate, the amount of digital data could grow to 35 zettabytes (1 zettabyte = 1 trillion gigabytes) by 2020 (Gantz & Reinsel, 2010).

Complex business processes are increasingly expecting to be executed through a variety of interconnected systems. Integrated sensors and probes not only enable continuous measurement of operational performance, the interconnectedness of many systems allows rapid communication and persistence of those measures. Every day, it is estimated that 15 petabytes of new information is being generated, 80% of which is unstructured (Bates et al., 2009).

We can conclude from these few examples of rapid expansion of the amount of digital information that exciting new vistas can be opened up as never before through combined analysis of structured and unstructured data. New and improved means of data analysis allow organizations to identify new business trends, innovate, assess the spread of disease, or even combat crime, among many other opportunities.

It appears that we are reaching the point where information is becoming the most significant focus of the business, where "statisticians mine the information output of the business for new ideas" (Bates et al., 2009). And these new ideas are not just lurking in structured databases. Rather the analysis must encompass unstructured data artifacts as well.

But as the volume of data grows, so does the complexity of finding those critical pieces of information necessary to make those business processes run at their optimized level. The issue is no longer the need to capture, store, and manage that data. Rather, the challenge is distilling out and delivering the relevant pieces of knowledge to the right people at the right to time to enhance the millions of opportunities for decision-making that occur on a daily basis.

Undoubtedly, big data brings big opportunities. The integration and analysis of big data can help enterprises glean deeper insights into the internal and external forces that affect their performance, anticipate development trends, and respond more quickly to changes. Until now, more and more companies have recognized that there is a lot of treasure contained in these huge datasets, indicating that big data adoption goes main stream in enterprises. According to IDC's latest survey in January, 2014, there are 70% of enterprises have either deployed or are planning to deploy big data related projects and programs, and the expense of every enterprise is expected to reach, on average, 8 million US dollars in the coming year.

Big data poses big challenges, including scalability and storage bottleneck, noise accumulation, spurious correlation, and error measurement. These challenges and opportunities associated with big data necessitate rethinking many aspects of data management software.

In essence, this can be summarized as the desire to integrate business intelligence in a pervasive manner into both the strategic and the operational processes across all functions and levels of the organization. And whether this means notifying senior management of emerging revenue opportunities, providing real-time insight into corporate performance indicators, or hourly realignment of field repair team schedules to best address customer service outages. The ability to accumulate, transform, and analyze information to provide rapid, trustworthy analyses to the right people at the right time can enhance growth opportunities and competitiveness, leading to a sustained open business model of value chain. All this can be done selecting the most appropriate BI system to the organization.

BUSINESS INTELLIGENCE

Some articles mention the term Business Intelligence (BI) was first introduced in 1989 by Howard Dresner, who defined BI as "a set of concepts and appropriate methods to support decision making, using the data provided by support systems to business process" (Power, 2007). However, some authors' claim Dresner re-appropriated the term to rebadged what was then called DSS-Decision Support Systems. They say H.P. Luhn actually invented the term, not in 1989, but in 1958 in an IBM Journal article that pretty accurately predicts BI systems today. The original definition of Business Intelligence from (Luhn, 1958) is: "business is a collection of activities carried on for whatever purpose, be it science, technology, commerce, industry, law, government, defense, et cetera. The communication facility serving the conduct of a business (in the broad sense) may be referred to as an intelligence system". The notion of intelligence is also defined here, in a more general sense, as "the ability to apprehend the interrelationships of presented facts in such a way as to guide action towards a desired goal".

Perhaps the first probable reference to BI was made in Sun Tzu's "Art of War" (Tzu, 1963), who was born five centuries BC, where he claimed that to succeed in war, full knowledge on one's strengths and weaknesses as well as the strengths and weaknesses of the enemy must be known. Applying this to the modern business world, BI becomes the art of wading and sieving through tons of data, and presenting the overloaded data as information that provides significant business value in improving the effectiveness of managerial decision-making (Turban et al., 2004). As such, BI is carried out not just for gaining sustainable competitive advantages, but it also has a valuable core competence in most instances. A variety of businesses have used BI for activities such as customer support and service, customer profiling, market research and segmentation, product profitability, inventory and distribution analysis, etc.

The concept of "business intelligence" and "analytics" include tools and techniques supporting a collection of user communities across an organization, as a result of collecting and organizing numerous (and diverse) data sets to support both management and decision making at operational, tactical, and strategic levels. Through data collection, aggregation, analysis, and presentation, business intelligence can be delivered to best serve a wide range of target users. Organizations that have matured their data warehousing programs allow those users to extract actionable knowledge from the corporate information asset and rapidly realize business value.

But while traditional data warehouse infrastructures support business analyst querying and canned reporting or senior management dashboards, a comprehensive program for information insight and intelligence can enhance decision-making process for all types of staff members in numerous strategic, tactical, and operational roles. Even better, integrating the relevant information within the immediate operational context becomes the differentiating factor. Offline customer analysis providing general sales strategies is one thing, but real-time business intelligence can provide specific alternatives to the sales person talking to a specific customer based on that customer's interaction history in ways that best serve the customer while simultaneously optimizing corporate profitability as well as the salesperson's commission. Maximizing overall benefit to all of the parties involved ultimately improves sales, increases customer and employee satisfaction, and improves response rate while reducing the cost of goods sold – a true win-win for everyone.

The wide ranges of analytical capabilities all help suggest answers to a series of increasingly valuable questions (Loshin, 2011):

- **What?:** Predefined reports will provide the answer to the operational managers, detailing what has happened within the organization and various ways of slicing and dicing the results of those queries to understand basic characteristics of business activity (e.g., counts, sums, frequencies, locations, etc.). Traditional BI reporting provides 20/20 hindsight – it tells what has happened, it may provide aggregate data about what has happened, and it may even direct individuals with specific actions in reaction to what has happened.
- **Why?:** More comprehensive *ad hoc* querying coupled with review of measurements and metrics within a time series enables more focused review. Drilling down through reported dimensions lets the business client get answers to more pointed questions, such as the sources of any reported issues, or comparing specific performance across relevant dimensions.
- **What If?:** More advanced statistical analysis, data mining models, and forecasting models allow business analysts to consider how different actions and decisions might have impacted the results, enabling new ideas for improving the business.
- **What Next?:** By evaluating the different options within forecasting, planning, and predictive models, senior strategists can weigh the possibilities and make strategic decisions.
- **How?:** By considering approaches to organizational performance optimization, the senior managers can adapt business strategies that change the way the organization does business.

Information analysis makes it possible to answer these questions. Improved decision-making processes depend on supporting business intelligence and analytic capabilities that increase in complexity and value across a broad spectrum for delivering actionable knowledge (as shown in Figure 1). As the analytical functionality increases in sophistication, the business client can gain more insight into the mechanics of optimization. Statistical analysis will help in isolating the root causes of any reported issues as well as provide some forecasting capabilities should existing patterns and trends continue without adjustment. Predictive models that capture past patterns help in projecting "what-if" scenarios that guide tactics and strategy towards organizational high performance.

Intelligent analytics and business intelligence are maturing into tools that can help optimize the business. That is true whether those tools are used to help (Loshin, 2011):

- C-level executives (CEO, CIO, CFO, …) review options to meet strategic objectives;
- Senior managers seeking to streamline their lines of business, or
- Operational decision-making in ways never thought possible.

These analytics incorporate data warehousing, data mining, multidimensional analysis, streams, and mash-ups to provide a penetrating vision that can enable immediate reactions to emerging opportunities while simultaneously allowing one to evaluate the environment over time to discover ways to improve and expand the business.

Business Intelligence and Decision Making

A BI system allows an organization to gather, store, access and analyze corporate data to aid in decision-making. Generally, these systems will illustrate business intelligence in the areas of customer profiling, customer support, market research, market segmentation, product profitability, statistical analysis, and inventory and distribution analysis to name a few.

Most companies collect a large amount of data from their business operations. To keep track of that information, a business would need to use a wide range of software programs, such as Excel, Access and different database applications for various departments throughout their organization. Using multiple software programs makes it difficult to retrieve information in a timely manner and to perform analysis of the data.

Figure 1. A range of techniques benefits a variety of consumers for analytics

Benefits of Business Intelligence

Initially, BI reduces IT infrastructure costs by eliminating redundant data extraction processes and duplicate data housed in independent data marts across the enterprise. For example, 3M justified its multimillion-dollar data warehouse platform based on the savings from data mart consolidation (Watson et al. 2004).

BI also saves time for data suppliers and users because of more efficient data delivery. End users ask questions like "What has happened?" as they analyze the significance of historical data. This kind of analysis generates tangible benefits like headcount reduction that are easy to measure; however, these benefits typically have local impact.

Over time, organizations evolve to questions like "Why has this happened?" and even "What will happen?" As business users mature to performing analysis and prediction, the level of benefits become more global in scope and difficult to quantify. For example, the most mature uses of BI might facilitate a strategic decision to enter a new market, change a company's orientation from product-centric to customer-centric, or help launch a new product line.

The spectrum of BI benefits can be summarized in the following (Ponniah, 2010):

- Cost savings from data mart consolidation
- Time savings for data suppliers
- Time savings for users
- More and better information
- Better decisions
- Improvement of business processes
- Support for the accomplishment of strategic business objectives.

However, success with BI isn't automatic and organizations are more likely to be successful when certain facilitating conditions exist. According to (Henschen, 2008) the top Roadblocks to BI Success are the complexity of BI tools and interfaces and the cost of BI software and per-user licenses.

BI RESOURCES

Resources on BI are freely available on the Web for both practitioners and academics. Here, we only describe three well-known resources: Teradata University Network, TDWI-The Data Warehousing Institute and Kimball University.

TUN - Teradata University Network

Teradata University Network (www.teradatauniversitynetwork.com) is a web-based portal for faculty and students in data warehousing, business intelligence/decision support, and database that is provided at no cost. This teaching portal is composed of practitioners and renowned academics recruited from around the world, united by their dedication to sharing innovative, proactive applications of authentic technology for data-driven decisions (Teradata, 2014).

The portal also support introduction to IT courses at the undergraduate and graduate levels. Teradata University Network (TUN) offers various free BI-related resources: course syllabi used by other faculty, book chapters, articles, research reports, cases, projects, assignments, PowerPoint presentations, software, large data sets, Web seminars, Web-based courses, discussion forums, podcasts, and certification materials.

Via the companion Teradata Student Network web site, professors design assignments using databases with millions of records — all without the issue of scale. TUN also provides students with resources that would normally be prohibitively expensive for a university to develop and maintain, thereby creating opportunities to learn realistic business intelligence using Teradata data warehousing technology. The software such as the Teradata database is available through an application service provider arrangement so that schools do not have to install and maintain BI software.

The Teradata University Network currently has more than 3,700 registered faculty members, from more than 1700 universities, in 98 countries, with thousands of student users, according to its web site.

TDWI - The Data Warehousing Institute

TDWI (The Data Warehousing Institute), a division of 1105 Media, is the premier provider of in-depth, high-quality education and research in the business intelligence, data warehousing, and analytics industry according to the information in its web site (TDWI, 2014). TDWI provides BI training, research, and networking opportunities to its members around the world.

Starting in 1995 with a single conference, TDWI is now a comprehensive resource for industry information and professional development opportunities. TDWI offers vendor-neutral educational opportunities at quarterly conferences, on-site classes, and regional events and through its web site. Each year, TDWI sponsors a BI best practices competition that recognizes organizations that have achieved significant success in BI. TDWI offers five major World Conferences, topical seminars, onsite education, a worldwide membership program, business intelligence certification, live Webinars, resourceful publications, industry news, an in-depth research program, and a comprehensive Web site: tdwi.org. The TDWI Business Intelligence publications provide fresh ideas and perspectives to help organizations operate more intelligently. They also provide actionable insight on how to plan, build, and deploy business intelligence and data warehousing solutions.

The Kimball University

Kimball University, operated by the Kimball Group, offers public and on-site data warehouse classes based on their best-selling books and extensive hands-on consulting experience (Kimball, 2014). The Kimball Group is a focused team of senior consultants specializing in the design of effective data warehouses to deliver enhanced business intelligence. Through consulting, education, and writing, they help organizations leverage the information that's collected by their operational systems to make better business decisions.

Kimball University Kimball University is a source for dimensional data warehouse and business intelligence education offering public classes in venues around the US and internationally. In addition, they teach classes on-site at client locations. All classes content are vendor neutral with the exception of the Microsoft-centric course (Kimball, 2014).

The Kimball Group delivers practical techniques via their monthly email Design Tips, along with reminders about upcoming worldwide classes and events. They have written over 250 articles for InformationWeek, Intelligent Enterprise, DBMS, Information Management and DM Review, that are available to download in the web site.

OPEN SOURCE MODEL

An economic shift has occurred in the past decades, introduced with the rise of the Internet. The Internet provides connectivity, which in turn connects demand to supply; this removes the capital equation and shifts conditions in the market. People with computers all over the world provide the means of conduction, and with easy ways for these people to connect they can easily collaborate on projects with very little infrastructure. This, in turn, led to the popularity of Open Source.

A variety of authors (e.g. (Pollock, 2009); (Lakhani & von Hippel, 2003); (Bessen, 2006)) have pointed out that an open-source approach may offer substantial efficiency advantages – for example by allowing users to participate directly in adding features and fixing bugs – and this is particularly true where the information good is complex and transaction costs are high.

Open Source has had many consequences for the enterprise software market, primarily by making it a commodity market and by driving down price. It also allows people who have a desire to do something to make money from doing it. Production inputs are widely distributed and the raw materials are there to produce things in new ways. Many argue that this shift has been about software licensing, but actually it is largely about the production and distribution of software; it is therefore a change that is more about economics than about ideology. That economic base – the combination of connectivity, of easier ways to market, produce and distribute software, and the fact that the Internet acts as a giant copying machine – changes the conditions under which software can be sold. That is why Open Source continues to disrupt the market and to force vendors to come up with new ways to cope with it. Enterprise software is not going away; rather, it has been forced to shift.

A 2008 survey by North Bridge Venture Partners (Skok, 2008) asked: "Which sector of the software industry is most vulnerable to disruption by Open Source?" At the top of the resulting list was web publishing and content management, a market that's currently highly fragmented and therefore perfect for introducing Open Source products. The second sector was social software, an entirely new category that has been difficult to define, and difficult currently for commercial vendors to make money from; again, Open Source is the ideal solution.

Business Intelligence was the third sector listed in the North Bridge survey. This is understandable, since BI tools and data warehousing tools are exactly that: tools. While end users consume the outputs, they're not themselves often put into the hands of end users; rather, IT sets up the meta-data, defines metrics, etc. Which means Open Source is targeted at the right audience; there is a platform in a data warehouse that has multiple layers, any one of which can be Open Source or proprietary. Those modular boundaries make Open Source an ideal fit.

Why Open Source?

In addition to examining the sectors left vulnerable by Open Source, the North Bridge Venture survey also asked: "What makes Open Source attractive?" Price was the most popular answer. In addition to the capital cost of licensing, Open Source drives down acquisition cost, as companies no longer have to go through heavy proof of concept. It's also easier to trial things, and if license costs are less then maintenance costs are also less. Finally, unbundling maintenance support and service means that businesses can choose from a menu of services instead of being forced into the traditional approach of a 20 percent single lump fee.

The study also showed that companies found that Open Source offered freedom from vendor lock-in. In addition, it is flexible, with easy access to commodity code, in order to develop, embed and build content into websites.

Another 2008 study, by (The 451 Group, 2008), gave a list of what organizations saw as benefits to Open Source once it was already introduced. At that point, flexibility came out over cost. In this instance, though, the definition of flexibility was different; respondents were impressed by the fact that there is no vendor that dictates when they have to upgrade, how they have to upgrade, and why they have to upgrade. For a commercial vendor at end of life or desupporting versions of their software, a sales and marketing schedule will often require a release every Q1, whether they are ready or not. As a result, companies will be forced into an upgrade they don't want, that was released simply because marketing dictated it and not necessarily because it was ready. Open Source is typically not under those same types of pressures.

Buyers were also impressed by scaling costs; if an organization has 50 initial licenses and pushes it out to 150 more people, in BI lowered costs come in beyond the initial capital costs. As well, companies are not dependent on vendors for service or for additional pieces of technology.

However, misconceptions still exist around Open Source, based largely on the idea that these projects are being developed by teenagers in their parents' basement; a myth that is more than a decade outdated, as today Open Source projects are generally run by commercial Open Source providers with paid developers. Still, a lack of information can prove a problem for organizations introducing Open Source. This often plays out in the legal department, which reviews all contracts and may not be informed when it comes to Open Source software licenses. An Open Source license will be missing half the standard clauses the lawyers are used to; clauses of restriction that dictate how to deploy, what can be deployed, where it can be deployed, and how the software can be used. Most Open Source licenses do not have these same clauses and lawyers will want to know why they're missing. That can be another road bump in getting the software acquired.

Support can also be more confusing. Most major projects have commercial vendor support behind them. But unbundling is also available, which means buyers don't have to purchase support, but instead can buy the subscription model that covers only bug fixes, integrated patch testing and certification against databases. This is because enterprise support is often overrated; more often than not internal support solves more problems than the vendor does.

(Chesbrough & Crowther, 2006) also proclaim the benefits of openness and at the same time it is closely related to entrepreneurship by focusing on new knowledge creation, too. The authors support the idea of transferring the open source development philosophy to entrepreneurship, i.e. the concept of open innovation. Open innovation at its core is the increasing usage of external sources for creating and developing new ideas, which lead to innovation. In contrast to a closed innovation paradigm, companies try to include customers, users, universities and even competitors in different stages of their new product development processes (Chesbrough, 2003). As every open source software innovation process is based on the desire of integrating external knowledge, it is not astonishing that open source development is often referred to the open innovation paradigm (Dahlander & Magnusson, 2005; West & Gallagher, 2006; West & Lakhani, 2008) and extends open business strategies.

OPEN BI SOLUTIONS

In this section we present the open source BI systems from the vendors that follow the open source model. We will describe the top open source BI tools accordingly to the rankings of Business Intelligence software vendors published by Dresner Advisory Services in its Wisdom of Crowds Business Intelligence Market Study (Dresner, 2014). In this study vendors were ranked using 32 different criteria, on a 5-point scale for each. Criteria covered:

- Sales/acquisition experience – 8 criteria
- Value for price paid (Excellent – Poor)
- Quality and usefulness of product – 12 criteria
- Quality of technical support – 5 criteria
- Quality and value of consulting services – 5 criteria
- Whether vendor is recommended (Yes/No)

The result is a stacked ranking with an average score for every one of the six categories and an overall average score for each vendor.

It is important to understand the scale that they used in scoring the industry and vendors. The scale used is the following:

- 5.0 = Excellent
- 4.0 = Very Good
- 3.0 = Adequate
- 2.0 = Poor
- 1.0 = Very Poor

The next section provides a discussion on the systems presented by Dresner as the best on the open source world

Open Source Business Intelligence Systems

In this section we present the ranking of Open Source BI based on the ranking presented in (Dresner, 2014), we examine 4 open source tools: Jaspersoft (JasperSoft, 2014), Jedox (Jedox, 2015), Pentaho (Pentaho, 2014) and Actuate/BIRT (Actuate, 2014) which according to the study, have higher scores. Table 1 shows the ranking for Open Source BI vendors.

These are all top BI solutions that organizations can choose according to their dimension, requirements and budget.

JasperSoft

JasperSoft is a well-established brand in the open source BI market. Founded in 2001, the company was bought in 2014 by TIBCO software. Nevertheless, Jaspersoft, now under the name TIBCO Jaspersoft claims itself as "the market leader in open-source BI" with more than 12,000 commercial customers worldwide and more than 11 million product downloads (Jaspersoft, 2014). Still, that claim is difficult

Table 1. Open Source Business Intelligence Vendors: Stacked Rankings

Vendor	Average Score
Jaspersoft www.jaspersoft.com	4.45
Jedox www.jedox.com	4.38
Pentaho www.pentaho.com	4.13
Actuate/BIRT www.actuate.com	4.02

to substantiate as many open-source vendors are quoting large numbers of product downloads, often hundreds of thousands or even millions, while the number of production deployments of their community editions is unclear.

TIBCO Jaspersoft provides a Web-based, open, and modular approach to the evolving business intelligence needs of the enterprise, providing a first-in-class, multi-tenant BI environment while providing a common platform for on-premise, virtualized, SaaS, and cloud deployments. The JasperSoft product family includes JasperServer, JasperReports, the JasperStudio report designer, the JasperAnalysis OLAP analysis server and JasperETL, which is based on the open-source ETL engine from Talend.

JasperSoft has established a partner network that includes companies such as Sun Microsystems, MySQL, Novell, Red Hat Unisys. JasperSoft attempts to extend its community into the world of applications with specific solutions for salesforce.com, SugarCRM and Oracle eBusiness Suite (Jaspersoft, 2014). Many small independent software vendors are also including JasperReports as the reporting component in their respective software packages.

The Jaspersoft Business Intelligence Suite offers a number of ways for end users to perform interactive analysis. The two primary tools dedicated to analysis within the Jaspersoft suite are JasperAnalysis and the integrated In-Memory Analysis tool within JasperServer. JasperAnalysis is a traditional OLAP (Online Analytical Processing) tool, based on the popular open source Mondrian engine. OLAP tools perform analytic tasks on specialized, analysis-tuned data collections commonly called "cubes."

JasperServer provides an integrated suite of BI capabilities, including ad-hoc query and reporting, dashboarding and analysis. All capabilities are delivered based on a common metadata and security layer and are delivered via the same Web 2.0-style user interface. To create a query, users simply drag and drop data objects of interest from a business view of the data into a query builder window, with the option to add filters and parameter groups. The query results can then be laid out and formatted to produce a report that can be saved, shared, scheduled and distributed through the JasperServer platform.

Dashboards, including features like URL-based mashups and live refresh, can also be created through the same drag-and-drop interface. Flash charts and maps enhance the look and interactivity of the dashboards. Figure 2 shows an example of a dashboard with some of these features.

Jaspersoft offers a suite of analysis capabilities covering a broad range of user and organizational profiles, delivered chiefly within JasperAnalysis and in the integrated In-Memory Analysis tool within JasperServer. Big Data Analytics can be a challenging concept with multiple sources, a number of different ways to connect and users wanting insight faster than ever.

Figure 2. A JasperSoft dashboard sample
source: www.jaspersoft.com

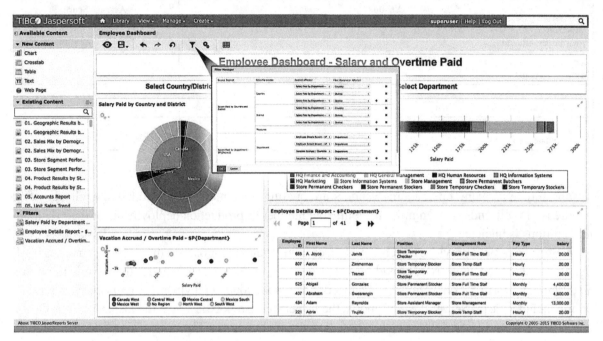

Jaspersoft has recently released Visualize.js, a JavaScript framework for advanced embedding of visualizations and reports in applications. The new framework, which is included in the newly released TIBCO Jaspersoft 5.6 product, delivers more control, simplicity and power for application developers by combining the power of the complete Jaspersoft analytic server with the simplicity and control of JavaScript. In addition to Visualize.js, Jaspersoft introduced a series of updates to its flagship platform. Version 5.6 of the Jaspersoft platform includes virtualized blending of relational and Big Data sources such as MongoDB, Hadoop and Cassandra, more powerful analytic calculations and visualizations, and new interactive reporting features. Furthermore, the company now partners with Hortonworks, Amazon AWS and Cloudera to provide Analytics as a Service (AaaS), enabling data visualization at reduced cost.

Jedox

Jedox Corporation was founded in Germany in 2002 by Kristian Raue and soon released its first product: The Worksheet Server, which "seamlessly publishes Excel planning and reporting to Jedox web applications". By 2003 the company released the first version of PALO, which remains, since then as its premium software edition. Later, in 2008, eCAPITAL Partners and Wecken & Cie. Invested in Jedox, leveraging its business and allowing it to expand globally and become a very well-known enterprise within BI.

Jedox offers a modular structure that relies on its OLAP server and several connectors that provide integration with ERP and CRM modules (such as SAP ERP and SAP BI); and cloud services (such as Amazon and Azure). Furthermore it also provides a broad variety of ways to present data. Among them are the Jedox Excel and Power Point Add-ins, the Jedox Web (see Figure 3) and the Jedox mobile.

Figure 3. Jedox Web Example
source: www.jedox.com

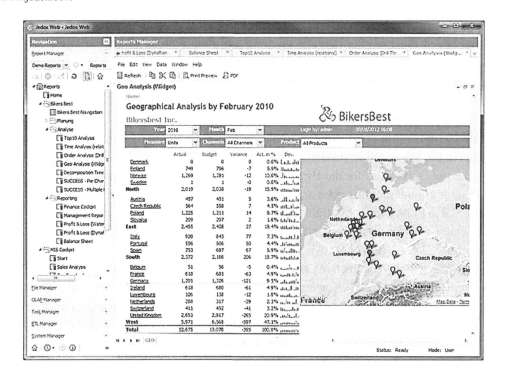

Jedox claims that its OLAP Server provides a "highly-scalable analytical appliance that delivers real-time performance over volatile enterprise data" (Jedox, 2015), complex planning and forecasting with in-memory rules modelling, predictive analytics with powerful statistical heuristics and instant consolidations and reporting over large multi-dimensional datasets. By providing Jedox Excel and Power Point Add-ins, the company ensures integration between its software and Microsoft's Excel and PowerPoint – some of the most used software for data visualization and presentation – leveraging the use of Jedox software in a broad way. In addition, with Jedox Mobile, the company is able to provide report and dashboarding capabilities on-the-fly, looking forward to fulfill business' needs.

Furthermore, Jedox provide their so called OLAP Accelerator that leverage computing power by using NVIDIA Tesla graphic cards in parallel GPU processing to provide consistent scalable performance over extreme data modelling scenarios. This technology, developed in cooperation with the University of Freiburg and the University of Western Australia in Perth was highly recognized by Gartner that awarded Jedox with the "Cool Vendor" award.

Regarding License, Jedox provides a double licensing option. Its open source option provides the OLAP Server and a functionally restricted version of the Excel add-in. The premium (PALO and PalO-OCa – for open office) version contains all software components and additional provider services such as technical support. In addition, Jedox was brought to the cloud and is now provided as a service both on Amazon AWS and Microsoft Azure flavors, providing availability to its users.

Pentaho

Pentaho was founded in 2004 and is one the best-known open-source BI platforms in the market. Pentaho provides a breadth of functionality that can be considered the closest match to commercial offerings from companies such as Business Objects, Cognos or Oracle.

Pentaho's offerings include a simple reporting solution and the more comprehensive Pentaho BI suite, which also includes analysis, dashboard and data mining capabilities. For both offerings, customers can purchase a subscription. The subscription also enables access to additional BI platform functionality (for example, system auditing, performance monitoring as well as single sign-on or clustering), which is not available in the open-source version.

To round out the capabilities for the BI platform, Pentaho has acquired the assets and hired the lead developers of some complementing open-source projects, such as Mondrian or Kettle, for online analytical processing (OLAP) or extraction, transformation and loading (ETL) technology, respectively. The BI platform, which runs on most popular Windows versions, Linux distributions and even Mac OS, is based on server-side Java, a thin client Ajax front-end and an Eclipse-based design environment.

Pentaho provides a highly interactive and easy to use web-based design interface for the casual business user to create simple and *ad hoc* operational reports. Pentaho has also rich and highly interactive dashboards that help business users to easily identify the business metrics that are on track, and the ones that need attention. With no prior training, users can create personalized dashboards to turn organizational metrics into visual and interactive representations as seen in Figure 4.

Figure 4. Pentaho interactive dashboards
source: www.pentaho.com

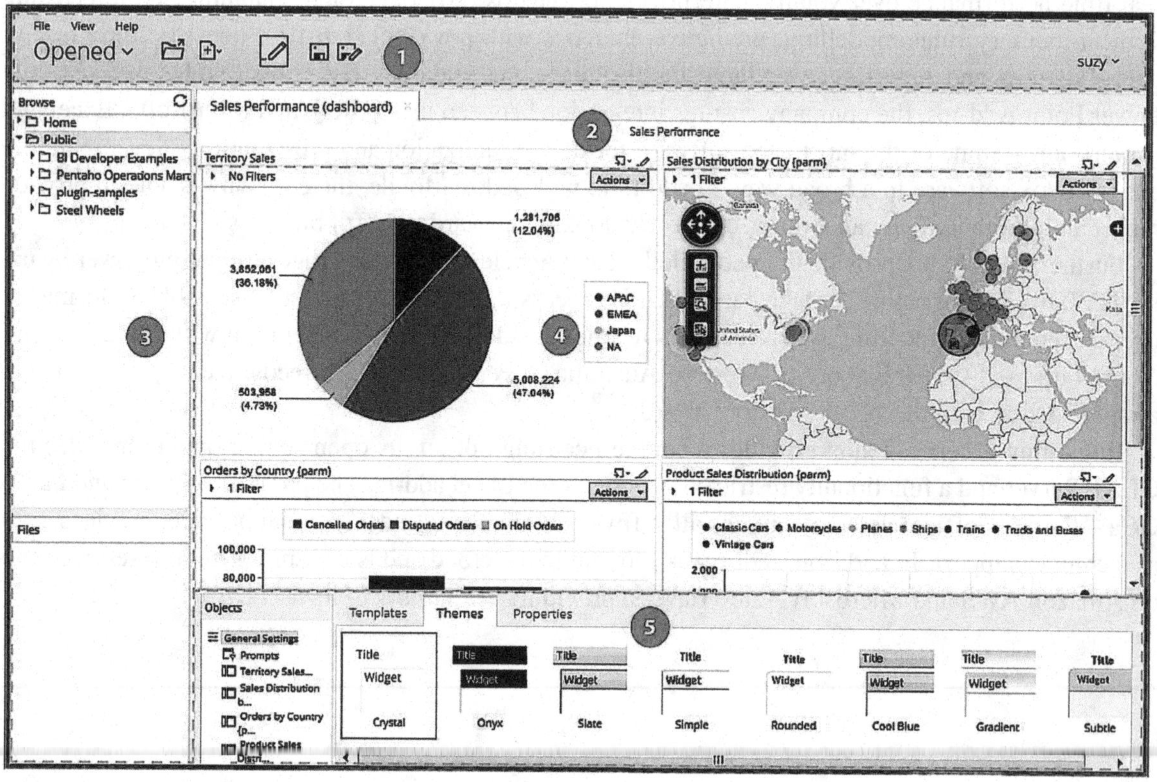

Pentaho 5.4, the last version of its business analytics and data integration platform, offers companies enhanced capabilities to scale up their big data operations and accelerates the delivery of value from any data by unleashing the power of highly scalable Big Data analytics.

This last version enables integration with SAP HANA and several Big Data systems such as Apache Spark and Hadoop, including Amazon Elastic MapReduce and YARN (MapReduce 2.0). Furthermore, it provides API to access Google Analytics' and enables business intelligence on-demand by partnering with Amazon Web Services (AWS) in order to provide Pentaho in the cloud. These new functionalities empower organizations to rapidly blend and analyze the highest volumes of data, ultimately speeding the time to a 360-degree business view.

The Pentaho 5.4 platform enables companies, large or small, to take full advantage of big data without having to endure a lengthy, specialized process that often proves a barrier to entry to big data.

Actuate/BIRT

Actuate Corporation was founded in 1993 and has been selling commercial BI software since its formation. In 2004, Actuate became the first public BI software company to enter the open-source space by petitioning for membership into the Eclipse Foundation and proposing a new open XML report design specification and accompanying toolset.

The Business Intelligence and Reporting Tool (BIRT), founded and co-lead by Actuate, is based on the Eclipse framework. Under the BIRT project, Actuate is making a small subset of its commercial enterprise reporting solution available under an open-source license.

For BIRT, Actuate offers a variety of products and services, supporting users through an annual subscription model for the open-source version, which has limited capabilities compared to the full Actuate platform. As such, the BIRT offering must be considered an attempt to attract highly technical do-it-yourself audiences and get a "foot in the door". Customers looking for the full functionality BI platform are required to upgrade to the commercial Actuate license.

BIRT's advanced and highly interactive reporting functionality, made highly scalable and function-rich with Actuate commercial extensions, propel Actuate BIRT to the leadership position. Actuate is also expanding its offering into end-to-end document management (or ILM — Information Life-cycle Management) capabilities. Producing reports often starts a report life cycle, where a report needs to be distributed, stored, secured, and archived.

Eclipse's BIRT project is a flexible, open source, and 100% pure Java reporting tool for building and publishing reports against data sources ranging from typical business relational databases, to XML data sources, to in-memory Java objects. BIRT is developed as a top-level project within the Eclipse Foundation and leverages the rich capabilities of the Eclipse platform and a very active open source community of users. Using BIRT, developers of all levels can incorporate powerful reporting into their Java, J2EE and Eclipse-based applications as illustrated in Figure 5.

BIRT has two main components: a report designer based on Eclipse, and a runtime component that we can use to integrate BIRT reports into our applications. BIRT also has a charting engine that lets include charts into BIRT reports or add stand alone charting capabilities to Java applications.

BIRT has also the Spreadsheet Designer, an Excel-like authoring environment that gives report developers and Excel experts the power to automate the task of creating and updating Excel spreadsheets with the latest data (see Figure 6). BIRT Spreadsheet automates and centralizes spreadsheet production,

Figure 5. BIRT report design
source: www.actuate.com

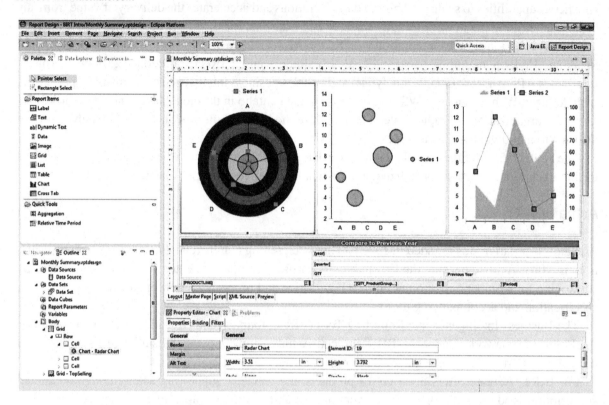

maintenance, archiving, and security, eliminating version discrepancies and curbing the proliferation of multiple silos of Excel workbook data.

BIRT Analytics, a visual data mining and predictive analytics tool for identifying customer insights within the organization, provides business users with fast, free-form visual data mining and predictive analytics. The uniqueness of BIRT Analytics results from a combination of the ease of use of data discovery tools with the power and sophisticated analytic products typically reserved for data scientists, and the operational and management reach of BIRT iHub 3.

Actuate's BIRT iHub 3 simplifies the delivery of personalized analytics and insights via a single platform that integrates BIRT based, visually appealing, interactive application services, predictive analytics services, and customer content services. This release also enhances the productivity of the application developer and the administrator in efficiently building applications that leverage traditional and Big Data sources to serve personalized insights securely to millions of end users, on any device at any time. With BIRT iHub 3 integration, BIRT Analytics customers can leverage common shared services, resulting in improved IT efficiency and faster time to value.

In the latest versions, BIRT introduced support for a broad range of report output formats (e.g.: HTML, paginated HTML, DOC, XLS, Postscript, PPT, PDF, ODP, ODS, and ODT formats). The software can now be integrated with several Big Data platforms such as Apache Cassandra and Hadoop, providing the ability to access virtually any data source that is structured or contains an API. Furthermore, BIRT

Figure 6. BIRT Spreadsheet Designer
source: www.actuate.com

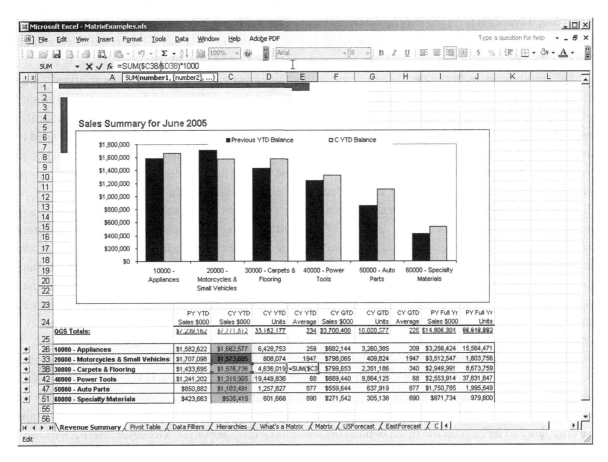

can now be purchased as platform as a service (PaaS) through BIRT onDemand, which came provide an easy and available way to use BIRT-based BI applications in a plug-and-play way.

FUTURE RESEARCH DIRECTIONS

Big Data

Many of today's enterprises are encountering the Big Data problems. A Big Data problem has four distinct characteristics (so called 4V features): the data volume is huge (Volume); the data type is diverse meaning a mixture of structured data, semi-structured data and unstructured data (Variety); the streaming data is very high (Velocity); and uncertain or imprecise data (Veracity). These 4V features pose a grand challenge to traditional data processing systems since these systems either cannot scale to the huge data volume in a cost effective way or fail to handle data with variety of types (Abouzeid et al., 2008; Chattopadhyay, 2011).

With the increasingly large amount of data, building separate systems to analyze data becomes expensive and infeasible, caused by not only the cost and time of building the systems, but also the required professional knowledge on big data management and analysis. Therefore, it is necessary to have a single infrastructure which provides common functionality of big data management, and flexible enough to handle different types of big data and big data analysis tasks (Agrawal et al., 2014).

Although current technologies such as cloud computing provide infrastructure for automation of data collection, storing, processing and visualization, big data impose significant challenges to the traditional infrastructure, due to the characteristics of volume, velocity and variety. Modern Internet and scientific research project produce a huge amount of data with complex inter-relationship. These big data need to be supported by a new type of Infrastructure tailored for big data, which must have the performance to provide fast data access and process to satisfy users' just in time needs (Slack, 2012). Moreover, community standards for data description and exchange are also crucial (Lynch, 2008).

Nowadays, users are accessing multiple data storage platforms to accomplish their operational and analytical requirements (Horey et al., 2012). Efficient integration of different data sources is important (Devlin et al., 2012). For example, an organization may purchase storage from different vendors and need to combine data with different format stored on systems from different vendors (Slack, 2012). Data integration, which plays an important role for both commercial and scientific domains, combines data from different sources and provides users with a unified view of these data (Lenzerini, 2002). How to make efficient data integration with the 4V (volume, velocity, variety, and veracity) characteristics is a key research direction for the big data platforms.

Although big data infrastructure and platform are critical, they can't create the same long-term value as various big data analytics software which apply big data to accelerate a market (Rouse, 2012). Big data analytics is the process of examining large amounts of data of various types to uncover hidden patterns, unknown correlations and other useful information (Analytics, 2014a). The big data analytics algorithms are complex and far beyond the reach of most organization's IT capabilities. Moreover, there are too few skilled big data practitioners available for every organization. Therefore, more and more organizations turn to Big Data Analytics Software-as-a-Service to obtain the business intelligence (BI) service that turns their unstructured data into an enhanced asset (O'Brien, 2012).

Big Data Analytics Software-as-a-Service exploits massive amounts of structured and unstructured data to deliver real-time and intelligent results, allowing users to perform self-service provisioning, analysis, and collaboration. Big Data Analytics Software-as-a-Service is typically Web-hosted, multi-tenant and use Hadoop, NoSQL, and a range of pattern discovery and machine learning technologies (Analytics, 2014b). Users would typically execute scripts and queries that data scientists and programmers developed for them to generate reports and visualizations (EMC, 2012). Various big data analytics approaches can be implemented and encapsulated into services. By this way, users will be able to interact with Web-based analytics services easily without worrying about the underlying data storage, management, and analyzing procedures.

Considering the 4-V characteristics of big data (Roos et al., 2011), and the requirements for enterprises' application development, in order to overcome the challenges big data caused, and to help enterprises seize the opportunities big data brings, these platforms are desired to provide the following functions:

- **Scalability:** Data storage should always be considerately designed in data-intensive application development. Traditionally, we always preferably choose a relational database management system (RDBMS) in that several decades of successful application has proved that the system is reliable, effective and robust. Al-though it could be scaled up or scaled out to some extent, there are also many bottlenecks on its scale and speed when processing trillions of data (Lee, 2004; Leavitt, 2010).

- **Multi-Typed Data Supported:** Besides existing relational databases, documents, e-mails and attachment, photos and videos, and Internet search indexes, log files and social media become the primary data sources that need to be stored, processed and utilized by enterprises. It is difficult for those rigidly-defined and schema-based existing approaches used by relational databases to quickly incorporate these unstructured and semi-structured data (Blumberg & Atre, 2003), which requires the products de-signed for unstructured data as well as structured data.
- **Business Driven and Agile Development:** In order to adapt to rapidly changing business requirements, data-intensive applications are no longer complex and all-in-one, and this requires the products should be designed to be simpler and lighter than ever before, and could be adjusted rapidly to meet the needs of business development.

Open Source Business Intelligence Systems

The increasing focus on open-source software has reached the mainstream business intelligence market. As some organizations are looking to reduce costs in their BI deployments, they are hoping that open source gives them greater leverage for their money. Other open-source BI deployments are initiated by application developers that are looking for a way to embed BI functionality into their applications. Similarly, companies often cannot afford to roll out BI technology to hundreds or maybe thousands of users, even from their preferred vendor, because of steep licensing costs and are therefore considering an open-source solution to complement the current infrastructure.

There are about a dozen vendors or projects that can be considered offering open-source BI, although quite a few of those same companies also provide commercial versions of the software, often with significant enhancements over the "free" version. The currently available offerings are effectively split into two camps: the BI platform approach, supported by a commercial vendor, which mainly generates its revenue by providing professional services around the BI platform. Alternatively, there are open-source projects, backed by a few individuals, who maintain a small community, but do not have any commercial interests otherwise. Almost all platforms, tools and source code, in their various open-source versions, are freely available for download at SourceForge (http://sourceforge.net) the largest open-source software development Web site, which currently maintains over 160,000 projects and over 1.7 million registered users.

As future work, we propose to evaluate a prototype in a real enterprise application environment using the open source BI platforms described in this chapter.

CONCLUSION

Big Data represents a fundamental shift in business decision-making. Organizations are accustomed to analyzing internal data – sales, shipments, and inventory. Now they are increasingly analyzing external data too, gaining new insights into customers, markets, supply chains and operations: the perspective of "outside-in view". We believe it is Big Data and the outside-in view that will generate the biggest opportunities for differentiation over the next years. The key to winning in the Information Age is making decisions that are consistently better and faster than the competition. Using big data for decision-making will lead to better decisions, better consensus, and better execution.

Business intelligence is an approach to managing business that is dedicated to providing competitive advantage through the execution of fact-based decision-making. At a tactical level, business intelligence allows to achieve this goal by applying a decision-making cycle of analyzing information, gaining insight, taking action, and measuring results. At a strategic level, business intelligence allows to use the results of analysis to create superior corporate strategies that outsmart competitors.

Business intelligence essentially means putting relevant information at the fingertips of decision makers at all levels of the organization – functional areas, business units, and executive management. Technologies exist today to make this possible for all companies – large and small. The BI technologies presented in this paper become valuable only when they are used to positively impact organization behavior. Successful BI solutions provide businesspeople with the information they need to do their jobs more effectively.

According to (Dresner, 2014), Jaspersoft is the best open source solution so far. However, Jedox is also very good but its open source license is very limitative, as it only provides a small subset of functionalities. On the contrary, Jaspersoft, Pentaho and Actuate BIRT provide lots of functionalities, including cloud support, consisting in better options regarding the scope of functionalities.

In our opinion Open Source Business Intelligence platforms are mature from the functional and business model point of view to become a solid option to meet and exceed the business intelligence needs of an organization, especially among SMEs to enter into the new market and operate on a national and global scale. Nowadays with the new techno-economic paradigm, the SMEs can also improve their competitiveness using open BI as an open innovation strategy. Thus, the use of open source BI systems in organizations can trigger immense possibilities of accelerating knowledge acquisition, innovation, intensifying entrepreneurship development and improving business skills, therefore, leading to business sustainability.

Data is now the fourth factor of production, as essential as land, labor and capital. It follows that tomorrow's winners will be the organizations that succeed in exploiting Big Data, for example by applying advanced predictive analytic techniques in real time using Business Intelligence tools.

REFERENCES

Abouzeid, A., Bajda-Pawlikowski, K., Abadi, D. J., Rasin, A., & Silberschatz, A. (2009). HadoopDB: An Architectural Hybrid of MapReduce and DBMS Technologies for Analytical Workloads. *The Proceedings of the VLDB Endowment*, 2(1), 922–933. doi:10.14778/1687627.1687731

Actuate Corporation. (2014). Actuate/BIRT BI. Retrieved from **Error! Hyperlink reference not valid.** http://www.actuate.com/

Adrian, M. (2010). Exploring the Extremes of Database Growth. IBM Data Management, Issue 1.

Agrawal, D., ... (2014). Challenges and opportunities with big data. Leading researchers across the United States, Tech. Rep., Retrieved from http://www.cra.org/ccc/files/docs/init/bigdatawhitepaper.pdf

Analytics. (2014a). Why big data analytics as a service? Analytics as a Service. Retrieved from http://www.analyticsasaservice.org/why-big-data-analytics-as-a-service/

Analytics. (2014b). What is Big Data? Analytics as a Service in the Cloud. Analytics as a Service. Retrieved from http://www.analyticsasaservice.org/what-is-big-data-analytics-as-a-service-in-the-cloud/

Arsham, H. (2015). Applied Management Science: Making Good Strategic Decisions. Retrieved from http://home.ubalt.edu/ntsbarsh/opre640/opre640.htm

Bates, P., Biere, M., Weideranders, R., Meyer, A., & Wong, B. (2009). New Intelligence for a Smarter Planet. Retrieved from http://www-01.ibm.com/common/ssi/cgi-bin/ssialias?infotype=PM&subtype=BK&appname=SWGE_IM_DD_USEN&htmlfid=IMM14055USEN&attachment=IMM14055USEN.PDF

Bessen, J. (2006). Open Source Software: Free Provision of Complex Public Goods. In J. Bitzer & P. J. H. Schröder (Eds.), *The Economics of Open Source Software Development*. Elsevier B.V. doi:10.1016/B978-044452769-1/50003-2

Blumberg, R., & Atre, S. (2003). The problem with unstructured data. *DM Review*, *13*(2), 42–49.

Burstein, F., & Holsapple, C. W. (2008). *Handbook on Decision Support Systems 2*. Berlin, Heidelberg: Springer Berlin Heidelberg.

Chamoni, P., & Gluchowski, P. (2004). Integration trends in business intelligence systems-An empirical study based on the business intelligence maturity model. *Wirtschaftsinformatik*, *46*(2), 119–128. doi:10.1007/BF03250931

Chattopadhyay, B., Lin, L., Liu, W., Mittal, S., Aragonda, P., Lychagina, V., & Wong, M. et al. (2011). Tenzing a SQL Implementation on the MapReduce Framework. *The Proceedings of the VLDB Endowment*, *4*(12), 1318–1327.

Chesbrough, H. (2003). Open Innovation: How Companies Actually Do It. *Harvard Business Review*, 81(7), 12-14.

Chesbrough, H. & Crowther, A. K. (2006). Beyond high tech: early adopters of open innovation in other industries. *R&D Management*, 36(3), 229-236.

Cisco (2011). Big Data in the Enterprise: Network Design Considerations. Retrieved from http://www.cisco.com/c/en/us/products/collateral/switches/nexus-5000-series-switches/white_paper_c11-690561.pdf

Cukier, K. (2010, February 21). Data, data everywhere. *The Economist*. Retrieved from http://www.economist.com/node/15557443?story_id=15557443)

Dahlander, L., & Magnusson, M. G. (2005). Relationships between open source software companies and communities: Observations from Nordic firms. *Research Policy*, 34(4), 481–493.

Devlin, B., Rogers, S., & Myers, J. (2012). Big data comes of age. *IBM*. Retrieved from http://www-03.ibm.com/systems/hu/resources/big_data_comes_of_age.pdf

Dresner Advisory Services. (2014). Wisdom of Crowds Business Intelligence Market Study. Retrieved from http://www.actuate.com/download/analyst-papers/Wisdom_of_Crowds_BI_Market_Study_Findings_2011.pdf

EMC. (2012). Big data-as-a-service: A market and technology perspective. EMC Solution Group. Retrieved from http://www.emc.com/collateral/software/white-papers/h10839-big-data-as-a-service-perspt.pdf

Evelson, B., & Norman, N. (2008). Topic overview: business intelligence. Forrester Research. Retrieved from http://www.forrester.com/Topic+Overview+Business+Intelligence/fulltext/-/E-RES39218

Evelson, B., & Norman, N. (2008). *Topic overview: business intelligence*. Forrester.

Gantz, J., & Reinsel, D. (201, May0). The Digital Universe Decade – Are You Ready? The IDC 2010 Digital Universe Study. Retrieved from http://idcdocserv.com/925

Henschen, D. (2008, October 13). BI Efforts Take Flight. InformationWeek.

Horey, J., Begoli, E., Gunasekaran, R., Lim, S.-H., & Nutaro, J. (2012). Big data platforms as a service: challenges and approach.*Proceedings of the 4th USENIX conference on Hot Topics in Cloud Computing, HotCloud'12* (p. 16).

Jaspersoft (2014). Jaspersoft Business Intelligence. Retrieved from http://www.jaspersoft.com/

Jedox (2015). Jedox Business Intelligence. Retrieved from http://www.jedox.com/en/

Kimball University. (2014). Kimball Group. Retrieved from http://www.kimballgroup.com/data-warehouse-business-intelligence-courses/

Kimberling, E. (2006). In search of business value: how to achieve the benefits of ERP technology (White paper). *Panorama Consulting Group*, Denver, CO.

Lakhani, K. R., & von Hippel, E. (2003). How open source software works: "Free" user-to-user assistance. *Research Policy*, *32*(6), 923–943. doi:10.1016/S0048-7333(02)00095-1

Leavitt, N. (2010). Will NoSQL databases live up to their promise? *IEEE Computer*, *43*(2), 12–14. doi:10.1109/MC.2010.58

Lee, R. (2004). Scalability report on triple store applications. Retrieved from http://simile.mit.edu/reports/stores/

Lenzerini, M. (2002). Data integration: A theoretical perspective.*Proceedings of the 21st ACM SIGMOD-SIGACT-SIGART Symposium on Principles of Database Systems* (pp. 233–246).

Lin, Y. H., Tsai, K. M., Shiang, W. J., Kuo, T. C., & Tsai, C. H. (2009). Research on using ANP to establish a performance assessment model for business intelligence systems. *Expert Systems with Applications*, *36*(2), 4135–4146. doi:10.1016/j.eswa.2008.03.004

Loshin, D. (2011). *The Analytics Revolution 2011: Optimizing Reporting and Analytics to Optimizing Reporting and Analytics to Make Actionable Intelligence Pervasive*. Knowledge Integrity, Inc.

Luhn, H. P. (1958). A Business Intelligence System. *IBM Journal of Research and Development*, *2*(4), 314–319. doi:10.1147/rd.24.0314

Lynch, C. (2008). Big data: How do your data grow? *Nature*, *455*(7209), 28–29. doi:10.1038/455028a PMID:18769419

Mearian, L. (2010, November 2). Data growth remains IT's biggest challenge, Gartner says. *Computerworld*. Retrieved from http://www.computerworld.com/s/article/9194283/Data_growth_remains_IT_s_biggest_challenge_Gartner_says

O'Brien, P. (2012). The future: Big data apps or web services? Retrieved from http://blog.fliptop.com/blog/2012/05/12/the-future-big-data-apps-or-web-services/

Pentaho Corporation. (2014). Pentaho Open Source BI. Retrieved from http://community.pentaho.com/

Pollock, R. (2009). Innovation, Imitation and Open Source. *International Journal of Open Source Software & Processes*, 1(2), 114-127.

Ponniah, P. (2010). *Data Warehousing Fundamentals for IT Professionals* (2nd ed.). New York: John Wiley & Sons, Inc. doi:10.1002/9780470604137

Popovič, A., Turk, T., & Jaklič, J. (2010). Conceptual model of business value of business intelligence systems. *Management*, 15(1), 5–30.

Power, D. J. (2007). A Brief History of Decision Support Systems, version 4.0. *DSSResources.COM*. Retrieved from http://DSSResources.COM/history/dsshistory.html

Roos, D., Eaton, C., Lapis, G., Zikopoulos, P., & Deutsch, T. (2011). *Understanding Big Data: Analytics for Enterprise Class Hadoop and Streaming Data*. McGraw-Hill Osborne Media.

Rouse, M. (2012). Definition of big data analytics. Retrieved from http://searchbusinessanalytics.techtarget.com/definition/big-data-analytics

Skok, M. (2008). *The Future of Open Source: Exploring the Investments, Innovations, Applications, Opportunities and Threats*. North Bridge Venture Partners.

Slack, E. (2012). Storage infrastructures for big data workflows. Storage Switzerland White Paper. Retrieved from https://iq.quantum.com/exLink.asp?8615424OJ73H28I34127712

. The Data Warehousing Institute (TDWI). (2014). Retrieved from http://tdwi.org/Home.aspx

Teradata University Network. (2014). Retrieved from http://www.teradatauniversitynetwork.com/

The 451 Group (2008). Open Source Is Not a Business Model. The 451 Commercial Adoption of Open Source (CAOS) Research Service.

Turban, E., King, D., Lee, J. K., & Viehland, D. (2004). *Electronic Commerce 2004: A Managerial Perspective* (3rd ed.). Prentice Hall.

Turban, E., Sharda, R., Aronson, J. E., & King, D. (2008). *Business Intelligence: a managerial approach*. Upper Saddle River, N.J.: Pearson Prentice Hall.

Tzu, S. (1963). *The Art of War. United Sates of America*. Oxford University Press.

Watson, H. J., Wixom, B. H., & Goodhue, D. L. (2004). Data Warehousing: The 3M Experience. In H. R. Nemati & C. D. Barko (Eds.), *Org. Data Mining: Leveraging Enterprise Data Resources for Optimal Performance* (pp. 202–216). Idea Group Publishing. doi:10.4018/978-1-59140-134-6.ch014

West, J., & Gallagher, S. (2006). Patterns of Open Innovation in Open Source Software. In H. Chesbrough, W. Vanhaverbeke, & J. West (Eds.), *Open Innovation: Researching a New Paradigm* (pp. 82–106). Oxford: Oxford University Press.

West, J., & Lakhani, K. (2008). Getting Clear About the Role of Communities in Open Innovation. *Industry and Innovation, 15*(2), 223–231. doi:10.1080/13662710802033734

Wit, B., & Meyer, R. (2003). *Strategy: Process, Content, Context* (3rd ed.). Cengage Learning Business Press.

ADDITIONAL READING

Al-Aqrabi, H., Liu, L., Hill, R., & Antonopoulos, N.Al-Aqrabi. (2015, February). H., Liu, L.; Hill, R. & Antonopoulos, N. Cloud BI: Future of business intelligence in the Cloud. *Journal of Computer and System Sciences, 81*(1), 85–96. doi:10.1016/j.jcss.2014.06.013

Arefin, S., Hoque, R., & Bao, Y. (2015). The impact of business intelligence on organization's effectiveness: An empirical study. *Journal of Systems and Information Technology, 17*(3), 263–285. doi:10.1108/JSIT-09-2014-0067

Arora, S., Nangia, V. K., & Agrawal, R. (2015). Making strategy process intelligent with business intelligence: An empirical investigation. *International Journal of Data Analysis Techniques and Strategies, 7*(1), 77. doi:10.1504/IJDATS.2015.067702

Back, W. D., Goodman, N., & Hyde, J. (2013). *Mondrian in Action: Open source business analytics* (1st ed.). Manning Publications.

Bell, J. (2014). *Machine Learning: Hands-On for Developers and Technical Professionals* (1st ed.). Wiley. doi:10.1002/9781119183464

Bulusu, L. (2012). *Open Source Data Warehousing and Business Intelligence* (1st ed.). CRC Press. doi:10.1201/b12671

Casters, M. Bouman & Dongen, J. V. (2010). Pentaho Kettle Solutions: Building Open Source ETL Solutions with Pentaho Data Integration (1st ed.). Wiley.

Chang, Y., Hsu, P., & Wu, Z. (2015). Exploring managers' intention to use business intelligence: The role of motivations. *Behaviour & Information Technology, 34*(3), 273–285. doi:10.1080/0144929X.2014.968208

Clausen, N. (2009). Open Source Business Intelligence (2nd edition). BoD.

Flach, P. (2012). *Machine Learning: The Art and Science of Algorithms that Make Sense of Data* (1st ed.). Cambridge University Press.

Grossmann, W., & Rinderle-Ma, S. (2015). *Fundamentals of Business Intelligence*. Springer Berlin Heidelberg. doi:10.1007/978-3-662-46531-8

Gudfinnsson, K., Strand, M., & Berndtsson, M. (2015). Analyzing business intelligence maturity. *Journal of Decision Systems, 24*(1).

Höpken, W., Fuchs, M., Keil, D., & Lexhagen, M. (2015, June). Business intelligence for cross-process knowledge extraction at tourism destinations. *Information Technology & Tourism., 15*(2), 101–130. doi:10.1007/s40558-015-0023-2

Howson, C. (2013). Successful Business Intelligence (2nd ed.). McGraw-Hill Education.

Hubbard, D. W. (2010). *How to Measure Anything: Finding the Value of Intangibles in Business*. Wiley. doi:10.1002/9781118983836

Khan, A. (2011). *Business Intelligence & Data Warehousing Simplified: 500 Questions, Answers, & Tips*. Mercury Learning & Information.

Kimball, R., Ross, M., Thornthwaite, W., & Mundy, J. (2010). *The Kimball Group Reader: Relentlessly Practical Tools for Data Warehousing and Business Intelligence*. Wiley.

Kolb, J. M. (2013). *Business Intelligence in Plain Language: A practical guide to Data Mining and Business Analytics*. CreateSpace Independent Publishing Platform.

Laursen, G., & Thorlund, J. (2010). *Business Analytics for Managers: Taking Business Intelligence Beyond Reporting*. Wiley and SAS Business Series. doi:10.1002/9781118983812

Leimeister, J. M. (2010). Collective Intelligence.[BISE]. *Business & Information Systems Engineering*, 2(4), 245–248. doi:10.1007/s12599-010-0114-8

Loshin, D. (2012). Business Intelligence (2nd edition). Morgan Kaufmann

Madsen, L. B. (2012). *Healthcare Business Intelligence, + Website: A Guide to Empowering Successful Data Reporting and Analytics* (1st ed.). Wiley. doi:10.1002/9781119205326

Maheshwari, A. (2014). Data Analytics Made Accessible.

Minelli, M., Chambers, M., & Dhiraj, A. (2013). *Big Data, Big Analytics: Emerging Business Intelligence and Analytic Trends for Today's Businesses* (1st ed.). Wiley. doi:10.1002/9781118562260

Moro, S., Cortez, P., & Rita, P. (2015, February 15). Business intelligence in banking: A literature analysis from 2002 to 2013 using text mining and latent Dirichlet allocation. *Expert Systems with Applications*, 42(3), 1314–1324. doi:10.1016/j.eswa.2014.09.024

O'Reilly Media Inc. (2012). *Big Data Now: 2012 Edition* (2nd ed.). O'Reilly Media.

Orgaz, G. B., Barrero, D. F., R-Moreno, M. D., & Camacho, D. (2015). Acquisition of business intelligence from human experience in route planning. *Enterprise Information Systems*, 9(3).

Provost, F., & Fawcett, T. (2013). *Data Science for Business: What you need to know about data mining and data-analytic thinking* (1st ed.). O'Reilly Media.

Sabherwal, R., & Becerra-Fernandez, I. (2013). *Business Intelligence: Practices, Technologies, and Management* (1st ed.). Wiley.

Shan, C., Chen, W., Wang, H., & Song, M. (2015). *The Data Science Handbook: Advice and Insights from 25 Amazing Data Scientists*. Data Science Bookshelf.

Sharda, R., Delen, D., & Turban, E. (2014). *Business Intelligence and Analytics: Systems for Decision Support* (10th ed.). Prentice Hall.

Sharda, R., Delen, D., Turban, E., & King, D. (2013). *Business Intelligence: A Managerial Perspective on Analytics* (3rd ed.). Prentice Hall.

Sherman, R. (2014). *Business Intelligence Guidebook: From Data Integration to Analytics* (1st ed.). Morgan Kaufmann.

Shollo, A. (2011). *Using Business Intelligence in IT Governance Decision Making. Governance and Sustainability in Information Systems.*

Su, S. I., & Chiong, R. (2011). Business Intelligence. In Encyclopedia of Knowledge Management (pp. 72-80). doi:10.4018/978-1-59904-931-1.ch008

Turban, E., Sharda, R., & Delen, D. (2010). *Decision Support and Business Intelligence Systems* (9th ed.). Prentice Hall.

Turban, E., Sharda, R., Delen, D., & King, D. (2010). *Business Intelligence* (2nd ed.). Prentice Hall.

Wise, L. (2012). *Using Open Source Platforms for Business Intelligence: Avoid Pitfalls and Maximize ROI* (1st ed.). Morgan Kaufmann.

KEY TERMS AND DEFINITIONS

Big Data: Big Data has four distinct characteristics (so called 4V features): the data volume is huge (Volume); the data type is diverse meaning a mixture of structured data, semi-structured data and unstructured data (Variety); the streaming data is very high (Velocity); and uncertain or imprecise data (Veracity).

BI Tools: Represents the tools and systems that play a key role in the strategic planning process of the organization. These systems allow a company to gather, store, access and analyze corporate data to aid in decision-making. Generally, these systems will illustrate business intelligence in the areas of customer profiling, customer support, market research, market segmentation, product profitability, statistical analysis, and inventory and distribution analysis to name a few.

Business Intelligence: Business intelligence is a broad category of applications and technologies for gathering, storing, analyzing, and providing access to data to help enterprise users make better business decisions. BI applications include the activities of decision support systems, query and reporting, online analytical processing (OLAP), statistical analysis, forecasting, and data mining. BI refers to a management philosophy and tool that help organizations to manage and refine business information to make effective decisions.

Cloud: Cloud consist in a distributed environment that uses resource virtualization to unify and abstract resource management and provide several high performance, available and redundant services in a pay-as-you-go model that allows cloud service provider's clients not to worry about IT concerns and focus mainly in their business needs.

Data Warehousing: Analytical databases focused on providing decision support information and deriving business intelligence for enterprises. According to Kimball definition, "a data warehouse is a copy of transaction data specifically structured for query and analysis". This is a functional view of a data warehouse. Typically, a data warehouse is a massive database (housed on a cluster of servers, or a mini or mainframe computer) serving as a centralized repository of all data generated by all departments and units of a large organization. Advanced data mining software is required to extract meaningful information from a data warehouse.

Decision Support Systems (DSS): Decision Support Systems are a specific class of computerized information system that supports business and organizational decision-making activities. A properly designed DSS is an interactive software-based system intended to help decision makers compile useful information from raw data, documents, personal knowledge, and/or business models to identify and solve problems and make decisions.

Infrastructure as a Service (IaaS): Which allow clients to purchase resources on demand; Platform as a Service (PaaS) where platform instances are hired as a service, trusting the cloud provider to maintain servers; Software as a Service (SaaS), which is used to deploy software in a scalable and available way; Big Data as a Service – a specification of PaaS – that provides cloud's customers a way to store, manage and process big volumes of data; Analytics and Business Intelligence as a Service (AaaS and BIaaS) enables users to mine data to find interesting patterns, correlations and trends.

Information and Communications Technology (ICT): ICT refers to technologies that provide access to information through telecommunications. It is similar to Information Technology (IT), but focuses primarily on communication technologies. This includes the Internet, wireless networks, cell phones, and other communication mediums. In the past few decades, information and communication technologies have provided society with a vast array of new communication capabilities. For example, people can communicate in real-time with others in different countries using technologies such as instant messaging, voice over IP (VoIP), and video-conferencing.

Information Technology (IT): set of tools, processes, and methodologies (such as coding/programming, data communications, data conversion, storage and retrieval, systems analysis and design, systems control) and associated equipment employed to collect, process, and present information. In broad terms, IT also includes office automation, multimedia, and telecommunications. It refers to anything related to computing technology, such as networking, hardware, software, the Internet, or the people that work with these technologies. Many companies now have IT departments for managing the computers, networks, and other technical areas of their businesses. IT jobs include computer programming, network administration, computer engineering, Web development, technical support, and many other related occupations. Since we live in the "information age," information technology has become a part of our everyday lives.

Open Source: Open source doesn't just mean access to the source code. The distribution terms of open-source software must comply with the following criteria: 1. Free Redistribution; 2. Source Code; 3. Derived Works; 4. Integrity of The Author's Source Code; 5. No Discrimination Against Persons or Groups; 6. No Discrimination Against Fields of Endeavor; 7. Distribution of License; 8. License Must Not Be Specific to a Product; 9. License Must Not Restrict Other Software; 10. License Must Be Technology-Neutral. For the complete definition see http://opensource.org/docs/osd.

Open Source Software (OSS): Open source software refers to software that is developed, tested, or improved through public collaboration and distributed with the idea that the must be shared with others, ensuring an open future collaboration. The collaborative experience of many developers, especially those in the academic environment, in developing various versions of the UNIX operating system, Richard Stallman's idea of Free Software Foundation, and the desire of users to freely choose among a number of products - all of these led to the Open Source movement and the approach to developing and distributing programs as open source software.

Chapter 7
Essential E Learning Tools, Techniques and Open CourseWare for E Learners and Trainers

Sarika Sawant
SHPT School of Library Science, SNDT Women's University, India

ABSTRACT

E-learning includes several types of media that deliver text, audio, images, animation, and streaming video, and includes technology applications and processes such as audio or video tape, satellite TV, CD-ROM, and computer-based learning, as well as local intranet/extranet and web-based learning. E learning is a learner-friendly mode of learning, offering alternative, self-paced and personalised ways of studying. The present chapter explains the synchronous and asynchronous mode of e learning with its features. It also defines and summarises the impact of open source software on teaching and learning process. The numerous open source e learning tools are discussed with examples such as Open source LMS, Open source authoring tools, Open source audio editing software, Open source social bookmarking tools, Open source CMS etc. It also throws light on free e learning tools useful in e learning such as Slideshare, Youtube, Wikis, RSS, Wordpress etc. The search engines especially for academic purpose and for Open CourseWear are also discussed in the chapter. It identifies open courseware around the world spanning various subjects. The chapter concludes with e learning initiatives in India.

E LEARNING: DEFINITION AND ITS TYPES

E – learning concept has revolutionarised education system. E-learning includes several types of media that deliver text, audio, images, animation, and streaming video, and includes technology applications and processes such as audio or video tape, satellite TV, CD-ROM, and computer-based learning, as well as local intranet/extranet and web-based learning (Wikipedia, 2014). E- learning is commonly referred to the intentional use of networked information and communications technology in teaching and learning.

DOI: 10.4018/978-1-5225-0556-3.ch007

E learning term is used interchangeably with the number of other terms. They include online learning, virtual learning, distributed learning, network and web based learning. (Sawant, 2013). Fundamentally, they all refer to educational processes that utilize information and communications technology to mediate asynchronous as well as synchronous mode of learning and teaching activities. In this e learning environment, the web is used as the medium for communication, collaboration, content hosting, and assessments. E learners could be a kid, college goers or adult.

In the synchronous learning model (Online model), the students can attend 'live' lectures at the scheduled hour from wherever they are irrespective of their location forming a virtual classroom. The lectures by the teacher are accessible to all registered students over the net. A synchronous learning includes text-based conferencing, and one or two-way audio and videoconferencing. But due to bandwidth constraints, these do not normally broadcast live video feed of the faculty; instead they restrict to audio and slides, and in some cases a whiteboard with live marking. The second method is asynchronous (Offline model) where the notion of classroom lectures is not included. They may be held in the traditional way in addition to the elearning setup (generally called blended learning). The typical example of this kind of activity include on-line discussions via electronic mailing lists.

The asynchronous mode of elearning generally offers the following facilities.

1. Teacher can post study material – downloaded files, web links, own notes and articles, videos, etc – for anytime anywhere access by the students. It is generally possible to check if and when students have accessed these materials.
2. Announcements and calendar online
3. Assignment posting, submission, and evaluation with feedback can be done online. Rich control is often possible to restrict what can be submitted and when.
4. Encourage student-student interaction, discussion of issues, etc. through discussion boards and chats.
5. Keeping track of student performance and grades.

To achieve the asynchronous learning requires Learning Management System (LMS). An LMS is an integrated software environment supporting all these functionalities along with some mechanism for student enrolment into courses, general user management (including administrator, teacher, and student) and some important system functions like backup and restore.

WHAT IS OPEN SOURCE SOFTWARE?

The Open Source Initiative ("OSI") defines Open Source as software providing the following rights and obligations:

1. **Unrestricted Distribution:** No royalty or other fee imposed upon redistribution.
2. **Source Code Distribution:** Availability of the source code of of the entire open source product
3. **Modifications:** Right to create modifications and derivative works.
4. **Author's Source Code Integrity:** May require modified versions to be distributed as the original version plus patches.

5. **No Personal Discrimination:** No discrimination against persons or groups.
6. **No Restriction On Application:** No discrimination against fields of endeavor or purpose.
7. **License Distribution:** All rights granted must flow through to/with redistributed versions.
8. **License Must Not Be Product-Specific:** The license applies to the program as a whole and each of its components.
9. **No Restriction On Other Software:** The license must not restrict other software, thus permitting the distribution of open source and closed source software together (Webbink, 2003).
10. **Technology Neutrality.** Licenses should not be issued on the basis of the specific technology involved (Lakhan & Jhunjhunwala, 2008).

OPEN SOURCE APPLICATIONS AND ITS IMPACT ON TEACHING AND LEARNING

Open source e learning software's has emerged as a viable solution to many school, college and university administrators, particularly universities. The advantages of use of open source e learning software's are as follows:

- **Free Availability:** Most universities annually pay large sums to software companies to use their products, but open source licenses are free. For example colleges the and universities pay to Microsoft for each license copy of operating system as well as office. But because of advent of Linux operating system and Open office which are freely available can cut the cost of annual subscription at a huge level.
- **Documentation:** All help and documentation required to use and run the open source software is available on the respective software's site. So no need to purchase books or manuals to use such software's. As well as these software's communities provide continuous help in a form of FAQ or posting query on their blogs with immediate reply.
- **Flexibility:** Open source products are customizable and can involve third parties. New features and tools can be imported from the open source community.
- **Service:** The huge collaborative network of the open source community minimizes, although it does not eliminate, the risk of discontinued service. Volunteer help is available through open source support systems such as forums.
- **Continuous Improvement:** Extensive collaboration ensures that software products keep improving. Programmers from different institutions and organizations, along with volunteers, contribute freely to projects.
- **Tax Benefits:** Governments of many countries have implemented tax-exemption policies to boost open source projects, although the governmental role in promoting open source software is controversial. It has not yet been implemented in India but definitely going for open source software's remove the VAT and other taxes that every institution has to pay after every purchase of such material. In India for educational purchase octri charges are waved on one condition if such a certificate is issued.

E learning tools can be divided into two types according to its availability

- Open source e learning tools whose source code is available free of cost on their websites
- Free e elearning tools without source code available freely on Internet.

OPEN SOURCE E-LEARNING TOOLS

Open Source LMS

Moodle (https://moodle.org/)

Moodle (Modular Object-Oriented Dynamic Learning Environment) Moodle is a Course Management System (CMS), also known as a Learning Management System (LMS) or a Virtual Learning Environment (VLE). It is an Open Source e-learning web application that educators can use to create effective online learning sites.

There are a range of potential applications of Moodle technology in education and training, delivery of learning materials and collaboration.

The basic features of Moodle include tools for creating resources and activities. These in turn provide the teacher managing the course various useful options. The Resources tab offers the teacher a choice of creating labels which are simply headings for each topic or week, creating text pages or web pages with a combination of text, images and links. Creating links to files or web sites/pages which can link to podcasts, videos and other files, creating directories which are folders one creates with a multitude of different files to be accessed by students or staff.

Another useful and collaborative section is the Activities tab which includes: assignments, chat, choice (one question with a choice of answers – answers are logged so statistics can be deducted), database which is a table created by the teacher and which is filled in by the students creating a database. Forum where everyone can post in response to discussion threads, glossary is a type of dictionary created by the teacher with terms used and their meanings.

Glossaries can also be an enjoyable, collaborative activity as well as a teaching tool. Lessons offer the flexibility of a web page, the interactivity of a quiz and branching capabilities. Quiz enables the creation of various types of quizzes, survey is a questionnaire which gathers feedback from students, wiki is a web page edited collaboratively.

Claroline (http://www.claroline.net/)

Claroline is a collaborative eLearning and eWorking platform (Learning Management System) released under the GPL Open Source license. It allows hundreds of organizations worldwide ranging from universities to schools and from companies to associations to create and administer courses and collaboration spaces over the web. The platform is used in more than 100 countries and is available in 35 languages. The management is simple, intuitive and requires no special skills.

Claroline is compatible with GNU/Linux, Mac OS and Microsoft Windows. It is based on open-source technologies like PHP and MySQL.

The Claroline platform is organized around the concept of space associated to a course or a pedagogical activity. Each course space provides a list of tools enabling the teacher to:

- Write a course description
- Publish documents in any format (text, PDF, HTML, video, etc...)
- Administer public or private forums
- Create learning paths (compatible with SCORM)
- Create groups of users
- Compose exercises (compatible with IMS / QTI standard 2)
- Structure an agenda with tasks and deadlines
- Post notifications (also by email)
- Propose home work to make online
- View statistics of attendance and completion exercises
- Use the wiki to write collaborative documents

Open Source Authoring Tool

Course Builder (https://code.google.com/p/course-builder/)

Course Builder contains software and instructions for presenting the course material, which can include lessons, student activities, and assessments. It also contains instructions for using other Google products to create a course community and to evaluate the effectiveness of the course. To use Course Builder, one should have some technical skills at the level of a web master. In particular, should have some familiarity with HTML and JavaScript.

eXe (http://exelearning.org/)

It is a Open Source authoring application to assist teachers and academics in the publishing of web content without the need to become proficient in HTML or XML markup. Resources authored in eXe can be exported in IMS Content Package, SCORM 1.2, or IMS Common Cartridge formats or as simple self-contained web pages.

Open Source Audio/Video Editing Software

Audacity (http://audacity.sourceforge.net/about/)

Audacity is a free, easy-to-use and multilingual audio editor and recorder for Windows, Mac OS X, GNU/Linux and other operating systems. You can use Audacity to:

- Record live audio.
- Convert tapes and records into digital recordings or CDs.
- Edit Ogg Vorbis, MP3, WAV or AIFF sound files.
- Cut, copy, splice or mix sounds together.
- Change the speed or pitch of a recording.

Matterhorn (http://opencast.org/matterhorn/)

Matterhorn is a free, open-source platform to support the management of educational audio and video content. Institutions use the Matterhorn to produce lecture recordings, manage existing video, serve designated distribution channels, and provide user interfaces to engage students with educational videos.

Open Source Social Bookmarking Tool

Scuttle (http://en.wikipedia.org/wiki/Scuttle)

Scuttle is a PHP/MySQL-based open source social bookmarking application. It contains code from other PHP-based projects such as Drupal and jQuery.

Scuttle offers the same functionality as most of the social bookmarking websites such as tagging, RSS, multiple languages and security settings (public and private). It also supports bookmark imports from delicious and the delicious API, which means that all programs or widgets might also work. Backups are available via XML or MySQL Backend. It lacks an administrator backend, although there is one commercially available called *"Scuttle Plus"*. The more advanced *semantic scuttle* provides anti-spam protection structured tags and collaborative tag description.

Open Source Wikis: Server Software

Twiki (http://twiki.org/)

It is a flexible, powerful, and easy to use enterprise wiki, enterprise collaboration platform, and web application platform. It is a structured Wiki, typically used to run a project development space, a document management system, a knowledge base, or any other groupware tool, on an intranet, extranet or the Internet. Users without programming skills can create web applications.

Open Source CMS

Joomla (http://www.joomla.org/)

Joomla is an award-winning content management system (CMS), which enables to build Web sites and powerful online applications. Many aspects, including its ease-of-use and extensibility, have made Joomla the most popular Web site software available. Joomla is used all over the world to power Web sites of all shapes and sizes. For example:

- Corporate intranets and extranets
- Corporate web tools or portals
- Online magazines, newspapers, and publications
- E-commerce and online reservations
- Government applications
- Small business Web sites
- Non-profit and organizational Web sites

- Community-based portals
- School and church Web sites
- Personal or family homepages

Web Conferencing Tools

BigBlueButton - (Web Conferencing) (http://www.bigbluebutton.org/)

BigBlueButton is built for Higher Education. It enables universities and colleges to deliver a high-quality learning experience to remote students. The project is hosted at Google. BigBlueButton is an active open source project that focuses on usability, modularity, and clean design — both for the user and the developer BigBlueButton is built by combining over fourteen open source components.

OpenMeetings(https://code.google.com/p/openmeetings/)

OpenMeetings is a free browser-based software that allows one to set up instantly a conference in the Web. One can use microphone or webcam, share documents on a white board, share screen or record meetings. It is available as hosted service or just download and install a package on the server with no limitations in usage or users.

Desktop Publishing Tools

Open Source Office Suite: OpenOffice (http://www.openoffice.org/)

It is an open source Office suite to download and is a great alternative to MS Office. It contains word processing, presentation, spreadsheet and database software and runs on both Macs and PCs. Two particular features are

- can convert word processed documents into PDFs within it, and
- can convert OO presentations into Flash-based versions, which provides a much more effective way of distributing them. So a very useful tool to create job aids or presentations.

LibreOffice (http://www.libreoffice.org/)

LibreOffice is a powerful office suite; its clean interface and powerful tools let you unleash your creativity and grow your productivity. LibreOffice embeds several applications that make it the most powerful Free & Open Source Office suite on the market: Writer, the word processor, Calc, the spreadsheet application, Impress, the presentation engine, Draw, our drawing and flowcharting application, Base, our database and database frontend, and Math for editing mathematics.

PDFCreator (http://sourceforge.net/projects/pdfcreator/)

Open source desktop application that creates PDFs from any Windows program. It has following features

- Convert your Documents to PDF, JPG, PNG, TIF and more
- Merge multiple documents to one file
- Profiles make frequently used settings available with one click
- Compress and resize images to reduce the file size
- Encrypt your PDFs with AES and protect them with a password

E-Book Management

calibre (http://calibre-ebook.com/)

calibre is a free and open source e-book library management application developed by users of e-books for users of e-books. It has a cornucopia of features divided into the following main categories:

- Library Management
- E-book conversion
- Syncing to e-book reader devices
- Downloading news from the web and converting it into e-book form
- Comprehensive e-book viewer
- Content server for online access to your book collection
- E-book editor for the major e-book formats

E-Portfolio

An ePorfolio allows for building in reflective activities for learners and staff, through blog functions and the creation of 'Critical incident diaries' in which users reflect on their learning and experiences over a given period or activity.

Mahara (https://mahara.org)

Mahara is an open source ePortfolio and social networking web application created by the government of New Zealand. It provides users with tools to create and maintain a digital portfolio of their learning, and social networking features to allow users to interact with each other. Mahara content management system provides users with blogs, a resume builder, a file manager and a view creator - a tool to help users create arrangements of their content in a particular way for others to see. It can also be easily integrated with different CMS, CRM and customized systems. Mahara also features interoperability with the Moodle LMS

Classroom Management

iTALK (http://italc.sourceforge.net/)

iTALC is a nd powerful didactical tool for teachers. It lets you view and control other computers in your network in several ways. It supports Linux and Windows XP, Vista and 7 and it even can be used transparently in mixed environments!

iTALC has been designed for usage in school. Therefore it offers a lot of possibilities to teachers, such as

- See what's going on in computer-labs by using overview mode and make snapshots
- Remote control computers to support and help other people
- Show a demo (either in fullscreen or in a window) - the teacher's screen is shown on all student's computers in realtime
- Lock workstations for moving undivided attention to teacher
- Send text messages to students
- Powering on/off and rebooting computers per remote
- Remote logon and logoff and remote execution of arbitrary commands/scripts
- Home schooling - iTALC's network-technology is not restricted to a subnet and therefore students at home can join lessons via VPN-connections just by installing iTALC client

Furthermore, iTALC is optimized for usage on multi-core systems (by making heavy use of threads). No matter how many cores you have, iTALC can make use of all of them.

Reading Lists

LORLS(http://blog.lboro.ac.uk/)

Loughborough Online Reading List System (LORLS) is a resource/reading list management system developed by the Systems Team at Loughborough University Library and made available as open source. It enables students to access reading lists and easily check availability of recommended resources, allows appropriate staff to create and maintain lists and informs the Library of changes made to lists to support collection development.

Tools for Religious Studies

The SWORD Project (http://www.crosswire.org/sword)

The SWORD Project is the CrossWire Bible Society's free Bible software project. Its purpose is to create cross-platform open-source tools-- covered by the GNU General Public License-- that allow programmers and Bible societies to write new Bible software more quickly and easily. They also create Bible study software for all readers, students, scholars, and translators of the Bible, and have a growing collection of over 200 texts in over 50 languages.

Zekr Qur'an (http://zekr.org/quran/)

Zekr Qur'an is a cross-platform tool for Qur'an study

Film MEDIA PRODUCTION

Kdenlive (https://kdenlive.org)

Kdenlive is a free open-source video editor for GNU/Linux and FreeBSD, which supports DV, AVCHD and HDV editing. It helps to mix different media without prior import & Support for a wide range of codecs and formats.

Interactive Content Creation

Xerte(http://www.nottingham.ac.uk/xerte/)

The Xerte Project provides a suite of award-winning open-source tools for elearning developers and content authors producing interactive learning materials including multimedia content and interactive exercises.

Interactive Whiteboard Software

Open-Sankoré (http://open-sankore.org/)

The Open-Sankoré program is an interactive, free, and Open-Source digital teaching program with high value added. In addition to being able to comment, draw, and highlight, the Open-Sankoré program gives you the option of enriching the course content by importing flash animations, images, audio, videos, or by including existing .pdf or .ppt documents.

Teachers can captivate audience by embedding dynamic content into their course: apps from widgets, Wikipedia, or Google Maps).

The Open-Sankoré program also offers tools for the different phases of a lesson: one can display only the essential part, with appropriate tools such as dynamic screen management or infinite zoom, etc.

Lastly, one can share the resources by publishing them in .PDF document form or as podcasts, or on the web by exporting them to the http://planete.sankore.org portal.

Open Source Referencing Tools

Zotero (http://www.zotero.org/)

Zotero is free, open source bibliographic software. It is a research tool for managing online references developed by the Center for History and New Media at George Mason University, Zotero is a Firefox extension that provides users with automated access to bibliographic information for resources viewed online. Online researchers can quickly and easily gather the information they will need later to review and cite references and create bibliographies. Zotero includes features to manage sources, and users can also manually enter sources. The result is a centralized location for gathering and storing references, significantly streamlining the research process.

FREE E LEARNING TOOLS

There are plenty of free e learning tools such as slideshare, youtube, blogs, e mails, mailing lists, news groups, bulletin boards, instant messaging, online polling, quizmakers etc. Few important e learning tools general and subject wise are described below.

Presentation Hosting Site

Slideshare (http://www.slideshare.net/)

This is a free service to host presentations (created with PowerPoint, OpenOffice Impress or Keynote). It also supports slidecasting, which means teacher/student can synchronise an audio file with a set of slides. It's also a great source of presentations that might be of use to the organisation. There is need to go to Slideshare to view a presentation or they can be embedded in your own blog, web or wiki page.

Video-Sharing Site

YouTube (http://www.youtube.com/)

This is a free online video streaming service. You will need a device to create your video, e.g. a camcorder, digital camera or webcam. You then copy your video to your computer and upload it to YouTube, where, if you prefer, you can make it "private" only to be viewed by those you select. Then, like Slideshare, people can either view your videos directly in YouTube or you can embed them in your web, blog or wiki page.

Photosharing Site

Flickr (https://www.flickr.com/)

Flickr is the best way to store, sort, search and share photos online with limit of 1 Terabyte of online storage. With a Flickr account, one can upload photos up to 200MB in size, or videos of up to 1GB for each video. One can keep photo album Public, Visible to friends, Visible to family, or Private.

Blogging

WordPress (http://wordpress.com/)

This is free blogging software. It is available both as a online service or as open source software to download or install on internal servers. If you opt for the online service, users can set up either public or private blogs where they can share information about their activities for others in the organisation, e.g. R&D might want to share information about products under development. It is important tool for information sharing.

Wiki Hosting Platform

Wikis (http://www.wikispaces.com/)

Wikis are websites where visitors can not only read content but also add their own content or edit the content added by others through a web browser. Both wikis and blogs are web browser technologies that greatly reduce technical barriers to web content creation. Both provide an editable and interactive web environment where visitors can easily create and contribute online. A primary goal of many wikis is to encourage many authors to participate. Everyone can contribute by adding, changing or commenting on the content. The collaborative nature of wikis promotes reflective, collaborative and constructive learning as they enact knowledge building with and for others, with the focus being on the community rather than on the individual learner. (Arezel Online, n.d.)

Online Collaboration and Sharing

Podio (https://students.podio.com/)

Podio makes it easy to work in real-time online with classmates to coordinate study groups, work on class projects, and organize research. You'll work more effectively, together.

RSS Reader

Google Reader (http://www.google.com/reader/view/)

The term RSS has three different meanings RDF (resource document frame work) site summary, rich site summary or really simple syndication RSS uses XML- formatted file to push content to subscribers. Each time the RSS file is updated, the subscriber is notified that new contents are available for viewing. There are several advantages for users in subscribing to RSS feeds.

Online Office Suite

Google Docs/Drive (www.google.com/docs)

Google Docs is a hosted service where you can create, store and share documents, spreadsheets and presentations and online forms. You can work on your own or collaboratively. You can also import docs from MS Office and Open Office.

Online Noticeboard

Padlet (https://padlet.com/)

It is an online notice board maker. It offers following features such as Personal note taking, To-do lists, Party Invitations, Feedback, Collection, Wishing people on occasions, like birthdays, anniversaries etc.

Collaborative Authoring Tool

TypeWith.me (www.typewithme.com)

Formally known as Etherpad, this collaborative authoring tool allows multiple people to create and edit a single document in real time. Files can be exported as Microsoft Word, PDF, HTML.

Conference Alert

Lanyrd.com (http://lanyrd.com/)

Most events on Lanyrd have at least one speaker, but professional networking events are appropriated as well. You can add conferences, workshops, unconferences, evening events with talks, conventions, trade shows and so forth. The site is geared towards knowledge sharing events with sessions and participants of some sort

Some more examples are as follows

http://conferencehound.com/
http://www.conferensum.com/Proceedings
http://www.conferencealerts.com/

Editing Image

GIMP (http://www.gimp.org/)

GIMP is an acronym for GNU Image Manipulation Program. It is a freely distributed program for tasks such as photo retouching, image composition and image authoring

Posters and Slides

F1000Posters (http://f1000.com/)

It is an open access poster repository, provides a permanent, structured environment for the deposition of posters as well as a trustworthy venue for ongoing discussion and development of the information being presented.

Online Storage and Sharing

4shared (http://www.4shared.com/)

4shared is a free online file-sharing service that provides storage for music, video and photo files. Upon registering for an account 4shared will provide users with 10-GB of online storage space.

Dropbox (www.dropbox.com)

Dropbox is an online storage site for all your photos, docs, videos, and files. Anything one add to Dropbox will automatically show up on all computers, phones and even the Dropbox website — so one can access stuff from anywhere. It come with free 2GB basic account.

Animation and Comic Strips

Blabberize (http://blabberize.com/)

It allows one to quickly animate any image to make it talk, by simply adding audio and specifying the bottom lip or jaw section. Within minutes one can have a talking photo and the novelty factor of this will never wear thin for students. They absolutely love Blabberize. Make a famous person speak, give an animal a voice, even add a mouth to an inanimate object like a hamburger and discuss its nutritional value.

Comic Master (https://www.comicmastersonline.com/)

A free web application teaching tool that allows one to easily create comics (graphic novels) online. Thought and speech bubbles, props, special effects, and caption boxes are easily added with a simple click-and-drag.

3DProjects

Blender (http://www.blender.org/)

Blender is a free and open source 3D animation suite. It supports the entirety of the 3D pipeline—modeling, rigging, animation, simulation, rendering, compositing and motion tracking, even video editing and game creation. Blender is cross platform and runs equally well on Linux, Windows and Macintosh computers. Its interface uses OpenGL to provide a consistent experience. As a community-driven project, it is available under the GNU General Public License (GPL)

Language Learning Tools

Babbel (http://www.babbel.com/)

It is a interactive online language courses to improve your grammar, vocabulary and pronunciation skills Babbel gives everything one need to speak, write, and understand a new language. Each lesson only takes a few minutes and strengthens ones language skills according to themes and topics that are chosen. Babbel listens, speak and helps to correct pronunciation, and the Review Manager makes sure that everything that you learn sticks in your memory.

Lingro (http://lingro.com/)

A unique website that helps language learners read foreign web pages or documents and build their vocabulary at the same time.

Games, Quizzes, and Educational Activities

Gnowledge (http://www.gnowledge.com/)

Teacher can create his/her own test paper on Gnowledge that students can take. These test papers last forever, so teacher can use it for your classes in the future too. Gnowledge marks and records test papers automatically. Teacher share tests with students, peers and children. Help them improve their grades and accelerate their academic prowess and growth. Students can Practice as much as they like. Randomized question and answer orders allow themto repeat the same tests over and over again, promoting understanding over rote memorization.

Hot Potatoes (http://hotpot.uvic.ca/)

The Hot Potatoes suite includes six applications, enabling you to create interactive multiple-choice, short-answer, jumbled-sentence, crossword, matching/ordering and gap-fill exercises for the World Wide Web. Hot Potatoes is freeware, and anyone may use it for any purpose or project you like.

Classtools (http://www.classtools.net/)

Create free educational games, quizzes, activities and diagrams in seconds.One can host them on own blog, website or intranet. No signup, no passwords, no charge is required.

Mathematics Applications

GNU Octave (https://www.gnu.org/)

GNU Octave is a high-level interpreted language, primarily intended for numerical computations. It provides capabilities for the numerical solution of linear and nonlinear problems, and for performing other numerical experiments. It also provides extensive graphics capabilities for data visualization and manipulation. Octave is normally used through its interactive command line interface, but it can also be used to write non-interactive programs. The Octave language is quite similar to Matlab so that most programs are easily portable. Octave is distributed under the terms of the GNU General Public License.

Maxima (http://maxima.sourceforge.net/)

Maxima allows to manipulate symbolic and numerical expressions, including differentiation, integration, Taylor series, Laplace transforms, ordinary differential equations, systems of linear equations, polynomials, and so on. Maxima yields high precision numeric results by using exact fractions, arbitrary precision integers, and arbitrarily precision floating point numbers. It can plot functions and data in two and three dimensions. It is the only system based on that effort still publicly available and with an active user community, thanks to its open source nature.

YACAS(http://yacas.sourceforge.net/)

YACAS is an easy to use, general purpose Computer Algebra System, a program for symbolic manipulation of mathematical expressions. It uses its own programming language designed for symbolic as well as arbitrary-precision numerical computations. The system has a library of scripts that implement many of the symbolic algebra operations; new algorithms can be easily added to the library. YACAS comes with extensive documentation (hundreds of pages) covering the scripting language, the functionality that is already implemented in the system, and the algorithms we used.

Statistical Applications

PSPP (https://www.gnu.org/software/pspp/)

PSPP is a stable and reliable application. It can perform descriptive statistics, T-tests, anova, linear and logistic regression, measures of association, cluster analysis, reliability and factor analysis, non-parametric tests and more. Its backend is designed to perform its analyses as fast as possible, regardless of the size of the input data. You can use PSPP with its graphical interface or the more traditional syntax commands.

A brief list of some of the PSPP's features follows below.

- Support for over 1 billion cases.
- Support for over 1 billion variables.
- Syntax and data files which are compatible with those of SPSS.
- A choice of terminal or graphical user interface.
- A choice of text, postscript, pdf, opendocument or html output formats.
- Inter-operability with Gnumeric, LibreOffice, OpenOffice.Org and other free software.
- Easy data import from spreadsheets, text files and database sources.
- The capability to open, analyse and edit two or more datasets concurrently. They can also be merged, joined or concatenated.
- A user interface supporting all common character sets and which has been translated to multiple languages.
- Fast statistical procedures, even on very large data sets.
- No license fees.
- No expiration period.
- No unethical "end user license agreements".
- A fully indexed user manual.
- Freedom ensured; It is licensed under the GPLv3 or later.
- Portability; Runs on many different computers and many different operating systems

Academic Search Engines

Google Scholar (https://scholar.google/)

Google Scholar provides a simple way to broadly search for scholarly literature. From one place, you can search across many disciplines and sources: articles, theses, books, abstracts and court opinions, from academic publishers, professional societies, online repositories, universities and other web sites. Google Scholar helps you find relevant work across the world of scholarly research.

ERIC (http://eric.ed.gov/)

ERIC - the Education Resources Information Center - is an online digital library of education research and information. ERIC is sponsored by the Institute of Education Sciences (IES) of the U.S. Department of Education. ERIC provides ready access to education literature to support the use of educational research and information to improve practice in learning, teaching, educational decision-making, and research.

BASE (http://www.base-search.net/)

BASE is one of the world's most voluminous search engines especially for academic open access web resources. BASE is operated by Bielefeld University Library. As the open access movement grows and prospers, more and more repository servers come into being which use the "Open Archives Initiative Protocol for Metadata Harvesting" (OAI-PMH) for providing their contents. BASE collects, normalises, and indexes these data. BASE provides more than 70 million documents from more than 3,000 sources. One can access the full texts of about 70% of the indexed documents. The index is continuously enhanced by integrating further OAI sources as well as local sources.

Open CourseWare (OCW)

OCW is an open and a free publication of formal course materials through the Internet. Course material includes Syllabus, Calendar, Lecture Notes. Other basic components such as Readings, Assignments, Exams. As well as recently Lecture Video or Audio (including pod casting) . While OCW initiatives typically do not provide a degree, credit, certification, or access to instructors, the materials are made available, for free, under open licenses for use and adaption by educators and learners around the world (UCI OpenCourseWare Project).

NPTEL (http://nptel.ac.in/)

NPTEL India (National Programme on Technology Enhanced Learning) provides E-learning through online Web and Video courses in Engineering, Science and humanities streams. The mission of NPTEL is to enhance the quality of engineering education in the country by providing free online courseware for more than 1100 courses.

Japan Opencourseware Consortium (JOCW) (http://www.jocw.jp/)

JOCW is a consortium of Japanese universities which provide OCW contents and activities in Japan. OCW is an open free publication of formal course materials of universities on the Internet.

Utah State OpenCourseWare (http://ocw.usu.edu/)

Utah State OpenCourseWare is a collection of educational material used in our formal campus courses, and seeks to provide people around the world with an opportunity to access high quality learning opportunities. More than 50 course materials are available. *National Science Digital Library* (https://nsdl. oercommons.org/)

National Science Digital Library provides high quality online educational resources for teaching and learning, with current emphasis on the sciences, technology, engineering, and mathematics (STEM) disciplines—both formal and informal, institutional and individual, in local, state, national, and international educational settings. The NSDL collection contains structured descriptive information (metadata) about web-based educational resources held on other sites by their providers. These providers have contribute this metadata to NSDL for organized search and open access to educational resources via this website and its services. Most resources in the library adhere to principles of Open Educational Resource (OER) access, although some resources are restricted to provider site membership, or may have a cost associated with them (indicated in the full record of the resource).

Open Learning Initiative (http://oli.cmu.edu/)

The Open Learning Initiative (OLI) is a grant-funded group at Carnegie Mellon University, offering innovative online courses to anyone who wants to learn or teach. Their aim is to create high-quality courses and contribute original research to improve learning and transform higher education. It offers more than 25 open and free courses and course materials.

Webcast.berkeley (http://webcast.berkeley.edu/)

Webcast.berkeley is the campus program for recording and publishing course and campus events for students and learners around the globe. Audio and video recordings of class lectures and special events are processed and made available to viewers, typically through UC Berkeley's YouTube and iTunes U distribution channels (though instructors can request that their lectures be viewable only to their students). The webcast.berkeley program leverages technology to lower the overall cost of production and distribution, and make it easy for faculty to webcast their courses. It offers course materials of more than 100 courses.

UCI OpenCourseWare (http://ocw.uci.edu/)

The University of California, Irvine's OCW is a web-based repository of various UC Irvine courses and video lectures from UC Irvine faculty, seminar participants, and instructional staff. While the great majority of courses are drawn from graduate, undergraduate, and continuing education programs, some were originally produced under grant funding to serve specific needs in California and elsewhere. UC

Irvine's OCW is open and available to the world for free. The University launched its OpenCourseWare initiative in November 2006. Since then, it has rapidly grown to become one of the premiere sites in the United States. Today, its YouTube channel, is viewed more than a million minutes per month. Around course materials of 40 courses and 100 lectures are available.

UMass Boston OCW(http://ocw.umb.edu/)

The University of Massachusetts Boston OCW is a free and open educational resource for faculty, students, and self-learners world wide. More than 50 course materials are available.

Open Yale Courses (http://oyc.yale.edu/)

Open Yale Courses (OYC) provides lectures and other materials from selected Yale College courses to the public free of charge via the Internet. The courses span the full range of liberal arts disciplines, including humanities, social sciences, and physical and biological sciences. More than 40 course materials are available.

U-Now(http://unow.nottingham.ac.uk/)

U-Now is The University of Nottingham's collection of open educational materials that have been openly licenced for anyone to use. The materials range from complete modules to smaller-scale learning objectives and highlight a range of teaching and learning activities from across the University. More than 240 course materials are available.

USQ OpenCourseWare(http://ocw.usq.edu.au/)

The University of Southern Queensland's OpenCourseWare (USQ OCW) provides access to free and open educational resources for faculty members, students, and self-learners throughout the world. More than 10 course materials are available.

Berklee Shares(http://www.berkleeshares.com/)

Berklee Shares, a collection of free music lessons from Berklee Online, the award-winning online extension school of Berklee College of Music. Watch, read, download, and share this free and open resource for the world's music community.

OEDb (http://oedb.org/)

Open Education Database is the most comprehensive collection of online college rankings and free courses anywhere online. We welcome learners of all levels to explore their interests and prepare for exciting new careers, build on existing foundations of education and experience, or just satisfy a craving to learn something completely new.

Open CourseWare (http://www.ocwconsortium.org)

Open CourseWare Consortium is a free and open digital publication of high quality educational materials, for colleges and universities, organized as courses contributed by over 200 higher education institutions. At present five LIS course materials are available from various universities.

Open.Michigan (https://open.umich.edu)

Open.Michigan is a University of Michigan initiative to create and share knowledge, resources, and research with the global learning community. Open.Michigan is committed to open content licensing and supporting the use, redistribution, and remixing of educational materials.

Their mission is directly related to Open Educational Resource (OER) production and publishing in some form. OER are learning materials and tools offered freely and openly for anyone to use and under some licenses to adapt, improve, and redistribute. There are about 5-6 courses and their course materials are available which are listed under the category-information (https://open.umich.edu/education/si)

Curruki (http://www.curriki.org/)

This site aims to distribute free curricula and educational resources to teachers around the world. Curriki encourages collaboration of diverse experiences from around the world to develop "best of breed" learning resources (peer-reviewed and classroom tested) and to create a culture of continuous improvement.

TU Delft OpenCourseWare (http://ocw.tudelft.nl/)

Delft University of Technology has joined the OpenCourseWare Consortium in offering the world free access to certain course content online. Currently content of more than 25 science and technology based course are available.

Stanford Engineering Everywhere (SEE) (http://see.stanford.edu/)

Stanford is offering some of its most popular engineering classes free of charge to students and educators around the world.

Harvard Medical School Open Courseware Initiative (http://mycourses.med.harvard.edu/)

Harvard Medical School Open Courseware Initiative is to exchange knowledge from the Harvard community of scholars to other academic institutions, prospective students, and the general public. Through the MyCourses initiative, Harvard has created a web-enabled distance learning environment for the four years of medical school.

MIT OpenCourseWare (OCW) (http://ocw.mit.edu/)

MIT OpenCourseWare (OCW) is a web-based publication of virtually all MIT course content. OCW is open and available to the world and is a permanent MIT activity. More than 200 course contents are available on their website.

Tufts OCW (http://ocw.tufts.edu/)

Tufts University is a leader in the Open Educational Resources (OER) movement, bringing access to educational content, tools, and infrastructure to educators, students, and self-learners. Approximately 60 course contents are available on their website.

Sofia Open Content Initiativ: (http://sofia.fhda.edu/)

The Sofia initiative is led by Foothill College's Learning Technology & Innovations program. There are about 8 course contents are available on their website.

JHSPH OpenCourseWare (http://ocw.jhsph.edu/)

OCW offers open materials and images from more than a hundred courses developed by the faculty of John Hopkins School of Public Health (JHSPH), the world's foremost institution of public health education and research.

Notre Dame OCW (http://ocw.nd.edu/)

It is a free and open educational resource for faculty, students, and self-learners throughout the world. There are about 54 course contents are available on their website.

Open Courseware Search Engines

Following search engines help to find more open educational course materials and resources.

Open Tapestry (http://www.opentapestry.com/)

Search for courses and other resources by keyword. Open Tapestry is all about discovering, adapting, and sharing learning resources, whether you're a teacher, an instructor, a professor, a corporate trainer, a learner, or just a curious mind

Open CourseWare Consortium (http://www.oeconsortium.org/)

The Open Education Consortium is a worldwide community of hundreds of higher education institutions and associated organizations committed to advancing open education and its impact on global education. It allows open education resources, tools and practices that employ a framework of open sharing to improve educational access and effectiveness worldwide.

DiscoverEd (http://wiki.creativecommons.org/)

DiscoverEd is a search prototype developed by Creative Commons to explore metadata enhanced search, specifically for OER.

E-LEARNING INITIATIVES IN INDIA

After realising the importance of e- learning in distance education the Indira Gandhi National Open University (IGNOU) and various state open universities in India are already testing its feasibility. Even the distance education departments of traditional universities are also working to use the e- learning for their distance learning programmes. VidyaOnline9 is one of such up-coming e- learning programme for the LIS education. It is a venture of Vidysagar University. Librarians Digital Library (LDL) developed by the DRTC (Documentation Training and Research Centre, Bangalore) provides digital resources to those interested in e- learning. (Chandwani, Lihitkar, & Anilkumar, 2010). LIS departments from the traditional universities in India are not far behind to introduce need-based, short-term e-learning courses. In fact SNDT Women's universities LIS dept has started 2 four credit online courses on school / children librarianship and Archives management in 2014.

The National Programme on Technology Enhanced Learning (NPTEL) is a project funded by the Ministry of Human Resource Development (MHRD). The operational objective of NPTEL is to make high quality learning material available to students of engineering institutions across the country by exploiting the advances in information and communication technology. Consortium for Educational Communication (CEC)(www.cec-ugc.org/) was set-up as a nodal agency at the national level to address the educational needs of the country through the use of electronic media. CEC has about more than 15000 educational video programmes in 50 subjects developed by different educational multimedia research centers spread across various universities and institutions across India. Virtual Learning Environment, Institute of Life-long Learning (ILLL) (www.vle.du.ac.in) is a unique and innovative initiative of the University of Delhi to provide Open Educational Resources (OER) to the teaching and learning community. VLE provides the courses in Commerce, Humanities and Social Sciences, History, Sciences, Interviews and Podcast. e-Contentof Fermentation Technology is a dedicated project for student of microbiology specifically in the area of industrial microbiology (Thakur, Kumar, Pallavi, 2013). e-PG Pathshala. is a project of MHRD, under its National Mission on Education through ICT (NME-ICT), which assigned work to the UGC for development of e-content in 77 subjects at postgraduate level. The content and its quality is the key component of education system. High quality, curriculum-based, interactive content in different subjects across all disciplines of social sciences, arts, fine arts & humanities, natural & mathematical sciences, linguistics and languages is being developed under this initiative.

CONCLUSION

There are plenty of open source as well as free e learning tools available on the web. It is a duty of every trainers/teacher to try to know and learn these applications. This can be used for the teaching in turn will enhance the learning process in students. It is true that no such customized training according to the subject is given to individual teachers but self orientation is the best practice in such a case. With available documentation, teachers can start to learn and implement in teaching to become real 21ˢᵗ century teacher. In today's' fast moving world one need to move on to the next level of teaching to enhance the learning process and achieve the goal of the profession. It is a demand to learn and flourish otherwise finish.

REFERENCES

Chandwani, A., Lihitkar, S., & Anilkumar, S. (2010). E-Learning Initiatives in India. In *Modern Practices in Library and Information Services*. Nagpur, India. Retrieved from http://eprints.rclis.org/15721/6/E-learning.pdf

Claroline. (2015). *Wikipedia.* Retrieved from http://en.wikipedia.org/wiki/Claroline

Johnson, J. (2014). Open Source Options For Education. Retrieved from http://oss-watch.ac.uk/resources/ossoptionseducation

Lakhan, S. E., & Jhunjhunwala, K. (2008, April–June). Open source softwares in education. *EDUCAUSE Quarterly, 31*(2). Retrieved from http://www.educause.edu/EDUCAUSE+Quarterly/EDUCAUSEQuarterlyMagazineVolum/OpenSourceSoftwareinEducation/162873

Naidu, S. (2006). E Learning: a guidebook of principles, procedures and practices. Commonwealth Educational Media Center for Asia. Retrieved from http://cemca.org/e-learning_guidebook.pdf

Natarajan, M. (2007). Blogs: A powerful tool for accessing information. *DESIDOC Bulletin of Information Technology, 27*(3). Retrieved from http://knowgate.niscair.res.in/jspui/bitstream/123456789/81/3/BLOGS_A%20POWERFUL%20TOOL.pdf

Online, A. (n.d.). Are traditional teaching methods still effective. retrieved February 18, 2014, from http://arzelonline.wordpress.com/2012/06/25/are-traditional-teachingmethods-still-effective/

Optimising technological tools in promoting LIS education. Education Essay. Retrieved from http://www.ukessays.com/essays/education/optimisingtechnological-tools-in-promoting-lis-education-education-essay.php

Sawant, S. (2013). E- learning: Use of Moodle by academic institutions in Mumbai.*Proceedings of International conference on redefining education: expanding horizons* (pp. 75-81).

Thakur, A, Kumar, A. & Pallavi. (2013). E-Learning: Initiatives in India. Open Journal of Education, 1(3), p. 61-69. Retrieved from http://manuscript.sciknow.org/uploads/oje/pub/oje_1363512069.pdf

UCI OpenCourseWare Project. (n. d.). A little info on my blog. Retrieved from http://sites.uci.edu/opencourseware/about/

Web 2.0 teaching tools. (2011). *Edjudo.com.* Retrieved from http://edjudo.com/web-2-0-teaching-tools-links#anchor14

Webbink, M. (2003). Understanding Open Source Software. Retrieved from http://www.groklaw.net/articlebasic.php?story=20031231092027900

E learning. (2014). Wikipedia. Retrieved from http://en.wikipedia.org/wiki/E-learning#cite_note-1

ADDITIONAL READING

Adeleke, A. A., & Olorunsola, R. (2010). ICT and library operations. *The Electronic Library*, 28(3), 453–462. doi:10.1108/02640471011052025

Bader, L., & Köttstorfer, M. (2013). E learning from a student's view with focus on Global Studies. *Multicultural Education & Technology Journal*, 7(2/3), 176–191. doi:10.1108/17504971311328062

Bennet, A., & Bennet, D. (2008). eLearning as energetic learning. *Vine*, 38(2), 206–220. doi:10.1108/03055720810889842

Berger, E. (2007). Podcasting in engineering education: A preliminary study of content, student attitudes, and impact. *Innovate: Journal of Online Education*, 4(1). Retrieved from http://www.innovateonline.info/index.php?view=article&id=426

Bracken, F., Earls, D., Madders, C., O'Leary, F., Ronan, S., Ward, C., & Wusteman, J. et al. (2014). The potential use of online tools for scientific collaboration by biology researchers. *Aslib Journal of Information Management*, 66(1), 13–37. doi:10.1108/AJIM-02-2013-0009

Bradshaw, P., Younie, S., & Jones, S. (2013). Open education resources and higher education academic practice. *Campus-Wide Information Systems*, 30(3), 186–193. doi:10.1108/10650741311330366

Collaborative Learning 2.0: Open Educational Resources. (2013). Online Information Review, 37(4), 658–658. Doi:10.1108/OIR-05-2013-0113

Czerniewicz, L., & Brown, C. (2009). A virtual wheel of fortune? Enablers and constraints of ICTs in Higher Education in South Africa. In S. Marshall, W. Kinuthia, & W. Taylor (Eds.), *Bridging the Knowledge Divide* (pp. 57–76). Charlote, NC: Information Age Publishing.

Dogoriti, E., Pange, J., & Anderson, G. S. (2014). The use of social networking and learning management systems in English language teaching in higher education. *Campus-Wide Information Systems*, 31(4), 254 263. doi:10.1108/CWIS-11-2013-0062

Edwards, G., & Mosley, B. F. (2011). Technology integration can be delicious: Social bookmarking as a technology integration tool. In Educating Educators with Social Media (Vol. 1, pp. 207–225). Emerald Group Publishing Limited. Retrieved from http://www.emeraldinsight.com/doi/abs/10.1108/S2044-9968%282011%290000001013 doi:10.1108/S2044-9968(2011)0000001013

Fernandez, P. (2011). Zotero: Information management software 2.0. *Library Hi Tech News*, 28(4), 5–7. doi:10.1108/07419051111154758

Homol, L. (2014). Web-based Citation Management Tools: Comparing the Accuracy of Their Electronic Journal Citations. *Journal of Academic Librarianship*, 40(6), 552–557. doi:10.1016/j.acalib.2014.09.011

Kai-Wah Chu, S. (2009). Using Wikis in Academic Libraries. *Journal of Academic Librarianship*, 35(2), 170–176. doi:10.1016/j.acalib.2009.01.004

Kinshuk, & Nian-Shing Chen. (2006). Synchronous methods and applications in e-learning. *Campus-Wide Information Systems*, 23(3). Doi:10.1108/cwis.2006.16523caa.001

Laughton, P. (2011). The use of wikis as alternatives to learning content management systems. *The Electronic Library*, 29(2), 225–235. doi:10.1108/02640471111125186

Lenis Zapata, J., Tilano Tilano, S., Jaramillo Bustos, A., & Valencia Arias, A. (2014) Motivations for choosing virtual learning tools in students of technology management of metropolitan institute of technology of medellin. Proceedings of INTED2014 (pp. 2411-2417).

Lewinson, J. (2005). Asynchronous discussion forums in the changing landscape of the online learning environment. *Campus-Wide Information Systems*, 22(3), 162–167. doi:10.1108/10650740510606162

Lwoga, E. (2012). Making learning and Web 2.0 technologies work for higher learning institutions in Africa. *Campus-Wide Information Systems*, 29(2), 90–107. doi:10.1108/10650741211212359

Macgregor, G., & McCulloch, E. (2006). Collaborative tagging as a knowledge organisation and resource discovery tool. *Library Review*, 55(5), 291–300. doi:10.1108/00242530610667558

Macpherson, A., Homan, G., & Wilkinson, K. (2005). The implementation and use of elearning in the corporate university. *Journal of Workplace Learning*, 17(1/2), 33–48. doi:10.1108/13665620510574441

Masrom, M. (2007). Technology Acceptance Model and E-learning. *Proceedings of the 12th International Conference on Education*, Sultan Hassanal Bolkiah Institute of Education, Brunei Darussalam (pp. 21-24).

McKinney, D., Dyck, J. L., & Luber, E. S. (2009). iTunes university and the classroom: Can podcasts replace professors? *Computers & Education*, 52(3), 617–623. doi:10.1016/j.compedu.2008.11.004

Miscione, G., & Johnston, K. (2010). Free and Open Source Software in developing contexts. *Journal of Information. Communication and Ethics in Society*, 8(1), 42–56. doi:10.1108/14779961011024800

Morgan, L. (2012). Generation Y, learner autonomy and the potential of Web 2.0 tools for language learning and teaching. *Campus-Wide Information Systems*, 29(3), 166–176. doi:10.1108/10650741211243184

Mu, C. (2008). Using RSS feeds and social bookmarking tools to keep current. *Library Hi Tech News*, 25(9), 10–11. doi:10.1108/07419050810946196

Nanayakkara, C. (2007). A Model of User Acceptance of Learning Management Systems: a study within Tertiary Institutions in New Zealand. *Paper presented at EduCause Australasia*. Retrieved from http://www.caudit.edu.au/educauseaustralasia07/authors_papers/Nanayakkara-361.pdf

Olofsson, A. D., Lindberg, J. O., & Stödberg, U. (2011). Shared video media and blogging online. *Campus-Wide Information Systems*, 28(1), 41–55. doi:10.1108/10650741111097287

Ossiannilsson, E. S. I. (2012). Quality enhancement on e-learning. *Campus-Wide Information Systems*, 29(4), 312–323. doi:10.1108/10650741211253903

Oye, N. D., Salleh, M., & Iahad, N. A. (2011). Challenges of E-learning in Nigerian University Education Based on the Experience of Developed Countries. *International Journal of Managing Information Technology*, 3(2), 39–48. doi:10.5121/ijmit.2011.3204

Paradise, A. (2012). Chapter 13 Picture Perfect? College Students' Experiences and Attitudes Regarding their Photo-Related Behaviors on Facebook. In *Misbehavior Online in Higher Education* (Vol. 5, pp. 261–292). Emerald Group Publishing Limited. Retrieved from http://www.emeraldinsight.com/doi/abs/10.1108/S2044-9968%282012%290000005015

Peter, S. E., Bacon, E., & Dastbaz, M. (2010). Adaptable, personalised e-learning incorporating learning styles. *Campus-Wide Information Systems*, 2(27), 91–100. doi:10.1108/10650741011033062

Porter, G. W. (2013). Free choice of learning management systems. *Interactive Technology and Smart Education*, 10(2), 84–94. doi:10.1108/ITSE-07-2012-0019

Raaij, E. M., & Schepers, J. J. L. (2008). The Acceptance and Use of a Virtual Learning Environment in China. *Computers & Education*, 50(3), 838–852. doi:10.1016/j.compedu.2006.09.001

Roffe, L. (2002). E-learning: Engagement, enhancement and execution. *Quality Assurance in Education*, 10(1), 40–50. doi:10.1108/09684880210416102

Ruppel, M. (2008). Blended learning: Tools for teaching and training, Barbara Allan. Facet, London (2007), ISBN: 978-1-85604-614-5. *Journal of Academic Librarianship*, 34(4), 372–373. doi:10.1016/j.acalib.2008.05.014

Samuel, K. W. C., & Kennedy, D. M. (2011). Using online collaborative tools for groups to co construct knowledge. *Online Information Review*, 35(4), 581–597. doi:10.1108/14684521111161945

Sawant, S. (2012). The study of the use of Web 2.0 tools in LIS education in India. *Library Hi Tech News*, 29(2), 11–15. doi:10.1108/07419051211236549

Sawant, S. (2013). Open access resources useful in LIS education. *Library Hi Tech News*, 30(7), 16–20. doi:10.1108/LHTN-05-2013-0029

Shroff, R. H., & Vogel, D. R. (2009). Assessing the factors deemed to support individual student intrinsic motivation in technology supported online and face-to-face discussions. *Journal of Information Technology Education*, 8, 59–85. Retrieved from http://www.jite.org/documents/Vol8/JITEv8p059-085Shroff416.pdf

Simmering, M., Posey, C., & Piccoli, G. (2009). Computer self-efficacy and motivation to learn in a selfdirected online course. *Decision Sciences Journal of Innovative Education*, 7(1), 99–121. doi:10.1111/j.1540-4609.2008.00207.x

Singh, A., Mangalaraj, G., & Taneja, A. (2010). Bolstering teaching through online tools. *Journal of Information Systems Education*, 21(3), 299–311.

Smart, K. L., & Cappel, J. J. (2006). Students' perceptions of online learning: A comparative study. *Journal of Information Technology Education*, 5, 201–219. Retrieved from http://www.jite.org/documents/Vol5/v5p201-219Smart54.pdf

Smith, P. J., Murphy, K. L., & Moheney, S. E. (2003). Towards identifying factors underlying readiness for online learning: An experimental study. *Distance Education*, 24(1), 57–67. doi:10.1080/01587910303043

Ssekakubo, G., Suleman, H., & Marsden, G. (2013). Designing mobile LMS interfaces: Learners' expectations and experiences. *Interactive Technology and Smart Education*, *10*(2), 147–167. doi:10.1108/ITSE-12-2012-0031

Stensaker, E. A., Maassen, P., Borgan, M., Oftebro, M., & Karseth, B. (2007). Use, updating and integration of ICT in Higher Education: Linking purpose, people and pedagogy. *Higher Education*, *54*(3), 417–433. doi:10.1007/s10734-006-9004-x

Traphagan, T., Kucsera, J. V., & Kishi, K. (2010). Impact of class lecture Webcasting on attendance and learning. *Educational Technology Research and Development*, *58*(1), 19–37. doi:10.1007/s11423-009-9128-7

Tseng, M. L., Lin, R. J., & Chen, H. P. (2011). Evaluating the effectiveness of e-learning system in uncertainty. *Industrial Management & Data Systems*, *111*(6), 869–889. doi:10.1108/02635571111144955

Vujovic, S., & Ulhøi, J. P. (2008). Online innovation: The case of open source software development. *European Journal of Innovation Management*, *11*(1), 142–156. doi:10.1108/14601060810845268

Walls, S. M., Kucsera, J. V., Walker, J. D., Acee, T. W., McVaugh, N. K., & Robinson, D. H. (2010). Podcasting in education: Are students as ready and eager as we think they are? *Computers & Education*, *54*(2), 371–378. doi:10.1016/j.compedu.2009.08.018

Wan, Z., Wang, Y., & Haggerty, N. (2008). Why people benefit from e-learning differently: The effects of psychological processes on e-learning outcomes. *Information & Management*, *45*(8), 513–521. doi:10.1016/j.im.2008.08.003

Wang, Q., Zhu, Z., Chen, L., & Yan, H. (2009). E-learning in China. *Campus-Wide Information Systems*, *26*(2), 77–81. doi:10.1108/10650740910946783

Weil, S., McGuigan, N., Kern, T., & Hu, B. (2013). Using asynchronous discussion forums to create social communities of practice in financial accounting. *Pacific Accounting Review*, *25*(1), 30–57. doi:10.1108/01140581311318959

Wood, J., Scorpo, A. L., Taylor, S., Rahman, M., Bell, E., & Matthews-Jones, L. (2014). Making Historians Digitally: Social Bookmarking and Inquiry-Based Learning in History in Higher Education in the UK. In *Inquiry-Based Learning for the Arts, Humanities, and Social Sciences: A Conceptual and Practical Resource for Educators* (Vol. 2, pp. 393–412). Emerald Group Publishing Limited. Retrieved from http://www.emeraldinsight.com/doi/abs/10.1108/S2055-364120140000002024

Yuen, H. K. A., & Ma, W. W. K. (2008). Exploring Teacher Acceptance of e-learning Technology. *Asia-Pacific Journal of Teacher Education*, *36*(3), 229–243. doi:10.1080/13598660802232779

KEY TERMS AND DEFINITIONS

Asynchronous Learning Model: In an asynchronous mode of elearning generally the teacher can post study materials, have announcements and calendars online, post assignments, submissions, and evaluations with feedback etc.

Blog: A regularly updated website or web page, typically one run by an individual or small group, that is written in an informal or conversational style.

Collaborative Authoring Tool: Collaborative Authoring tool is a web-based tool to create a document (word processing file, wiki page, presentation, spreadsheet, etc.), which can be edited by the multiple members of a group in an online environment.

Conference Alert: Is an online service where events such as conference/seminar can be added, promoted and subscribed by individual users.

Content Management System: It is a computer application that allows publishing, editing and modifying content, organizing, deleting as well as maintenance from a central interface.

Creative Commons: Creative Commons develops, supports, and stewards legal and technical infrastructure that maximizes digital creativity, sharing, and innovation.

Document Management System: It is a system used to track, manage and store documents. Most are capable of keeping a record of the various versions created and modified by different users

E-Learning: It is commonly referred to the intentional use of networked information and communications technology in teaching and learning.

Learning Management System: An LMS is an integrated software environment supporting all these functionalities along with some mechanism for student enrolment into courses, general user management (including administrator, teacher, and student) and some important system functions like backup and restore.

MIT Open CourseWare Consortium: MIT OpenCourseWare (OCW) is a web-based publication of virtually all MIT course content. OCW is open and available to the world and is a permanent MIT activity.

Online Learning/Virtual Learning/Distributed Learning/Web Based Learning: It refer to educational processes that utilize information and communications technology to mediate asynchronous as well as synchronous mode of learning and teaching activities.

Online Referencing Tool: It helps users to collect, organize, cite, and share research sources.

Open Education Consortium: The Open Education Consortium is a worldwide community of hundreds of higher education institutions and associated organizations committed to advancing open education and its impact on global education.

Open Educational Resource: Open Educational Resources (OERs) are any type of educational materials that are in the public domain or introduced with an open license. The nature of these open materials means that anyone can legally and freely copy, use, adapt and re-share them. OERs range from textbooks to curricula, syllabi, lecture notes, assignments, tests, projects, audio, video and animation.

Search Engines: A computer program that search information on the Internet

Online Noticeboard: Online notice boards are a neat way of getting a shared space to collect ideas from class for a brainstorm. Or for a teacher to post resources for a topic. Students could ask questions about a topic which you (or each other) can then answer.

Open Source Initiative: The Open Source Initiative (OSI) is a global non-profit that supports and promotes the open source movement. Among other things, we maintain the Open Source Definition, and a list of licenses that comply with that definition.

Open source Office Suite: Open Source Office Suite is the FREE alternative to other, more expensive productivity and office suites. Open Office offers many of the same features completely FREE such as Word Processing, Spreadsheet creation, Slide show creation and so much more.

Open Source Software: Open source software is software that can be freely used, changed, and shared (in modified or unmodified form) by anyone. Open source software is made by many people, and distributed under licenses that comply with the Open Source Definition.

Social Bookmarking: A social bookmarking service is a centralized online service which enables users to add, annotate, edit, and share bookmarks of web documents.

Synchronous Learning Model: In the synchronous learning model (Online model), the students can attend 'live' lectures at the scheduled hour from wherever they are irrespective of their location forming a virtual classroom.

Web Conferencing: Web conferencing is a form of real-time communications (RTC) in which multiple computer users, all connected to the Internet, see the same screen at all times in their Web browsers. Some Web conferencing systems include features such as texting, VoIP (voice over IP) and full-motion video.

APPENDIX

Websites Referred for Key Terms and Definitions

http://creativecommons.org/
http://www.oeconsortium.org/
http://www.unesco.org/new/en/communication-and-information/access-to-knowledge/open-educational-
    resources/what-are-open-educational-resources-oers/
http://ocw.mit.edu/
http://www.conferencealerts.com/
https://digitalresearchtools.pbworks.com/w/page/17801651/Collaborative%20Authoring
http://www.oxforddictionaries.com/
http://www.whiteboardblog.co.uk/2011/09/8-online-noticeboards-wallwisher-and-more/
http://www.openoffice.us.com/
https://www.zotero.org/
http://en.wikipedia.org/wiki/Document_management_system
http://en.wikipedia.org/wiki/Content_management_system
http://searchunifiedcommunications.techtarget.com/definition/Web-conferencing
http://en.wikipedia.org/wiki/Social_bookmarking
http://opensource.org/

Chapter 8

ICT as an Engine for Community Participation:
An Assessment of Uganda's Community Media

Brian Semujju
Uganda Christian University, Uganda & University of Kwazulu-Natal, South Africa

ABSTRACT

This chapter discusses two issues prevalent in community media: Information communication technology (ICT) and Community participation. While several studies have explored community media and ICT in Uganda (Nassanga, 2003, 2009a, 2009b), the view that ICT has changed the way media operate to an extent of reversing the agenda-setting role to the listeners (McQuail, 2006, pp. 38-39; Straubhaar & Larose 2002, p. 386) needed investigation. Using Kagadi-Kibale Community radio (KKCR), the chapter shows how ICT is spreading in one Ugandan region and the relationship that technology has with participation in community media activities. Findings show that there is need to redefine the relationship between ICT and geographically defined community media as usage of ICT is dependent on forces that still require decades to harmonize. The chapter therefore suggests that an alternative to community media, herein called Basic Media, is best suited to match the communication patterns of a developing world.

INTRODUCTION

Although ICT eases the way people participate in media activities, the original models of study were designed based on the dominant paradigm that advocated for transfer of technology from the developed world to the periphery (Hamelink, 2001). Therefore, such a transfer did not cater for access to ICT for all among poor nations. Instead, it created a vertical ICT access pat-tern where control was (is) at the top (North/ West/cities), while the bottom (South/villages/ communities) remains underprivileged. For example, Uganda, which has 35.4 million people (Uganda Bureau of Statistics (UBOS), 2013), has an estimated 6.8 million internet users (Uganda Communications Commissions (UCC), 2013). Mobile phone subscribers on the other hand are 16.6 million (UCC, 2013; UBOS, 2013). This is testimony to

DOI: 10.4018/978-1-5225-0556-3.ch008

what Sharma (2010) calls a divided world into 'highly developed, developed, developing, and poorly developed'. The view that because of ICT listeners determine media agenda (McQuail, 2006, pp. 38-39; Straubhaar & Larose 2002, p. 386) is an over ambitious one when it fails to consider the number of people in local communities that can participate in community media and the realities of their daily lives like bad governance, civil wars, lack of capital to invest in hybrid ICTs, low literacy levels, lack of electricity and other disadvantages which are instead escalated by and have escalated the digital divide (Pringle & David, 2002). For any ICT-participatory initiative to foster development, it would have to be less prone to most but not only one of the above problems. That is the reason why the Organization for Economic Co -operation and Development (OECD, 2003) warns that ICT is not a 'silver bullet' to terminate poverty.

This paper therefore put the underlying problems facing ownership and access to ICT into perspective and tried to re-examine the effectiveness of ICT towards community participation. The intention was to see what effect ICT has on community participation in the developing world. That purpose was achieved by answering the following research questions: Which ICTs have been integrated in community media? How many people have access to ICTs in the community? How do ICTs influence participation? What are the challenges of ICT and community participation in com-munity media? How can ICT be better utilized to enhance community participation?

Generally, the paper begins with a discussion of ICT and community participation, in which a basic understanding of the two concepts is given and the status of the ICT area in Uganda. The second part puts ICT and community participation into a theoretical perspective arguing that to understand that combination, the complexity theory has to be applied. The same part also provides an insight into the methods employed by the research to meet its objectives. In the findings, presented in part three, the paper shows that Uganda's community media is riddled with problems that cannot be solved within a decade and this breaks the combination of ICT and community participation. Therefore, the paper concludes that alternative forms to community media may be used to achieve participation of communities. The paper introduces Basic Media as one of such forms.

ICT AND COMMUNITY PARTICIPATION

ICT is the technology used in conveying, manipulating and storing of data by electronic means. It includes, but not limited to: satellite, internet, computer, and digital storage devices (Hang, 2005). In the West, where there is more advanced technology, Williams and Carpini (2004, p. 212) say that, the growth of 'cable and satellite television, the internet and the World Wide Web, the availability of video cassette recorders and remote TV- controls', and so on, now define what Marshal McLuhan's 1953 article on Harold Innis (Peters, 2009, p. 16) and later in 1960 (McQuail, 2006, p. 36), called new media. In Uganda, with 6.8 million people using the internet (UCC, 2013), there is a certain minority consuming media on-line especially print, as most newspapers in Uganda are online.

On the African continent, the United Nations is therefore embracing a move to help (or not) Africa to move from the agricultural to an information society. However, like the modernization theory in the past, the ICT policy has been questioned by several African scholars like Banda (2010) and Berger (2010). Knowing that there are mandatory efforts from the UN to digitalize African media (Berger, 2010), and yet the efforts are not consumer-oriented, raises questions. Digitalization in Africa needs to be taken with caution as most communities for which ICT is assumed to be beneficial are illiterate. It is possible that the UN's approach to slap a deadline on Africa to digitalize by 2015 is producer-oriented (Berger, 2010).

The need to look at the global south as an ICT market has proved Manuel Castell's fore-cast of the creation of the Fourth World. "This new world is made up of the working poor who are excluded from the network society and the social movement that rise to advocate for equal network opportunity" (O'donnell et al. 2006). Their counterparts in the city meanwhile are being turned into giant ICT addicts through massive adverts. The era of 'virtual presence', as Youngs (2002) calls it, has created a growing concern of the new world information disorder. Besides, there is little correlation between ICT investment and overall productivity in the developing world (Pohjola, 2003).

Theoretical Framework and Research Methodology

To explain the phenomenon of ICT in media, the complexity theory can be appropriately applied. According to Qvortrup (2006, p. 350), this theoretical approach suggests that the basic function of media is to manage social complexity. In other words, media is supposed to unravel the mysteries of our world for us. To do this job well, a local community requires a local media that can understand all complements of that community while an international com-munity requires communication means with an international platform. On the other hand, these two worlds (local and international) are becoming a complex global setting that ICT only can bind together. In McLuhan (1987)'s words, the world has become a global village. The globalized society can only be reached by a globalized media.

Community Participation

Participation was integrated into communication based on the ideas of Paulo Freire who advocated for the involvement of the people for whom the development was intended, using the image of a teacher who gives instructions to a pupil when the pupil is only a recipient. In his *Pedagogy of the Oppressed*, Freire (1970) raises a significant question: 'who suffer the effects of oppression more than the oppressed? The pedagogy (teaching) of the oppressed, Freire says, must be 'forged *with, not for,* the oppressed.'

Fortunately, while the idea of community media was becoming synonymous with development com-munication, there was political will to foster participation, in order to attain development at its fullest. Participation received political capital when, in 1990s, as Wanyeki (2000) observes, the United Nations adopted the 1990 African Charter for Popular Participation in Development and Transformation. The charter stipulates that

The political context of socio-economic development has been characterised in many instances by over-centralisation of power and impediments to the effective participation of the overwhelming majority of the people in social, political and economic development. As a result, the motivation of the majority of the African people and their organisations to contribute to the development process, and to the betterment of their well-being as well as their say in national development has been severely constrained and curtailed and their collective and individual creativity has been undervalued and under-utilised.

This basis meant that if a country commissioned resources to develop people through, for example, communication structures, the communication had to be participatory. In community media terms, the view was that 'common sense should be valued over expertise' (Carpentier, 2001, pp. 210), while airing out development programs.

Community participation is further based on the idea that local people as key stake holders can have an impact on issues that specifically affect them (Burns & Taylor, 2000). It increases a sense of responsibility and consciousness about local issues while at the same time, as Zakus and Lysack (1998) note, maintains a powerful citizenry due to acquisition of new skills that can help them control different aspects of their lives. In a way, resources will be appropriated to the needs of the community through monitoring.

However, there are problems associated with the concept of community participation. For example, the definition of community is diverse. When for instance government wants to release funds for a community, it (government) has to define which community to aim at. In such a way, it is hard to satisfy all the prevailing communities. Besides, members in the same community may have differences in characteristics and attitude about a particular issue. Burns and Taylor (2000) also recognize the presence of several threats to this kind of approach where the participating members could have a negative perception that nothing will change even when they get involved.

In that case, one needs to define the needs, problems and solutions based on the community that the project is going to serve. Additionally, some projects, like a farmers' radio, require ample time and commitment of all parties involved and resources. Otherwise, handled well, community participation can facilitate democratization of opinions. Since 'citizen participation is a categorical name for citizen power', as Arnstein (1969) notes, who then has the real power? Are people really participating or participation is just a name given for acceptance in community media realms? Arnstein also notes that citizen participation, also called citizen control has been 'waged largely in terms of exacerbated rhetoric and misleading euphemisms' with very little or no action.

Nowadays, participation has evolved into e-participation thanks to ICT. Loosely connected to e-governance and e-democracy, e-participation still suffers the nature of hindrances suffered by the creation of virtual communities among village settings. While the concepts are different although related (virtual community and e-participation), the realities that determine the operationalisation of both concepts are still the same. The new version (e-participation) has been "intended to transform traditional bureaucratic systems to participatory, autocratic to democratic, and exclusive to inclusive, empowering, open, transparent and trustworthy (Islam, 2008). In Uganda, this assertion is still a normative concept and even then, there is little evidence to suggest progress. In this case, Macintosh (2004)'s observation can better suit the normative state through which most developing countries consider e-participation. She argues that there has been "a gradual awareness of the need to consider the innovative application of ICTs for participation that enables a wider audience to contribute to democratic debate and where contributions themselves are broader and deeper". Unlike several studies, Macintosh (2004) puts in mind the lack of access to ICT in the developing world and so, in her three levels of participation, she includes e-enabling alongside e-engaging(communication from top seeks to engage the bottom) and e-empowering(where the top provides real support to advance the participation of the bottom). E-enabling, on the other hand, which in Uganda must come before the debate of how effective the entire participation practice is, pays attention to getting the technology (ICT) to the person before that person is expected to participate (Macintosh, 2004). Only after e-enabling can we certainly talk about reversing the agenda-setting role from the sender to the receiver.

Research Methodology

The data for this paper was part of a bigger research project studying the impact of ICT on rural radio activities and listeners' behaviour, sponsored by Carleton University and the International Development Research Centre.

The research was conducted at KKCR in Kibale District. Kibale is found in the south western part of Uganda. Contrary to broad-casting Council regulations, KKCR's signal interferes with most radios' frequencies which makes the listeners within a mile's radius miss out on other stations' programs until midnight when KKCR goes off-air. Therefore, it was hard to determine whether or not participation in the choice of radio among the locals was done at will. The researcher included two more areas where the signal was not too strong. The two extra areas: Muhorro and Kyenzige were in a distance of seven and 10 km away from Kagadi Town Council respectively and the listeners there had a variety of stations to choose from at will. The Government's recognition of in-formation as a resource that activates various sectors of the economy is seen in the media and communication infrastructure that the country has. By 2013, according to UCC, one that is tasked with managing communications in the country, there were 251 operational radio stations. Only one (Mama FM), is licensed as a community radio station. Two more stations (KKCR and Radio Apac), although not licensed as community radios, are widely accepted by media and communication scholars (Scmujju, 2013), as community radios because of access, self-management and participation. Of the several applications that were received to establish TV services, 68 had been approved and so these were operational TV channels (UCC, 2013).

The Telecommunication infrastructure on the other hand is provided for in the 1997 Communications Act which created two National Telephone Providers. One was public (Uganda Telecom Limited-UTL), while the other was private (Mobile Telephone Network-MTN). Currently, Uganda has seven telecommunication companies including: Uganda Telecom, MTN, Airtel, Warid, Orange, Smile Telecom, and K2. This surge has led to a tremendous increase in both talk time and subscribers of mobile and fixed line telephony. It is this growth in the ICT sector that forms the basis of the argument that participation has been made easy in community media.

Population Sample and Justification

KKCR has an estimated audience of 1.8 million people across five districts (Kibale, Kyenjojo, Hoima, Masindi, and Fort-portal) in western Uganda. The listeners in Kibale district had higher chances of being selected because very few of them experience signal loss since they live near the station. Therefore, 250 KKCR listeners were chosen to represent the radio population. The Radio management committee, two policy makers at district level: the Mayor of Kagadi Town Council and the area MP (who were the most powerful politicians in the area by virtue of their offices), two community volunteers (the volunteers with most hours at the station) administrative posts) constituted the population sample of the research. This choice of respondents intended to find out how the community accesses and uses ICT in radio activities and to know how ICT affects that participation. The researcher also interviewed two ICT/community media personnel at national level. These were the secretaries of Uganda Communication Commission and Uganda Media Council respectively. They helped the researcher to understand how the ICT-led participation affects KKCR in terms of the law and regulation of media. Since the sample of listeners chosen included all age groups (from 18 and above), both sexes, people with different economic and education status, the findings are representative of the community media audience in Uganda.

Data Collection Methods and Instruments

Survey: A survey was carried out using a questionnaire, key informant interviews, and focus group discussions. With a questionnaire, data from 250 listeners was collected in a door - to - door approach, picking a house randomly, followed by the house after next, alternating between male and female respondents to ensure gender balance in the sample. Additionally, an interview guide was used to collect data through key informant interviews while a focus group outline was very vital during the focus group discussion.

FINDINGS AND DISCUSSION

This section shows which ICTs have been integrated in community media, how those ICTs influence participation, and the challenges of the ICTs to community participation.

Integrated ICTs in Community Media

ICT ownership was the first consideration as it would inform access (although people who did not own ICTs also accessed them). The attention was put on major ICTs like the mobile phone, radio set, TV-set, printer, laptop, fax, landline, smart phone, email address, webpage, internet and ipad. As it turned out, the most owned ICT was the mobile phone owned by 109 (43.6%) people of the total sample chosen. This was followed by the radio-set at 104 (41.6%). The Television-set came next with 16 (6.4%) while there was only 1(0.4%) personal computer and printer. The rest of the above ICT indicators were inactive in the area. This is summarized in Table 1:

ICT Access by the Community

The trick with mobile phones, unlike most ICTs, is that while a community member might listen to a radio in the neighbourhood, especially when his/her set is faulty, the same person with a faulty mobile phone might find it difficult to get a person willing to share. This is because mobile phones require constant credit to be used to send information. To save money, one has to be economical in the way of using and so a person would not want to give such a money-consuming ICT out for free. The above fact

Table 1. ICT ownership in the Kagadi-Kibale community

ICT Indicator	Frequency	Percentage
Radio	104	41.6%
TV	16	6.4%
Mobile phone	109	43.6%
Computer/printer	1	0.4%
Refused to answer	20	8%
Total	250	100%

was put into consideration and so the mobile phone was analysed along two major factors: number of times accessed and reason for accessing mobile phone.

The time people gave to usage of mobile phones was different. The people who owned them used them every day, although they would also be limited by factors such as electricity (for charging) low signal strength, and cost of airtime. These problems were then shifted to the others who used friends or family members' phones. However, there were those who never used mobile phones. Some of them had no money to purchase one; others had no one to call, while others thought they were too old to consider using such a complicated technology. Otherwise, 138 (55.2%) respondents said they used mobile phones every day.

In terms of access to mobile phone technology, people in the category of 'a few times a year', 'not sure', 'less than once a month', 'a few times a month' were still far from realizing the full potential of the mobile phone. For example, most of the respondents were farmers, while others did retail business. Convergence has gone to another level such that sometimes, one who has a mobile phone has access to, at least, breaking news. This could benefit farmers who may take their products to where the price is favourable. The consumer can also know market information and hence save money in the exchange of goods. A person who does not access a mobile phone regularly can miss out on all those opportunities.

Mobile Phone and Purpose for Which It Is Used: The major purpose for the mobile phone differed. The majority of users made calls (national). These were 63 (25.2%). Another 56 (23.6%) admitted to being able to send an SMS. Like in the first category of 'times used', the reason for which a mobile phone is used sheds some light on information access in the community. Some people used phones for advanced banking services. It is quite likely such people will use the phone for other developmental purposes like internet access. With internet, they can receive in-formation but most importantly, they can seek clarification on the received information using search engines. If information is really a key ingredient of development, it remains upon them to decide on how to use the information received. While there is an urgent need to make mobile phones accessible to all by reducing taxes on new mobile phones and airtime, it is also important for the community to be taught how to use phones at their full potential. Otherwise, development will remain for the privileged few (see Table 2).

Table 2. Major functions of a mobile phone in the KKCR community

Mobile Phone Function	Number of People	Percentage
Making national calls	63	25.2
International calls	3	1.2
Sending SMS	59	23.6
Access Internet	4	1.6
Listen to music	4	1.6
Listen to radio	31	12.4
Use it for banking	1	0.4
Others purposes	12	4.8
Don't use phones	73	29.2
Total	250	100

Table 3. Radio access points of the Kagadi-Kibale community

Radio Access Points	Frequency	Percentage
At home	206	82.4
Work place	2	0.8
Family /friend's house	12	4.8
Others	8	3.2
No access	22	8.8
Total	250	100

Access to Radio: While some people did not own radio-sets, they could access the service. This means that the number of people who own radio sets does not strictly represent that of people who actually listen to radio. A radio-set can be borrowed from another family since some homes have more than one radio. Other people listened to a neighbour's radio for a specific pro-gram. Access to radio was high enough although a certain percentage, 8.8% (22 people) did not have them. Radio is the oldest ICT available in the community and until when convergence started, it was the most owned. This is still a fact in some African villages (See Table 3).

Access to TV: While 27(10.8%) people watched TV at home, (although not all of them owned these TV-sets), 64(25.6%) people watched from a family friend's house. Others watched from school, work places, community media centre, and other places. Nevertheless, 98(39.2%) people did not have access to TV. To make matters worse, the community radio centre that provides TV services only shows English Premier League to the public on weekends. While this programming is good for the youths to relax, it excludes so many categories of people. Therefore, one can only conclude that the available TV teaches the area foreign cultures instead of working as a mirror in which the image of that community can be reflected. Such an ICT might fail to develop the community.

Access to Computers: Computer was not much accessed either. Before identifying the number of people who accessed computers, the study looked at the number of people who could use computers for any purpose (some people used computers to browse but couldn't operate a computer as a separate gadget). The majority of the respondents, which was 198 people (79.2%), did not know how to use computers. Some of these had never seen one. There were 13 respondents (5.2%) who said that they learnt computer from school. Learning from school therefore reduced computer literacy to be for only those who went to school. Another 2 respondents (0.8%) who said had taught themselves had access to a computer either at work place or at friend's place.

Access to Internet: 172 respondents- (68.8%) did not use internet while 42 respondents (16.8%) had never heard of the internet. Some of them said if they had heard about it, they did not pay attention to it. Of the internet's 36(14.4%) users, news was the basic activity followed by sports, education, music, while social network sites like Facebook and Twitter came at the very bottom. Table 4 gives an illustration.

The Influence of ICT on Participation

Using ICTs could determine how a person and at what rate they engaged in radio activities. Like owner-ship and usage of ICT, participation did not exist in a vacuum. It was influenced by several factors. The first level of participation was choice of radio. Although this study also considered Arnstein (1969)'s

Table 4. Internet access and number of users

Internet Access	Frequency	Percentage
Don't access Internet	172	68.8
News	20	8.0
Sports	3	1.2
Education	4	1.6
Music	4	1.6
Social	2	0.8
Business	3	1.2
Never heard of Internet	42	16.8
Total	250	100

ladder of citizen participation, it must be noted that her ladder looks at participation at managerial level where people move from learning to taking decisions at the top. This study's version of the ladder has three rungs so that the ladder can include all community activities in radio. It starts with listening, goes to reaction, and then to involvement.

Out of the 197(78.8%) respondents inter-viewed in Kagadi Town Council, 190(76%) said that they listened to KKCR because it was the only station they could receive unless they waited for it to close at midnight for other station to stream in. Seven respondents (2.8%) said they could receive other stations because of their advanced radio sets and these shared preference of KKCR with other commercial stations. Those seven people also pointed out KKCR only as their first channel for local news broadcasts. The respondents from the other two comparative places (Kyenzige and Muhorro) where KKCR competes with other stations in reception, divided best choice station between KKCR and Radio Hoima, Kyenjojo FM, Life FM, and Radio Endigito (these other radios are also located within the neighbouring districts, broadcasting in the same dialect like KKCR but are commercial).

Categories were further divided into listening hours. The unemployed were not the most listeners as one would assume because of having enough time to spare. Actually the category of people that listened for the most hours was that of the self-employed. They were the best listeners falling under the 10-18hrs a day category (highest). Other categories included: the 5-10hrs, 3-5hrs, and the less than an hour category (least category). In total, there were 101(40.4%) self-employed people who listened to the radio. The reason for their heavy listening was because they were their own bosses and did casual labour. Some of them ran local village restaurants where the radio was on all the time and it was the only source of entertainment for them and their customers. There were those in salons, while others operated shops and small vegetable stores. Apart from the shop business that was unisex, the above mentioned trades (restaurant, salons, vending) were dominated by women.

Because of their daily business of going to class, the students listened less in all categories followed by those employed part time. Part time employment meant that after work, that person went to do another job or he/she went back home to the garden. The unemployed listened to radio for three hours. For example, a woman who was unemployed was a house wife. Every day, she woke up and prepared breakfast for her husband and when he went for work, the woman went to the garden. After gardening, she would then wash clothes, clean the house and cook food. All the women in this category said that they preferred to do all their chores first before they sat down to listen to their favourite program. The house wives, the unemployed and students listened less because of the batteries that they could not afford to buy.

However, 170(68%) people said that they replaced the batteries within a day of expiry. Three percent said that their radio spent more than a month without batteries as they were still looking for the money to buy new ones. This division was created by employment differences. The group (under more than a month category) also said that within that time, they were completely green about KKCR activities. The category of people who used other sources of power like generators (these were mainly for business and so they listened while at work), had their own problems too. In a small salon, using a generator would mean that there is too much noise for one to listen to radio. Genera-tor users were also staggering under the heavy weight of prices of fuel. Prices of generator fuel rose almost every day during the time of the study. According to the Consumer Price Index (CPI) data from the Uganda Bureau of Statistics, the country was suffering from a 14% level of inflation (Kulabako, 2011). Table 5 for battery-radio relationship.

With the presence of mobile phones now, one cannot neglect the number of people who have been reunited with radio by the converging technologies of radio and mobile phones. This is not cheap though. Apart from the battery that needs charging all the time, not all people were educated to manage the functions of such a complicated phone, if they could afford it.

Analysing community participation re-quires looking at ICTs on all sides. From the sender's side (radio station workers and volunteers), the station uses the phone as a major ICT for participation. An idea is introduced on air and then the community is asked to make comments on a given phone number. On average, the Station Manager, Anthony Lwanga, said that the station receives approximately 50 calls per day. The computer is another ICT that is vital to community participation. When messages are sent, they are received on the studio computer and transcribed. The presenter can read the message as the program goes on. However, because of the digital divide, messages are very few compared to calls. Some people may not be able to send messages due to complexity of the technology. Without a phone at both ends, participation would never be immediate.

Volunteers and ICT: Ntuti, 70, who does a family program from 9:30 pm every Tuesday to midnight, said that she uses computer, and phones to gather support for the program from the community. As a volunteer, Ntuti has managed to learn the basics of operating ICTs. When she had just started the program, she had problems locating jingles to play between programs and looking for songs that matched

Table 5. Time spent without radio due to batteries

Battery Life	Frequency	Percentage
Less than a day	170	68
1-3 days	13	5.2
3-7 days	8	3.2
1-2 days	9	3.6
2 weeks- 1 month	4	1.6
More than a month	9	3.6
Others	37	14.8
Total	250	100

the themes of her program (Ntuti, 2011, personal communication). She said she would get a negative reaction from listeners if she talked about a shocking idea and played a feasting song to accompany it. It is very evident from her explanation that ICTs can change a listeners' mood. A presenter's failure to manipulate ICTs will in return determine the community's opinion about the program. Evelyn Mirembe, 42, also a volunteer, uses her experience as an HIV-positive person to tell pregnant mothers ways of avoiding unborn babies contracting HIV/AIDS during birth (Mirembe, 2011, personal communication). However, she does not know how to operate ICTs except a phone. This, as she admitted, reduces her chances of finding vital information off the internet. As a result, her participation is limited only to life experiences some of which might have had wrong approaches.

Calling in: On Monday, for example, during the morning program, there is a time left specifically for participation. In between the morning program, there is *Greeting Card*, a program in which listeners call-in and send greetings and also talk about their plans for the week and what they did over the weekend. Another participatory moment comes the following day, Tuesday, during an afternoon program about cultural awareness and a few more times during the rest of the week.

Phones on the other hand make participation to be limited to only a few people. Out of the 60 phone calls the station said it receives every- day, one caller may be recorded as having called more than two times. Other problems include semantic and other types of noise. Presenters also said that some callers go through and fail to say anything. This congests the line. Instead of having 60 or 50 callers a day, only about 30 people participate, not to mention the quality of participation that leaves a lot to be desired.

Nevertheless, ICTs, especially phones, make interaction easy and fast. The alternative for nearby community members would be to walk to the studio and give their views. ICTs also minimize the need for more space to host all the participants which the station would never have. It is evident that ICTs, especially a mobile phone, have profound effects on com-munity participation.

CHALLENGES FACING COMMUNITY PARTICIPATION

It is to be remembered that the challenges facing ICT (discussed later in this chapter) in turn affect participation. However, besides challenges ushered in by ICT, participation faces several other challenges like distance. Since the radius coverage of the radio is 40km, ICT's failure to mediate between distance and the individual means enduring long distances to the station for participants. This might prove difficult in an area with barely two taxis a day. According to the area MP, "there are very few taxis connecting the station to villages and when they are available, they charge a hefty sh.5000 ($25)" (Besisira, 2011, personal communication). In addition, all the programs that end at night will be interfered with for security reasons.

Also, participation faces political and commercial interests. Some program participants like the area mayor complained about the station's failure to cut itself loose from the ruling party cords. "Any program that has divergent political or economic views from those of government will be sabotaged" (Kasaija, 2011, personal communication).

The Mayor, who participates in a weekly program on behalf of the Town Council, also said that he has been some times denied access to the radio because of political wrangles. The KKCR Station Manager however said that "there can never be political conflict of interest here (at the station) because all of us here belong to the ruling party" (Lwanga, 2011, personal communication). KKCR also fails to resist the temptation to invite adverts. While community media associates with the phrase 'free for all', it is not very free after all. The Town Council pays sh500, 000($250) yearly for its weekly program. For the Town Council, participation means that the community can be rallied into general cleanliness, hard work, support of education programs, and others. If community media is for uplifting communities, are those not the major concerns?

Challenges of using ICT

- **Unreliable Electricity:** Power that goes-off all the time means that the station has to incur expenses of buying diesel for the generator. It is only on weekend that the area gets a stable power supply. The generator, as the Station Manager explained, consumes 100 litres of diesel daily. At a current price of sh3000 per litre, the station would need sh300, 000 per day to run. This power problem is intensified by lack of resources to buy a new generator. The station's existing generator is too old that when it breaks down sometimes, it will not come back until weeks. During the study, the radio spent two weeks without broadcasting as power was off and the generator was down.
- **Slow Internet**: All of the journalists talked to said that sometimes the webpage takes very long to display. This consumes time. It is more costing especially if one wanted to use the internet to do research and gave up because of the slowness.
- **Faulty Phone Lines:** There are two lines in the studio and one of them does not work. This introduces more problems to participation. The only working one will be jammed with calls and at last, the presenter will be able to allow only a few people to contribute in the interest of time. The jamming process itself makes it hard for callers to go through.
- **No Signal:** Besides calling on faulty lines, callers face problems with phone networks. Kibale District is generally a hilly area. The listeners therefore have a difficult time finding a signal whenever they want to call-in. The area MP said that in his village, people have to climb anthills for signal reception.
- **Complexity of Mobile Phones:** Calling is easier for some community members than sending text messages as the latter has a lengthy process that includes instructions in English. Mirembe said that most of her listeners complain that during her program, they would like to contribute but they do not know how to send messages. Calling as an option is costly.

The problems that face community participation and ICT make community media seem an over ambitious idea to an African community. We need a smaller media that the local person (in an African context) does not find intimidating. One that will be taken near the village person since ICTs may not take the media to the village person. Such an alternative to community media should extend the problems of ICTs to solvable limits. This alternative to community media could run on, for example, 20 litres in case power is off as opposed to 100 litres that KKCR uses a day. Such media should not take for granted that people will use the ICTs to participate because people cannot afford to buy or maintain the ICTs and yet they should have access to information. One should be able to walk by the station without having to worry about transport. Such an alternative is discussed further below.

Alternative to Community Media: Basic Media.

Basic media is operated using locally-made horn speakers. Three speakers are tied together each facing an opposite direction and then hung up on a pole. The speakers are then connected to a communication device down the pole, which has a microphone and a power source. Even when power goes off, a small-size generator would run it.

Basic Media can be defined as community accessible media that provides on-time information about people's basic needs and suggests immediate solutions. This media is concerned with the fundamental elements of people's survival. It would point out the price of food on the market as opposed to better farming methods. It gets concerned when there is a broken well instead of advocating for tap water. The reason for this is that basic media can gather people to fix their wells. For community or any other media to beg government to extend tap water to the community in Uganda takes several decades.

Since I first suggested the idea of basic media (Semujju, 2013), I have observed the media further in my PhD research project which is still underway. From observation done over a period of ten days at two basic media locations in Ugandan communities (one rural and the other semi-urban), basic media use the following technology: horn speakers (about three or four) hoisted on top of long dry polls next to a small room that has an amplifier, microphone and a DVD player for playing music. Every day, there are mainly two narrowcasts. These are at 6:30am up to 7am and then at 9:30 pm up to 10pm. This routine is broken down when there is an emergence like if someone loses a child or property. The rule applies also if police have something to say about security, if thieves break into someone's house or place of work and other emergencies. As in radio broadcasts, basic media presenters too begin by greeting listeners, identifying the name of the basic media that has started to narrowcast and telling the community from which location the media is narrowcasting. On the first day of observation at 6:30am, the rural basic media, had lost-and-found announcements, local sports competitions that would take place that week, death announcement, an announcement thanking those who attended a previous funeral for the recently buried member of the community, Eid day special adverts, lost children and ended with music at the end of the narrowcast. The evening narrowcast followed the same format.

The following day, it was still the same format except that the basic media started narrowcasting at 28 minutes to 7 in the morning and stopped at 7:13am with announcements, followed by music until 7:20am when the morning narrowcast was done. There was no new information given. It was as if the previous evening's information had been recorded except that this time, there was more emphasis. After the narrowcast on the second day, two community members came in to give the presenter information that he would narrowcast in the evening. The third person came to inquire when his information was going to be narrowcast. The evening of the second day had specifically information about the dead, lost children and property. This format ran across the week with each announcement lasting between two to three minutes.

Rationale for Basic Media: The Purpose of Development Communication

The development communication theory notes that communication should be used after identifying a target. After this process, the messages addressing the point of concern can then be modeled to suit the intended purpose. 'It's a process of strategic intervention towards social change initiated by institutions and communities' (Baran & Davis, 2003). The phrase 'strategic intervention' calls for planning of information packages to uplift communities.

Instead of using ICTs for commercial gains and/or political activism, the theory advocates for 'advancing socially beneficial goals' (Baran & Davis, 2003). This theory's sole purpose has been summarized by Waisbord (2001) that 'the ultimate goal of development communication is to raise the quality of life of populations'. Waisbord believes that among the examples of how development communication can do its job include: increasing the community members' income and well-being, eradicating social injustice, promoting land reform and freedom of speech, and establishing community centers for leisure and entertainment. The above analysis of development communication is a measure to show that development communication through community media needs more effort in Uganda. The process which basic media go through can better accommodate the requirements of development communication than community media.

Understanding community media's ineffectiveness to the village person can best be achieved by identifying their limitations in communities. Community media as we currently know them fail to fit into several Ugandan communities. To begin with, there are changes in terms as used in community media literature and practice in Uganda. For example, while the workers at the community radios in the West are referred to as volunteers and they are indeed volunteers, at KKCR, these are staff members who get a salary (even though it might not be much). The term volunteer at KKCR refers to community members who come to participate in different programs. These ones are not paid at all but they work alongside 15 staff members.

Another example is that of having community members at management committees as literature suggests. This does not happen at KKCR and besides, to get quality opinions, it would require people with a basic level of literacy. Bearing in mind the low standards of education among some village schools in Uganda, a person who went half-way through secondary school might not attain the same knowledge about life in general like his/her counterpart in the city who studied with text books and other necessary requirements.

Basic media's current operationalisation brings back some of the requirements set aside for community media. Besides, the people have already realised the relevancy of basic media in their communities. People said in one of the areas visited that several thieves had been intercepted because of this media. Basic media shares this information with every household but not with only those with batteries and radio sets. This can be useful especially in an area where for a person to make a complaint to police, that person has to buy a book in which a statement must be written and sometimes provide transport for the police.

If we can put such media at each community centre or trading centre, since it broadcasts within 1000 meters, everyone then knows where to get news and other information from, without having to worry about batteries, computer literacy, phone network and complexity, distance, transport and insecurity. A person can walk in and say whatever it is he/she wants to say to the community. Besides, this media is way cheaper than community radio to operate. If we put into consideration the benefits of this media, then we may borrow programming from community media.

The assumption by this chapter is that if we get a computer, internet and other ICTs that have failed community radio and give them to the operators of basic media, they can get information from all corners and pass it on to the community. The community member has nothing to worry about in terms of spending. In Uganda so far, Basic Media has been used in more than 10 districts. There are more basic media facilities in the country than there are community media. However, the most pressing need that must be addressed is that in its current form, basic media is manned by community members with personal interests while it is also not facilitated yet to handle community participation.

However, if we are to succeed with basic media, we need to first of all subject its processes to a careful study that community media has gone through for the last 20 or more years. There is need to know how to avoid personalization of these media, and also, we should demarcate distance between one station and another to avoid interference. However, since we cannot give alternative power sources to everyone or buy batteries for every community member or still buy a radio set for everyone, the best way to promote access to information and community participation is to resort to basic media.

Need to Contextualize Community: If community media is based on the definition of community, then we should look at community from Uganda's perspective. Community media has been successful on European and American continents. The communities found on those continents are different from the Kagadi-Kibale Community. The Kagadi-Kibale Community has three taxis working every day. The first taxi to the capital (260km) leaves at 3 am. The second one leaves at 12pm, while the third leaves at 3pm. Sometimes it stays back to become the first to leave the following day. The road is only smooth for 160km from the capital (Kampala). The rest of the 100km to Kagadi town is cloud-dusty during the dry season and too slippery for cars to move on a rainy day.

The community has no free -to-air TV like most parts of the country. To access the two local channels (WBS TV and NTV) that have extended their services through the digital satellite TV Company (Multichoice), one needs to have a decoder, which requires a subscription and a monthly payment. Both channels are commercial and are on a free-to-air basis in other parts of the country. The area has no public service broadcasting channels. Except bars which subscribe to boost business, there are six homesteads that have managed to subscribe privately in the community to get TV.

Is the current ICT-boosted community media therefore designed to meet the participatory needs of the likes of the KKCR community? Scholars have nevertheless advanced ICT as a component crucial for participation even when the phone and internet penetration is in cities while community media (In Uganda) is mostly in villages. For example, Carpentier et al (2001) note that the trendy way of dis-cussing the notion of community is far from geographically defined spaces. Carpentier et al (2001) continue, communities are 'formed in cyber space-for example usergroups'. At KKCR, it is the opposite. The community has no usergroup, cyber space or mailing list. Even though mobile phones are beginning to spread, there is no 'calling or texting list' among the listeners specifically exchanging ideas about community media or KKCR.

Such changes in community had been foreseen by Tonnies (1887), when he said that 'the growth of capitalism, industrialization and urbanization had profoundly altered the relationship between the individual and society, resulting in the loss of community'. This prophecy of the demise of community has not come to pass in Uganda which means, we can still live within the limits of the old community not society. Uganda specifically is between communism and capitalism. The government for instance is the sole provider of water, military hardware, rail transport and it also controls several other resources. Nevertheless, we have liberalization in media and other sectors. Second on Tonnies' list is industrialization. Out of the total population (35.4 million people), 87% live in villages and most of them are farmers. The third factor that can wash away community for society is urbanisation but Uganda has 6.4 million people living in urban areas (UBOS, 2013) of the total population.

Why then do we still define community media communities in Uganda (listeners) as participatory communities because of ICTs?

By doing this, we assume that wherever there is community media, people have access to ICT and maybe it is only their resources that affect the usage. This is not the case at Kagadi. There is only one internet café which has eight computers and this is supposed to serve over 10,000 people in the Town Council. Others in the villages do not even mind about internet. Internet goes off all the time and the level of education is not enough to allow the community members to understand usage of other ICT gadgets than a mobile phone (mostly for the literate teenagers) and radio. Even then, this study for example established that 90% of radio owners in Kagadi-Kibale have the locally-assembled Makula-Sembule radio-set that is easy to use. It has no complication like cassette player, CD or DVD player, just a radio with two bands and no remote control.

Limitations of Basic Media

Basic media have challenges that need to be dealt with. For example, basic media have no control over noise. However, the position of the law is not well pronounced for or against basic media. Instead, the government uses the general broadcasting law that governs other platforms like radio and TV to regulate (control) basic media. Although this law (UCC Act 2013) does not mention or refer to basic media, it is invoked if government wants to close basic media whenever someone complains about the noise. Contrary to government actions, some local leaders have come out to speak for basic media, noting that government needs to sit and create a law that can be used to regulate basic media and that such a law should take into special consideration the uniqueness of the media (Luwaga, 2012). As a solution to the lack of law and policy problem, the local leaders have come up to decide what times basic media should go on air, and how many times a day (Bakalu, 2014). How many times basic media go on air differs from community to community.

The other limitation is that basic media remove the freedom of choice of stations that community media are able to provide. However, currently for the KKCR community, that provision too has been taken away by KKCR's dominance of other stations. Besides, basic media only work a few times a day. At most, they are on two times a day. Between these two times, community members can seek information from other communication platforms.

CONCLUSION

The opportunity created by ICT towards participation undoubtedly is generous. Specifically, mobile phones and radio continue to lead among ICT dominance in Kagadi-Kibale community. This is because more than half of the community has access to these two particular ICTs, a triumph of time over distance in rhetoric. However, the general contention in this paper is that ICT cannot solely claim responsibility for community participation in the developing world unless unconditional attention has been paid to e-enabling. Under that general umbrella, several ICT constraints like electricity shortage, network problems, complexity of gadgets and many others may be tackled. If not, these problems will continue to ravage any opportunity the presence of ICT may have created for participation. With such troubled community participation and lack of self-management, there remains a very thin line between community and commercial media. Since there is lack of political will while the civil society is pushing for community media and ICT in their current form, it is imperative that an alternative to community media, here in the paper referred to as Basic Media, be adopted for the developing world.

ACKNOWLEDGMENT

Appreciation goes to Carleton University and the International Development Research Centre (IDRC) for funding the project. Special thank you to Dr. Linje Manyozo (formerly of London School of Economics), and to Associate Professor Nassanga Goretti, Department of Journalism and Communication, Makerere University, who started and paved the way.

REFERENCES

Arnstein, S. (1969). A ladder of citizen participation. *Journal of the American Institute of Planners*, *37*(7), 216–224. doi:10.1080/01944366908977225

Bakalu, B. (2014). Luweero passes law on 'radios'. *Cpanel Observer*. Retrieved from http://www.cpanel. observer.ug/index.php?option=com_content&view=article&id=30177:-luweero-passes-law-on-radios &catid=34:news&Itemid=114

Baliamoune-Lutz, M. (2003). An analysis of the determinants and effects of ICT diffusion in developing countries. *Information Technology for Development*, *10*(1), 151–169. doi:10.1002/itdj.1590100303

Banda, F. (2010). *Citizen journalism and democracy in Africa: An exploratory study*. Grahamstown, South Africa: Highway Africa.

Baran, S., & Davis, D. (2003). *Mass Communication Theory: Foundation, Ferment, and Future*. California: Wordsworth.

Berger, G. (2010). *Challenges and perspectives of digital migration for Africa*. Dakar: Panos West Africa.

Burns, D., & Taylor, M. (2000). *Auditing community participation: An assessment handbook*. Bristol, UK: The Policy Press.

Carpentier, N. (2001). Managing Audience Participation: The Construction of Participation in an Audience Discussion Programme. *European Journal of Communication*, *16*(2), 209–232. doi:10.1177/0267323101016002004

Carpentier, N., Lie, R., & Servaes, J. (2001, July). Community media – Muting the democratic media discourse?*Proceedings of the International Social Theory Consortium Second Annual Conference*, Brighton, UK.

Freire, P. (1970). *Pedagogy of the oppressed*. London: Penguin.

Hamelink, C. J. (2001). The planning of communication technology: Alternatives for the periphery. In S. Melkote & S. Rao (Eds.), *Critical issues in communication: Looking forward for answers*. New Delhi, India: Sage.

Hang, D. (2005). *Effects of ICT on media transformation, education and training in Cambodia, Lao PDR and Viet Nam*. Retrieved from http://www.comminit.com/en/node/287055/307

Islam, S. M. (2008). Towards a sustainable e-participation implementation model. *European Journal of ePractice*. Retrieved from www. epracticejournal.eu

Kulabako, F. (2011, March). Inflation rises to 14 percent. *Daily Monitor*, *22*, 3.

Luwaga, B. (2012). Closure of Community Radio Stations lives Luwero Quiet. Retrieved from http://ugandaradionetwork.com/a/story.php?s=39811

Macintosh, A. (2004). Characterizing e-participation in policy-making.*Proceedings of the 37th Hawaii International Conference on System Sciences*.

McQuail, D. (2006). *McQuail's mass communication theory*. London, UK: Sage.

Nassanga, L. G. (2003). Is there a place for community media in East Africa in the context of globalisation? In G. Nassanga (Ed.), *The East African media and globalisation: Defining the public interest* (pp. 184–202). Kampala, Uganda: Makerere University.

Nassanga, L. G. (2009a). An assessment of the changing community media parameters in East Africa. *African Journalism Studies*, *30*(1), 42–57. doi:10.3368/ajs.30.1.42

Nassanga, L. G. (2009b). Participatory discussion programs as 'hybrid community media' in Uganda. *International Journal of Media and Cultural Politics*, *5*(1 & 2), 119–124.

O'Donnell, S., McIver, W. J., & Rideout, V. (2006, September). Community media and networking and ICT.*Proceedings of the Canadian Communication Association Annual Conference*, Toronto, Canada, York University.

Organisation for Economic Co-operation and Devel-opment. (2003). Integrating information and communication technologies in development programmes. Retrieved from www.oecd.org/bookshop

Peters, B. (2009). And lead us not into thinking the new is new: A bibliographic case for new media history. *New Media & Society*, *11*(13), 13–30. doi:10.1177/1461444808099572

Pohjola, M. (2003). *The adoption and diffusion of ICT across countries: Patterns and determinants, The new economy handbook*. Helsinki, Finland: Academic Press.

Pringle, I., & David, M. J. R. (2002). Rural com-munity ICT applications: The Kothmale model. *The Electronic Journal on Information Systems and Development*, *8*(4), 1–14.

Qvortrup, L. (2006). Understanding new digital media: Medium theory or complexity. *European Journal of Communication*, *21*(345), 345–356. doi:10.1177/0267323106066639

Semujju, B. (2013). ICT as an engine for community participation: An assessment of Uganda's community media. *International Journal of Information Communication Technologies and Human Development*, *5*(1), 20–36. doi:10.4018/jicthd.2013010102

Semujju, B. (2014). Participatory media for a non-participating community: Western media for Southern communities. *The International Communication Gazette*, *76*(2), 197–208. doi:10.1177/1748048513504166

Sharma, A. (2010). *Use of ICT at community level around the globe*. Retrieved from http://www.telecentremagazine.net/news/newsde-tails.asp?newsid=15808

Straubhaar, J., & Larose, R. (2002). *Media now: Communication media in the Information Age*. Wadsworth Group.

Tonnies, F. (1887). *Community and society: Gemeinschaft und gesellschaft* (C. P. Loomis, Trans. & Ed.). Lansing, MI: Michigan State University Press.

Uganda Bureau of Statistics. (2013). *Statistical Abstract*. Kampala: UBOS.

Uganda Communications Commission. (2013). *Annual Market Review*. Kampala: UCC.

Wanyeki, M. L. (2000). The Development of Community Media in East and Southern Africa. In S. T. K. Boafo (Ed.), *Promoting Community media in Africa* (pp. 25–41). Paris: UNESCO.

Williams, B., & Carpini, M. (2004). Monica and Bill all the time and everywhere: The collapse of gate keeping and agenda setting in the new media environ-ment. *The American Behavioral Scientist, 47*(1208), 1208–1230. doi:10.1177/0002764203262344

Wong, P. (2002). ICT production and diffusion in Asia Digital dividends or digital divide? *Information Economics and Policy, 14*(11), 167–187. doi:10.1016/S0167-6245(01)00065-8

Youngs, G. (2002). Virtual communities. In C. New-bold, O. Boyd-Barret, & H. Van den Bulk (Eds.), *The Media Book*. London, UK: Arnold Publications.

Zakus, L., & Lysack, C. L. (1998). Revisiting community participation. *Health Policy and Planning, 13*(1), 1–12. doi:10.1093/heapol/13.1.1 PMID:10178181

ADDITIONAL READING

Collins, P. H. (2010). The New Politics of Community. *American Sociological Review, 75*(1), 7–30. doi:10.1177/0003122410363293

Hamelink, C. J. (2001). The planning of communication technology: Alternatives for the periphery. In S. Melkote & S. Rao (Eds.), *Critical issues in communication: Looking forward for answers*. New Delhi, India: Sage.

Hang, D. (2005). *Effects of ICT on media transformation, education and training in Cambodia, Lao PDR and Viet Nam*. Retrieved from http://www.comminit.com/en/node/287055/307

Islam, S. M. (2008). Towards a sustainable e-participation implementation model. *European Journal of ePractice*. Retrieved from www. epracticejournal.eu

Litho, P. K. (2007). *Information and communication technologies and the" empowerment" of women in rural Uganda* [Doctoral dissertation]. University of East London.

Nassanga, G. L. (2009). An assessment of the changing community media parameters in East Africa. *Ecquid Novi, 30*(1), 42–57. doi:10.3368/ajs.30.1.42

Nassanga, G. L., Manyozo, L., & Lopes, C. (2013). ICTs and radio in Africa: How the uptake of ICT has influenced the newsroom culture among community radio journalists. *Telematics and Informatics, 30*(3), 258–266. doi:10.1016/j.tele.2012.04.005

Nassanga, L. G. (2009a). An assessment of the changing community media parameters in East Africa. *African Journalism Studies*, *30*(1), 42–57. doi:10.3368/ajs.30.1.42

Nassanga, L. G. (2009b). Participatory discussion programs as 'hybrid community media' in Uganda. *International Journal of Media and Cultural Politics*, *5*(1 & 2), 119–124.

Semujju, B. (2014). ICT as an engine for community participation: An assessment of Uganda's community media . In Digital Arts and Entertainment: Concepts, Methodologies, Tools, and Applications (Ch. 40, pp. 839-854). Hershey, PA, USA: IGI-Global Publishing.

Semujju, B. (2014). Participatory media for a non-participating community: Western media for Southern communities. *The International Communication Gazette*, *76*(2), 197–208. doi:10.1177/1748048513504166

Semujju, R. B. (2012). *The impact of ICT on community participation in community media: case study of Kagadi-Kibaale Community Radio* [MA Thesis]. Makerere University, Kampala.

Ssewanyana, J., & Busler, M. (2007). Adoption and usage of ICT in developing countries: Case of Ugandan firms. *International Journal of Education and Development using ICT*, *3*(3).

Ssewanyana, J. K. (2007). ICT access and poverty in Uganda. *International Journal of Computing and ICT Research*, *1*(2), 10–19.

KEY TERMS AND DEFINITIONS

Basic Media: The media that localizes community needs down to basic life survival needs. Such media concern themselves with basic needs like water and food. For example, these media do not discuss better farming methods. The instead talk about which market has good prices for a certain kind of food. Basic media also talk about a broken well, which community members should go and fix instead of calling for government to extend tap water to communities.

Community: A group that shares physical or digital space or idea as an interest that binds members together. While community changes as society undergoes several geographical and technological changes, the underlying idea of having a unifying factor like space, or idea is important to the understanding of community.

Community Media: This refers to a communication platform which is run by the local geographical (mostly) communities for the local community. Community media distinguish themselves using three main principles: access, participation and self-management.

Community Participation: The idea that local efforts lead and maintain the development efforts intended to develop the same people. In community media discourse, such local people would act as volunteers at the stations while the same people would be used to relay their experiences about an issue of contentions, other than bringing in expert opinions.

Information Communication Technology (ICT): The technology used in conveying, manipulating and storing of data by electronic means. This includes computers and all their components that help in handling information at different levels, the internet which transmits large volumes of data at terrific speeds, and several others.

Chapter 9
Research Dimensions of Open Innovation in Small and Medium Enterprises

Hakikur Rahman
BRAC University, Bangladesh

ABSTRACT

Innovation is treated as a recognized driver of economic prosperity of a country through the sustained growth of its entrepreneurships. Moreover, recently coined term open innovation is increasingly taking the lead in enterprise management in terms of value addition. Foci of academics, researchers and practitioners nowadays are revolving around various innovation models, comprising innovation methods, processes and strategies. This chapter seeks to find out open innovation researches and practices that are being carried out circumscribing development of entrepreneurships, particularly the sector belonging to the small and medium enterprises (SMEs) through a longitudinal study. Along this context the chapter put forwards part of a continuous study investigating into researches in the area of open innovation for entrepreneurship development that are being carried out by leading researchers and research houses across the globe, and at the same time it also investigating open innovation practices that are being carried out for the development of entrepreneurships, emphasizing SMEs. Before conclusion the chapter has tried to develop a framework to instigate future research.

INTRODUCTION

Innovation is not any more just a research topics, but it has become a significant driver for prosperity, growth and sustained profitability to global entrepreneurships. Innovation along its route to the current period exhaled new methods or tools in terms of products, processes or organizational management. As far as this literature review and research go, from its early inception inscribing issues of economic development (Schumpeter, 1934; 1942; 1950), patents and licensing (Von Hippel, 1988), organizational networking (Powell, 1990), process innovation (Davenport, 1993), co-opetition (Brandenburger and Nalebuff, 1996), management of intellectual capital (Grindley and Teece, 1997) till the coining up of

DOI: 10.4018/978-1-5225-0556-3.ch009

its features in more familiar ways framing on the utilization of information technologies, such as open innovation (Chesbrough 2003a; 2003b), innovation never stayed stalled. Furthermore, due to opening up the innovation processes and combining internally and externally developed technologies and strategies to create economic value the innovation has crossed the boundary of closed innovation to open innovation (Rahman and Ramos, 2010; 2012).

Traditionally, firms used to prefer the so-called, closed innovation strategies in developing their own products internally, and with limited interactions with the external world (Lichtenthaler, 2011). In recent years, researchers and practitioners are showing interests in open innovation research and practices that are visible during the literature review in various publications, and conference proceedings. This has also been observed in contemporary literatures that innovation researches are shifting from the closed and controlled environment of the corporate entrepreneurs towards more open and flexible model, based on cooperation and coordination among various parties. Knowledge and new technologies are no longer remaining sole properties of major monopoly corporations (Caetano and Amaral, 2011; Westergren and Holmstrom, 2012).

In this aspect, the business sector belonging to the small and small enterprises (SMEs[1]) play important role in networking and making innovation clusters in association with universities and research houses, being recognized as major driving forces in the open innovation paradigm.

SMEs also play a crucial role in raising investments in spin offs, start ups, or research and development (R&D) and making countries more competitive, which is true for not only the European Union but also in other countries (European Union, 2005). Moreover, the majority of the developing and transitional economies have acknowledged that SMEs are the potential engine of economic growth and source of sustainable development, which are essential for industrial reformation, new job creation, and revenue generation of the population at large (Koyuncugil & Ozgulbas, 2009).

However, this research observes that utilization of open innovation strategies for the development of SMEs remains low in terms of researches and practices (Chesbrough 2003a; 2003b; West, Vanhaverbeke & Chesbrough, 2006; Lichtenthaler & Ernst, 2009; Lindermann, Valcareel, Schaarschmidt & Von Kortzfleisch, 2009; Van de Vrande, de Jong, Vanhaverbeke & de Rochemont, 2008; 2009), especially finding interpretative results justifying through empirical studies. Only a limited number of literatures are there to support the introduction of OI strategies in SMEs.

This study while conducting an empirical study in Portugal among some selected SMEs, has tried to synthesize various research dimensions by carrying out a longitudinal study. In doing so, a thorough literature review has been conducted emphasizing researches conducted by leading researchers and practitioners through two most comprehensive search engines (Sciencedirect, and Scopus), though hardly these could be recognized as cent percent contribution towards SMEs growth. While investigating into the open innovation aspects of SMEs, the study covered characteristics of individual firms, and group of firms (by human aspect, financial aspect, and issues of challenges in adopting OI strategies) taken at national or regional contexts. The intention is to prepare a report by mapping the issues of challenges, and on adoption of OI strategies in Portugal. However, this chapter restrains only within the theoretical contexts on various research dimensions that the study has encountered during the initial stage of the research, including the conduction of the pilot survey and extension of the survey in a few other countries of similar socio-economic status.

The chapter has been divided into five sections. Introducing about generic perspectives of open innovation in SMEs, the next section discusses specific research aspects of open innovation. The third section is the main thrust of the chapter, which discusses about the literature search using two search engines with relevant observation from the research group. Thereafter, before concluding this particular aspect of the study with the findings, it put forward a few research hints for future research and dialogue in this particular area of research.

BACKGROUND

Open Innovation and SMEs

Innovative entrepreneurship need to be treated as a utility with purpose, meaning, and accountability; not a glitch. The task can be fulfilled by an individual alone or by teaming up with one or more partners, or with the support from other firms or similar ventures. If the task is performed in a collaborative platform, even a large group of firms can function as partners in the entrepreneurship. The entrepreneur is the one who brings together the necessary resources (financial, logistic, managerial and personnel) that the innovation calls for. The entrepreneur is the one who finds the place of application and directs the execution of the alteration. Sometimes a long time may pass before a promising invention is taken up by a true entrepreneur. Probably it may happen that an invention or discovery and an entrepreneur do not match immediately. Fortunately in the realm of technology advancement, it is quite frequent that the match is made without much difficulty. However, in most cases the Schumpeterian entrepreneur drives the innovation process during the first realization of any revolutionary innovation. Furthermore, the process following the pioneering innovation (also known as diffusion), is also mostly driven by entrepreneurs and majority of the initiative appears at the beginning of the entrepreneurship sequence (Kornai, 2010). The entire collaborative functions can be familiarized as a part and parcel of innovation, or rather open innovation. Also, in recent days, not only innovative entrepreneurs are there who are initiating innovative ventures, or looking for a partner of similar attitude, but also there are successful intermediaries with knowledge and expertise in this field, and assisting each individual firms or group of firms utilizing the innovative information technology platforms.

The most important benefit of open innovation to entrepreneurship is that it provides a flexible and extended base of knowledge; with new ideas and technologies based on sources internal or external partners, such as clients, suppliers, researchers, practitioners, staffs and all others who are involved in producing productive input in the value addition process. Main motive of joining forces is not to compete, but to seize new business opportunities by sharing risks and resources (OECD, 2008b; Sousa, 2008). The open innovation approach assumes that the firm is no longer the sole place of innovation, nor the lone entity in reaping the benefits of research, development and innovation. In contrast to the closed innovation where each entity used to treat others with either suspicion, who could take away useful knowledge; or at least thought to be another competitor, who could reduce the profit margin; in the open innovation paradigm, each and every entities are being taken as partners, and regarded as potential contributors of crucial piece of information needed to the value addition process. This process is open ended and collaborative, thus assists in reducing RDI costs, risks, and technology costs, and essentially becoming important driver of economic growth (Lemola and Lievonen, 2008; Rahman and Ramos, 2012-research model).

Various school of thoughts support the idea of benefitting from open innovation for the small and medium scale business firms, which may lead to product innovation or process innovation including employment generation (Roper and Hewitt-Dundas, 2004). But, in reality this newly opened paradigm is relatively challenging, as the society is yet to confirm the impact of open innovation in SMEs, in spite of claims on enhanced collaboration and employment generation (Nahlinder, 2005). Thus, not only improving the competitive advantage of SMEs is essential to the individual firm or the group of firms, but also the impact at the national economy is need to be visible (Tilley and Tonge, 2003). However, except surveys conducted at the institutional levels, like OECD Science Technology and Industry Scoreboard, OECD SME and Entrepreneurship Outlook, only a few literatures exist illustrating empirical studies on SMEs and the impact of open innovation in collaboration of more than one researchers, such as de Jong, Orietta Marsili, 2006; van de Vrande, de Jong, Vanhaverbeke and de Rochemont, 2009; Dahlander and Gann, 2010; Gassmann, Enkel and Chesbrough, 2010; Lee, Park, Yoon& Park, 2010; and others. Apart from them several researches are being conducted at individual level, such as Lichtenthaler, 2006; 2007a; 2007b; 2008a; 2008b; 2008c; 2008d; 2008e; 2008f; 2009a; 2009b; 2009c; 2010a; 2010b; 2010c; 2011a; 2011b; von Hippel, 1975; 1978; 1986; 1987; 1990; 1994; 1998; 2001a; 2001b; 2005; 2007; 2010. Hence, this study suggests that further researches are required to map the impact of open innovation at the group level, individual level, country level, or cross-country level.

Open Innovation Researches on SMEs

Innovation is an essential element among other functionalities for enterprises and entrepreneurships, especially surviving within the current economic situation, and at the same time planning for sustainable growth relative to their competitors, locally and globally. It is not a luxury, but essentiality. Though not plenty, but tools exist to assist the entrepreneurs to measure their propensity to innovate and increase their capability for innovation or their innovation performance. However, this research finds that the situation is scanty for SMEs, due to the fact that majority of those tools are being applicable at corporate level, not for small enterprises who could not afford such tools due to various challenges, such as a lack of awareness, funding and capacity which causes apprehension about innovation, open innovation, intellectual property and other strategies (Gassmann, 2006; Van de Vrande, de Jong, Vanhaverbeke & de Rochemont, 2009). Furthermore, amongst SMEs who have been subjected to relevant researches there is persuasive evidence that innovation tends to be a domestic affair with more developments coming from existing resources rather than coming from outside sources (Bevis and Cole, 2010).

It has been observed that most of the researches on open innovation remain restricted towards targeting common stakeholders through major corporate houses or their alliances. In addition, it is a fact that a few of those corporate are controlling the entire global market or system of open innovation chain through process modification, product differentiation, or diversification of resources. Moreover, despite immense potentiality to reach out the stakeholders at the grass roots through open ended demand, diversity of product variation, and scale of economic capacity majority of the contemporary researches are confined towards generic pattern-oriented clients (Rahman & Ramos, 2010). It is good sign that the scenario is rapidly transforming in the recent decade. Innovation is no longer remains within a vertically integrated company with everything remaining in-house. With the advent of open innovation concept and new information technologies, open and flexible cooperation among business houses, research centers and universities is being treated as the most beneficial approach for business development, especially start-offs, spin-offs, or kick-starting joint ventures. In this new business model different actors are applying their principles in addition to other partners through interactive participations to bring out an acceptable outcome for value addition (Chesbrough, 2003a; Maijers, Vokurka, van Uffelen, & Ravensbergen, 2005; Wijffels, 2009; Rahman and Ramos, 2012).

The other fact is that SMEs are being accepted as the global drivers of technological innovation and economic development and represent the deep, broad and fertile platform that nourishes, sustains, and regenerates the global economic ecosystem (Kowalski, 2009). At the same time, to engage the open innovation strategies, research and development (R&D, taken as a key innovation indicator) is increasingly being outsourced to lower the cost of production (Dehoff & Sehgal, 2006; 2008). Apart from the cooperation, coordination and collaboration, open innovation strategies involve vigorous networking with partner companies, interaction with start-up ventures, public research institutes, universities and external suppliers; thus sharing and accessing of outside information and technology, IP management, knowledge management, creative entrepreneurship thinking, making strategic alliances and above all leading to be global visionary (Kowalski, 2009; Lichtenthaler, 2011a). All these factors resonate for integrated and enhanced researches on the aspect of SME development through open innovation strategies.

The current section serves as a broad background on the concept of open innovation that has been observed by this research along while carrying out the literature review. However, the research hypothesis is to find out contemporary researches following a respectable search from a dependable repository. The study has taken various approaches in this aspect, but mainly depended on contents from the ScienceDirect, a concern of Elsevier B.V, Scopus, Google Scholar, and the university's integrated online library search. Due to the subscription status of the researchers own institute, it was easy to obtain cross reference materials easily from other subscribed sources. The main literature review has been conducted across various research dimensions, and they have been presented in the next section. The next section discusses about various research dimensions that have been carried out by contemporary researchers in the field of open innovation for the development of SMEs.

RESEARCHES DIMENSIONS: THE REVIEW

By far the open innovation (authors prefer it to be seen as a form of collaborative innovation) is becoming the central topics surrounding business strategy and innovation (Huizingh, 2009) and open innovation is being claimed to be the new breed of innovation requiring enterprises to look beyond the boundaries of their organizations, thus using external and internal knowledge for successful value creation (Thoben, 2008). In the eyes of an open innovator on entrepreneurship development, economic prosperity is expected to result from exploiting the innovation capacity of an enterprise by improving the competitiveness and thus enhancing the productivity (BVCA, 2005). However, as observed during this longitudinal study, open innovation has so far been adopted mainly in high-tech and multinational companies. Though open innovation has received increasing attention in the scientific research arena, but so far it has mainly been investigated in corporate and high-tech multinational enterprises (MNEs) based on instruments, such as in-depth interviews and case studies (Chesbrough, 2003b; Kirschbaum, 2005; Lichtenthaler, 2010a). Moreover, when searching for cases or examples, most of them are found to be focusing on very specific industries, for example open source software (Henkel, 2006) or tabletop role-playing games (Lecocq & Demil, 2006) or crafts industries (Santisteban, 2006) or tourism (Novelli, Schmitz & Spencer, 2006; Hjalager, 2010). Even if a large sample of enterprises is being explored by various researchers, their focuses remain on specific issues rather than the full open innovation model (Van de Vrande, de Jong, Vanhaverbeke & de Rochemont, 2009). Perhaps, the reason could be that the open innovation strategies depend on the very specific cases, applications, sectors or environments, and cannot be generalized, as such. Or, the open innovation maturity model has not been reached at such a stage that can be generalized.

The review has, however observed that open innovation researches also exist in smaller organizations (Van de Vrande, de Jong, Vanhaverbeke & de Rochemont, 2009) and this trend is increasing (Gassmann, Enkel & Chesbrough, 2010; Saarikoski, 2006; Dahlander & Gann, 2010; Fredberg, Elmquist & Ollila, 2008). To find out further detail about the research trends on open innovation for SMEs development, several searches were conducted among the contemporary researchers, their research and research practices carried out by reputed organizations like OECD, European Union, European Commission and others in the field of open innovation, especially targeted for SMEs development. Following the search methodology of Saarikoski (2006, p. 24) and supported by similar methodology on structured litera-ture review of Fredberg, Elmquist and Ollila (2008, p. 10), a search into the Internet (Google) with the search string 'open innovation research AND SMEs development' (empirical setting of the research) was conducted and it yield 3,580,000 hits (though the string ["open innovation research" AND "SMEs development"] resulted only 2 hits). With the later string, Google Scholar returns only 1 hit. These hits included contents on this aspect incorporating all those mentioned entities (researchers, researches, research organizations, and academia, national and international organizations). However, to keep the search less generalized and focused to specific search settings and foremost to have an overview on the contemporary research works including practices on open innovation, the search for this study was conducted on a content provider namely, ScienceDirect, and Scopus. This search has been carried out on ScienceDirect by using the search formulae set_1.

Search in ScienceDirect

The Search Formulae set_1:

1. (open AND innovation for all fields and research AND SMEs for all fields) [(All Sources) (All Sciences) (All Years*)]
2. (open AND innovation for all fields and research AND SMEs for all fields) [(All Sources) (Business, Management and Accounting) (All Years*)]
3. (open AND innovation AND research for all fields and SMEs for all fields) [All Sources (Business, Management and Accounting) (All Years*)]
4. (open AND innovation for titles and research AND SMEs for all fields) [All Sources (Business, Management and Accounting) (All Years*)]

* Since 2002.

The search string (1) brings 2,394 counts; search string (2) brings 1,496 counts and search string (3) brings 1,496 counts; while search string (4) brings only 17 counts.

Search string (3) (with 1,496 counts) has been taken as the entry point of this longitudinal study and among them 1,353 were journal articles, 143 books and 4 were tagged as reference works. Table 1 shows their publication pattern considering major number of publication (here the minimum count is 40) and Table 2 shows their years of publication (here the data has been given from 2000 till the date of the search, which is October 21, 2010). Noteworthy to mention that the search was conducted applying

Table 1. Number of entries in different journals: Search string (3) with minimum count of 40

Name of Journal	Number of Entries
Technovation	205
Research Policy	191
Technological Forecasting and Social Changes	70
Industrial Marketing Management	66
International Business Review	64
European Management Journal	61
Journal of Business Venturing	53
World Patent Information	46
Journal of Business Research	40

(counts were taken since 2002 till the date of the search, which is October 08, 2012)

to all fields. But, when the search was modified with 'open innovation' in the title and 'research+smes' within the fields, the result returned only 10 journal articles and books.

Table 2 shows that the trend of researches using open innovation strategies for SMEs development is growing after the term 'open innovation' has been coined by Prof. Henry Chesbrough. This table also reveals that the trend of using OI strategies was there as number of articles before 2002 with the available data from the ScienceDirect is significant. However, the main purpose of this study is to find out thematic patterns or themes of researches obtained from most relevant contents of these searches. To be more specific, the most relevant contents were separated from these search using search string (iii). Also, the main notion of using ScienceDirect is to provide the first impression of freely available content without being subscribed, notwithstanding other arguments.

Table 2. Number of publications in various years on oi researches for SMEs

Year of Publication	Number of Publications
2012	248
2011	164
2010	131
2009	122
2008	124
2007	107
2006	97
2005	93
2004	56
2003	55
2002 and earlier since 1992	303

(counts were taken since 2003 till the date of the search, which is October 08, 2012)

Search in Scopus

On Scopus, the following search string has been used (termed as the Search Formulae set_2):

- (open AND innovation AND research for all Titles, Abstracts and Keywords) [All documents] (All Years*)]

* Since 2003.

The Search Formulae set_2 resulted in 42 counts with ALL documents type and Subject Areas belonging to Life Sciences (with more than 4,300 titles), Physical Sciences (>7,200 titles), health Sciences (>6,800 titles), and Social Sciences and Humanities (>5,300 titles).

Another set of search was carried out among the publication of the leading researchers and practitioners in this field. Among them, the book, "Open Innovation: The New Imperative for Creating and Profiting from Technology" (Chesbrough, 2003a, being the most cited author on 'open innovation' (Fredberg, Elmquist & Ollila, 2008)); "Open Innovation: Practice, Trends, Motives and bottlenecks in the SMEs" (De Jong, 2006); "Open Innovation: Researching a new Paradigm" (Chesbrough, Vanhaverbeke & West, 2006); Journal articles written by Van de Vrande, de Jong, Vanhaverbeke & de Rochemont, 2008; 2009; De Jong, Vanhaverbeke, Kalvet & Chesbrough, 2008; Gassman, 2006; and Gasmann, Enkel & Chesbrough, 2010 were included. The first book was selected as the most cited book in this sector, the second article was selected as the most relevant search return each time made on search engines, and the rest were selected by the authors after careful observations from various search strings and citation index.

As a fourth check, contribution of forerunners on the concept of open innovation in the form of books were also included in the categorization, such as Schumpeter (1934; 1942; 1950), Von Hippel (1986; 1987; 1988) and Davenport (1993a; 1993b; 1994). Noteworthy to mention that there were several others books (available in the references), but they are not being included here, as separate entities. And, unless they provide fundamental concepts on open innovation research, literatures earlier than 2003 were less emphasized.

Finally, to avail the information about open innovation researches in SMEs, this study looked at various publications from international organizations like, OECD, European Union, and European Commission; individual organizations like, Vinnova, Vision Era-Net; portals like, OpenInnovation dot net, Innocentive dot com, Ideaconnection dot com; and articles from special issues from journals like, MIT Sloan Management Review, Technovation, Research Policy, and Harvard Business Review.

After several round of iterations, the following research themes were taken into consideration for exploration, pending further research impact on these themes and extended debate on their substances in relation to the development of smaller firms serving at the grass roots. Table-3 is showing the selected research themes, which are being discussed in the next sub-section in terms of their relevancies.

RESEARCHES AND RESEARCHERS: RESEARCH THEMES

Ranging from the conceptualization, policy initiation, and establishment of research model to development of business model, adaptation of strategies, measurement of the impact and development of tools for use and dissemination of the strategies, this study emphasizes on seven distinct research themes. One may argue about this setting of the research theme, but this study observed that without an appropriate

Table 3. Synthesized Research Themes on Oi for the SMEs

Research Themes	Literatures from the Search
Conceptualization of open innovation (and policy initiation)	Savioz & Blum, 2002; Amara, Landry, Becheikh & Ouimet, 2008; Chesbrough, 2003a; Lee, Park, Yoon & Park, 2010; Huizingh, 2011
Establishment of research model (and action research)	Major & Cordey-Hayes, 2000; Chesbrough, 2003b; 2006; Edwards, Delbridge & Munday, 2005; Lawson, Longhurst & Ivey, 2006; Thorgren, Wincent & Örtqvist, 2009; Raymond & St-Pierre, 2010; Rhee, Park & Lee, 2010
Development of business model (and framework development)	Cooke, 2005; Chesbrough, 2006; De Jong, 2006; Partanen, Möller, Westerlund, Rajala & Rajala, 2008; Freel & De Jong, 2009; Lee, et al., 2010; Belussi, Sammarra & Sedita, 2010; Carlos de Oliveira and Kaminski, 2012
Opportunities and challenges of open innovation (and action plan to combat the situation)	Hoffman, Parejo, Bessant & Perren, 1998; Levy, Powell & Galliers, 1999; Del Brío & Junquera, 2003; Tödtling & Trippl, 2005; Van de Vrande, de Jong, Vanhaverbeke, & Rochemont, 2009; Groen & Linton, 2010; Knudsen & Mortensen, 2010; Rahman & Ramos, 2010
Adoption of OI strategies and technologies (and the impact at the ground reality)	Bougrain & Haudeville, 2002 ; Izushi, 2003; De Jong & Marsili, 2006; Dickson, Weaver & Hoy, 2006; Ferneley & Bell, 2006; O´Regan, Ghobadian & Sims, 2006; Laforet, 2008; Van de Vrande et al., 2009; Leiponen & Byma, 2009; Zeng, Xie & Tam, 2010; Lichtenthaler, 2010; Lee & Lan, 2011; Mention, 2010; Hjalager, 2010; O'Regan, De Jong & Hippel, 2009; Spithoven, Clarysse and Knockaert, 2010
Measuring the impact of OI strategies (and taking actions to improve the situation)	Huang, Soutar & Brown 2004 ; Massa & Testa, 2008; Woodhams & Lupton, 2009; Grupp & Schubert, 2010; Liao and Rice, 2010; Raymond and St-Pierre, 2010; Caetano and Amaral, 2011; Gredel, Kramer and Bend, 2012; Fu, 2012; Nunes, Serrasqueiro and Leitão, 2012
Development of tools or instruments based on OI strategies (and piggybacking on any existing tools or instruments that are available in the market)	Kaufmann & Tödtling, 2002; Kohn & Hüsig, 2006; Descotes, Walliser, Holzmüller and Guo, 2011; Ramos, Acedo and Gonzalez, 2011; Hervas-Oliver, Garrigos and Gil-Pechuan, 2011; Kang and Park, 2012; Love and Ganotakis, 2012;

conceptualization of the innovation process (and certainly without the involvement of the policy initiators), it cannot be established, and similarly next stages are invariably dependent (even inter-dependent within the internal processes) on the previous stages, such as without learning about the opportunities and challenges behind the strategies, the methodologies cannot be adopted, or without learning about the impact of the open innovation strategies, the tools cannot be developed, and so forth. Another school of thoughts could be how much these themes are relevant or appropriate to the SMEs. These researchers argue that adoption of open innovation strategies to small scale enterprises are yet to reach the level of maturity in even developed nations or nations who are leaders in doing so, hence these themes are also need to be investigated extensively at the grass roots level and these call for comprehensive research, especially in marginal or critically affected socio-economic environments.

Conceptualization of Open Innovation Strategies in Entrepreneurship Development

Though the concept of open innovation was in the market for many years before the term was newly introduced and popularized by Prof. Henry Chesbrough in 2003, this study finds many researchers are still researching on modernizing the concepts of open innovation strategies or advancing the degree of novelty of innovation. With the adoption of OI strategies in the entrepreneurship development, many researchers have initiated extended studies to reach out to the market by breaking the boundary of the firm. Terms like, innovation merchants, innovation architects, innovation missionaries, innovation intermediaries, business angels, or outsourcing R&Ds, use of venture capital, technology intelligence, licensing management, intellectual property management started gaining their acceptance and popularity to fill an ever-existing gap between the producer and the user (Chesbrough, 2003a; Lee, Park, Yoon & Park, 2010; Savioz & Blum, 2002; Amara, Landry, Becheikh & Ouimet, 2008). Apart from the mentioned terms, such as 'Users-as-innovators', 'customers-as-innovators', 'suppliers-as-innovators' (von Hippel 1986; 1988), 'networked coordination' (Powell, 1990), 'co-opetition' (Brandeburger & Nalebuff 1996), 'communities of practice' (Wenger 1998), and the 'private-collective innovation model' (Von Hippel & Von Krogh 2003), there are many other visible concepts that have been observed and they need to be scrutinized according to their importance to contribute for the entrepreneurship development. At the same time the research dimension has also been shifted from 'closed boundaries to networked paradigm' (Livieratos & Papoulias, 2009; Rahman & Ramos, 2010), which need extended investigation, especially at the local level of the value chain.

It has also been observed that due to lack of appropriate interventions from the national level, open innovation strategies are not being flourished at the local level, in spite of several distinct regional and global agencies are acting in this arena. Furthermore, due to lack of ability to access external resources with minimal technology assets (Narula, 2004), more inclined towards external intervention than engage themselves within to look for external sources (Edwards, Delbridge and Munday, 2005), lack of knowledge in open innovation acquisition process (Vanhaverbeke and Cloodt, 2006) keep them away from open innovation incentives at the early stage of their development.

Establishment of Research Model

With the term 'open innovation' is being popularized, majority of the researchers are trying to launch various research models, especially incorporating the role of external partners (SMEs, academia, research house, universities and intermediaries) to achieve improved performance and efficiency on product, process, service and organizational innovation. Along the path to the paradigm shift, as indicated by majority of the researchers, various research models have tried to validate the role of internal R&D, effect of the firm's size, the linkage between R&D activities and innovation exposition, and looked into various channels of open innovation thus mainstreaming open innovation research in the entrepreneurships through illustrating the conceptual arguments and conceptual frameworks incorporating various drivers of innovativeness (Chesbrough, 2003b; 2006; Raymond & St-Pierre, 2010; Edwards, Delbridge & Munday, 2005; Thorgren, Wincent & Örtqvist, 2009; Lawson, Longhurst & Ivey, 2006; Major & Cordey-Hayes, 2000; Rhee, Park & Lee, 2010).

Furthermore, SME networking and alliances have attracted considerable research attention based on collaboration models such as, bi-firm networks and include alliances with and outsourcing to other firms (Lee et al., 2010). Researchers also claim that SMEs are more flexible to adopt to open innovation due to their ability to utilize external networks more efficiently (Rothwell and Dodgson, 1994). More importantly, inter-firm collaboration is particularly important for SMEs with their limited technology assets (Lichtenthaler, 2005). In this aspect, Lee et al. (2010) proposes a collaborative model based on three distinct patterns, such as outsourcing depending on customer and supplier to explore funding and licensing; partnership depending on strategic alliance to explore joint-venture and R&D partnership; and networking depending on inter-firm alliance to explore networking and collaboration.

Development of Business Model

Since the mid-1980s a novel systemic model of innovation has emerged by incorporating a number of factors, such as externality, transferability, modularity, and network structure, which are not included in the previously dominant linear model (Livieratos & Papoulias, 2009). In this respect, innovation is considered as a systemic, path dependent and knowledge-centric social process influenced by the institutional environment (Chesbrough, 2003a). However, Livieratos and Papoulias (2009) argue that, within the open innovation model the innovation process becomes more complex and fragmented, actors are increasingly heterogeneous and more interdependent, and the period from conceptualization to commercialization is shorter (shorter life time cycle). Livieratos & Papoulias (2009) further argue that, this model has created porous boundaries between the an innovative firm and its surrounding environment by changing the inter- and intra-organizational modes of coordination and triggering new answers to Coase's (1937) question as to, 'what determines the boundaries of the organization'.

Similar to finding an integrated open innovation research model, there is a lack in finding an integrated open innovation business model. Chesbrough (2003a) while introducing this open innovation model, however, argued on the fact that larger firms have better capability to develop and commercialize technologies internally, though due to labor mobility, abundant venture capital, and widely dispersed knowledge across industries lead them to go beyond their peripheries. Hence, open innovation business model adopts both internal and external pathways to exploit technologies and at the same time acquire knowledge from outside (van de Vrande et al., 2009; Lee et al., 2010).

Lee et al. (2010) mentioned about various business models according to their nature, such as product innovation, process innovation, radical innovation, incremental innovation, systemic innovation, component innovation, technology-push and market-pull, including closed innovation and open innovation. Lee et al. (2010) also referred to other business models according to their innovation processes (such as, linear models, or chain-linked models), or according to the fitness for developed or developing countries. Hence, open innovation business models no longer remain restricted by the simple boundary of its own firm, or inter-intra-connected firms.

While investigating the existence and the performance of an Open Regional Innovation System (ORIS model) characterized by the firms' adoption of an open innovation strategy Belussi, Sammarra & Sedita (2010) argue that in terms of adopting open innovation strategies, it overcomes not only the boundaries of the firms, but also the boundaries of the region. Furthermore, Damaskopoulos & Evgeniou (2003) find that open innovation strategy based business models adopt frameworks comprising three interrelated levels of analysis, such as the level of the firm, the level of the market and industrial structures and the regulatory environment.

Literatures portrayed adoption of framework or business model incorporating OI strategies, such as Triple Helix or ORIS, Open Business Model articulating value creation or value addition by emphasizing the role of social capital (Wang, Jaring & Wallin, 2009; West, 2006; Chesbrough, 2006; De Jong, 2006; Partanen, Möller, Westerlund, Rajala & Rajala, 2008; Freel & De Jong, 2009; Cooke, 2005; Belussi, Sammarra & Sedita, 2010; Mortara and Minshall, 2011).

OPPORTUNITIES AND CHALLENGES ON ADOPTING OPEN INNOVATION STRATEGIES

Among many opportunities the availability of public research seems to be the best opportunity factor for the SMEs, as this not only provides chances for innovation, but also produces a pool of experts (researchers, academics, staffs, and consulting firms) with strongly localized knowledge appropriation (Autant-Bernard, Fadairo and Massard, 2012). However, creation and administration of an effective innovative network often remain as critical challenges for SMEs (Lazzarotti, Manzini & Pizzurno, 2008). It has been observed that SMEs are more open to open innovation due to their limited size and resources. At the same time, intense competition and more demanding customers are also tend to be the major motivation for open innovation. But, the most important bottleneck for open innovation is differences in organization and culture between the individual partners (De Jong, 2006).

While researchers are carrying out researches to develop innovation opportunity framework (Levy, Powell & Galliers, 1999; Wang, Jaring & Wallin, 2009; Rahman & Ramos, 2010), but at the same time, the review observes that some other researchers are finding open innovation as challenges for the SMEs development. Groen & Linto (2010) raised a challenge, as whether the term open innovation hindering any growth in research and understanding about the entrepreneurship, and if so should the term be used as it is currently, or be it renamed? Knudsen & Mortensen (2010) chart an unnoticed theme in the current debate on open innovation, as a foundational question, as whether increasing openness is beneficial at all. They further investigate that, with increasing degrees of openness the product development projects are slower than the average in the industry, and these projects are slower than what is usual for the firm's traditional projects and had higher cost than the average in the industry and the firm's usual projects, as well.

In terms of capacity development, Hoffman, Parejo, Bessant & Perren (1998) mention that, despite the strong commitment to support innovation within SMEs at both regional and local level, the actual processes whereby small firms undertake innovative activity remain unclear at the grass roots. Further in this context, Tödtling & Trippl (2005) argue that, there is no "ideal model" or "generic model" so far to be adopted within the innovation policy as innovation activities differ strongly between central, peripheral and old industrial areas. Foremost, the context dependency of open innovation has found to be one of the least understood topics in this arena and further research is needed on the internal and external environment characteristics affecting the overall performance of an organization (Huizingh, 2011).

Strategies and Technologies

During the recent economic crisis, many firms are attempting to capture additional value from their technologies through utilization of open innovation strategies (Lichtenthaler, 2010c). Majority of the research documents are found to be discussing on adoption of open innovation strategies in the form of practices or applications incorporating innovation technologies. These strategies include inter-firm cooperation, cooperation with intermediary institutions, and cooperation with research organization (Zeng, Xie & Tam, 2010; Izushi, 2003; Leiponen & Byman, 2009; Mention, 2010); changes in management attitude, planning and external orientation (De Jong & Marsili, 2006); technology licensing (Teece, 2006; Huston and sakkab, 2006); technology-product integration (Caetano and Amaral, 2011); linking technology intelligence to open innovation (Veugelers, Bury and Viaene, 2010); creation of absorptive capacity (Wang, Vanhaverbeke and Roijakkers, 2012); venture capital investment (Ferrary, 2010); R&D

outsourcing through acquisition strategy (Ferrary, 2011) and enhanced R&D alliances (Dickson, Weaver & Hoy, 2006). It has been observed that these strategies are providing significant impact on the innovation performances for SMEs. There are researches on the introduction of tools, such as, bricolage (Ferneley & Bell, 2006); or taxonomies, like, fruit flies approach (De Jong & Marsili, 2006); or terminologies, like, technology exploitation (van de Vrande, de Jong, Vanhaverbeke, & Rochemont, 2009; Lichtenthaler, 2010c) or technology exploration (van de Vrande et al., 2009).

In these contexts, O'Regan, Ghobadian and Sims (2006) emphasize that close association between strategy, organizational culture, leadership and novelty plays important role in achieving successful innovation. However, Lee & Lan (2011) argue that adoption of knowledge management is becoming an emerging agenda in developing company strategies, and thus leading towards the knowledge based economy. They further argue that, implementation depends on a harmonious amalgamation of infrastructure and process capabilities, including technology, culture and organizational formation. Furthermore, based on a random sample of 500 South Yorkshire non-hi-tech manufacturing SMEs, Laforet (2008) finds that the size, strategy and market orientation are also associated with innovation. Hence, strategies and technologies behind the open innovation are getting complex, dynamic and time dependent.

Measuring the Impact of OI Strategies

Strategies to optimize investments in the recognized technologies becomes of vital importance if an organization would like to match knowledge and ideas that are originating from outside of the organization but with internal core competences (Veugelers, Bury and Viaene, 2010). However, as the OI strategies are being increasingly adopted at all levels of the entrepreneurships, especially for the SMEs, researchers engaged themselves in finding the ultimate benefits of their utilization by measuring their impact. Massa and Testa (2008) points out to various indicators of the innovation measurements. Rejeb, Morel-Guimarães, Boly and Assiélou (2009) argue that innovation, being a competitive economic factor, is a process that compels a continuous, evolving and matured management. Therefore, innovative companies need to measure their innovation capacity as they grow further. In this aspect, innovation indicators have been used largely by "innovation scholars", a community that comprised of researchers from a variety of disciplines (ranging from engineering, and information science to sociology, and political science), who have a common research focus on technological innovation (Grupp & Schubert, 2010). However, Huang, Soutar and Brown (2004) indicated that four major factors underline the commonly used success measurement in an organization, such as financial performance, objective market acceptance, subjective market acceptance and product-level measures. They also mention that these four factors are interrelated and can be used as well to predict the overall measurement.

Tools and Instruments

Regarding use of software in the innovation process for SMEs, Kohn & Hüsig (2006) during their investigation have found that a large variety of software products are available in the market. Their research, while trying to address the issue of how far these products are specifically being used in practice, they find that these software products are rarely used to support the innovation process in German SMEs. Kaufmann & Tödtling (2002) mention that, the problem that most SMEs hardly interact with knowledge providers from outside the business sector (for example, universities, research houses or intermediaries) and the interaction is not reduced by the support instruments. Further, SMEs perform insufficiently the function of interfaces to innovation-related resources and information from outside the environment. Kaufmann & Tödtling (2002) also argue that, there is a lack of proactive consultancy concerning strategic, organizational and technological weaknesses which is necessary because most of the time, the firms are not aware of such deficiencies within themselves.

Caetano and Amaral (2011) mention about technology road mapping (TRM) as a method that assists organizations plan their technologies by describing the path to be followed in order to integrate a given technology into products and services. However, they state that other road mapping methods that are found in the literature were created to suit the large corporations, which combine R&D and product development structures, such as organizations that mainly adopt the market pull strategy and closed innovation to define technologies to be developed based on very specific market needs. A generic search on Google with string "open innovation tool" yields over 88,000 counts. However, a few are being cited here after going through their home pages. A list of those tools is being given below:

- **innogetCloud** [2] : Mentioned as an open innovation tool that is marketed branding as "Software as a Service" (SaaS). It has been stated that using innogetCloud, organizations are able to build an open innovation marketplace where the members can interact and collaborate by posting technology offers and requests;
- **Qmarkets** [3] : Described as a idea management software that allows their users to effectively manage their innovation process end to end - from idea generation and collection to idea selection and implementation;
- **IdeaNet** [4] : Indicated to provide a combination of software tools for innovation and consultants by facilitating idea challenges, problem solving challenges and knowledge challenges to generate vibrant innovation and knowledge communities; and
- **Innovator** [5] : Mentioned as an Enterprise Management System with enterprise innovation and intellectual property management solution to enhance idea management, decision management, invention disclosure/IP management and innovation and IP security;

Furthermore, there exist companies, like NineSigma, Ideaconnection, and Innocentive who are providing various supports to firms and individuals through open innovation tools and technologies.

However, in spite of the emergence of outsourcing R&D and it's emphasize by early introducers of open innovation in the entrepreneurship enhancement, this study does not find significant contributions from the researchers or practitioners illustrating the application of R&D outsourcing for SMEs development. Outsourcing R&D is mainly adopted by corporate houses. Hence, there is a visible gap in applying OI strategies in practice, especially for SMEs. Van de Vrande et al. (2009) conducted a study, which they claim as the first, explorative one to address this gap by focusing on SMEs. Their study tried to measure the extent of application of OI practices by SMEs and find out whether there is any positive trend on adoption of OI model over the time. Along this route, this study has tried to the above mentioned seven themes that have been found to be distinct and visible, and it is expected that future research on these perspectives will promote open innovation practices among SMEs. Next a few future research hints have been discussed for further dialogues and debates.

FUTURE RESEARCH

Within the research areas of open innovation in SMEs, awareness on the effective utilization of OI strategies, the timely intervention of opportunities for technologies outside the core business process, and skilled management of the OI strategies are essential for the successful entrepreneurship. However, these are particularly challenging for SMEs due to their lack of specialized knowledge base and also limited financial resources that can be devoted to innovation activities (Bianchi, Campodall'Orto, Frattini & Vercesi, 2010).

Furthermore, in spite of the enormous growth in research on open innovation, there are several openings of further research that this study has observed; such as linking open innovation research with other management areas, like marketing, human resources, change process, product diversification, and especially intellectual property management (Van de Vrande, Vanhaverbeke & Gassman, 2010; Rahman and Ramos, 2012). In addition to those factors, to match the global demand, increased competition and increasing supply of innovation, businesses need to internationalize their innovation activities through collaboration with external partners, such as customers, suppliers, universities, research houses and intermediaries (De Backer & Cervantes, 2008). Foremost, the understanding of open innovation at the outermost periphery of the business chain, driving factors of global innovation networking across different SMEs sub-sectors, accessibility and relationship of open innovation strategies with the implementing firms deserves further attention and in-depth research.

As mentioned in the problem statement of this study, and reiterated within the texts in the literature review, it is worthy to mention for the sake of future research that the concentration on open innovation researches are primarily focused to corporate businesses or large entrepreneurships and it is yet unclear whether these findings can be generalized to SMEs (Pedersen, Sondergaard & Esbjerg, 2009). Following a few success cases, small sized pilot projects may be initiated in a few backlogging countries with similar social and economic patterns to learn about the incubation of OI strategies before making a further leap to standardize a common platform for a larger number of countries within a region, or prescribe a generalized model at the global level.

Based on the study findings, this research sets out a future research framework involving products, processes, services and organizational transformations. Listed below are summarizes the framework:

- Need to improve the current understanding of open innovation in SMEs, especially while adopting the different strategies
- Need to focus on the nature of innovation and the extent to which open innovation is embedded in SMEs
- Should investigate how entrepreneurs engage in open innovation during their growth phases, and particularly what managerial implication can be derived
- Need to find out the characteristics of SMEs that are more likely to get benefit from collaboration, particularly via an intermediary, whether it could be a non-profit, or not-for-profit entity
- Should be carried out by minimizing the screening questions which may opt out, especially start-ups and micro-enterprises, as these enterprises have been identified as the sources of breakthrough innovations and challengers of contemporary innovation actors
- Should attempt to survey open innovation in broader samples of enterprises in more detailed and exploratory way

- Should focus on the requirement of OI on differences in culture, structure and decision making among partners of different sizes and sectors
- May incorporates findings of OI strategies in improving innovation cooperation for SMEs in emerging economies and developing countries and extend the generalizations of the findings
- Need to focus in identifying different segments within the population of every stakeholder (the entrepreneurs could be segmented by industry or geographic location and the academics by discipline)
- Need to pay more attention to the outflows of knowledge, which is intellectual property management
- Should emphasize on National Innovation System (NIS) inter-relating the national, economic, institutional and social environment
- Should restructure to establish the communication channels in facilitating knowledge sharing with the external entities such as business partners and government agencies

Ref: Massa & Testa, 2008; Van de Vrande, de Jong, Vanhaberbeke & Rochemont, 2009; Lee, Park, Yoon & Park, 2010; Zeng, Xie & Tam, 2010; Rahman and Ramos, 2010; Lee and Lan, 2011; Samara, Georgiadis and Bakouros, 2012

CONCLUSION

In the recent economic crisis, many firms attempt to capture additional value by adopting open innovation strategies (Lichtenthaler, 2010c). It has also been observed that the small firms that do innovate are among those who could successfully increase their chances of survival (Cofis and Marsili, 2003) and growth (De Jong, Vermeulen & O'Shaughnessy, 2004). However, the behavior of small firms can vary substantially. Some small firms survive by competing in a market niche, while others pursue more radical innovations and eventually, become the market leaders (De Jong & Marsili, 2006).

This study finds the evidence of clustered researches in various segments of SMEs sectors (especially, manufacturing), but likes to deduce that a continued research covering major categories of SMEs sectors (such as service, process, or product) is a demanding field of open innovation. Along the study, the significant research themes have been explored, including their nature, number, exposition and effectiveness. The study concludes that a huge research gap exists at the periphery of the entrepreneurship where most of the businesses nourish among the developed economies, which are the SMEs. The study also concludes that there is a broadening gap in terms of applying results of empirical researches in the form of practices aiming at SMEs in the arena of open innovation. This study has already conducted a test survey among a few selected Portuguese SMEs (due to the nature of the title of the chapter, it has not been include here, but it forms a separate chapter in this book) and finds that majority of the surveyed SMEs are adopting OI strategies just by replicating others, but not solely dependent on any concrete empirical researches. This validates the conclusion about further enhanced researches among the peripheral SMEs on the adoption, utilization, and impact of open innovation.

REFERENCES

Amara, N., Landry, R., Becheikh, N., & Ouimet, M. (2008). Learning and novelty of innovation in established manufacturing SMEs. *Technovation*, *28*(7), 450–463. doi:10.1016/j.technovation.2008.02.001

Autant-Bernard, C., Fadairo, M. & Massard, N. (2012). Knowledge diffusion and innovation policies within the European regions: Challenges based on recent empirical evidence. Original Research Article, Research Policy, In Press, Corrected Proof, Available online 10 August 2012.10.1016/j.respol.2012.07.009

Belussi, F., Sammarra, A., & Sedita, S. R. (2010). Learning at the boundaries in an "Open Regional Innovation System": A focus on firms' innovation strategies in the Emilia Romagna life science industry. *Research Policy*, *39*(6), 710–721. doi:10.1016/j.respol.2010.01.014

Bianchi, M., Campodall'Orto, S., Frattini, F., & Vercesi, P. (2010). Enabling open innovation in small- and medium-sized enterprises: How to find alternative applications for your technologies. *R & D Management*, *40*(4), 414–431. doi:10.1111/j.1467-9310.2010.00613.x

Bougrain, F., & Haudeville, B. (2002). Innovation, collaboration and SMEs internal research capacities. *Research Policy*, *31*(5), 735–747. doi:10.1016/S0048-7333(01)00144-5

Brandenburger, A., & Nalebuff, B. (1996). *Co-Opetition*. New York: Doubleday.

Caetano, M., & Amaral, D. C. (2011, July). Roadmapping for technology push and partnership: A contribution for open innovation environments Original Research Article. *Technovation*, *31*(7), 320–335. doi:10.1016/j.technovation.2011.01.005

Carlos de Oliveira, A. & Kaminski, P.C. (2012). A reference model to determine the degree of maturity in the product development process of industrial SMEs Original Research Article

Technovation, In Press, Corrected Proof, Available online 28 September 2012

Chesbrough, H. W. (2003a). The era of open innovation. *MIT Sloan Management Review*, *44*(3), 35–41.

Chesbrough, H. W. (2003b). *Open Innovation: The New Imperative for Creating and Profiting from Technology*. Boston, MA: Harvard Business School Press.

Chesbrough, H. W. (2006). *Open Business Models: How to Thrive in the New Innovation Landscape*. Harvard Busines School Press Books.

Coase, R. (1937). The Nature of the Firm. *Economica*, *4*(16), 386–405. doi:10.1111/j.1468-0335.1937.tb00002.x

Cofis, E., & Marsili, O. (2003) Survivor: The role of innovation in firm's survival, No. 03-18. WPT. Koopmans Institute, USE, Utrecht University

Cooke, P. (2005). Regionally asymmetric knowledge capabilities and open innovation: Exploring 'Globalisation 2'—A new model of industry organisation. *Research Policy*, *34*(8), 1128–1149. doi:10.1016/j.respol.2004.12.005

Dahlander, L., & Gann, D. M. (2010). How open is innovation? *Research Policy*, 2010.

Damaskopoulos, P., & Evgeniou, T. (2003). Adoption of New Economy Practices by SMEs in Eastern Europe. *European Management Journal*, *21*(2), 133–145. doi:10.1016/S0263-2373(03)00009-4

Davenport, T. H. (1993a). *Process Innovation*. Boston, MA: Harvard Business School Press.

Davenport, T. H. (1993b). *Process Innovation: reengineering work through information technology, Ernst & Young*. Harvard Business School Press.

Davenport, T. H. (1994). Managing in the New World of Process. *Public Productivity & Management Review*, *18*(2), 133–147. doi:10.2307/3380643

De Backer, K., & Cervantes, M. (2008). *Open innovation in global networks*. OECD.

Dehoff, K. & Sehgal, V. (2006) Innovators without Borders, *strategy+business*, Autumn 2006

Dehoff, K. & Sehgal, V. (2008) Beyond Borders: The Global Innovation 1000, *strategy+business*, Winter 2008

Del Brío, J. Á., & Junquera, B. (2003, December). A review of the literature on environmental innovation management in SMEs: Implications for public policies. *Technovation*, *23*(12), 939–948. doi:10.1016/S0166-4972(02)00036-6

De Jong, J. P. J. (2006). *Open Innovation: Practice, Trends, Motives and bottlenecks in the SMEs (Meer Open Innovatie: Praktijk, Ontwikkelingen, Motieven en Knelpunten in het MKB)*. Zoetermeer: EIM.

De Jong, J.P.J., Vermeulen, P.A.M. & O'Shaughnessy, K.C. (2004) Effects of Innovation in Small Firms, *M & O*, 58(1): 21-38

De Jong, J. P. J., & Marsili, O. (2006). The fruit flies of innovations: A taxonomy of innovative small firms. *Research Policy*, *35*(2), 213–229. doi:10.1016/j.respol.2005.09.007

De Jong, J. P. J., Vanhaverbeke, W., Kalvet, T., & Chesbrough, H. (2008), Policies for Open Innovation: Theory, Framework and Cases, Research project funded by VISION Era-Net, Helsinki: Finland.

De Jong, J. P. J., & von Hippel, E. (2009, September). Transfers of user process innovations to process equipment producers: A study of Dutch high-tech firms. *Research Policy*, *38*(7), 1181–1191. doi:10.1016/j.respol.2009.04.005

Descotes, R. M., Walliser, B., Holzmüller, H., & Guo, X. (2011, December). Original Research Article. *Journal of Business Research*, *64*(12), 1303–1310.

Dickson, P. H., Weaver, K. M., & Hoy, F. (2006, July). Opportunism in the R&D alliances of SMES: The roles of the institutional environment and SME size. *Journal of Business Venturing*, *21*(4), 487–513. doi:10.1016/j.jbusvent.2005.02.003

Edwards, T., Delbridge, R., & Munday, M. (2005). Understanding innovation in small and medium-sized enterprises: A process manifest. *Technovation*, *25*(10), 1119–1127. doi:10.1016/j.technovation.2004.04.005

European Union (2005) *EU-Summary*. The joint Japan-EU Seminar on R&D and Innovation in Small and Medium size Enterprises (SMEs), Tokyo, November 18, 2004

Ferrary, M. (2011). Specialized organizations and ambidextrous clusters in the open innovation paradigm. *European Management Journal*, *29*(3), 181–192. doi:10.1016/j.emj.2010.10.007

Ferneley, E., & Bell, F. (2006). Using bricolage to integrate business and information technology innovation in SMEs. *Technovation*, *26*(2), 232–241. doi:10.1016/j.technovation.2005.03.005

Fredberg, T., Elmquist, M., & Ollila, S. (2008). *Managing Open Innovation: Present Findings and Future Directions*, Report VR 2008:02, VINNOVA - Verket för Innovationssystem/Swedish Governmental Agency for Innovation Systems.

Freel, M. & De Jong, J.P.J. (2009) Market novelty, competence-seeking and innovation networking. *Technovation, 29*(12), 873–884.

Fu, X. (2012, April). How does openness affect the importance of incentives for innovation? Original Research Article. *Research Policy, 41*(3), 512–523. doi:10.1016/j.respol.2011.12.011

Gassmann, O. (2006). Opening up the innovation process: Towards an agenda[Blackwell Publishing Ltd.]. *R & D Management, 36*(3), 223–228. doi:10.1111/j.1467-9310.2006.00437.x

Gassmann, O., Enkel, E., & Chesbrough, H. (2010). The future of open innovation. *R & D Management, 40*(3), 213–221. doi:10.1111/j.1467-9310.2010.00605.x

Gredel, D., Kramer, M., & Bend, B. (2012, September–October). Original Research Article. *Technovation, 32*(9–10), 536–549. doi:10.1016/j.technovation.2011.09.008

Grindley, P. C., & Teece, D. J. (1997). Managing intellectual capital: Licensing and cross-licensing in semiconductors and electronics. *California Management Review, 39*(2), 1–34. doi:10.2307/41165885

Groen, A. J., & Linton, J. D. (2010). Is open innovation a field of study or a communication barrier to theory development? *Technovation, 30*(11-12), 554. doi:10.1016/j.technovation.2010.09.002

Grupp, H., & Schubert, T. (2010, February). Review and new evidence on composite innovation indicators for evaluating national performance. *Research Policy, 39*(1), 67–78. doi:10.1016/j.respol.2009.10.002

Huang, X., Soutar, G. N., & Brown, A. (2004). Measuring new product success: An empirical investigation of Australian SMEs. *Industrial Marketing Management, 33*(2), 117–123. doi:10.1016/S0019-8501(03)00034-8

Izushi, H. (2003). Impact of the length of relationships upon the use of research institutes by SMEs. *Research Policy, 32*(5), 771–788. doi:10.1016/S0048-7333(02)00085-9

Henkel, J. (2006). Selective revealing in open innovation processes: The case of embedded Linux. *Research Policy, 35*(7), 953–969. doi:10.1016/j.respol.2006.04.010

Hervas-Oliver, J. L., Garrigos, J. A., & Gil-Pechuan, I. (2011, September). Original Research Article. *Technovation, 31*(9), 427–446. doi:10.1016/j.technovation.2011.06.006

Hjalager, A.-M. (2010, February). A review of innovation research in tourism. *Tourism Management, 31*(1), 1–12. doi:10.1016/j.tourman.2009.08.012

Huang, X., Soutar, G.N. & Brown, A. (2004) Review and new evidence on composite innovation indicators for evaluating national performance, *Research Policy,* 39(1), 67-78.

Hoffman, K., Parejo, M., Bessant, J., & Perren, L. (1998). Small firms, R&D, technology and innovation in the UK: A literature review. *Technovation, 18*(1), 39–55. doi:10.1016/S0166-4972(97)00102-8

Huizingh, E. K. R. E. (2009, June 21-24). The future of innovation. *Proceedings of the XX International Society for Professional Innovation Management ISPIM Conference '09.*

Huston, L., & Sakkab, N. (2006). Connect and develop: Inside Procter & Gamble's new model for innovation. *Harvard Business Review, 84*, 58–66.

Huizingh, E. K. R. E. (2011, January). Original Research Article. *Technovation, 31*(1), 2–9. doi:10.1016/j. technovation.2010.10.002

(2012, January). Kang, Kyung-Nam & Park, H. (2012). Original Research Article. *Technovation, 32*(1), 68–78.

Kaufmann, A., & Tödtling, F. (2002, March). How effective is innovation support for SMEs? An analysis of the region of Upper Austria. *Technovation, 22*(3), 147–159. doi:10.1016/S0166-4972(00)00081-X

Kirschbaum, R. (2005). Open innovation in practice. *Research on Technology Management, 48*, 24–28.

Knudsen, M.P. & Mortensen, T.B. (2010) Some immediate – but negative – effects of openness on product development performance. *Technovation.*

Kohn, S., & Hüsig, S. (2006, August). Potential benefits, current supply, utilization and barriers to adoption: An exploratory study on German SMEs and innovation software. *Technovation, 26*(8), 988–998. doi:10.1016/j.technovation.2005.08.003

Kowalski, S. P. (2009, December 10-11). SMES, Open Innovation and IP Management: Advancing Global Development. *Presentation at the WIPO-Italy International Convention on Intellectual Property and Competitiveness of Micro, Small and Medium-Sized Enterprises (MSMEs)*, Rome, Italy.

Koyuncugil, A. S., & Ozgulbas, N. (2009). Risk modeling by CHAID decision tree algorithm. *ICCES, 11*(2), 39–46.

Laforet, S. (2008) Size, strategic, and market orientation affects on innovation, *Technovation, 25*(10), 1119-1127.

Laursen, K., & Salter, A. (2006). Open for innovation: The role of openness in explaining innovation performance among UK manufacturing firms. *Strategic Management Journal, 27*(2), 131–150. doi:10.1002/smj.507

Lawson, C. P., Longhurst, P. J., & Ivey, P. C. (2006). The application of a new research and development project selection model in SMEs. *Technovation, 26*(2), 242–250. doi:10.1016/j.technovation.2004.07.017

Lazzarotti, V., Manzini, R., & Pizzurno, E. (2008). Managing innovation networks of SMEs: a case study.*Proceeding of the International Engineering Management Conference: managing engineering, technology and innovation for growth (IEMC Europe 2008)*, Estoril, Portugal (pp. 521-525). doi:10.1109/ IEMCE.2008.4618024

Lecocq, X., & Demil, B. (2006). Strategizing industry structure: The case of open systems in low-tech industry. *Strategic Management Journal, 27*(9), 891–898. doi:10.1002/smj.544

Lee, S., Park, G., Yoon, B., & Park, J. (2010). Open innovation in SMEs—An intermediated network model. *Research Policy, 39*(2), 290–300. doi:10.1016/j.respol.2009.12.009

Lee, M. R., & Lan, Y.-C. (2011, January). Toward a unified knowledge management model for SMEs. *Expert Systems with Applications*, *38*(1), 729–735. doi:10.1016/j.eswa.2010.07.025

Leiponen, A., & Byma, J. (2009, November). If you cannot block, you better run: Small firms, cooperative innovation, and appropriation strategies. *Research Policy*, *38*(9), 1478–1488. doi:10.1016/j.respol.2009.06.003

Lemola, T. & Lievonen, J. (2008). The role of innovation policy in fostering open innovation activities among companies. Vision ERAnet.

Levy, M., Powell, P., & Galliers, R. (1998). Assessing information systems strategy development frameworks in SMEs. *Information & Management*, *36*(5), 247–261. doi:10.1016/S0378-7206(99)00020-8

Liao, Tung-Shan & Rice, J. (2010). *Original Research Article Research Policy*, *39*(1), 117–125.

Lichtenthaler, U. (2005). External commercialization of knowledge: Review and research agenda. *International Journal of Management Reviews*, *7*(4), 231–255. doi:10.1111/j.1468-2370.2005.00115.x

Lichtenthaler, U. (2006). Technology exploitation strategies in the context of open innovation, International Journal of Technology Intelligence and Planning, Volume 2. *Number*, *1/2006*, 1–21.

Lichtenthaler, U. (2007a). Hierarchical strategies and strategic fit in the keep-or-sell decision. *Management Decision*, *45*(Iss: 3), 340–359. doi:10.1108/00251740710744990

Lichtenthaler, U. (2007b). The drivers of technology licensing: An industry comparison. *California Management Review*, *49*(4), 67–89. doi:10.2307/41166406

Lichtenthaler, U. (2008a). Open Innovation in Practice: An Analysis of Strategic Approaches to Technology Transactions. *IEEE Transactions on Engineering Management*, 55(1), 148–157.

Lichtenthaler, U. (2008b, May/June). Integrated roadmaps for open innovation. *Research Technology Management*, *51*(3), 45–49.

Lichtenthaler, U. (2008c, September). Relative capacity: Retaining knowledge outside a firm's boundaries. *Journal of Engineering and Technology Management*, *25*(3), 200–212. doi:10.1016/j.jengtecman.2008.07.001

Lichtenthaler, U. (2008d, April). Leveraging technology assets in the presence of markets for knowledge. *European Management Journal*, *26*(2), 122–134. doi:10.1016/j.emj.2007.09.002

Lichtenthaler, U. (2008e, July). Externally commercializing technology assets: An examination of different process stages. *Journal of Business Venturing*, *23*(4), 445–464. doi:10.1016/j.jbusvent.2007.06.002

Lichtenthaler, U. (2008f, July). Externally commercializing technology assets: An examination of different process stages Original Research Article. *Journal of Business Venturing*, *23*(4), 445–464. doi:10.1016/j.jbusvent.2007.06.002

Ulrich Lichtenthaler Lichtenthaler, U. (2009a, April). RETRACTED: The role of corporate technology strategy and patent portfolios in low-, medium- and high-technology firms. *Research Policy* (Special Issue: Innovation in Low- and Medium-Technology Industries), *38*(3), 559–569. doi:10.1016/j.respol.2008.10.009

Lichtenthaler, U. (2009b, August). Absorptive capacity, environmental turbulence, and the complementarity of organizational learning processes. *Academy of Management Journal, 52*(4), 822–846. doi:10.5465/AMJ.2009.43670902

Lichtenthaler, U. (2009c, September). Outbound open innovation and its effect on firm performance: Examining environmental influences. *R & D Management, 39*(4), 317–330. doi:10.1111/j.1467-9310.2009.00561.x

Lichtenthaler, U. (2010a, July–August). Original Research Article. *Technovation, 30*(7–8), 429–435. doi:10.1016/j.technovation.2010.04.001

Lichtenthaler, U. (2010b, November). Organizing for external technology exploitation in diversified firms. *Journal of Business Research, 63*(11), 1245–1253. doi:10.1016/j.jbusres.2009.11.005

Lichtenthaler, U. (2010c, July-August). Technology exploitation in the context of open innovation: Finding the right 'job' for your technology. *Technovation, 30*(7-8), 429–435. doi:10.1016/j.technovation.2010.04.001

Lichtenthaler, U. (2011a, February–March). 'Is open innovation a field of study or a communication barrier to theory development?' A contribution to the current debate. *Technovation, 31*(2–3), 138–139. doi:10.1016/j.technovation.2010.12.001

Lichtenthaler, U. (2011b, February). Open Innovation: Past Research, Current Debates, and Future Directions. *The Academy of Management Perspectives, 25*(1), 75–93. doi:10.5465/AMP.2011.59198451

Lichtenthaler, U., & Ernst, H. (2009). Opening Up the Innovation Process: The Role of Technology Aggressiveness. *R & D Management, 39*(1), 38–54. doi:10.1111/j.1467-9310.2008.00522.x

Lindermann, N., Valcareel, S., Schaarschmidt, M., & Von Kortzfleisch, H. (2009). SME 2.0: Roadmap towards Web 2.0- Based Open Innovation in SME-Network- A Case Study Based Research Framework. In G. Dhillon, B. C. Stahl, & R. Baskerville (Eds.), *CreativeSME2009, IFIP International Federation for Information Processing, IFIP AICT 301* (pp. 28–41). doi:10.1007/978-3-642-02388-0_3

Livieratos, A. D., & Papoulias, D. B. (2009) *Towards an Open Innovation Growth Strategy for New*, Technology-Based Firms, National Technical University of Athens, Retrieved from http://www.ltp.ntua.gr/uploads/GJ/eK/GJeKw8Jf5RqjCO9CWapm4w/Growth.pdf

Love, J.H. & Ganotakis, P. (2012). Original Research Article. *International Business Review*.

Lundvall, B. (1995). *National systems of innovation: Towards a theory of innovation and interactive learning*. London: Biddles Ltd.

Maijers, W., Vokurka, L., van Uffelen, R. & Ravensbergen, P. (2005) Open innovation: symbiotic network, Knowledge circulation and competencies for the benefit of innovation in the Horticulture delta. *Presentation IAMA Chicago 2005*.

Major, E. J., & Cordey-Hayes, M. (2000). Engaging the business support network to give SMEs the benefit of foresight. *Technovation, 20*(11), 589–602. doi:10.1016/S0166-4972(00)00006-7

Massa, S., & Testa, S. (2008, July). Innovation and SMEs: Misaligned perspectives and goals among entrepreneurs, academics, and policy makers. *Technovation, 28*(7), 393–407. doi:10.1016/j.technovation.2008.01.002

Mention, A.-L. (2010). Co-operation and co-opetition as open innovation practices in the service sector: Which influence on innovation novelty? *Technovation.*

Mortara, L., & Minshall, T. (2011). How do large multinational companies implement open innovation? *Technovation, 31*(10-11), 586–597. doi:10.1016/j.technovation.2011.05.002

Nahlinder, J. (2005). *Innovation and Employment in Services: The Case of Knowledge Intensive Business Services in Sweden* [Doctoral Thesis]. Department of technology and Social Change, Linköping University, Sweden.

Nagaoka, S., & Kwon, H. U. (2006). The incidence of cross-licensing: A theory and new evidence on the firm and contract level determinants. *Research Policy, 35*(9), 1347–1361. doi:10.1016/j.respol.2006.05.007

Narula, R. (2004). R&D collaboration by SMEs: New opportunities and limitations in the face of globalisation. *Technovation, 25*(2), 153–161. doi:10.1016/S0166-4972(02)00045-7

Novelli, M., Schmitz, B., & Spencer, T. (2006, December). Networks, clusters and innovation in tourism: A UK experience. *Tourism Management, 27*(6), 1141–1152. doi:10.1016/j.tourman.2005.11.011

Nunes,P.M., Serrasqueiro, Z. & Leitão, J. (2010). Is there a linear relationship between R&D intensity and growth? Empirical evidence of non-high-tech vs. high-tech SMEs. *Research Policy, 41*(1), 36-53.

OECD. (2008). *Open Innovation in Global Networks, Policy Brief, OECD Observer*. Paris: OECD.

O'Regan, N., Ghobadian, A., & Sims, M. (2006, February). Fast tracking innovation in manufacturing SMEs. *Technovation, 26*(2), 251–261. doi:10.1016/j.technovation.2005.01.003

Partanen, J., Möller, K., Westerlund, M., Rajala, R., & Rajala, A. (2008, July). Social capital in the growth of science-and-technology-based SMEs. *Industrial Marketing Management, 37*(5), 513–522. doi:10.1016/j.indmarman.2007.09.012

Pedersen, M., Sondergaard,and H.A., Esbjerg, L. (2009, June 21-24). Network characteristics and open innovation in SMEs. In K.R.E. Huizingh, S. Conn, M. Torkkeli, & I. Bitran (Eds.), *Proceedings of The XX ISPIM Conference*, Vienna, Austria.

Powell, W. (1990). Neither market nor hierarchy: network forms of organization. In B. Stow & L. L. Cummings (Eds.), *Research in Organizational Behavior*. Greenwich: JAI Press.

Rahman, H., & Ramos, I. (2010). Open Innovation in SMEs: From Closed Boundaries to Networked Paradigm. *Issues in Informing Science and Information Technology, 7*, 471–487.

Rahman, H., & Ramos, I. (2012, June 22-27). Open Innovation in Entrepreneurships: Agents of Transformation towards the Knowledge-Based Economy.*Proceedings of the Issues in Informing Science and Information Technology Education Conference*, Montreal, Canada.

Ramos, E., Acedo, F. J., & Gonzalez, M. A. (2011, October–November). Internationalisation speed and technological patterns: A panel data study on Spanish SMEs. Original Research Article. *Technovation*, *31*(10–11), 560–572. doi:10.1016/j.technovation.2011.06.008

Rejeb, H. B., Morel-Guimarães, L., Boly, V., & Assiélou, N. G. (2009). Measuring innovation best practices: Improvement of an innovation index integrating threshold and synergy effects. *Technovation*, *28*(12), 838–854. doi:10.1016/j.technovation.2008.08.005

Raymond, L., & St-Pierre, J. (2010). R&D as a determinant of innovation in manufacturing SMEs: An attempt at empirical clarification. *Technovation*, *30*(1), 48–56. doi:10.1016/j.technovation.2009.05.005

Rhee, J., Park, T., & Lee, D. H. (2010). Drivers of innovativeness and performance for innovative SMEs in South Korea: Mediation of learning orientation. *Technovation*, *30*(1), 65–75. doi:10.1016/j.technovation.2009.04.008

Rothwell, R., & Dodgson, M. M. (1994). The Handbook of Industrial Innovation. Edward Elgar, Cheltenham.

Roper, S., & Hewitt-Dundas, N. (2004). Innovation persistence: survey and case - study evidence (Working Paper). Aston Business School, Birmingham, UK.

Saarikoski, V. (2006). *The Odyssey of the Mobile Internet- the emergence of a networking attribute in a multidisciplinary study* [Academic dissertation]. TIEKE, Helsinki.

Samara, E., Georgiadis, P., & Bakouros, I. (2012). The impact of innovation policies on the performance of national innovation systems: A system dynamics analysis. *Technovation*, *32*, 624–638.

Santisteban, M. A. (2006). Business Systems and Cluster Policies in the Basque Country and Catalonia (1990-2004). *European Urban and Regional Studies*, *13*(1), 25–39. doi:10.1177/0969776406059227

Savioz, P., & Blum, M. (2002). Strategic forecast tool for SMEs: How the opportunity landscape interacts with business strategy to anticipate technological trends. *Technovation*, *22*(2), 91–100. doi:10.1016/S0166-4972(01)00082-7

Schumpeter, J. A. (1934). *The Theory of Economic Development*. Cambridge: Harvard University Press.

Schumpeter, J. A. (1942). *Capitalism, Socialism, and Democracy*. NY: Harper & Row.

Schumpeter, J. A. (1950). *Capitalism, Socialism, and Democracy* (3rd ed.). NY: Harper.

Sousa, M. C. (2008). Open innovation models and the role of knowledge brokers. *Inside Knowledge magazine*, 11(6), 1–5.

Spithoven, A., Clarysse, B., & Knockaert, M. (2010). Building absorptive capacity to organize inbound open innovation in traditional industries. *Technovation*, *30*(2), 130–141. doi:10.1016/j.technovation.2009.08.004

Teece, D. J. (2006). Reflections on "Profiting from Innovation". *Research Policy*, *35*(8), 1131–1146. doi:10.1016/j.respol.2006.09.009

Thoben, K. D. (2008, 23-25). A new wave of innovation in collaborative networks.*Proceedings of the 14th international conference on concurrent enterprising: ICE 2008*. Lisbon, Portugal (pp. 1091-1100).

Thorgren, S., Wincent, J., & Örtqvist, D. (2009). Designing interorganizational networks for innovation: An empirical examination of network configuration, formation and governance. *Journal of Engineering and Technology Management, 26*(3), 148–166. doi:10.1016/j.jengtecman.2009.06.006

Tilley, F., & Tonge, J. (2003). Introduction. In O. Jones & F. Tilley (Eds.), *Competitive Advantage in SME's: Organising for Innovation and Change*. John Wiley & Sons.

Tödtling, F., & Trippl, M. (2005). One size fits all?: Towards a differentiated regional innovation policy approach. *Research Policy, 34*(8), 1203–1219. doi:10.1016/j.respol.2005.01.018

Van de Vrande, V., de Jong, J. P. J., Vanhaverbeke, W., & de Rochemont, M. (2008, November). Open innovation in SMEs: Trends, motives and management challenges, a report published under the SCALES-initiative (SCientific AnaLysis of Entrepreneurship and SMEs), as part of the 'SMEs and Entrepreneurship programme' financed by the Netherlands Ministry of Economic Affairs, Zoetermeer 2008.

Van de Vrande, V., de Jong, J. P. J., Vanhaverbeke, W., & de Rochemont, M. (2009, June-July). Open innovation in SMEs: Trends, motives and management challenges. *Technovation, 29*(6-7), 423–437. doi:10.1016/j.technovation.2008.10.001

Van de Vrande, V., Vanhaverbeke, W., & Gassman, O. (2010). Broadening the scope of open innovation: Past research, current state and future directions. *International Journal of Technology Management, 52*(3-4), 221–235. doi:10.1504/IJTM.2010.035974

Van Hemel, C., & Cramer, J. (2002, October). Barriers and stimuli for ecodesign in SMEs. *Journal of Cleaner Production, 10*(5), 439–453. doi:10.1016/S0959-6526(02)00013-6

Vanhaverbeke, W., & Cloodt, M. (2006). Open innovation in value networks. In H. Chesbrough, W. Vanhaverbeke, & J. West (Eds.), *Open Innovation: Researching a New Paradigm*. NY: Oxford University Press.

Veugelers, M., Bury, J., & Viaene, S. (2010). Linking technology intelligence to open innovation. *Technological Forecasting and Social Change, 77*(2), 335–343. doi:10.1016/j.techfore.2009.09.003

Hippel, V. (1975). *The Dominant Role of Users in the Scientific Instrument Innovation Process, WP 764-75*. NSF.

Hippel, V. (1978, January). Successful Industrial Products from Customer Ideas. *Eric von Hippel Journal of Marketing, 42*(1), 39–49.

Von Hippel, E. (1986). Lead users: A source of novel product concepts. *Management Science, 32*(7), 791–805. doi:10.1287/mnsc.32.7.791

Von Hippel, E. (1987). Cooperation between rivals: Informal Know-how trading. *Research Policy, 16*(6), 291–302. doi:10.1016/0048-7333(87)90015-1

Von Hippel, E. (1988) The Sources of Innovation, Oxford University Press, New York.

Von Hippel, E. (1990). Task Partitioning: An Innovation Process Variable. *Research Policy, 19*, 407–418.

Von Hippel, E. (1994). "Sticky Information" and the Locus of Problem Solving: Implications for Innovation. Management Science, 40(4), 429-439.

Von Hippel, E. (1998). Economics of product development by users: The impact of `sticky' local information. Management Science, 44(5), 629-644.

VonHippel, E. (2001, Summer). 2001a Innovation by User Communities: Learning from Open-Source Software, MIT. *Sloan Management Review, 42*(4), 82–86.

VonHippel, E. (2001). 2001b PERSPECTIVE: User toolkits for innovation. *Journal of Product Innovation Management, 18*(4), 247–257. doi:10.1111/1540-5885.1840247

von Hippel, E. (2005). Democratizing innovation: The evolving phenomenon of user innovation. *Journal für Betriebswirtschaft, 55*(1), 63–78. doi:10.1007/s11301-004-0002-8

Hippel, V. (2007, April). 2007 Horizontal Innovation Networks--By and for Users. *Industrial and Corporate Change, 16*(2), 293–315. doi:10.1093/icc/dtm005

Von Hippel, E., & Von Krogh, G. (2003). Open source software and the "private – collective" innovation model: Issues for organization science. *Organization Science, 14*(2), 209–223. doi:10.1287/orsc.14.2.209.14992

Wang, L., Jaring, P., & Wallin, A. (2009) Developing a Conceptual Framework for Business Model Innovation in the Context of Open Innovation.*Proceedings of the Third IEEE International Conference on Digital Ecosystems and Technologies (IEEE DEST 2009)* (pp. 460-465).

Wang, Y., Vanhaverbeke, W., & Roijakkers, N. (2012). Exploring the impact of open innovation on national systems of innovation - A theoretical analysis. *Technological Forecasting and Social Change, 79*(3), 419–428. doi:10.1016/j.techfore.2011.08.009

Wenger, E. (1998). *Communities of Practice: Learning, Meaning and Identity*. Cambridge University Press. doi:10.1017/CBO9780511803932

West, J. (2006) Does Appropriability Enable or Retard Open Innovation? In H. Chesbrough, W. Vanhaverbeke, & J. West (Eds.), Open Innovation: Researching a New Paradigm. London: Oxford University Press.

West, J., Vanhaverbeke, W., & Chesbrough, H. (2006). Open Innovation: A Research Agenda. In H. Chesbrough, W. Vanhaverbeke, & J. West (Eds.), Open Innovation: Researching a New Paradigm. London: Oxford University Press.

Westergren, U. H., & Holmström, J. (2012). Exploring preconditions for open innovation: Value networks in industrial firms. *Information and Organization, 22*(4), 209–226. doi:10.1016/j.infoandorg.2012.05.001

Wijffels, H. (2009). *Leadership, sustainability and levels of consciousness. A speech at the conference on the Leadership for a Sustainable World, June 5, 2009*. Den Haag, the Netherlands: Grote Kerk.

Woodhams, C., & Lupton, B. (2009, June). Analysing gender-based diversity in SMEs. *Scandinavian Journal of Management, 25*(2), 203–213. doi:10.1016/j.scaman.2009.02.006

Zeng, S. X., Xie, X. M., & Tam, C. M. (2010). Relationship between cooperation networks and innovation performance of SMEs. *Technovation, 30*(3), 181–194. doi:10.1016/j.technovation.2009.08.003

ADDITIONAL READING

Alshawi, S., Missi, F. & Irani, Z. (2010). Organisational, technical and data quality factors in CRM adoption - SMEs perspective, *Industrial Marketing Management, In Press, Corrected Proof, Available online 15 September 2010.*

Bayraktar, E., Demirbag, M., Koh, S. C. L., Tatoglu, E., & Zaim, H. (2009, November). A causal analysis of the impact of information systems and supply chain management practices on operational performance: Evidence from manufacturing SMEs in Turkey. *International Journal of Production Economics, 122*(1), 133–149. doi:10.1016/j.ijpe.2009.05.011

Bevis, K. I., & Cole, A. (2010, June). Open Innovation Readiness: a Tool. *Proceedings of ISPIM XXIth International Conference*, Bilbao. International Society for Professional Innovation Management.

Bianchi, M., Cavaliere, A., Chiaroni, D., Frattini, F. & Chiesa, V. (2010). Organisational modes for Open Innovation in the bio-pharmaceutical industry: An exploratory analysis. *Technovation.*

Bidault, F. (2004). Global licensing strategies and technology pricing. *International Journal of Technology Management, 27*(2/3), 295–305. doi:10.1504/IJTM.2004.003959

Bougrain, F., & Haudeville, B. (2002, July). Original Research Article. *Research Policy, 31*(5), 735–747. doi:10.1016/S0048-7333(01)00144-5

BVCA. (2005). *Creating success from University Spin-outs, A Review conducted by Library House on behalf of the BVCA, BVCA (British Venture Capital Association)*. Library House.

Chesbrough, H.W. (2003c). The Era of Open Innovation. *Sloan Management Review*, 44, 3 (Spring): 35-41.

Chesbrough, H.W. (2003d). Open Innovation: How Companies Actually Do It. *Harvard Business Review*, 81(7), 12-14.

Chesbrough, H.W. (2003e). Open Platform Innovation: Creating Value from Internal and External Innovation. *Intel Technology Journal*, 7(3), 5-9.

Chesbrough, H.W. (2004). Managing Open Innovation: Chess and Poker. *Research-Technology Management*, 47(1), 23-26.

Chesbrough, H. W. (2006). Open Innovation: A New Paradigm for Understanding Industrial Innovation. In H. Chesbrough, W. Vanhaverbeke, & J. West (Eds.), *Open Innovation: Researching a New Paradigm* (pp. 1–12). Oxford: Oxford University Press.

Chesbrough, H. W. (2006). New Puzzles and New Findings. In H. Chesbrough, W. Vanhaverbeke, & J. West (Eds.), *Open Innovation: Researching a New Paradigm* (pp. 15–34). Oxford: Oxford University Press.

Chesbrough, H. W. (2006). *Open Business Models: How to Thrive in the New Innovation Landscape*. Boston: Harvard Business School Press.

Chesbrough, H. W., Vanhaverbeke, W., & West, J. (Eds.), (2006). Open innovation: Researching a new paradigm. Oxford University Press: London.

Chesbrough, H.W. (2007). The market for innovation: implications for corporate strategy. *California Management Review*, 49(3), 45–66.

Chesbrough, H.W., & Crowther, A.K. (2006). Beyond high tech: early adopters of open innovation in other industries. R&D Management, 36(3), 229-236.

Chesbrough, H. W. (2007). Business model innovation: It's not just about technology anymore. *Strategy and Leadership*, *35*(6), 12–17. doi:10.1108/10878570710833714

Davenport, T. H., & Short, J. E. (1990, Summer). The New Industrial Engineering: Information Technology and Business Process Redesign. *Sloan Management Review*, 1990, 11–27.

Davenport, T. H., & Stoddard, D. B. (1994, July). Reengineering: Business Change of Mythic Proportions? *Management Information Systems Quarterly*, *18*(2), 121–127. doi:10.2307/249760

Davenport, T. H., & Beers, M. C. (1995). Managing Information About Processes. *Journal of Management Information Systems*, *12*(1), 57–80. doi:10.1080/07421222.1995.11518070

Davenport, T. H., & Harris, J. G. (2005). Automated decision making comes of age. *MIT Sloan Management Review*, *46*(4), 83–89.

Davenport, T.H. (1998) Putting the enterprise into the enterprise system, *Harvard Business Review*, 76(4), 121–131.

EIRMA. (2005). Responsible Partnering: A Guide to Better Practices for Collaborative Research and Knowledge Transfer between Science and Industry. *Proceedings of EIRMA, EUA, EARTO, ProTon Europe*, version 1.0.

EIRMA. (2009, October). Joining Forces in a World of Open Innovation: Guidelines for Collaborative Research and Knowledge Transfer between Science and Industry. *Proceedings of EIRMA, EUA, EARTO, ProTon Europe*, version 1.1.

Ferrary, M. (2010). Syndication of venture capital investment: The art of resource pooling. Entrepreneurship. *Theory into Practice*, *34*(5), 885–907.

Fernández-Viñé, M. B., Gómez-Navarro, T., & Capuz-Rizo, S. F. (2010, May). Eco-efficiency in the SMEs of Venezuela. Current status and future perspectives. *Journal of Cleaner Production*, *18*(8), 736–746. doi:10.1016/j.jclepro.2009.12.005

Kaivanto, K., & Stoneman, P. (2007, June). Public provision of sales contingent claims backed finance to SMEs: A policy alternative. *Research Policy*, *36*(5), 637–651. doi:10.1016/j.respol.2007.01.001

Kollmer, H., & Dowling, M. (2004). Licensing as a commercialisation strategy for new technology-based firms. *Research Policy*, *33*(8), 1141–1151. doi:10.1016/j.respol.2004.04.005

Kornai, J. (2010). *Innovation and Dynamism: Interaction between Systems and Technical Progress.*

Kühne, B., Vanhonacker, F., Gellynck, X., & Verbeke, W. (2010, September). Innovation in traditional food products in Europe: Do sector innovation activities match consumers' acceptance? *Food Quality and Preference*, *21*(6), 629–638. doi:10.1016/j.foodqual.2010.03.013

Jones, O., & Macpherson, A. (2006) Inter-organizational Learning and Strategic Renewal in SMEs: Extending the 4I Framework. *Long Range Planning*, 39, 155-175.

Kohn, S., & Hüsig, S. (2006, August). Original Research Article. *Technovation*, *26*(8), 988–998. doi:10.1016/j.technovation.2005.08.003

Raymond, L., & St-Pierre, J. (2010, January). Original Research Article. *Technovation*, *30*(1), 48–56. doi:10.1016/j.technovation.2009.05.005

Spithoven, A., Clarysse, B., & Knockaert, M. (2010). Building absorptive capacity to organise inbound open innovation in traditional industries. *Technovation*, *30*(2), 130–141. doi:10.1016/j.technovation.2009.08.004

Tilley, F., & Tonge, J. (2003). Introduction. In O. Jones & F. Tilley (Eds.), *Competitive Advantage in SME's: Organising for Innovation and Change*. John Wiley & Sons.

Ziedonis, A. A. (2007). Real options in technology licensing. *Management Science*, *53*(10), 1618–1633. doi:10.1287/mnsc.1070.0705

KEY TERMS AND DEFINITIONS

Open Innovation Concepts: Concept that uses the purposive inflows and outflows of knowledge to accelerate internal innovation, as well as external innovation and expand the markets for increased use of innovation.

Open Innovation Practices: Practices carried out by the entrepreneurships incorporating open innovation researches and methods.

Open Innovation Researches: Researches utilizing open innovation concepts, methods and strategies.

Open Innovation Strategies: Strategies that incorporate fresh perspectives, knowledge and inspiration from the inside and outside of an entrepreneurship, thus allowing to go beyond day-to-day thinking and opens up the way to entirely new possibilities for any value addition.

SMEs Development: Development of the small and medium enterprises sector of the business arena; in terms of economic, knowledge, human skills and other forms of value additions.

ENDNOTES

[1]   Small and Medium scale Enterprises (SMEs) by definition are small firms with a small number of headcounts and the turnover fall below a certain limit. In terms of headcounts, they vary from country to country and regions to regions. In Europe, the headcounts are less than 250 and the turnover is less than 50 million Euros; http://ec.europa.eu/enterprise/policies/sme/facts-figures-analysis/sme-definition/index_en.htm. The study has adopted this definition.

[2]   https://www.innogetcloud.com/news/sale-al-mercado-la-primera-herramienta-de-open-innovation-en-formato-cloud/1

[3]   http://www.qmarkets.net/home

[4]   http://www.innovationfactory.eu/services/ideanet/

[5]   http://www.mindmatters.net/Software/INNOVATOREnterprise.aspx

Chapter 10
Managing Seven Dimensions of ICT4D Projects to Address Project Challenges

Devendra Potnis
University of Tennessee at Knoxville, USA

ABSTRACT

A large number of ICT for development (ICT4D) projects experience a variety of challenges, especially when conducting field research with disadvantaged communities in developing nations. Using cluster analysis, this chapter identifies the six most common factors associated with a majority of ICT4D project challenges, and depicts the inter-relationship between these factors and over 100 distinct challenges reported by existing literature. In addition, based on the secondary analysis of 380 research artifacts in the ICT4D literature, this chapter proposes ways to manage the scope, time, costs, quality, human resources, communication, and risks for addressing ICT4D project challenges. Findings inform researchers of best practices for conducting ICT4D research with disadvantaged communities in developing nations.

BACKGROUND

Projects which (a) design information and communication technology (ICT) solutions for disadvantaged communities, (b) test ICT prototypes with disadvantaged communities, (c) deploy ICT solutions in disadvantaged communities, or (d) assess the impact of ICT solutions on the development of disadvantaged communities in developing nations are known as ICT4D projects (Potnis, 2014). A large number of ICT4D projects experience a variety of challenges, especially when conducting field research with disadvantaged communities in developing nations. In addition, most ICT4D projects have limited resources, including time and money, which are often subjected to identified or unforeseen risks.

ICT4D researchers are always in search of systematic guidance for addressing project challenges. As a result, a number of studies published by top journals in the ICT4D area, including *IT for Development* (e.g., Krauss, 2013; Krishna & Walsham, 2005; Madon, Reinhard, Roode, & Walsham, 2009; Walsham & Sahay, 2006, etc.), *IT and International Development* (Abraham, 2006; Anokwa et al., 2009; Medhi

DOI: 10.4018/978-1-5225-0556-3.ch010

& Toyama, 2007, etc.), *Electronic Journal of Information Systems in Developing nations* (e.g., Touray, Salminen, & Murso, 2013), *International Journal of ICT and Human Development* (e.g., Mathur & Sharma, 2009; Rahman & Ramos, 2013), and books or book chapters (e.g., Chib & Harris, 2012; De, 2012; Krishna & Madon, 2003, Vaidya, Myers, & Gardner, 2013, etc.), discuss the challenges associated with ICT4D field research at great length. This multidisciplinary guidance available for conducting ICT4D field research equips researchers collecting, analyzing, and reporting data in multiple formats from the field.

However, this guidance is not systematic or structured. As a result, it requires significant experience or a relevant academic background for interpretation and application. For instance, a team of computer scientists (Brewer et al., 2006) advise researchers to "plan hard but remain flexible." But how does one remain flexible in ICT4D field research? What exactly does it mean to plan hard in the context of ICT4D projects in developing nations? Also, there hardly exists any theoretical foundation of the guidance for addressing ICT4D project challenges, which makes the problem worse for researchers with no prior experience or training.

This study proposes applying project management principles to address ICT4D project challenges. Project management is a scientifically designed approach for managing scope, time, cost, quality, human resources, communications, and risks related to a variety of projects. Table 1 presents seven project management principles (PMP) and related activities.

However, PMP, which are codified by standards, tools, and techniques, cannot be applied "as is" to address ICT4D project challenges since PMP rely extensively on assumptions of economic rationality. For instance, increasing profit margins and controlling cost factors are the two prime objectives of PMP, which are typically not the goals of ICT4D projects; scaling, sustainability, and benefiting disadvantaged communities without undesired outcomes are typically the goals of ICT4D projects. There are fundamental differences in some of the goals of PMP and ICT4D projects. Due to the differences in the business environment in developing and developed countries (Roztocki & Weistroffer, 2011), PMP grounded in the West cannot be applied "as is" in the developing world. Hence, it becomes necessary to customize PMP for addressing ICT4D project challenges.

This chapter addresses the following two research questions: (A) what are the factors responsible for ICT4D project challenges? And (B) how can PMP developed in the West be customized to address the challenges experienced by ICT4D projects in developing nations?

The next section synthesizes various ways to customize PMP for a variety of development projects aiming to create social, economic, and human development in developing nations. The following section presents study findings. The concluding section discusses key contributions, limitations, and implications of this study.

GUIDANCE TO CUSTOMIZE PMP IN DEVELOPING NATIONS

Typically, researchers serve as project managers for ICT4D projects. Hence, irrespective of their personality and training they should be able to manage seven dimensions of ICT4D projects in order to address project challenges. ICT4D researchers could learn from the following observations and advice for customizing PMP for development projects in developing nations.

The operating conditions in the developing world as characterized by contextual factors make traditional PMP in the developed world less appropriate and applicable (Blunt, 1992). These contextual

Table 1. Project management principles

Scope management	Scope planning	Documentation of how the project scope will be defined, verified, controlled, and how the work will be broken down in a structured way
	Scope definition	Defining a project statement useful for future decisions
	Creating a work breakdown structure	Subdividing project into smaller, more manageable components
	Scope verification	Formalizing acceptance of completed project deliverables
	Scope control	Controlling changes to the project scope
Time management	Activity definition	Identifying specific schedule activities
	Activity sequencing	Identifying and documenting dependencies among schedule activities
	Activity resource estimating	Estimating the type and quantities of resources required for each activity
	Activity duration estimating	Estimating the number of work periods needed to complete schedule activities
	Schedule development	Analyzing activity sequences, durations, resource requirements, and schedule constraints
	Schedule control	Controlling changes to the schedule
Cost management	Cost estimating	Developing an approximation of the costs of the resources needed to complete project activities
	Cost budgeting	Aggregating estimated costs of individual activities to establish cost baseline
	Cost control	Influencing factors creating cost variances and controlling cost changes
Quality management	Quality planning	Identifying quality standards relevant to the project and deciding how to satisfy them
	Perform quality assurance	Applying the planned systematic quality activity to ensure that the project employs processes necessary to meet requirements
	Perform quality control	Monitoring project results to make sure they comply with relevant quality standards and identifying ways to eliminate cases of unsatisfactory performance
Human resource management	Human resource planning	Identifying and documenting roles, responsibilities, and reporting relationships
	Acquire project team	Obtaining human resources
	Develop project team	Improving competencies and interaction of team members
	Manage project team	Tracking team member performance, providing feedback, resolving issues, and coordinating changes to enhance project performance
Communications management	Communications planning	Determining the information and communications needs of the project stakeholders
	Information distribution	Making needed information available to project stakeholders in a timely manner
	Performance reporting	Collecting and distributing performance information
	Manage stakeholders	Managing communications to satisfy the requirements of and resolve issues with project stakeholders
Risk management	Risk management planning	Deciding how to approach, plan, and execute the risk management activities
	Risk identification	Determining which risks might affect the project and documenting their characteristics
	Risk analysis	Prioritizing risks for subsequent analysis and assessing and combining the probability of occurrence and impact
	Risk response planning	Developing options and actions to enhance opportunities and to reduce threats to project objectives
	Risk monitoring and control	Tracking identified risks, monitoring current risks, identifying new risks, executing risk response plan, and evaluating their effectiveness throughout the project life cycle

Source: PMBOK, 2003

factors include geographic and cultural differences between project actors, technologically challenged operating conditions, and unpredictable socio-political environments. The challenges of managing a team of diverse stakeholders are exacerbated as a result of the varied political, cultural, and linguistic differences faced by development projects (Cleland & Ireland, 2008). In an ICT4D field research team, in addition to disadvantaged communities and local mediators, researchers may have to work with local technical support personnel, local gatekeepers, and government officials. It is necessary for researchers to identify and address the motives and agendas of various actors participating in field research so that various ICT4D project challenges can be managed appropriately.

To manage challenges in development projects in the developing world, the project management literature strongly advises considering the "need to cope with political and community demands on project resources, recognition that economic rationality and efficiency, assumed as a basis for many project management tools and techniques does not reflect local realities; and that use of such tools and techniques will not enhance project success if they run counter to cultural and work values" (Muriithi & Crawford, 2003, p. 309). A contemporary view of project management acknowledges the influence of culture on the management of project challenges (Shore & Cross, 2005; Wang & Liu, 2007).

Project managers are accountable for managing cultural factors affecting the success of projects. Most importantly, they need to be culturally sensitive, i.e., they should understand the mentality of others, but that can be achieved only if they understand their own mentality as it comes across to others (Hofstede, 1997). A project manager's ability to decode and encode messages when communicating with everyone involved in the project holding different beliefs grounded in varied national and organizational cultural values plays a critical role in managing challenges (Henderson, 2008). Biases of project managers affect their ability to manage and make decisions, leading to project failures (Shore, 2008). A project management study conducted by Yanwen (2012) illustrates how project managers could assess the project environment, maintain flexibility, and be competent to analyze the nature of associated problems in geographically dispersed projects. ICT4D researchers need to be sensitive and responsive to the various cultural factors and habits of the disadvantaged communities with whom they conduct field research.

METHODS

This study builds on an empirical base of 380 artifacts. The artifacts include journal articles, books, master's theses and doctoral dissertations, national and international conference proceedings, newspaper articles, and project reports submitted to grantees. The artifacts are authored by scholars from academia, public organizations (e.g., World Bank, Ford Foundation, and the Bill and Melinda Gates Foundation), and private companies (e.g., Yahoo and Microsoft Research). The artifacts can be categorized into empirical study findings, observations from ICT-prototype pilot studies, reviews of ICT designed for a particular disadvantaged community, and comparisons of ICT-based practices in developing nations.

Rationale for Selecting the Sources

The author commenced the study by compiling peer-reviewed articles published by top-tier ICT4D journals. Proceedings from conferences like ICT4D, ITU World Telecom Development Conference,

Mobile Communications for Development, and conferences held by IFIP, with acceptance rates of 40% or less also enriched the collection. In the second phase, a snowball sampling approach was adopted to access artifacts from a variety of journals (e.g., MIS Quarterly, IT and People, Communications of the ACM, etc.) in the disciplines related to and outside of ICT4D. On multiple occasions the EBSCO, ERIC, ProQuest Dissertations, and Google Scholar databases were used to retrieve academic artifacts other than journal articles. Search engines of public agencies/institutions and private sector firms including Google were instrumental in locating practitioner reports and non-academic artifacts published since 2000.

Data Analysis

The author analyzed 380 artifacts using cluster analysis technique and grounded theory principles.

Cluster Analysis: A Lens for Identifying and Depicting Factors Responsible for ICT4D Project Challenges. Cluster analysis is a data visualization technique used for depicting complex phenomena or describing the world for analyzing data (Tan, Steinbach & Kumar, 2006). Cluster analysis divides data objects into groups that are meaningful, useful, or both. Each cluster is a collection of objects that share common characteristics. The greater the similarity within a group and the greater the difference between groups, the better or more distinct the cluster becomes. Visual representation of clusters consists of the following methods: Conceptual, density-based, well-separated, prototype-based, and graph-based. This chapter employs graph-based cluster analysis where nodes are objects and links represent connections among objects. The graph-based visualization represents clusters as connected components.

Grounded theory is a method for conducting qualitative research originally conceptualized by sociologists Barney Glaser and Anselm Strauss (1967). The data analysis for this study is based upon the method as explained by Glaser and Strauss. The open coding, i.e. line-by-line coding, of more than 150 challenges documented within the 380 artifacts led to more than 50 axial codes that were further clustered into 7 select codes. For instance, the author recommends managing the scope of data collection based on two axial codes, namely, setting unrealistic goals for data collection and a lack of planning for data collection. The axial codes were derived from open codes such as: lack of time, money, and other context-specific resources, inflexible schedules for data collection, selection of research sites without maps or transportation, and uncoordinated data collection at multiple research sites in the same research project. In another instance, the author identified insufficient funds for data collection, abrupt discontinuation of funds during data collection, and sudden increases in the cost of hardware devices and other resources during data collection as some of the open codes which led him to propose the following three axial codes: insufficient operational budget, unreliable sources of funding, and unpredictable operational cost; the axial codes underscore the significance of managing cost during data collection.

Table 2 demonstrates the process of deriving seven clusters of challenges extracted from the ICT4D literature considered for analysis. The analysis of these challenges suggests that the inability of researchers to manage *scope, time, cost, quality, human resources, communication,* and *risks* related to data collection makes ICT4D field research challenging.

Table 2. Analyzing ICT4D project challenges

Open Coding Sample Data Points (Challenges)	Axial Coding Clustering of Challenges	Selective Coding
Lack of time, money, and other context-specific resources (e.g., appropriate housing, etc.) to complete ongoing data collection	Unrealistic goals set for data collection	Lack of scope management
Inflexible schedule for data collection		
Selecting research sites without maps or transportation, etc.	Lack of planning for data collection	
Uncoordinated efforts including data collection at multiple research sites of a single research project		
Too short or too long duration of data collection	Inappropriate duration of data collection	Lack of time management
Too many questions in a single survey or interview		
Collecting data during draught or monsoon	Wrong timing of data collection	
Insufficient funds negatively affecting the scope, duration, or any other factor related to data collection	Insufficient operational budget	Lack of cost management
Abrupt reduction or discontinuation of funding for data collection	Unreliable sources of funding	
Sudden increase in the cost of ICT during data collection	Unpredictable operational cost	
Incorrect data, data entry errors by local assistants or researchers, etc.	Poor quality of data	Lack of quality management
Ambiguous data collected by local assistants or researchers		
Noisy communication channels and interrupted communications	Poor communication channels	
Recruitment of assistants who are unable to communicate in a local dialect spoken by disadvantaged communities	Inappropriate composition of research team	Lack of human resources management
Sudden disappearance of local assistants from data collection sites, irresponsible behavior of researchers, etc.	Lack of accountability among team members	
Disadvantaged communities wary of talking to outsiders	Cultural and contextual barriers to communication	Lack of communication management
Lack of trust in ICT and trust in personnel involved in data collection		
Differences in researchers and disadvantaged communities creating misunderstandings, hostility, or other negative feelings	Demographic and social barriers to communication	
Flood, earthquake, wildfire, etc.	Unexpected natural calamities	Lack of risk management
Unwillingness of participants to share their personal stories related to sensitive, embarrassing, or controversial research topics	Sensitive, embarrassing, or controversial research topics	
Riots, political rallies, elections, epidemics, etc. during data collection	Changes in local circumstances	

FINDINGS

Six Factors Associated with ICT4D Project Challenges

Outside researchers, disadvantaged communities, local assistants, ICTs, contextual factors, and research methods are associated with the challenges, barriers, and issues facing ICT4D projects.

1. **Outside Researchers:** Cross-cultural working, adapting to local culture, and understanding the needs and customs of disadvantaged communities are the most frequent challenges faced by *outside researchers* (Blom, Chipchase & Lehikoinen, 2005; Walsham & Sahay, 2006). Visible dis-

parities between disadvantaged communities and researchers often lead to misunderstandings that could create suspicions regarding the researchers' intentions. Their assumptions, preconceptions, and limitations, including the inability to understand local concerns, needs, and realities create hurdles in their field projects (Krauss & Turpin, 2013). For instance, as part of a study conducted in Kenya, researchers brought expensive computers into a resource-starved community during a time of drought when the community was barely capable of producing enough food. This upset the community affecting their study participation (Hewett, Erulkar, & Mensch, 2004).

2. **Disadvantaged Communities:** Psychological, physical, cultural, and several other issues associated with *disadvantaged communities* negatively affect their interest and ability to participate in field research. For instance, Straub, Loch & Hill (2001) found that the cultural beliefs and values in Arab society are strong predictors of their resistance to new information and communication technologies. Disadvantaged communities often have to go through difficult cultural transitions to understand new or culturally-foreign ICT, and to interpret it within their community and context (Krauss, 2013). Detailed effort and attention to the involvement of multiple stakeholder groups play an important role for the successful implementation of ICT projects (Krishna & Walsham, 2005); failure to do so discourages potential study participants, diminishing the quality and quantity of responses. Lack of trust for ICTs or research teams often appears to be another core issue impeding the implementation of ICT4D projects (Vaidya et al., 2013). Sometimes community and political leaders pressure potential participants not to cooperate with outside researchers to demonstrate their "loyalty" toward the community (Hewett et al., 2004). Also, disadvantaged communities living in remote, thinly populated areas pose logistical and technical problems making data collection cumbersome (Elahi, 2008).

3. **Local Assistants:** Sometimes *local assistants* unintentionally create or are unable to help researchers solve ICT4D project problems. Their abrupt disappearance from research sites could create uncertainty for field research (Brewer et al., 2006). Violation of project protocol and data collection policies by local assistants affects the quality of data collected. For instance, local assistants, who were assigned to conduct face-to-face and self-administered interviews, went over an allocated time period in the hope that by conducting more in-depth interviews they would be looked on favorably for possible future employment (Hewett et al., 2004). Sometimes financial incentives are not lucrative enough for local assistants to continue working on field projects (Elahi, 2008). A lack or low degree of engagement from the IT industry with the transformative ICT4D discourse in developing nations fails to produce skilled IT workers with a passion to work for development programs (Avgerou, 2008). As a result, ICT4D projects are forced to utilize local assistants who lack technical expertise for addressing technical issues, stalling the projects.

4. **ICT:** Typical *ICT*-related issues including power outages and interruptions (Anokwa et al., 2009; Brewer et al., 2006), noisy communication channels, and the several unpredictable technological problems prevalent in developing nations creating hardware and software problems, delaying or interrupting the execution of ICT4D projects. The limited technical resources available for ICT4D projects inhibit the development and management of innovative information systems for developing nations (Avgerou, 2008).

5. **Contextual Factors:** Contextual factors frequently affect the following dimensions of ICT4D projects: information, technology, processes, objectives and values, staffing and skills, management systems and structures, and valuable project resources like time and money (Heeks, 2002). In addition, bureaucratic systems, government policies, organizational norms, and processes in

developing nations shape the research design for worse or delay the implementation of ICT4D projects (Krishna & Walsham, 2005). For instance, the government organizations implementing agricultural marketing information systems tend to be ridden with rigid bureaucracies, corruption and inefficient project management (Islam & Grönlund, 2010). Contextual problems like intermittent political interference, a lack of supporting policies crafted by organizations or governments, and deeply ingrained unfair local practices (Vaidya et al., 2013) also challenge the implementation of information systems in developing nations.

6. **Research Methods:** Data collection, an important dimension of *research methods*, is often affected severely by challenges, barriers, and issues associated with ICT4D projects. For instance, conservative social values and cultural norms made it difficult to get honest feedback from disadvantaged populations in Pakistan, Tanzania, Rwanda, and Ghana (Anokwa et al., 2009). In a similar experience, Evangelical Christian groups made it almost impossible for unmarried Kenyan adolescent boys and girls to participate in a survey seeking information about family planning and sexual behavior (Hewett et al., 2004). Conflicts among upper management, unions, and middle management make it difficult for collecting data from public servants working in government-funded organizations in developing nations (Tarafdar & Vaidya, 2005). Due to the official ban on recording interviews with government officers in India, Puri & Sahay (2007) could not tape their interviews with the officials as part of their research project studying the role of ICTs in participatory development in rural parts of the country. Intentional tampering with data by local IT staff and data theft are two more key threats affecting the quality of data in ICT4D projects (Brewer et al., 2006). Research questions like "what, how, why, and when people carry what they do" require device researchers to study the user in an everyday mobile environment. This type of data collection is particularly challenging when observing female mobile phone users in developing nations (Blom et al., 2005).

The above cluster analysis portrays the association of six factors (human and non-human) with challenges related to ICT4D projects. The factors, which are identified by the literature dedicated to ICT4D project problems, are as follows: ICTs, disadvantaged communities, outside researchers, local assistants, data collection, and contextual factors. Each cluster (see Figure 1) is labelled by the factor responsible for or associated with the challenges, barriers, and issues in the cluster.

The cluster analysis also identifies the inter-relationship among six clusters. Several challenges, barriers, and issues are associated with one, two, or three factors at a time. For instance, "fear & inhibitions to communicate with outsiders" is related to two factors, namely, outside researchers and disadvantaged communities. A majority of challenges are associated with disadvantaged communities followed in order by information technologies, contextual factors, disadvantaged communities, outside researchers, and local assistants.

The next sub-section illustrates the ways to manage the seven dimensions drawn from the literature on ICT4D projects successful in addressing ICT4D project challenges in the past, the lessons learnt by researchers, and their advice for collection data from disadvantaged communities in developing nations.

Managing Seven Dimensions of ICT4D Projects

Considering the variation in contextual factors related to developing nations, it is important to remember that a successful practice in one context does not guarantee the same level of success in other contexts. Researchers may need to make appropriate changes to a practice successful in one context when applying

Figure 1. Visualizing ICT4D field research challenges

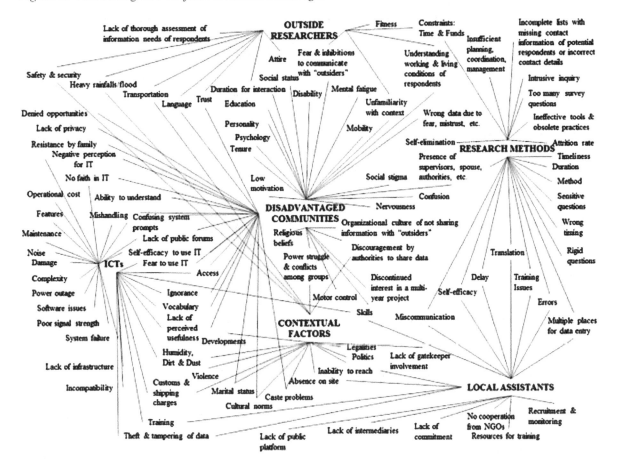

it to other contexts. Failures and shortcomings documented in past studies are helpful for understanding what not to do or how mistakes could be avoided during data collection.

The following sub-sections illustrate the utility of PMP for addressing ICT4D project challenges. It is important to note that a majority of the existing guidance for addressing ICT4D project challenges is similar or related to the literature on customizing PMP for development projects in developing nations. For instance, the lessons learnt and the guidance offered by experienced researchers (e.g., Braa, Monteiro & Sahay, 2004; Heeks & Bhatnagar, 1999; Heeks, 2009; Krishna & Walsham, 2005; Sahay & Walsham, 2006) for managing data collection efforts in ICT4D projects *overlap* with the PMP.

1. **Managing Scope of Data Collections:** While planning and defining the scope of data collection, past ICT4D studies advise to take into consideration contextual factors including socio-cultural inequalities and religious beliefs that could possibly threaten the execution of data collection (Braa et al., 2004; Walsham & Sahay, 2006). Researchers break down the scope of ambitious ICT4D projects into manageable objectives and deliverables for synchronous data collection at multiple sites. The Technology & Social Change Group at the University of Washington undertook a global study to learn the ways in which trust and perceptions shape uses of ICT at public access venues like libraries, telecentres, and cybercafés in 25 developing nations (Gomez & Gould, 2010). They

developed a shared research design to form local research teams and appoint team leaders to conduct surveys, visit over 500 sites, and interview over 25,000 respondents in different types of public access venues in the selected countries. The systematic planning and delegation of tasks and responsibilities to various teams allowed the Group to collect data synchronously and meet the objectives set for this ambitious research project. To facilitate synchronous data collection at different sites, multiple teams consisting of local gatekeepers were formed.

Periodic verification of the scope of data collection could help researchers manage the challenges associated with access to research sites and ICT. Poor transportation infrastructure makes it difficult for researchers to reach respondents living in remote rural parts of any developing country. For instance, Vodafone Research Team (Samuel, Shah, & Hadingham, 2005) found that roads to 11 communities and 9 businesses in Tanzanian villages were sealed. Considering the resources at hand, the researchers eliminated potential respondents from the inaccessible villages. In a similar instance, accessing and keeping track of nomadic respondents living in informal settlements posed a unique set of challenges for data collection. While collecting data from urban migrants in South Africa, Mathee et al. (2010) found that in informal settlements, maps were either not available or considerable change had occurred between the time of map production and the time of data collection. The researchers considered using aerial photographs to improve sampling accuracy, but the cost of commissioning dedicated aerial photography was prohibitively expensive. In such unexpected circumstances and with limited resources at hand, they decided to eliminate potential respondents from the inaccessible sites.

Researchers cannot address ICT4D project challenges alone; the involvement and cooperation of local assistants is critical for outside researchers to be able to address the pre-existing context-specific barriers and subsequent ICT4D project challenges.

2. **Time Management:** Appropriate timing and duration (i.e. not too short or long duration) of data collection is critical in shaping the interaction of researchers with disadvantaged communities. Aggressive ICT prototype development timelines often limit time spent by the HCI researchers in the field. For instance, the small amount of time that HCI researchers were able to spend in the field did not give them enough opportunities to understand local culture and possible ways in which their system would be adopted by locals in a developing nation (Chetty & Grinter, 2007). Long durations of collecting responses on sensitive personal and social issues could adversely impact data collection. For instance, semi- and low-literate users from Botswana experienced mental fatigue while revealing HIV/AIDS related health information (Sharma-Grover, Plauche, Barnard, & Kuun, 2009).

To address duration-related challenges, researchers advise others to identify, define, and prioritize data collection activities. They also advocate for estimating and utilizing the type and quantities of resources available to complete the activities (Chetty & Grinter, 2007; Sharma-Grover et al., 2009). Better informed decisions about data collection schedules can be made after gathering the information related to time durations, resource requirements, and schedule constraints.

Fifth grade students from government-run schools in India were expected to participate in an ICT-prototype testing experiment aimed at improving multi-user sharing of existing educational applications. However, the study was conducted during a swine flu scare in 2008. This issue, coupled with widespread absenteeism in government-run Indian schools, led to absence rates approaching 75% on specific days of data collection (Heimerl, Vasudev, Buchanan, Parikh, & Brewer, 2010). Researchers cannot predict the natural or man-made calamities that might be faced by study participants; hence, to handle such unexpected challenges resulting from the *wrong timing* for data collection, researchers need to have contingency plans or a plan B for data collection (Heimerl et al., 2010). To address timing-lead ICT4D project challenges, it is advisable to undertake pilot studies to estimate appropriate timelines, durations, and the frequencies of data collection in ICT4D projects.

3. **Managing Costs of Data Collection:** The costs of one-time investments in ICT, recurring maintenance costs (e.g., electric bills, etc.) for devices supporting ICT, and ongoing operational expenses for recruiting skilled personnel could be three areas of financial investment in the data collection phase of ICT4D projects. The exorbitant cost for access to the Internet constrained monetary planning for a qualitative study which examined how professionals in Nairobi, Kenya, use ICT in their everyday lives (Wyche, Smyth, Chetty, Aoki, & Grinter, 2010). Large sampling requirements and longitudinal designs often incur high financial costs (Duncombe, 2011). Limited funding assigned for studying rural farmers in China prevented Wang & Chen (2010) from conducting large surveys with farmers and farm-workers in rural China.

Researchers can manage their scarce funds available for ICT4D projects by (a) estimating the costs of the resources needed to complete data collection activities, and (b) aggregating the estimated costs of individual activities to establish a cost baseline (Mathee et al., 2010; Wang & Chen, 2010; Wyche et al., 2010). This approach is likely to control changes to the budget for data collection. Careful planning of field activities for data collection can save monetary resources and help researchers address challenges arising from having limited funds available for completing data collection. For instance, if their budget is small, researchers should not plan to undertake massive quantitative surveys but conduct qualitative interviews or semi-structured surveys with quick turnarounds, producing presentable results acceptable to the ICT4D community; they might not able to produce valid statistical inferences but being able to capture the impact of ICT from the perspective of disadvantaged communities is always better than having small quantitative samples with inconclusive or limited causation (Duncombe, 2011).

4. **Quality Management:** Data quality is valuable to ICT4D projects since it may shape the ability of researchers to make sense of the expectations, needs, and experiences of disadvantaged communities using ICT solutions. Researchers advise managing decisions, activities, and external circumstances that deteriorate data quality. In a study observing parental perspectives on computers in rural India, unannounced visits by researchers at the respondents' homes were considered intrusive and unethical, straining the interactions between the researchers and the respondents (Pal, Lakshmanan, & Toyama, 2007). Tense interactions with participants could deteriorate the quality of information shared by study participants. Hence, researchers should avoid any such decision and action jeopardizing their relation with disadvantaged communities.

Researchers periodically monitor data collection results to decide whether the planned processes need to be adjusted for collecting the highest quality data. Sometimes it becomes difficult for respondents to answer certain questions in the presence of supervisors, spouses, or teachers if the responses are collected at workplaces, homes, or schools. For instance, the lack of privacy provided to Ghanaian HIV/AIDS patients adversely affected the quality of information shared by them in front of their families (Paik et al., 2009). Kuriyan, Ray, & Toyama, (2008) warn researchers of not approaching disadvantaged communities as a way to get "the true story," but to understand their perspective for interpreting issues and possible solutions. This approach suggests researchers be empathetic with respondents and the context in which they respond to ICT and make use of ICT while pursuing their daily information needs.

The mere act of observing a group could influence the group's reaction to the observation, especially if the group is aware that they have been "chosen," which is also known as the *Hawthorne effect* (Adair, 1984). Paik et al. (2009) made a different arrangement to collect data from respondents in the absence of family members. Lima & Brown (2007) also observed that children and teens attending schools and colleges in Brazil were not comfortable participating in a study in the presence of their teachers. They changed their original data collection plan to make students comfortable sharing their stories in the absence of teachers. Thus researchers attuned data collection procedures to eliminate the causes of deteriorated quality of responses.

Datasets related to market prices for commodities, ICT adoption by disadvantaged communities, and small business owners are useful to jumpstart data collection in unfamiliar contexts. However, a lack of systematically collected historical data is a common problem when studying informal markets and unorganized communities. For instance, Abraham (2006) could not locate historical data on fish prices since few formal records were kept and many people hid or distorted any written records they did keep. In such circumstances, researchers must develop data quality standards and eliminate sources and data that do not meet the standards. To understand the impact of subsidies on the sustainability of tele-centers in Kyrgyzstan, it was essential to get hold of datasets on the low-income citizens receiving Internet coupons (Best, Thakur, & Kolko, 2009). However, incomplete lists with missing or incorrect contact information for beneficiaries forced the researchers to adopt convenience sampling which did not represent the entire population.

Without active participation and training of local assistants it is almost impossible for outside researchers to overcome language barriers, data entry errors, and the Hawthorne effect. Research methods should be designed in such a way that they respect the privacy of disadvantaged communities; it is necessary for researchers to learn local norms of privacy, etiquette, and decent behavior while working with disadvantaged communities, improving the likelihood of success in data collection.

5.   **HR Management:** Local assistants, a key human resource for data collection, often play a multipurpose role in the data collection phase of ICT4D projects. For instance, they might be responsible for arranging transportation to research sites in remote rural parts of developing nations, introducing outside researchers to the gatekeepers of local communities, translating context and communications, conducting interviews with disadvantaged communities, addressing technology issues, helping researchers scale information systems, or catering to unexpected logistic requirements of data collection (Sahay & Walsham, 2006).

Due to their critical role in data collection, it is important that local assistants speak the same dialect and not just the same language as that of respondents. Researchers studying the speech-based access to health information by low-literate users in Pakistan assumed that local assistants would be able to speak the same language as that of the low-literate users. The researchers did not realize that health workers who could not speak Urdu would be of no use in collecting responses from the Sindhi speaking user population (Sherwani et al., 2007). The assumption made by outside researchers regarding local assistants delayed the data collection process. Hence, it is important to involve local assistants, right from the beginning, i.e. the planning phase of data collection.

The shortage of local experts on software development, maintenance, and operation is a more long-term complicated problem than the difficulties associated with hardware purchases (Ewusi-Mensah, 2012). Many times locally recruited technical assistants fail to operate technology platforms or programming languages selected for software to be tested in the field. Sometimes local assistants flounder when asked to fix ICT. Also, many local assistants lack basic computing knowledge and of expertise in network administration. This means that each time the wireless network fails it stays down until a network administrator fixes it. To manage these issues, researchers must plan ahead of time for recruiting assistants with specific ICT skills required to collect data during ICT4D projects (Blom et al., 2005; Hewett et al., 2004). However, developing technology skills and expertise among local assistants requires a significant amount of training and education, which is generally out of the scope of ICT4D projects. Direct recruitment of undergraduate and graduate students in Western universities and residents of developing nations living in the West, who have the requisite technology expertise and skills (Ewusi-Mensah, 2012), is a possible solution to the shortage of ICT skills required for data collection.

For addressing HR related challenges, researchers should (a) identify and document roles, responsibilities, and reporting relationships for staff members, (b) improve the interaction of staff members to improve their performance in the field, and (c) track staff performance by providing feedback and coordinating changes to enhance their overall performance. Without cooperation of local assistants it is almost impossible for outside researchers to streamline their process of recruiting and retaining the local talent necessary for completing data collection.

6. **Managing Communication:** Non-verbal communication between researchers and disadvantaged communities is equally or perhaps more important than verbal communication in data collection. Socioeconomic and demographic differences between respondents and researchers reflected through researchers' attire, perfume, eyewear, etc. reinforce their outsider status, and could eventually distort the way respondents perceive the researchers. For instance, women from indigenous communities in remote, rural parts of Australia shied away from researchers due to their feeling of "shame" for talking to outsiders (McCallum & Papandrea, 2009). Trust in ICT and trust in personnel involved in data collection also shapes the involvement of disadvantaged communities in data collection. For instance, in a study with housemaids from urban India, perceived mistrust for technology led respondents to be hesitant towards touching the technology or to self-eliminate from the study (Medhi & Toyama, 2007). Sometimes researchers are being told what their respondents think the researchers want to hear, instead of being told the "real truth." In many cultures – and often exacerbated by the perceived power distances between researchers and locals – it is considered a courtesy to tell "guests" what they want to hear; it is rude to inform guests about real issues or problems. The locals are trying to please the researchers and want to support them in reaching their perceived research objectives.

Building a bond of trust with study participants is a major step toward addressing communication-related challenges for researchers. For instance, researchers can overcome the communication challenges by determining the information and communication needs of the disadvantaged communities with the help of local assistants, and making needed information available to them in a timely manner.

Sometimes when study participants do not trust the ability of ICT, it becomes necessary for researchers to convince the participants of the utility and benefits of using ICT for their betterment. If convinced, the disadvantaged communities are likely to participate actively in data collection exercises. Without active participation of local assistants it is almost impossible for outside researchers to gain the trust of disadvantaged communities, which in return, would help them portray a positive image to seek maximum possible cooperation from disadvantaged communities.

7. **Managing Inherent Risks:** When researchers test ICT prototypes with disadvantaged communities, there are some obvious risks associated with the experiments. Typical risks are related to the fear of, unfamiliarity with, or lack of efficacy of respondents for using ICT. A team of researchers testing a multimedia application for information dissemination in disadvantaged communities found that fear and inhibitions among respondents towards using the application kept the communities away from it (Chu et al., 2009). The nervous state of respondents towards using ICT discouraged respondents from participating in a project that tested the impact of touchtone vs. speech recognition on HIV health information access (Sharma-Grover et al., 2009). In a similar case, the negative perceptions of disadvantaged communities towards newly introduced ICT and their unfamiliarity with text-based technology discouraged them from participating in a study assessing the vulnerability of their communities after surviving disasters in rural Asia (Chib & Komathi, 2009). Researchers should never blame disadvantaged communities for their inability to operate ICT prototypes. Instead they should empathetically analyze the fear and any other psychological barriers that lead to the inability of study participants to use ICT, and should encourage the participants with the help of various incentives, including financial compensation.

Sensitive, embarrassing, or controversial research topics could jeopardize data collection. The social stigma associated with victims of HIV/AIDS often makes it difficult for data collection teams to reach out to the victims for data collection. For instance, Angolan patients were hesitant and reluctant to give personal information regarding their HIV/AIDS and sexual behavior (Cheng, Ernesto & Truong, 2008). Questions related to alcohol and drug consumption, contraceptive practices, pregnancies, induced abortions, and illegitimate child births cause a similar setback for data collection. Assuring the privacy of study participants during data collection and guaranteeing the confidentiality of data collected are common strategies for collecting data on sensitive, embarrassing, or controversial research topics (Cheng et al., 2008; Paik et al., 2009).

The issue of safety vs. the ability to operate on research sites is often faced during data collection. The safety of participants and research teams is paramount but each environment comes with its own set of risks. Mathee et al. (2010) experienced verbal abuse, racial slurs, and physical assault (or threats of it) while conducting interviews in South Africa. The risk of offensive behavior and physical assault was elevated over weekends when the consumption of alcohol and substance abuse were at a peak. Moreover, conflicts with local organizations could also result in high rates of crime, challenging the safety of research teams. It is always advisable to avoid collecting data in risky sociocultural environments.

Researchers should identify and determine which risks might affect their data collection and their staff members, and document the risk characteristics. Prioritizing risks based on the probability of their occurrence and impact is another strategy implemented during data collection. It is important to analyze the effect of identified risks on overall data collection objectives, developing options and actions to reduce threats to data collection objectives, tracking and monitoring identified risks, and recognizing new risks and evaluating their effect on data collection.

FUTURE RESEARCH DIRECTIONS

This chapter breaks silos between the ICT4D and project management communities, ushering in a new era where both communities could engage to benefit each other and disadvantaged communities in developing nations. The ICT4D community could learn from the applications of PMP for managing projects in developing nations. For instance, the project management literature advises managers to (a) assess and adapt to local realities, cultural values, organizational norms, and work practices (Nguyen, 2007), (b) revitalize the sluggish and ineffective management practices in organizations (Stuckenbruck & Zomorrodian, 1987), and (c) acquire and retain skilled IT professionals in developing nations (Mia & Ramage, 2011).

PMP could help researchers adopt innovative process-based and technology-driven solutions to collect, store, and process different types of data (i.e. text, audio, video, tactile, etc.). Research focusing on the inter-relationship between contextual factors (e.g., policy frameworks, environmental conditions, culture, etc.), research methods, and local assistants in ICT4D field research could enrich this dialog between ICT4D researchers and project management professionals.

The project management community could undertake consulting assignments with the World Bank, United Nations, etc. to help them conceptualize, plan, execute, and report findings from ICT4D projects with disadvantaged communities in developing nations, thereby increasing the success rates of ICT4D projects and possibly saving millions of dollars' worth of donations and taxpayer money.

Finally, the visualization of ICT4D project challenges depicted in this chapter would help the ICT4D community to (a) synthesize a wide variety of ICT4D project challenges at one place (similar to a snapshot), (b) identify trends, indirect relationships, or hidden patterns among the challenges, which might not be possible otherwise in the text format, and (c) analyze new challenges, which are not depicted in figure 1, by correlating the new challenges with one or more of the six factors in order to devise a solution.

CONCLUSION

Success stories, failures, and shortcomings in projects documented in past ICT4D studies suggest a strong correlation between the management of the seven dimensions of ICT4D projects listed above and the ability to address project challenges. For instance, researchers who broke down the scope of ambitious data collection conducted at multiple sites in different developing nations were successful in collecting data synchronously with the help of teams of local assistants (Gomez & Gould, 2010; Samuel et al., 2005). These examples and similar others illustrated in this chapter support the author's claim regarding managing the seven dimensions to address ICT4D project challenges.

Some of the key contributions made by this chapter are as follows.

1. This chapter informs researchers by providing an argument in terms of how to think about and address ICT4D project challenges. Key areas of interest for researchers covered in the chapter include challenges in eliciting participation, gathering data, and working with participants in developing

nations. Exploring possible ways of managing the seven dimensions associated with data collection provides a greater learning experience for researchers.

2. The overall guidance to manage the seven dimensions is based on past ICT4D studies. The studies included both failures and successful case examples. Considering the differences in contextual factors in developing nations, this chapter asks researchers to make appropriate modifications in the ways they manage the seven dimensions as illustrated by the past studies successful in addressing ICT4D project challenges.

3. The existing ICT4D literature rarely offers any structured guidance to conduct field research with disadvantaged communities in developing nations. This chapter fills the gap by illustrating the utility of PMP for addressing project challenges. The generalizability of these dimensions would be of immense value to ICT4D researchers in the future.

Limitation

The challenges discussed in this chapter are reported by academic researchers, who may have very different motivations and resources to address the challenges than that of practitioners. Hence, practitioners may not find the study findings useful or applicable. Also, this chapter does not present a comprehensive list of challenges, but it proposes ways to address a large number of ICT4D project challenges rarely documented and analyzed in a single artifact.

ACKNOWLEDGMENT

I would like to thank Dr. Hakikur Rahman for inviting me to extend my manuscript titled "Addressing Data Collection Challenges in ICT for Development Projects" published earlier by the International Journal of ICT and Human Development. Informal discussions with researchers and practitioners in the US, India, China, Saudi Arabia, Mexico, Ghana, and Ethiopia in the past enriched this chapter.

REFERENCES

Abraham, R. (2006). Mobile phones and economic development: Evidence from the fishing industry in India. *Information Technologies and International Development, 4*(1), 5–17.

Adair, J. (1984). The Hawthorne effect: A reconsideration of the methodological artifact. *The Journal of Applied Psychology, 69*(2), 334–345. doi:10.1037/0021-9010.69.2.334

Anokwa, Y., Smyth, T., Ramachandran, D., Sherwani, J., Schwartzman, Y., Luk, R., & DeRenzi, B. (2009). Stories from the field: Reflections on HCI4D experiences. *Information Technologies and International Development, 5*(4), 101–115.

Avgerou, C. (2008). Information systems in developing countries: A critical research review. *Journal of Information Technology, 23*(3), 133–146. doi:10.1057/palgrave.jit.2000136

Best, M., Thakur, D., & Kolko, B. (2009). The contribution of user-based subsidies to the impact and sustainability of telecenters – The eCenter Project in Kyrgyzstan. *Paper presented at the 3rd International Conference on Information and Communication Technologies and Development*, Education City, Doha, Qatar.

Blom, J., Chipchase, J., & Lehikoinen, J. (2005). Contextual and cultural challenges for user mobility research. *Communications of the ACM, 48*(7), 37–41. doi:10.1145/1070838.1070863

Blunt, P., & Jones, M. L. (1992). *Managing Organisations in Africa*. Berlin: Walter de Gruyter. doi:10.1515/9783110850031

Braa, J., Monteiro, E., & Sahay, S. (2004). Networks of action: Sustainable health information systems across developing nations. *Management Information Systems Quarterly, 28*, 337–362.

Brewer, E., Demmer, M., Ho, M., Honicky, R., Pal, J., Plauche, M., & Surana, S. (2006). The challenges of technology research for developing regions. *IEEE Pervasive Computing / IEEE Computer Society [and] IEEE Communications Society, 5*(2), 15–23. doi:10.1109/MPRV.2006.40

Cheng, K., Ernesto, F., & Truong, K. (2008). Participant and interviewer attitudes toward handheld computers in the context of HIV/AIDS programs in sub-Saharan Africa. *Paper presented at the proceeding of the 26th annual SIGCHI Conference on Human Factors in Computing Systems*, Florence, Italy. doi:10.1145/1357054.1357175

Chetty, M., & Grinter, R. (2007). HCI4D: HCI challenges in the global south. *Paper presented at the Extended Abstracts Proceedings of the 2007 Conference on Human Factors in Computing Systems*, San Jose, California. doi:10.1145/1240866.1241002

Chib, A., & Harris, R. (2012). *Linking research to practice: Strengthening ICT for development research capacity in Asia*. Singapore: ISEAS Publishing.

Chib, A., & Komathi, A. (2009). Extending the technology-community-management model to disaster recovery: Assessing vulnerability in rural Asia. *Paper presented at the 3rd International Conference on Information and Communication Technologies and Development*, Education City, Doha, Qatar. doi:10.1109/ICTD.2009.5426694

Chu, G., Satpathy, S., Toyama, K., Gandhi, R., Balakrishnan, R., & Menon, S. (2009). Featherweight multimedia for information dissemination. *Paper presented at the 3rd International Conference on Information and Communication Technologies and Development*, Education City, Doha, Qatar. doi:10.1109/ICTD.2009.5426695

Cleland, D., & Ireland, L. (2008). *Project Manager's Handbook: Applying Best Practices Across Global Industries*. New York, NY: McGraw Hill.

De, R. (2012). Messy methods for ICT4D research. In A. Chib & R. Harris (Eds.), *Linking research to practice: Strengthening ICT for development research capacity in Asia* (pp. 58–67). Singapore: ISEAS Publishing.

Duncombe, R. (2011). Researching impact of mobile phones for development: Concepts, methods and lessons for practice. *Information Technology for Development, 17*(4), 268–288. doi:10.1080/0268110 2.2011.561279

Elahi, A. (2008). Challenges of data collection in developing nations – the Pakistani experience as a way forward. *Statistical Journal of the IAOS, 25,* 11–17.

Ewusi-Mensah, K. (2012). Problems of information technology diffusion in sub-Saharan Africa: The case of Ghana. *Information Technology for Development, 18*(3), 247–269. doi:10.1080/02681102.201 2.664113

Glaser, B., & Strauss, A. (1967). *The discovery of grounded theory: Strategies for qualitative research.* New York, NY: Aldine de Gruyter.

Gomez, R., & Gould, E. (2010). The "cool factor" of public access to ICT. *Information Technology & People, 23,* 247–264.

Heeks, R. (2002). Information systems and developing nations: Failure, success, and local improvisations. *The Information Society, 18*(2), 101–112. doi:10.1080/01972240290075039

Heeks, R. (2009). *The ICT4D 2.0 manifesto: Where next for ICTs and international development?* Manchester: Development Informatics Group.

Heeks, R., & Bhatnagar, S. (1999). Understanding (information systems) success and failures in information age reform. In R. Heeks (Ed.), *Reinventing government in the information age: International practice in ICT-enabled public sector reform* (pp. 49–75). London: Routledge. doi:10.4324/9780203204962

Heimerl, K., Vasudev, J., Buchanan, K., Parikh, T., & Brewer, E. (2010). Metamouse: Improving multi-user sharing of existing educational applications. *Paper presented at theInternational Conference on Information and Communication Technologies and Development,* London. doi:10.1145/2369220.2369237

Henderson, L. (2008). The impact of project managers' communication competencies: Validation and extension of a research model for virtuality, satisfaction, and productivity on project teams. *Project Management Journal, 39*(2), 48–59. doi:10.1002/pmj.20044

Hewett, P., Erulkar, A., & Mensch, B. (2004). The feasibility of computer-assisted survey interviewing in Africa: Experience from two rural districts in Kenya. *Social Science Computer Review, 22*(3), 319–334. doi:10.1177/0894439304263114

Hofstede, G. (1997). *Cultures and organizations: Software of the mind.* New York, NY: McGraw Hill.

Islam, M. S., & Grönlund, Å. (2010). Agriculture market information services (AMIS) in the least Developed Countries (LDCs): Nature, Scopes, and Challenges. In M.A. Wimmer, J.-L. Chappelet, M. Janssen, H.J. Scholl (Eds.), Proceedings of EGOV '10, LNCS (Vol. 6228, pp. 109–120). Heidelberg: Springer

Krauss, K. (2013). Collisions between the worldviews of international ICT policy makers and a deep rural community in South Africa: Assumptions, interpretation, implementation, and reality. *Information Technology for Development, 19*(4), 296–318. doi:10.1080/02681102.2013.793167

Krauss, K., & Turpin, M. (2013). The emancipation of the researcher as part of information and communication technology for development work in deep rural South Africa. *The Electronic Journal of Information Systems in Developing Nations, 59*(2), 1–21.

Krishna, S., & Madon, S. (2003). Introduction: Challenges of ICT in the development context. In S. Krishna & S. Madon (Eds.), *The Digital Challenge: Information Technology in the Development Context* (pp. 1–12). Burlington, VT: Ashgate. doi:10.1016/B978-012426297-3.50027-8

Krishna, S., & Walsham, G. (2005). Implementing public information systems in developing nations: Learning from a success story. *Information Technology for Development, 11*(2), 123–140. doi:10.1002/itdj.20007

Kuriyan, R., Ray, I., & Toyama, K. (2008). Information and communication technologies for development: The bottom of the pyramid model in practice. *The Information Society, 24*(2), 93–104. doi:10.1080/01972240701883948

Lima, C., & Brown, S. (2007). ICT for development: Are Brazilian students well prepared to become global citizens? *Educational Media International, 44*(2), 141–153. doi:10.1080/09523980701295141

Madon, S., Reinhard, N., Roode, D., & Walsham, G. (2009). Digital Inclusion Projects in Developing Countries: Processes of Institutionalization. *Information Technology for Development, 15*(2), 95–107. doi:10.1002/itdj.20108

Mathee, A., Harpham, T., Naicker, N., Barnes, B., Plagerson, S., Feit, M., & Naidoo, S. et al. (2010). Overcoming fieldwork challenges in urban health research in developing nations: A research note. *International Journal of Social Research Methodology, 13*(2), 171–178. doi:10.1080/13645570902867742

Mathur, M., & Sharma, S. (2009). Strategic metamorphoses of ICT sector for human development in India. *International Journal of Information Communication Technologies and Human Development, 1*(4), 16–29.

McCallum, K., & Papandrea, F. (2009). Community business: The internet in remote Australian indigenous communities. *New Media & Society, 11*(7), 1230–1251. doi:10.1177/1461444809342059

Medhi, I., & Toyama, K. (2007). Full-context videos for first-time, non-literate PC users. *Information Technologies and International Development, 4*(1), 37–50. doi:10.1162/itid.2007.4.1.37

Mia, M., & Ramage, M. (2011). IT project management in developing nations: Approaches and factors affecting success in the microfinance sector of Bangladesh. *Paper presented at theproceedings of the 6th International Research Workshop on IT Project Management*, Milan, Italy.

Muriithi, N., & Crawford, L. (2003). Approaches to project management in Africa: Implications for international development projects. *International Journal of Project Management, 21*(5), 309–319. doi:10.1016/S0263-7863(02)00048-0

Nguyen, N. (2007). The challenges of transferring modern project management principles and methodologies to developing nations. *Paper presented at theproceedings of the 2007 Project Management Institute Global Congress*, Hong Kong.

Paik, M., Sharma, A., Meacham, A., Quarta, G., Smith, P., Trahanas, J., & Subramanian, L. (2009). The case for SmartTrack. *Paper presented at the 3rd International Conference on Information and Communication Technologies and Development, Education City*, Doha, Qatar. doi:10.1109/ICTD.2009.5426683

Pal, J., Lakshmanan, M., & Toyama, K. (2007). My child will be respected: Parental perspectives on computers in rural India. *Information Systems Frontiers, 11*(2), 129–144. doi:10.1007/s10796-009-9172-1

PMBOK. (2003). *Project Management Body of Knowledge*. Washington, D.C.: Project Management Institute.

Potnis, D. (2014). Managing gender-related challenges in ICT4D field research. *The Electronic Journal of Information Systems in Developing Nations, 65*(2), 1–26.

Puri, S., & Sahay, S. (2007). Role of ICTs in participatory development: An Indian experience. *Information Technology for Development, 13*(2), 133–160. doi:10.1002/itdj.20058

Rahman, H., & Ramos, I. (2013). Implementation of e-Commerce at the grassroots: Issues of challenges in terms of human-computer interaction. *International Journal of Information Communication Technologies and Human Development, 5*(2), 1–19. doi:10.4018/jicthd.2013040101

Roztocki, N., & Weistroffer, H. (2011). Information technology success factors and models in developing and emerging economies. *Information Technology for Development, 17*(3), 163–167. doi:10.1080/02681102.2011.568220

Sahay, S., & Walsham, G. (2006). Scaling of health information systems in India: Challenges and approaches. *Information Technology for Development, 12*(3), 185–200. doi:10.1002/itdj.20041

Samuel, J., Shah, N., & Hadingham, W. (2005). Mobile Communications in South Africa, Tanzania and Egypt: Results from community and business surveys. *Africa: The Impact of Mobile Phones. The Vodafone Policy Paper Series, 2*, 44–52.

Sharma-Grover, A., Plauché, M., Barnard, E., & Kuun, C. (2009). *HIV health information access using spoken dialogue systems: Touchtone vs. speech.Paper presented at the 3rd International Conference on Information and Communication Technologies and Development*, Education City, Doha, Qatar.

Sherwani, J., Ali, N., Mirza, S., Fatima, A., Memon, Y., Karim, M., & Rosenfeld, R. (2007). HealthLine: Speech-based access to health information by low-literate users. *Paper presented at the2nd IEEE/ACM International Conference on Information and Communication Technologies and Development*, Bangalore, India. doi:10.1109/ICTD.2007.4937399

Shore, B. (2008). Systematic biases and culture in project failures. *Project Management Journal, 39*(4), 5–16. doi:10.1002/pmj.20082

Shore, B., & Cross, B. (2005). Exploring the role of national culture in the management of large-scale international science projects. *International Journal of Project Management, 23*(1), 55–64. doi:10.1016/j.ijproman.2004.05.009

Straub, D., Loch, K., & Hill, C. (2001). Transfer of information technology to the Arab world: A test of cultural influence modeling. *Journal of Global Information Management, 9*(4), 6–48. doi:10.4018/jgim.2001100101

Stuckenbruck, L., & Zomorrodian, A. (1987). Project management: The promise for developing nations. *International Journal of Project Management, 5*(3), 167–175. doi:10.1016/0263-7863(87)90022-6

Tan, P.-N., Steinbach, M., & Kumar, V. (2006). *Introduction to data mining*. USA: Addison-Wesley Publishing.

Tarafdar, M., & Vaidya, S. (2005). Adoption and implementation of IT in developing nations: Experiences from two public sector enterprises in India. *Cases on Information Technology, 7*(1), 440–464.

Touray, A., Salminen, A., & Mursu, A. (2013). ICT barriers and critical success factors in developing nations. *Electronic Journal of Information Systems in Developing Nations, 56*(7), 1–17.

Vaidya, R., Myers, M., & Gardner, L. (2013). Major issues in the successful implementation of information systems in developing nations. In Y. Dwivedi, H. Zinner, H. Wastell, & R. De (Eds.), *Grand Successes and Failures in ICT. Public and Private Sectors* (pp. 151–163). Berlin: Springer. doi:10.1007/978-3-642-38862-0_10

Walsham, G., & Sahay, S. (2006). Research on information systems in developing nations: Current landscape and future prospects. *Information Technology for Development, 12*(1), 7–24. doi:10.1002/itdj.20020

Wang, F., & Chen, Y. (2010). *From potential users to practical users: Use of E-government service by Chinese migrant farmer workers. Paper presented at the 4th International Conference on Theory and Practice of Electronic Governance*, Beijing, China. doi:10.1145/1930321.1930380

Wang, X., & Liu, L. (2007). Cultural barriers to the use of Western project management in Chinese enterprises: Some empirical evidence from Yunnan Province. *Project Management Journal, 38*(3), 61–73. doi:10.1002/pmj.20006

Wyche, S., Smyth, T., Chetty, M., Aoki, P., & Grinter, R. (2010). Deliberate interactions: Characterizing technology use in Nairobi, Kenya. *Paper presented at the 28th International Conference on Human Factors in Computing Systems*, Atlanta, Georgia. doi:10.1145/1753326.1753719

Yanwen, W. (2012). The study on complex project management in developing countries. *Physics Procedia, 25*, 1547–1552. doi:10.1016/j.phpro.2012.03.274

ADDITIONAL READING

Anker, R. (1983). Female labour force participation in developing countries: A critique of current definitions and data collection methods. *Int'l Lab. Rev., 122*, 709. PMID:12266775

Ashenfelter, O. (1986). *Collecting Panel Data in Developing Countries: Does It Make Sense? Living Standards Measurement Study Working Paper No. 23*.

Barry, M. (1988). Ethical considerations of human investigation in developing countries: The AIDS dilemma. *The New England Journal of Medicine, 319*(16), 1083–1085. doi:10.1056/NEJM198810203191609 PMID:3173436

Batra, R., Ramaswamy, V., Alden, D. L., Steenkamp, J. B. E., & Ramachander, S. (2014). Effects of brand local and non-local origin on consumer attitudes in developing countries. *Journal of Consumer Psychology, 9*(2), 83–95. doi:10.1207/S15327663JCP0902_3

Bilsborrow, R. E. (1997). *International migration statistics: Guidelines for improving data collection systems.* International Labour Organization.

Corbin, J., & Strauss, A. (2014). *Basics of qualitative research: Techniques and procedures for developing grounded theory.* Sage publications.

Déglise, C., Suggs, L. S., & Odermatt, P. (2012). SMS for disease control in developing countries: A systematic review of mobile health applications. *Journal of Telemedicine and Telecare, 18*(5), 273–281. doi:10.1258/jtt.2012.110810 PMID:22826375

Denny, S. G., Silaigwana, B., Wassenaar, D., Bull, S., & Parker, M. (2015). Developing Ethical Practices for Public Health Research Data Sharing in South Africa The Views and Experiences From a Diverse Sample of Research Stakeholders. *Journal of Empirical Research on Human Research Ethics; JERHRE, 10*(3), 290–301. doi:10.1177/1556264615592386 PMID:26297750

Heeks, R. (2014). ICT4D 2016: New Priorities for ICT4D Policy, Practice and WSIS in a Post-2015 World.

Islam, D., Ashraf, M., Rahman, A., & Hasan, R. (2015). Quantitative Analysis of Amartya Sen's Theory: An ICT4D Perspective. *International Journal of Information Communication Technologies and Human Development, 7*(3), 13–26. doi:10.4018/IJICTHD.2015070102

Kearney, P. M., Whelton, M., Reynolds, K., Muntner, P., Whelton, P. K., & He, J. (2005). Global burden of hypertension: Analysis of worldwide data. *Lancet, 365*(9455), 217–223. doi:10.1016/S0140-6736(05)70151-3 PMID:15652604

Mohan, L., Potnis, D., & Mattoo, N. (2013). A pan-India footprint of microfinance borrowers from an exploratory survey: Impact of over-indebtedness on financial inclusion of the poor. *Enterprise Development & Microfinance Journal., 24*(1), 55–71. doi:10.3362/1755-1986.2013.006

Patel, V., Rodrigues, M., & DeSouza, N. (2014). Gender, poverty, and postnatal depression: A study of mothers in Goa, India. *The American Journal of Psychiatry.* PMID:11772688

Potnis, D. (2015). Addressing data collection challenges in ICT for development projects. *International Journal of ICT and Human Development, 7*(3), 36–55.

Potnis, D. (2015). Beyond access to information: Understanding the Use of information by poor female mobile users in rural India. *The Information Society, 31*(1), 83–93. doi:10.1080/01972243.2014.976687

Potnis, D. (2016). Culture's consequences: Economic barriers to owning mobile phones experienced by women in India. *Telematics and Informatics, 33*(2), 356–369. doi:10.1016/j.tele.2015.09.002

Sekaran, U. (1983). Methodological and theoretical issues and advancements in cross-cultural research. *Journal of International Business Studies, 14*(2), 61–73. doi:10.1057/palgrave.jibs.8490519

Sinha, C., Elder, L., & Smith, M. (2012). Improve the Field of ICT4D. *Linking research to practice: Strengthening ICT for development research capacity in Asia,* 12.

Touray, A., Salminen, A., & Mursu, A. (2013). ICT barriers and critical success factors in developing countries. *The Electronic Journal of Information Systems in Developing Countries*, *56*, 1–16.

KEY TRENDS AND DEFINITIONS

Culture: Culture can be defined as the values and belief systems held by a group of individuals, learned early in life, and difficult to change (Hofstede, 1997).

Development: Human development can be defined as "a process of enlarging people's choices" (UNDP, 1990, p.10).

Project: The project management literature defines the term project as an endeavor undertaken to create a unique product, service, or result. Ideally, every project has a definite beginning and a definite end (PMBOK, 2003).

Chapter 11
Open Innovation in Small and Medium Enterprises:
Perspectives of Developing and Transitional Economies

Hakikur Rahman
BRAC University, Bangladesh

ABSTRACT

In spite of the increased acceptance by most of the corporate business houses around the world, the adaptation of strategies and concepts belonging to the newly evolved dimension of entrepreneurships, the open innovation (OI), countries in the East, West or South are yet to adapt appropriate strategies in their business practices, especially in order to reach out to the grass roots communities, or to the masses. So far, firms belonging to the small and medium sized enterprises (SMEs) sector, irrespective of their numbers and contributions towards their national economies are lagging behind far in accepting open innovation strategies for their business advancements. While talking about this newly emerged business dimension, it comprises of complex and dynamically developed concepts like, management of various aspects of intellectual property, administration of patents, copyright and trademark issues or supervision of market trend for minute details related to knowledge acquisition. All these issues are largely responsible to add value to the business plan in terms of economy or knowledge gain, and organizations acting in this aspect deserve comprehensive researches and investigations. As most of the developed countries are already in their advanced stage in adopting open innovation strategies, finding this as a weak link in terms of entrepreneurships in less developed countries, this chapter intends to seek answers related to the mentioned issues focusing adaption of open innovation strategies in developing and transitional economies. It is a study on business houses or national efforts from countries belonging to these categories, deducting from a longitudinal literature review. The chapter goes on looking into other aspects of business development incorporating various OI concepts, synthesizes to build a reasonable framework to be applicable in the target economies, points out to some future research aspects and concludes the finding of this research. This study expects to enhance knowledge of entrepreneurs, academics and researchers by gaining specific knowledge on trend of open innovation strategies in developing and transitional countries.

DOI: 10.4018/978-1-5225-0556-3.ch011

INTRODUCTION

Innovation is no more an experimentation, but a genuine reality within the business processes, given the circumstances of economic crisis, global competition and novelties of technologies. Perplexing further to face the reality and overcome crises, firms are day by day adopting newly developed ideas, concepts, and perceptions to fit into the business dimension from within and outside the boundaries of their own entities, thus channeling the entrepreneurships through the paradigm of open innovation (OI). By far, majority of the corporate business houses and multi-national enterprises are competing or collaborating with a common goal in promoting value added products, processes, or services. Notwithstanding, they are transforming the entire business development infrastructure to face the reality and move ahead (Van Hemert & Nijkamp, 2010).

Furthermore, it has been observed that over the past two decades, there has been a substantial shift in the global innovation landscape. Multinationals from developed economies are increasingly globalizing their research and development (R&D) activities and are developing an open innovation model to source innovations from outside the firm, including from emerging economies such as those in Africa and Asia. In addition, emerging economy enterprises, which traditionally have played a secondary role in the global innovation landscape, have now begun to catch up in developing their own innovative capabilities (Li and Kozhikode, 2009).

However, it has also been observed that a major portion of the business community that belongs to the small and medium enterprises (SMEs) sector, in spite of their justified contribution to economic growth and employment generation, is not always in advantageous situations in the arena of open innovation due to many factors, seen, unseen, attended, un-attended, researched, un-researched, and deserves further research (United Nations, 2006; World Business Council, 2007).

In this context, Edwards, Delbridge and Munday (2005) argue that, in spite of increasing attention being given to the role of SMEs and innovation, there is a gap between what is understood by way of the general innovation literature and the extant literature on innovation for SMEs. They further argue that studies of innovation in SMEs have largely failed to reflect advances in the innovation literature. Supporting these arguments, this study has tried to find out relevance of open innovation among SMEs, and particularly the emergence of OI strategies in developing and transitional economies.

There are a considerable number of literatures that are available about innovation, and in recent years various models have been suggested to describe its nature. Models have also be divided according to their innovation processes (such as, linear models, chain-linked models, triple-helix, Coventry University Enterprises Limited model, Rahman and Ramos model and others), or according to the fitness for developed or developing countries (Lee, Park, Yoonc and Park, 2010; Rahman and Ramos, 2013).

When one talks about cross-boundary issues on business concerns, innovation requires not only harvesting and transferring knowledge, but also an effective absorption capacity within the entity. However, the main components of this, in terms of organization, resources, and culture are in principal similar both in the domestic and international arenas. Furthermore, internationalization poses particular challenges in terms of openness and the tolerance or, encouragement of diversity if knowledge is to be absorbed successfully, and translated into innovation (Zahra and George, 2002; English-Lucek, Darrah and Saveri, 2002; Williams and Shaw, 2011).

To advance into the context of this trend of research this study has observed that, countries ranking as developed economies are ahead in the race adopting open innovation in their business development, while countries among the developing and transitional economies are struggling to fit into the race of the champions. This chapter based on a study, though not a specific case of one country, has tried to illustrate a few discrete scenarios from five developing countries through longitudinal literature review. The chapter has tried to provide a generic context of innovation (inclined to open innovation) in those randomly selected countries, and present challenges they are facing, including some recommendations, before concluding for further extensive research. Along this route, the chapter has tried to build a framework synthesizing the aspects of the findings. It is expected that this study will contribute to enhance knowledge of readers in refreshing the basic concept of open innovation and application of OI strategies among SMEs in developing countries. Furthermore, as majority of OI strategies nowadays are mainly dependent on utilization of information technologies, this study could form a start up literature or a guide towards future open innovation practices adopting strategic and pragmatic business processes.

BACKGROUND

Joseph Schumpeter (1883–1950), one of the first theorists who studied the economy through the innovative eye, stated that innovation is about new ways of doing things by combining existing elements into new products through a creative process (De Jong, Vanhaverbeke, Kalvet & Chesbrough, 2008). Along this route, innovation through the creation, dissemination and utilization of knowledge has become a key driver of economic growth. However, factors influencing innovation performance have changed in this globalized knowledge based economy, partly due to the advent of new information and communication technologies (ICTs), and partly due to the increased global competition. Innovation results from increasingly complex interactions at the local, national, regional and global levels among individuals, firms, industries and other knowledge institutions. Moreover, governments exert a strong influence on the innovation processes through financing and steering of public bodies which are directly responsible for knowledge creation and dissemination (universities, public and private labs, research houses or intermediaries), and through the provision of financial and regulatory inducements (Carayannis, Popescu, Sipp & Steward, 2006).

In this context, firstly, the new ICTs; secondly, the government and its politics; thirdly, universities and research houses; fourthly, entrepreneurs, suppliers, vendors, and partners; and finally, consumers have roles in forming environments pertaining to the launching of innovation within and among entrepreneurships. By far, all these actors need to collaborate and actively participate to create the environment, thus even, turning the innovation processes from traditional or closed ended towards rather non-traditional or open ended, terming it as open innovation.

However, due to the close acquaintance and strong industry-university relationship, including familiarity with new ICTs and exploring their benefits, developed countries are much on the lead in creating and commercializing new knowledge. On the contrary, though developing nations are familiarizing their entrepreneurships through university spin-offs and increased intensification of industry-university relation to commoditize ready-made knowledge, but the situation is far behind to compete with the developed world. This applies both to the standardization of university-industry relationship and to the competency of the university, which need further investigation (Kroll and Liefner 2008). In this aspect, Savitskaya (2009) argues that the contribution to the understanding of open innovation practices in developing countries resides in demonstrated role of the government for creating favorable conditions for entrepreneurs to open up and integrate into innovation system in the country. She assumed that open innovation system needs a certain level of governmental support to emerge in developing economies.

Furthermore, when comes to the question of introducing open innovation in entrepreneurships, the focus directly or indirectly goes to developed countries, even so towards large and corporate business houses. But a prospective observation this study has made is that, with increased relationship between public funded research houses and entrepreneurs, including government initiatives, the sector of business entities that belongs to the SMEs are catching up in the run by adopting open innovation, mainly in developed countries, and very recently in a few developing countries. To set the benchmarking of a post doctoral research on assessing current scenario of open innovation dynamics in developing countries this study incorporates some specific observations along this context and this chapter is the result of a horizontal study on a few countries of that category who are trying in adopting open innovation (rather, trying to be innovative) in their businesses.

Apart from the entrepreneurship development, due to the very basic inheritance of the marginal societies in developing nations, a considerable interest of the entrepreneurs among SMEs has focused on their roles in the alleviation of widespread poverty. However, looking beyond the immediate, pressing concern of the poor, Andrew Warner (2001) has advanced the concept that SMEs are the building blocks of innovation and sustainable growth in developing countries, such as SMEs represent foci of technological creativity. Supporting Kowalski (2009) this study accepts that, these concepts are linked as sustained economic growth, which can alleviate real poverty. Hence, as SME development drives economic growth in a country, there is a concomitant reduction in poverty. Now the question appears as what could be an acceptable approach in establishing a sustained business environment in developing countries' perspective in the longer run? And, what could be the appropriate strategies they should adopt to enter into the open innovation paradigm? Moreover, as long as the developing countries are trying to adopt novel ideas and strategies as a booster of economic activity, especially by adopting open innovation strategies for the development of small and medium enterprises, the study has find that these concepts are relatively unfamiliar in developing countries.

Though Lee et al. (2010) mentioned, there is considerable literature about innovation, and various models have been suggested to describe its nature, such as product innovation and process innovation; radical innovation and incremental innovation; systemic innovation and component innovation; technology push and market pull; and more recently closed innovation, open innovation, collaborative or crowdsourcing innovation. Models can also be divided according to their innovation processes or according to the fitness for developed or developing countries, etc. but, this research argues that models as such on developing countries perspectives are scant.

Following these observations, this study explores the role and impact of SMEs in the developing and transitional economies, and discusses about a few countries' context focusing the emancipation of SMEs policies and practices accommodating open innovation (rather, innovation). The study observes that to roll out open innovation at the grass roots level of developing and transitional countries, it needs more additional input in addition to just being innovative. Next section looks into some details about innovation in business sector in developing countries.

INNOVATION AND DEVELOPING COUNTRIES

Based on the arguments made above, there arise several issues in terms of implementing open innovation for SMEs development in developing countries. Firstly, it must be understood that the term "developing countries" comprises a wide variety of nations that are at very different stages of economic development, have very heterogeneous levels of technological capabilities, and have very diversified cultural differences. Hence, the innovation appropriability dynamics will be very different, for example, in advanced developing countries such as some Latin American or Asian economies where industrial, export and innovation capabilities are more or less strong, *vis à vis* most least developed countries (LDCs), mainly rely on traditional agricultural activities and have poorer productive and technological capabilities. Predominantly, there is a reasonable innovation gap in between them.

Secondly, it is often thought that developing countries are mainly imitators or adopters of technologies and knowledge developed elsewhere. Hence, the debate on introducing OI strategies in developing countries is often focused on whether environments are more favorable for technological changes in those countries. While lax or strong intellectual property rights (IPRs) are thought to favor imitation, copy and reverse engineering; and hence are seen by some authors as a favorable factor for the deployment of learning processes that could lead in the medium and long run to the creation of genuine innovation capabilities in those countries; it is often stated that strong IPRs are a condition for developing countries to receive updated technology transfers by means of licenses and foreign direct investment (López, 2009).

Thirdly, reasonable policy update is desired at national and local contexts in transforming business environments in favor of open innovation. Developing countries are yet to be familiarized with the newly evolved OI strategies. To enhance OI adoption and to create a sustained platform of OI, developing countries should come up with policies at their national levels, emphasizing local businesses.

Fourthly, one has to recognize that, SMEs are critical to the economies of all countries, especially the developing ones (Payne, 2003), and encouraging innovation in SMEs remains at the heart of policy initiatives for stimulating economic development at the local, state, national and regional levels (Jones & Tilley, 2003; Edwards, Delbridge & Munday, 2005). According to Ernst, Mytelka and Ganiatsos (1994), innovation in developing countries is based on the continuous and incremental upgrading of existing technologies or on a new combination of them.

Fifthly, majority of the developing countries and LDCs (Least Developing Countries) are suffering from the weakness of the basic infrastructure necessary for economic activities. Activities for innovation and the use of intellectual property for promoting investment and R&D (research and development) in those countries are faced with additional difficulties caused by the lack of basic infrastructure and a "knowledge infrastructure" (Takagi and Czajkowski, 2012).

Realizing these issues, in recent years, there is a considerable interest among entrepreneurs in establishing SMEs in developing countries. There are probably two main reasons for this. One is the belief that SME development may prove to be an effective antipoverty initiation. The second is the belief that SME development is one of the building blocks of innovation and sustainable growth. These two reasons are of course inter-linked because most of the research evidence says that growth and real poverty reduction go hand in hand. If SMEs development helps growth, more than likely it helps reduce poverty as well (Warner, 2001).

Finally, organizational approaches (with patronage from the highest corners of the government) in the form of providing assistance in finding funds, knowledge and technologies are meant to be common practices at the beginning of the innovation cycle, till it matures to take over on its own both at the local level and national level.

Evidently, across Southeast and South Asia, the contribution of SMEs to the overall economic growth and the GDP is relatively high. Some examples include;

- Bangladesh where SMEs contribute 50% of industrial GDP and provide employment to 82% of the total industrial sector employment;
- India, where SMEs' contribution to GDP is 30%;
- Indonesia, where SMEs accounted to 99.985% of the total number of enterprises with their output contributed to 53.28% of GDP in 2006 and SMEs account for 96.18% of the total employment;
- Nepal, where SMEs constitute more than 98% of all establishments and contribute 63% of the value-added segment;
- Thailand, where SMEs account for more than 90% of the total number of establishments, 65% of employment and 47% of manufacturing value-added; and
- The Philippines, where SMEs comprise 99% of the total manufacturing establishments and contribute 45% of employment and 18% of value added in the manufacturing sector (Kowalski, 2009).

However, when comes the question of finding good cases or case studies or national initiatives on adoption of open innovation for SMEs development at the context of developing countries, they are rare. Although, the phenomenon on innovation of SMEs has captured the interest of many scholars, few studies have been found on studying the issue from the developing countries' perspective.

Literature on innovation indicates that over the last two decades, there has been a systematic and fundamental change in the way firms undertake innovating activities. Particularly, there has been a tremendous growth in the use of external networks by firms of all sizes. Innovation is seen as a process which results from various interactions among different actors. Inter-organizational and cross-sectoral networks, which facilitate the accelerated flows of information, resources and trust necessary to secure and diffuse innovation, have emerged as leaders. However, as SMEs with scarce resources, have less R&D, and generally face more uncertainties and barriers to innovation, networks represent a complementary response to insecurity arising from development and use of new technologies, while reducing uncertainties in innovation. Moreover, in the era of "open innovation", according to Chesbrough (2003), firms consistently rely on external sources of innovation by emphasizing the ideas, resources and individuals flowing in and out of organizations, searching for and using a wider range of external ideas, knowledge and resources, networks, which are becoming essential for the creation of successful innovations for SMEs (Zeng, Xie & Tam, 2010), but seems unfamiliar in developing countries.

Furthermore, in the perspective of innovation systems in developing countries, production and exchange of knowledge (mainly technical; internal or external or both) and information are not the only prerequisites for innovation; several additional factors play as key roles, such as policy, legislation, infrastructure, funding, and market developments (Klein-Woolthuis, Lankhuizen & Gilsing, 2005). In addition to these, the concept of knowledge absorption is often used related to intra- and inter- firm knowledge transfer and ability to implement the acquired knowledge, and the notion of absorptive capacity can be related to cross-region or cross-country knowledge exchange. This is most relevant to developing countries, who are believed to be imitators, rather than innovators, and their innovative development happens in terms of adaptation of existing technologies to satisfy local realities (Savitskaya, 2009).

This chapter likes to discuss a few SMEs development initiatives in five developing countries in terms of adopting innovative approaches. The study has tried to collect researches or examples based on policies and practices adopting open innovation. The selection criterion follows random sampling and availability of searched literature within accessible search engines.

CASE DESCRIPTIONS

Small and medium enterprises are being recognized in different ways in different countries. Most countries have adopted the benchmarks of employment. Some classify them in terms of assets, a few in terms of sales and others, in terms of fund. In a few countries, a hybrid definition is used, such as employment and assets or turnover. Although definition differ across countries, they have one thing in common; the vast majority of SMEs are relatively small and over 95% of SMEs in Asia employ less than 100 people. Based on this, broad comparison on the characteristics and role of SMEs is still possible even with differing definitions (Pandey & Shivesh, 2007).

This study has considered six countries from Africa and Asia. Among them the two countries in Africa, South African one is based on the Sekhukhune Living Labs experience and Ugandan one is showing the national contexts focusing SMEs development. Among the four Asian countries; from Bangladesh, India, Indonesia and China, the national policy perspectives have been illustrated, which show evolution of entrepreneurships towards innovation paradigm. Countries in this section have been selected at random basis, however, the intention is to find out the trend of doing any innovative (rather open innovative) entrepreneurships among these countries, any initiative taken by their governments to promote innovative entrepreneurships, and to find out any catalytic agents in this aspect. They are being described next following alphabetical order.

Bangladesh

Government of Bangladesh formulated the National Industrial Policy 2005 by giving emphasize for developing Small and Medium Enterprises[1] as a thrust sector for balanced and sustainable industrial development in the country with the vision for facing the challenges of free market economy and globalization. In the policy strategies, smooth and sustainable development of SMEs all over the country has been considered as one of the vehicles for accelerating national economic growth including poverty alleviation, and generation of employment. Most of the industrial enterprises in Bangladesh are typically SME in nature. Generally, SMEs are found to be labor intensive with relatively low capital intensity. SMEs also possess a character of privilege as cost effective and comparative cost advantages by nature. In this aspect, the SME policy strategies have been formulated in line with the acknowledged principles for achieving the Millennium Development Goals (MDGs) by the Government (Govt. of Bangladesh, 2005a).

Furthermore, the provisions of facilities for attracting foreign investments have been envisaged in the Industrial Policy. The government has taken an initiative to formulate a separate SME policy to provide entrepreneurs with necessary guidance and strategic support in respect of the establishment of SME industries all over the country (Govt. of Bangladesh, 2005b).

A few of the broad objectives of the SME policy strategies are to:

- Accept SMEs as an indispensable player in growth acceleration and poverty reduction, worthy of their total commitment in the requisite overall policy formulation and execution;

- SME policy strategies shall essentially be linked with broad based and integrated manner in line with the poverty reduction strategy paper (PRSP) of the Government of Bangladesh;
- Encourage and induce private sector development and promote the growth of foreign direct investment (FDI), develop a code of ethics and establish good governance, ICT based knowledge management and customer supremacy in the market alliances;
- Identify and establish the network of infrastructure and institutional delivery mechanisms that facilitate the promotion of SMEs;
- Re-orient the existing fiscal and regulatory framework and government sponsored institutions supporting the goals of SME policy;
- Have credible management teams in terms of the delivery of needed services, leadership, initiation, counseling, mentoring and tutoring;
- Create innovative but rewarding arrangements so that deserving and especially enterprises with desired entrepreneurial qualifications and promise can be offered financial incentives within industries prescribed on some well-agreed bases;
- Assist implement dispute settlement procedures that proactively shield small enterprises especially from high legal costs and insidious harassments;
- Take measures to create avenues of mobilizing debt without collaterals to match (either using *debt-guarantee schemes* or mapping *intellectual-property* capital into pseudo-*venture capital*) in order to assist small enterprises in dealing with their pervasive lack of access to finance (Govt. of Bangladesh, 2005a).

This study notes that use of debt-guarantee scheme, mapping of intellectual property or concept of venture capital are very basic ingredients of open innovation strategies.

For promotional support the following booster sectors has been identified and the list has been set to be reviewed every three years:

- Electronics and Electrical,
- Software Development,
- Light Engineering,
- Agro-processing and related business,
- Leather and Leather goods,
- Knitwear and Ready Made Garments,
- Plastics and other synthetics,
- Healthcare and Diagnostics,
- Educational Services,
- Pharmaceuticals/ Cosmetics/ Toiletries,
- Fashion-rich personal effects, wear and consumption goods (Govt. of Bangladesh, 2005a).

Moreover, the government has established an SME Foundation as a pivotal platform for the delivery of all planning, developmental, financing, awareness-raising, evaluation and advocacy services in the name of SME development as one of the crucially-important element of poverty alleviation. The Foundation supposed to provide a one-window delivery of all administrative facilities, including some resources needed for capacity-building in appropriate industry association(s), for SMEs in Bangladesh (Govt. of Bangladesh, 2005a; 2005b)

China

China is attempting to catch-up in terms of innovating their entrepreneurships, which is fundamentally different from earlier latecomers like Japan and Korea. The basic elements of Chinese catching up strategy are: market size, market-oriented innovation, global alliance and open innovation, spillover of FDI and role of government. Moreover, the core capability of Chinese company is an integration capability of market knowledge, outsourcing and learning (Liu, 2008).

Since the realization of the open policy in 1978, China has made great efforts to change from a highly centralized planned state to the near market economy. The role of SMEs has been expanding in the changing socio-political context. They not only play a greater role in the economies (accounting for more than 99% of all firms being SMEs), but also contribute in a large extent to the increased levels of business activity and employment (Siu, 2005). Zeng, Xie & Tam (2010) argue that, the manufacturing industry is the main driving force of social development and economic growth in developing countries. In this context, Zeng, Xie & Tam (2010) mention that China, with more than two decades of market oriented reform, there has been a rapid growth in the manufacturing industry. Hence, it is necessary to explore the external cooperation network of manufacturing SMEs in order to help them improve their industrial competitiveness. However, there is a paucity of studies on the impact of external cooperation network on the innovation of Chinese manufacturing SMEs. *This study notes that collaborative networking is one of the most effective preconditions for adopting OI strategies.*

Using a structured questionnaire survey, Zeng, Xie & Tam (2010) examine the innovation networking activities of some surveyed SMEs in Shanghai, the largest city and economic center in China. Their study aims to explore the relationships between different cooperation networks and innovation performance of SME. Based on a survey of 137 Chinese manufacturing SMEs, they empirically explore the relationships between different cooperation networks and innovation performance of SME using the technique of structural equation modeling (SEM). Their study finds that there are significant positive relationships between inter firm cooperation, cooperation with intermediary institutions, cooperation with research organizations and innovation performance of SMEs, of which inter firm cooperation has the most significant positive impact on the innovation performance of SMEs.

This study supports the above mentioned parameters as the basic building block in establishing a platform of open innovation. However, the result of Zeng, Xie & Tam (2010) reveals that the linkage and cooperation with government agencies do not demonstrate any significant impact on the innovation performance of SMEs. Moreover, their findings confirm that the vertical and horizontal cooperation with customers, suppliers and other firms plays a more distinct role in the innovation process of SMEs than horizontal cooperation with research institutions, universities or colleges, and government agencies, which is quite opposite to the context of developed countries. This study suggests that further studies need to be carried out to re-confirm this hypothesis or find out any future diversions.

India

In India, the term small scale industries (SSIs[2]), is used far more often than SMEs and is based upon investment in assets[3] (Saini & Budhwar, 2008). However, despite various liberalizations and schematic changes to meet the emerging requirements of the business sector, availability of finance continues to be a major problem for small enterprises in India. Realizing this fact, some of the development financial institutions (DFIs) and forward looking commercial banks have put in operation a number of innovative schemes, and among them the Small Industries Development Bank of India (SIDBI) has taken the lead. The majority of the experiments have started showing good results. The SSI sector plays a significant role in the Indian economy. For the past one decade, it has been consistently registering about three per cent higher real growth rate in terms of GDP (8.9 per cent during 1999–2000) compared to the growth recorded by the industrial sector as a whole. The SSI sector contributes over 41 per cent of the total industrial production, 31 per cent of the country's total exports, and jointly with traditional industries (for example Khadi, handloom, handicrafts, sericulture, and coir) the relative percentage goes up to 58 per cent (Narain, 2001).

In terms of finance, transaction lending such as asset based lending, factoring and leasing have been in use to fund SMEs for some time, and there is some evidence of relationship lending in India. Moreover, in developing countries, the private economy would comprise largely of family businesses. It is estimated that in India, family businesses account for 70% of the total sales and net profits of the biggest 250 private-sector companies (Economist, 1996), and almost all the micro-small-and-medium-enterprise (MSME) would be family firms. Inter-family relationships and family succession play an important role in the performance of family firms, and financial institutes would need to take this into account in their credit decisions. A study by Marisetty, Ramachandran & Jha (2008) finds that family businesses in India where succession takes place without fights and splits show higher profitability (Thampy, 2010). *This study notes that India is accepting several strategies towards open innovation, such as providing financial supports; liberalizing market conditions; adopting lending, factoring and leasing; and foremost promoting networking.*

Indonesia

Based on Indonesian Presidential Decree no. 99/1998, Small Enterprise is being defined as "Small scale people economical activities with major business category in small business activities and need to protect from unhealthy business competition". However, the government of Indonesia defines small enterprises as firms with total asset up to RP. 200 million (1 USD is equivalent to 9887 Indonesian Rupee as on June 17, 2013) excluding land and building, the total annual sales are not more than Rp. 1 billion owned by Indonesian citizens, not subsidiary or branch of medium or large enterprise, personal firm. While medium enterprises are firms with total asset more than Rp. 200 million but not exceed Rp. 10 billion excluding land and buildings. Apart from these definitions, Biro Pusat Statistik (Statistic Center Body) defined SMEs based on number of employee. Small enterprises employ 5 to 19 people, while medium enterprises employ 20-99 people (Hamdani and Wirawan, 2012).

Similar to other countries, SMEs in Indonesia also play an important role in social and economic growth of the country, due to great number of industry, GDP contribution, and total employment. SME's characteristics have been found to be more agile and adaptable with capability to survive and raise their performance during economical crisis than larger firm. But with the increase of business competition, in particular against large and modern competitor, SMEs are being placed in a vulnerable situation. Hence, the development of sustainable SMEs has become an important step to strengthen and sustain Indonesian economy. According to the statistics 43.22 million SMEs accounted to 99.985% of the total number of enterprises in Indonesia in 2006. Their output contributed 53.28% of GDP in 2006, and, with over 85.42 million workers, SMEs account for 96.18% of the total employment in Indonesia. The role of SMEs has become more important, because according to research by AKATIGA, the Center for Micro and Small Enterprise Dynamic (CEMSED), and the Center for Economic and Social Studies (CESS)

2000, SMEs have the unique ability to survive and raise performance during economic crisis, due to their flexibility in adapting production process, ability to develop with their own capital, capacity to pay high interest loan and only a little get involve with the bureaucracy. It is expected that with this vital stance in the economy, the development of SMEs would contribute to economic and social development through economic diversification and accelerated structural changes that promote stable and sustainable long-term economic growth (Padmadinata, 2007; Hamdani and Wirawan, 2012)

It has been observed that the success factors of Indonesian SMEs are capital access, marketing and technology, while legality was a challenge to business success. Education and source of capital were related significantly to business accomplishment. However, these later two factors seemed to need moderating variables since poor operational explanations were needed to link these two with business achievement. Increasing business competition, in particular against large and modern competitors, put SMEs in a vulnerable position. In Indonesia, most SMEs operate along traditional lines in production and marketing. They also have several challenges such as lack of knowledge, lack of qualified human resource as well as quantity, non-conducive atmosphere, lack of facility, limitation of market and information access, and bureaucracy (Indarti and Langenber, 2004; Hamdani and Wirawan, 2012).

South Africa

In European context, supporting open innovation among SMEs, Living Labs are providing significant input in terms of co-creation, exploration, experimentation and evaluation[4]. As a knowledge centre of the European Network of Living Labs (ENoLL), the Sekhukhune Living Lab focuses on small, medium and micro-enterprises (SMMEs) which are regarded as important growth engines in South Africa. However, several barriers are inhibiting rural entrepreneurship and access to mainstream or global supply chains and markets. Schaffers et al. (2007), in their research mentions that, long distances, high transport/transaction costs and low economies of scale are the consequences of typical rural conditions such as physical remoteness and low economic activity levels there. Furthermore, the problems associated with these barriers worsen dramatically if roads are poor, telecommunications bandwidth is limited or expensive, and many rural entrepreneurs have limited computer literacy and do not own a truck, motorcar or computer. These are the typical complexities faced by rural entrepreneurs in most of the developing countries, and in South Africa's "deep rural areas" such as Sekhukhune.

Through ENoLL, Sekhukhune Living Lab introduces a range of services through the facilitation of so called Infopreneurs, which are micro, self-sustainable service enterprises that channel and deliver services for local SMMEs and citizens into the community. These Infopreneurs are the 1st tier target SMME group of the work and interventions of the C@R Living Lab. They provide knowledge-based services such as cross-organizational business process enabling, SWOT analysis and logistics brokerage to assist start-up, grow and cluster other SMME's in various sectors (for example, health, mining, construction).

These Infopreneurs are being deployed in existing infrastructure and getting benefit from ongoing local initiatives supported by the South-African government. Franchise-like agreements are shaping the collaboration among partners. However, the focus of Living Lab development is on establishing collaboration tools and processes, particularly addressing the accessibility of knowledge-based services that are relevant to local SMME businesses, in harnessing increased mobile connectivity and enabling rural service channels that enhance effective collaboration amongst SMMEs in communities and between first and second economy enterprises.

The ubiquitous infrastructure shortcomings of South-Africa (such as, constricted bandwidth) are being taken into account when setting up these knowledge service agents. By forming clustered enterprises via Infopreneur services, consolidation of supply chain volumes is achieved with lower transaction and transportation costs. The strategy is to create Infopreneur service bundles to enhance local business and geo-economic intelligence that helps SMMEs to seamlessly interoperate among each other and first economy enterprises (Schaffers et al., 2007). *Intermediaries are an essential element of promoting open innovation dynamics in diverse and difficult environments, as such this study notes.*

Uganda

In Uganda, SMEs[5] are increasingly taking the role of the primary vehicles for the creation of employment and income generation through self-employment, and treated as tools for poverty alleviation. SMEs also provide the economy with a continuous supply of ideas, skills and innovation necessary to promote competition and at the same time, efficient allocation of scarce resources.

Furthermore, mentioned by Kasekende (2001), a few strong SMEs in Uganda, like Capital Radio, Kabira International School, Masaba Cotton Co. Ltd and Africa Basic Foods were formed through *joint venture* arrangements with foreign partners from the United Kingdom and the United States. These and other SMEs have provided domestic linkages, comprising link between agriculture and industry and between SMEs and large-scale industries. This has created opportunities for employment and income generation both in rural and urban areas at relatively low cost, thus ensuring a more equitable income distribution. In turn, the stimulation of activities in both rural and urban areas has mitigated some of the problems that unplanned urbanization tends to create, thus offering an efficient and progressive decentralization of the economy. In this aspect, SMEs play a crucial role in creating opportunities to achieve equitable and sustainable growth. SMEs in Uganda are providing employment and income generation opportunities to low income sectors of the economy.

However, due to their characteristics and nature, SMEs in Uganda suffer from constraints that lower their resilience to risk and prevent them from growing and attaining economies of scale. The challenges are not only in the areas of financial investment and working capital, but also in *human resource development*, *market access*, and *access to modern ICTs*. Furthermore, *access to financial resources* is constrained by both internal and external factors. Internally, most SMEs lack creditworthiness and management capacity, so they have trouble securing funds for their business activities, for example procuring raw materials and products, and investing in plant and equipment. From the external viewpoint, SMEs are regarded as insecure and costly businesses to deal with because they lack required collateral and have the capacity to absorb only small amount of funds from financial institutions. Foremost, due to high intermediate costs, including the cost of monitoring, they are rationed in their access to credits and having difficulties in enforcing loan contracts (Kasenkende, 2001).

To overcome such constraints, the government and other players such as the Bank of Uganda (BOU) have designed programmes and policies to support SMEs that are market driven and non-market distorting. The government has created stable macroeconomic conditions, liberalized the economy, and encouraged the growth of the micro-financing business. In conjunction with donors, the government has designed a medium-term competitive strategy and a Rural Financial Services Programme to benefit SMEs. However, the challenge to SMEs in accessing financial services will remain dependent on how they themselves increase their creditworthiness (Kasekende, 2001). *This study observes that to widen OI strategies at the national and local level, Uganda has been moving in the appropriate direction.*

SYNTHESIS AND THE FRAMEWORK

Synthesizing the countries of this study provides different dimensions of business growth in their countries, accommodating innovation. Ranging from policy initiation to networking, to liberization, to institutionalization are significantly observable there. Table 1 shows various aspects of the synthesis in the form of a framework, however, this does not mean that any country is superseding another.

CURRENT CHALLENGES

This section starts using a quote of Saini and Budhwar about the understanding on SMEs, saying "The concept of SME itself is quite problematic" (2008: 417). This study finds another important quote from their paper, where Storey notes, "there is no single, uniformly acceptable, definition of a small firm. There are differences as to size, shape and capital employed. In the USA there is no standard definition of small business. Even a firm employing up to 1500 employees is considered as small by American Small Business Administration. The concept in USA is industry-specific; mostly income and persons employed will determine whether a firm falls in the category of small business or not" (1994: 8).

The European Commission classifies firms according to the number of employees as: micro (0–9), small (10–99) and medium (100–499). However, in Oslo Manual (OECD, 2005) the EC has incorporated turn over, in addition to the number of employees. In China, it includes companies employing less than 200 persons; and in Japan those employing less than 300 persons are considered to be SMEs (Srivas-tava, 2005: 166). Even, sometimes the definition of SMEs depends on the stage of national economic development and the broad policy purposes for which the definition is required. But, the essential fact is that, whatever may be the definitional problems, SMEs occupy an important place in the economy of most countries; especially they are favored in developing countries due to their employment potential (Saini and Budhwar, 2008).

Table 1. Observed Tendencies on SMEs development

Country	Pattern at National Context	Observed Tendency
Bangladesh	Policy initiation	Awareness development, acceptance of policy, initiation of policy, and patronization from the government
China	Action through vertical and horizontal integration	Cooperation among customers, suppliers, other firms, partners, research institutions, universities and government agencies; Market driven initiation accommodating global competition, dependency on FDI (foreign direct investment), and patronization from the government
India	Identification	Identify the potential business sector where thrust should be given
Indonesia	Translation	Conceptualization, awareness development, adoption of appropriate policy, recognizing challenges in the formulation process
South Africa	Clusterization and Institutionalization	Build a sustainable infrastructure serving local community at local context
Uganda	Utilization	Application of appropriate strategies at designated levels of enterprises

Furthermore, access to finance has been identified as a key element for SMEs to succeed in their drive to build productive capacity, compete, create job opportunities and contribute to poverty alleviation in developing countries. Without finance, SMEs cannot acquire or absorb new technologies nor they can expand to compete in global markets or even establish business linkages with larger firms. Finance has been identified in many business surveys as the most important factor determining the survival and growth of SMEs in both developing and developed countries. Access to finance allows SMEs to undertake productive investments to expand their businesses and acquire the latest technologies, thus ensuring their competitiveness. Poorly functioning financial systems can seriously undermine the microeconomic environment of a country, resulting in lower growth in income and employment (UNCTAD Secretariat, 2001)

Despite their dominant numbers and importance in job creation, SMEs face difficulty in obtaining formal credit or equity. For example, maturities of commercial bank loans made available to SMEs are often limited to a period far too short to pay off any sizeable investment. Meanwhile, access to competitive interest rates is reserved for only a few selected blue-chip companies while loan interest rates offered to SMEs always remain high. Moreover, banks in many developing countries traditionally lent overwhelmingly to the government, which are less risky and offer higher returns. Such practices have congested most private sector borrowers and increased the cost of capital for them. Governments cannot expect to have a dynamic private sector as long as they absorb the bulk of private savings. In the case of venture capital funds (an essential ingredient of open innovation entrepreneurship), governments have been concentrated in high technology sectors. Similarly, the international financial institutions have ignored the plight of SMEs. These preferences and tendencies have aggravated the lack of financing for SMEs (UNCTAD Secretariat, 2001).

Technological advancements have contributed to remarkable changes to the nature of current production systems. This has also created impact on the nature of work, workers and skills involved. SMEs may take benefit from these advancements in their operations, but they do not recognize the critical role of effective human resource policies for their success. Furthermore, the need for a skilled workforce in SMEs certainly becomes apparent during periods of such technological changes. Particularly, SMEs have to undergo some changes when they compete with global companies and other large buyers, as they are dependent on supply contracts from the same. This puts substantial pressure on SMEs to control both their costs and quality and meet the different legal requirements. Moreover, this poises a serious challenge for SMEs, especially for those operating in developing countries with labor-intensive technologies, where labor cost is a major concern. Many of them resort to disputed practices, such as employment of child labor to reduced labor costs and violation of labor standards including denial of minimum wage, and other minimum-work conditions. Majority of them also lack access to relevant data and information about new markets, legal provisions regulating their working, and product innovations, which hinders their survival. In addition to these, it has been found that their accessibility to professional management tools is almost absent (Zeng, Xie and Tam, 2010).

In terms of innovation, not all countries have the opportunity or ability to capitalize on the opportunity to catch up. For a developing country, it is not easy to proceed from stage of imitation to stage of innovation (Zeng, et. al., 2010). Bell and Pavitt (1993) pointed out, just installing large plants with foreign technology and foreign assistance will not assist in the building of technological capability. The prevailing fact is that the relation between competition patterns, productive structures and innovation in developing countries are very different from that in developed countries, and hence one should also expect to find differences in the pattern of use of intellectual property rights (IPRs) and other innovation mechanisms. Furthermore, there are differences when comparing developing countries at different stages of industrial and technological development (López, 2009). Hence, researching into open innovation focusing SMEs development in developing countries requires further intensive study and research.

This section concludes with a final sentence that, among these five nations, being driven by geographical, cultural, economical and most of all economical aspects, are very different from each other in achieving innovation in their entrepreneurships, which is a challenge to develop a generic framework for developing countries. However, as this research continues, efforts will be given to include a few more countries of similar socio-economic-cultural contexts and in-depth study will be carried out.

RECOMMENDATIONS AND FUTURE RESEARCH

From this study on a few country specific aspects of SMEs development, if one likes to interpret them towards the dimension of open innovation, the question will arrive, as how important open innovation thinking should be at the national level to guide the policy makers and other decision support systems in policymaking. In terms of adopting open innovation, especially in developing countries, there may be other priorities in policymaking due to the relatively modest absorptive capacity of incumbent enterprises and under-developed innovation institutions. In such countries it would probably easier to start with the relatively simple guidelines with simpler framework, for example developing basic innovation and interaction skills, rather than starting with more sophisticated interventions to enhance technology markets or stimulate corporate entrepreneurship (matured stages of technology exploration or technology exploitation). Future work may explore if there is an optimal sequence in the innovation system as how to adopt various open innovation policy guidelines, and if the developed framework needs to be refined for this purpose (De Jong, Vanhaverbeke, Kalvet and Chesbrough, 2008; Rahman & Ramos, 2010; Gassmann, Enkel and Chesbrough, 2010).

In the recent years banks in developed countries have launched a number of initiatives that both improve the profitability of lending to SMEs, and provides SMEs with better access to finance and financial products that are better tailored to their needs. A number of leading banks have demonstrated that providing financial services to SMEs can be turned into a profitable business. Although the business environments in developing countries and developed countries differ in many respects, the problems of servicing SME customers remain similar, such as high perceived risk, problems with information asymmetry and high administrative costs. Hence, recent innovations in developed countries to improve SMEs access to credit may provide valuable insights for developing country banks to become more SME-oriented and increase the volume and the quality of their services (Warner, 2001).

Davidsson (2006) forwarded the idea of the Small Business Innovation Program, and suggested that, perhaps in one way to adjust the conditions and challenges of a developing country one can pursue the following focus areas;

- Education, training and skill development programmes for entrepreneurship;
- Routines, initiations and contacts for initiating start-ups;
- Communication with government officials to better understand legislation and regulation in the area of entrepreneurships, including marketing environments;
- Availability of skills those are useful for potential consumer markets;
- Improving online access by skills and resources;
- Access to financial resource and contacts for foreign direct investments;

- Strengthen the technological capacity;
- Successful e-business models; and
- Establish stronger, more effective representation of small enterprises' interests at local, and national government and international level.

Foremost, there is an urgent need to make the best out of the public and private resources invested in fundamental and applied research. Both budget pressures and the need to solve crucial challenges, such as transitioning to an environmentally sustainable economy and supporting the equitable growth of developing countries mean that science will be required to generate technology at an ever-increased rate to maintain the continuous stream of social and market driven innovations (Ruiz, 2010).

CONCLUSION

The emerging global market has become the focus of sustained research in the past two decades due to several reasons. Firstly, the emerging markets comprise the majority of the world's population and land, and they continue to grow faster than the developed world. Secondly, the emerging markets are increasingly being recognized as a diverse set of business, cultural, economic, financial, institutional, legal, political and social environments within which to test, reassess and renew acquired wisdoms about how the business works, to gain deeper insights into prevailing theories and their supporting evidence, and to make new discoveries that enhances human welfare in all environments including the world's poorest countries, the developing economies, the transitional countries and the developed world (Kearney, 2012).

SMEs are in general initiated by a single entrepreneur or a small group of people, and are often managed by owner–managers. Their organizational structures are typically flat. SMEs do not have many layers (mainly due to small number of both employees/supervisors and specializations in human skills) because the owner/s is/are mostly at the top of decision making affairs (which still keeps them bureaucratic as most of the times employees do not dare to challenge the supervisors/owner/s). However, the good thing come from this nature is that it adds to their flexibility. Many researchers argue that entrepreneurs mostly seek to derive several advantages by undertaking operations at a smaller level in terms of flexibility, informality, sustainability, and structural adaptability (Zeng, Xie & Tam, 2010).

However, this study argues that, to observe the rolling out of innovation processes in developing and transitional economies, a multi-facet research has to be carried out, including broader aspects of the entire context of open innovation dynamics and incorporating larger sample size. The discussions presented so far, is an attempt to overview the open innovation paradigm and relevant public policy context in a developing country. The indicative remarks may offer insights for future research in the fields of open innovation and innovation policy initiation not only in the developing economies, but also in the transitional economies. This study had its limitations. Scant literature and lack of necessary tools, such as survey or interview or other instruments are among them. Nevertheless, introducing these tools is expected to bring along opportunities for further research.

REFERENCES

Bell, M., & Pavitt, K. L. R. (1993). Technological accumulation and industrial growth: Contrasts between developed and developing countries. *Industrial and Corporate Change*, 2(1), 157–210. doi:10.1093/icc/2.1.157

Carayannis, E. G., Popescu, D., Sipp, C., & Steward, M. (2006). Technological learning for entrepreneurial development (TL4ED) in the knowledge economy (KE): Case studies and lessons learned. *Technovation*, 26(4), 419–443. doi:10.1016/j.technovation.2005.04.003

Chesbrough, H. W. (2003). *Open innovation: The new imperative for creating and profiting from technology*. Boston: Harvard Business School Press.

Davidsson, J. (2006). *Small Business Innovation Program: Business development and entrepreneurial training with intellectual property in developing countries*. B-Open Nordic AB.

De Jong, J. P. J., Vanhaverbeke, W., Kalvet, T., & Chesbrough, H. (2008), Policies for Open Innovation: Theory, Framework and Cases. Research project funded by VISION Era-Net, Helsinki: Finland.

Edwards, T., Delbridge, R., & Munday, M. (2005). Understanding innovation in small and medium-sized enterprises: A process manifest. *Technovation*, 25(10), 1119–1127. doi:10.1016/j.technovation.2004.04.005

English-Lucek, J. A., Darrah, C. N., & Saveri, A. (2002). Trusting strangers: Work relationships in four high-tech communities. *Information Communication and Society*, 5(1), 90–108. doi:10.1080/13691180110117677

Ernst, D., Mytelka, L., & Ganiatsos, T. (1994). *Technological Capabilities: A Conceptual Framework, Mimeo*. Geneva: UNCTAD.

Gassmann, O., Enkel, E., & Chesbrough, H. (2010). The future of open innovation. *R & D Management*, 40(3), 213–221. doi:10.1111/j.1467-9310.2010.00605.x

Govt. of Bangladesh. (2005a). *Policy Strategies for Small & Medium Enterprises (SME) Development in Bangladesh*, Ministry of Industries, Government of the People's Republic of Bangladesh, January 2005

Govt. of Bangladesh. (2005b). *Bangladesh Industrial Policy 2005*, Ministry of Industries, Government of the People's Republic of Bangladesh.

Hamdani, J., & Wirawan, C. (2012). Open Innovation Implementation to Sustain Indonesian SMEs. *Procedia Economics and Finance*, 4, 223–233. doi:10.1016/S2212-5671(12)00337-1

Indarti, N., & Langenberg, M. (2004, April 19-21). Factors Affecting Business Success Among SMEs: Empirical Evidences from Indonesia. *Proceedings of the Second Bi-annual European Summer University*, University of Twente, Encschode, Netherland.

Jones, O., & Tilley, F. (Eds.). (2003). *Competitive Advantage in SMEs: organizing for innovation and change*. Chichester: Wiley.

Kasekende, L. (2001). Financing SMEs: Uganda's Experience. In *Improving the Competitiveness of SMEs in Developing Countries: The Role of Finance to Enhance Enterprise Development* (pp. 97–107). New York, Geneva: United Nations.

Kearney, C. (2012). Emerging markets research: Trends, issues and future directions. *Emerging Markets Review, 13*(2), 159–183. doi:10.1016/j.ememar.2012.01.003

Klein-Woolthuis, R., Lankhuizen, M., & Gilsing, V. (2005). A system failure framework for innovation policy design. *Technovation, 25*(6), 609–619. doi:10.1016/j.technovation.2003.11.002

Kowalski, S. P. (2009, December 10-11). SMES, Open Innovation and IP Management: Advancing Global Development, A presentation paper on the Theme 2: The Challenge of Open Innovation for MSMEs - SMEs, Open Innovation and IP Management - Advancing Global Development. *WIPO-Italy International Convention on Intellectual Property and Competitiveness of Micro, Small and Medium-Sized Enterprises (MSMEs)*, Rome, Italy.

Kroll, H., & Liefner, I. (2008). Spin-off enterprises as a mean of technology commercialisation in a transforming economy – evidence from three universities in China. *Technovation, 28*(5), 298–313. doi:10.1016/j.technovation.2007.05.002

Lee, S., Park, G., Yoonc, B., & Park, J. (2010). Open innovation in SMEs—An intermediated network model. *Research Policy, 39*(2), 290–300. doi:10.1016/j.respol.2009.12.009

Li, J., & Kozhikode, R. K. (2009). Developing new innovation models: Shifts in the innovation landscapes in emerging economies and implications for global R&D management. *Journal of International Management, 15*(3), 328–339. doi:10.1016/j.intman.2008.12.005

Liu, X. (2008). *China's Development Model: An Alternative Strategy for Technological Catch-Up*, SLPTMD Working Paper Series No. 020, University of Oxford, UK.

López, A. (2009, January). Innovation and Appropriability, Empirical Evidence and Research Agenda. In The Economics of Intellectual Property: Suggestions for Further Research in Developing Countries and Countries with Economies in Transition.

Marisetty, V., Ramachandran, K., & Jha, R. (2008). *Wealth effects of family succession: A case of Indian family business groups*. Working Paper. Indian School of Business.

Narain, S. (2001). Development Financial Institutions' and Commercial banks' Innovation Schemes for Assisting SMEs in India. In *Improving the Competitiveness of SMEs in Developing Countries: The Role of Finance to Enhance Enterprise Development* (pp. 81–87). Geneva: United Nations.

OECD. (2005). *Oslo Manual: Guidelines for Collecting and Interpreting Innovation Data* (3rd ed.). Paris: Organization for Economic Co-operation and Development.

Padmadinata, F. Z. S. (2007, April 3-4). Quality Management System and Product Certification Process and Practice for SME in Indonesia. *Proceedings of the National Workshop on Subnational Innovation Systems and Technology Capacity Building Policies to Enhance Competitiveness of SMEs*, UN-ESCAP and Indonesian Institute of Science (LIPI), Jakarta, Indonesia.

Pandey, A.P. & Shivesh (2007, December). *Indian SMEs and their uniqueness in the country*, Munich Personal RePEc Archive, MPRA Paper No. 6086. Retrieved from http://mpra.ub.uni-muenchen.de/6086/

Payne, J. E. (2003). E-Commerce Readiness for SMEs in Developing Countries: a Guide for Development Professionals. Retrieved from http://learnlink.aed.org/Publications/Concept_Papers/ecommerce_readiness.pdf

Rahman, H., & Ramos, I. (2010). Open Innovation in SMEs: From Closed Boundaries to Networked Paradigm. *Issues in Informing Science and Information Technology*, 7, 471–487.

Rahman, H., & Ramos, I. (2013). Open Innovation Strategies in SMEs: Development of a Business Model. In Small and Medium Enterprises: Concepts, Methodologies, Tools, and Applications (Vols. 1–4). pp. 281–293). USA: Information Resources Management Association. doi:10.4018/978-1-4666-3886-0.ch015

Ruiz, P. P. (2010). *Technology & Knowledge Transfer Under the Open Innovation Paradigm: a model and tool proposal to understand and enhance collaboration-based innovations integrating C-K Design Theory, TRIZ and Information Technologies* [Dissertation for the Master of Science in Innovation and Technology]. Management School of Management, University of Bath, UK.

Saini, D. S., & Budhwar, P. S. (2008). Managing the human resource in Indian SMEs: The role of indigenous realities. *Journal of World Business*, *43*(4), 417–434. doi:10.1016/j.jwb.2008.03.004

Savitskaya, I. (2009). *Towards open innovation in regional Innovation system: case St. Petersburg, Research Report 214*. Lappeenranta: Lappeenranta University of Technology.

Schaffers, H., Cordoba, M. G., Hongisto, P., Kallai, T., Merz, C., & van Rensburg, J. (2007, June 4-6). Exploring business models for open innovation in rural living labs. *Paper from the13th International Conference on Concurrent Enterprising*, Sophia-Antipolis, France.

Siu, W. S. (2005). An institutional analysis of marketing practices of small and medium-sized enterprises (SMEs) in China, Hong Kong and Taiwan. *Entrepreneurship and Regional Development*, *17*(1), 65–88. doi:10.1080/08985620052000330306

Srivastava, D. K. (2005). Human resource management in Indian mid size operations. In Datta (Ed.), Indian mid-size manufacturing enterprises: Opportunities and challenges in a global economy. Gurgaon: Management Development Institute.

Storey, D. (1994). *Understanding the small business sector*. London: International Thomson Business Press.

Takagi, Y., & Czajkowski, A. (2012). WIPO services for access to patent information - Building patent information infrastructure and capacity in LDCs and developing countries. *World Patent Information*, *34*(1), 30–36. doi:10.1016/j.wpi.2011.08.002

Thampy, A. (2010). Financing of SME firms in India Interview with Ranjana Kumar, Former CMD, Indian Bank. Vigilance Commissioner, Central Vigilance Commission. doi:10.1016/j.iimb.2010.04.011

The family connection. (1996, October 05). Economist, 341(7986): 62

UNCTAD Secretariat. (2001). Best Practices in Financial Innovations for SMEs. In *Improving the Competitiveness of SMEs in Developing Countries: The Role of Finance to Enhance Enterprise Development* (pp. 3–58). New York, Geneva: United Nations.

United Nations. (2006). *Globalization of R&D and Developing Countries, United Nations Conference on Trade and Development.*

Van Hemert, P., & Nijkamp, P. (2010). Knowledge investments, business R&D and innovativeness of countries: A qualitative meta-analytic comparison. *Technological Forecasting and Social Change, 77*(3), 369–384. doi:10.1016/j.techfore.2009.08.007

Warner, A. (2001, October 22-24). Small and Medium Sized Enterprises and Economic Creativity. A paper presented at UNCTAD's intergovernmental Expert Meeting on *"Improving the Competitiveness of SMEs in Developing Countries: the Role of Finance, Including E-finance, to Enhance Enterprise Development*, Geneva (pp. 61-77).

Williams, A. M., & Shaw, G. (2011). Internationalization and innovation in Tourism. *Annals of Tourism Research, 38*(1), 27–51. doi:10.1016/j.annals.2010.09.006

World Business Council. (2007). *Promoting Small and Medium Enterprises for Sustainable Development* (Development Focus Area. *I Issue Brief*, 2007.

Zahra, A. Z., & George, G. (2002). Absorptive capacity: A review, reconceptualization, and extension. *Academy of Management Review, 27*(2), 185–203.

Zeng, S. X., Xie, X. M., & Tam, C. M. (2010). Relationship between cooperation networks and innovation performance of SMEs. *Technovation, 30*(3), 181–194. doi:10.1016/j.technovation.2009.08.003

ADDITIONAL READING

Albuquerque, E. M. (2007). Inadequacy of technology and innovation systems at the periphery. *Cambridge Journal of Economics, 31*(5), 669–690. doi:10.1093/cje/bel045

Alcorta, L., & Peres, W. (1998). Innovation systems and technological specialization in Latin America and Caribbean. *Research Policy, 26*(7–8), 857–881. doi:10.1016/S0048-7333(97)00067-X

Alexander, N., & Dawson, J. (1994). Internationalisation of retailing operations. *Journal of Marketing Management, 10*(4), 267–282. doi:10.1080/0267257X.1994.9964274

Bell, R. M., & Albu, M. (1999). Knowledge systems and technological dynamism in industrial clusters in developing countries. *World Development, 27*(9), 1715–1734. doi:10.1016/S0305-750X(99)00073-X

Bougrain, F., & Haudeville, B. (2002). Innovation, collaboration and SMEs internal research capacities. *Research Policy, 31*(5), 735–747. doi:10.1016/S0048-7333(01)00144-5

Buckley, P. J., & Casson, M. C. (1985). *The economic theory of multinational enterprise*. London: Macmillan. doi:10.1007/978-1-349-05242-4

Cook, I., & Horobin, G. (2006). Implementing eGovernment without promoting dependence: Open source software in developing countries in Southeast Asia. *Public Administration and Development, 26*(4), 279–289. doi:10.1002/pad.403

Dodgson, M., Gann, D., & Salter, A. (2008). *The management of technological innovation: Strategy and practice*. Oxford: Oxford UP.

Edwards, T., Delbridge, R., & Munday, M. (2005). Understanding innovation in small and medium-sized enterprises: A process manifest. *Technovation, 25*(10), 1119–1120. doi:10.1016/j.technovation.2004.04.005

Ernst, D. (2006). Innovation offshoring: Asia's emerging role in global innovation networks. *East-West Center Special Reports, 10*, 1–50.

Jacob, M., & Groizard, J. L. (2007). Technology transfer and multinationals: The case of Balearic hotel chains' investments in two developing economies. *Tourism Management, 28*(4), 976–992. doi:10.1016/j.tourman.2006.08.013

Jaeger, A. (1990). The applicability of western management techniques in developing countries: a cultural perspective. In A. Jaeger & R. Kanungo (Eds.), *Management in Developing Countries* (pp. 131–145). London: Routledge.

James, J. (2002). Low-cost information technology in developing countries: Current opportunities and emerging possibilities. *Habitat International, 26*(1), 21–31. doi:10.1016/S0197-3975(01)00030-3

Jones, O., & Tilley, F. (Eds.). (2003). *Competitive Advantage in SMEs: organizing for Innovation and Change*. Chichester: Wiley.

Lall, S. (2000). The technological structure and performance of developing country manufactured exports, 1985–1998. *Oxford Development Studies, 28*(3), 337–369. doi:10.1080/713688318

Lall, S., & Teubal, M. (1998). Market stimulating technology policies in developing countries: A framework with examples from East Asia. *World Development, 26*(8), 1369–1385. doi:10.1016/S0305-750X(98)00071-0

Lundvall, B.-A. (Ed.). (1992). *National Systems of Innovation: Towards a Theory of Innovation and Interactive Learning*. London, UK: Pinter.

Maranto-Vargas, D., & Gómez-Tagle Rangel, R. (2007). Development of internal resources and capabilities as sources of differentiation of SME under increased global competition: A field study in Mexico. *Technological Forecasting and Social Change, 74*(1), 90–99. doi:10.1016/j.techfore.2005.09.007

Narula, R. (2004). R&D collaboration by SMEs: New opportunities and limitations in the face of globalisation. *Technovation, 25*(2), 153–161. doi:10.1016/S0166-4972(02)00045-7

NESTA. (2008). *UK global innovation: Engaging with new countries, regions and people*. London: NESTA.

Niosi, J. (2008). Technology, development and innovation systems: An introduction. *The Journal of Development Studies, 44*(5), 613–621. doi:10.1080/00220380802009084

Prashantham, S. (2008). *The internationalization of small firms: A strategic entrepreneurship perspective*. Abingdon: Routledge.

Rusinovic, K. (2008). Transnational embeddedness: Transnational activities and networks among first- and second-generation immigrant entrepreneurs in the Netherlands. *Journal of Ethnic and Migration Studies*, *34*(3), 431–451. doi:10.1080/13691830701880285

KEY TERMS AND DEFINITIONS

Developed Economies: While there is no one set definition, but typically a developed economy refers to a country with a relatively high level of economic growth and security. Some of the most common criteria for evaluating a country's degree of development are its per capita income or gross domestic product (GDP), the level of industrialization, general standard of living and the amount of widespread infrastructure. Increasingly other non-economic factors are included in evaluating an economy or country's degree of development, such as the Human Development Index (HDI) which reflects relative degrees of advancement in education, literacy and health.

Developing Economies: Comprise low- and middle-income countries where most people have lower standard of living with access to fewer goods and services than most people in high-income countries. Developing countries are broadly split into two categories, the middle-income and the low-income groups.

Emerging Economies: The most economically progresses of developing countries. In terms of GNP per capita, they correspond to the medium-low and medium-high country groups but are characterized by a regulated and functioning securities exchange, or in the process of developing one, and the fact that shares traded on the stock exchanges must be available for purchase by foreign investors, even if subject to certain restrictions.

Entrepreneurs: An entrepreneur is a person who has possession of a new enterprise, venture or idea organizes, operates a business or businesses and assumes significant accountability for the inherent risks and the outcome.

Entrepreneurships: It is the process of discovering new ways of blending resources. When the market value generated by this new blending of resources is greater than the market value these resources can generate elsewhere individually or in some other combination, then the entrepreneur makes a profit.

First Economy Enterprises: These are the enterprises that are comprised of established businesses in sustained form.

Second Economy Enterprises: These are the form of enterprises that are mainly belong to the working poor, or marginalized communities, and working in the informal economy.

ENDNOTES

[1] Enterprises shall be categorized using the following definition (fixed investment implies exclusion of land and building, and valuation on the basis of current replacement cost only): Small enterprise: an enterprise should be treated as *small* if, in today's market prices, the replacement cost of plant, machinery and other parts/components, fixtures, support utility, and associated technical services by way of capitalized costs (of turn-key consultancy services, for example), etc., excluding land

and building, were to be up to Tk. 15 million; Medium enterprise: an enterprise would be treated as *medium* if, in today's market prices, the replacement cost of plant, machinery, and other parts/components, fixtures, support utility, and associated technical services (such as turn-key consultancy), etc., excluding land and building, were to be up to Tk. 100 million; a. For non-manufacturing activities (such as trading or other services), the Taskforce defines: Small enterprise: an enterprise should be treated as *small* if it has less than 25 workers, in full-time equivalents; Medium enterprise: an enterprise would be treated as *medium* if it has between 25 and 100 employees.

[2] In India, the industrial sector has two broad segments viz., (a) Small Scale Industries (SSI) and (b) Others (i.e. medium and large industries). The Government of India notifies the definition of small-scale industry from time to time based on the investment ceiling. The present definition is, "an industry in the small scale sector shall have investment in plant and machinery not exceeding INR 10 million" (approx. US$22,000). A sub-component of micro enterprises, known as the "Tiny Sector" forms part of the overall SSI sector. Medium sized industries are out of the purview. India, thus, follows the concept of SSIs and not SMEs.

[3] In India, until recently there has been no formal concept of SME or medium enterprises. However, the term small scale industry (SSI) is well known; this is different from the SME sector in other countries. The Government of India had a policy of providing assistance of different types to SSIs through various state agencies. Lately, Indian Parliament has enacted the Micro, Small and Medium Enterprises Development Act, 2006.1 As per this Act, medium manufacturing or production enterprises are those which have an investment in plant and machinery between Rs. 50 million and 100 million (1$ US = Rupees 40.10 approximately in July 2007). The investment referred to in this definition is that in ''initial fixed assets'' i.e., the plant and machinery (which excludes land & building). Under this Act, a micro enterprise has been defined as one where the investment in plant and machinery does not exceed Rs. 2.5 million and a small enterprise as one where such investment is more than Rs. 2.5 million but does not exceed Rs. 50 million. Whereas, a medium enterprise is one in which the investment limit is between Rs. 50 million and Rs. 100 million. In this Act there is no reference to the term SME. One may, however, combine the definitions of small and medium enterprises to derive a concept of SME. This would mean that an SME in the Indian context is an enterprise in which the investment in plant and machinery is between 2.5 million and 100 million.2 The definition of the terms ''small'' and ''medium'' enterprise in India is investment specific, while in the rest of the world it reflects a combination of factors including terms of employment, assets or sales or combination of these factors (Saini & Budhwar, 2008).

[4] http://www.openlivinglabs.eu_.

[5] SMEs are widely defined in terms of their characteristics, which include the size of capital investment, the number of employees, the turnover, the management style, the location, and the market share. Country context plays a major role in determining the nature of these characteristics, especially, the size of investment in capital accumulation and the number of employees. For developing countries, small-scale generally means enterprises with less than 50 workers and medium-size enterprises would usually mean those that have 50–99 workers. In Uganda, a small-scale enterprise is an enterprise or a firm employing less than 5 but with a maximum of 50 employees, with the value of assets, excluding land, building and working capital of less than Ugshs. 50 million (USD 30,000), and an annual income turnover of between Ugshs. 10–50 million (USD 6,000–30,000). A medium-size enterprise is considered a firm, which employs between 50–100 workers. Other characteristics have not been fully developed.

Chapter 12

Open Innovation:
Reaching out to the Grass Roots through SMEs – Exploring Issues of Opportunities and Challenges to Reach Economic Sustainability

Hakikur Rahman
BRAC University, Bangladesh

ABSTRACT

While talking about successful entrepreneurship and value addition within an enterprise through innovation, one could realize that the innovation paradigm has been shifted from simple introduction of new ideas and products to accumulation of diversified actions, actors and agents along the process. Furthermore, when the innovation process is not being restricted within the closed nature of it, the process takes many forms during its evolution. Innovations have been seen as closed innovation or open innovation, depending on its nature of action, but contemporary world may have seen many forms of innovation, such as technological innovation, products/service innovation, process/production innovation, operational/management/organizational innovation, business model innovation or disruptive innovation, though often they are strongly interrelated.

Definition of innovation has also adopted many transformations along the path, incorporating innovations within the products, process or service of an enterprise to organizational, marketing, or external entities and relations. Nature and scope of agents and actors even varies widely within the innovation dynamics, when the open innovation techniques are being applied to enterprises, designated as the small and medium enterprises (SMEs).

Researching in this paradigm, one has to look for some underlying issues that should be attended through responding to research questions as the research continues. Among many of the fundamental questions on innovation advancement for SMEs development there are a few, how to acquire precise information

DOI: 10.4018/978-1-5225-0556-3.ch012

on the flow-chart of their business operations, gain knowledge on specific parameters of their business processes, utilize existing potential capacities to extend their knowledge towards successful innovation acquisition and dissemination, and extend their knowledge platform through various capacity development initiatives. They aggregate further, when issues of opportunities and challenges are being researched along the path of SME development through open innovation.

Rationale of this research is to ascertain diverse aspects of opportunities and challenges surrounding the open innovation processes, and design action plans to empower SMEs in reaching out to the grass roots communities utilizing open innovation strategies. Primary focus of this research is to enable SMEs in finding out their innovation potentiality and empower them through various capacity development initiatives. However, the specific focus will adhere to adaptable technology transfer through open innovation.

Along the route to justify the research potential and validate the research hypotheses (whether this research will add any economic value or knowledge gain), this study will conduct extensive literature review on various patterns of open innovation (crowdsourcing or collaborative), investigate case studies to learn about intricate issues surrounding their operational strategies (conducted by European Commission, OECD and similar institutions) and conduct surveys among selected SMEs (email, web based, egroups) in several phases. Research design includes formulation of strategies to resolve acquired research questions; collection and recording of the evidences obtained from the literature review or case studies or surveys; processing and analyzing gathered data and their appropriate interpretations; and publication of results. Analysis will include both qualitative (descriptive and exploratory) and quantitative (inferential statistics) methods.

INTRODUCTION

The initial effort of this research was in fact to find a focus area to empower small and medium enterprises (SMEs[1]) through open innovation strategies. Due to the open and collaborative nature of this newly evolved concept, the primary research focus has been kept within crowdsourcing innovation[2], but not limited to other collaborative innovation, though it is not easy to put a restrictive boundary between them. Being new in the research arena, on one hand the concept of open innovation has been flourished very progressively within a short span of time (Chesbrough, 2003a; Chesbrough, Vanhaverbeke & West, 2006; Gassmann, 2006), but at the same time, it has evolved through various growth patterns in diversified directions involving different factors and parameters (Christensen, Olesen & Kjaer, 2005; Chesbrough & Crowther, 2006; Dodgson, Gann & Salter, 2006; Gassmann, 2006; Vanhaverbeke, 2006; West & Gallagher, 2006). Furthermore, as this research is related to SMEs[3], which are the steering factor of economic growth in the European countries, and especially in Portugal where they comprise of almost 99.9% (EC, 2008) of the entrepreneurships, the problem statements were constructed following multiple studies along this aspect, though much work towards the improvement of knowledge factors on SMEs development have not been found.

Problem statements or the main purpose of this study lies within the intrinsic definition of innovation itself. Innovation is a way of performing something new. It may refer to incremental and emergent or radical and revolutionary changes in thinking, products, process development, or organizational development. Innovation, as seen by Schumpeter (1934; 1982) incorporates way of producing new products, new methods of production, new sources of supply, opening of new markets, and new ways of organizing businesses. OECD (1992; 1996; 2005), after several adjustment has come into this argument, that innovation is the implementation of a new or significantly improved product (good or service), or process, a new marketing method, or a new organizational method in business practices, workplace organization or external relations.

However, other scholars and researchers in the field of innovation, has put forward definition of innovation in various formats and perspectives. Some definitions or arguments are being included below:

The creation of new ideas/processes which will lead to change in an enterprise´s economic and social potential (Drucker, 1998: 149)

This research will look into the economic and social aspect of innovation process, but at the same time look into any technology parameters that are involved within the processes.

Tidd, Bessant & Pavitt (2005) and Bessant & Tidd (2007) argued that there are four types of innovation, i.e., the innovator has four routes of innovation paths, such as product innovation (changes in the products or services [things] which an organization offers), process innovation (changes in the ways in which products or services are created and delivered), positioning innovation (changes in the context in which the products or services are introduced) and paradigm innovation (changes in the underlying mental models which outline what the organization does)[4].

This research would argue that these are the areas of innovation through which innovation takes place in an enterprise.

However, in terms of the types of innovation, Darsø (2001) argued that innovation can be

incremental (improvements of processes, products and methods, often found by technicians or employees during their daily work), radical (novel, surprising and different approach or composition), social (spring from social needs, rather than from technology, and are related to new ways of interaction) and quantum (refers to the emergence of qualitatively new system states brought by small incremental changes).

Furthermore, talking about types of innovation, Henderson & Clark (1990) identified four:

incremental innovation- improves component knowledge and leaves architectural knowledge unchanged; modular innovation- architectural knowledge unchanged, component knowledge of one or more components reduced in value; architectural innovation- component knowledge unchanged, architectural knowledge reduced in value; and radical innovation[5]- both component knowledge and architectural knowledge reduced in value.

These are the natures of innovation in which innovation belongs.

Thus, innovation can be termed as introduction of new idea into the marketplace in the form of a new product or service, or an improvement in organization or process[6].

This definition enables one to concentrate on demand driven innovation, or innovation may be re-termed as a:

Process by which an idea or invention is translated into good or service for which people will pay. (Businessdictionary.com[7])

The above definition leads to the very basic parameters of innovation, where there are goods or services between buyer and the seller.

Hence, a functional equation (innovation as the most probable or prominent function of the mentioned parameters in above definitions and arguments) can be deducted:

A context diagram from the above equation sets the primary problem statements of this research. If one argues that innovation generates new or improved products, process or services, then the following diagram can be derived:

This research would like to carry out investigation into these three aspects of innovation. However, it will set its boundary within the various business processes through organizational transformations and

Figure 1. A functional equation mapping various definitions and arguments

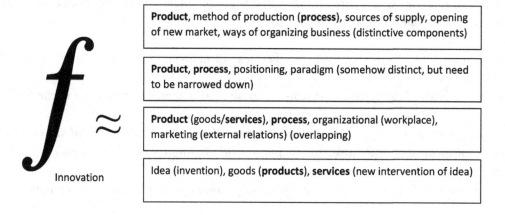

Figure 2. A context diagram derived from the functional equation

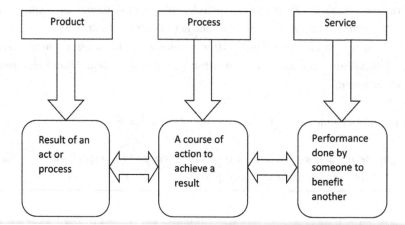

capacity development initiatives incorporating crowdsourcing methods to empower SMEs. Furthermore, it will emphasize on technology diffusion and issues of technical nature to enable the SMEs community to innovate further in reaching out to their grass roots stakeholders.

LITERATURE REVIEW

Open Innovation and SMEs

In search of finding different patterns of innovation and their relationships with SMEs, initial part of the research spent sufficient period of time (over a year or so) in literature review. Review was restricted to definite search strings, but was not confined to specific journals or search engines. However, to keep the credibility of the searched content most of the searches were limited to highly ranked journals and databases. Similarly, case studies were conducted and survey reports were being studied that were being operationalized or established or implemented by well reputed national and international agencies or institutes, such as European Commission, OECD, World Bank, UNDP, Vinnova, Innocentive and others. Moreover, literature review emphasized on empirical studies and cases illustrating activities on SMEs in reaching out to their broad based grass roots clientele.

Innovation, being latent within the product, process and service in an entrepreneurship grows naturally if these three could be intermingled further, such as incorporating new idea and changes through product development, process development and service development. In its simplest sense, innovation will grow in an enterprise, if the bonding among them increases. As f(P1, P2,S) moves inwards, bonding increases, and innovation grows (see Figure 5).

Given the potentiality of open innovation in an enterprise through improvement of the three parameters as shown in Figure-3, especially small and medium scale enterprises (SMEs), literature review gave primary focus to gather knowledge on opportunities and challenges that are being faced by SMEs when they are opening their windows of business processes through open innovation methods. Furthermore, to

Figure 3. Bonding of the three parameters of innovation management

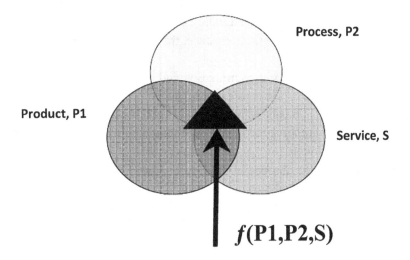

f(P1,P2,S)

design an appropriate action plan for empowering them, a thorough literature review has been conducted on existing success cases utilizing open innovation strategies. These eventually assisted in developing the research design and survey methods.

However, before progressing further, this study would like to give an insight into the product, process and service innovation, but not reinventing the wheel. Researchers mention that *product innovation* is linked to the analysis of changes and innovations within the product category. Product innovation allows one to map out changes in one´s enterprise´s product. It compels to determine how a product should evolve to meet needs of the client and be competitive in the future. Essentially, it may include any or some or all of the features of product innovation as mentioned below:

- A product may come out with an entirely new idea;
- A product may offer improved performance against an existing function or desire or need;
- It may provide a new approach for an existing product;
- The product may provide additional functions or features;
- It may be an existing product, but targeting to a new segment of the market;
- The product may have a new price or value mix (promotion or other value addition);
- It may have improved packaging;
- The product may have changes in appearance or forms (Crawford, 1983; Hiebing Jr. & Cooper, 2003).

Process innovation combines the adoption of a new view of the business process with the application of innovation into key processes. The novel and distinctive feature of this combination is its enormous potential to assist an organization in achieving major reductions in process cost or process time, or major improvements in quality, flexibility, and service levels. In this perspective, the business must be viewed not in terms of functions, divisions, or products, but of key processes, they may include redesigning key processes from the beginning to the end, and employing whatever innovative technologies and organizational resources are available. However, a major challenge in process innovation is to make a successful transition to a continuous improvement in environment. Referring to Davenport (1993), this research purview that, if a company that does not institute continuous improvement after implementing process innovation is likely to revert to old ways of doing business. Framework for process innovation may comprise of; identifying processes for innovation, identifying transformation enablers, developing a business vision and process objectives, understanding and measuring existing processes, and designing and creating a prototype of the new process. In essence, the process innovation;

- Should respond to the need for better coordination and management of functional interdependencies (relative independence);
- Is intended to achieve radical business improvement (notable breakthrough);
- May seem to be a discrete initiative but must be combined with other initiatives for ongoing transformations (integrated actions);
- Can seldom be achieved in the absence of a carefully considered combination of both technological and human catalysts (intricately designed), and
- Must suit the business culture (localized one) (Zuboff, 1988; Walton, 1989; Davenport, 1993).

Service innovation systems are dynamic configurations of *people, technologies, organizations* and *shared information* that create and deliver value to customers, providers and partners through services. They are forming a growing proportion of the world economy and are becoming central activity for the businesses, governments, families and individuals. Nowadays, firms do not consider themselves to be ´services´ or ´manufacturing´ but providing solutions for customers that involve a combination of products and services. Preferably, service innovation can happen across all service sectors and one should look at all possible *service activities* rather than looking at specific *service sectors* (Van Ark, Broersma & Den Hertog, 2003; Miles, 2005; IfM & IBM, 2008). Service innovation is more closely related to the depth than breadth (vertical than horizontal), and a deep relationship with external sources, such as customer needs of target markets are essential for service innovation (Lee et al., 2010). Service innovation referring SMEs development may:

- Establish a common language and shared framework;
- Adopt interdisciplinary approach for research and education on service systems;
- Promote learning programmes on service science, management and engineering;
- Develop modular template-based platform of common interests;
- Provide solutions for challenges on service systems research;
- Develop appropriate organizational arrangements to enhance industry-academic collaboration; and
- Work with partners within a sustainable framework (IfM and IBM, 2008)[8].

Open Innovation Opportunities among SMEs

In recent years open innovation models have become an integral part of the innovation strategies and business models of enterprises. The most important benefit of open innovation has been seen as it provides a larger base of ideas and technologies. Enterprises look at open innovation as a close collaboration with external partners; customers, consumers, researchers or other intermediaries that may have an input to the future of their company. The main motives for joining forces between companies is to grasp new business opportunities, share risks, join complementary resources and achieve synergies. Thus, enterprises recognize open innovation as a strategic tool to explore new growth opportunities at a lower risk, and open technology sourcing offers them higher flexibility and responsiveness without necessarily incurring huge investments (OECD, 2008).

The open innovation approach assumes that innovating enterprise is no longer the sole locus of innovation, nor it is the only means for reaping the benefits of research, development and innovation (RDI). In comparison to a closed innovation model, where external actors are viewed with suspicion, who could take away useful knowledge to other competitors, an open innovation environment sets a common platform to its users, customers, suppliers, public knowledge institutions, individual inventors and even competitors and regarded as potential contributors of crucial pieces of information. In addition to this, through collaboration, innovating partners can enhance their own technologies or reduce RDI costs, which is an important driver of open innovation (Lemola & Lievonen, 2008). One may term it as economization of RDI.

Another driver of open innovation is knowledge augmentation. As Chesbrough (2006a) mentioned that even larger companies applies a fraction of the total knowledge that is generated in a particular sector of company. In that case, it is better to keep doors open to external knowledge. Increasingly corporate entities are seeking out collaborative relationships with a variety of innovative organizations, universities, research institutes and other intermediaries.

Chesbrough (2006b) further emphasized on obtaining external resources in contrast to internal ones, spin-offs and licensing to gain commercial benefits of innovation in contrast to aim solely at new products by innovating oneself, utilizing available commercial knowledge to eliminate false positives and false negatives in contrast to experiment on an unsuccessful venture, fostering outflows of knowledge and technology to arrange better intellectual property management in contrast to situated under a controlled environment, and promoting innovation intermediaries as cheaper sources of innovation managers in contrast to rely on age old methods and technologies.

Life-Cycle of Technology Exploration and Technology Exploitation

As evolved from the very basic, but comprehensive definition of open innovation (Chesbrough, Vanhaverbeke & West, 2006:1), it is "the use of purposive inflows to accelerate internal innovation" and "the use of purposive outflows to expand the markets for external use of innovation", and thus, it comprises of outside-in and inside-out flow of ideas, knowledge and technologies. The outside-in movements may be termed as technology acquisition or technology exploration, while the inside-out movements may be termed as technology dissemination or technology exploration (Lichtenthaler, 2008; Van de Vrande, De Jong, Vanhaverbeke & De Rochemont, 2009). Through technology exploration, SMEs can get acquainted with outside information, gain knowledge and utilize them for their empowerment by enhancing existing technology platform. On the other hand, through technology exploitation, SMEs can empower themselves by raising their knowledge platform Chesbrough & Crowther, 2006; Lichtenthaler, 2008). Inter-firm collaborations (strategic alliances and joint ventures) are becoming essential instruments to improve competitiveness of enterprises in complex and critical environments (Hoffman & Schlosser, 2001).

Along these two routes of open innovation, SMEs have the opportunities of increased customer involvement, external participation, networking among other partners, outsourcing of R&D and inward licensing of intellectual property (IP) through technology exploration, and they may have the opportunities of augmented venturing, inclusion of all-out staff involvement within the R&D processes and outward licensing of IP through technology exploitation (Van de Vrande, De Jong, Vanhaverbeke & De Rochemont, 2009).

In the context of technology exploration and technology exploitation, parameters as mentioned above need further investigation. A few important activities under the category of technology exploration are being discussed next.

- **Increased Customer Involvement:** Researchers on open innovation recognize increased customer involvement as an essential element to expedite internal innovation process (Gassmann, 2006). Apart from Von Hippel´s (2005) initiating work, this has been supported by many other researchers (Olson & Bakke, 2001; Lilien et al., 2002; Bonner & Walker, 2004). Emphasis has been given to increased involvement of the customers at the beginning of the innovation process (Brockhoff, 2003; Von Hippel, 1998; 2005; Enkel et al., 2005). Firms may benefit from their customers´ ideas, thoughts and innovations by developing better products that are currently offered or by producing products based on the designs of customers (Van de Vrande et al., 2009).

- **External Networking:** Another essential activity to innovate through open and collaborative innovation (Chesbrough, Vanhaverbeke and West, 2006), which includes acquiring and maintaining connections with external sources of social capital, organizations and individuals (Van de Vrande et al., 2009). External networking allows enterprises to acquire specific knowledge without spending time, effort or money but to connect to external partners. Such collaborative network among non-competing entities can be utilized to create R&D alliances and acquire technological capabilities (Gomes-Casseres, 1997; Lee, et al., 2010). Within the limited resources of SMEs, they must find ways to achieve production of economies of scale to market their products effectively, and at the same time provide satisfactory support services to their customers. Lee et al. (2010) observed that SMEs are flexible and more innovative in new areas, but lack in resources and capabilities. On the other hand, larger firms may be less flexible, but have stronger trend to develop inventions into products or processes. These resources often attract SMEs to collaborate with large firms (Barney & Clark, 2007). But stronger ties with larger firms may limit opportunities and alternatives for SMEs, and they prefer to make external networks with other SMEs or institutions, such as universities, private research establishments or other forms of non-competitive intermediaries (Rothwell, 1991; Torkkeli, et al., 2007; Herstad, et al., 2008; Lee, et al., 2010).

- **External Participation:** In fact this may refer to crowdsourcing in terms of open innovation strategies and it enables one to look into the minute details of innovation sequences in an enterprise which may seemingly unimportant or not promising before (Van de Vrande et al., 2009). A company's competitiveness is increasingly depending on its capabilities beyond the internal boundaries (Prügl & Schreier, 2006).During the start up stages, an enterprise can invest by keeping eyes on potential opportunities (Keil, 2002; Chesbrough, 2006b), and then explore for further increase the knowledge platform through external collaboration (Van de Vrande et al., 2009). Within the innovation process, companies are intensifying relationships and cooperation with resources located outside the firm, ranging from customers, research institutes, intermediaries and business partners to universities (Howells, James and Malek, 2003; Linder, Jarvenpaa and Davenport, 2003).

- **Outsourcing R&D:** Nowadays, enterprises are outsourcing R&D activities to acquire external knowledge and technical service providers, such as engineering firms or high-tech organizations are taking lead in the open innovation arena (Van de Vrande et al., 2009). The basic assumption is that enterprises may not be able to conduct all R&D activities by themselves, but capitalize on external knowledge through outsourcing, either by collaboration, or taking license or purchasing (Gassmann, 2006). In this context, collaborative R&D is a useful means by which strategic flexibility can be increased and access to new knowledge can be realized (Pisano, 1990; Quinn, 2000; Fritsch and Lukas, 2001). While R&D outsourcing has been targeted to cost savings in most companies, more and more managers are discovering the value of cooperative R&D to achieve higher innovation rates. Collaborative R&D are being utilized to make systematic use of the competences of suppliers, customers, universities and competitors in order to share risks and costs, enlarge the knowledge base, access the complementary tangible and intangible assets, keep up with market developments and meet customer demands (Nalebuff & Brandeburger, 1996; Boiugrain & Haudeville, 2002; Van Gils & Zwart, 2004; Christensen, Olesen and Kjaer, 2005; De Jong, Vanhaverbeke, Van de Vrande and De Rochemont, 2007). Furthermore, the not-invented-here syndrome, a severe barrier to innovation, can also be mitigated if external partners are increasingly involved in the R&D processes (Katz and Allen, 1982) and the most important factor is that, in the open innovation paradigm, it is considered totally acceptable to acquire key development outside the organizational boundary (Prencipe, 2000).

- **Inward Licensing of Intellectual Property:** Intellectual Property (IP) can be termed as creative ideas and expressions of the human mind that have commercial value[9] or it can be seen as an idea, invention, formula, literary work, presentation, or other knowledge asset owned by an organization or individual[10]. The major legal mechanisms for protecting intellectual property rights are copyrights, patents, and trademarks. IP rights enable owners to select who may access and use their property and to protect it from unauthorized use[11]. As Chesbrough (2006a) has mentioned IP as a catalyst of open business model, an enterprise can acquire intellectual property including the licensing of patents, copyrights or trade marks. This has been supported by Van de vrande et al. (2009), as this process may strengthen one's business model and gear up the internal research engines. Inward licensing tend to be less costly than conducting in-house R&D, the licensing payment can be used to control risks by prudent payment scheme, reduces time to bring new products into market and lowers risk when an invention of similar nature has already been commercialized (Box, 2009; Darcy, Kraemer-Eis, Gnellec and Debande, 2009).
- Other issues like user innovation, non-supplier integration or external commercialization of technology fall under this category, but hardly have they formed any definitive trend channeling separate research aspects other than the activities mentioned above. However, as this research progress, efforts will be given to extract contents of similar interest and highlight them.

Before proceeding next, a few activities on technology exploitation are being discussed below:

- **Venturing:** A venture can be seen as an agreement among people to do things in service of a purpose and according to a set of values, and in this context, an entrepreneur is a venturer that carries primary responsibility for operating a venture[12]. Hence, venturing is the process of establishing and developing a venture, and can be defined as starting up new entrepreneurships drawing on internal knowledge, which implies spin-off and spin-out processes. In most cases, support from the parent organization includes finance, human capital, legal advice, or administrative services (Van de vrande, et al., 2009). Keil (2002) suggests that external corporate venturing unites both physical and intellectual assets of an enterprise by extending and exploiting the internal capabilities for continual regeneration and growth. Though earlier studies on open innovation have primarily focused on venturing activities in large enterprises (Chesbrough, 2003a; Lord, Mandel and Wager, 2002), but the potential of venturing activities is regarded to be as enormous. Chesbrough (2003a) illustrated that the total market value of 11 projects which turned into new ventures exceeding that of their parent company, Xerox, by a factor of two.
- **Outward Licensing of Intellectual Property:** As mentioned earlier, IP plays a crucial role in open innovation as a result of the in-and out flows of knowledge (Arora, 2002; Chesbrough, 2003a, 2006a; Lichtenthaler, 2007). Enterprises have opportunities to out-license their IP through commercialization to obtain more value from it (Gassmann, 2006; Darcy et al., 2009). Darcy et al. (2009) mention that out-licensing of IPs bring opportunity of high profitability, allow multiple licensees to work together at the same time, seem less riskier than Foreign Direct Investment (FDI), simple to operate when less technology components exist, and especially suited for SMEs as this process lowers risk by eliminating need for downstream production facilities. Out-licensing of IPs allow them to profit from their IPs when other firms with different business models find them as profitable, and in this way IPs route to the market through external paths (Van de vrande et al.,

2009). By means of out-licensing, many firms have begun to actively commercialize technology. This increase in inward and outward technology transactions reflects the new paradigm of open innovation (Vujovic & Ulhøi, 2008; Lichtenthaler & Ernst, 2009). However, the decision of firms to license out depends on anticipated revenues and profit-dissipation effects (Arora, Fosfuri and Gambardella, 2001), as whether the outward licensing generates revenues in the form of licensing payments, but current profits might decrease when licensees use their technology to compete in the same market (Van de vrande, et al., 2009). Moreover, these new forms of knowledge exploitation and creation of technology markets require the design of appropriate financial instruments to support the circulation and commercialization of knowledge (Darcy et al., 2009).

- **Involvement of Non-R&D Employees:** By capitalizing on the initiatives and knowledge of internal employees, active or non-active with the R&D exercises, an enterprise can be benefited (Van de vranda, et al., 2009). Chesbrough et al. (2006) has conducted case studies which illustrate the significance of informal ties of employees of one enterprise with employees of other enterprises, which are crucial in understanding of arrival of new products in the market and also the commercialization processes. Earlier researches (Van de ven, 1986), also support this view that innovation by individual employees within an enterprise who are not involved in R&D, but involved in new idea generation could be effective in fostering the success of an enterprise. Moreover, along the context of currently evolved knowledge society, employees need to be involved in innovation processes in diversified ways, such as by encouraging them to generate new ideas and suggestions, exempting them to take initiatives beyond organizational boundaries, or introducing suggestion schemes such as idea boxes and internal competitions (Van Dijk and Van den Ende, 2002);
- There are other activities like spin-off (Ndonzuau, Pirnay and Surlemont, 2002), selling of results (OECD, 2008), transfer of technology (OECD, 2008), transfer of know-how (OECD, 2008).

In the perpetual scenario, one can portrait a picture as shown in Figure-4, as SMEs are acting as catalysts in the process of technology exploration and technology exploitation performing the necessary actions. But, in reality, they need to be under a strategically guided and managed environment to achieve their innovativeness and competitiveness to attain a sustainable economic platform (Sautter & Clar, 2008). This research would argue that a third party in between them is essential to take necessary initiatives, strategies and action plans for providing appropriate guidance, support and directives at the field level in tackling issue, difficulties and challenges on behalf of them. Furthermore, this form of support should be carried out from a platform that would be institutional, so that in time of need, SMEs may rely on and feel dependable. In addition to these, if this institutional support comes from a locally generated perspective, they would feel confident and comfortable to be working with.

Moreover, the life-cycle of technology exploration and technology exploitation (see Figure-4) is not a perpetual one and demands a catalytic agent to make it roll or put in action. This research would like to put forward action plans in accomplishing the life-cycle management of the mentioned open innovation phenomena. It also affirms that a third party or agent of innovation can play the most important role in ascertaining pre-requisites at each entrepreneurship level, their networked level, or even at the level of their human skills. Among various action plans, establishment of a networked environment is pertinent. Utilizing ICT, an extended platform of communication and knowledge sharing can be established (Walther and D´Adderio, 2001; Antonelli, 2005), which can be physical or virtual.

However, apart from the mentioned benefits or opportunities mentioned above, as Professor Henry Chesbrough (2003a; 2003b; 2006a; 2006b; 2007) claims a fundamental shift in innovation paradigm from

Figure 4. Life-cycle of technology exploration and technology exploitation in SMEs

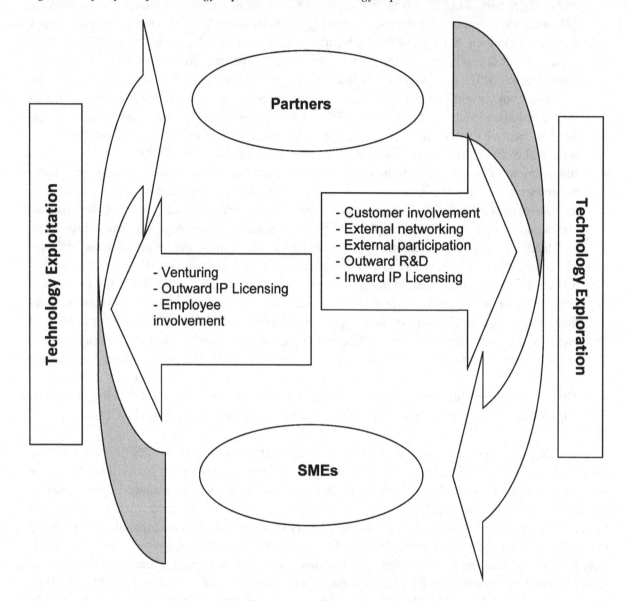

closed to open innovation and advocates collaborative and open innovation strategies and open business models to take the full benefit from collaborating with external partners, this research would continue building on the paradigm shift. It would explore to develop a sustainable business model adopting open innovation strategies to be applicable for SMEs operating at the grass roots. Furthermore, as mentioned by Sautter & Clar (2008), this research would support that, it is beneficial to avail the competences of external partners meeting the challenges of increased complexity of research, technological development and innovation (RTDI), and growing global competition. Along this context, a few challenges are being mentioned next.

Open Innovation Challenges for SMEs

Innovation is an essential element in wealth creation and employment generation for enterprises and entrepreneurs in all regions and sub-regions of the world (Tourigny & Le, 2003), and reflects a critical way in which organizations respond to either technological or market challenges (Hage, 1999). However, dispersal of innovation is a classical view of social systems (Rogers, 1962) that has been revisited by many in various aspects of innovation (Moore, 1991; 2006; Evangelista, 2000; Tilley & Tonge, 2003; Toivonen, 2004; Nählinder, 2005; Maes, 2009) as one advances through the era of rapidly changing technology (MacGregor, Bianchi, Harnandez & Mandibil, 2007). But, the real challenge is not to diffuse in increasing amount of products and services, but to ensure that the diffusion process follow a more responsible and sustainable approach throughout the life cycle. It is not easy to achieve (Hoffman et al. 1998). Hoffman et al. (1998) further argues that though innovative effort appears to be widespread, this does not translate directly into improved firm performance and, ultimately, greater profitability.

Moreover, within the context of this research, when applying innovation in a open paradigm, especially dedicated to small and medium enterprises, situation face various challenges often unpredictable and unfamiliar (De Jong, Vanhaverbeke, Kalvet and Chesbrough, 2008; Van de Vrande et al., 2009). SMEs are characterized by stretched resources, which puts them in particular jeopardy from increasing globalization and rapid technological change. One might expect that SMEs would draw extensively on alliances to overcome their resource constrains and increase their viability in hard times. But, studies show that SMEs´ propensity to co-operate is significantly less than that of large companies (Haagedorn & Schakenraad, 1994; Hoffman & Schlosser, 2001). Hoffman & Schlosser (2001), further state that empirical findings show that SMEs do not fully utilize alliances to improve their competitive position. Furthermore, it is assumed that the reported reluctance of SMEs to collaborate is due not only to emotional and cultural barriers, but also to a lack of knowledge about the specific success factors of alliances.

Moreover, the key issue facing many SMEs relates to how they can foster effective innovation using organizational supporting mechanisms (McEvily, Eisenhardt and Prescott, 2004), and their needs including their decision-making processes often differ significantly from those of larger firms (Shrader, Mulford and Blackburn, 1989). If one would like to investigate in-depth, there is a dearth of research on what encourages and drives product development, management practices and process technologies deployment from a strategic orientation perspective (Tidd, Bessant and Pavitt, 2001). Also, it is difficult to find empirical research examining the association between strategic orientation and deployment of leading management practices or new process technologies (O´Regan & Ghobadian, 2005).

Tools like ERP (Enterprise Resource Planning) or groupware, which are considered crucial to increase process transparency and gain control on distributed networks at global level, are less diffused in SMEs (Di Maria & Micelli, 2008). Often the grass roots entrepreneurs are not aware of complexities of the global market (Tapscot & Wimmiams, 2007), which lead innovation researchers unaware of the local economic and social systems (Di Maria & Micelli, 2008). In terms of collaborative innovation, modularity and codification widens circulation and utilization of knowledge across contexts, but at the same time complicates the codification for promoting sophisticated sharing strategies based on pragmatic collaboration (Helper, MacDuffie & Sabel, 2000; Di Maria & Micelli, 2008).

Apart from these, Chesbrough & Crowther (2006) identified the not-invented-here (NIH) syndrome and lack of internal commitment as main hampering factors. The NIH syndrome has been previously found to be a prominent barrier for external knowledge acquisition (Katz & Allen, 1982). Although open innovation focuses on the external acquisition of knowledge, its underlying antecedents are also applicable to technology exploitation, leading to the only-used-here´ (OUH) syndrome (Lichtenthaler & Ernst, 2006). Boschma (2005) identified various forms of ´proximity´ which are essential for effective collaboration. These include cognitive, organizational, cultural and institutional differences between collaboration partners, implying that potential problems may arise due to insufficient knowledge, cultures or modes of organization, or bureaucratic elements. Other potential challenges include lacking of financial resources, scant opportunities to recruit specialized workers, lack of appropriate information inflow, market entry barriers, increased competition, dynamic shifting of market, free-riding behavior, and problems with contracts (Boer, Hill & Krabbendam, 1990; Mohr & Spekman, 1994; Coughlan, Harbison, Dromgoole & Duff, 2001; Hoffman & Schlosser, 2001; Van de Vrande, De Jong, Vanhaverbeke & De Rochemont, 2009; Lee et al., 2010).

Role of Intermediaries

Systems of innovation are conceptualized as a complete set of institutions and organizations along with sub-sets of relationships among them. These relationships could be among firms, universities, industry associations, scientific societies, professional bodies, regulatory agencies, higher education institutes, research organizations, support entities and dedicated intermediaries (Lopez-vega, 2009) on sub-sets of common habits and practices, routine or established practices, or established rules or laws regulating the relationships and interactions (Edquist & Johnson, 1997). Intermediaries can take the role of adapting specialized solutions on the market as per demand of individual user firms by linking players within a technological system and on transforming relations (Stankiewicz, 1995), or encourage creation of organizations through collaboration and create technology centers or other forms of inter-fir clearing houses for exchange of innovations (Lundvall, Johnson, Andersen and Dalum, 2002), or play a role in policy terms within the innovation system by increasing the connectedness and designing new possibilities (Howells, 2006).

Within the context of open innovation, emphasizing SMEs development highlight the role of a intermediary (Watkins & Horley, 1986) or third party (Mantel & Rosegger, 1987) or broker (Aldrich & von Glinow, 1992) or consultant (Bessant & Rush, 1995) or knowledge mediator (Millar & Choi, 2003), though the role of intermediary for innovation and technology development was already existed in other sectors (Howells, 2006). The introducer of open innovation (Chesbrough, 2003a) has supported the idea of collaborating with an intermediary and mentioned that the time for developing a new technology can be drastically reduced through this process. Diener & Piller (2009), put forward an extensive literature review on the role, functionalities and characteristics of intermediaries, and mentioned that intermediaries connect an enterprise with different sources of knowledge. However, Diener & Piller (2009) also mentioned that, the brokering job as an intermediary is complex, and requires translation of information, communication, and manipulation of diversified perspectives, including legitimacy. But, Datta (2007) added another feature for them to act as multiple value-added service providers, which this research supports.

Intermediaries can act as an interface between the demand side (end-users or firms or other intermediaries) and supply side (knowledge intensive business services, KIBS or other R&D providers) (Klerkx, 2008). Innovation intermediaries are an integral component of the innovation chain (Mehra, 2009), and as mentioned before, in the paradigm of open innovation they could be private entities, NGOs, professional bodies, research organizations, academic institutes, trade unions and individuals (Clarke, 2007). Howells (2006) termed them as an organization or body that acts as agent or broker in any aspect of the innovation process between two or more parties, and Klerkx (2008) further elaborated their functionaries, which include providing information about potential collaborators; brokering a transaction between two or more parties acting as a mediator, or go-between, bodies or organizations that are already collaborating; and helping find advice, funding and support for the innovation outcomes of such collaborations.

Other literatures on intermediaries indicates their role through fulfilling a variety of functions from connecting companies that accelerate technological outputs to others engaged in transfer of technologies (Bessant & Rush, 1995; Mehra, 2009); knowledge co-creation (Turpin, Garrett-Jones and Rankin, 1996); mediation between science, policy and governance (Cash, 2001; Gereffi, Humphrey and Sturgeon, 2005); promotion of neutral space for development of new technologies (Winch & Courtney, 2007); product or functionality upgradation through acquiring new functions in the value chain (Humphrey & Schmitz, 2000; Pietrobelli & Rabellotti, 2006; Rahman and Ramos, 2010); communities of practice (Brown & Duguid, 2000; 2001); R&D collaboration (Narula, 2004); networking (Kirkels & Duysters, 2010); and creation of new possibilities and dynamism with the system (Howells, 2006) by maximizing chances of innovation and increase the likelihood of success in developing new products and services (Lee, et al., 2010).

Development of a Sustainable Business Model

A business model may be seen as the totality of how a company selects its clients, defines and differentiates its responses; classifies those tasks it will perform itself and those it will outsource; configures its resources, goes to market, creates utility for clients; and get hold of profits. It is the entire system for delivering utility to clients and gaining a profit from that activity (Pourdehnad, 2007). Figure 5 shows a relationship diagram with the various actors or stakeholders involved in a business model. This evidently envisages the clear bonding among visible groups of stakeholders among the business communities.

Triple Helix Model (see Figure 6) is another highly discussing model in this arena. According to this model, a spiral of innovation involves government, university, and industry in multiple reciprocal relationships, to create a flexible overlapping innovation system (CSR Europe, 2008b).

This research would like to point out to another business model that may be utilized in SMEs OI process, which has been developed incorporating mixed approach (Shorthouse, 2008). Figure 7 shows

Figure 5. Relationship with the stakeholders in a business model
(Adopted from Pourdehnad, 2007)

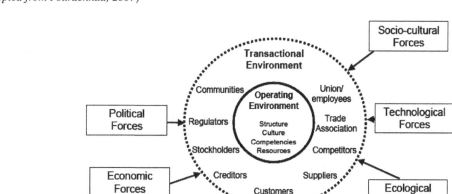

Figure 6. The triple helix model
(Adopted from CSR Europe, 2008b)

a mixed approach (closed and open innovation) business model. Shorthouse (2008) has adopted a joint effort to reach the niche market through using both closed and open innovation business model.

For a business model, using partnership approach as mentioned earlier, Fredberg, Elmquist and Ollila (2008) underline the following flow chart, illustrating the partnership approach in an enterprise (see Box 1).

Based on the above arguments and arguments made by Chesbrough and Rosenbloom (2002), authors like to introduce another flow chart (see Box 2) illustrating the formulation of innovation strategy in an open innovation business model.

Provided the appropriate articulation, however, to attain a sustainable business model in SMEs open innovation, one need to follow the flowchart indicated in Box 3.

Finally, a sustainable business model should also follow to what is shown in Box 4.

Hence, the business model should incorporate inclusion of SMEs inclusive in the following dimension:

The proposed business model (to be adopted in a few selected SMEs) emphasizes on two other tiers of relationship; among the core partners in the network and among the peripheral partners in the network. However, both the segments need not to be isolated from each other. Rather they may remain as active member of the entire community. Eventually, for sustained entrepreneurship the entire group must interact to the grass roots for effective dissemination of open innovation strategies promoting economic and value gain.

Figure 7. A mixed approach business model
(Adopted from Shorthouse, 2008)

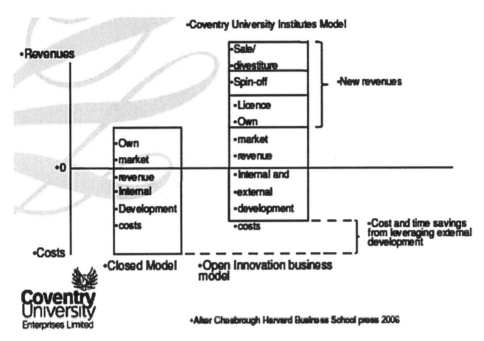

Box 1. Illustrating the partnership approach in an entrepreneurship

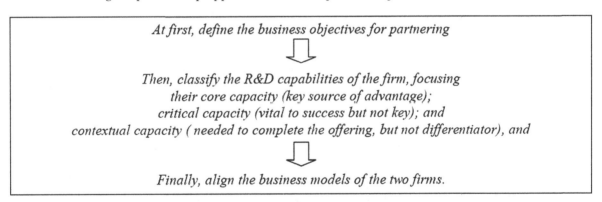

Development of Tools for SMEs Empowerment

Most of the researches in open innovation paradigm focus targeting common stakeholders through major global entrepreneurs or their alliances. In addition, a few of those global business houses are controlling the entire market or system of open innovation development through process modification or diversification of resources or other activities. Despite immense potentiality to reach out the stakeholders at the grass roots through open ended demand, diversity of product variation and scale of economic capacity, major contemporary researches are confined towards generic pattern-oriented clients (Rahman & Ramos, 2010).

In these contexts, the SMEs who always deal with the clients at the grass roots and they have to satisfy the client base the most, though seldom they produce the product. Moreover, despite the globalization

Box 2. Shows the formulation of innovation strategies

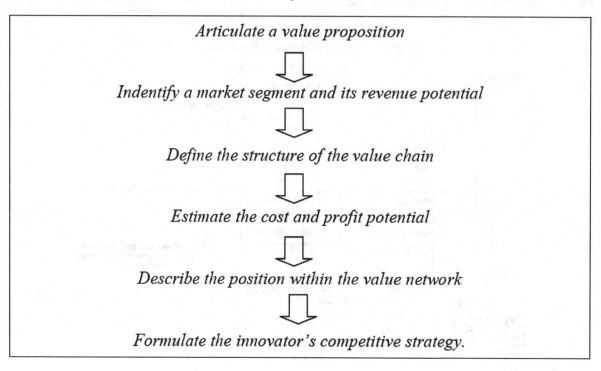

Articulate a value proposition

Indentify a market segment and its revenue potential

Define the structure of the value chain

Estimate the cost and profit potential

Describe the position within the value network

Formulate the innovator's competitive strategy.

Box 3. Empowerment of the stakeholders

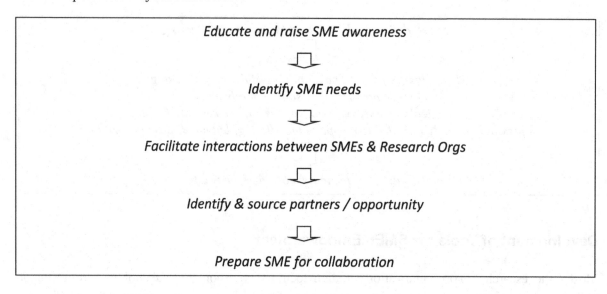

Educate and raise SME awareness

Identify SME needs

Facilitate interactions between SMEs & Research Orgs

Identify & source partners / opportunity

Prepare SME for collaboration

that offers unprecedented opportunities and challenges for SMEs, but seemingly they are thinking of mere survival in the context of global economy, marketing, value promotion, job creation and expansion (CSR Europe, 2008a; b). SMEs in Europe comprises of about 23M€ investment market that account for 99% of all businesses and represent 2/3rd of the total employment (Renaud, 2008). However, in spite of being key contributor to the global economy accounting for approximately 50% of local and national

Box 4. Implementation of a sustained business model

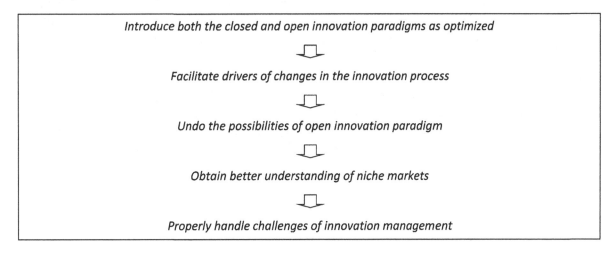

Figure 8. Building block of the proposed business model (Rahman and Ramos model)

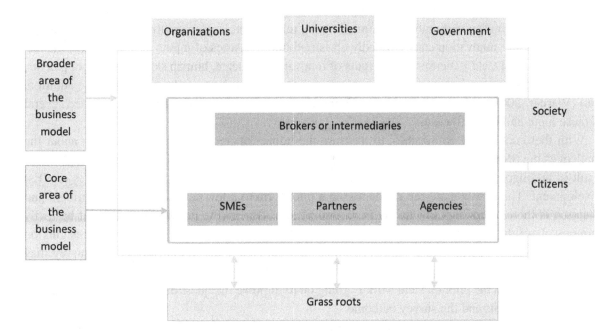

GDP, 30% of export and 10% of FDI[13] most of the SMEs communities are lagging behind promoting their products at the national level, and at the global level (OECD, 2006).

This research argues that, time has come to transform the process of innovation system (through organized deregulation, wider knowledge distribution, focused training, and capacity development) to put SMEs at the heart of the technology transfers as they represent a privileged source for the innovations in a competitive context in which large companies prefer to concentrate on their core competencies. So, SMEs play an important role and distinct part in the innovative activity whereas many large firms are acting as just a systems integrator. However, the challenge remains, particularly as delicate as before, because

SMEs do not exists in this global environment by themselves, they require stronghold interoperability to larger entrepreneurs for better opportunities, to intermediaries for improving their capacities, and to the grass roots clients for offering better services. Hence, there are scope of promoting open innovation to reach out the grass roots, not only through the SMEs, but also through a combination of SMEs, agencies of corporate entrepreneurs, research centres, team of university researchers, and other catalytic factors.

The research further argues that by establishing a common platform of communication as a tool of interaction for the SMEs, can enhance their knowledge about open innovation practices happening around their communities and abroad; establish dialogues among themselves, partners and the intermediaries for initiating improved open innovation strategies; and engage themselves by introducing adoptive open innovation models for sustained business growth. A few tools are being discussed next, which this research would like to develop and utilize.

The Survey

Although it is rationally clear what innovation is, but it is obviously not a simple thing to measure precisely, especially the effect of it on SMEs. Most people would naturally grasp after a few minutes of reflection that innovative ideas usually emerge in the minds of people and then go through some degree of the following: further elaboration, communication, refinement, implementation and replication. Attempts to measure innovation can be broadly classified into measures of inputs to innovation (finance, human skills, R&D, etc.), measures of outputs of innovation (finance, human skills, number of patents, copyright, etc.), and measures of by-products or symptoms of innovation (knowledge, value addition, etc.) (Warner, 2001). Porter and Bond (1999) presented an innovation measure that combined several of these input and output measures.

With these contextual approaches, to measure the impact of open innovation and learn about the challenges the SMEs are facing at the grass roots, a survey questionnaire has been developed. It is the result of an ongoing research work on Open Innovation and Small and Medium Enterprises (SMEs) development. The survey has been conducted in a pilot form to a few selected SMEs in Portugal and intention is there to conduct the survey in several phases. During the preliminary phase, it basically enquires about the general characteristics of firms that are active in the sector of SMEs, insights on business constraints, competition, human resources problem and data on innovation. The survey may be divided into two broad categories; the questionnaire and the interview. The survey questionnaire has been tested through the pilot one and work is going on to improve the questionnaire as per the feedback from the respondents and the survey outcome.

Broad objectives of the survey is to acquire knowledge about the current status of SMEs active in open innovation practices in Portugal. The focus is to know the general and financial characteristics of the enterprises belonging to this category, and learn about their inclusion in innovation in terms of financial, technological, managerial, policy issues and other relevant contexts. This survey could lead to;

- Know about the actual state of affairs in the business sector focusing SMEs,
- Foster understanding of developments taking place in various sectors of SMEs in business development within the country,
- Analyze basic characteristics of those enterprises,
- Acquire knowledge on best practices and innovation,
- Identify and recommend the best practices for policy makers and other beneficiaries,

- Write a report justifying those analysis to bring up a coherent environment conducive to national SME innovation, and
- Put forward recommendations suggesting efforts and activities to resolve impediments of SME innovation.

Similar survey has been carried out in Turkey and a comparative study will soon be published. Efforts are there to conduct such surveys in India and Israel.

FUTURE RESEARCH DIRECTIONS

Despite lack of empirical evidence of its relevance (Batterlink, 2009), benefit (Chesbrough and Crowther, 2006), extent (Batterlink, 2009) and geographical spread (Chesbrough, 2006a) to small and medium enterprises, open innovation has launched a new paradigm (Gassmann, Enkel and Chesbrough, 2010) in business development. Batterlink (2009) mentions about its relevance and extent related mainly to large and high tech industries, and Chesbrough and Crowther (2006) supported them. Moreover, Chesbrough (2006a) pointed about its relevance and geographical spread more or less within the US-based firms.

At this moment, if one investigates over the question, as how far will open innovation go reaching the grass roots clientele of SMEs and what would be the long term impact in terms of economic sustainability, this research observes that future research works need to be carried out to find out above mentioned aspects and issues in relation to SMEs in Europe and for this case, in Portugal.

Gassmann et al. (2010) suggested a few parameters of investigation that would set a new baseline for future research, such as to observe the extent of

- Industry penetration focusing pioneers to mainstream,
- R&D intensity focusing high to low tech industries,
- Structure and composition of partnerships,
- Content and other value added incentives.

It has been observed that the strength of the European economy during the past century has mostly been dependent on large and established firms. Furthermore, most of these firms operate multi-nationally, moving their activities where knowledge, technology and market conditions are most favorable. This implies a new competitive landscape for Europe. In this aspect, SMEs are becoming increasingly important as transformational agents in the economy, as important channels for commercialization of research and as sources of new growth companies. However, the solutions addressing these challenges are predominantly based on a European Added Value perspective, especially when it comes to public support to SMEs, since assessment of growth potential and competencies of SMEs applying for support often requires local knowledge and proximity (Brogren, 2009). Further researches are desired in this area to learn about the behavior of exposed SMEs and implement similar ideas in other regions or countries.

Future research would also need to examine the conditions for change or transformations with the effect that proactive agents have on the reminder of the population. This would constitute a significant research effort, and while future research should aim to uncover clues in this area, and the focus would be on disseminating and improving innovation tool for SMEs at the grass roots (MacGregor, Bianchi, Hernandez. & Mendibil, 2007).

CONCLUSION

It is apparent that there are a range of potential contribution that SMEs can make to economic development at the national and regional levels, that include employment generation (new job creation), acting as supplier to larger companies (in terms of skills, knowledge or physical products or services) and contributing to a more diversified economic strength through the development of new activities, especially through the formation of newly established firms in service sector (Smallbone et. al., 2003). However, as it has been observed, SMEs are in lack of supports, such as finance, organizational or knowledge, in addition to policy issues.

In terms of policy function, it has been observed that there are several un-chartered areas (predominantly visible), where policy involvements are necessary, such as user innovation at the grass roots, technology marketing at the enterprise level, corporate entrepreneurship in incumbent enterprises, balanced (career, work, knowledge, skill) incentives for scientific researches and setting of standard for various innovation processes. There are a cluster of SMEs, who are in lack of conceptual basis of open innovation strategies and for them this sort of sophisticated interventions would not be the ideal approach. Rather to be start with, they could be involved in basic open innovation and interaction skills, and as they grows under a managed innovation umbrella, other strategies could be applied to them. In addition to these, there are also remote policy areas (often seems invisible), such as labour market and skill development, where policy initiation could lead to rapid adoptability to open innovation strategies (De Jong, et. al, 2008).

Furthermore, for majority of the SMEs, especially those operating in an increased dynamic and digitized environment, mere survival becomes the prime factor, rather than being added with knowledge parameters, which are indispensable and important resource for innovation. These include establishment of trusted relations to the community or society (including all partners), and formation of collaborative network among all the stakeholders (Hafkesbrink and Scholl, (2010). Undoubtedly the ability to innovate and to bring innovation successfully to market is the crucial determinant of the global competitiveness of nations over the coming decade. Fortunately, there is a growing awareness among policymakers that innovative activity is the main driver of economic advancement and organizational well-being, as well as a latent factor in meeting the dynamic global challenges (OECD, 2007).

REFERENCES

Aldrich, H. E., & von Glinow, M. A. (1992). Business start-ups: the HRM imperative. In S. Birley & I. C. MacMillan (Eds.), *International Perspectives on Entrepreneurial Research* (pp. 233–253). New York: North-Holland.

Antonelli, C. (2005). Models of knowledge and systems of governance. *Journal of Institutional Economics, 1*(1), 51–73. doi:10.1017/S1744137405000044

Arora, A. (2002). Licensing tacit knowledge: Intellectual property rights and the market for know-how. *Economics of Innovation and New Technology, 4*(1), 41–59. doi:10.1080/10438599500000013

Arora, A., Fosfuri, A., & Gambardella, A. (2001). Markets for technology and their implications for corporate strategy. *Industrial and Corporate Change, 10*(2), 419–450. doi:10.1093/icc/10.2.419

Artemis. (2009). Multi-Annual Strategic Plan and Research Agenda 2009.

Barney, J., & Clark, D. (2007). *Resource-based Theory: Creating and Sustaining Competitive Advantage*. NY: Oxford University Prass.

Batterlink, M. (2009) Profiting from external knowledge: How companies use different knowledge acquisition strategies to improve their innovation performance [PhD thesis]. Wageningen University.

Bessant, J., & Rush, H. (1995). Building bridges for innovation: The role of consultants in technology transfer. *Research Policy*, *24*(1), 97–114. doi:10.1016/0048-7333(93)00751-E

Bessant, J., & Tidd, J. (2007). *Innovation and Entrepreneurship*. Wiley.

Boer, H., Hill, M., & Krabbendam, K. (1990). FMS implementation management: Promise and performance. *International Journal of Operations & Production Management*, *10*(1), 5–20. doi:10.1108/01443579010004994

Boiugrain, F., & Haudeville, B. (2002). Innovation, collaboration and SMEs internal research capacities. *Research Policy*, *31*(5), 735–747. doi:10.1016/S0048-7333(01)00144-5

Bonner, J., & Walker, O. (2004). Selecting influential business-to-business customers in new product development: Relational embeddedness and knowledge heterogeneity considerations. *Journal of Product Innovation Management*, *21*(3), 155–169. doi:10.1111/j.0737-6782.2004.00067.x

Boschma, R. A. (2005). Proximity and innovation: A critical assessment. *Regional Studies*, *39*(1), 61–74. doi:10.1080/0034340052000320887

Box, S. (2009). OECD Work on Innovation- A Stocktaking of Existing Work. OECD Science, Technology & Industry Working Papers.

Brockhoff, K. (2003). Customers' perspectives of involvement in new product development. *International Journal of Technology Management*, *26*(5/6), 464–481. doi:10.1504/IJTM.2003.003418

Brogren, C. (2009). *Comments from VINNOVA: Public consultation on Community Innovation Policy, VINNOVA*. Stockholm.

Brown, J. S., & Duguid, P. (2000). *The Social Life of Information*. Cambridge: Harvard Business School Press.

Brown, J. S., & Duguid, P (2001). Knowledge and Organization: A Social-PracticePerspective. *Organization Science*, *12*(2), 198–213.

Cash, D. W. (2001). In order to aid in diffusion useful and practical information: Agricultural extension and boundary organizations. *Science, Technology & Human Values*, *26*(4), 431–453. doi:10.1177/016224390102600403

Chesbrough, H. (2003a). *Open Innovation: The New Imperative for Creating and Profiting from Technology*. Boston, MA: Harvard Business School Press.

Chesbrough, H. (2003b). The era of open innovation. *MIT Sloan Management Review*, *44*(3), 35–41.

Chesbrough, H. (2006a). Open Innovation: A New Paradigm for Understanding Industrial Innovation. In H. Chesbrough, W. Vanhaverbeke, & J. West (Eds.), Open Innovation: Researching a New Paradigm (pp. 1-27). Oxford: Oxford University Press.

Chesbrough, H. (2006b). *Open Business Models: How to Thrive in the New Innovation Landscape.* Boston, MA: Harvard Business School Press.

Chesbrough, H. (2007). The market for innovation: Implications for corporate strategy. *California Management Review, 49*(3), 45–66. doi:10.2307/41166394

Chesbrough, H., & Crowther, A. K. (2006). Beyond high tech: Early adopters of open innovation in other industries. *R & D Management, 36*(3), 229–236. doi:10.1111/j.1467-9310.2006.00428.x

Chesbrough, H., Vanhaverbeke, W., & West, J. (2006). (Eds.). Open innovation: Researching a new paradigm, Oxford University Press: London

Christensen, J. F., Olesen, M. H., & Kjær, J. S. (2005). The Industrial Dynamics of Open Innovation: Evidence from the transformation of consumer electronics. *Research Policy, 34*(10), 1533–1549. doi:10.1016/j.respol.2005.07.002

Clarke, I. (2007). The role of intermediaries in promoting knowledge flows within global value chains [PhD Doctoral Symposium]. Brunel University, UK.

Coughlan, P., Harbison, A., Dromgoole, T., & Duff, D. (2001). Continuous improvement through collaborative action learning. *International Journal of Technology Management, 22*(4), 285–301. doi:10.1504/IJTM.2001.002965

Crawford, C. M. (1983). *New Products Management, Homewood II.* Richard D. Irwin, Inc.

Darcy, J., Kraemer-Eis, H., Guellec, D., & Debande, O. (2009). Financing Technology Transfer, Working paper 2009/002. EIF Research & Market Analysis, European Investment Fund, Luxemburg.

Darsø, L. (2001). *Innovation in the Making.* Frederiksberg, Denmark: Samfundslitteratur.

Datta, P. (2007). An agent-mediated knowledge-in-motion model. *Journal of the Association for Information Systems, 8*(5), 288–311.

Davenport, T. H. (1993). *Process innovation: reengineering work through information technology.* Ernst & Young.

De Jong, J. P. J., Vanhaverbeke, W., Kalvet, T., & Chesbrough, H. (2008). *Policies for Open Innovation: Theory, Framework and Cases.* Helsinki: VISION Era-Net.

De Jong, J. P. J., Vanhaverbeke, W., Van de Vrande, V., & De Rochemont, M. (2007) Open innovation in SMEs: trends, motives and management challenges. *Proceeding of EURAM Conference*, Paris.

Di Maria, E., & Micelli, S. (2008). SMEs and Competitive Advantage: A Mix of Innovation, Marketing and ICT. The Case of "Made in Italy". Marco Fanno Working Paper No. 70, Università degli Studi di Padova, Padova, Italy.

Diener, K. & Piller, F. (2009). The Market for Open Innovation: Increasing the efficiency and effectiveness of the innovation process. Open Innovation Accelerator Survey 2009, RWTH Aachen University, TIM Group.

Dodgson, M., Gann, D., & Salter, A. (2006). The role of technology in the shift towards open innovation: The case of Procter & Gamble. *R & D Management, 36*(3), 333–346. doi:10.1111/j.1467-9310.2006.00429.x

Drucker, P. (1998). The Discipline of Innovation. *Harvard Business Review*, (Nov-Dec): 149.

EC (2008). SBA Fact Sheet Portugal, European Commission: Enterprise and Industry.

Edquist, C., & Johnson, B. (1997). Institutions and organizations in systems of innovation. In C. Edquist (Ed.), *Systems of Innovation: Technologies, Institutions and Organizations.* London: Routledge.

Enkel, E., Kausch, C., & Gassmann, O. (2005). Managing the risk of customer integration. *European Management Journal, 23*(2), 203–213. doi:10.1016/j.emj.2005.02.005

CSR Europe. (2008a, March 4). The European Alliance for CSR Progress Review 2007: Making Europe a Pole of Excellence on CSR, European Commission, Brussels.

CSR Europe. (2008b). *R&D Open Innovation: Networks with SME.* Open Innovation Network.

Evangelista, R. (2000). Sectoral Patterns of Technological Change in Services. *Economics of Innovation and New Technology, 9*(3), 183–221. doi:10.1080/10438590000000008

Fritsch, M., & Lukas, R. (2001). Who cooperates on R&D? *Research Policy, 30*(2), 297–312. doi:10.1016/S0048-7333(99)00115-8

Gassmann, O. (2006). Opening up the innovation process: Towards an agenda[Blackwell Publishing Ltd.]. *R & D Management, 36*(3), 223–228. doi:10.1111/j.1467-9310.2006.00437.x

Gassmann, O., Enkel, E., & Chesbrough, H. (2010). The future of open innovation. *R & D Management, 40*(3), 213–221. doi:10.1111/j.1467-9310.2010.00605.x

Gereffi, G, Humphrey, J & Sturgeon, T (2005) The governance of global value chains

Gereffi, G., Humphrey, J., & Sturgeon, T. (2005, February). The governance of global value chains. *Review of International Political Economy, 12*(1), 78–104. doi:10.1080/09692290500049805

Gomes-Casseres, B. (1997). Alliance strategies of small firms. *Small Business Economics, 9*(1), 33–44. doi:10.1023/A:1007947629435

Haagedorn, J., & Schakenraad, J. (1994). The effect of strategic technology alliances on company performance. *Strategic Management Journal, 15*(4), 291–309. doi:10.1002/smj.4250150404

Hafkesbrink, J., & Scholl, H. (2010) Web 2.0 Learning- A Case Study on Organizational Competences in Open Content Innovation. In J. Hafkesbrink, H.U. Hoppe, & J. Schlichter (Eds.), Competence Management for Open Innovation- Tools and IT-support to unlock the potential of Open Innovation.

Hage, J. T. (1999). Organizational Innovation and Organizational Change. *Annual Review of Sociology, 25*(1), 597–622. doi:10.1146/annurev.soc.25.1.597

Helper, S., MacDuffie, J. P., & Sabel, C. M. (2000). Pragmatic collaboration: Advancing knowledge while controlling opportunism. *Industrial and Corporate Change, 9*(3), 443–488. doi:10.1093/icc/9.3.443

Henderson, R. M., & Clark, K. B. (1990). Architectural Innovation: The Reconfiguration of Existing Product Technologies and the Failure of Established Firms. *Administrative Science Quarterly, 35*(1), 9–30. doi:10.2307/2393549

Herstad, S.J., Bloch, C., Ebersberger, B. & van de Velde, E. (2008). Open innovation and globalisation: Theory, evidence and implications. VISION Era.net.

Hiebing, R. G. Jr, & Cooper, S. W. (2003). *The Successful Marketing Plan: A Disciplined and Comprehensive Approach*. The McGraw-Hill Companies, Inc.

Hoffman, H., Parejo, M., Bessant, J., & Perren, L. (1998). Small firms, R&D, technology and innovation in the UK: A literature review. *Technovation, 18*(1), 39–55. doi:10.1016/S0166-4972(97)00102-8

Hoffman, W. H., & Schlosser, R. (2001). Success factors of strategic alliances in small and medium-sized enterprises: An empirical study. *Long Range Planning, 34*(3), 357–381. doi:10.1016/S0024-6301(01)00041-3

Howells, J. (2006). Intermediation and the role of intermediaries in innovation. *Research Policy, 35*(5), 715–728. doi:10.1016/j.respol.2006.03.005

Howells, J., James, A., & Malek, K. (2003). The sourcing of technological knowledge: Distributed innovation processes and dynamic change. *R & D Management, 33*(4), 395–409. doi:10.1111/1467-9310.00306

Humphrey, J., & Schmitz, H. (2000). *Governance and Upgrading: Linking industrial cluster and global value chain research*. IDS Working Paper 120.

IfM and IBM. (2008). *Succeeding through service innovation: A service perspective for education, research, business and government*. Cambridge, UK: University of Cambridge Institute for Manufacturing.

Katz, R., & Allen, T. J. (1982). Investigating the not-invented-here (NIH)- syndrome: A look at performance, tenure and communication patterns of 50 R&D project groups. *R & D Management, 12*(1), 7–19. doi:10.1111/j.1467-9310.1982.tb00478.x

Keil, T. (2002). *External Corporate Venturing: Strategic Renewal in Rapidly Changing Industries*. Westport, CT: Quorum.

Kirkels, Y., & Duysters, G. (2010). Brokerage in SME networks. *Research Policy, 39*(3), 375–385. doi:10.1016/j.respol.2010.01.005

Klerkx, L. W. A. (2008, October 26-29). Establishment and embedding of innovation brokers at different innovation system levels: insights from the Dutch agricultural sector.*Proceedings of the Conference Transitions towards sustainable agriculture food chains and peri-urban areas*, Wageningen, Wageningen University.

Lee, S., Park, G., Yoon, B., & Park, J. (2010). Open innovation in SMEs- An intermediated network model. *Research Policy, 39*(2), 290–300. doi:10.1016/j.respol.2009.12.009

Lemola, T., & Lievonen, J. (2008, April 16-17). The role of Innovation Policy in Fostering Open Innovation Activities Among Companies *Proceedings of European Perspectives on Innovation and Policy Programme for the VISION Era-Net Workshop*, Stockholm.

Lichtenthaler, U. (2007). The drivers of technology licensing: An industry comparison. *California Management Review, 49*(4), 67–89. doi:10.2307/41166406

Lichtenthaler, U. (2008). Open innovation in practice: An analysis of strategic approaches to technology transactions. *IEEE Transactions on Engineering Management, 55*(1), 148–157. doi:10.1109/TEM.2007.912932

Lichtenthaler, U., & Ernst, H. (2006). Attitudes to externally organizing knowledge management tasks: A review, reconsideration and extension of the NIH syndrome. *R & D Management, 36*(4), 367–386. doi:10.1111/j.1467-9310.2006.00443.x

Lichtenthaler, U., & Ernst, H. (2009). Opening up the Innovation Process: The Role of Technology Aggressiveness. *R & D Management, 39*(1), 38–54. doi:10.1111/j.1467-9310.2008.00522.x

Lilien, G. L., Morrison, P. D., Searls, K., Sonnack, M., & von Hippel, E. (2002). Performance assessment of the lead user idea-generation process for new product development. *Management Science, 48*(8), 1042–1059. doi:10.1287/mnsc.48.8.1042.171

Linder, J.C., Jarvenpaa, S., & Davenport, T.H. (2003) Toward an Innovation Sourcing Strategy. *MIT Sloan Management Review*.

Lopez-vega, H. (2009, January 22-24). How demand-driven technological systems of innovation work?: The role of intermediary organizations. *Paper from the DRUD-DIME Academy Winter 2009 PhD Conference on Economics and Management of Innovation Technology and Organizational Change*, Aalborg, Denmark.

Lord, M. D., Mandel, S. W., & Wager, J. D. (2002). Spinning out a star. *Harvard Business Review, 80*, 115 121.

Lundvall, B. A., Johnson, B., Andersen, E. S., & Dalum, B. (2002). National Systems of production and competence building. *Research Policy, 31*(2), 213–231. doi:10.1016/S0048-7333(01)00137-8

MacGregor, S., Bianchi, M., Hernandez, J. L., & Mendibil, K. (2007, October 29-30). Towards the tipping point for social innovation. *Proceedings of the 12th International Conference on Towards Sustainable Product Design (Sustainable Innovation 07)*, Farnham, Surrey, UK (pp. 145-152).

Maes, J. (2009). *SMEs´ Radical Product Innovation: the Role of the Internal and External Absorptive Capacity Spheres. Job Market Paper*.

Mantel, S. J., & Rosegger, G. (1987). The role of third-parties in the diffusion of innovations: a survey. In R. Rothwell & J. Bessant (Eds.), *Innovation: Adaptation and Growth* (pp. 123–134). Amsterdam: Elsevier.

McEvily, S. K., Eisenhardt, K. M. M., & Prescott, J. E. (2004). The global acquisition, leverage, and protection of technological competencies. *Strategic Management Journal, 25*(8/9), 713–722. doi:10.1002/smj.425

Mehra, K. (2009). Role of Intermediary Organisations in Innovation Systems- A Case from India. *Proceedings of the 6th Asialics International Conference*, Hong Kong.

Miles, I. (2005). Innovation in Services. In. J. Fagerberg, D.C. Mowery, & R.R. Nelson (Eds.), The Oxford Handbook of Innovation (pp. 433-458). Oxford University Press.

Millar, C. C. J. M., & Choi, C. J. (2003). Advertising and knowledge intermediaries: Managing the ethical challenges of intangibles. *Journal of Business Ethics*, *48*(3), 267–277. doi:10.1023/B:BUSI.0000005788.90079.5d

Mohr, J., & Spekman, R. (1994). Characteristics of partnership success: Partnership attributes, communication behavior and conflict resolution techniques. *Strategic Management Journal*, *15*(2), 135–152. doi:10.1002/smj.4250150205

Moore, G. A. (1991). *Crossing the Chasm*. New York, NY: Harper Business.

Moore, G. A. (2006). *Dealing with Darwin: How Great Companies Innovate at Every Phase of Their Evolution*. Chichester: UK Capstone Publishing.

Nählinder, J. (2005). *Innovation and Employment in Services: The case of Knowledge Intensive Business Services in Sweden* [PhD Thesis]. Department of Technology and Social Change, Linköping University, Sweden, Unitryck Linköping.

Nalebuff, B. J., & Brandeburger, A. M. (1996). *Co-opetition*. London: Harper Collins.

Narula, R. (2004). R&D collaboration by SMEs: New opportunities and limitations in the face of globalization. *Technovation*, *24*(2), 153–161. doi:10.1016/S0166-4972(02)00045-7

Ndonzuau, F. N., Pirnay, F., & Surlemont, B. (2002). A stage model of academic spin-off creation. *Technovation*, *22*(5), 281–289. doi:10.1016/S0166-4972(01)00019-0

O'Regan, N., & Ghobadian, A. (2005). Innovation in SMEs: The impact of strategic orientation and environmental perceptions. *International Journal of Productivity and Performance Management*, *54*(2), 81–97. doi:10.1108/17410400510576595

OECD. (1992). Oslo Manual (1st ed.). DSTI, Organization for Economic Co-operation and Development (OECD), Paris

OECD. (1996). Oslo Manual (2nd ed.). DSTI, OECD, Paris.

OECD. (2005). Oslo Manual (3rd ed.). DSTI, OECD, Paris.

OECD. (2006). *The Athens Action Plans for Removing Barriers to SME Access to International Markets*. Adopted at the OECD-APEC Global Conference in Athens, on 8 November 2006, OECD Report, Paris.

OECD. (2007). *Innovation and Growth: Rationale for an Innovation Strategy, OECD Report*. Paris: OECD.

OECD. (2008). *Open Innovation in Global Networks, Policy Brief, OECD Observer*. Paris: OECD.

Olson, E., & Bakke, G. (2001). Implementing the lead user method in a high technology firm: A longitudinal study of intentions versus actions. *Journal of Product Innovation Management*, *18*(2), 388–395. doi:10.1016/S0737-6782(01)00111-4

Pietrobelli, C., & Rabellotti, R. (Eds.), (2006). Upgrading to Compete: Global Value Chains, Clusters, and SMEs in Latin America. Washington: Inter-American Development Bank.

Pisano, G. P. (1990). The R&D boundaries of the firm: An empirical analysis. *Administrative Science Quarterly, 35*(1), 153–176. doi:10.2307/2393554

Porter, M. E., & Bond, G. C. (1999). The Global Competitiveness Report 1999. In *World Economic Forum* (pp. 54-65).

Pourdehnad, J. (2007, October). Idealized Design - An "Open Innovation" Process. *Presentation from the annual W.Edwards Deming Annual Conference*, Purdue University, West Lafayette, Indiana.

Prencipe, A. (2000). Breadth and depth of technological capabilities in CoPS: The case of the aircraft engine control system. *Research Policy, 29*(7-8), 895–911. doi:10.1016/S0048-7333(00)00111-6

Prügl, R., & Schreier, M. (2006). Learning from leading-edge customers at *The Sims*: Opening up the innovation process using toolkits. *R & D Management, 36*(3), 237–250. doi:10.1111/j.1467-9310.2006.00433.x

Quinn, J. B. (2000). Outsourcing innovation: The new engine of growth. *Sloan Management Review, 41*, 4, 13–28.

Rahman, H., & Ramos, I. (2010). Open Innovation in SMEs: From Closed Boundaries to Networked Paradigm. *Issues in Informing Science and Information Technology, 7*, 471–487.

Renaud, P. (2008, February 25-26). Open Innovation at Oseo Innovation: Example of the Passerelle Programme (A tool to support RDI collaboration between innovative SME's and large enterprises). *Presentation at the OECD Business Symposium on Open Innovation in Global Networks*, Copenhagen.

Rogers, E. M. (1962). *Diffusion of Innovations*. New York, NY: Free Pres.

Rothwell, R. (1991). External networking and innovation in small and medium-sized manufacturing firms in Europe. *Technovation, 11*(2), 93–112. doi:10.1016/0166-4972(91)90040-B

Sautter, B., & Clar, G. (2008). Strategic Capacity Building in Clusters to Enhance Future-oriented Open Innovation Processes, *Foresight Brief* No. 150, The European Foresight Monitoring Network, www.efmn.info

Schumpeter, J. A. (1934). *The Theory of Economic Development*. Cambridge, Mass.: Harvard University Press.

Schumpeter, J. A. (1982). *The Theory of Economic Development: An Inquiry into Profits, Capital, Credit, Interest, and the Business Cycle (1912/1934)*. Transaction Publishers.

Shorthouse, S. (2008, May 29). Innovation and Technology Transfer. *Presentation from the International Conference DISTRICT 2008. International Conference Centre*, Dresden.

Shrader, C., Mulford, C., & Blackburn, V. (1989). Strategic and operational planning, uncertainty and performance in small firms. *Journal of Small Business Management, 27*(4), 45–60.

Smallbone, D., North, D., & Vickers, I. (2003). The role and characteristics of SMEs in innovation. In B.T. Asheim, A. Isaksen, C. Nauwelaers, & F. Tödtling (Eds.), Regional Innovation Policy for Small-Medium Enterprises. Edward Elgar. doi:10.4337/9781781009659.00010

Stankiewics, R. (1995). The role of the science and technology infrastructure in the development and diffusion of industrial automation in Sweden. In B. Carlsson (Ed.), *Technological systems and economic performance: The case of the factory automation* (pp. 165–210). Dordrecht, The Netherlands: Kluwer Academic Publishers. doi:10.1007/978-94-011-0145-5_6

Tapscott, D., & Williams, A. D. (2007). *Wikinomics: How mass collaboration changes everything*. New York: Penguin Book.

Tidd, J., Bessant, J., & Pavitt, K. (2001). *Managing Innovation*. New York, NY: John Wiley.

Tidd, J., Bessant, J., & Pavitt, K. (2005). *Managing Innovation: Integrating Technological, Market and Organizational Change* (3rd ed.). Chichester: John Wiley & Sons Ltd.

Tilley, F., & Tonge, J. (2003). Introduction. In O. Jones & F. Tilley (Eds.), *Competitive Advantage in SME's: Organising for Innovation and Change*. John Wiley & Sons.

Toivonen, M. (2004). *Expertise as Business: Long-term development and future prospects of knowledge-intensive business services (KIBS)* [Doctoral Dissertation]. Laboratory of Industrial Management, Helsinki University of Technology.

Torkkeli, M., Tiina Kotonen, T., & Pasi Ahonen, P. (2007). Regional open innovation system as a platform for SMEs: A survey. *International Journal of Foresight and Innovation Policy*, *3*(4), 2007. doi:10.1504/IJFIP.2007.016456

Tourigny, D., & Le, C. D. (2004). Impediments to Innovation Faced by Canadian Manufacturing Firms. *Economics of Innovation and New Technology*, *13*(3), 217–250. doi:10.1080/10438590410001628387

Turpin, T., Garrett-Jones, S., & Rankin, N. (1996). Bricoleurs and boundary riders: Managing basic research and innovation knowledge networks. *R & D Management*, *26*(3), 267–282. doi:10.1111/j.1467-9310.1996.tb00961.x

Van Ark, B., Broersma, L. & Den Hertog, P. (2003). *Service Innovation, Performance and Policy: A Review*. Structural Information Provision on Innovation in Services SIID for the Ministry of Economic Affairs of the Netherlands.

Van de Ven, A. H. (1986). Central problems in the management of innovation. *Management Science*, *32*(5), 590–607. doi:10.1287/mnsc.32.5.590

Van de Vrande, V., De Jong, J. P. J., Vanhaverbeke, W., & De Rochemont, M. (2009). Open innovation in SMEs: Trends, motives and management challenges. *Technovation*, *29*(6-7), 423–437. doi:10.1016/j.technovation.2008.10.001

Van Dijk, C., & Van den Ende, J. (2002). Suggestion systems: Transferring employee creativity into practicable ideas. *R & D Management*, *32*(5), 387–395. doi:10.1111/1467-9310.00270

Van Gils, A., & Zwart, P. (2004). Knowledge Acquisition and Learning in Dutch and Belgian SMEs: The Role of Strategic Alliances. *European Management Journal, 22*(6), 685–692. doi:10.1016/j.emj.2004.09.031

Vanhaverbeke, W. (2006). The Inter-organizational Context of Open Innovation. In H. Chesbrough, W. Vanhaverbeke, & J. West (Eds.), *Open Innovation: Researching a New Paradigm* (pp. 205–219). Oxford: Oxford University Press.

Von Hippel, E. (1998). Economics of product development by users: The impact of 'Sticky' local information. *Management Science, 44*(5), 629–644. doi:10.1287/mnsc.44.5.629

Von Hippel, E. (2005). *Democratizing Innovation.* Boston, MA: MIT Press.

Vujovic, S., & Ulhøi, J. P. (2008). *Opening up the Innovation Process: Different Organizational Strategies* (Vol. 7). Springer, US: Information and Organization Design Series. doi:10.1007/978-0-387-77776-4_8

Walther, J., & D'Addario, K. (2001). The Impacts of Emoticons on Message Interpretation in Computer-Mediated Communication. *Social Science Computer Review, 19*(3), 324–347. doi:10.1177/089443930101900307

Walton, R. E. (1989). *Up and Running: Integrating Information Technology and the Organization.* Boston, MA: Harvard Business School Press.

Warner, A. (2001, October 22-24). Small and Medium Sized Enterprises and Economic Creativity. *Paper presented at UNCTAD's intergovernmental Expert Meeting on "Improving the Competitiveness of SMEs in Developing Countries: the Role of Finance, Including E-finance, to Enhance Enterprise Development"*, Geneva (pp. 61-77).

Watkins, D., & Horley, G. (1986). Transferring technology from large to small firms: the role of intermediaries. In T. Webb, T. Quince, & D. Watkins (Eds.), *Small Business Research* (pp. 215–251). Aldershot: Gower.

West, J., & Gallagher, S. (2006). Challenges of open innovation: The paradox of firm investment in open-source software. *R & D Management, 36*(3), 319–331. doi:10.1111/j.1467-9310.2006.00436.x

Winch, G. M., & Courtney, R. (2007). The organization of innovation brokers: An international review. *Technology Analysis and Strategic Management, 19*(6), 747–763. doi:10.1080/09537320701711223

Zhang, J., & Zhang, Y. (2009). Research on the Process Model of Open Innovation Based on Enterprise Sustainable Growth. *Proceeding of the International Conference on Electronic Commerce and Business Intelligence*, Beijing, China (pp. 318-322).

Zuboff, S. (1988). *In the Age of the Smart Machine: The Future of Work and Power.* New York, NY: Basic Books.

ADDITIONAL READING

Ackerman, M. (1994). Definitional and contextual issues in organizational and group memories. *Proceedings of the 27th annual Hawaii international conference on system sciences* (pp. 191–200). IEEE Computer Society Press. doi:10.1109/HICSS.1994.323444

Ahuja, G. (2000). Collaboration networks, structural holes, and innovation: A longitudinal study. *Administrative Science Quarterly*, *45*(3), 425–455. doi:10.2307/2667105

Alavi, M., & Leidner, D. E. (1999). Knowledge management systems: Emerging views and practices from the field. *Proceedings of the 32nd Hawaii international conference on system sciences* (pp. 7009). IEEE Computer Society. doi:10.1109/HICSS.1999.772754

Asheim, B. T., & Isaksen, A. (2002). Regional innovation systems: The integration of local 'sticky' and global 'ubiquitous' knowledge. *The Journal of Technology Transfer*, *27*(1), 77–86. doi:10.1023/A:1013100704794

Baum, J. A., Calabrese, T., & Silverman, B. S. (2000). Don't go it alone: Alliance network composition and startups' performance in Canadian biotechnology. *Strategic Management Journal*, *21*(3), 267–294. doi:10.1002/(SICI)1097-0266(200003)21:3<267::AID-SMJ89>3.0.CO;2-8

Blaauw, G., & Boersma, S. (1999). The control of crucial knowledge. In M. Khosrowpour (Ed.), *Proceedings of the 1999 IRMA international conference* (pp. 1098–1108).

Bohn, R. (1994). Measuring and managing technological knowledge. *Sloan Management Review*, *36*(1), 61–73.

Boschma, R. A., & ter Wal, A. L. J. (2007). Knowledge networks and innovative performance in an industrial district: The case of a footwear district in the South of Italy. *Industry and Innovation*, *14*(2), 177–199. doi:10.1080/13662710701253441

Chan, I., & Chao, C. (2008). Knowledge management in small and medium-sized enterprises. *Communications of the ACM*, *51*(4), 83–88. doi:10.1145/1330311.1330328

Chesbrough, H. (2002). Making sense of corporate venture capital. *Harvard Business Review*, 2002, 4–11.

Coenen, L., Moodysson, J., & Asheim, B. T. (2004). Nodes, networks and proximities: On the knowledge dynamics of the Medicon Valley biotech cluster. *European Planning Studies*, *12*, 1003–1018.

Cowan, R., & Harison, E. (2001). Protecting the Digital Endeavour: Prospects for Intellectual Property Rights in the Information Society. Dutch Advisory Board on Technological Policy (AWT). Background Study, No. 22.

Dahlander, L., & Mckelvey, M. (2005, December). The occurrence and spatial distribution of biotech firms in Gothenburg, Sweden. *Technology Analysis and Strategic Management*, *17*(4), 409–431. doi:10.1080/09537320500357202

Desouza, K. C., & Awazu, Y. (2006). Knowledge management at SMEs: Five peculiarities. *Journal of Knowledge Management*, *10*(1), 32–43. doi:10.1108/13673270610650085

Gertler, M. S., & Levitte, Y. M. (2005). Local nodes in global networks: The geography of knowledge flows in biotechnology innovation. *Industry and Innovation, 12*(4), 487–507. doi:10.1080/13662710500361981

Henkel, J. (2006). Selective revealing in open innovation processes: The case of embedded Linux. *Research Policy, 35*(7), 953–969. doi:10.1016/j.respol.2006.04.010

Jennex, M., & Olfman, L. (2002). Organizational memory/knowledge effects on productivity, a longitudinal study.*Proceedings of the 35th Hawaii international conference on system sciences, HICSS35.* IEEE Computer Society. doi:10.1109/HICSS.2002.994053

Koruna, S. (2004). External technology commercialization policy guideline. *International Journal of Technology Management, 27*(2/3), 241–254. doi:10.1504/IJTM.2004.003954

Laursen, K., & Salter, A. (2006). Open for innovation: The role of openness in explaining innovation performance among UK manufacturing firms. *Strategic Management Journal, 27*(2), 131–150. doi:10.1002/smj.507

Lazzarotti, V., Manzini, R., & Pizzurno, E. (2008). Managing innovation networks of SMEs: a case study. *Proceeding of the International Engineering Management Conference: managing engineering, technology and innovation for growth (IEMC Europe 2008)*, Estoril, Portugal (pp. 521-525).

Lecocq, X., & Demil, B. (2006). Strategizing industry structure: The case of open systems in low-tech industry. *Strategic Management Journal, 27*(9), 891–898. doi:10.1002/smj.544

Lee, M., & Grossman, M. (2007). A culture-based knowledge sharing model for innovation incubators. *Proceedings of 13th cross-strait academic conference on development & strategies of information management* (pp. 239–242).

Niosi, J. (2003). Alliances are not enough explaining rapid growth in biotechnology firms. *Research Policy, 32*(5), 737–750. doi:10.1016/S0048-7333(02)00083-5

Nonaka, I., Toyama, R., & Nagata, A. (2000). A firm as a knowledge creating entity: A new perspective on the theory of the firm. *Industrial and Corporate Change, 9*(1), 1–20. doi:10.1093/icc/9.1.1

Owen-Smith, J., & Powell, W. W. (2004). Knowledge networks as channels and conduits: The effects of spillovers in the Boston biotechnology community. *Organization Science, 15*(1), 5–21. doi:10.1287/orsc.1030.0054

Robertson, P., & Smith, K. (2008). Distributed knowledge bases in low-and mediumtechnology industries. In H. Hirsh-Kreinsen & D. Jacobson (Eds.), *Innovation in Low-Tech Firms and Industries*. Cheltenham: Elgar. doi:10.4337/9781848445055.00015

Ruggles, R. (1998). The state of the notion: Knowledge management in practice. *California Management Review, 40*(3), 80–89. doi:10.2307/41165944

Swedish presidency of the EU. (2009, June 12). Industry views on Research, Innovation and Education (Conference summary). Government of Sweden.

Traveter, K., & Wagner, G. (2005). Towards Radical Agent-Oriented Software Engineering Processes Based on AOR Modeling. In B. Henderson-Sellers & P. Giorgini (Eds.), Agent-Oriented Methodologies (pp. 277–316). Hershey, PA, USA: IGI Publishing. doi:10.4018/978-1-59140-581-8.ch010

Valentin, F., & Jensen, R. L. (2003). Discontinuities and distributed innovation: The case of biotechnology in food processing. *Industry and Innovation, 10*(3), 275–310. doi:10.1080/1366271032000141652

Wensley, A. (2000). Tools for knowledge management. In BPRC conference on knowledge management: Concepts and controversies. doi:10.1016/B978-0-7506-7247-4.50008-2

Yu, S.-H., Kim, Y.-G., & Kim, M.-Y. (2004). Linking organizational knowledge management drivers to knowledge management performance: An exploratory study. *Proceedings of the 37th Hawaii international conference on system sciences, HICSS36* (pp. 1–10). IEEE Computer Society.

KEY TERMS AND DEFINITIONS

Open Innovation: Open innovation is the use of useful inflows and outflows of knowledge to accelerate internal innovation, and at the same time, expand the markets for external use of innovation.

Crowdsoucing Innovation: Crowdsourcing innovation is the practice of obtaining needed services, ideas, or content by imploring contributions from a large group of people or individual, and especially from an online community, rather than from traditional employees or suppliers. This form of innovation is often used to subdivide tedious work or to fund-raise startup companies and charities, and this process may take place both online and offline.

Collaborative Innovation: This sort of innovation takes place in collaboration with clients, suppliers, universities, research houses, intermediaries and other partners in a collaborative ways with shared ideas, but envisioned goals.

Collaborative Innovation Network: A collaborative innovation network is a social construct that is used to describe innovative teams. It can be seen as a cyber-team of self-motivated people with a collective vision, enabled by the Web technologies to collaborate in achieving a common goal by sharing ideas, information, knowledge and work.

SMEs Empowerment: It is meant by the real connotation to enhance the knowledge dimension of the enterprises belonging to this sector in terms of knowledge, capacity, and human skills and thereby empowering themselves to face various obstacles or making them capable to tackle challenges to reach out to the grass roots communities.

Organizational Well-Being: Well-being can be seen as a state of complete physical, mental, and social health and not merely the absence of disease or infirmity of an individual. Organizational well-being, along this way can be seen as the organization's ability to promote and maintain the physical, psychological and social workers wellbeing at all levels and for every job.

ENDNOTES

[1]   There is no single agreed definition of a SME. A variety of definitions are applied among OECD and APEC economies, and employee number is not the sole defined criterion. SMEs are considered to be non-subsidiary, independent firms which employ less than a given number of employees.

[2]   Crowdsourcing is a form of open innovation (and in some cases, user innovation) that attempts to involve a large pool of outsiders to solve a problem. Product recommendations at Amazon etc. are probably the most often seen example (Chesbrough, Vanhaverbeke & West, 2006)

[3]   Small and médium enterprises (also SMEs, small and medium businesses, SMBs, and variations thereof) are companies whose headcount or turnover falls below certain limits (http://en.wikipedia.org/wiki/SMEs)

[4]   About Types of Innovation: Tidd et al (2005) argue that there are four types of innovation; consequently the innovator has four pathways to investigate when searching for good ideas, such as: a) Product Innovation - new products or improvements on products (example- the new Mini or the updated VX Beetle, new models of mobile phones and so on.); b) Process Innovation - where some part of the process is improved to bring benefit (example- Just in Time); c) Positioning Innovation – for example- Lucozade used to be a medicinal drink but the was repositioned as a sports drink; and d) Paradigm Innovation - where major shifts in thinking cause change (example- during the time of the expensive mainframe, Bill Gates and others aimed to provide a home computer for everyone) (http://ezinearticles.com/?Types-of-Innovation&id=38384).

[5]   Radical innovation concerns technology breakthrough, user embracement as well as new business models (Artemis, 2009).

[6]   http://www.mjward.co.uk/Businesses-phrases-terms-jargon/Business-Phrases-Terms-1.html

[7]   http://www.businessdictionary.com/definition/innovation.html#

[8]   Examples of service innovation may include: On-line tax returns, e-commerce, helpdesk outsourcing, music download, loyalty programs, home medical test kits, mobile phones, money market funds, ATMs and ticket kiosks, bar code, credit cards, binding arbitration, franchise chains, instalment payment plans, leasing, patent system, public education and compound interest saving accounts (IfM and IBM, 2008: 17).

[9]   http://www.c7.ca/glossary

[10]   www.uen.org/core/edtech/glossary.shtml

[11]   www.c7.ca/glossary

[12]   http://igniter.com/post56

[13]   This refers to firms in the formal sector only.

Chapter 13
The Absence of One-Size-Fits-All in the Day Labour Organisations ICT4D Designs

Christopher Chepken
University of Nairobi, Kenya

ABSTRACT

This chapter covers design experiences gained by working with two Non-Governmental organizations and one day-labour organization for the informal job seekers and employers—day-labour market (DLM). The three design architectures implemented for the DLM organizations are presented. On critically discussing the designs, it is found that even when users are portrayed as similar in the way they work and the things they do, their Information Management Systems (IMS) functional software requirements remain contextual up to the details. The synthesis of the designs shows that there is need to focus on the different functional information needs, including the ones that may seem insignificant even where non-functional requirements may be the same for seemingly similar users. From this argument, it is important that information systems designers, especially for Day labour market organizations, should go deeper into their users and beyond the "about us" information to understand the unique features and requirements of each user group. In conclusion, designers should not assume that seemingly similar organizations/ users can be approached from the "one size fits all" IMS perspective.

INTRODUCTION

Designing systems in an ICT4D context is challenging. It involves making compromises in an effort to compensate for scarce resources (Brewer, Demmer, Ho, Honicky, Pal, Plauche, & Surana, 2006); Agarwal, Kumar, Nanavati, & Rajput, 2009). These challenges get worse when designing for NGOs and other seemingly similar organizations in the developing world. Most NGOs in - underdeveloped regions usually have limited funding and limited capacity. For example, in the experience reported in this book chapter, with two NGOs working for the informal job-seekers and employers—Day-labour Market (DLM), it was found that the NGOs Information Management Systems (IMSs) were donated by well wishers. As the NGOs evolved, they acquired fragmented software applications, which made it challenging to understand and, hence, design any other system or improve the existing systems. When

DOI: 10.4018/978-1-5225-0556-3.ch013

the systems used by the NGOs were critically examined, it was noted that as the NGOs evolved, their functions changed. However, the overall descriptions of what the NGOs did and how they operated remained similar. As a result, at first, it was thought that the different NGOs having similar functions (and another one being a spin off from the first one) may require the same IMS. This was not the case, as is described in this book chapter.

The design experiences for two Non-Governmental organisations and one day-labour organisation working for the informal job seekers and employers in the DLM sector are presented in this chapter. The main components are present the three design architectures implemented for the organisations. In presenting these design architectures and experiences, it is shown that even when users are portrayed as similar in the way they work and what they do, their IMS functional software requirements remain contextual to the details i.e. they still have small important differences which needs to be considered during software design. It is evident that although non-functional requirements may be the same for seemingly similar users, there is need for different functional information needs. Consequently, designers need to know more about their users than what is given by "about us" descriptions. The key lesson drawn from this work is the need to pay attention to specific functional details of each organisation regardless of how similar it is to other known organisations working in seemingly similar contexts. In the end, the argument for this work is the absence of "one size fits all" in the IMS by describing the designs and showing their perceived organisational similarities, actual similarities and the differences as seen from the field work and engagement with the organisations.

The organization of this chapter is that after the abstract and the introduction, a summary of related work is presented in section two. An overview of the day-labour market (DLM) is in Section three while Section four details why there was the need to build applications for the NGOs. Section five gives the design process, followed by the design architectures and discussions in Section six and seven respectively. Finally the conclusion is presented in section eight.

RELATED WORK

Even though reports on Information systems requirements have had mixed reactions, there is a current trend and agreement which point to the fact that context is an important factor. This trend is however in different perspectives. The argument for the work presented in this chapter is the absence of "one size fits all" in the IMS. Other researches in this area have, in a general way, supported this argument. In their work, McPhail, Costantino, Bruckmann, Barclay & Clement, (1998) showed that computers and computer applications must be considered in the context of their workplace. Wilson (2000), pointed out the need to put the Information Systems design process in the wider context of the user. Similarly, way back in 1981, Wilson (1981) had brought out the improtance of context in information needs of a user. Avgerou (2008) has advocated for Research development towards considering context in Information Systems. In this work Avgerou has shown the risks of paying relatively little attention to developing theory on the interplay between IS innovation and its socio-economic context. In their research focusing on the need to balance standardization and local flexibility/localization, Braa & Hedberg, (2002), acknowledged that there exists tension between standardization and localization. Walsham & Sahay (2006), confirmed this and pointed out that, although there is need to standardize for efficiency and comparability, it makes it difficult for the same standards to be applied to diverse local contexts. This is in turn is what this chapter of the book is showing.

For the work closely related, in terms of case studies and context, to the one described in this chapter, many studies, for example Chang, Liao, Wang, & Chang. (2010); Raman, Ryan, & Olfman. (2011), used single case studies or single NGOs. Studies such as Chang et al. (2010); have given good insights on how to use action research and participatory methodologies to introduce e-services in NGOs working for disadvantaged groups. Medhi, Sagar, & Toyama (2006) describe work to design job search and a generic map for a community of illiterate domestic labourers. Medhi, Sagar, & Toyama key objective was to study user interface for illiterate or semi-illiterate workers. Ghayur (1994) describes how a Labour Market Information System (LMIS) can be developed for the Informal Sector (IFS). Medhi, Menon, & Toyama (2008) described work done in implementing a paper-based system that provides the intended functionality of helping match low-income domestic workers from an urban slum with potential middle-class employers in Bangalore, India. Kishore (2009) gives very close arguments to those advanced here in terms of possible ways of using ICTs to help reduce the number of lower-class job-seekers. It emphasises on using ICTs as a training platform to increase the employability of job-seekers. Another similar work is by Kumar et al. (2008) who describe the *VoiAvatar* system which could be used by micro-businessmen (who include job-seekers) to create their own virtual avatars by making a phone call.

Closely related studies on methodology reflection and designs are those by Mcphail, et al. (1998) and Lewis and Madon (2004). Mcphail, et al. (1998) carried out a study to explore the use of participatory design (PD) in a non-profit volunteer setting to reflect on the experience of learning and applying participatory methodologies. In their case, Lewis and Madon (2004), identified a set of critical issues for information systems research that can be fruitfully explored through the study of NGOs in developing countries. They also identified what they called contextual factors that influence the effectiveness of information systems and the overall management of NGOs. Examples included the importance of local culture and context on information systems.

Another study looking at context was by Avgerou (2001). It emphasised the significance of considering the context of Information System innovation in developing countries. However, the argument for Avgerou is that of a situation where Information systems innovations involve the transfer of technologies and organisational practices which were originally designed and proved useful in other socio-organisational contexts, which may not be seen as very similar. In the experience presented here, the cases had close socio-organisation but proved to have different unnoticeable differences which needed close examination for designs transfer from one context to another. Many other researchers have written about the importance of context and PD. For example, Puri, Byrn, Nhampossa, & Quraishi, (2004) reported the importance of context in PD. Steen, Kuijt-Evers, & Klok, (2007) gave a comprehensive definition of methods and practices of early user involvement and human-centred design. Their discussion was on which methods or practice would be most appropriate for which kind of project, or for which goal. They discussed methods such as participatory design, ethnographic fieldwork, contextual design and empathic design. In all these discussions, what is clear is that the user needs must be understood at all costs.

As a summary of the previous work done on this area, it was concluded that there were two main fundamental things lacking in previous studies. One was the use of single organisations or intermediary organisations as case studies. Seeing the small difference and hence appreciating contextual designs and differences in functional requirements when using a single case study becomes challenging. The second issue is that many studies which emphasised the importance of participatory methods such as contextual design process in NGOs (and especially DLM) are theoretical. Although practical works applying multiple case studies have been described, they were done in other subjects such as health (for example Kimaro & Nhampossa, 2005) and special groups, for example work by Blake, William,

Meryl and Adinda (2012). Although some researchers, such as Braa & Hedberg (2002), have argued for the importance of standardization, they have in fact pointed out that there is need for flexibility to allow for successful localization/contextulization. This chapter continues this argument of localization/contextulization by showing the importance of contextual design process and understanding the NGOs by describing three cases of the DLM.

BACKGROUND INFORMATION: DLM AND TECHNOLOGY

In this section, an overview of the context of our study is given. This will be followed by a description of the big picture of the study being described in this chapter and then narrowed down to the specifics that relate to the systems which are used to show the importance of context even where user requirements appear similar to designers.

The Day-Labour Market

The term "day labour" refers to a type of employment arrangement not covered or regulated by formal labour laws (Blaauw & Pretorius, 2007; Melendez, Valenzuela Jr, Theodore, Visser, & Gonzalez, 2009). Day labour workers are workers whose job contracts are mainly on a daily basis. Evidence from the field findings for this study showed that contracts may go for one week, one month, six months or, at most, one year. A day labourer can be described as someone who waits at a street corner, an official or non-official hiring site, or other spots to sell his/her labour for the day, hour, or for a particular job (Valenzuela, 2001). Day labour workers can be described as non-office workers, working on elementary occupations (Wills, 2009) which include carpentry, electric works, plumbing, ship surveying, driving, nursing and home-health care. In this line of work, mobility is required due to the nature of the work activities (Skattør, Berntzen, Engvig & Hasvold 2007).

The day labour market (DLM) consists of three primary actors: the employers, the job seekers – also referred to as day labourers - and labour market intermediary organizations. Day labourers are considered blue-collar workers (Luff & Heath 1998; Brodie & Perry, 2001) whenever they are at work. When day labour workers are out of work, they are mainly job seekers and cannot be considered as employees and, hence, not as blue-collar workers. Intermediary organizations are those organizations and/or individuals positioned between employers and job seekers (Mehta & Theodore, 2006). They are mainly non-governmental organizations, local government agencies, church groups and, sometimes, individuals. Day labour employers hire day labour workers, either directly or through intermediaries. The day labour market provides opportunities for low-skilled, low-literate job seekers. For worker-hire sites to accrue benefits to workers, the other two major stakeholders—the employer and the intermediary body—of the day labour market must also benefit from the DLM arrangement.

Day Labour Worker Collection Points

Day labour worker collection points are usually open air places where workers congregate every morning whenever they are out of work and ready to be picked up for jobs by employers. However, in other places, they can be closed shades or buildings. These spots go by different names such as 'worker collection points', 'worker centres', 'worker corners' (Valenzuela Jr, Theodore, Meléndez, & Gonzalez, 2006) and even, informally, as 'open air labour market'. Figure 1 shows two types of the worker collection points.

Figure 1. (a): An examples of a day-labour worker collection point with a shade; (b): An examples of a day-labour worker collection point in an open place

(a)

(b)

Worker Hire Sites in Africa

There are millions of day-labourers in South Africa and Africa in general (Blaauw, Louw, & Schenck, 2006). These men and women stand at the various worker hire sites every day seeking work (Harmse, Phillip & Rinie, 2009). Even though the field study used as a case in this chapter was not quantitative, field observations from Kenya (Nairobi); South Africa (Cape Town and Johannesburg) and Namibia (Windhoek) gave indications of these large numbers of day-labourers and many worker collection points.

The collection points are in different types. One type is made up of those that are run and controlled by intermediary organisations. The DLM associated with the intermediary-organised worker collection points is categorised as *intermediary-organised* DLM. Although employers may interact directly with workers in the intermediary organised DLM, they mainly interact through the organisations. The second is run and controlled by workers themselves. Workers control such sites through an association of workers. In this study, these worker hire sites run by workers are referred to as *self-organizing*. In *self-organizing* worker hiring sites, employers interact directly with workers or through contractors. In either of the cases, a triangular relationship between the three DLM major stakeholders exists. Figure 2 shows the triangular relationship between the day labour market stakeholders. Figure 3 shows the different forms of DLM.

Figure 2. (a): Intermediary organised DLM; (b): Self-organised DLM

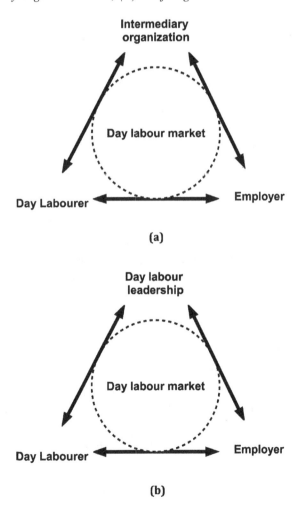

Figure 3. Different types of the DLM

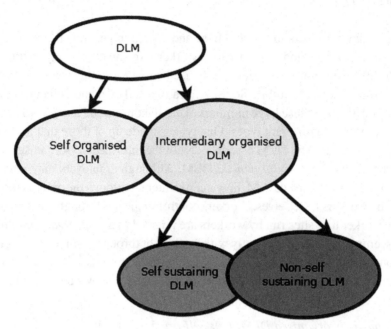

The triangular relationship for the DLM stakeholders. Figure 2 (a) shows a relationship where an intermediary organisation comes in between the day-labourers and the employers. In Figure 2 (b), a self-organising day-labour stakeholder relationship is shown. The day-labour leadership is optional in some DLMs.

The DLM is the general day-labour market as seen in the case studies. Intermediary-organised is run by an organisation, mainly NGOs and can either be self-sustaining or non-self- sustaining. The DLM can also be made up of a self-organised DLM

The Organisations and the NGOs

This study focused on the day-labour market in four African cities, namely: Nairobi (Kenya), Windhoek (Namibia) and Cape Town and Johannesburg (South Africa). In South Africa and Namibia, the study was mediated by non-governmental organisations working for day-labour workers. These organisations are Men on the Side of the Road South Africa (abbreviated MSRSA in this study) and Men on the Side of the Road Namibia (abbreviated MSRNA). In Kenya, it was found that there was no organisation working for the day-labour market, save for commercial institutions in the formal economy.

MSRSA is an NGO based in South Africa and headquartered in Cape Town. MSRNA is Namibian, with their only office in Windhoek, the capital city of Namibia. The two day-labour intermediary organisations were set up in a similar structure and operation model. However, during the course of this study, MSRNA changed their operation model to function as a profit making NGO. Initially, they were non-profit organisations involved in the organisation of unemployed workers by managing worker collection points. The management of worker collection points is done through the field officers who are employees of the intermediary organisations. Field officers are representatives of the NGO at the worker collection points. The same Field officers organise workers and sometimes talk to potential employers on behalf of the job-seekers.

According to MSRSA management, the worker membership, both registered and non-registered, was estimated to be over one hundred thousand men and women. The total number of workers in the MSRSA database was at 19523 while that of employers had reached above 100. The number of workers registered with MSRSA was almost half the total number of workers who were said to stand at worker collection points in South Africa. MSRNA had about 707 registered workers and 47 employers (most of them being corporate clients).

The DLM NGOs studied in this work were MSRSA and MSRNA. Their key objective was to alleviate some of the challenges faced by unskilled unemployed day-labourers. The NGOs were formed as non-profit organisations, being supported through donations. They organised workers through running the worker collection points. MSRSA was formed with the aim of bridging the gap between the growing South African economy and unemployed people with low skills—day-labourers. Their key objective was to increase the ability of people to earn a sustainable income by being employed even on a short term basis. MSRNA was later formed under the same operation model as MSRSA. Both MSRSA and MSRNA used the same IMS, donated by a well-wisher.

Among other things, the NGOs managed the unemployed by registering them as their members and placing them with employers in an organised manner. Their services were free to the unemployed and members of the public as all their costs were covered by donors. Other objectives for which MSRSA and MSRNA intermediary organisations were created include carrying out a nationwide assessment of the workers' skills, implementing training for workers and providing mentored opportunities in focused teams. They also provided a unified voice for members' skills in the day labour market place through communication with contractors, employers, government, the public and the media.

Organised Worker Collection Points

The NGOs facilitated order and structure at the collection point, with the objective of preventing workers from mobbing potential employers. The end result was expected to be an environment where employers are able to request and get the right worker services with ease. According to MSRSA and MSRNA, the impact of an organised worker collection point is significant especially in the small business and domestic employment market. Employers collecting worker members were also brought into the loop. Every time an employer utilized a members' service, MSRSA collected that information and used it to build up a profile of the members' work experience. To support all the operations, MSRSA operated a call centre while MSRNA had one dedicated office-based employee handling work and worker search related activities, which included the following:

1. Supporting the organised worker collection point field officers by confirming details of workers, employers and specific jobs.
2. Handling over-the-phone employer booking enquiries.
3. Engaging in marketing and promotional activities related to job search, for instance by updating members, especially employers, about their free services. The updates were mainly through emails, fliers and media advertisements.
4. Carrying out data entry for worker and employer field registrations.

5. Updating worker ratings. Call centre officers do this by contacting employers and capturing the response on their web based system.
6. Forwarding (via email and phone calls) work booking enquiries to placement officers.

Worker and Employer Registration and Confirmation/Verification

Employers and the job seekers registered as the intermediary organisation members, which is paper based. Most of the registrations take place at the worker collection points or at the employers by the field officer/coordinator. At the end of the registration, filled forms are returned to the office for data entry into *workerhire* system (MSR, 2009). Worker confirmation may be needed during work placement and especially in the field. This is done by making phone calls to office-based employees who then search for the same in the database.

Marketing: Aka Job Hunting Initiative

Both MSRSA and MSR NA would get involved in marketing to create a brand name. Their aim was to reach as many potential employers as possible. Their marketing has a promotional pack with the following items: Skills list, Stickers, Newsletters and script cards (mainly for field officers who interacted with the general public). Field officers, day labourers and sometimes regional managers got involved.

Worker Job Allocation

The intermediary organisations play a central role when matching workers to employers. When placing workers on jobs requiring low skills, placement officers are required to be fair, i.e. no one member should be frequently placed at the expense of others except for cases where there is an express request from employers. For jobs that require particular skills, only members with verified skills can be placed using a flexible round robin formula. Preferences are given to members at the top of the queue but with the highest skills ratings. In all the cases, members are contacted either through a phone call (mobile phone) by the placement officer or are picked up at the worker collection point with recommendations from field officers. However, about 50% of workers picked up are not with the filed officer's recommendations.

THE NEED TO DESIGN AND WHY THE NGOS AND SELF-ORGANISED DLMS

The problems associated with DLMs are diverse. Individual stakeholders face unique problems mainly associated with commuting, and job and worker search. Workers use most of their earnings in job search activities (Chepken, Blake & Marsden, 2011). Even when the workers are employed at any given time, they might not be employed the following day. They are, therefore, continually faced with the problems of being unemployed. As a result, they have very low income, which is not always enough to cover for their daily expenditure (Kumar, Rajput, Agarwal, Chakraborty, & Nanavati, 2008).

The DLM potential employers spend time and money when looking for workers. They drive through heavy traffic jams in developing world cities such as Nairobi in search of workers. In search of workers, employers may pick the wrong-skilled or, even worse, pick criminal workers for a job.

When running the DLM, intermediary organisations spend money and time in linking employers and workers. They also have other challenges associated with job allocation such as when a field officer favours some workers.

The Overall Study Objective

Following the identified DLM challenges, an objective which was to find out the kind of Information and Communication technology (ICT) systems that can help improve the efficiency and effectiveness of the day-labour market (DLM) was developed. The key aim was to collect user requirements from both the NGOs and design ICT systems based on the requirements collected.

The key informants were the two (MSRSA and MSRNA) NGOs working for the DLM. These NGOs acted as intermediaries to members of the DLM (workers and employers). The choice to work with the NGOs was mainly because of previous researches which have shown that NGOs serve as human access points to the community and help in understanding the situation on the ground (Gitau & Marsden, 2009). They have also been shown to be important as mediating agents both for communication and avoiding marginalization (Madon & Sahay, 2002; Eevi Beck, Madon & Sahay, 2004).

RESEARCH DESIGN

The research design took an exploratory approach (Smyth, Etherton, & Best, 2010) applying Action Research (AR) model. The exploratory approach allowed the researchers to gain knowledge about the DLMs as the study progressed. AR is the term which describes the integration of action (implementing a plan) with research (developing an understanding of the effectiveness of the implementation) (Susman & Evered, 1978; Avison, Baskerville & Myers, 2001). It has five steps, namely: diagnosing, action planning, action taking, evaluating, and specifying learning or reflection (Susman & Evered, 1978).

In this study, there were four AR cycles involving three case studies, MSRSA, MSRNA and the Nairobi DLMs. The main field finding was that the key challenge of the DLM was travelling around in search of jobs and workers by job seekers and employers respectively. As a result, the study sought to concentrate on finding out designs that would reduce distance at the same time still achieving the DLMs' objectives. The study commenced with MSRSA because of its proximity to the primary researcher and the support received from them. Initial requirements gathering revealed two types of software applications: mobile applications and Web-based database application. The other two, MSRNA and Nairobi, followed a similar trend albeit the fact that it was noticed later on that, even though the DLM operated in a similar manner, the details of their operations required tailor-made designs.

The Participants

During the entire study period, over 100 day-labourers; 23 intermediary organisations' employees (11 from MSRSA Cape Town; eight from MSRSA Johannesburg; and four from MSRNA Namibia); and the DLM employers (three from Cape Town; five from Nairobi, Kenya) were interviewed and observed. Other stakeholders included (Wiwallet (the organisation which was running the MSRSA payments systems) =1; Author of Day-labourers' characteristics in Namibia (Gonzo, & Plattner, 2003). Also involved in the study were many friends, colleagues and family members, some of who were employers of the day-labourers.

In South Africa and Namibia, the research focused mostly on the intermediary organisations and workers—both members and non-members—of the intermediary organisations. In Kenya, only workers without any affiliation to any intermediary organisation—self-organising day-labour workers were studied. The self-organised group which worked with the researchers in Kenya consisted of about 600 members, gathering in a street pavement (Moi Avenue) as their worker collection point. The figure of 600 is according to the chairman of the self-organising group. The chairman is the elected leader of the workers and is charged with the responsibility of running the worker collection points. There was no any intermediary organisation identified in Kenya. Instead of field officers in a self-organised group in Kenya, contractors or job brokers served the purpose of looking for jobs on behalf of workers. This model has served to the disadvantage of the workers as most contractors are middlemen and do their work on commission (sometimes earning more than the workers earn).

The Action Research Process

Figure 4 gives a summary of how the AR steps proceeded. The target group is represented as NBI (Nairobi DLM); CT (Cape Town—MSRSA); WDK (Windhoek—MSRNA) and JNB (Johannesburg and Pretoria—MSRSA). Although the places indicated may refer to the case studies, they mostly represent the group of DLM studied. For example, diagnosis NBI/CT means data was collected from DLM stakeholders in the specific Nairobi worker collection point and the Cape Town MSRSA organisation and its members (workers and employers). Action CT/NBI/WDK means that interventions were being designed, prototyped and/or tested for the specific community of DLM involved.

Although a number of prototype applications employing mobile based and web applications (shown in Table 1) were tried, this chapter concentrates on web-based database applications and how they supported the overall architecture of the proposed DLM systems design. The architectures show how the three designs had different functional requirements despite the seemingly similar operational models of the DLM organisations.

Figure 4. How our action research proceeded
The case study is represented as NBI (Nairobi DLM); CT (Cape Town—mainly MSRSA); WDK (Windhoek MSRNA) and JNB (Johannesburg and Pretoria)

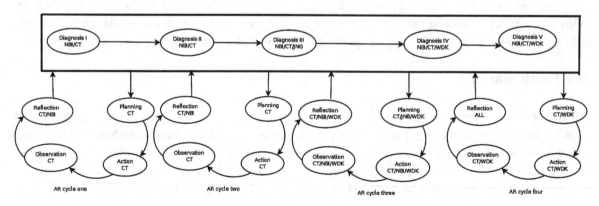

Table 1. The design process of the prototype applications within our different AR cycles

Prototype Applications				
Time line	2009-2010	2010-2011	2011-2012	2012
Case study	AR cycle One	AR cycle Two	AR cycle Three	AR cycle Four
South Africa—MSRSA	• Mobile application: Field registrar I • Web verification module	• Field Registrar II • verification module	• MSRVoice	• MSRVoice • Field Registrar II • Download upload module
Kenya—Nairobi DLM		• integrated web-based Database • worker/employer mobile applications	• integrated web-based Database • worker/employer mobile applications	
Namibia—MSRNA			• MSRNA integrated web-based Database	• Mobile application: Field registrar

THE ARCHITECTURAL DESIGNS

In this section, the various architectural designs carried out during the study are presented. As a start, a generalized design based on the general understanding of the DLM was developed. On being specific to self-organised and intermediary-organised, the generalised design was split into two. Thereafter, the intermediary organised designs were contextulised to fit the MSRSA and MSRNA DLMs.

The Generalised DLM Application Design

The researchers had a pilot study where from these initial field study findings and brainstorming with MSRSA, there was an indication of an architecture that would include a mobile application. The mobile phone application would allow field officers to optionally work from the field. The findings were backed by literature on the use of hand held devices, which show that the use of hand-held computers to collect and check data is more accurate and efficient than paper based data collection (Forster, Behrens, Campbell, & Byass, 1991; Parikh, Javid, Sasikumar, Ghosh, & Toyama, 2006 and Mourão and Okada, 2009). The aim here was then to empower field officers to use mobile phones to carry out registration and worker search from the field without making phone calls to the office. This would reduce on the cost of operation in terms of time and money by minimizing traveling. The response time to employers would be reduced by replicating some of the functionalities that were being offered through the web based application in a mobile phone.

Prior to the study, MSRSA had a web-based database application. To achieve the aim of incorporating the mobile phone applications into the existing web based applications, there was need to extend and modify the existing web based systems. The system in use prior the research intervention had a number of challenges which made it inefficient for the NGOs to match workers and employers. For example, in cases where field officers wanted to confirm a worker, they would have to call the office-based employees. This would mean a cost in calling charges and a waiting time. Besides extending the functionality of the system, there was need to also improve the functionalities of the current system. Some of the functions that MSRSA identified as needing modification included the referencing and worker rating functionality. They also reported a problem with the data validation using the old system. The web-based data capture system did not have enough validation measures to ensure accurate data entry. Amid all these system weaknesses, MSRSA could not commission a better system because the donation terms and conditions of the software indicated that the company which donated the software would only improve the software whenever they had extra resources.

The initial design architecture came up as a result of the MSRSA's need to understand the key research objective in the whole study process. The NGO representatives needed to have an idea of what the research had in mind. Even though the research team insisted on first studying them and then going through a co-design process, they insisted on the researcher describing what they had in mind. This left the researchers with only one design option which was to use data collected from Cape Town and Nairobi, Kenya on the DLM. Considering the characteristics and needs of the DLM and both the software and manual systems they were using at that time, the researchers came up with the conceptual system design architecture shown in Figure 5. The design architecture was used as a mock up design thereafter.

Figure 5 is the conceptual architecture encompassing different modules. It consists of coordinators, employers, administrators and job-seekers as users. The use of SMS and Internet based connections from the server application logic to the users was anticipated. This architecture was used to mock up the design participants who were mainly MSRSA.

Figure 5. Initial conceptual system design architecture for the DLM

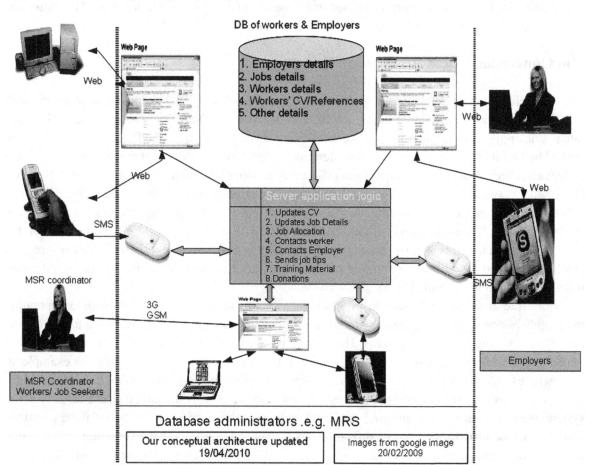

The Self- and Intermediary-Organised DLM Application Design

On further data collection in Nairobi and Cape Town, it was found that there was a difference between self-and intermediary-organised DLM. Their mode of operation and the existing systems brought about two different designs. The design for MSRSA was co-designed with the MSRSA field officers and the office employees. The intermediary organised design was majorly based on the MSRSA operation model and their functional requirements.

On the other hand, the architectural design for the self-organised was done using the Nairobi findings and the comparisons with the intermediary-organised, MSRSA. Many of the characteristics of the Intermediary-organised DLM came out during the design and implementation process of a mobile application with MSRSA (an intermediary organised DLM) and the field studies in Cape Town and Nairobi. Therefore, the differences for the intermediary- and self-organised may be contextual to the Nairobi DLM and MSRSA. The comparisons are presented in Table 2. Figure 6 and Figure 7 shows the design architecture for the intermediary- and self-organised respectively.

Figure 6 shows an initial design architecture for MSRSA. It costs of paper based registration form (1) and the mobile application for worker and employer registration and search (4 and 7). It also has the functionality of uploading data from the local MSRSA database to the placementpartner cloud database (2). Summarised data can also be downloaded from the placement partner.

Figure 6 shows the different modules the MSRSA intermediary organised design had. It had the MSRSA database (MSRSA DB) for storing data captured from the field through either mobile based application or manual paper registrations. The payment database stores payment information of workers and employers. The payment database was out of the scope of the research designs. However, it was a requirement to include an interface that would link to it through MSRSA. *Placementpartner* is a database application for uploading all the data captured about workers and employers. It was a proprietary application that one could only develop an interface to allow for the data upload and download. The need to have an interface to the *placementpartner* was to allow for data collected from the field using the mobile application to be verified before uploading.

Table 2. The difference in operations between the self- and intermediary organised DLM

	Self-Organised	Intermediary-Organised
1	Did not have the support of the field officers.	Used field officers to find jobs on behalf of workers.
2	They did not have computerised systems although they used minimal manual systems.	MSRSA and MSRNA had a functional web based database application for running the daily activities of the organisation.
3	The workers interacted directly with employers.	Employers interacted through the NGO hence a good means of verifying skills.
4	They had no job allocation problems.	The field officers faced the job allocation problem.
5	They did not have existing records of employers.	The NGOs kept a list of employers and workers.
6	There was no champion responsible for collecting data such as work allocations and skills.	The NGOs were responsible for collecting information about the relationship between employers and workers

Figure 6. MSRSA design (mainly for intermediary-organised DLM)

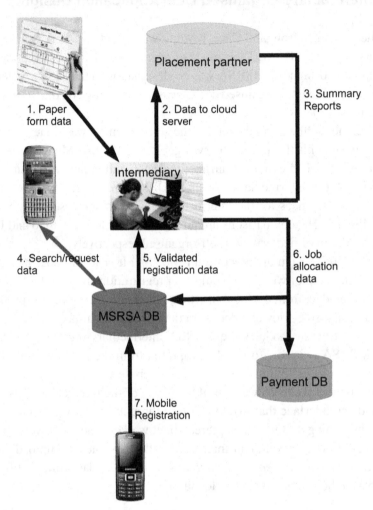

The Nairobi DLM Design

As a result of its characteristics, the Nairobi DLM required functions to allow for automatic data collection and use by workers, employers and members of the public. It also required the means of having the primary users (day-labourers) directly access the system as opposed to using mediators as was the case in intermediary organisations (e.g. MSRSA and MSNA).

Data from Nairobi revealed that there was a possibility of implementing a design that would include other stakeholders such as members of the public and independent system administrators. The self-organised design needed to be flexible in order to allow for system management by various members of the day-labour organisation and, hence, the system administrator module. In the self-organised design architecture, most of the functionalities indicated in the boxes, were to be implemented as both web-based and on the mobile phone.

Figure 7. Generalised design architecture for the self-organised DLM
The DLM central database—the conceptual design after user requirements gathering—stores all the job-seekers and employer details such as skills, job allocations etc. It can be accessible through mobile phone applications or through Internet via a web browser. The users of the DLM central database are employers, job-seekers, field officers, the general public and the system administrator.

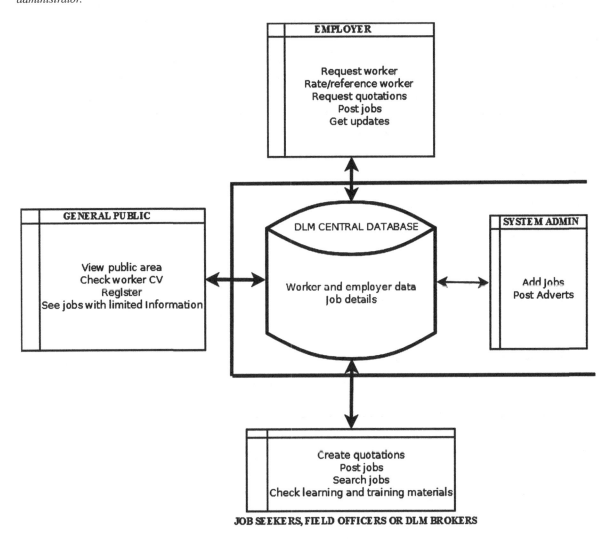

The other difference in the Nairobi DLM design was that the verification module for the Nairobi DLM was part of the web based application rather than separately as had been done for the MSRSA. In addition, the payment module was not necessary for the Nairobi DLM.

The Difference in the Intermediary-Organised

After the intermediary-organised DLM design architecture was agreed upon with the MSRSA representatives, there was a plan to design and implement the different components of the architecture. The design and implementation started with the remote mobile application because the thinking was that the existing web based database application owned by MSRSA, but which was also being used by MSRNA as a back-end server application would be used hence eliminating the need to develop a new one. And because of their similar characteristics, it was initially assumed that it would be possible to design one remote mobile application, connect it with the back-end server application and be deployed for both MSRSA and MSRNA. This was until we started prototyping for each of the NGOs.

The design process involving linking the mobile phone application to the MSRSA server-side revealed many small requirements that needed the extension of the server side. This brought about the verification module and the payment module interface. The verification module had the process of saving verified data into a payment database. The payment database was an external database (out of control of MSRSA) and was being introduced by MSRSA for their newly adopted model of operation. In the new operation model, MSRSA would link workers to jobs and handle the payment process using a mobile phone payment system. For that to happen, they needed a service provider for the payment process. The service provider provided them with a user interface to enter worker payment details through a web interface. However, on introduction of the new systems by the researchers, MSRSA director proposed a design where the data captured either from the field or in the office would also be transmitted to the payment database. That is why the verification module design included the payment database interface.

Figure 8 shows a design of the verification module which would be used by the MSRSA office based employees.

Figure 8 shows the verification design architecture that includes the verification module and the payment module. The web-based validation interface provides a means to upload the data to either the payment database or MSRSA main database.

THE MSRNA PROTOTYPING

After designing the mobile applications and the payment module, and the validation interfaces for the MSRSA, the assumption was that the same was going to be needed for MSRNA. To validate the design, which now consisted of the mobile application (the field registrar) and the payment interface and vali-

Figure 8. MSRSA design architecture with the web-based verification module

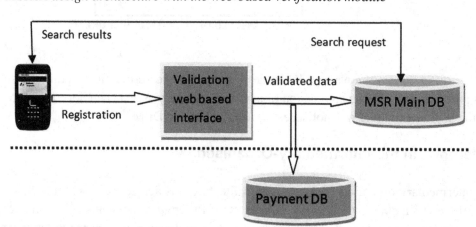

dation module, it was implemented for MSRNA. Before implementing the design for MSRNA, it was presented it to the MSRNA director (head of the organisation) and the three employees. Apart from the mobile application for registering and searching of workers and employers remotely, the payment and verification modules advocated for by MSRSA (Figure 8), was described to them. From the findings through field observations, document review and interviewing the three MSRNA employees and over 40 day-labourers, it was becoming apparent that the MSRNA requirements were different from MSRSA. This, in essence, meant that although MSRSA and MSRNA were using the same back-end web-based application to manage their records and having a similar set of the DLM, their internal operations were different. Table 3 shows the key difference in the two DLMs.

Although the original design architecture for the intermediary organisation DLM remained for both MSRSA and MSRNA, there were individual design differences that had to be considered for the two DLMs. As for MSRSA, the existing DLM database application was used together with additional modules (payment and verification module) to support the developed remote mobile application. The MSRSA design process took longer than expected and involved many extra modules which made the researchers presume that it would have been easy to design a new database and web application altogether from scratch. Having this MSRSA design experience, the limitations of their current database application (which it was sharing with MSRNA) and the requirements findings from MSRNA, a new complete web-based application design to MSRNA representatives was proposed. The idea was to consolidate all the requirements for MSRNA and include the interface to the proposed mobile application without adding new interfaces. The design architecture for the MSRNA applications is shown in Figure 9. It has all the modules adopted from MSRSA design except the payment and the verification modules. As can be depicted in the designs, the architectures look the same but with a number of differences in functionalities. The functionalities were dictated by the internal operations of the various NGOs.

DISCUSSION

In the study reported in this chapter, a number of software design issues came up. These issues and lessons learnt were mainly inferred from the evaluation and implementation outcome of the architectures presented. In this section these lessons, as discussions, are presented.

Table 3. The difference between MSRSA and MSRNA

	MSRSA	**MSRNA**
1	Kept payment details for workers and employers.	Did not keep any payment details.
2	Had no training material requirements. Their focus was only daily work related activities.	Had a training requirement for the workers. In addition to work related activities, their focus was capacity building and skills development.
3	Occasionally collected information about the employers.	Did not collect any employer information. However, it decided to do so after our recommendations.
4	Had many DLM branches in different towns of South Africa.	Had a single DLM branch in Windhoek, South Africa.
5	Used to keep track of job allocations and skills change and verification.	Only kept details of workers but rarely followed up on skills change and verification.

Figure 9. Design architecture for MSRNA

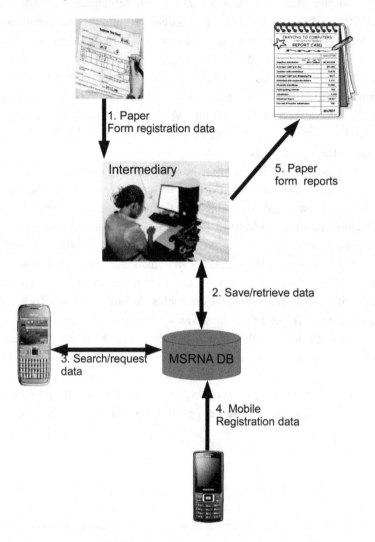

The Seemingly Similar Characteristics

The three different cases of the DLM exhibited seemingly similar characteristics. Even though all the three DLM organisations (Nairobi DLM, MSRSA and MSRNA) appeared like they were similar in all aspects, they were still different in the way they carried out their operations. It is believed that, had the study not gone deep into understanding the organisations, the researchers would have assumed a one-size fits all principle for their application designs. Informal setup organisations evolve and designers must pay attention to specific functional details of organisations as they evolve. This study proposes that it is important to be part of the organisation as that is the only way one can get to know the minute details of the daily happenings and which may affect design. An example was the difficulty of realising the difference between MSRSA and MSRNA, as their websites (even the newly designed ones) still gave indications of NGOs working for workers free of charge.

During the design and implementation process, the NDLM systems were not adopted. They did not go beyond the testing stage. This was blamed on two things:

- The complexity of the DLM: the DLM was being run by an organisation formed by workers, which was very informal in its operations. As a result, the researchers may have missed to model some of their operations correctly.
- The lack of a champion: For MSRSA and MSRNA, the NGOs took charge of the software systems and pushed for their continued design and use. In the process, the researchers managed to understand their requirements and hence redesigned the systems to fit them. On the contrary, NDLM had no one to push for the system usage, and hence collapsed after testing.

The fact that MSRNA systems worked and had continuous changes was interpreted to mean that the researchers understood its context well and, hence, emphasising the importance of context in design.

Monitoring Gradual Organizational Change

The second lesson picked was monitoring the kind of change organisations take. While others take gradual approach, others prefer a total overhaul of their systems. In this case under study, MSRSA decided to extend the *workerhire* system as they abandoned it gradually. MSRNA went for a total redesign based on the *workerhire* system. Although each of these organisations came from using the same software systems, they chose different design options. The choices are related to the small differences in terms of their operations. It looked like, while MSRSA was still following their original vision and, therefore, still wanted to maintain original applications, MSRNA looked like they had adopted inappropriate applications when they started and, hence, wanted to rectify their designs. Generally, they might not have been working in a similar way as MSRSA even though they reported that MSRNA was formed using MSRSA model.

As reported by other researchers, for example Madon, & Sahay (2002), mediating agencies, play an important role in participatory design. It was only possible in this study to understand the changes and, hence, design appropriately, through the organisations mediating for the DLM stakeholders. The process was co-designing with MSRSA throughout and, hence, understing their change requirements. Monitoring the organisation change by being part of it was, therefore, regarded as an important point in designing for DLM organisations.

Checking the Moving Goal Posts

As the MSRSA study continued, it kept evolving. For example, when data collection about them was started, they were not interested in payment details between the employer and the worker. However, in the course of the study, they added their functions to include acting as a payment mediator. Consequently, in the course of the design, MSRSA introduced two new proprietary systems. This necessitated the design and implementation of new interfaces to link the three systems (*workerhire*, payment system and the *placementpartner* cloud based system). This change in the MSRSA operations brought about the design challenge for organisations that change their operations model during the design process (Harker, Eason,

& Dobson, 1993). In order to monitor the moving goal posts and react appropriately, one way designers can do it is to recognize the importance of the local context and doing design from the users' environment (Parikh, Ghosh & Chavan, 2003). This argument agrees with Puri, Byrne, Nhampossa, & Quraishi (2004) on the importance of context in Participatory Design (PD). In fact, the study argues that, even if a designer is doing participatory design without any contextual approach, such minor but important changes for organisations may pass without being noticed. One way of monitoring the changes, which was applied here, is by reflective monitoring concept (Bjørn & Boulus, 2011).

The Non-Functional Requirements

While the functional requirements of the various DLM organizations changed, the non-functional requirements remained the same for all the three DLMS. The non-functional requirements included the cost of using the applications; the amount of time for using the system; the security and accuracy of the data captured and disseminated; and the cost of maintaining the system. For this observation, the lesson learnt is that though the specific functional requirements for seemingly similar users may differ, non-functional requirements are likely to remain the same.

System Alternatives

For MSRNA, because of them having the system which was designed as part of this study as the primary system, their system uptake was faster compared to MSRSA. MSRSA, having had the proprietary system as their key system was slow in adopting and using the system designed in this study. For example, despite MSRSA being bigger than MSRNA, within two months of the deployment, they registered about 100 workers and employers. With the same deployment time, MSRNA registered over 150 workers and employers. This can mean that organisations that have other systems as alternatives are likely to be slower in adopting a new system than those which do not have other options.

CONCLUSION

In this book chapter, a design experience with two intermediary NGOs and one self-organised organisation working for the DLM was presented. The lessons learnt throughout the design process can be summarized as: IS design for seemingly similar user organisations still requires separate contextual design processes. According to the experiences gained, even those organisations working in almost similar contexts have hidden operational differences. It was found that the operational differences mainly affect functional user requirements and less of non-functional requirements. As, Puri, Byrne, Nhampossa, & Quraishi, (2004) concluded, contextual nature of participatory design emerges as the most strong strategy used in various designs. In this chapter, it is concluded that Puri, Byrne, Nhampossa, & Quraishi, (2004) conclusion applies to the seemingly similar DLM organisations working in seemingly similar contexts. The close relationship forged between the organisation and the designer will help the designer/ researcher to notice the small differences and changes that are likely to occur during the usually long study periods using action research.

REFERENCES

Agarwal, S. K., Kumar, A., Nanavati, A. A., & Rajput, N. (2009). Content creation and dissemination by-and-for users in rural areas. *Proceedings of the 2009 International Conference on Information and Communication Technologies and Development (ICTD)* (pp. 56-65). IEEE. doi:10.1109/ICTD.2009.5426702

Avgerou, C. (2001). The significance of context in information systems and organizational change. *Information Systems Journal*, *11*(1), 1365–2575. doi:10.1046/j.1365-2575.2001.00095.x

Avgerou, C. (2008). Information systems in developing countries: A critical research review. *Journal of Information Technology*, *23*(3), 133–146. doi:10.1057/palgrave.jit.2000136

Avison, D., Baskerville, R., & Myers, M. (2001). Controlling action research projects.[MCB UP Ltd]. *Information Technology & People*, *14*(1), 28–45. doi:10.1108/09593840110384762

Beck, E., Madon, S., & Sahay, S. (2004). On the margins of the "information society": A comparative study of mediation. *The Information Society*, *20*(4), 279–290. doi:10.1080/01972240490481009

Bjørn, P., & Boulus, N. (2011). Dissenting in reflective conversations: Critical components of doing action research. *Action Research*, *9*(3), 282–302. doi:10.1177/1476750310396949

Blaauw, D., Louw, H., & Schenck, R. (2006). The employment history of day labourers in South Africa and the income they earn. a case study of day labourers in Pretoria. *South African Journal of Economic and Management Sciences*, *9*(4), 458–471.

Blaauw, P. F., & Pretorius, A. M. (2007). Day labourers in Pretoria – entrepreneurial spirit in action or survivors in a cul de sac? *SA Journal of Human Resource Management*, *5*(1), 65–70. doi:10.4102/sajhrm.v5i1.109

Blake, E. H., Tucker, W. D., Glaser, M., & Freudenthal, A. (2011). Deaf telephony: Community-based co-design. In *Interaction design: beyond human-computer interaction* (pp. 412-413).

Braa, J., & Hedberg, C. (2002). The struggle for district-based health information systems in South Africa. *The Information Society*, *18*(2), 113–127. doi:10.1080/01972240290075048

Brewer, E., Demmer, M., Ho, M., Honicky, R. J., Pal, J., Plauche, M., & Surana, S. (2006). The challenges of technology research for developing regions. *Pervasive Computing, IEEE*, *5*(2), 15–23. doi:10.1109/MPRV.2006.40

Brodie, J., & Perry, M. (2001). Designing for mobility, collaboration and information use by blue-collar workers. *ACM SIGGROUP Bulletin*, *22*(3), 22–27. doi:10.1145/567352.567356

Chang, Y. J., Liao, R. H., Wang, T. Y., & Chang, Y. S. (2010). Action research as a bridge between two worlds: Helping the NGOs and humanitarian agencies adapt technology to their needs.[Springer]. *Systemic Practice and Action Research*, *23*(3), 191–202. doi:10.1007/s11213-009-9154-8

Chepken, C., Blake, E., & Marsden, G. (2011). Day labour mobile electronic data capture and browsing system. *Proceedings of the South African Institute of Computer Scientists and Information Technologists Conference on Knowledge, Innovation and Leadership in a Diverse, Multidisciplinary Environment* (pp. 69-76). ACM. doi:10.1145/2072221.2072230

Forster, D., Behrens, R. H., Campbell, H., & Byass, P. (1991). Evaluation of a computerized field data collection system for health surveys. *Bulletin of the World Health Organization*, *69*(1), 107–111.

Ghayur, S., & Haque, I. (1994). Developing Labour Market Information System for Informal Sector in Pakistan[with Comments]. *Pakistan Development Review*, *33*(4), 1357–1370.

Gitau, S., & Marsden, G. (2009). Fair Partnerships–Working With NGOs. In *Human-Computer Interaction–INTERACT 2009* (pp. 704–707). Springer Berlin Heidelberg. doi:10.1007/978-3-642-03655-2_77

Gonzo, W., & Plattner, I. E. (2003). *Unemployment in an African country: a psychological perspective (No. 5)*. University of Namibia.

Harker, S. D., Eason, K. D., & Dobson, J. E. (1993). The change and evolution of requirements as a challenge to the practice of software engineering. *Proceedings of IEEE International Symposium onRequirements Engineering '93* (pp. 266-272). IEEE.

Harmse, A., Blaauw, P., & Schenck, R. (2009, November). Day labourers, unemployment and socio-economic development in South Africa. *Urban Forum*, 20(4), 363-377. doi:10.1007/s12132-009-9067-8

Kimaro, H. C., & Nhampossa, J. L. (2005). Analyzing the problem of unsustainable health information systems in less-developed economies: Case studies from Tanzania and Mozambique. *Information Technology for Development*, *11*(3), 273–298. doi:10.1002/itdj.20016

Kimaro, H. C., & Nhampossa, J. L. (2005). Analyzing the problem of unsustainable health information systems in less-developed economies: Case studies from Tanzania and Mozambique. *Information Technology for Development*, *11*(3), 273–298. doi:10.1002/itdj.20016

Kishore, A. (2009). ICTs for Employability in India. *peopleslabsorg*. Retrieved from http://www.peopleslabs.org/docs/ICTs_for_Employability_in_India.pdf

Kumar, A., Rajput, N., Agarwal, S., Chakraborty, D., & Nanavati, A. A. (2008). Organizing the unorganized-employing IT to empower the under-privileged.*Proceedings of the 17th international conference on World Wide Web* (pp. 935-944). ACM. doi:10.1145/1367497.1367623

Lewis, D., & Madon, S. (2004). Information systems and nongovernmental development organizations: Advocacy, organizational learning, and accountability. *The Information Society*, *20*(2), 117–126. doi:10.1080/01972240490423049

Luff, P., & Heath, C. (1998, November 14-18). Mobility in Collaboration. *Proceedings of Conference on Computer Supported Cooperative Work*, Seattle, Washington, USA (pp. 305-314). New York: ACM. doi:10.1145/289444.289505

Madon, S., & Sahay, S. (2002). An information-based model of NGO mediation for the empowerment of slum dwellers in Bangalore. *The Information Society*, *18*(1), 13–19. doi:10.1080/01972240252818199

McPhail, B., Costantino, T., Bruckmann, D., Barclay, R., & Clement, A. (1998). CAVEAT exemplar: Participatory design in a non-profit volunteer organisation. *Computer Supported Cooperative Work*, *7*(3-4), 223–241. doi:10.1023/A:1008631020266

Medhi, I., Menon, G., & Toyama, K. (2008). Challenges in computerized job search for the developing world. Proceedings of CHI'08: extended abstracts on Human factors in computing systems (pp. 2079-2094). ACM. doi:10.1145/1358628.1358640

Medhi, I., Sagar, A., & Toyama, K. (2006). Text-free user interfaces for illiterate and semi-literate users. *Proceedings of the ACM/IEEE International Conference on Information and Communication Technologies and Development* (ICTD '06) (pp. 72-82). IEEE. doi:10.1109/ICTD.2006.301841

Mehta, C., & Theodore, N. (2006). Workplace Safety in Atlanta's Construction Industry: Institutional Failure in Temporary Staffing Arrangements. *Working USA. Journal of Labor and Society, 9*, 59–77.

Melendez, E., Valenzuela, A., Jr., Theodore, N., Visser, A., & Gonzalez, A. L. (2009). Differences in the Types of Operations, Capacities and Approaches of Day Labor Worker Centers. *Centre for study of urban poverty.* Retrieved from http://www.csup.ucla.edu/publications/Differences%20in%20Types%20 of%20Operations.pdf/view

Mourão, S., & Okada, K. (2009). Mobile Phone as a Tool for Data Collection in Field Research. *World Academy of 75 Science. Engineering and Technology, 70*(43), 222–226.

MSR. (2009). Operation Manual for use by regional and worker collection points.

Parikh, T., Ghosh, K., & Chavan, A. (2003). Design studies for a financial management system for micro-credit groups in rural India. *ACM SIGCAPH Computers and the Physically Handicapped, 73(74), 15-22.* doi:10.1145/957205.957209

Parikh, T. S., Javid, P., Ghosh, K., & Toyama, K. (2006). Mobile phones and paper documents: evaluating a new approach for capturing microfinance data in rural India.*Proceedings of the SIGCHI conference on Human Factors in computing systems* (pp. 551—560). ACM. doi:10.1145/1124772.1124857

Puri, S. K., Byrne, E., Nhampossa, J. L., & Quraishi, Z. B. (2004). Contextuality of participation in IS design: a developing country perspective.*Proceedings of the eighth conference on Participatory design: Artful integration: interweaving media, materials and practices (Vol. 1,* pp. 42—52). ACM. doi:10.1145/1011870.1011876

Raman, M., Ryan, T., & Olfman, L. (2006). Knowledge management system for emergency preparedness: an action research study. *Proceedings of the 39th Annual Hawaii International Conference onSystem Sciences HICSS '06 (Vol. 2,* p. 37b). IEEE. doi:10.1109/HICSS.2006.244

Sheetal, K. A., Ketki, D., Aupam, J., Abhishek, K., Srijit, M., Nitendra, R., . . . Saurabh, S. (2010). Organizational, social and operational implications in delivering ICT solutions: a telecom web case-study. *Proceedings of the 4th ACM/IEEE International Conference on Information and Communication Technologies and Development* (ICTD '10). ACM.

Skattør, B., Berntzen, L., Engvig, T., & Hasvold, P. (2007). A framework for mobile services supporting mobile non-office workers. In Human-Computer Interaction. HCI Applications and Services (pp. 742-751). Springer Berlin Heidelberg. doi:10.1007/978-3-540-73111-5_83

Smyth, T. N., Etherton, J., & Best, M. L. (2010). MOSES: exploring new ground in media and post-conflict reconciliation.*Proceedings of the SIGCHI conference on Human Factors in computing systems* (pp. 1059—1068). ACM. doi:10.1145/1753326.1753484

Steen, M., Kuijt-Evers, L., & Klok, J. (2007). Early user involvement in research and design projects–A review of methods and practices. *Proceedings of the 23rd EGOS Colloquium, Vienna*. Citeseer.

Susman, G. I., & Evered, R. D. (1978). An assessment of the scientific merits of action research. *Administrative Science Quarterly*, *23*(4), 582–603. doi:10.2307/2392581

Valenzuela, A. Jr. (2001). Day labourers as entrepreneurs? *Journal of Ethnic and Migration Studies*, *27*(2), 335–352. doi:10.1080/13691830020041642

Valenzuela, A., Jr., Theodore, K., Meléndez, E., & Gonzalez, A. L. (2006). ON THE CORNER: Day Labor in the United States. Chicago: University of Illinois Chicago Center for Urban Economic Development. Retrieved from http://www.sscnet.ucla.edu/issr/csup/uploaded_files/Natl_DayLabor-On_the_Corner1.pdf

Walsham, G., & Sahay, S. (2006). Research on information systems in developing countries: Current landscape and future prospects. *Information Technology for Development*, *12*(1), 7–24. doi:10.1002/itdj.20020

Wills, G. (2009). South Africa's Informal Economy: A Statistical Profile. Urban Policies Research Report, No. 7.

Wilson, T. D. (2000). Human information behavior. *Informing Science*, *3*(2), 49–56.

Wilson, T. D. (1981). On user studies and information needs. *The Journal of Documentation*, *37*(1), 3–15. Retrieved from http://www.inclusivecities.org/research/RR7_Wills.PDF

ADDITIONAL READING

Addas, S. (2010). A Call for Engaging Context in HCI/MIS Research with Examples from the Area of Technology Interruptions. *AIS Transactions on Human-Computer Interaction*, *2*(4), 178–196.

Baresi, L., Di Nitto, E., & Ghezzi, C. (2006). Toward open-world software: Issue and challenges. *Computer*, *39*(10), 36–43. doi:10.1109/MC.2006.362

Blake, E. (2010, May). Software engineering in developing communities.*Proceedings of the 2010 ICSE Workshop on Cooperative and Human Aspects of Software Engineering* (pp. 1-4). ACM. doi:10.1145/1833310.1833311

Boehm, B., & Beck, K. (2010). Perspectives[The changing nature of software evolution; The inevitability of evolution]. *Software, IEEE*, *27*(4), 26–29. doi:10.1109/MS.2010.103

Chavan, A. L. (2005, July). Another culture, another method.*Proceedings of the Human Computer Interaction International Conference* (Vol. 21, No. 2).

Franz, C. R., & Robey, D. (1986). Organizational context, user involvement, and the usefulness of information systems. *Decision Sciences*, *17*(3), 329–356. doi:10.1111/j.1540-5915.1986.tb00230.x

He, H. A., Greenberg, S., & Huang, E. M. (2010, April). One size does not fit all: applying the transtheoretical model to energy feedback technology design.*Proceedings of the SIGCHI Conference on Human Factors in Computing Systems* (pp. 927-936). ACM. doi:10.1145/1753326.1753464

Kaiser, K. M., & Bostrom, R. P. (1982). Personality characteristics of MIS project teams: An empirical study and action-research design. *Management Information Systems Quarterly*, *6*(4), 43–60. doi:10.2307/249066

Kelly, D. (2006). A study of design characteristics in evolving software using stability as a criterion. *IEEE Transactions on* Software Engineering, *32*(5), 315–329.

Meissner, F., & Blake, E. (2011, October). Understanding culturally distant end-users through intermediary-derived personas. *Proceedings of the South African Institute of Computer Scientists and Information Technologists Conference on Knowledge, Innovation and Leadership in a Diverse, Multidisciplinary Environment* (pp. 314-317). ACM. doi:10.1145/2072221.2072266

Rohracher, H. (2009). Intermediaries and the governance of choice: The case of green electricity labelling. *Environment & Planning A*, *41*(8), 2014–2028. doi:10.1068/a41234

Sein, M., Henfridsson, O., Purao, S., Rossi, M., & Lindgren, R. (2011). Action design research.

Stonebraker, M., & Çetintemel, U. (2005, April). "One size fits all": an idea whose time has come and gone. *Proceedings of the 21st International Conference on Data Engineering ICDE '05* (pp. 2-11). IEEE.

van Reijswoud, V. (2009). Appropriate ICT as a Tool to Increase Effectiveness in ICT4D: Theoretical considerations and illustrating cases. *The Electronic Journal of Information Systems in Developing Countries, 38*.

Whyte, W. F. E. (1991). *Participatory action research*. Sage Publications, Inc.

Zhang, C., & Budgen, D. (2012). What do we know about the effectiveness of software design patterns? *IEEE Transactions on* Software Engineering, *38*(5), 1213–1231.

KEY TERMS AND DEFINITIONS

Day Labour Market: This is a market environment which is made up of three primary main actors: the employers, the job-seekers, (day-labourers) and optionally the intermediary organisations.

Day-Labourers: Are non-skilled, low-skilled, illiterate or semi-literate workers whose contracts are on a daily basis. They work in a type of employment arrangement not covered or regulated by formal labour laws.

Design Context: A design (mainly software) environment which exhibits a unique set of characteristics which may seem similar to other context especially when not critically examined.

Job-Seeker: Is described as someone who is unemployed and are actively involved in job search activities such as availing themselves to a worker collection point with the intention of securing a job.

One-Size-Fits-All: This is a software design description which means that a software application can be designed for one organization and then deployed for many similar organizations regardless of their context.

Compilation of References

Advanced Online Collaboration. (n. d.). Where Creative Minds Meld. Retrieved from http://www.yorku.ca/dzwick/what_is_octopz.htm

(2012, January). Kang, Kyung-Nam & Park, H. (2012). Original Research Article. *Technovation*, *32*(1), 68–78.

. The Data Warehousing Institute (TDWI). (2014). Retrieved from http://tdwi.org/Home.aspx

Abouzeid, A., Bajda-Pawlikowski, K., Abadi, D. J., Rasin, A., & Silberschatz, A. (2009). HadoopDB: An Architectural Hybrid of MapReduce and DBMS Technologies for Analytical Workloads. *The Proceedings of the VLDB Endowment*, *2*(1), 922–933. doi:10.14778/1687627.1687731

Abraham, R. (2011). The poor are no different from us. *The Economist*. Retrieved from http://www.economist.com/blogs/banyan/2011/10/reuben-abraham-market-solutions

Abraham, R. (2006). Mobile phones and economic development: Evidence from the fishing industry in India. *Information Technologies and International Development*, *4*(1), 5–17.

Acemoglu, D., & Robinson, A. J. (2013). *Why nations fail: The origins of power, prosperity and poverty*. London: Profile Books.

Actuate Corporation. (2014). Actuate/BIRT BI. Retrieved from **Error! Hyperlink reference not valid.**http://www.actuate.com/

Adair, J. (1984). The Hawthorne effect: A reconsideration of the methodological artifact. *The Journal of Applied Psychology*, *69*(2), 334–345. doi:10.1037/0021-9010.69.2.334

Adrian, M. (2010). Exploring the Extremes of Database Growth. IBM Data Management, Issue 1.

Agarwal, S. K., Kumar, A., Nanavati, A. A., & Rajput, N. (2009). Content creation and dissemination by-and-for users in rural areas. *Proceedings of the 2009 International Conference on Information and Communication Technologies and Development (ICTD)* (pp. 56-65). IEEE. doi:10.1109/ICTD.2009.5426702

Aggarwal, A., & Bento, R. (2002). Web-Based Education. Hershey, PA, USA: IGI Global.

Agrawal, D., ... (2014). Challenges and opportunities with big data. Leading researchers across the United States, Tech. Rep., Retrieved from http://www.cra.org/ccc/files/docs/init/bigdatawhitepaper.pdf

Aldrich, H. E., & von Glinow, M. A. (1992). Business start-ups: the HRM imperative. In S. Birley & I. C. MacMillan (Eds.), *International Perspectives on Entrepreneurial Research* (pp. 233–253). New York: North-Holland.

Alexander, S. (2001). E-learning developments and experiences. *Education + Training*, *43*(4-5), 240-248.

Al-Fahad, F. (2009). Students' attitudes and perceptions towards the effectiveness of mobile learning in king Saud University, Saudi Arabia. *The Turkish Online Journal of Educational Technology, 8*(2). Retrieved November 18, 2012, from http://www.tojet.net/articles/8210.pdf

Alkire, S., Roche, M. J., & Sumner, A. (2013). Where do the world's multidimensionally poor people live? *Oxford University Department of International Development OPHDI Working Papers No 61.* Retrieved from http://www.ophi. org.uk/resources/ophi-working-papers/

Alkire, S. et al.. (2015). *Multidimensional poverty index: Measurement and analysis.* New York, NY: Oxford University Press. doi:10.1093/acprof:oso/9780199689491.001.0001

Amara, N., Landry, R., Becheikh, N., & Ouimet, M. (2008). Learning and novelty of innovation in established manufacturing SMEs. *Technovation, 28*(7), 450–463. doi:10.1016/j.technovation.2008.02.001

Aminuzzaman, M. S. (2002). Cellular phones in rural Bangladesh: A study of the Village Pay Phone of Grameen Bank. In A. Goldstein & D. O'Connor (Eds.), *Electronic commerce for development* (pp. 161–178). Paris: OECD.

Aminuzzaman, S., Baldersheim, H., & Jamil, I. (2003). Talking back! Empowerment and mobile phones in rural Bangladesh: A study of the village phone scheme of Grameen Bank. *Contemporary South Asia, 12*(3), 327–348. doi:10.1080/0958493032000175879

Analytics. (2014a). Why big data analytics as a service? Analytics as a Service. Retrieved from http://www.analyticsasaservice.org/why-big-data-analytics-as-a-service/

Analytics. (2014b). What is Big Data? Analytics as a Service in the Cloud. Analytics as a Service. Retrieved from http://www.analyticsasaservice.org/what-is-big-data-analytics-as-a-service-in-the-cloud/

Andersen, K. (2011, December 14). The protestor. *Time.*

Anokwa, Y., Smyth, T., Ramachandran, D., Sherwani, J., Schwartzman, Y., Luk, R., & DeRenzi, B. (2009). Stories from the field: Reflections on HCI4D experiences. *Information Technologies and International Development, 5*(4), 101–115.

Antonelli, C. (2005). Models of knowledge and systems of governance. *Journal of Institutional Economics, 1*(1), 51–73. doi:10.1017/S1744137405000044

Argyriades, D. (2010). From bureaucracy to debureaucratization? *Public Organization Review, 10*(3), 275–297. doi:10.1007/s11115-010-0136-1

Armstrong, K. (2001). *Buddha.* New York, NY: Penguin.

Arnason, P. J. (2002). Multiple modernities and civilizational contexts: Reflections on the Japanese experience. In J. P. Arnason (Ed.), *The peripheral centre: Essays on Japanese history and civilization* (pp. 132–157). Melbourne, Australia: Trans Pacific Press.

Arnstein, S. (1969). A ladder of citizen participation. *Journal of the American Institute of Planners, 37*(7), 216–224. doi:10.1080/01944366908977225

Arora, A. (2002). Licensing tacit knowledge: Intellectual property rights and the market for know-how. *Economics of Innovation and New Technology, 4*(1), 41–59. doi:10.1080/10438599500000013

Arora, A., Fosfuri, A., & Gambardella, A. (2001). Markets for technology and their implications for corporate strategy. *Industrial and Corporate Change, 10*(2), 419–450. doi:10.1093/icc/10.2.419

Arsham, H. (2015). Applied Management Science: Making Good Strategic Decisions. Retrieved from http://home.ubalt. edu/ntsbarsh/opre640/opre640.htm

Artemis. (2009). Multi-Annual Strategic Plan and Research Agenda 2009.

Ashraf, Q. H., Weil, D. N., & Wilde, J. (2013). The effect of fertility reduction on economic growth. *Population and Development Review*, *39*(1), 97–130. doi:10.1111/j.1728-4457.2013.00575.x PMID:25525283

Autant-Bernard, C., Fadairo, M. & Massard, N. (2012). Knowledge diffusion and innovation policies within the European regions: Challenges based on recent empirical evidence. Original Research Article, Research Policy, In Press, Corrected Proof, Available online 10 August 2012.10.1016/j.respol.2012.07.009

Avgerou, C. (2001). The significance of context in information systems and organizational change. *Information Systems Journal*, *11*(1), 1365–2575. doi:10.1046/j.1365-2575.2001.00095.x

Avgerou, C. (2008). Information systems in developing countries: A critical research review. *Journal of Information Technology*, *23*(3), 133–146. doi:10.1057/palgrave.jit.2000136

Avison, D., Baskerville, R., & Myers, M. (2001). Controlling action research projects.[MCB UP Ltd]. *Information Technology & People*, *14*(1), 28–45. doi:10.1108/09593840110384762

Bakalu, B. (2014). Luweero passes law on 'radios'. *Cpanel Observer*. Retrieved from http://www.cpanel.observer.ug/index.php?option=com_content&view=article&id=30177:-luweero-passes-law-on-radios&catid=34:news&Itemid=114

Baker, M. (2006). Translation and activism: Emerging patterns of narrative community. *The Massachusetts Review*, *47*(3), 462–484.

Baliamoune-Lutz, M. (2003). An analysis of the determinants and effects of ICT diffusion in developing countries. *Information Technology for Development*, *10*(1), 151–169. doi:10.1002/itdj.1590100303

Banda, F. (2010). *Citizen journalism and democracy in Africa: An exploratory study*. Grahamstown, South Africa: Highway Africa.

Bank for the poor. (2014). *Grameen Bank*. Retrieved from http://www.grameen.com/

Baran, S., & Davis, D. (2003). *Mass Communication Theory: Foundation, Ferment, and Future*. California: Wordsworth.

Barney, J., & Clark, D. (2007). *Resource-based Theory: Creating and Sustaining Competitive Advantage*. NY: Oxford University Prass.

Barth, M. et al. (2000). Developing Key Competencies for Sustainable Development in Higher Education. *International Journal of Sustainability in Higher Education*.

Bates, P., Biere, M., Weideranders, R., Meyer, A., & Wong, B. (2009). New Intelligence for a Smarter Planet. Retrieved from http://www-01.ibm.com/common/ssi/cgi-bin/ssialias?infotype=PM&subtype=BK&appname=SWGE_IM_DD_US EN&htmlfid=IMM14055USEN&attachment=IMM14055USEN.PDF

Bates, T. R. (1975). Gramsci and the theory of hegemony. *Journal of the History of Ideas*, *36*(2), 351–366. doi:10.2307/2708933

Batterlink, M. (2009) Profiting from external knowledge: How companies use different knowledge acquisition strategies to improve their innovation performance [PhD thesis]. Wageningen University.

Beck, E., Madon, S., & Sahay, S. (2004). On the margins of the "information society": A comparative study of mediation. *The Information Society*, *20*(4), 279–290. doi:10.1080/01972240490481009

Becker. (2000). *The Digital Disconnect: The Widening Gap Between Internet-Savvy Students and Their Schools*.

Bell, M., & Pavitt, K. L. R. (1993). Technological accumulation and industrial growth: Contrasts between developed and developing countries. *Industrial and Corporate Change, 2*(1), 157–210. doi:10.1093/icc/2.1.157

Bell, S., & Shank, J. (2007). *Academic Librarianship by Design: A Blended Librarian's Guide to the Tools and Techniques*. Chicago: ALA.

Belussi, F., Sammarra, A., & Sedita, S. R. (2010). Learning at the boundaries in an "Open Regional Innovation System": A focus on firms' innovation strategies in the Emilia Romagna life science industry. *Research Policy, 39*(6), 710–721. doi:10.1016/j.respol.2010.01.014

Berger, G. (2010). *Challenges and perspectives of digital migration for Africa*. Dakar: Panos West Africa.

Berger, L. P., Berger, B., & Kellner, H. (1973). *The homeless mind: Modernization and consciousness*. Oxford, UK: Penguin.

Bernal, M. (2000). Animadversions in the origins of Western science. In M. H. Shank (Ed.), *The scientific enterprise in Antiquity and the Middle Ages* (pp. 72–83). Chicago: Chicago University Press.

Berthon, H., & Webb, C. (2000). The Moving Frontier: Archiving, Preservation and Tomorrow's Digital Heritage. Paper presented at VALA 2000 - 10th VALA Biennial Conference and Exhibition, Melbourne, Victoria, 16 - 18 February, 2000. Retrieved from http://www.nla.gov.au/nla/staffpapers/hberthon2.html

Bessant, J., & Rush, H. (1995). Building bridges for innovation: The role of consultants in technology transfer. *Research Policy, 24*(1), 97–114. doi:10.1016/0048-7333(93)00751-F

Bessant, J., & Tidd, J. (2007). *Innovation and Entrepreneurship*. Wiley.

Bessen, J. (2006). Open Source Software: Free Provision of Complex Public Goods. In J. Bitzer & P. J. H. Schröder (Eds.), *The Economics of Open Source Software Development*. Elsevier B.V. doi:10.1016/B978-044452769-1/50003-2

Best, M., Thakur, D., & Kolko, B. (2009). The contribution of user-based subsidies to the impact and sustainability of telecenters – The eCenter Project in Kyrgyzstan. *Paper presented at the 3rd International Conference on Information and Communication Technologies and Development*, Education City, Doha, Qatar.

Bianchi, M., Campodall'Orto, S., Frattini, F., & Vercesi, P. (2010). Enabling open innovation in small- and medium-sized enterprises: How to find alternative applications for your technologies. *R & D Management, 40*(4), 414–431. doi:10.1111/j.1467-9310.2010.00613.x

Bilby, M. (2014, June 17-22). Collaborative Student Research with Google Drive: Advantages and Challenges. *Presentation at the annual conference of the American Theological Library Association*, New Orleans, LA. Retrieved from http://lanyrd.com/sctzbt

Björk, B.-C., Welling, P., Laakso, M., Majlender, P., Hedlund, T., ... (2010). Open Access to the Scientific Journal Literature. *PLoS ONE, 5*(6). Retrieved from www.plosone.org/article/info:doi/10.1371/journal.pone.0011273

Bjørn, P., & Boulus, N. (2011). Dissenting in reflective conversations: Critical components of doing action research. *Action Research, 9*(3), 282–302. doi:10.1177/1476750310396949

Blaauw, D., Louw, H., & Schenck, R. (2006). The employment history of day labourers in South Africa and the income they earn. a case study of day labourers in Pretoria. *South African Journal of Economic and Management Sciences, 9*(4), 458–471.

Blaauw, P. F., & Pretorius, A. M. (2007). Day labourers in Pretoria – entrepreneurial spirit in action or survivors in a cul de sac? *SA Journal of Human Resource Management, 5*(1), 65–70. doi:10.4102/sajhrm.v5i1.109

Blake, E. H., Tucker, W. D., Glaser, M., & Freudenthal, A. (2011). Deaf telephony: Community-based co-design. In *Interaction design: beyond human-computer interaction* (pp. 412-413).

Blom, J., Chipchase, J., & Lehikoinen, J. (2005). Contextual and cultural challenges for user mobility research. *Communications of the ACM, 48*(7), 37–41. doi:10.1145/1070838.1070863

Blumberg, R., & Atre, S. (2003). The problem with unstructured data. *DM Review, 13*(2), 42–49.

Blunt, P., & Jones, M. L. (1992). *Managing Organisations in Africa*. Berlin: Walter de Gruyter. doi:10.1515/9783110850031

BOAI: Budapest Open Access Initiative. (Last revised December 16, 2011). Frequently Asked Questions. Retrieved from http://www.earlham.edu/~peters/fos/boaifaq.htm

Bobish, G. (2011). Participation and Pedagogy: Connecting the Social Web to ACRL Learning Outcomes. *Journal of Academic Librarianship, 37*(1), 54–63. doi:10.1016/j.acalib.2010.10.007

Boer, H., Hill, M., & Krabbendam, K. (1990). FMS implementation management: Promise and performance. *International Journal of Operations & Production Management, 10*(1), 5–20. doi:10.1108/01443579010004994

Bonner, J., & Walker, O. (2004). Selecting influential business-to-business customers in new product development: Relational embeddedness and knowledge heterogeneity considerations. *Journal of Product Innovation Management, 21*(3), 155–169. doi:10.1111/j.0737-6782.2004.00067.x

Borlaug, E. N. (2000b). *The Green Revolution revisited and the road ahead*. Retrieved from http://nobelprize.org/nobel_prizes/peace/laureates/1970/borlaug-lecture.pdf

Borlaug, E. N. (2000a). Ending world hunger: The promise of biotechnology and the threat of antiscience zealotry. *Plant Physiology, 124*(2), 487–490. doi:10.1104/pp.124.2.487 PMID:11027697

Boschma, R. A. (2005). Proximity and innovation: A critical assessment. *Regional Studies, 39*(1), 61–74. doi:10.1080/0034340052000320887

Bougrain, F., & Haudeville, B. (2002). Innovation, collaboration and SMEs internal research capacities. *Research Policy, 31*(5), 735–747. doi:10.1016/S0048-7333(01)00144-5

Box, S. (2009). OECD Work on Innovation- A Stocktaking of Existing Work. OECD Science, Technology & Industry Working Papers.

Braa, J., & Hedberg, C. (2002). The struggle for district-based health information systems in South Africa. *The Information Society, 18*(2), 113–127. doi:10.1080/01972240290075048

Braa, J., Monteiro, E., & Sahay, S. (2004). Networks of action: Sustainable health information systems across developing nations. *Management Information Systems Quarterly, 28*, 337–362.

Brandenburger, A., & Nalebuff, B. (1996). *Co-Opetition*. New York: Doubleday.

Brewer, E., Demmer, M., Ho, M., Honicky, R., Pal, J., Plauche, M., & Surana, S. (2006). The challenges of technology research for developing regions. *IEEE Pervasive Computing / IEEE Computer Society [and] IEEE Communications Society, 5*(2), 15–23. doi:10.1109/MPRV.2006.40

Brockhoff, K. (2003). Customers' perspectives of involvement in new product development. *International Journal of Technology Management, 26*(5/6), 464–481. doi:10.1504/IJTM.2003.003418

Brodie, J., & Perry, M. (2001). Designing for mobility, collaboration and information use by blue-collar workers. *ACM SIGGROUP Bulletin, 22*(3), 22–27. doi:10.1145/567352.567356

Brogren, C. (2009). *Comments from VINNOVA: Public consultation on Community Innovation Policy, VINNOVA.* Stockholm.

Brown, J. S., & Duguid, P (2001). Knowledge and Organization: A Social-PracticePerspective. *Organization Science, 12*(2), 198–213.

Brown, J. S., & Duguid, P. (2000). *The Social Life of Information.* Cambridge: Harvard Business School Press.

Brownlee-Conyers, J. (1996). Voices from networked classrooms. *Educational Leadership, 54*(3), 34–37.

Buenstorf, G. (Ed.). (2012). *Evolution, organization, and economic behavior.* Northampton, MA: Edward Elgar. doi:10.4337/9780857930897

Burke, P. (1999). *The European Renaissance: Centres and peripheries.* New York, NY: Blackwell.

Burns, D., & Taylor, M. (2000). *Auditing community participation: An assessment handbook.* Bristol, UK: The Policy Press.

Burstein, F., & Holsapple, C. W. (2008). *Handbook on Decision Support Systems 2.* Berlin, Heidelberg: Springer Berlin Heidelberg.

Caetano, M., & Amaral, D. C. (2011, July). Roadmapping for technology push and partnership: A contribution for open innovation environments Original Research Article. *Technovation, 31*(7), 320–335. doi:10.1016/j.technovation.2011.01.005

Carayannis, E. G., Popescu, D., Sipp, C., & Steward, M. (2006). Technological learning for entrepreneurial development (TLED) in the knowledge economy (KE): Case studies and lessons learned. *Technovation, 26*(4), 419–443. doi:10.1016/j.technovation.2005.04.003

Carlos de Oliveira, A. & Kaminski, P.C. (2012). A reference model to determine the degree of maturity in the product development process of industrial SMEs Original Research Article

Carpentier, N. (2001). Managing Audience Participation: The Construction of Participation in an Audience Discussion Programme. *European Journal of Communication, 16*(2), 209–232. doi:10.1177/0267323101016002004

Carpentier, N., Lie, R., & Servaes, J. (2001, July). Community media – Muting the democratic media discourse? *Proceedings of the International Social Theory Consortium Second Annual Conference,* Brighton, UK.

Cash, D. W. (2001). In order to aid in diffusion useful and practical information: Agricultural extension and boundary organizations. *Science, Technology & Human Values, 26*(4), 431–453. doi:10.1177/016224390102600403

Castells, M. (Ed.), (2010). The information age: Economy, society and culture (Vol 1, 2nd ed., with a new preface). Malden, MA: Blackwell.

Center for Teaching Excellence. Carnegie Mellon University. (2009). Collaboration tools. Teaching with Technology White Paper. Carnegie Mellon university. Retrieved from https://www.cmu.edu/teaching/technology/whitepapers/CollaborationTools_Jan09.pdf

Chambers, R., & Von Medeazza, G. (2013). Sanitation and stunting in India: Undernutrition's blind spot. *Economic and Political Weekly, 48*(25), 15–18.

Chamoni, P., & Gluchowski, P. (2004). Integration trends in business intelligence systems-An empirical study based on the business intelligence maturity model. *Wirtschaftsinformatik, 46*(2), 119–128. doi:10.1007/BF03250931

Chandra, R. (2015). Collaborative Learning for Educational Achievement. *IOSR Journal of Research & Method in Education, 5*(3), 04-07. Retrieved from http://www.iosrjournals.org/iosr-jrme/papers/Vol-5%20Issue-3/Version-1/B05310407.pdf

Chandwani, A., Lihitkar, S., & Anilkumar, S. (2010). E-Learning Initiatives in India. In *Modern Practices in Library and Information Services*. Nagpur, India. Retrieved from http://eprints.rclis.org/15721/6/E- learning.pdf

Chang, Y. J., Liao, R. H., Wang, T. Y., & Chang, Y. S. (2010). Action research as a bridge between two worlds: Helping the NGOs and humanitarian agencies adapt technology to their needs.[Springer]. *Systemic Practice and Action Research*, *23*(3), 191–202. doi:10.1007/s11213-009-9154-8

Chattopadhyay, B., Lin, L., Liu, W., Mittal, S., Aragonda, P., Lychagina, V., & Wong, M. et al. (2011). Tenzing a SQL Implementation on the MapReduce Framework. *The Proceedings of the VLDB Endowment*, *4*(12), 1318–1327.

Cheng, K., Ernesto, F., & Truong, K. (2008). Participant and interviewer attitudes toward handheld computers in the context of HIV/AIDS programs in sub-Saharan Africa. *Paper presented at theproceeding of the 26th annual SIGCHI Conference on Human Factors in Computing Systems*, Florence, Italy. doi:10.1145/1357054.1357175

Chenoweth, N. A., Ushida, E., & Murday, K. (2006). Students learning in hybrid French and Spanish courses: An overview of language online. *CALICO Journal*, *24*(1), 115–145.

Chen, X. (2009). The power of "troublemaking". *Comparative Politics*, *41*(4), 451–471. doi:10.5129/00104150 9X12911362972557

Chepken, C., Blake, E., & Marsden, G. (2011). Day labour mobile electronic data capture and browsing system. *Proceedings of the South African Institute of Computer Scientists and Information Technologists Conference on Knowledge, Innovation and Leadership in a Diverse, Multidisciplinary Environment* (pp. 69-76). ACM. doi:10.1145/2072221.2072230

Chesbrough, H. & Crowther, A. K. (2006). Beyond high tech: early adopters of open innovation in other industries. *R&D Management*, *36*(3), 229-236.

Chesbrough, H. (2003). Open Innovation: How Companies Actually Do It. *Harvard Business Review*, 81(7), 12-14.

Chesbrough, H. (2006a). Open Innovation: A New Paradigm for Understanding Industrial Innovation. In H. Chesbrough, W. Vanhaverbeke, & J. West (Eds.), Open Innovation: Researching a New Paradigm (pp. 1-27). Oxford: Oxford University Press.

Chesbrough, H., Vanhaverbeke, W., & West, J. (2006). (Eds.). Open innovation: Researching a new paradigm, Oxford University Press: London

Chesbrough, H. (2003b). The era of open innovation. *MIT Sloan Management Review*, *44*(3), 35–41.

Chesbrough, H. (2007). The market for innovation: Implications for corporate strategy. *California Management Review*, *49*(3), 45–66. doi:10.2307/41166394

Chesbrough, H. W. (2003). *Open innovation: The new imperative for creating and profiting from technology*. Boston: Harvard Business School Press.

Chesbrough, H. W. (2003a). The era of open innovation. *MIT Sloan Management Review*, *44*(3), 35–41.

Chesbrough, H. W. (2003b). *Open Innovation: The New Imperative for Creating and Profiting from Technology*. Boston, MA: Harvard Business School Press.

Chesbrough, H. W. (2006). *Open Business Models: How to Thrive in the New Innovation Landscape*. Harvard Business School Press Books.

Chesbrough, H., & Crowther, A. K. (2006). Beyond high tech: Early adopters of open innovation in other industries. *R & D Management*, *36*(3), 229–236. doi:10.1111/j.1467-9310.2006.00428.x

Chetty, M., & Grinter, R. (2007). HCI4D: HCI challenges in the global south. *Paper presented at theExtended Abstracts Proceedings of the 2007 Conference on Human Factors in Computing Systems*, San Jose, California. doi:10.1145/1240866.1241002

Chib, A., & Komathi, A. (2009). Extending the technology-community-management model to disaster recovery: Assessing vulnerability in rural Asia. *Paper presented at the 3rd International Conference on Information and Communication Technologies and Development*, Education City, Doha, Qatar. doi:10.1109/ICTD.2009.5426694

Chib, A., & Harris, R. (2012). *Linking research to practice: Strengthening ICT for development research capacity in Asia*. Singapore: ISEAS Publishing.

Christensen, J. F., Olesen, M. H., & Kjær, J. S. (2005). The Industrial Dynamics of Open Innovation: Evidence from the transformation of consumer electronics. *Research Policy*, *34*(10), 1533–1549. doi:10.1016/j.respol.2005.07.002

Chu, G., Satpathy, S., Toyama, K., Gandhi, R., Balakrishnan, R., & Menon, S. (2009). Featherweight multimedia for information dissemination. *Paper presented at the 3rd International Conference on Information and Communication Technologies and Development*, Education City, Doha, Qatar. doi:10.1109/ICTD.2009.5426695

Cibangu, K. S. (2013). A reconsideration of modernization theory: Contribution to ICT4D's research. *International Journal of Information Communication Technologies and Human Development*, *5*(2), 86–101. doi:10.4018/jicthd.2013040106

Cisco (2011). Big Data in the Enterprise: Network Design Considerations. Retrieved from http://www.cisco.com/c/en/us/products/collateral/switches/nexus-5000-series-switches/white_paper_c11-690561.pdf

Clark, A. D. (2007). Adaptation, poverty and well-being: Some issues and observations with special reference to the capability approach and development studies. *Work Paper Series 081 Global Poverty Research Group University of Manchester.* Retrieved from http://www.gprg.org/pubs/workingpapers/pdfs/gprg-wps-081.pdf

Clark, A. D. (Ed.), (2006). *The Elgar companion to development studies*. Northampton, MA: Edward Elgar. doi:10.4337/9781847202864

Clarke, I. (2007). The role of intermediaries in promoting knowledge flows within global value chains [PhD Doctoral Symposium]. Brunel University, UK.

Claroline. (2015). *Wikipedia.* Retrieved from http://en.wikipedia.org/wiki/Claroline

Cleland, D., & Ireland, L. (2008). *Project Manager's Handbook: Applying Best Practices Across Global Industries*. New York, NY: McGraw Hill.

Coase, R. (1937). The Nature of the Firm. *Economica*, *4*(16), 386–405. doi:10.1111/j.1468-0335.1937.tb00002.x

Cofis, E., & Marsili, O. (2003) Survivor: The role of innovation in firm's survival, No. 03-18. WPT. Koopmans Institute, USE, Utrecht University

Collaborative writing (n. d.). EdTechTeacher. Retrieved from http://tewt.org/collaborative-writing/

Cooke, P. (2005). Regionally asymmetric knowledge capabilities and open innovation: Exploring 'Globalisation 2'—A new model of industry organisation. *Research Policy*, *34*(8), 1128–1149. doi:10.1016/j.respol.2004.12.005

Cooper, B. B. (2015, November 18). The Science of Collaboration: How to Optimize Working Together. Retrieved from http://thenextweb.com/entrepreneur/2014/07/15/science-collaboration-optimize-working-together/

Copenhaver, P. B., & Schmitt, B. C. (2002). *Renaissance philosophy (Foreword by P.O. Kristeller)*. New York, NY: Oxford University Press.

Coughlan, P., Harbison, A., Dromgoole, T., & Duff, D. (2001). Continuous improvement through collaborative action learning. *International Journal of Technology Management*, 22(4), 285–301. doi:10.1504/IJTM.2001.002965

Crawford, C. M. (1983). *New Products Management, Homewood II*. Richard D. Irwin, Inc.

Crawford, W. (2011). *Open access: what you need to know now*. USA: ALA Publishing.

CSR Europe. (2008a, March 4). The European Alliance for CSR Progress Review 2007: Making Europe a Pole of Excellence on CSR, European Commission, Brussels.

CSR Europe. (2008b). *R&D Open Innovation: Networks with SME*. Open Innovation Network.

Cukier, K. (2010, February 21). Data, data everywhere. *The Economist*. Retrieved from http://www.economist.com/node/15557443?story_id=15557443)

Currie-Alder, B., Kanbur, R., Malone, M. D., & Medhora, R. (2014). The state of development thought. In B. Currie-Alder, R. Kanbur, D. M. Malone, & R. Medhora (Eds.), *International development: Ideas, experience, and prospects* (pp. 1–16). New York, NY: Oxford University Press. doi:10.1093/acprof:oso/9780199671656.003.0001

Dahlander, L., & Magnusson, M. G. (2005). Relationships between open source software companies and communities: Observations from Nordic firms. *Research Policy*, 34(4), 481–493.

Dahlander, L., & Gann, D. M. (2010). How open is innovation? *Research Policy*, 2010.

Damaskopoulos, P., & Evgeniou, T. (2003). Adoption of New Economy Practices by SMEs in Eastern Europe. *European Management Journal*, 21(2), 133–145. doi:10.1016/S0263-2373(03)00009-4

Darcy, J., Kraemer-Eis, H., Guellec, D., & Debande, O. (2009). Financing Technology Transfer, Working paper 2009/002. EIF Research & Market Analysis, European Investment Fund, Luxemburg.

Darsø, L. (2001). *Innovation in the Making*. Frederiksberg, Denmark: Samfundslitteratur.

Datta, P. (2007). An agent-mediated knowledge-in-motion model. *Journal of the Association for Information Systems*, 8(5), 288–311.

Davenport, T. H. (1993). *Process innovation: reengineering work through information technology*. Ernst & Young.

Davenport, T. H. (1993a). *Process Innovation*. Boston, MA: Harvard Business School Press.

Davenport, T. H. (1993b). *Process Innovation: reengineering work through information technology, Ernst & Young*. Harvard Business School Press.

Davenport, T. H. (1994). Managing in the New World of Process. *Public Productivity & Management Review*, 18(2), 133–147. doi:10.2307/3380643

Davidsson, J. (2006). *Small Business Innovation Program: Business development and entrepreneurial training with intellectual property in developing countries*. B-Open Nordic AB.

Dawson, S., Burnett, B., & O'Donohue, M. (2006). Learning Communities: An untapped sustainable comparative advantage for higher education. *International Journal of Educational Management*, 20(2), 127–139. doi:10.1108/09513540610646118

Day M. (1998). Electronic Access: Archives in the New Millennium. Reports on a conference held at the Public Record Office, Kew on 3-4 June 1998 *Ariadane (16)*.

De Backer, K., & Cervantes, M. (2008). *Open innovation in global networks*. OECD.

De Jong, J. P. J., Vanhaverbeke, W., Kalvet, T., & Chesbrough, H. (2008), Policies for Open Innovation: Theory, Framework and Cases, Research project funded by VISION Era-Net, Helsinki: Finland.

De Jong, J. P. J., Vanhaverbeke, W., Kalvet, T., & Chesbrough, H. (2008), Policies for Open Innovation: Theory, Framework and Cases. Research project funded by VISION Era-Net, Helsinki: Finland.

De Jong, J.P.J., Vermeulen, P.A.M. & O'Shaughnessy, K.C. (2004) Effects of Innovation in Small Firms, *M & O*, 58(1): 21-38

De Jong, J. P. J. (2006). *Open Innovation: Practice, Trends, Motives and bottlenecks in the SMEs (Meer Open Innovatie: Praktijk, Ontwikkelingen, Motieven en Knelpunten in het MKB)*. Zoetermeer: EIM.

De Jong, J. P. J., & Marsili, O. (2006). The fruit flies of innovations: A taxonomy of innovative small firms. *Research Policy*, 35(2), 213–229. doi:10.1016/j.respol.2005.09.007

De Jong, J. P. J., Vanhaverbeke, W., Kalvet, T., & Chesbrough, H. (2008). *Policies for Open Innovation: Theory, Framework and Cases*. Helsinki: VISION Era-Net.

De Jong, J. P. J., Vanhaverbeke, W., Van de Vrande, V., & De Rochemont, M. (2007) Open innovation in SMEs: trends, motives and management challenges. *Proceeding of EURAM Conference*, Paris.

De Jong, J. P. J., & von Hippel, E. (2009, September). Transfers of user process innovations to process equipment producers: A study of Dutch high-tech firms. *Research Policy*, 38(7), 1181–1191. doi:10.1016/j.respol.2009.04.005

Dehoff, K. & Sehgal, V. (2006) Innovators without Borders, *strategy+business*, Autumn 2006

Dehoff, K. & Sehgal, V. (2008) Beyond Borders: The Global Innovation 1000, *strategy+business*, Winter 2008

Del Brío, J. Á., & Junquera, B. (2003, December). A review of the literature on environmental innovation management in SMEs: Implications for public policies. *Technovation*, 23(12), 939–948. doi:10.1016/S0166-4972(02)00036-6

Denhardt, R. B. (2011). *Theories of Public Organization* (6th ed.). Boston: Wadsworth.

De, R. (2012). Messy methods for ICT4D research. In A. Chib & R. Harris (Eds.), *Linking research to practice: Strengthening ICT for development research capacity in Asia* (pp. 58–67). Singapore: ISEAS Publishing.

Descotes, R. M., Walliser, B., Holzmüller, H., & Guo, X. (2011, December). Original Research Article. *Journal of Business Research*, 64(12), 1303–1310.

Devlin, B., Rogers, S., & Myers, J. (2012). Big data comes of age. *IBM*. Retrieved from http://www-03.ibm.com/systems/hu/resources/big_data_comes_of_age.pdf

Di Maria, E., & Micelli, S. (2008). SMEs and Competitive Advantage: A Mix of Innovation, Marketing and ICT. The Case of "Made in Italy". Marco Fanno Working Paper No. 70, Università degli Studi di Padova, Padova, Italy.

Dickson, P. H., Weaver, K. M., & Hoy, F. (2006, July). Opportunism in the R&D alliances of SMES: The roles of the institutional environment and SME size. *Journal of Business Venturing*, 21(4), 487–513. doi:10.1016/j.jbusvent.2005.02.003

Diehl, A. R. (2004). *The Olmecs: America's first civilization*. London: Thames and Hudson.

Diener, K. & Piller, F. (2009). The Market for Open Innovation: Increasing the efficiency and effectiveness of the innovation process. Open Innovation Accelerator Survey 2009, RWTH Aachen University, TIM Group.

Diga, K. (2013a). Access and usage of ICTs by the poor (Part I). In L. Elder, H. Emdon, R. Fuchs, & B. Petrazzini (Eds.), *Connecting ICTs to development: The IDRC experience* (pp. 117–135). New York, NY: Anthem Press.

Diga, K. (2013b). Local and economic opportunities and ICTs: How ICTs affect livelihoods (Part II). In L. Elder, H. Emdon, R. Fuchs, & B. Petrazzini (Eds.), *Connecting ICTs to development: The IDRC experience* (pp. 137–160). New York, NY: Anthem Press.

Dirlik, A. (2003). Global modernity? Modernity in an age of global capitalism. *European Journal of Social Theory*, *6*(3), 275–292. doi:10.1177/13684310030063001

Diwan, P., Suri, R. K., & Kaushik, S. (2000). *IT Encyclopaedia.com* (Vol. 1-10). New Delhi: Pentagon Press.

Dlodlo, N. (2009). Access to ICT education for girls and women in rural South Africa: A case study. *Technology in Society*, *31*(2), 168–17. doi:10.1016/j.techsoc.2009.03.003

Dodgson, M., Gann, D., & Salter, A. (2006). The role of technology in the shift towards open innovation: The case of Procter & Gamble. *R & D Management*, *36*(3), 333–346. doi:10.1111/j.1467-9310.2006.00429.x

Don Dingsdag, D., Armstrong B. & Neil, D. (2000). *Electronic Assessment Software for Distance Education Students*.

Douglas, M., Praul, M., & Lynch, M. (2008). Mobile learning in higher education: an empirical assessment of a new educational tool. *The Turkish Online Journal of Educational Technology, 7*(3). Retrieved from http://www.tojet.net/articles/732.pdf\

Dresner Advisory Services. (2014). Wisdom of Crowds Business Intelligence Market Study. Retrieved from http://www.actuate.com/download/analyst-papers/Wisdom_of_Crowds_BI_Market_Study_Findings_2011.pdf

Drucker, P. (1998). The Discipline of Innovation. *Harvard Business Review*, (Nov-Dec): 149.

Dulani, B., Mattes, R., & Logan, C. (2013). After a decade growth in Africa, little change in poverty at the grassroots. *Afrobarometer Policy Paper No 1*. Retrieved from http://www.afrobarometer.org/files/documents/policy_brief/ab_r5_policybriefno1.pdf

Duncombe, R. (2012a). Understanding mobile phone impact on livelihoods in developing countries: A new research framework. *IDPM Development Informatics Working Paper no.48*. Retrieved from http://www.sed.manchester.ac.uk/idpm/research/publications/wp/di/index.htm

Duncombe, R. (2012b). Mobile phones for agricultural and rural development: A literature review and future research directions. *IDPM Development Informatics Working Paper no.50*. Retrieved from http://www.sed.manchester.ac.uk/idpm/research/publications/wp/di/index.htm

Duncombe, R. (2011). Researching impact of mobile phones for development: Concepts, methods and lessons for practice. *Information Technology for Development*, *17*(4), 268–288. doi:10.1080/02681102.2011.561279

Durkheim, E. (2007). *De la division du travail social*. Paris: PUF. (Original work published 1893)

Dwyer, D. (1996). A response to Douglas Noble: We're in this together. *Educational Leadership*, *54*(3), 24–27.

E learning. (2014). Wikipedia. Retrieved from http://en.wikipedia.org/wiki/E-learning#cite_note-1

EC (2008). SBA Fact Sheet Portugal, European Commission: Enterprise and Industry.

Edquist, C., & Johnson, B. (1997). Institutions and organizations in systems of innovation. In C. Edquist (Ed.), *Systems of Innovation: Technologies, Institutions and Organizations*. London: Routledge.

Edwards, T., Delbridge, R., & Munday, M. (2005). Understanding innovation in small and medium-sized enterprises: A process manifest. *Technovation*, *25*(10), 1119–1127. doi:10.1016/j.technovation.2004.04.005

Eisenstadt, S. N. (1966). *Modernization: Protest and change*. Englewood Cliffs, N.J: Prentice-Hall.

Eisenstadt, S. N. (1996). *Japanese civilization: A comparative view*. Chicago: University of Chicago Press.

Elahi, A. (2008). Challenges of data collection in developing nations – the Pakistani experience as a way forward. *Statistical Journal of the IAOS, 25*, 11–17.

eLearning 101 – concepts, trends, applications. (2014). Epignosis. Retrieved from http://www.talentlms.com/elearning/

Elliott, A. J. (2008). Development and social welfare/human rights. In V. Desai & R. B. Potter (Eds.), *The companion to development studies* (2nd ed., pp. 40–45). London: Hodder Education.

El-Mahdi, R. (2009). Enough! Egypt's quest for democracy. *Comparative Political Studies, 42*(8), 1011–1039. doi:10.1177/0010414009331719

EMC. (2012). Big data-as-a-service: A market and technology perspective. EMC Solution Group. Retrieved from http://www.emc.com/collateral/software/white-papers/h10839-big-data-as-a-service-perspt.pdf

English-Lucek, J. A., Darrah, C. N., & Saveri, A. (2002). Trusting strangers: Work relationships in four high-tech communities. *Information Communication and Society, 5*(1), 90–108. doi:10.1080/13691180110117677

Enkel, E., Kausch, C., & Gassmann, O. (2005). Managing the risk of customer integration. *European Management Journal, 23*(2), 203–213. doi:10.1016/j.emj.2005.02.005

Erixon, P (2010). School subject paradigms and teaching practice in lower secondary Swedish schools influenced by ICT and media in *Computers & Education*, 54(4), 1212-1221.

Ernst, D., Mytelka, L., & Ganiatsos, T. (1994). *Technological Capabilities: A Conceptual Framework, Mimeo*. Geneva: UNCTAD.

Escobar, A. (2009). Other worlds are (already) possible: Self-organization, complexity, and post-capitalist cultures. In J. Sen & P. Waterman (Eds.). *World social forum: Challenging empires* (pp. 393-404). New York, NY: Black Rose.

Escobar, A. (1992). Reflections on "development,": Grassroots approaches and alternatives politics in the Third World. *Futures, 24*(5), 411–436. doi:10.1016/0016-3287(92)90014-7

Escobar, A. (1995). *Encountering development: The making and unmaking of the Third World*. Princeton, NJ: Princeton University Press.

Escobar, A. (2005). Economics and the space of modernity: Tales of markets, production and labour. *Cultural Studies, 19*(2), 139–175. doi:10.1080/09502380500077714

Escobar, A. (2010). Latin America at crossroads: Alternative modernizations, post-liberalism, or post-development? *Cultural Studies, 24*(1), 1–65. doi:10.1080/09502380903424208

Esteva, G. (1987). Regenerating people's space. *Alternatives, 10*(3), 125–152. doi:10.1177/030437548701200106

Esteva, G., & Prakash, S. M. (1998). *Grassroots post-modernism: Remaking the soil of cultures*. London: Zed.

European Union (2005) *EU-Summary*. The joint Japan-EU Seminar on R&D and Innovation in Small and Medium size Enterprises (SMEs), Tokyo, November 18, 2004

Evangelista, R. (2000). Sectoral Patterns of Technological Change in Services. *Economics of Innovation and New Technology, 9*(3), 183–221. doi:10.1080/10438590000000008

Evans, P. (2007). The "movement of movements" for global justice. *American Sociological Association, 62*(6), 62–64.

Evelson, B., & Norman, N. (2008). Topic overview: business intelligence. Forrester Research. Retrieved from http://www.forrester.com/Topic+Overview+Business+Intelligence/fulltext/-/E-RES39218

Evelson, B., & Norman, N. (2008). *Topic overview: business intelligence.* Forrester.

Everywhere, P. live audience participation (2012). Retrieved from http://www.polleverywhere.com

Ewusi-Mensah, K. (2012). Problems of information technology diffusion in sub-Saharan Africa: The case of Ghana. *Information Technology for Development, 18*(3), 247–269. doi:10.1080/02681102.2012.664113

Farazmand, A. (1999). The elite question: Toward a normative elite theory of organization. *Administration & Society, 31*(3), 321–352. doi:10.1177/00953999922019166

Farazmand, A. (2012a). Institutionalized chaos and transformation of governance and public administration: Explaining the global crisis of capitalism. *Public Organization Review, 12*(4).

Farazmand, A. (2012b). Predatory globalization, global crisis of capitalism, and the deepening crisis of the state: Why has public administration failed to grasp its own identity? *Public Organization Review, 12*(4).

Farazmand, A. (2013). Conclusion: Can we go home now? Roads taken, targets met, and lessons learned on governance and organizational eclecticism in the public arena. *Public Organization Review, 13*(2), 219–228. doi:10.1007/s11115-013-0236-9

Ferneley, E., & Bell, F. (2006). Using bricolage to integrate business and information technology innovation in SMEs. *Technovation, 26*(2), 232–241. doi:10.1016/j.technovation.2005.03.005

Ferrary, M. (2011). Specialized organizations and ambidextrous clusters in the open innovation paradigm. *European Management Journal, 29*(3), 181–192. doi:10.1016/j.emj.2010.10.007

Filgueira, H. C. (2001). Social development. In N. J. Smelser & P. B. Baltes (Eds.), *International encyclopedia of the social and behavioral sciences* (Vol. 6, pp. 3583–3587). New York, NY: Elsevier. doi:10.1016/B0-08-043076-7/03343-X

Follet, M.P. (1926). The giving of orders. *Scientific foundations of business administration.* 29-37.

Forster, D., Behrens, R. H., Campbell, H., & Byass, P. (1991). Evaluation of a computerized field data collection system for health surveys. *Bulletin of the World Health Organization, 69*(1), 107–111.

Fredberg, T., Elmquist, M., & Ollila, S. (2008). *Managing Open Innovation: Present Findings and Future Directions,* Report VR 2008:02, VINNOVA - Verket för Innovationssystem/Swedish Governmental Agency for Innovation Systems.

Freedman, A. (1996). *The computer desktop encyclopedia.* New York: AMACOM.

Freel, M. & De Jong, J.P.J. (2009) Market novelty, competence-seeking and innovation networking. *Technovation, 29*(12), 873–884.

Freire, P. (1970). *Pedagogy of the oppressed.* London: Penguin.

Fritsch, M., & Lukas, R. (2001). Who cooperates on R&D? *Research Policy, 30*(2), 297–312. doi:10.1016/S0048-7333(99)00115-8

Fuchs, B. (2014). The Writing is on the Wall: Using Padlet for Whole-Class Engagement. LOEX Quarterly, 40(4), 7-9. Retrieved from http://uknowledge.uky.edu /libraries_facpub/240

Fuchs, R. (2013). From heresy to orthodoxy: ICT4D at IDRC. In L. Elder, H. Emdon, R. Fuchs, & B. Petrazzini (Eds.), *Connecting ICTs to development: The IDRC experience* (pp. 1–17). New York, NY: Anthem Press.

Fu, X. (2012, April). How does openness affect the importance of incentives for innovation? Original Research Article. *Research Policy, 41*(3), 512–523. doi:10.1016/j.respol.2011.12.011

Gantz, J., & Reinsel, D. (201, May0). The Digital Universe Decade – Are You Ready? The IDC 2010 Digital Universe Study. Retrieved from http://idcdocserv.com/925

Garrison, V. (2012, July 16). How I lost my fear of universal health care. RH Reality Check: Reproductive & Sexual Health and Justice News, Analysis & Commentary. Retrieved from http://www.rhrealitycheck.org/article/2012/07/12/how-i-lost-my-fear-universal-health-care

Gassmann, O. (2006). Opening up the innovation process: Towards an agenda[Blackwell Publishing Ltd.]. *R & D Management, 36*(3), 223–228. doi:10.1111/j.1467-9310.2006.00437.x

Gassmann, O., Enkel, E., & Chesbrough, H. (2010). The future of open innovation. *R & D Management, 40*(3), 213–221. doi:10.1111/j.1467-9310.2010.00605.x

Gaventa, J. (1980). *Power and Powerlessness: Quiescence and Rebellion in an Appalachian Valley.* Chicago: University of Illinois Press.

Geertz, C. (1973/2000). *The interpretation of cultures: Selected essays by Clifford Geertz.* New York: Basic Books.

Gereffi, G, Humphrey, J & Sturgeon, T (2005) The governance of global value chains

Gereffi, G., Humphrey, J., & Sturgeon, T. (2005, February). The governance of global value chains. *Review of International Political Economy, 12*(1), 78–104. doi:10.1080/09692290500049805

Ghayur, S., & Haque, I. (1994). Developing Labour Market Information System for Informal Sector in Pakistan[with Comments]. *Pakistan Development Review, 33*(4), 1357–1370.

Gitau, S., & Marsden, G. (2009). Fair Partnerships–Working With NGOs. In *Human-Computer Interaction–INTERACT 2009* (pp. 704–707). Springer Berlin Heidelberg. doi:10.1007/978-3-642-03655-2_77

Giugale, M. M. (2014). *Economic development: What everyone needs to know.* New York, NY: Oxford University Press.

Glaser, B., & Strauss, A. (1967). *The discovery of grounded theory: Strategies for qualitative research.* New York, NY: Aldine de Gruyter.

Gomes-Casseres, B. (1997). Alliance strategies of small firms. *Small Business Economics, 9*(1), 33–44. doi:10.1023/A:1007947629435

Gomez, R., & Gould, E. (2010). The "cool factor" of public access to ICT. *Information Technology & People, 23*, 247–264.

Gonzo, W., & Plattner, I. E. (2003). *Unemployment in an African country: a psychological perspective (No. 5).* University of Namibia.

Gooden, S., & Portillo, S. (2011). Advancing social equity in the Minnowbrook tradition. *Journal of Public Administration: Research and Theory, 21*(1), 1–14.

Govt. of Bangladesh. (2005a). *Policy Strategies for Small & Medium Enterprises (SME) Development in Bangladesh,* Ministry of Industries, Government of the People's Republic of Bangladesh, January 2005

Govt. of Bangladesh. (2005b). *Bangladesh Industrial Policy 2005,* Ministry of Industries, Government of the People's Republic of Bangladesh.

Gredel, D., Kramer, M., & Bend, B. (2012, September–October). Original Research Article. *Technovation, 32*(9–10), 536–549. doi:10.1016/j.technovation.2011.09.008

Greve, W. (2001). Successful human development: Psychological conceptions. In N. J. Smelser & P. B. Baltes (Eds.), *International encyclopedia of the social and behavioral sciences* (Vol. 10, pp. 6970–6974). New York, NY: Elsevier. doi:10.1016/B0-08-043076-7/01693-4

Grindley, P. C., & Teece, D. J. (1997). Managing intellectual capital: Licensing and cross-licensing in semiconductors and electronics. *California Management Review*, *39*(2), 1–34. doi:10.2307/41165885

Groen, A. J., & Linton, J. D. (2010). Is open innovation a field of study or a communication barrier to theory development? *Technovation*, *30*(11-12), 554. doi:10.1016/j.technovation.2010.09.002

Grupp, H., & Schubert, T. (2010, February). Review and new evidence on composite innovation indicators for evaluating national performance. *Research Policy*, *39*(1), 67–78. doi:10.1016/j.respol.2009.10.002

Haagedorn, J., & Schakenraad, J. (1994). The effect of strategic technology alliances on company performance. *Strategic Management Journal*, *15*(4), 291–309. doi:10.1002/smj.4250150404

Habermas, J. (1993). Modernity an incomplete project. In T. Docherty (Ed.), *Postmodernism: A reader* (pp. 98–109). New York, NY: Harvester Wheatsheaf.

Habermas, J., & Ben-Habib, S. (1981). Modernity versus postmodernity. *New German Critique, NGC*, *22*(22), 3–15. doi:10.2307/487859

Hafkesbrink, J., & Scholl, H. (2010) Web 2.0 Learning- A Case Study on Organizational Competences in Open Content Innovation. In J. Hafkesbrink, H.U. Hoppe, & J. Schlichter (Eds.), Competence Management for Open Innovation- Tools and IT-support to unlock the potential of Open Innovation.

Hage, J. T. (1999). Organizational Innovation and Organizational Change. *Annual Review of Sociology*, *25*(1), 597–622. doi:10.1146/annurev.soc.25.1.597

Hajer, M. A. (1993). Coalitions, practices and meaning in environmental politics: from acid rain to BSE. In D. Howarth & J. Torfing (Eds.), Discourse Theory in European Politics: Identity, Policy and Governance (Ch. 12, pp. 297-315). Hampshire, UK: Palgrave MacMillan.

Hamdani, J., & Wirawan, C. (2012). Open Innovation Implementation to Sustain Indonesian SMEs. *Procedia Economics and Finance*, *4*, 223–233. doi:10.1016/S2212-5671(12)00337-1

Hamelink, C. J. (2001). The planning of communication technology: Alternatives for the periphery. In S. Melkote & S. Rao (Eds.), *Critical issues in communication: Looking forward for answers*. New Delhi, India: Sage.

Hang, D. (2005). *Effects of ICT on media transformation, education and training in Cambodia, Lao PDR and Viet Nam*. Retrieved from http://www.comminit.com/en/node/287055/307

Harker, S. D., Eason, K. D., & Dobson, J. E. (1993). The change and evolution of requirements as a challenge to the practice of software engineering. *Proceedings of IEEE International Symposium onRequirements Engineering '93* (pp. 266-272). IEEE.

Harmse, A., Blaauw, P., & Schenck, R. (2009, November). Day labourers, unemployment and socio-economic development in South Africa. *Urban Forum*, *20*(4), 363-377. doi:10.1007/s12132-009-9067-8

Harris, M., & Butterworth, G. (2002). *Developmental psychology: A student's handbook*. New York, NY: Psychology Press.

Harrison, L., & Huntington, P. S. (2000). *Culture matters*. New York, NY: Basic Books.

Harriss, J. (2014). Development theories. In B. Currie-Alder, R. Kanbur, D. M. Malone, & R. Medhora (Eds.), *International development: Ideas, experience, and prospects* (pp. 35–49). New York, NY: Oxford University Press. doi:10.1093/acprof:oso/9780199671656.003.0003

Haughton, B. (2007). *Hidden history: Lost civilizations, secret knowledge, and ancient mysteries (foreword by F. Joseph).* Franklin Lakes, NJ: The Career Press.

He, J., & Brandweiner, N. (2014). The 20 best tools for online collaboration. *CreativeBloq.com.* Retrieved from http://www.creativebloq.com/design/online-collaboration-tools-912855

He, C. (2012a). Introduction. In C. He (Ed.), *Modernization science: The principles and methods of national advancement* (pp. 1–65). New York, NY: Springer. doi:10.1007/978-3-642-25459-8_1

He, C. (2012b). History of Modernization. In C. He (Ed.), *Modernization science: The principles and methods of national advancement* (pp. 153–180). New York, NY: Springer. doi:10.1007/978-3-642-25459-8_3

Heeks, R. (2006). Analysing the software sector in developing countries using competitive advantage theory. *IDPM Development Informatics Working Paper no.25.* Retrieved from http://www.sed.manchester.ac.uk/idpm/research/publications/wp/di/index.htm

Heeks, R. (2014a). From the MDGs to the post-2015 agenda: Analysing changing development priorities. *IDPM Development Informatics Working Paper no.56.* Retrieved from http://www.sed.manchester.ac.uk/idpm/research/publications/wp/di/index.htm

Heeks, R. (2014b). Future priorities for development informatics research from the post-2015 development agenda. *IDPM Development Informatics Working Paper no.57.* Retrieved from http://www.sed.manchester.ac.uk/idpm/research/publications/wp/di/index.htm

Heeks, R. (2014c). ICTs and poverty eradication: Comparing economic, livelihoods and capabilities models. *IDPM Development Informatics Working Paper no.58.* Retrieved from http://www.sed.manchester.ac.uk/idpm/research/publications/wp/di/index.htm

Heeks, R. (2014d). ICT4D 2016: New priorities for ICT4D policy, practice and WSIS in a post-2015 world. *IDPM Development Informatics Working Paper no.59.* Retrieved from http://www.sed.manchester.ac.uk/idpm/research/publications/wp/di/index.htm

Heeks, R., & Jagun, A. (2007). Mobile phones and development: The future in new hands? *Id21 Insights, 69,* p. 1. Retrieved from http://www.id21.org/insights/insights69/insights69.pdf

Heeks, R., & Molla, A. (2009). Impact assessment of ICT-for-development projects: A compendium of approaches. *IDPM Development Informatics Working Paper no.36.* Retrieved from http://www.sed.manchester.ac.uk/idpm/research/publications/wp/di/index.htm

Heeks, R., Subramanian, L., & Jones, C. (2013). Understanding e-waste management in developing countries: Building sustainability in the Indian ICT sector. *IDPM Development Informatics Working Paper no.52.* Retrieved from http://www.sed.manchester.ac.uk/idpm/research/publications/wp/di/index.htm

Heeks, R. (2002). Information systems and developing nations: Failure, success, and local improvisations. *The Information Society, 18*(2), 101–112. doi:10.1080/01972240290075039

Heeks, R. (2007). Theorizing ICT4D research. *Information Technologies and International Development, 3*(3), 1–4. doi:10.1162/itid.2007.3.3.1

Heeks, R. (2009). *The ICT4D 2.0 manifesto: Where next for ICTs and international development?* Manchester: Development Informatics Group.

Heeks, R. (2010a). Do information and communication technologies (ICTs) contribute to development? *Journal of International Development, 22*(5), 625–640. doi:10.1002/jid.1716

Heeks, R. (2010b). Development 2.0: The IT-enabled transformation of international development. *Communications of the ACM, 53*(4), 22–24. doi:10.1145/1721654.1721665

Heeks, R., & Bhatnagar, S. (1999). Understanding (information systems) success and failures in information age reform. In R. Heeks (Ed.), *Reinventing government in the information age: International practice in ICT-enabled public sector reform* (pp. 49–75). London: Routledge. doi:10.4324/9780203204962

Heimerl, K., Vasudev, J., Buchanan, K., Parikh, T., & Brewer, E. (2010). Metamouse: Improving multi-user sharing of existing educational applications. *Paper presented at theInternational Conference on Information and Communication Technologies and Development*, London. doi:10.1145/2369220.2369237

Helper, S., MacDuffie, J. P., & Sabel, C. M. (2000). Pragmatic collaboration: Advancing knowledge while controlling opportunism. *Industrial and Corporate Change, 9*(3), 443–488. doi:10.1093/icc/9.3.443

Hemenover, S. H. (2003). The good, the bad, and the healthy: Impacts of emotional disclosure of trauma on resilient self-concept and psychological distress. *Personality and Social Psychology Bulletin, 29*(10), 1236–1244. doi:10.1177/0146167203255228 PMID:15189585

Henderson, L. (2008). The impact of project managers' communication competencies: Validation and extension of a research model for virtuality, satisfaction, and productivity on project teams. *Project Management Journal, 39*(2), 48–59. doi:10.1002/pmj.20044

Henderson, R. M., & Clark, K. B. (1990). Architectural Innovation: The Reconfiguration of Existing Product Technologies and the Failure of Established Firms. *Administrative Science Quarterly, 35*(1), 9–30. doi:10.2307/2393549

Henderson, V. J., Storeygard, A., & Weil, N. D. (2012). Measuring economic growth from outer space. *The American Economic Review, 102*(2), 994–1028. doi:10.1257/aer.102.2.994 PMID:25067841

Henkel, J. (2006). Selective revealing in open innovation processes: The case of embedded Linux. *Research Policy, 35*(7), 953–969. doi:10.1016/j.respol.2006.04.010

Henschen, D. (2008, October 13). BI Efforts Take Flight. InformationWeek.

Herman, J. (1997). *Trauma and recovery: The aftermath of violence – from domestic abuse to political terror.* New York: BasicBooks.

Herstad, S.J., Bloch, C., Ebersberger, B. & van de Velde, E. (2008). Open innovation and globalisation: Theory, evidence and implications. VISION Era.net.

Hewett, P., Erulkar, A., & Mensch, B. (2004). The feasibility of computer-assisted survey interviewing in Africa: Experience from two rural districts in Kenya. *Social Science Computer Review, 22*(3), 319–334. doi:10.1177/0894439304263114

Hidreth, C. (2001). Accounting for user's inflated assessment of online catalogue search performance and usefulness an experimental study. *Information Research, 6* (2). Retrieved from http://www.informationR.net/ir/6-2/paper101.html

Hiebing, R. G. Jr, & Cooper, S. W. (2003). *The Successful Marketing Plan: A Disciplined and Comprehensive Approach.* The McGraw-Hill Companies, Inc.

Hippel, V. (1975). *The Dominant Role of Users in the Scientific Instrument Innovation Process, WP 764-75.* NSF.

Hippel, V. (1978, January). Successful Industrial Products from Customer Ideas. *Eric von Hippel Journal of Marketing*, *42*(1), 39–49.

Hippel, V. (2007, April). 2007 Horizontal Innovation Networks--By and for Users. *Industrial and Corporate Change*, *16*(2), 293–315. doi:10.1093/icc/dtm005

Hjalager, A.-M. (2010, February). A review of innovation research in tourism. *Tourism Management*, *31*(1), 1–12. doi:10.1016/j.tourman.2009.08.012

Hoffman, K., Parejo, M., Bessant, J., & Perren, L. (1998). Small firms, R&D, technology and innovation in the UK: A literature review. *Technovation*, *18*(1), 39–55. doi:10.1016/S0166-4972(97)00102-8

Hoffman, W. H., & Schlosser, R. (2001). Success factors of strategic alliances in small and medium-sized enterprises: An empirical study. *Long Range Planning*, *34*(3), 357–381. doi:10.1016/S0024-6301(01)00041-3

Hofmeyr, J. (2013). *Africa rising? Popular dissatisfaction with economic management despite the decade of growth. Afro Barometer Policy Paper No2*. Retrieved from http://www.afrobarometer.org/files/documents/policy_brief/ab_r5_poli-cybriefno2.pdf

Hofstede, G. (1997). *Cultures and organizations: Software of the mind*. New York, NY: McGraw Hill.

Hong, P. Y. P., & Song, I. H.In Han Song. (2010). Glocalization of social work practice: Global and local responses to globalization. *International Social Work*, *53*(5), 656–670. doi:10.1177/0020872810371206

Horey, J., Begoli, E., Gunasekaran, R., Lim, S.-H., & Nutaro, J. (2012). Big data platforms as a service: challenges and approach.*Proceedings of the 4th USENIX conference on Hot Topics in Cloud Computing, HotCloud'12* (p. 16).

Hovious, A. (2013). 5 Free Real-Time Collaboration Tools. *Designer Librarian*. Retrieved from https://designerlibrarian.wordpress.com/2013/09/15/5-free-real-time-collaboration-tools/

Howells, J. (2006). Intermediation and the role of intermediaries in innovation. *Research Policy*, *35*(5), 715–728. doi:10.1016/j.respol.2006.03.005

Howells, J., James, A., & Malek, K. (2003). The sourcing of technological knowledge: Distributed innovation processes and dynamic change. *R & D Management*, *33*(4), 395–409. doi:10.1111/1467-9310.00306

Hsu, S. (2011). Who assigns the most ICT activities? Examining the relationship between teacher and student usage. *Computers & Education*, *56*(3), 847–855. doi:10.1016/j.compedu.2010.10.026

Huang, X., Soutar, G.N. & Brown, A. (2004) Review and new evidence on composite innovation indicators for evaluating national performance, *Research Policy*, 39(1), 67-78.

Huang, X., Soutar, G. N., & Brown, A. (2004). Measuring new product success: An empirical investigation of Australian SMEs. *Industrial Marketing Management*, *33*(2), 117–123. doi:10.1016/S0019-8501(03)00034-8

Huizingh, E. K. R. E. (2009, June 21-24). The future of innovation. *Proceedings of the XX International Society for Professional Innovation Management ISPIM Conference '09*.

Humphrey, J., & Schmitz, H. (2000). *Governance and Upgrading: Linking industrial cluster and global value chain research*. IDS Working Paper 120.

Huntington, P. S. (1968). *Political order in changing societies*. New Haven, CT: Yale University Press.

Huston, L., & Sakkab, N. (2006). Connect and develop: Inside Procter & Gamble's new model for innovation. *Harvard Business Review*, *84*, 58–66.

IfM and IBM. (2008). *Succeeding through service innovation: A service perspective for education, research, business and government*. Cambridge, UK: University of Cambridge Institute for Manufacturing.

Indarti, N., & Langenberg, M. (2004, April 19-21). Factors Affecting Business Success Among SMEs: Empirical Evidences from Indonesia. *Proceedings of the Second Bi-annual European Summer University*, University of Twente, Encschode, Netherland.

International Telecommunication Union (ITU). (2013). *The world in 2013: ICT facts and figures*. Retrieved from https://www.itu.int/en/ITU-D/Statistics/.../facts/ ICTFactsFigures2014-e.pdf

Islam, M. S., & Grönlund, Å. (2010). Agriculture market information services (AMIS) in the least Developed Countries (LDCs): Nature, Scopes, and Challenges. In M.A. Wimmer, J.-L. Chappelet, M. Janssen, H.J. Scholl (Eds.), Proceedings of EGOV '10, LNCS (Vol. 6228, pp. 109–120). Heidelberg: Springer

Islam, S. M. (2008). Towards a sustainable e-participation implementation model. *European Journal of ePractice*. Retrieved from www. epracticejournal.eu

Izushi, H. (2003). Impact of the length of relationships upon the use of research institutes by SMEs. *Research Policy*, *32*(5), 771–788. doi:10.1016/S0048-7333(02)00085-9

Jacobsen, J. (2015). Revisiting the modernization hypothesis: Longevity and democracy. *World Development*, *67*, 174–185. doi:10.1016/j.worlddev.2014.10.003

Jagun, A. (2007). Micro-enterprise and the "mobile divide": New benefits and old inequalities in Nigeria's informal sector. *Id21 Insights, 69*, p. 2. Retrieved from http://www.id21.org/insights/insights69/insights69.pdf

Jarrett, S. (2013). From poverty traps to indigenous philanthropy: Complexity in a rapidly changing world. *University of Sussex IDS [Institute of Development Studies] Working Paper No 425*. Retrieved from http://www.ids.ac.uk/files/dmfile/Wp425.pdf

Jaspersoft (2014). Jaspersoft Business Intelligence. Retrieved from http://www.jaspersoft.com/

Jedox (2015). Jedox Business Intelligence. Retrieved from http://www.jedox.com/en/

Johnson, J. (2014). Open Source Options For Education. Retrieved from http://oss-watch.ac.uk/resources/ossoptionseducation

Johnson, L., Smith, R., Willis, H., Levine, A., & Haywood, K. (2011). *The 2011 Horizon Report*. Austin, Texas: The New Media Consortium.

Johnston. (2002). *Assessing the Impact of Technology in Teaching and Learning Changing the Conversation about Teaching, Learning and Technology: A Report on 10 Years of ACOT Research*.

Jones, O., & Tilley, F. (Eds.). (2003). *Competitive Advantage in SMEs: organizing for innovation and change*. Chichester: Wiley.

Kalsched, D. (2013). *Trauma and the soul: A psycho-spiritual approach to human development and its interruption*. New York, NY: Routledge.

Kanbur, R. (2002). Economics, social science and development. *World Development*, *30*(3), 477–486. doi:10.1016/S0305-750X(01)00117-6

Kanugo, S. (1999). *Making IT work*. New Delhi: Sage Publications.

Kasekende, L. (2001). Financing SMEs: Uganda's Experience. In *Improving the Competitiveness of SMEs in Developing Countries: The Role of Finance to Enhance Enterprise Development* (pp. 97–107). New York, Geneva: United Nations.

Katz, R., & Allen, T. J. (1982). Investigating the not-invented-here (NIH)- syndrome: A look at performance, tenure and communication patterns of 50 R&D project groups. *R & D Management, 12*(1), 7–19. doi:10.1111/j.1467-9310.1982. tb00478.x

Kaufmann, A., & Tödtling, F. (2002, March). How effective is innovation support for SMEs? An analysis of the region of Upper Austria. *Technovation, 22*(3), 147–159. doi:10.1016/S0166-4972(00)00081-X

Kearney, C. (2012). Emerging markets research: Trends, issues and future directions. *Emerging Markets Review, 13*(2), 159–183. doi:10.1016/j.ememar.2012.01.003

Keil, T. (2002). *External Corporate Venturing: Strategic Renewal in Rapidly Changing Industries.* Westport, CT: Quorum.

Khona, Z. (2000, September18). Copyright: A safeguard against piracy. *Express Computer, 11*(28), 15.

Kiely, R. (2006). Modernization theory. In D. A. Clark (Ed.), *The Elgar companion to development studies* (pp. 395–399). Northampton, MA: Edward Elgar.

Kimaro, H. C., & Nhampossa, J. L. (2005). Analyzing the problem of unsustainable health information systems in less-developed economies: Case studies from Tanzania and Mozambique. *Information Technology for Development, 11*(3), 273–298. doi:10.1002/itdj.20016

Kimball University. (2014). Kimball Group. Retrieved from http://www.kimballgroup.com/data-warehouse-business-intelligence-courses/

Kimberling, E. (2006). In search of business value: how to achieve the benefits of ERP technology (White paper). *Panorama Consulting Group*, Denver, CO.

Kirkels, Y., & Duysters, G. (2010). Brokerage in SME networks. *Research Policy, 39*(3), 375–385. doi:10.1016/j.respol.2010.01.005

Kirschbaum, R. (2005). Open innovation in practice. *Research on Technology Management, 48*, 24–28.

Kishore, A. (2009). ICTs for Employability in India. *peopleslabsorg*. Retrieved from http://www.peopleslabs.org/docs/ICTs_for_Employability_in_India.pdf

Kleine, D. (2009). ICT4What? Using the choice framework to operationalise the capability approach to developemnt. *Proceedings of the Doha Conference.* Retrieved from http://www.cs.washington.edu/education/courses/cse590f/09sp/ictd09/Kleine.pdf

Kleine, D. (2013). *Technologies of choice: ICTs, development, and the capabilities approach.* Cambridge, MA: MIT.

Klein-Woolthuis, R., Lankhuizen, M., & Gilsing, V. (2005). A system failure framework for innovation policy design. *Technovation, 25*(6), 609–619. doi:10.1016/j.technovation.2003.11.002

Klerkx, L. W. A. (2008, October 26-29). Establishment and embedding of innovation brokers at different innovation system levels: insights from the Dutch agricultural sector.*Proceedings of the Conference Transitions towards sustainable agriculture food chains and peri-urban areas*, Wageningen, Wageningen University.

Knudsen, M.P. & Mortensen, T.B. (2010) Some immediate – but negative – effects of openness on product development performance. *Technovation.*

Kohn, S., & Hüsig, S. (2006, August). Potential benefits, current supply, utilization and barriers to adoption: An exploratory study on German SMEs and innovation software. *Technovation, 26*(8), 988–998. doi:10.1016/j.technovation.2005.08.003

Kole, E. S. (2001). Internet Information for African Women's Empowerment. Paper presented at the seminar 'Women, Internet and the South', organized by the Vereniging Informatie en International Ontwikkeling (Society for Information and International Development, VIIO), 18 January 2001, Amsterdam. Retrieved from http://www.xs4all.nl/~ekole/public/endrapafrinh.html

Kolnick, J. (2012, September 26). Redistribution of wealth has gone upward, not down, since early '80s. *MinnPost*. Retrieved from http://www.minnpost.com/community-voices/2012/09/redistribution-wealth-has-gone-upward-not-down-early-80s

Kowalski, S. P. (2009, December 10-11). SMES, Open Innovation and IP Management: Advancing Global Development, A presentation paper on the Theme 2: The Challenge of Open Innovation for MSMEs - SMEs, Open Innovation and IP Management - Advancing Global Development. *WIPO-Italy International Convention on Intellectual Property and Competitiveness of Micro, Small and Medium-Sized Enterprises (MSMEs)*, Rome, Italy.

Kowalski, S. P. (2009, December 10-11). SMES, Open Innovation and IP Management: Advancing Global Development. *Presentation at the WIPO-Italy International Convention on Intellectual Property and Competitiveness of Micro, Small and Medium-Sized Enterprises (MSMEs)*, Rome, Italy.

Koyuncugil, A. S., & Ozgulbas, N. (2009). Risk modeling by CHAID decision tree algorithm. *ICCES, 11*(2), 39–46.

Krauss, K. (2013). Collisions between the worldviews of international ICT policy makers and a deep rural community in South Africa: Assumptions, interpretation, implementation, and reality. *Information Technology for Development, 19*(4), 296–318. doi:10.1080/02681102.2013.793167

Krauss, K., & Turpin, M. (2013). The emancipation of the researcher as part of information and communication technology for development work in deep rural South Africa. *The Electronic Journal of Information Systems in Developing Nations, 59*(2), 1–21.

Krishna, S., & Madon, S. (2003). Introduction: Challenges of ICT in the development context. In S. Krishna & S. Madon (Eds.), *The Digital Challenge: Information Technology in the Development Context* (pp. 1–12). Burlington, VT: Ashgate. doi:10.1016/B978-012426297-3.50027-8

Krishna, S., & Walsham, G. (2005). Implementing public information systems in developing nations: Learning from a success story. *Information Technology for Development, 11*(2), 123–140. doi:10.1002/itdj.20007

Kroll, H., & Liefner, I. (2008). Spin-off enterprises as a mean of technology commercialisation in a transforming economy – evidence from three universities in China. *Technovation, 28*(5), 298–313. doi:10.1016/j.technovation.2007.05.002

Krongard, S., & McCormick, J. (2013). Real Time Visual Analytics to Evaluate Online Collaboration. *Presentation at the annual conference of NERCOMP*, Providence, RI. Retrieved from http://www.educause.edu/nercomp-conference/2013/2013/real-time-visual-analytics-evaluate-online-collaboration

Kulabako, F. (2011, March). Inflation rises to 14 percent. *Daily Monitor, 22*, 3.

Kumar, A., ... (2010). An exploratory study of unsupervised mobile learning in rural India. Retrieved from http://www.cs.cmu.edu/~anujk1/ CHI2010.pdf

Kumar, A. (1999). *Mass Media*. New Delhi: Anmol.

Kumar, A., Rajput, N., Agarwal, S., Chakraborty, D., & Nanavati, A. A. (2008). Organizing the unorganized-employing IT to empower the under-privileged. *Proceedings of the 17th international conference on World Wide Web* (pp. 935-944). ACM. doi:10.1145/1367497.1367623

Kumar, H., et al. (2006). Using Blogs for Extending Library Services. *University News*, *48*(12), 16.

Kumar, K. (2005). *From post-industrial to post-modern society: New theories of the contemporary world* (2nd ed.). Malden, MA: Blackwell.

Kuriyan, R., Ray, I., & Toyama, K. (2008). Information and communication technologies for development: The bottom of the pyramid model in practice. *The Information Society*, *24*(2), 93–104. doi:10.1080/01972240701883948

Laforet, S. (2008) Size, strategic, and market orientation affects on innovation, *Technovation*, 25(10), 1119-1127.

Lakhani, K. R., & von Hippel, E. (2003). How open source software works: "Free" user-to-user assistance. *Research Policy*, *32*(6), 923–943. doi:10.1016/S0048-7333(02)00095-1

Lakhan, S. E., & Jhunjhunwala, K. (2008, April–June). Open source softwares in education. *EDUCAUSE Quarterly*, *31*(2). Retrieved from http://www.educause.edu/EDUCAUSE+Quarterly/EDUCAUSEQuarterlyMagazineVolum/Open-SourceSoftwareinEducation/162873

Lark, J. (n. d.). Collaboration Tools in Online Learning Environments. *ALN Magazine*. Retrieved from www.nspnvt.org/jim/aln-colab.pdf

Laursen, K., & Salter, A. (2006). Open for innovation: The role of openness in explaining innovation performance among UK manufacturing firms. *Strategic Management Journal*, *27*(2), 131–150. doi:10.1002/smj.507

Lawson, C. P., Longhurst, P. J., & Ivey, P. C. (2006). The application of a new research and development project selection model in SMEs. *Technovation*, *26*(2), 242–250. doi:10.1016/j.technovation.2004.07.017

Lazzarotti, V., Manzini, R., & Pizzurno, E. (2008). Managing innovation networks of SMEs: a case study.*Proceeding of the International Engineering Management Conference: managing engineering, technology and innovation for growth (IEMC Europe 2008)*, Estoril, Portugal (pp. 521-525). doi:10.1109/IEMCE.2008.4618024

Leavitt, L. (2013). A purple primaries protocol for progressive policy victories in "deep-red" American states. *Administrative Theory & Praxis*, *35*(3), 457–465. doi:10.2753/ATP1084-1806350306

Leavitt, N. (2010). Will NoSQL databases live up to their promise? *IEEE Computer*, *43*(2), 12–14. doi:10.1109/MC.2010.58

Lecocq, X., & Demil, B. (2006). Strategizing industry structure: The case of open systems in low-tech industry. *Strategic Management Journal*, *27*(9), 891–898. doi:10.1002/smj.544

Lee, R. (2004). Scalability report on triple store applications. Retrieved from http://simile.mit.edu/reports/stores/

Lee, M. R., & Lan, Y.-C. (2011, January). Toward a unified knowledge management model for SMEs. *Expert Systems with Applications*, *38*(1), 729–735. doi:10.1016/j.eswa.2010.07.025

Lee, S., Park, G., Yoon, B., & Park, J. (2010). Open innovation in SMEs—An intermediated network model. *Research Policy*, *39*(2), 290–300. doi:10.1016/j.respol.2009.12.009

Legge, J. (2014). La frontière la plus meurtrière au monde. *La Libre Belgique*. Retrieved from http://www.lalibre.be/actu/international/la-frontiere-la-plus-meurtriere-au-monde-52975d703570386f7f3695ab

Leiponen, A., & Byma, J. (2009, November). If you cannot block, you better run: Small firms, cooperative innovation, and appropriation strategies. *Research Policy*, *38*(9), 1478–1488. doi:10.1016/j.respol.2009.06.003

Lemola, T. & Lievonen, J. (2008). The role of innovation policy in fostering open innovation activities among companies. Vision ERAnet.

Lemola, T., & Lievonen, J. (2008, April 16-17). The role of Innovation Policy in Fostering Open Innovation Activities Among Companies *Proceedings of European Perspectives on Innovation and Policy Programme for the VISION Era-Net Workshop*, Stockholm.

Lenzerini, M. (2002). Data integration: A theoretical perspective. *Proceedings of the 21st ACM SIGMOD-SIGACT-SIGART Symposium on Principles of Database Systems* (pp. 233–246).

Lepore, S. J., Ragan, J. D., & Jones, S. (2000). Talking facilitates cognitive-emotional processes of adaptation to an acute stressor. *Journal of Personality and Social Psychology*, *78*(3), 499–508. doi:10.1037/0022-3514.78.3.499 PMID:10743876

Lerner, M. R. (2001). History of developmental sciences. In N. J. Smelser & P. B. Baltes (Eds.), *International encyclopedia of the social and behavioral sciences* (Vol. 11, pp. 3615–3620). New York, NY: Elsevier. doi:10.1016/B0-08-043076-7/00057-7

Lesk, M. (1995). *Keynote a*ddress: preserving digital objects: recurrent needs and challenges. Papers from the National Preservation Office Annual Conference - 1995 Multimedia Preservation: Capturing The Rainbow. Retrieved from http://community.bellcore.com/lesk/auspres/aus.html)

Levy, M., Powell, P., & Galliers, R. (1998). Assessing information systems strategy development frameworks in SMEs. *Information & Management*, *36*(5), 247–261. doi:10.1016/S0378-7206(99)00020-8

Lewis, D., & Madon, S. (2004). Information systems and nongovernmental development organizations: Advocacy, organizational learning, and accountability. *The Information Society*, *20*(2), 117–126. doi:10.1080/01972240490423049

Lewis, T. C., & Short, C. (1879). *A Latin dictionary: Founded on Andrews' edition of Freund's Latin dictionary: Revised, enlarged, and in great part rewritten*. Oxford, UK: Clarendon Press.

Liao, Tung-Shan & Rice, J. (2010). *Original Research Article Research Policy*, *39*(1), 117–125.

Lichtenthaler, U. (2008a). Open Innovation in Practice: An Analysis of Strategic Approaches to Technology Transactions. *IEEE Transactions on Engineering Management*, *55*(1), 148–157.

Lichtenthaler, U. (2005). External commercialization of knowledge: Review and research agenda. *International Journal of Management Reviews*, *7*(4), 231–255. doi:10.1111/j.1468-2370.2005.00115.x

Lichtenthaler, U. (2006). Technology exploitation strategies in the context of open innovation, International Journal of Technology Intelligence and Planning, Volume 2. *Number*, *1/2006*, 1–21.

Lichtenthaler, U. (2007a). Hierarchical strategies and strategic fit in the keep-or-sell decision. *Management Decision*, *45*(Iss: 3), 340–359. doi:10.1108/00251740710744990

Lichtenthaler, U. (2007b). The drivers of technology licensing: An industry comparison. *California Management Review*, *49*(4), 67–89. doi:10.2307/41166406

Lichtenthaler, U. (2008). Open innovation in practice: An analysis of strategic approaches to technology transactions. *IEEE Transactions on Engineering Management*, *55*(1), 148–157. doi:10.1109/TEM.2007.912932

Lichtenthaler, U. (2008b, May/June). Integrated roadmaps for open innovation. *Research Technology Management*, *51*(3), 45–49.

Lichtenthaler, U. (2008c, September). Relative capacity: Retaining knowledge outside a firm's boundaries. *Journal of Engineering and Technology Management*, *25*(3), 200–212. doi:10.1016/j.jengtecman.2008.07.001

Lichtenthaler, U. (2008d, April). Leveraging technology assets in the presence of markets for knowledge. *European Management Journal*, *26*(2), 122–134. doi:10.1016/j.emj.2007.09.002

Lichtenthaler, U. (2008e, July). Externally commercializing technology assets: An examination of different process stages. *Journal of Business Venturing*, *23*(4), 445–464. doi:10.1016/j.jbusvent.2007.06.002

Lichtenthaler, U. (2009b, August). Absorptive capacity, environmental turbulence, and the complementarity of organizational learning processes. *Academy of Management Journal*, *52*(4), 822–846. doi:10.5465/AMJ.2009.43670902

Lichtenthaler, U. (2009c, September). Outbound open innovation and its effect on firm performance: Examining environmental influences. *R & D Management*, *39*(4), 317–330. doi:10.1111/j.1467-9310.2009.00561.x

Lichtenthaler, U. (2010b, November). Organizing for external technology exploitation in diversified firms. *Journal of Business Research*, *63*(11), 1245–1253. doi:10.1016/j.jbusres.2009.11.005

Lichtenthaler, U. (2010c, July-August). Technology exploitation in the context of open innovation: Finding the right 'job' for your technology. *Technovation*, *30*(7-8), 429–435. doi:10.1016/j.technovation.2010.04.001

Lichtenthaler, U. (2011a, February–March). 'Is open innovation a field of study or a communication barrier to theory development?' A contribution to the current debate. *Technovation*, *31*(2–3), 138–139. doi:10.1016/j.technovation.2010.12.001

Lichtenthaler, U. (2011b, February). Open Innovation: Past Research, Current Debates, and Future Directions. *The Academy of Management Perspectives*, *25*(1), 75–93. doi:10.5465/AMP.2011.59198451

Lichtenthaler, U., & Ernst, H. (2006). Attitudes to externally organizing knowledge management tasks: A review, reconsideration and extension of the NIH syndrome. *R & D Management*, *36*(4), 367–386. doi:10.1111/j.1467-9310.2006.00443.x

Lichtenthaler, U., & Ernst, H. (2009). Opening Up the Innovation Process: The Role of Technology Aggressiveness. *R & D Management*, *39*(1), 38–54. doi:10.1111/j.1467-9310.2008.00522.x

Lichtheim, M. (1973). Ancient Egyptian literature.: Vol. 1. *The Old and Middle Kingdoms*. Berkeley, CA: University of California Press.

Liddell, G. H., & Scott, R. (1996). *A Greek-English lexicon* (9th ed.). New York, NY: Oxford University Press. (Original work published 1843)

Liddy, M. (2013). Education about, for, as development. *Policy and Practice: A Development. Educational Review*, *17*, 27–45.

Light, D., Menon, R., & Shulman, S. (2009). *Training teachers across a diversity of contexts: An analysis of international evaluation data on the Intel Teach Essentials Course, 2006*. New York: EDC/Center for Children and Technology.

Li, J., & Kozhikode, R. K. (2009). Developing new innovation models: Shifts in the innovation landscapes in emerging economies and implications for global R&D management. *Journal of International Management*, *15*(3), 328–339. doi:10.1016/j.intman.2008.12.005

Lilien, G. L., Morrison, P. D., Searls, K., Sonnack, M., & von Hippel, E. (2002). Performance assessment of the lead user idea-generation process for new product development. *Management Science*, *48*(8), 1042–1059. doi:10.1287/mnsc.48.8.1042.171

Lima, C., & Brown, S. (2007). ICT for development: Are Brazilian students well prepared to become global citizens? *Educational Media International*, *44*(2), 141–153. doi:10.1080/09523980701295141

Linder, J.C., Jarvenpaa, S., & Davenport, T.H. (2003) Toward an Innovation Sourcing Strategy. *MIT Sloan Management Review*.

Lindermann, N., Valcareel, S., Schaarschmidt, M., & Von Kortzfleisch, H. (2009). SME 2.0: Roadmap towards Web 2.0- Based Open Innovation in SME-Network- A Case Study Based Research Framework. In G. Dhillon, B. C. Stahl, & R. Baskerville (Eds.), *CreativeSME2009, IFIP International Federation for Information Processing, IFIP AICT 301* (pp. 28–41). doi:10.1007/978-3-642-02388-0_3

Linn, M. C. (1998). Instances of Distance Learning: Cognition and distance learning. *Journal of the American Society for Information Science, 47*(11), 826–842. doi:10.1002/(SICI)1097-4571(199611)47:11<826::AID-ASI6>3.0.CO;2-4

Lin, Y. H., Tsai, K. M., Shiang, W. J., Kuo, T. C., & Tsai, C. H. (2009). Research on using ANP to establish a performance assessment model for business intelligence systems. *Expert Systems with Applications, 36*(2), 4135–4146. doi:10.1016/j.eswa.2008.03.004

Liu, X. (2008). *China's Development Model: An Alternative Strategy for Technological Catch-Up,* SLPTMD Working Paper Series No. 020, University of Oxford, UK.

Livieratos, A. D., & Papoulias, D. B. (2009) *Towards an Open Innovation Growth Strategy for New,* Technology-Based Firms, National Technical University of Athens, Retrieved from http://www.ltp.ntua.gr/uploads/GJ/eK/GJeKw8Jf5Rqj-CO9CWapm4w/Growth.pdf

Lockner, O. A. (Ed.). (2013). Steps to local government reform: A guide to tailoring local government reforms to fit regional governance communities in democracies. Bloomington, IN: iUniverse.

López, A. (2009, January). Innovation and Appropriability, Empirical Evidence and Research Agenda. In The Economics of Intellectual Property: Suggestions for Further Research in Developing Countries and Countries with Economies in Transition.

Lopez-vega, H. (2009, January 22-24). How demand-driven technological systems of innovation work?: The role of intermediary organizations. *Paper from the DRUD-DIME Academy Winter 2009 PhD Conference on Economics and Management of Innovation Technology and Organizational Change,* Aalborg, Denmark.

Lord, M. D., Mandel, S. W., & Wager, J. D. (2002). Spinning out a star. *Harvard Business Review, 80,* 115–121.

Loshin, D. (2011). *The Analytics Revolution 2011: Optimizing Reporting and Analytics to Optimizing Reporting and Analytics to Make Actionable Intelligence Pervasive.* Knowledge Integrity, Inc.

Love, J.H. & Ganotakis, P. (2012). Original Research Article. *International Business Review.*

Luff, P., & Heath, C. (1998, November 14-18). Mobility in Collaboration. *Proceedings of Conference on Computer Supported Cooperative Work,* Seattle, Washington, USA (pp. 305-314). New York: ACM. doi:10.1145/289444.289505

Luhn, H. P. (1958). A Business Intelligence System. *IBM Journal of Research and Development, 2*(4), 314–319. doi:10.1147/rd.24.0314

Lundvall, B. (1995). *National systems of innovation: Towards a theory of innovation and interactive learning.* London: Biddles Ltd.

Lundvall, B. A., Johnson, B., Andersen, E. S., & Dalum, B. (2002). National Systems of production and competence building. *Research Policy, 31*(2), 213–231. doi:10.1016/S0048-7333(01)00137-8

Luwaga, B. (2012). Closure of Community Radio Stations lives Luwero Quiet. Retrieved from http://ugandaradionetwork.com/a/story.php?s=39811

Lv, J. (2011). ICT education in rual areas of southwest China: A case study of Zhongxian County, Chongqing. *Proceedings of the6th International Conference on Computer Science & Education* (pp. 681-685). IEEE doi:10.1109/ICCSE.2011.6028730

Lynch, C. (2008). Big data: How do your data grow? *Nature, 455*(7209), 28–29. doi:10.1038/455028a PMID:18769419

MacGregor, S., Bianchi, M., Hernandez, J. L., & Mendibil, K. (2007, October 29-30). Towards the tipping point for social innovation. *Proceedings of the 12th International Conference on Towards Sustainable Product Design (Sustainable Innovation 07),* Farnham, Surrey, UK (pp. 145-152).

Macintosh, A. (2004). Characterizing e-participation in policy-making.*Proceedings of the 37th Hawaii International Conference on System Sciences.*

Madon, S., Reinhard, N., Roode, D., & Walsham, G. (2009). Digital Inclusion Projects in Developing Countries: Processes of Institutionalization. *Information Technology for Development, 15*(2), 95–107. doi:10.1002/itdj.20108

Madon, S., & Sahay, S. (2002). An information-based model of NGO mediation for the empowerment of slum dwellers in Bangalore. *The Information Society, 18*(1), 13–19. doi:10.1080/01972240252818199

Maes, J. (2009). *SMEs´ Radical Product Innovation: the Role of the Internal and External Absorptive Capacity Spheres. Job Market Paper.*

Mahajan, S. L. (2002). Information Communication Technology in distance education in India: A challenge. *University News, 40*(19), 1-9.

Maijers, W., Vokurka, L., van Uffelen, R. & Ravensbergen, P. (2005) Open innovation: symbiotic network, Knowledge circulation and competencies for the benefit of innovation in the Horticulture delta. *Presentation IAMA Chicago 2005.*

Major, E. J., & Cordey-Hayes, M. (2000). Engaging the business support network to give SMEs the benefit of foresight. *Technovation, 20*(11), 589–602. doi:10.1016/S0166-4972(00)00006-7

Makrakis. (2012). ICTs in Education for Sustainable Development. *UNESCO Ministry of HRD.*

Mallon, M., & Bernsten, S. (2015). Collaborative Learning Technologies. Tips and Trends. ACRL Instruction Section, Instructional Technologies Committee, Winter. Retrieved from http://bit.ly/tipsandtrendswi15

Mantel, S. J., & Rosegger, G. (1987). The role of third-parties in the diffusion of innovations: a survey. In R. Rothwell & J. Bessant (Eds.), *Innovation: Adaptation and Growth* (pp. 123–134). Amsterdam: Elsevier.

Marisetty, V., Ramachandran, K., & Jha, R. (2008). *Wealth effects of family succession: A case of Indian family business groups.* Working Paper. Indian School of Business.

Marsh, M. R. (2014). Modernization theory, then and now. *Comparative Sociology, 13*(3), 261–283. doi:10.1163/15691330-12341311

Martinelli, A. (2015). Global modernization and multiple modernities. In A. Martinelli & C. He (Eds.), *Global modernization review: New discoveries and theories revisited* (pp. 5–24). Hackensack, NJ: World Scientific.

Martinez, R., Yacef, K., & Kay, J. (2010). Collaborative concept mapping at the tabletop. Technical Report 657. University of Sydney. Retrieved from http://sydney.edu.au/engineering/it/research/tr/tr657.pdf

Marx, K. (1955). *The poverty of philosophy.* Moscow: Progress Publishers. (Original work published 1847)

Marx, K. (1977). *Capital: A critique of political economy* (B. Fowkes, Trans.). New York, NY: Vintage. (Original work published 1867)

Massa, S., & Testa, S. (2008, July). Innovation and SMEs: Misaligned perspectives and goals among entrepreneurs, academics, and policy makers. *Technovation, 28*(7), 393–407. doi:10.1016/j.technovation.2008.01.002

Mathee, A., Harpham, T., Naicker, N., Barnes, B., Plagerson, S., Feit, M., & Naidoo, S. et al. (2010). Overcoming fieldwork challenges in urban health research in developing nations: A research note. *International Journal of Social Research Methodology, 13*(2), 171–178. doi:10.1080/13645570902867742

Mathur, M., & Sharma, S. (2009). Strategic metamorphoses of ICT sector for human development in India. *International Journal of Information Communication Technologies and Human Development, 1*(4), 16–29.

Mattes, R. (2008). The material and political bases of lived poverty in Africa: Insights from the Afrobarometer. *Afrobarometer Working Paper No. 98.* Retrieved from http://www.afrobarometer.org/files/documents/working_papers/AfropaperNo98.pdf

Mattes, R., & Bratton, M. (2009). Poverty reduction, economic growth and democratization in Sub-Saharan Africa. *Afrobarometer Briefing Paper No.68.* Retrieved from http://www.afrobarometer.org/files/documents/briefing_papers/AfrobriefNo68.pdf

Maximum security: a hacker's guide to protecting your internet site and network. (1998). New Delhi: Techmedia.

May, J., Dutton, V., & Munyakazi, L. (2014). Information and communication technologies as a pathway from poverty: Evidence from East Africa. In E. O. Adera, T. M. Waema, J. May, O. Mascarenhas, & K. Diga (Eds.), *ICT pathways to poverty reduction: Empirical evidence from East and Southern Africa* (pp. 33–52). Ottawa, Canada: IDRC. doi:10.3362/9781780448152.002

McCabe, L. (2010). What's a Collaboration Suite & Why Should You Care? *Small Business Computing.* Retrieved from http://www.smallbusinesscomputing.com/biztools/article.php/3890601/Whats-a-Collaboration-Suite--Why-Should-You-Care.htm

McCallum, K., & Papandrea, F. (2009). Community business: The internet in remote Australian indigenous communities. *New Media & Society, 11*(7), 1230–1251. doi:10.1177/1461444809342059

Mcconatha, D., Praul, M., & Lynch, M. (2008). Mobile learning in higher education: An empirical assessment of a new educational tool. *The Turkish Online Journal of Educational Technology – TOJET, 7* (3). Retrieved from http://davidwees.com/etec522/sites/default/files/mobile%20learning%20in%20higher%20education.pdf

McEvily, S. K., Eisenhardt, K. M. M., & Prescott, J. E. (2004). The global acquisition, leverage, and protection of technological competencies. *Strategic Management Journal, 25*(8/9), 713–722. doi:10.1002/smj.425

McGrath, B. (1998). Partners in learning: Twelve ways technology changes the teacher-student relationship. Technological Horizon. *Education, 25*(9), 58–62.

McPhail, B., Costantino, T., Bruckmann, D., Barclay, R., & Clement, A. (1998). CAVEAT exemplar: Participatory design in a non-profit volunteer organisation. *Computer Supported Cooperative Work, 7*(3-4), 223–241. doi:10.1023/A:1008631020266

McQuail, D. (2006). *McQuail's mass communication theory.* London, UK: Sage.

Mearian, L. (2010, November 2). Data growth remains IT's biggest challenge, Gartner says. *Computerworld.* Retrieved from http://www.computerworld.com/s/article/9194283/Data_growth_remains_IT_s_biggest_challenge_Gartner_says

Medhi, I., Menon, G., & Toyama, K. (2008). Challenges in computerized job search for the developing world. Proceedings of CHI'08: extended abstracts on Human factors in computing systems (pp. 2079-2094). ACM. doi:10.1145/1358628.1358640

Medhi, I., Sagar, A., & Toyama, K. (2006). Text-free user interfaces for illiterate and semi-literate users. *Proceedings of the ACM/IEEE International Conference on Information and Communication Technologies and Development* (ICTD '06) (pp. 72-82). IEEE. doi:10.1109/ICTD.2006.301841

Medhi, I., & Toyama, K. (2007). Full-context videos for first-time, non-literate PC users. *Information Technologies and International Development, 4*(1), 37–50. doi:10.1162/itid.2007.4.1.37

Mehra, K. (2009). Role of Intermediary Organisations in Innovation Systems- A Case from India. *Proceedings of the 6th Asialics International Conference,* Hong Kong.

Mehta, C., & Theodore, N. (2006). Workplace Safety in Atlanta's Construction Industry: Institutional Failure in Temporary Staffing Arrangements. *Working USA. Journal of Labor and Society, 9*, 59–77.

Melendez, E., Valenzuela, A., Jr., Theodore, N., Visser, A., & Gonzalez, A. L. (2009). Differences in the Types of Operations, Capacities and Approaches of Day Labor Worker Centers. *Centre for study of urban poverty.* Retrieved from http://www.csup.ucla.edu/publications/Differences%20in%20Types%20of%20Operations.pdf/view

Meltzer, S. E. (2001). Egyptology. In D. B. Redford (Ed.), *The Oxford encyclopedia of ancient Egypt* (Vol. 1, pp. 448–458). New York, NY: Oxford University Press.

Mention, A.-L. (2010). Co-operation and co-opetition as open innovation practices in the service sector: Which influence on innovation novelty? *Technovation.*

Mia, M., & Ramage, M. (2011). IT project management in developing nations: Approaches and factors affecting success in the microfinance sector of Bangladesh. *Paper presented at the proceedings of the 6th International Research Workshop on IT Project Management,* Milan, Italy.

Miles, I. (2005). Innovation in Services. In. J. Fagerberg, D.C. Mowery, & R.R. Nelson (Eds.), The Oxford Handbook of Innovation (pp. 433-458). Oxford University Press.

Millar, C. C. J. M., & Choi, C. J. (2003). Advertising and knowledge intermediaries: Managing the ethical challenges of intangibles. *Journal of Business Ethics, 48*(3), 267–277. doi:10.1023/B:BUSI.0000005788.90079.5d

Miller, H. T. (2004). The ideographic individual. *Administrative Theory & Praxis, 26*(4), 469–488.

Miller, H. T. (2012). *Governing narratives: Symbolic politics and policy change.* Tuscaloosa: University of Alabama Press.

Mohan, G. (2008). Participatory development. In V. Desai & R. B. Potter (Eds.), *The companion to development studies* (2nd ed., pp. 45–50). London: Hodder Education.

Mohr, J., & Spekman, R. (1994). Characteristics of partnership success: Partnership attributes, communication behavior and conflict resolution techniques. *Strategic Management Journal, 15*(2), 135–152. doi:10.1002/smj.4250150205

Moore, G. A. (1991). *Crossing the Chasm.* New York, NY: Harper Business.

Moore, G. A. (2006). *Dealing with Darwin: How Great Companies Innovate at Every Phase of Their Evolution.* Chichester: UK Capstone Publishing.

Morgan, G. (2006). *Images of organization, updated.* Thousand Oaks, CA: Sage.

Morgan, H. L. (1985). *Ancient society.* Tucson, AZ: University of Arizona Press. (Original work published 1877)

Morrison, J. (Ed.), (2000) On the Horizon: US Higher Education in Transition. The Technology Source, 11(1), 6-10.

Mortara, L., & Minshall, T. (2011). How do large multinational companies implement open innovation? *Technovation, 31*(10-11), 586–597. doi:10.1016/j.technovation.2011.05.002

Mosse, D. (2013). The anthropology of international development. *Annual Review of Anthropology, 42*(1), 227–246. doi:10.1146/annurev-anthro-092412-155553

Motlik, S. (2008). Mobile Learning in Developing Nations. *International Review of Research in Open and Distance Learning, 9*(2).

Mourão, S., & Okada, K. (2009). Mobile Phone as a Tool for Data Collection in Field Research. *World Academy of 75 Science. Engineering and Technology, 70*(43), 222–226.

Mouzelis, N. (1999). Modernity: A non-European conceptualization. *The British Journal of Sociology, 50*(1), 141–159. doi:10.1080/000713199358851 PMID:15266678

MSR. (2009). Operation Manual for use by regional and worker collection points.

Muriithi, N., & Crawford, L. (2003). Approaches to project management in Africa: Implications for international development projects. *International Journal of Project Management, 21*(5), 309–319. doi:10.1016/S0263-7863(02)00048-0

Murugan, S. (2013). User Education: Academic Libraries. *International Journal of Information Technology and Library Science Research, 1*(1), 1-6. Retrieved from http://acascipub.com/Journals.php

Muuro, M., Wagacha, W., Kihoro, R., & Oboko, J. (2014). Students' Perceived Challenges in an Online Collaborative Learning Environment: A Case of Higher Learning Institutions in Nairobi, Kenya. *The International Review of Research in Open and Distributed Learning, 15*(6). Retrieved from http://www.irrodl.org/index.php/irrodl/article/view/1768/3124

Nagaoka, S., & Kwon, H. U. (2006). The incidence of cross-licensing: A theory and new evidence on the firm and contract level determinants. *Research Policy, 35*(9), 1347–1361. doi:10.1016/j.respol.2006.05.007

Nahlinder, J. (2005). *Innovation and Employment in Services: The Case of Knowledge Intensive Business Services in Sweden* [Doctoral Thesis]. Department of technology and Social Change, Linköping University, Sweden.

Nählinder, J. (2005). *Innovation and Employment in Services: The case of Knowledge Intensive Business Services in Sweden* [PhD Thesis]. Department of Technology and Social Change, Linköping University, Sweden, Unitryck Linköping.

Naidu, S. (2006). E Learning: a guidebook of principles, procedures and practices. Commonwealth Educational Media Center for Asia. Retrieved from http://cemca.org/e-learning_guidebook.pdf

Nalebuff, B. J., & Brandeburger, A. M. (1996). *Co-opetition*. London: Harper Collins.

Narain, S. (2001). Development Financial Institutions' and Commercial banks' Innovation Schemes for Assisting SMEs in India. In *Improving the Competitiveness of SMEs in Developing Countries: The Role of Finance to Enhance Enterprise Development* (pp. 81–87). Geneva: United Nations.

Narula, R. (2004). R&D collaboration by SMEs: New opportunities and limitations in the face of globalisation. *Technovation, 25*(2), 153–161. doi:10.1016/S0166-4972(02)00045-7

Nassanga, L. G. (2003). Is there a place for community media in East Africa in the context of globalisation? In G. Nassanga (Ed.), *The East African media and globalisation: Defining the public interest* (pp. 184–202). Kampala, Uganda: Makerere University.

Nassanga, L. G. (2009a). An assessment of the changing community media parameters in East Africa. *African Journalism Studies, 30*(1), 42–57. doi:10.3368/ajs.30.1.42

Nassanga, L. G. (2009b). Participatory discussion programs as 'hybrid community media' in Uganda. *International Journal of Media and Cultural Politics, 5*(1 & 2), 119–124.

Natarajan, M. (2007). Blogs: A powerful tool for accessing information. *DESIDOC Bulletin of Information Technology*, 27(3). Retrieved from http://knowgate.niscair.res.in/jspui/bitstream/123456789/81/3/BLOGS_A%20POWERFUL%20 TOOL.pdf

National Curriculum Framework. (2005). *Ministry of HRD*. Government of India.

Ndonzuau, F. N., Pirnay, F., & Surlemont, B. (2002). A stage model of academic spin-off creation. *Technovation*, 22(5), 281–289. doi:10.1016/S0166-4972(01)00019-0

Nguyen, N. (2007). The challenges of transferring modern project management principles and methodologies to developing nations. *Paper presented at theproceedings of the 2007 Project Management Institute Global Congress*, Hong Kong.

Nine Tools for Collaboratively Creating Mind Maps. (2010). Retrieved from http://www.freetech4teachers.com/2010/03/ nine-tools-for-collaboratively-creating.html#.VubuNPl97IV

Nisbet, A. R. (1969). *Social change and history: Aspects of the Western theory of development*. New York, NY: Oxford University Press.

Nisbet, A. R. (1986). *The making of modern society*. New York, NY: Wheatsheaf.

Novelli, M., Schmitz, B., & Spencer, T. (2006, December). Networks, clusters and innovation in tourism: A UK experience. *Tourism Management*, 27(6), 1141–1152. doi:10.1016/j.tourman.2005.11.011

Nowaczyk, R. (1998). Student perception of multimedia in the undergraduate classroom. *International Journal of Instructional Media*, 25, 367–368.

Nunes,P.M., Serrasqueiro, Z. & Leitão, J. (2010). Is there a linear relationship between R&D intensity and growth? Empirical evidence of non-high-tech vs. high-tech SMEs. *Research Policy*, 41(1), 36-53.

O'Brien, P. (2012). The future: Big data apps or web services? Retrieved from http://blog.fliptop.com/blog/2012/05/12/ the-future-big-data-apps-or-web-services/

O'Donnell, S., McIver, W. J., & Rideout, V. (2006, September). Community media and networking and ICT.*Proceedings of the Canadian Communication Association Annual Conference*, Toronto, Canada, York University.

O'Regan, N., & Ghobadian, A. (2005). Innovation in SMEs: The impact of strategic orientation and environmental perceptions.*International Journal of Productivity and Performance Management*,54(2),81–97.doi:10.1108/17410400510576595

OECD. (1992). Oslo Manual (1st ed.). DSTI, Organization for Economic Co-operation and Development (OECD), Paris

OECD. (1996). Oslo Manual (2nd ed.). DSTI, OECD, Paris.

OECD. (2005). Oslo Manual (3rd ed.). DSTI, OECD, Paris.

OECD. (2005). *Oslo Manual: Guidelines for Collecting and Interpreting Innovation Data* (3rd ed.). Paris: Organization for Economic Co-operation and Development.

OECD. (2006). *The Athens Action Plans for Removing Barriers to SME Access to International Markets*. Adopted at the OECD-APEC Global Conference in Athens, on 8 November 2006, OECD Report, Paris.

OECD. (2007). *Innovation and Growth: Rationale for an Innovation Strategy, OECD Report*. Paris: OECD.

OECD. (2008). *Open Innovation in Global Networks, Policy Brief, OECD Observer*. Paris: OECD.

Olson, E., & Bakke, G. (2001). Implementing the lead user method in a high technology firm: A longitudinal study of intentions versus actions.*Journal of Product Innovation Management*,18(2),388–395.doi:10.1016/S0737-6782(01)00111-4

Online degree courses from India. (2016). *U18edu.in*. Retrieved from www.U18edu.in

Online, A. (n.d.). Are traditional teaching methods still effective. retrieved February 18, 2014, from http://arzelonline. wordpress.com/2012/06/25/are-traditional-teachingmethods-still-effective/

Optimising technological tools in promoting LIS education. Education Essay. Retrieved from http://www.ukessays.com/essays/education/optimisingtechnological-tools-in-promoting-lis-education-education-essay.php

O'Regan, N., Ghobadian, A., & Sims, M. (2006, February). Fast tracking innovation in manufacturing SMEs. *Technovation, 26*(2), 251–261. doi:10.1016/j.technovation.2005.01.003

Organisation for Economic Co-operation and Devel-opment. (2003). Integrating information and commu-nication technologies in development programmes. Retrieved from www.oecd.org/bookshop

Organski, F. K. A. (1965). *The stages of political development.* New York, NY: Alfred A. Knopf.

Padmadinata, F. Z. S. (2007, April 3-4). Quality Management System and Product Certification Process and Practice for SME in Indonesia. *Proceedings of the National Workshop on Subnational Innovation Systems and Technology Capacity Building Policies to Enhance Competitiveness of SMEs*, UN-ESCAP and Indonesian Institute of Science (LIPI), Jakarta, Indonesia.

Paik, M., Sharma, A., Meacham, A., Quarta, G., Smith, P., Trahanas, J., & Subramanian, L. (2009). The case for Smart-Track. *Paper presented at the 3rd International Conference on Information and Communication Technologies and Development, Education City*, Doha, Qatar. doi:10.1109/ICTD.2009.5426683

Pal, J., Lakshmanan, M., & Toyama, K. (2007). My child will be respected: Parental perspectives on computers in rural India. *Information Systems Frontiers, 11*(2), 129–144. doi:10.1007/s10796-009-9172-1

Palmer, I., Dunford, R., Rura-Polley, T., & Baker, E. (2001). Changing forms of organizing: Dualities in using remote collaboration technologies in film production. *Journal of Organizational Change Management, 14*(2), 190–212. doi:10.1108/09534810110388081

Pandey, A.P. & Shivesh (2007, December). *Indian SMEs and their uniqueness in the country*, Munich Personal RePEc Archive, MPRA Paper No. 6086. Retrieved from http://mpra.ub.uni-muenchen.de/6086/

Parikh, T. S., Javid, P., Ghosh, K., & Toyama, K. (2006). Mobile phones and paper documents: evaluating a new approach for capturing microfinance data in rural India.*Proceedings of the SIGCHI conference on Human Factors in computing systems* (pp. 551—560). ACM. doi:10.1145/1124772.1124857

Parikh, T., Ghosh, K., & Chavan, A. (2003). Design studies for a financial management system for micro-credit groups in rural India. *ACM SIGCAPH Computers and the Physically Handicapped, 73(74), 15-22.* doi:10.1145/957205.957209

Partanen, J., Möller, K., Westerlund, M., Rajala, R., & Rajala, A. (2008, July). Social capital in the growth of science-and-technology-based SMEs. *Industrial Marketing Management, 37*(5), 513–522. doi:10.1016/j.indmarman.2007.09.012

Payne, J. E. (2003). E-Commerce Readiness for SMEs in Developing Countries: a Guide for Development Professionals. Retrieved from http://learnlink.aed.org/Publications/Concept_Papers/ecommerce_readiness.pdf

Pedersen, M., Sondergaard,and H.A., Esbjerg, L. (2009, June 21-24). Network characteristics and open innovation in SMEs. In K.R.E. Huizingh, S. Conn, M. Torkkeli, & I. Bitran (Eds.), *Proceedings of The XX ISPIM Conference*, Vienna, Austria.

Peet, R., & Hartwick, E. (2015). *Theories of development: Contentions, arguments, alternatives* (3rd ed.). New York, NY: The Guilford Press.

Pentaho Corporation. (2014). Pentaho Open Source BI. Retrieved from http://community.pentaho.com/

Perkins, H. J. (1997). *Geopolitics and the Green Revolution: Wheat, genes, and the Cold War*. New York, NY: Oxford University Press.

Perry, C. D. (2001). Infrastructure investment. In N. J. Smelser & P. B. Baltes (Eds.), *International encyclopedia of the social and behavioral sciences* (Vol. 11, pp. 7486–7489). New York, NY: Elsevier. doi:10.1016/B0-08-043076-7/04411-9

Peters, B. (2009). And lead us not into thinking the new is new: A bibliographic case for new media history. *New Media & Society*, *11*(13), 13–30. doi:10.1177/1461444808099572

Pietrobelli, C., & Rabellotti, R. (Eds.), (2006). Upgrading to Compete: Global Value Chains, Clusters, and SMEs in Latin America. Washington: Inter-American Development Bank.

Piketty, T. (2014). *Capital in the Twenty-First Century*. Cambridge, Mass: Belknap Press. doi:10.4159/9780674369542

Pisano, G. P. (1990). The R&D boundaries of the firm: An empirical analysis. *Administrative Science Quarterly*, *35*(1), 153–176. doi:10.2307/2393554

Plato. (5-4th c. BC, 1921). Cratylus (Vol. 12, H.N. Fowler, Trans.). Cambridge, MA: Harvard University Press.

Plato. (5-4th c. BC, 1967). Laws (Vols. 10 & 11, R.G. Bury, Trans.). Cambridge, MA: Harvard University Press.

PMBOK. (2003). *Project Management Body of Knowledge*. Washington, D.C.: Project Management Institute.

Pohjola, M. (2003). *The adoption and diffusion of ICT across countries: Patterns and determinants, The new economy handbook*. Helsinki, Finland: Academic Press.

Pollock, R. (2009). Innovation, Imitation and Open Source. *International Journal of Open Source Software & Processes*, *1*(2), 114-127.

Ponniah, P. (2010). *Data Warehousing Fundamentals for IT Professionals* (2nd ed.). New York: John Wiley & Sons, Inc. doi:10.1002/9780470604137

Popovič, A., Turk, T., & Jaklič, J. (2010). Conceptual model of business value of business intelligence systems. *Management*, *15*(1), 5–30.

Porter, M. E., & Bond, G. C. (1999). The Global Competitiveness Report 1999. In *World Economic Forum* (pp. 54-65).

Potnis, D. (2014). Managing gender-related challenges in ICT4D field research. *The Electronic Journal of Information Systems in Developing Nations*, *65*(2), 1–26.

Potter, B. R., Binns, T., Smith, W. D., & Elliott, A. J. (2008). *Geographies of development: An introduction to development studies* (3rd ed.). London: Pearson.

Potter, R., Conway, D., Evans, R., & Lloyd-Evans, S. (2012). *Key concepts in development geography*. Thousand Oaks, CA: Sage. doi:10.4135/9781473914834

Pourdehnad, J. (2007, October). Idealized Design - An "Open Innovation" Process. *Presentation from the annual W.Edwards Deming Annual Conference*, Purdue University, West Lafayette, Indiana.

Powell, W. (1990). Neither market nor hierarchy: network forms of organization. In B. Stow & L. L. Cummings (Eds.), *Research in Organizational Behavior*. Greenwich: JAI Press.

Power, D. J. (2007). A Brief History of Decision Support Systems, version 4.0. *DSSResources.COM*. Retrieved from http://DSSResources.COM/history/dsshistory.html

Prahalad, K. C. (2005). *The fortune at the bottom of the pyramid: Eradicating poverty through profits.* Upper Saddle River, NJ: Pearson.

Prencipe, A. (2000). Breadth and depth of technological capabilities in CoPS: The case of the aircraft engine control system. *Research Policy, 29*(7-8), 895–911. doi:10.1016/S0048-7333(00)00111-6

Pringle, I., & David, M. J. R. (2002). Rural com-munity ICT applications: The Kothmale model. *The Electronic Journal on Information Systems and Development, 8*(4), 1–14.

Prügl, R., & Schreier, M. (2006). Learning from leading-edge customers at *The Sims*: Opening up the innovation process using toolkits. *R & D Management, 36*(3), 237–250. doi:10.1111/j.1467-9310.2006.00433.x

Puri, S. K., Byrne, E., Nhampossa, J. L., & Quraishi, Z. B. (2004). Contextuality of participation in IS design: a developing country perspective.*Proceedings of the eighth conference on Participatory design: Artful integration: interweaving media, materials and practices (Vol. 1*, pp. 42—52). ACM. doi:10.1145/1011870.1011876

Puri, S., & Sahay, S. (2007). Role of ICTs in participatory development: An Indian experience. *Information Technology for Development, 13*(2), 133–160. doi:10.1002/itdj.20058

Quinn, J. B. (2000). Outsourcing innovation: The new engine of growth. *Sloan Management Review, 41*, 4, 13–28.

Qvortrup, L. (2006). Understanding new digital media: Medium theory or complexity. *European Journal of Communication, 21*(345), 345–356. doi:10.1177/0267323106066639

Rahman, H., & Ramos, I. (2013). Open Innovation Strategies in SMEs: Development of a Business Model. In Small and Medium Enterprises: Concepts, Methodologies, Tools, and Applications (Vols. 1–4). pp. 281–293). USA: Information Resources Management Association. doi:10.4018/978-1-4666-3886-0.ch015

Rahman, H., & Ramos, I. (2010). Open Innovation in SMEs: From Closed Boundaries to Networked Paradigm. *Issues in Informing Science and Information Technology, 7*, 471–487.

Rahman, H., & Ramos, I. (2012, June 22-27). Open Innovation in Entrepreneurships: Agents of Transformation towards the Knowledge-Based Economy.*Proceedings of the Issues in Informing Science and Information Technology Education Conference*, Montreal, Canada.

Rahman, H., & Ramos, I. (2013). Implementation of e-Commerce at the grassroots: Issues of challenges in terms of human-computer interaction. *International Journal of Information Communication Technologies and Human Development, 5*(2), 1–19. doi:10.4018/jicthd.2013040101

Rainey, H. (2009). *Understanding and managing public organizations* (4th ed.). San Francisco, CA: John Wiley & Sons.

Raman, M., Ryan, T., & Olfman, L. (2006). Knowledge management system for emergency preparedness: an action research study. *Proceedings of the 39th Annual Hawaii International Conference onSystem Sciences HICSS '06 (Vol. 2*, p. 37b). IEEE. doi:10.1109/HICSS.2006.244

Ramos, E., Acedo, F. J., & Gonzalez, M. A. (2011, October–November). Internationalisation speed and technological patterns: A panel data study on Spanish SMEs. Original Research Article. *Technovation, 31*(10–11), 560–572. doi:10.1016/j.technovation.2011.06.008

Raymond, L., & St-Pierre, J. (2010). R&D as a determinant of innovation in manufacturing SMEs: An attempt at empirical clarification. *Technovation, 30*(1), 48–56. doi:10.1016/j.technovation.2009.05.005

Rejeb, H. B., Morel-Guimarães, L., Boly, V., & Assiélou, N. G. (2009). Measuring innovation best practices: Improvement of an innovation index integrating threshold and synergy effects. *Technovation*, *28*(12), 838–854. doi:10.1016/j.technovation.2008.08.005

Renaud, P. (2008, February 25-26). Open Innovation at Oseo Innovation: Example of the Passerelle Programme (A tool to support RDI collaboration between innovative SME's and large enterprises). *Presentation at the OECD Business Symposium on Open Innovation in Global Networks*, Copenhagen.

Rhee, J., Park, T., & Lee, D. H. (2010). Drivers of innovativeness and performance for innovative SMEs in South Korea: Mediation of learning orientation. *Technovation*, *30*(1), 65–75. doi:10.1016/j.technovation.2009.04.008

Richardson, J., & Swan, K. (2003). Examining social presence in online courses in relation to students' perceived learning and satisfaction. *Journal of Asynchronous Learning Networks*, *7*(1), 68–88.

Riggs, F. W. (1997). Modernity and bureaucracy. *Public Administration Review*, *4*(57), 347–353. doi:10.2307/977318

Rogers, S. (2011, November 14). Occupy protests around the world: full list visualised. *The Guardian*. Retrieved from http://www.guardian.co.uk/news/datablog/2011/oct/17/occupy-protests-world-list-map#

Rogers, E. M. (1962). *Diffusion of Innovations*. New York, NY: Free Pres.

Rojas, C. (2010). *The Great Wall: A cultural history*. Cambridge, MA: Harvard University Press.

Roos, D., Eaton, C., Lapis, G., Zikopoulos, P., & Deutsch, T. (2011). *Understanding Big Data: Analytics for Enterprise Class Hadoop and Streaming Data*. McGraw-Hill Osborne Media.

Roper, S., & Hewitt-Dundas, N. (2004). Innovation persistence: survey and case - study evidence (Working Paper). Aston Business School, Birmingham, UK.

Rostow, W. W. (1960). *The stages of economic growth: A non-communist manifesto*. New York, NY: Cambridge University Press.

Rothwell, R., & Dodgson, M. M. (1994). The Handbook of Industrial Innovation. Edward Elgar, Cheltenham.

Rothwell, R. (1991). External networking and innovation in small and medium-sized manufacturing firms in Europe. *Technovation*, *11*(2), 93–112. doi:10.1016/0166-4972(91)90040-B

Rouse, M. (2012). Definition of big data analytics. Retrieved from http://searchbusinessanalytics.techtarget.com/definition/big-data-analytics

Roztocki, N., & Weistroffer, H. (2011). Information technology success factors and models in developing and emerging economies. *Information Technology for Development*, *17*(3), 163–167. doi:10.1080/02681102.2011.568220

Ruggiero, K. J., Smith, D. W., Hanson, R. F., Resnick, H. S., Saunders, B. E., Kilpatrick, D. G., & Best, C. L. (2004). Is disclosure of childhood rape associated with mental health outcome? Results from the national women's study. Child Maltreatment. *Journal of the American Professional Society on the Abuse of Children*, *9*(1), 62–77.

Ruiz, P. P. (2010). *Technology & Knowledge Transfer Under the Open Innovation Paradigm: a model and tool proposal to understand and enhance collaboration-based innovations integrating C-K Design Theory, TRIZ and Information Technologies* [Dissertation for the Master of Science in Innovation and Technology]. Management School of Management, University of Bath, UK.

Saarikoski, V. (2006). *The Odyssey of the Mobile Internet- the emergence of a networking attribute in a multidisciplinary study* [Academic dissertation]. TIEKE, Helsinki.

Saez, E. (2012). *Striking it richer: the evolution of top incomes in the United States (updated with 2009 and 2010 estimates). Pathways Magazine.* Berkeley, CA: University of California – Berkley.

Sahay, S., & Walsham, G. (2006). Scaling of health information systems in India: Challenges and approaches. *Information Technology for Development, 12*(3), 185–200. doi:10.1002/itdj.20041

Saini, D. S., & Budhwar, P. S. (2008). Managing the human resource in Indian SMEs: The role of indigenous realities. *Journal of World Business, 43*(4), 417–434. doi:10.1016/j.jwb.2008.03.004

Salaberry, M. (2001). The use of technology for second language learning and teaching: A retrospective. *Modern Language Journal, 85*(1), 41–56. doi:10.1111/0026-7902.00096

Samara, E., Georgiadis, P., & Bakouros, I. (2012). The impact of innovation policies on the performance of national innovation systems: A system dynamics analysis. *Technovation, 32*, 624–638.

Samuel, J., Shah, N., & Hadingham, W. (2005). Mobile Communications in South Africa, Tanzania and Egypt: Results from community and business surveys. *Africa: The Impact of Mobile Phones. The Vodafone Policy Paper Series, 2,* 44–52.

Sandström, A., & Carlsson, L. (2008). The performance of policy networks: The relation between network structure and network performance. *Policy Studies Journal: the Journal of the Policy Studies Organization, 36*(4), 497–524. doi:10.1111/j.1541-0072.2008.00281.x

Sandum, A. (2010). *Economics evolving: A history of economic thought.* Princeton, NJ: Princeton University Press.

Santisteban, M. A. (2006). Business Systems and Cluster Policies in the Basque Country and Catalonia (1990-2004). *European Urban and Regional Studies, 13*(1), 25–39. doi:10.1177/0969776406059227

Sautter, B., & Clar, G. (2008). Strategic Capacity Building in Clusters to Enhance Future-oriented Open Innovation Processes, *Foresight Brief* No. 150, The European Foresight Monitoring Network, www.efmn.info

Savioz, P., & Blum, M. (2002). Strategic forecast tool for SMEs: How the opportunity landscape interacts with business strategy to anticipate technological trends. *Technovation, 22*(2), 91–100. doi:10.1016/S0166-4972(01)00082-7

Savitskaya, I. (2009). *Towards open innovation in regional Innovation system: case St. Petersburg, Research Report 214.* Lappeenranta: Lappeenranta University of Technology.

Sawant, S. (2013). E- learning: Use of Moodle by academic institutions in Mumbai. *Proceedings of International conference on redefining education: expanding horizons* (pp. 75-81).

Schaffers, H., Cordoba, M. G., Hongisto, P., Kallai, T., Merz, C., & van Rensburg, J. (2007, June 4-6). Exploring business models for open innovation in rural living labs. *Paper from the 13th International Conference on Concurrent Enterprising*, Sophia-Antipolis, France.

Schein, E. H. (2010). *Organizational Culture and Leadership* (4th ed.). San Francisco, CA: Jossey-Bass.

Schumpeter, J. A. (1934). *The Theory of Economic Development.* Cambridge: Harvard University Press.

Schumpeter, J. A. (1942). *Capitalism, Socialism, and Democracy.* NY: Harper & Row.

Schumpeter, J. A. (1982). *The Theory of Economic Development: An Inquiry into Profits, Capital, Credit, Interest, and the Business Cycle (1912/1934).* Transaction Publishers.

Schweller, R. L. (2014). *Maxwell's Demon and the Golden Apple: Global Discord in the New Millennium.* Baltimore, MD: Johns Hopkins University Press.

Semujju, B. (2013). ICT as an engine for community participation: An assessment of Uganda's community media. *International Journal of Information Communication Technologies and Human Development, 5*(1), 20–36. doi:10.4018/jicthd.2013010102

Semujju, B. (2014). Participatory media for a non-participating community: Western media for Southern communities. *The International Communication Gazette, 76*(2), 197–208. doi:10.1177/1748048513504166

Sen, K. A. (2011). L'euro fait tomber l'Europe. *Le monde.* Retrieved from http://www.lemonde.fr/imprimer/article/2011/07/02/1543995.html

Shafritz, J. M., & Russell, E. W. (2002). *Introducing Public Administration* (3rd ed.). New York: Longman.

Shank, H. M. (2000). Introduction. In M. H. Shank (Ed.), *The scientific enterprise in Antiquity and the Middle Ages* (pp. 1–19). Chicago: Chicago University Press. Random House.

Sharma, A. (2010). *Use of ICT at community level around the globe.* Retrieved from http://www.telecentremagazine.net/news/newsde-tails.asp?newsid=15808

Sharma-Grover, A., Plauché, M., Barnard, E., & Kuun, C. (2009). *HIV health information access using spoken dialogue systems: Touchtone vs. speech.Paper presented at the 3rd International Conference on Information and Communication Technologies and Development,* Education City, Doha, Qatar.

Sharpton, A. (Performer) (2011). Acceptable [YouTube Video]. Retrieved from http://www.youtube.com/watch?v=3HdrToihZc

Sheetal, K. A., Ketki, D., Aupam, J., Abhishek, K., Srijit, M., Nitendra, R., . . . Saurabh, S. (2010). Organizational, social and operational implications in delivering ICT solutions: a telecom web case-study. *Proceedings of the 4th ACM/IEEE International Conference on Information and Communication Technologies and Development* (ICTD '10). ACM.

Sheller, M. (2015). News now. *Journalism Studies, 16*(1), 12–26. doi:10.1080/1461670X.2014.890324

Sherwani, J., Ali, N., Mirza, S., Fatima, A., Memon, Y., Karim, M., & Rosenfeld, R. (2007). HealthLine: Speech-based access to health information by low-literate users. *Paper presented at the2nd IEEE/ACM International Conference on Information and Communication Technologies and Development,* Bangalore, India. doi:10.1109/ICTD.2007.4937399

Shore, B. (2008). Systematic biases and culture in project failures. *Project Management Journal, 39*(4), 5–16. doi:10.1002/pmj.20082

Shore, B., & Cross, B. (2005). Exploring the role of national culture in the management of large-scale international science projects. *International Journal of Project Management, 23*(1), 55–64. doi:10.1016/j.ijproman.2004.05.009

Shorthouse, S. (2008, May 29). Innovation and Technology Transfer. *Presentation from the International Conference DISTRICT 2008. International Conference Centre,* Dresden.

Shrader, C., Mulford, C., & Blackburn, V. (1989). Strategic and operational planning, uncertainty and performance in small firms. *Journal of Small Business Management, 27*(4), 45–60.

Shweder, R. A., & Good, G. (2005). *Clifford Geertz by his Colleagues.* Chicago.

Sinclair, B. (2009). The blended librarian in the learning commons: New skills for the blended library. *College & Research Libraries News, 70*(9), 504–516. http://crln.acrl.org/content/70/9/504.full Retrieved October 27, 2015

Singhal, A., Svenkerud, J. P., Malaviya, P., Rogers, M. E., & Krishna, V. (2005). Bridging digital divides: Lessons learned from the IT initiatives of the Grameen Bank in Bangladesh. In O. Hemer & T. Tufte (Eds.), *Media and glocal change: Rethinking communication for development* (pp. 427–433). Göteborg, Sweden: NORDICOM.

Singh, S. P., & Passi, A. (2014). Real Time Communication. *International Journal of Recent Development in Engineering and Technology, 2*(3). Retrieved from http://www.ijrdet.com/files/Volume2Issue3/IJRDET_0314_23.pdf

Siu, W. S. (2005). An institutional analysis of marketing practices of small and medium-sized enterprises (SMEs) in China, Hong Kong and Taiwan. *Entrepreneurship and Regional Development, 17*(1), 65–88. doi:10.1080/0898562052000330306

Skattør, B., Berntzen, L., Engvig, T., & Hasvold, P. (2007). A framework for mobile services supporting mobile non-office workers. In Human-Computer Interaction. HCI Applications and Services (pp. 742-751). Springer Berlin Heidelberg. doi:10.1007/978-3-540-73111-5_83

Skok, M. (2008). *The Future of Open Source: Exploring the Investments, Innovations, Applications, Opportunities and Threats.* North Bridge Venture Partners.

Skype. (n. d.). *Wikipedia.* Retrieved from https://en.wikipedia.org/wiki/Skype

Slack, E. (2012). Storage infrastructures for big data workflows. Storage Switzerland White Paper. Retrieved from https://iq.quantum.com/exLink.asp?8615424OJ73H28I34127712

Slideshare. (n. d.). *Wikipedia.* Retrieved from https://en.wikipedia.org/wiki/SlideShare

Smallbone, D., North, D., & Vickers, I. (2003). The role and characteristics of SMEs in innovation. In B.T. Asheim, A. Isaksen, C. Nauwelaers, & F. Tödtling (Eds.), Regional Innovation Policy for Small-Medium Enterprises. Edward Elgar. doi:10.4337/9781781009659.00010

Smith, C. L. (2013). The great Indian calorie debate: Explaining rising undernourishment during India's rapid economic growth. *University of Sussex Institute of Development Studies [IDS] Working Papers No 430.* Retrieved from http://opendocs.ids.ac.uk/opendocs/bitstream/handle/123456789/2877/Wp430.pdf?sequence=1

Smith, A. (1961). *An inquiry into the nature and causes of the wealth of nations.* London: Penguin. (Original work published 1776)

Smith, B. L., & MacGregor, J. T. (1992). What is collaborative learning? In A. S. Goodsell, M. R. Maher, & V. Tinto (Eds.), *Collaborative Learning: A Sourcebook for Higher Education. National Center on Postsecondary Teaching, Learning, & Assessment.* Syracuse University.

Smith, B. M. (2012). Reimagining development education for a changing geopolitical landscape. *Policy and Practice: A Development. Educational Review, 15,* 1–7.

Smyth, T. N., Etherton, J., & Best, M. L. (2010). MOSES: exploring new ground in media and post-conflict reconciliation. *Proceedings of the SIGCHI conference on Human Factors in computing systems* (pp. 1059—1068). ACM. doi:10.1145/1753326.1753484

Sousa, M. C. (2008). Open innovation models and the role of knowledge brokers. *Inside Knowledge magazine, 11*(6), 1–5.

Spithoven, A., Clarysse, B., & Knockaert, M. (2010). Building absorptive capacity to organize inbound open innovation in traditional industries. *Technovation, 30*(2), 130–141. doi:10.1016/j.technovation.2009.08.004

Srivastava, D. K. (2005). Human resource management in Indian mid size operations. In Datta (Ed.), Indian mid-size manufacturing enterprises: Opportunities and challenges in a global economy. Gurgaon: Management Development Institute.

Srivastava, K. (2004). Technology based training: Issues and concerns. In E learning and technology: New opportunities in training and development by Reddy, S. (ed.): Hyderabad: ICFAI Books, p. 3 – 18.

Stankiewics, R. (1995). The role of the science and technology infrastructure in the development and diffusion of industrial automation in Sweden. In B. Carlsson (Ed.), *Technological systems and economic performance: The case of the factory automation* (pp. 165–210). Dordrecht, The Netherlands: Kluwer Academic Publishers. doi:10.1007/978-94-011-0145-5_6

Statistics Canada. (2004). *Literacy Scores, human capital and growth across 14 OECD countries.*

Steen, M., Kuijt-Evers, L., & Klok, J. (2007). Early user involvement in research and design projects–A review of methods and practices. *Proceedings of the 23rd EGOS Colloquium, Vienna.* Citeseer.

Stein, J. (1964). *The fiddler on the roof.* New York: Crown Publishers.

Stepp- Greany, J. (2002). Student Perceptions on Language Learning in a Technological Environment: Implications for the New Millennium. *Language Learning & Technology, 6*(1), 165–180.

Stille, A. (2011, October 22). The paradox of the new elite. *New York Times.*

Stone, D. (2002). *Policy Paradox: The Art of Political Decision Making* (Revised ed.). New York: W.W. Norton.

Storey, D. (1994). *Understanding the small business sector.* London: International Thomson Business Press.

Straub, D., Loch, K., & Hill, C. (2001). Transfer of information technology to the Arab world: A test of cultural influence modeling. *Journal of Global Information Management, 9*(4), 6–48. doi:10.4018/jgim.2001100101

Straubhaar, J., & Larose, R. (2002). *Media now: Communication media in the Information Age.* Wadsworth Group.

Strigel, C. (2011). *ICT and the Early Grade Reading Assessment: From Testing to Teaching.* Retrieved from https://edutech-debate.org/reading-skills-in-primary-schools/ict-and-the-early-grade-reading-assessment-from-testing-to-teaching/

Stuckenbruck, L., & Zomorrodian, A. (1987). Project management: The promise for developing nations. *International Journal of Project Management, 5*(3), 167–175. doi:10.1016/0263-7863(87)90022-6

Susman, G. I., & Evered, R. D. (1978). An assessment of the scientific merits of action research. *Administrative Science Quarterly, 23*(4), 582–603. doi:10.2307/2392581

Takagi, Y., & Czajkowski, A. (2012). WIPO services for access to patent information - Building patent information infrastructure and capacity in LDCs and developing countries. *World Patent Information, 34*(1), 30 36. doi:10.1016/j.wpi.2011.08.002

Tan, P.-N., Steinbach, M., & Kumar, V. (2006). *Introduction to data mining.* USA: Addison-Wesley Publishing.

Tapscott, D., & Williams, A. D. (2007). *Wikinomics: How mass collaboration changes everything.* New York: Penguin Book.

Tarafdar, M., & Vaidya, S. (2005). Adoption and implementation of IT in developing nations: Experiences from two public sector enterprises in India. *Cases on Information Technology, 7*(1), 440–464.

Tas, E. M. (2011). ICT Education for Development- a case study. *Procedia Computer Science, 3,* 507–512. doi:10.1016/j.procs.2010.12.085

Task management. (n. d.). Retrieved from Wikipedia: https://en.wikipedia.org/wiki/Task_management

Technovation, In Press, Corrected Proof, Available online 28 September 2012

Teece, D. J. (2006). Reflections on "Profiting from Innovation". *Research Policy, 35*(8), 1131–1146. doi:10.1016/j.respol.2006.09.009

Teradata University Network. (2014). Retrieved from http://www.teradatauniversitynetwork.com/

Thakur, A, Kumar, A. & Pallavi. (2013). E-Learning: Initiatives in India. Open Journal of Education, 1(3), p. 61-69. Retrieved from http://manuscript.sciknow.org/uploads/oje/pub/oje_1363512069.pdf

Thampy, A. (2010). Financing of SME firms in India Interview with Ranjana Kumar, Former CMD, Indian Bank. Vigilance Commissioner, Central Vigilance Commission. doi:10.1016/j.iimb.2010.04.011

Thayer, F. C. (1973). *An end to hierarchy! an end to competition!* New York: New Viewpoints.

Thayer, F. C. (2002). Elite theory of organization: Building a normative foundation. In A. Farazmand (Ed.), *Modern Organizations: Theory and Practice* (2nd ed., pp. 97–132). Westport, CT: Praeger.

The 451 Group (2008). Open Source Is Not a Business Model. The 451 Commercial Adoption of Open Source (CAOS) Research Service.

The exam performance specialists (2012). *Tutor2u.net.* Retrieved from http://www.tutor2u.net

The family connection. (1996, October 05). Economist, 341(7986): 62

The Oxford American dictionary and language guide. (1999). New York, NY: Oxford University Press.

Thirlwall, P. A. (2008). Development and economic growth. In V. Desai & R. B. Potter (Eds.), *The companion to development studies* (2nd ed., pp. 37–40). London: Hodder Education.

Thoben, K. D. (2008, 23-25). A new wave of innovation in collaborative networks.*Proceedings of the 14th international conference on concurrent enterprising: ICE 2008*. Lisbon, Portugal (pp. 1091-1100).

Thomson, S. (2014). 6 Online Collaboration Tools and Strategies for Boosting Learning. Retrieved from http://elearningindustry.com/6-online-collaboration-tools-and-strategies-boosting-learning

Thorgren, S., Wincent, J., & Örtqvist, D. (2009). Designing interorganizational networks for innovation: An empirical examination of network configuration, formation and governance. *Journal of Engineering and Technology Management, 26*(3), 148–166. doi:10.1016/j.jengtecman.2009.06.006

Thornton, S. (2008). *Understanding human development: Biological, social and psychological processes from conception to adult life*. New York, NY: Palgrave Macmillan.

Tidd, J., Bessant, J., & Pavitt, K. (2001). *Managing Innovation*. New York, NY: John Wiley.

Tidd, J., Bessant, J., & Pavitt, K. (2005). *Managing Innovation: Integrating Technological, Market and Organizational Change* (3rd ed.). Chichester: John Wiley & Sons Ltd.

Tikam, M., & Lobo, A. (2012). Special Information Center for Visually Impaired Persons – A Case Study. *International Journal of Information Research, 1*(3), 42–49.

Tilley, F., & Tonge, J. (2003). Introduction. In O. Jones & F. Tilley (Eds.), *Competitive Advantage in SME's: Organising for Innovation and Change*. John Wiley & Sons.

Todaro, P. M. (1997). *Economic development* (6th ed.). New York, NY: Addison Wesley.

Todoist. (2015). Retrieved from http://www.pcmag.com/article2/0,2817,2408574,00.asp

Tödtling, F., & Trippl, M. (2005). One size fits all?: Towards a differentiated regional innovation policy approach. *Research Policy, 34*(8), 1203–1219. doi:10.1016/j.respol.2005.01.018

Toivonen, M. (2004). *Expertise as Business: Long-term development and future prospects of knowledge-intensive business services (KIBS)* [Doctoral Dissertation]. Laboratory of Industrial Management, Helsinki University of Technology.

Tonnies, F. (1887). *Community and society: Gemeinschaft und gesellschaft* (C. P. Loomis, Trans. & Ed.). Lansing, MI: Michigan State University Press.

Torkkeli, M., Tiina Kotonen, T., & Pasi Ahonen, P. (2007). Regional open innovation system as a platform for SMEs: A survey. *International Journal of Foresight and Innovation Policy*, *3*(4), 2007. doi:10.1504/IJFIP.2007.016456

Touray, A., Salminen, A., & Mursu, A. (2013). ICT barriers and critical success factors in developing nations. *Electronic Journal of Information Systems in Developing Nations*, *56*(7), 1–17.

Tourigny, D., & Le, C. D. (2004). Impediments to Innovation Faced by Canadian Manufacturing Firms. *Economics of Innovation and New Technology*, *13*(3), 217–250. doi:10.1080/10438590410001628387

Townsend, M., & Wheeler, S. (2004). Is there anybody out there? Teaching assistants' experiences of online learning. *The Quarterly Review of Distance Education*, *5*(2), 127–138.

Trakulhun, S., & Weber, R. (2015). Modernities: Editors' introduction. In S. Trakulhun & R. Weber (Eds.), Delimiting modernities: Conceptual challenges and regional responses (pp. ix-xxiv). Lanham, MD: Lexington Books.

Travis, J., & Price, K. (2005). Instructional culture and distance learning. *Journal of Faculty Development*, *20*(2), 99–103.

Traxler, J. (2007). Defining, discussing and evaluating mobile learning: The moving finger writes and having writ . . . *. International Review of Research in Open and Distance Learning*, *8*(2). Retrieved from http://www.irrodl.org/index. php/irrodl/ article/ view/346/875

Trilokekar, N. P. (2000). *A practical guide to information technology act, 2000: Indian cyber law*. Mumbai: Snow White Publications.

Tu, C.-H. (2004). *Online Collaborative Learning Communities: Twenty-One Designs to Building an Online Collaborative Learning Community* (p. 12). Libraries Unlimited Inc.

Turban, E., King, D., Lee, J. K., & Viehland, D. (2004). *Electronic Commerce 2004: A Managerial Perspective* (3rd ed.). Prentice Hall.

Turban, E., Sharda, R., Aronson, J. E., & King, D. (2008). *Business Intelligence: a managerial approach*. Upper Saddle River, N.J.: Pearson Prentice Hall.

Turpin, T., Garrett-Jones, S., & Rankin, N. (1996). Bricoleurs and boundary riders: Managing basic research and innovation knowledge networks. *R & D Management*, *26*(3), 267–282. doi:10.1111/j.1467-9310.1996.tb00961.x

Tzu, S. (1963). *The Art of War. United Sates of America*. Oxford University Press.

UCI OpenCourseWare Project. (n. d.). A little info on my blog. Retrieved from http://sites.uci.edu/opencourseware/about/

Uganda Bureau of Statistics. (2013). *Statistical Abstract*. Kampala: UBOS.

Uganda Communications Commission. (2013). *Annual Market Review*. Kampala: UCC.

Ulrich Lichtenthaler Lichtenthaler, U. (2009a, April). RETRACTED: The role of corporate technology strategy and patent portfolios in low-, medium- and high-technology firms. *Research Policy (*Special Issue: Innovation in Low- and Medium-Technology Industries), *38*(3), 559–569. doi:10.1016/j.respol.2008.10.009

UNCTAD Secretariat. (2001). Best Practices in Financial Innovations for SMEs. In *Improving the Competitiveness of SMEs in Developing Countries: The Role of Finance to Enhance Enterprise Development* (pp. 3–58). New York, Geneva: United Nations.

UNESCO. (2003). *Developing and Using Indicators of ICT Use in Education*. Paris.

UNESCO. (2006). *ICTs in education for people with special needs united nations educational, scientific and cultural organizationunesco institute for information technologies in education specialized training course*. Moscow: UNESCO. Retrieved from http://iite.unesco.org/pics/publications/en/files/3214644.pdf

UNESCO. (2009). *Guide to measuring Information and Communication Technologies (ICT) in education*. Canada: UNESCO Institute for Statistics.

UNESCO. (2015). Retrieved from http://unesco.org

United Nations. (2006). *Globalization of R&D and Developing Countries, United Nations Conference on Trade and Development*.

University of Waterloo. (n. d.). Collaborative online learning: fostering effective discussions. Retrieved from https://uwaterloo.ca/centre-for-teaching-excellence/teaching-resources/teaching-tips/alternatives-lecturing/discussions/collaborative-online-learning

Unwin, T. (2009a). Development agendas and the place of ICTs. In T. Unwin (Ed.), *ICT4D: Information and communication technology for development* (pp. 7–38). New York, NY: Cambridge University Press.

Unwin, T. (2009b). ICT4D implementation: Policies and partnerships. In T. Unwin (Ed.), *ICT4D: Information and communication technology for development* (pp. 125–175). New York, NY: Cambridge University Press.

Unwin, T. (2009c). Conclusions. In T. Unwin (Ed.), *ICT4D: Information and communication technology for development* (pp. 360–375). New York, NY: Cambridge University Press.

Unwin, T. (2009d). Information and communication in development practices. In T. Unwin (Ed.), *ICT4D: Information and communication technology for development* (pp. 39–75). New York, NY: Cambridge University Press.

Vaidya, R., Myers, M., & Gardner, L. (2013). Major issues in the successful implementation of information systems in developing nations. In Y. Dwivedi, H. Zinner, H. Wastell, & R. De (Eds.), *Grand Successes and Failures in ICT. Public and Private Sectors* (pp. 151–163). Berlin: Springer. doi:10.1007/978-3-642-38862-0_10

Valenzuela, A., Jr., Theodore, K., Meléndez, E., & Gonzalez, A. L. (2006). ON THE CORNER: Day Labor in the United States. Chicago: University of Illinois Chicago Center for Urban Economic Development. Retrieved from http://www.sscnet.ucla.edu/issr/csup/uploaded_files/Natl_DayLabor-On_the_Corner1.pdf

Valenzuela, A. Jr. (2001). Day labourers as entrepreneurs? *Journal of Ethnic and Migration Studies*, *27*(2), 335–352. doi:10.1080/13691830020041642

Valk, J., Rashid, A., & Elder, L. (2010). Using Mobile Phones to Improve Educational Outcomes: An Analysis of Evidence from Asia. *The International Review of Research in Open and Distance Learning*, *11*(1). Retrieved from http://www.irrodl.org/index.php/ irrodl/article/view/794/1487

Van Ark, B., Broersma, L. & Den Hertog, P. (2003). *Service Innovation, Performance and Policy: A Review*. Structural Information Provision on Innovation in Services SIID for the Ministry of Economic Affairs of the Netherlands.

Van de Ven, A. H. (1986). Central problems in the management of innovation. *Management Science*, *32*(5), 590–607. doi:10.1287/mnsc.32.5.590

Van de Vrande, V., de Jong, J. P. J., Vanhaverbeke, W., & de Rochemont, M. (2008, November). Open innovation in SMEs: Trends, motives and management challenges, a report published under the SCALES-initiative (SCientific AnaLysis of Entrepreneurship and SMEs), as part of the 'SMEs and Entrepreneurship programme' financed by the Netherlands Ministry of Economic Affairs, Zoetermeer 2008.

Van de Vrande, V., de Jong, J. P. J., Vanhaverbeke, W., & de Rochemont, M. (2009, June-July). Open innovation in SMEs: Trends, motives and management challenges. *Technovation*, *29*(6-7), 423–437. doi:10.1016/j.technovation.2008.10.001

Van de Vrande, V., Vanhaverbeke, W., & Gassman, O. (2010). Broadening the scope of open innovation: Past research, current state and future directions. *International Journal of Technology Management*, *52*(3-4), 221–235. doi:10.1504/IJTM.2010.035974

Van den Ham, A. (2004). Local area development planning and management in the province of West Java and the province of the special territory of Aceh, Indonesia. In A. Van den Ham & J. Veenstra (Eds.), *Shifting logic in area development practices* (pp. 255–340). Burlington, VT: Ashgate.

Van Dijk, C., & Van den Ende, J. (2002). Suggestion systems: Transferring employee creativity into practicable ideas. *R & D Management*, *32*(5), 387–395. doi:10.1111/1467-9310.00270

Van Gils, A., & Zwart, P. (2004). Knowledge Acquisition and Learning in Dutch and Belgian SMEs: The Role of Strategic Alliances. *European Management Journal*, *22*(6), 685–692. doi:10.1016/j.emj.2004.09.031

Van Hemel, C., & Cramer, J. (2002, October). Barriers and stimuli for ecodesign in SMEs. *Journal of Cleaner Production*, *10*(5), 439–453. doi:10.1016/S0959-6526(02)00013-6

Van Hemert, P., & Nijkamp, P. (2010). Knowledge investments, business R&D and innovativeness of countries: A qualitative meta-analytic comparison. *Technological Forecasting and Social Change*, *77*(3), 369–384. doi:10.1016/j.techfore.2009.08.007

Vanhaverbeke, W. (2006). The Inter-organizational Context of Open Innovation. In H. Chesbrough, W. Vanhaverbeke, & J. West (Eds.), *Open Innovation: Researching a New Paradigm* (pp. 205–219). Oxford: Oxford University Press.

Vanhaverbeke, W., & Cloodt, M. (2006). Open innovation in value networks. In H. Chesbrough, W. Vanhaverbeke, & J. West (Eds.), *Open Innovation: Researching a New Paradigm*. NY: Oxford University Press.

Verzola, R. (2006). Technology issues and the new ICTs. *Leonardo*, *39*(4), 311–313. doi:10.1162/leon.2006.39.4.311

Veugelers, M., Bury, J., & Viaene, S. (2010). Linking technology intelligence to open innovation. *Technological Forecasting and Social Change*, *77*(2), 335–343. doi:10.1016/j.techfore.2009.09.003

Von Hippel, E. (1988) The Sources of Innovation, Oxford University Press, New York.

Von Hippel, E. (1994). "Sticky Information" and the Locus of Problem Solving: Implications for Innovation. Management Science, 40(4), 429-439.

Von Hippel, E. (1998). Economics of product development by users: The impact of `sticky' local information. Management Science, 44(5), 629-644.

Von Hippel, E. (1986). Lead users: A source of novel product concepts. *Management Science*, *32*(7), 791–805. doi:10.1287/mnsc.32.7.791

Von Hippel, E. (1987). Cooperation between rivals: Informal Know-how trading. *Research Policy*, *16*(6), 291–302. doi:10.1016/0048-7333(87)90015-1

Von Hippel, E. (1990). Task Partitioning: An Innovation Process Variable. *Research Policy*, *19*, 407–418.

Von Hippel, E. (1998). Economics of product development by users: The impact of 'Sticky' local information. *Management Science*, *44*(5), 629–644. doi:10.1287/mnsc.44.5.629

Von Hippel, E. (2005). *Democratizing Innovation*. Boston, MA: MIT Press.

von Hippel, E. (2005). Democratizing innovation: The evolving phenomenon of user innovation. *Journal für Betriebswirtschaft*, *55*(1), 63–78. doi:10.1007/s11301-004-0002-8

Von Hippel, E., & Von Krogh, G. (2003). Open source software and the "private – collective" innovation model: Issues for organization science. *Organization Science*, *14*(2), 209–223. doi:10.1287/orsc.14.2.209.14992

VonHippel, E. (2001). 2001b PERSPECTIVE: User toolkits for innovation. *Journal of Product Innovation Management*, *18*(4), 247–257. doi:10.1111/1540-5885.1840247

VonHippel, E. (2001, Summer). 2001a Innovation by User Communities: Learning from Open-Source Software, MIT. *Sloan Management Review*, *42*(4), 82–86.

Vrettos, T. (2001). *Alexandria*. New York, NY: The Free Press.

Vujovic, S., & Ulhøi, J. P. (2008). *Opening up the Innovation Process: Different Organizational Strategies* (Vol. 7). Springer, US: Information and Organization Design Series. doi:10.1007/978-0-387-77776-4_8

Vygotsky, L. S. (1978). *Mind in society: The development of higher psychological processes*. Cambridge, UK: Harvard University Press.

Wagner, P. (2001). Modernity: One or many? In J. R. Blau (Ed.), *The Blackwell companion to sociology* (pp. 30–42). Malden, MA: Blackwell.

Waight, C. et al.. (2004). Recurrent themes in e-learning: A narrative analysis of major e-learning report. *The Quarterly Review of Distance Education*, *5*(3), 195–203.

Waldron, N. A. (1983). The problem of the Great Wall of China. *Harvard Journal of Asiatic Studies*, *43*(2), 643–663. doi:10.2307/2719110

Waldron, N. A. (1990). *The Great Wall of China: From history to myth*. Cambridge, MA: Harvard University Press.

Walsham, G., & Sahay, S. (2006). Research on information systems in developing nations: Current landscape and future prospects. *Information Technology for Development*, *12*(1), 7–24. doi:10.1002/itdj.20020

Walsh, J. (2012). *What's the matter with white people: Why we long for a golden age that never was*. Hoboken, NJ: John Wiley & Sons.

Walther, J., & D'Addario, K. (2001). The Impacts of Emoticons on Message Interpretation in Computer-Mediated Communication. *Social Science Computer Review*, *19*(3), 324–347. doi:10.1177/089443930101900307

Walton, R. E. (1989). *Up and Running: Integrating Information Technology and the Organization*. Boston, MA: Harvard Business School Press.

Wang, F., & Chen, Y. (2010). *From potential users to practical users: Use of E-government service by Chinese migrant farmer workers. Paper presented at the4th International Conference on Theory and Practice of Electronic Governance*, Beijing, China. doi:10.1145/1930321.1930380

Wang, L., Jaring, P., & Wallin, A. (2009) Developing a Conceptual Framework for Business Model Innovation in the Context of Open Innovation.*Proceedings of the Third IEEE International Conference on Digital Ecosystems and Technologies (IEEE DEST 2009)* (pp. 460-465).

Wang, X., & Liu, L. (2007). Cultural barriers to the use of Western project management in Chinese enterprises: Some empirical evidence from Yunnan Province. *Project Management Journal*, *38*(3), 61–73. doi:10.1002/pmj.20006

Wang, Y., Vanhaverbeke, W., & Roijakkers, N. (2012). Exploring the impact of open innovation on national systems of innovation - A theoretical analysis. *Technological Forecasting and Social Change*, *79*(3), 419–428. doi:10.1016/j.techfore.2011.08.009

Wanyeki, M. L. (2000). The Development of Community Media in East and Southern Africa. In S. T. K. Boafo (Ed.), *Promoting Community media in Africa* (pp. 25–41). Paris: UNESCO.

Warner, A. (2001, October 22-24). Small and Medium Sized Enterprises and Economic Creativity. A paper presented at UNCTAD's intergovernmental Expert Meeting on *"Improving the Competitiveness of SMEs in Developing Countries: the Role of Finance, Including E-finance, to Enhance Enterprise Development*, Geneva (pp. 61-77).

Warner, A. (2001, October 22-24). Small and Medium Sized Enterprises and Economic Creativity. *Paper presented at UNCTAD's intergovernmental Expert Meeting on "Improving the Competitiveness of SMEs in Developing Countries: the Role of Finance, Including E-finance, to Enhance Enterprise Development"*, Geneva (pp. 61-77).

Watkins, D., & Horley, G. (1986). Transferring technology from large to small firms: the role of intermediaries. In T. Webb, T. Quince, & D. Watkins (Eds.), *Small Business Research* (pp. 215–251). Aldershot: Gower.

Watson, H. J., Wixom, B. H., & Goodhue, D. L. (2004). Data Warehousing: The 3M Experience. In H. R. Nemati & C. D. Barko (Eds.), *Org. Data Mining: Leveraging Enterprise Data Resources for Optimal Performance* (pp. 202–216). Idea Group Publishing. doi:10.4018/978-1-59140-134-6.ch014

Web 2.0 teaching tools. (2011). *Edjudo.com*. Retrieved from http://edjudo.com/web-2-0-teaching-tools-links#anchor14

Webbink, M. (2003). Understanding Open Source Software. Retrieved from http://www.groklaw.net/articlebasic.php?story=20031231092027900

Weil, N. D. (2012). *Economic growth* (3rd ed.). New York, NY: Pearson.

Weiss, J. (1994). Keeping up with the research. *Technology and Learning*, *14*(5), 30–34.

Wenger, E. (1998). *Communities of Practice: Learning, Meaning and Identity*. Cambridge University Press. doi:10.1017/CBO9780511803932

West, J. (2006) Does Appropriability Enable or Retard Open Innovation? In H. Chesbrough, W. Vanhaverbeke, & J. West (Eds.), Open Innovation: Researching a New Paradigm. London: Oxford University Press.

West, J., Vanhaverbeke, W., & Chesbrough, H. (2006). Open Innovation: A Research Agenda. In H. Chesbrough, W. Vanhaverbeke, & J. West (Eds.), Open Innovation: Researching a New Paradigm. London: Oxford University Press.

WestEd (2002), *The e Learning Return on our Educational Technology Investment—A Review of Findings from Research*

Westergren, U. H., & Holmström, J. (2012). Exploring preconditions for open innovation: Value networks in industrial firms. *Information and Organization*, *22*(4), 209–226. doi:10.1016/j.infoandorg.2012.05.001

West, J., & Gallagher, S. (2006). Challenges of open innovation: The paradox of firm investment in open-source software. *R & D Management*, *36*(3), 319–331. doi:10.1111/j.1467-9310.2006.00436.x

West, J., & Gallagher, S. (2006). Patterns of Open Innovation in Open Source Software. In H. Chesbrough, W. Vanhaverbeke, & J. West (Eds.), *Open Innovation: Researching a New Paradigm* (pp. 82–106). Oxford: Oxford University Press.

West, J., & Lakhani, K. (2008). Getting Clear About the Role of Communities in Open Innovation. *Industry and Innovation, 15*(2), 223–231. doi:10.1080/13662710802033734

Wijffels, H. (2009). *Leadership, sustainability and levels of consciousness. A speech at the conference on the Leadership for a Sustainable World, June 5, 2009.* Den Haag, the Netherlands: Grote Kerk.

Wiki. (n. d.). Retrieved from Wikipedia: http://wiki.org/wiki.cgi?WhatIsWiki

Wilkes, R. (2006). The protest actions of indigenous peoples: A Canadian-U.S. comparison of social movement emergence. *The American Behavioral Scientist, 50*(4), 510–525. doi:10.1177/0002764206294059

Williams, A. M., & Shaw, G. (2011). Internationalization and innovation in Tourism. *Annals of Tourism Research, 38*(1), 27–51. doi:10.1016/j.annals.2010.09.006

Williams, B., & Carpini, M. (2004). Monica and Bill all the time and everywhere: The collapse of gate keeping and agenda setting in the new media environ-ment. *The American Behavioral Scientist, 47*(1208), 1208–1230. doi:10.1177/0002764203262344

Williams, D. (2014). The study of development. In B. Currie-Alder, R. Kanbur, D. M. Malone, & R. Medhora (Eds.), *International development: Ideas, experience, and prospects* (pp. 21–34). New York, NY: Oxford University Press. doi:10.1093/acprof:oso/9780199671656.003.0002

Williams, H. (2001). Hindsight after the Cold War: Samuel Huntington, the social sciences and development paradigms. *Dialectical Anthropology, 26*(3/4), 311–324. doi:10.1023/A:1021224219580

Wills, G. (2009). South Africa's Informal Economy: A Statistical Profile. Urban Policies Research Report, No. 7.

Wilmot, A. (1896). *Monomotapa (Rhodesia): Its monuments, and its history from the most ancient times to the present century (with preface by H.R. Haggard).* London: Fisher Unwin.

Wilson, T. D. (1981). On user studies and information needs. *The Journal of Documentation, 37*(1), 3–15. Retrieved from http://www.inclusivecities.org/research/RR7_Wills.PDF

Wilson, T. D. (2000). Human information behavior. *Informing Science, 3*(2), 49–56.

Winch, G. M., & Courtney, R. (2007). The organization of innovation brokers: An international review. *Technology Analysis and Strategic Management, 19*(6), 747–763. doi:10.1080/09537320701711223

Wit, B., & Meyer, R. (2003). *Strategy: Process, Content, Context* (3rd ed.). Cengage Learning Business Press.

Wong, P. (2002). ICT production and diffusion in Asia Digital dividends or digital divide? *Information Economics and Policy, 14*(11), 167–187. doi:10.1016/S0167-6245(01)00065-8

Woodhams, C., & Lupton, B. (2009, June). Analysing gender-based diversity in SMEs. *Scandinavian Journal of Management, 25*(2), 203–213. doi:10.1016/j.scaman.2009.02.006

World Bank. (2002). *Information and Communication Technologies: a World Bank group strategy.* Washington: World Bank.

World Business Council. (2007). *Promoting Small and Medium Enterprises for Sustainable Development* (Development Focus Area. *I Issue Brief,* 2007.

Wright, R. K., & Zegarra, V. A. (2000). *Machu Picchu: A civil engineering marvel.* Reston, VA: ASCE. doi:10.1061/9780784404447

Wyche, S., Smyth, T., Chetty, M., Aoki, P., & Grinter, R. (2010). Deliberate interactions: Characterizing technology use in Nairobi, Kenya. *Paper presented at the28th International Conference on Human Factors in Computing Systems,* Atlanta, Georgia. doi:10.1145/1753326.1753719

Xiong, B., Ren, K., Shu, Y., Chen, Y., Shen, B., & Wu, H. (2014). Recent developments in microfluidics for cell studies. *Advanced Materials, 26*(31), 5525–5532. doi:10.1002/adma.201305348 PMID:24536032

Yadava, J. S., & Mathur, P. (1998). Mass communication: the basic concepts: Vol. 1 & 2. New Delhi: Kanishka.

Yamarik, S., & Ghosh, S. (2015). Broad versus regional integration: What matters more for economic development? *The Journal of International Trade & Economic Development: An International and Comparative Review, 24*(1), 43–75. doi:10.1080/09638199.2013.868024

Yancey, K. (2005). The people's university. *Change,* (March-April), 13.

Yanow, D. (2000). *Conducting interpretive policy analysis.* Thousand Oaks, CA: Sage. doi:10.4135/9781412983747

Yanwen, W. (2012). The study on complex project management in developing countries. *Physics Procedia, 25,* 1547–1552. doi:10.1016/j.phpro.2012.03.274

Yen, L. Yuyun, Sandra, Shameen, and Rajen. (2013). SMU Libraries' Role in Supporting SMU's Blended Learning Initiatives. Retrieved from http://library.smu.edu.sg/sites/default/files/library/pdf/Librarys_Role_in_Blended_Learning.pdf

Youngs, G. (2002). Virtual communities. In C. New-bold, O. Boyd-Barret, & H. Van den Bulk (Eds.), *The Media Book.* London, UK: Arnold Publications.

Yunus, M. (2007). *Creating a world without poverty: Social business and the future of capitalism.* New York, NY: Public Affairs.

Zahra, A. Z., & George, G. (2002). Absorptive capacity: A review, reconceptualization, and extension. *Academy of Management Review, 27*(2), 185–203.

Zakus, L., & Lysack, C. L. (1998). Revisiting community participation. *Health Policy and Planning, 13*(1), 1–12. doi:10.1093/heapol/13.1.1 PMID:10178181

Zeng, S. X., Xie, X. M., & Tam, C. M. (2010). Relationship between cooperation networks and innovation performance of SMEs. *Technovation, 30*(3), 181–194. doi:10.1016/j.technovation.2009.08.003

Zhang, J., & Zhang, Y. (2009). Research on the Process Model of Open Innovation Based on Enterprise Sustainable Growth. *Proceeding of the International Conference on Electronic Commerce and Business Intelligence,* Beijing, China (pp. 318-322).

Zuboff, S. (1988). *In the Age of the Smart Machine: The Future of Work and Power.* New York, NY: Basic Books.

About the Contributors

Hakikur Rahman is an academic with over 27 years having served leading education institutes and established various ICT4D projects funded by ADB, UNDP and World Bank in Bangladesh. He is currently serving BRAC University, Bangladesh as an Associate Professor. Before joining BRAC University he was doing his Post-Doctoral Research at the University of Minho, Portugal under the Centro Algoritmi. He has written and edited over 25 books, more than 50 book chapters and contributed over 100 articles on computer education, ICTs, knowledge management, open innovation, data mining and e-government research in newspapers, journals and conference proceedings. Graduating from the Bangladesh University of Engineering and Technology in 1981, he completed his Master's of Engineering at the American University of Beirut in 1986 and completed his PhD in Computer Engineering at Ansted University, BVI, UK in 2001.

* * *

Jorge Bernardino received a PhD degree in computer science from the University of Coimbra in 2002. He is a Coordinator Professor at ISEC (Instituto Superior de Engenharia de Coimbra) of the Polytechnic of Coimbra, Portugal. His main research fields are big data, data warehousing, business intelligence, open source tools, and software engineering, subjects in which he has authored or co-authored dozens of papers in refereed conferences and journals. Jorge Bernardino has served on program committees of many conferences and acted as a referee for many international conferences and journals. He was President of ISEC from 2005–2010. During 2014, he was General Chair of the IDEAS conference and a visiting professor at Carnegie Mellon University (CMU).

Sylvain K. Cibangu earned his PhD degree in 2016 in Information Science/Technology in the Centre for Information Management, in the School of Business and Economics at Loughborough University, UK. He has a Master's degree in Communication and a Master's degree in Information Science from the University of Washington, Seattle. He also has a Master's degree in Social Sciences from Regis University, Denver, Colorado. His research interests include research methods, qualitative research, quantitative research, social sciences, international development, minorities and Black populations, race and diversity, communication studies, and foundations of information studies.

Robert Hindle is a lecturer in Education & Economics at the University of Manchester, an author and an associate with Tutor2U.

Lester Leavitt is a doctoral candidate in the School of Public Administration at Florida Atlantic University. Prior to returning to university in 2009 to complete a bachelor's degree in multimedia journalism, he had been an accountant and business consultant in public practice for 25 years, with a special interest in franchise development. Leavitt's interest in devising a mechanism for improving the effectiveness of protest narratives stems directly from his involvement in social equity activism that began in 2006 and gradually expanded to include all progressive causes. In 2010, he began his work with inner-city populations, where he has a particular interest in America's historically segregated black communities. Leavitt has four grown children from a previous 25-year marriage to a woman. In 2007, he met Mickey Rowe, and in 2009 they travelled to Connecticut so that they could be married.

Geeta Nair is the Head & Associate Professor of Department of Business Economics and Ph.D. Centre in Business Economics at H.R. College of Commerce & Economics. She is also Member of Board of Studies in Business Economics at the University of Mumbai. Geeta has presented and published several research papers and is a recipient of the Marquis-Who's Who Award in Economics, and 2 Indo-French Postdoctoral Awards. Her Ph.D. in the arena of gender economics is published in a book entitled, "Revisiting Globalization through the Gender Lens', 2008 with her post-doctoral work on Globalization and Higher Education to be published as a Palgrave Pivot shortly.

Sarika Sawant -- Expertise in teaching Cataloging, Reference Sources and Services, Information Storage & Retrieval T & P at MLISc level Career Highlights as an Assistant Professor - Since Sept 2004 - Research Publications Total 21, Journal research publications 17, in international peer-reviewed indexed journals out of it 3 are in high impact factor journals (Below 1). 4 research publications in Indian peer-reviewed journals, 10 research papers have received 34 citations & H-index as per Google scholar is 3. 13 papers in conference proceedings, 3 papers in edited books. Research guidance/projects: Recognised PhD guide, currently guiding 4 students, MLISc project guidance 10 students from 2009-10 onwards. One minor research project completed sponsored by UGC, Center for Canadian Studies (2012). Numerous consultancy projects for developing database & library undertaken but not in terms of money, International Collaboration Member of Editorial board of the international peer-reviewed journal International Information & Library Review, a Taylor & Francis Pub (ISSN: 1057-2317). Member of Editorial board of the international peer reviewed open access journal SAGE Open (Online ISSN: 2158-2440).

Brian Semujju lectures at Uganda Christian University and is currently doing a PhD at the University of Kwazulu-Natal South Africa, where he is stationed. His academic interests fall under media law, mass communication theory and community media.

Madhuri Vikram Tikam is working as the Chief Librarian of H.R. College of Commerce & Economics in Mumbai. She also worked at a multinational multimedia company as an "Information Scientist" where she developed Information product manuals, directories, brochures, and other publicity materials. She is involved in various research projects and published several articles in different national and international books and journals. She authored a book *Measuring Value of Academic Library: Few Examples*. She provided consultancy to more than 150 colleges on NAAC and computerization and promotion of library activities. Her research interests are in the field of Education, Automation and Promotion of library services and Special libraries.

Index

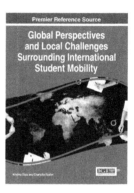
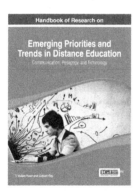

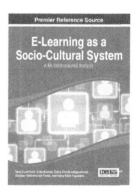